THE FACTS ON FILE

Companion to

Shakespeare

VOLUME IV

THE FACTS ON FILE

Companion to
Shakespeare

VOLUME IV

WILLIAM BAKER AND KENNETH WOMACK

Facts On File
An Infobase Learning Company

The Facts On File Companion to Shakespeare

Copyright © 2012 William Baker and Kenneth Womack

Facts On File, Inc.
An imprint of Infobase Learning
132 West 31st Street
New York NY 10001

Library of Congress Cataloging-in-Publication Data
Baker, William, 1944–
    The facts on file companion to Shakespeare / William Baker and Kenneth Womack.
        p. cm.
    Includes bibliographical references and index.
    ISBN 978-0-8160-7820-2 (acid-free paper) 1. Shakespeare, William, 1564–1616—Encyclopedias.
I. Womack, Kenneth. II. Title.
    PR2892.B26 2011
    822.3'3—dc22   2010054012

Facts On File books are available at special discounts when purchased in bulk quantities for businesses, associations, institutions, or sales promotions. Please call our Special Sales Department in New York at (212) 967-8800 or (800) 322-8755.

You can find Facts On File on the World Wide Web at http://www.infobaselearning.com

Text design by Annie O'Donnell
Composition by Hermitage Publishing Services
Cover printed by Yurchak Printing, Landisville, Pa.
Book printed and bound by Yurchak Printing, Landisville, Pa.
Date printed: January 2012

Printed in the United States of America

10 9 8 7 6 5 4 3 2 1

This book is printed on acid-free paper.

Contents

Measure for Measure

INTRODUCTION

Measure for Measure is one of Shakespeare's most ambiguous plays, which makes it especially interesting and popular in both performance and study. The subject matter is contentious and potentially salacious, encompassing blackmail, the sacrifice of sexual honor, justice, the control of the state, and extensive deception and manipulation. All of this raises many moral questions—none of which are answered definitively.

Such questions are not, however, confined to those of personal decisions and morality. The world offered up for scrutiny in *Measure for Measure* is sexually permissive and yet at odds with this: Images of venereal disease, violence, perversity, and disgust abound among all characters, whether they profit financially from the sex industry (though, notably, we meet no actual prostitutes), visit brothels and public houses recreationally, indulge in sexual misbehavior without the sanctity of marriage, or have chosen to be celibate. This suggests a society that *needs* the strict laws banning fornication to be enforced and marks the intersection of the private or personal and the political, where personal sexuality is necessarily regulated by the state in order to maintain the social and moral order of both society and the individuals within that society. The brothels in the Vienna city suburbs, so redolent of the outskirts of London at that time, are destroyed, but the pimps, prostitutes, tapsters, bawds, and bored young men are dispersed only briefly, gathering again in the prison. The state seems unable to fully eradicate the problem, and the Duke's return to power offers no promise of enforcement of the law.

Measure for Measure was probably written in 1604, after Shakespeare's early romantic comedies and around the time of some of his great tragedies. Indeed, some critics consider the mixed or tragicomic nature of the play as indicative of a shift in production. The play's ambiguity led to its early classification by critics as being an example of what were known as the "problem plays" or "dark comedies," along with *Troilus and Cressida* (1602) and *All's Well That Ends Well* (1603–04). The problems or questions raised by the text (more recent criticism prefers to consider the "problem plays" as being plays *about* problems) are various and comprehensive, including all dramatic components: genre (comedy, tragedy, tragicomedy, etc.), structure, character, and plot.

The play's ambiguity largely arises from the combination of comedy and serious, almost tragic, matters. The central plot—a sister offered a chance to save her brother from death by compromising her honor—is certainly nothing to laugh about, but this is balanced by comic scenes and overseen by a sympathetic figure of authority. In addition, the play's structure, with the central dramatic irony of the disguised ruler and the finale promising four marriages, would suggest, following contemporary theatrical convention, that the play is intended to be a comedy, yet the comic scenes are based to a large extent on jokes about venereal disease and

Froth and Pompey explain their case before Angelo and Escalus in Act II, Scene 1 of *Measure for Measure*. This is a print from the Boydell Shakespeare Gallery project, which was conceived in 1786 and lasted until 1805. *(Painting by Robert Smirke; engraving by Thomas Ryder)*

sexual puns that focus on sex as something sinful and disgusting. Additionally, the marriages that are arranged at the conclusion are obviously problematic, with two unwilling bridegrooms and an unanswered proposal. The dramatic solution is further complicated by both its uneasy relation to the rest of the play and by Isabella's unscripted response to the Duke's proposition. Productions have to decide how to interpret this through action so that the final scene can reverberate retrospectively throughout the rest of the play. Similarly, judgments of the characters involved in this shadowy world of sexual licentiousness and surveillance are difficult to summarize and open to greater performative interpretation than is perhaps usual: Is Isabella unreasonable in her determined chastity? Does she need to learn the difference between abstract ideals and their application in real life? Moreover, is she hypocritical in allowing another to undergo the same ordeal? Is the Duke a savior or a masterful manipulator who could have circumvented a good deal of deception and anguish but chooses instead to play with his subjects' lives? Is he guilty of the same attitude toward Isabella as Angelo?

BACKGROUND

The title of *Measure for Measure* would have immediately conveyed certain ideals to its contemporary audience more familiar with the Bible than a modern secular audience. The phrase is taken from Jesus' Sermon on the Mount, in the opening verses of the seventh chapter of Saint Matthew's gospel: "Judge not, that ye not be judged. For with what judgment ye judge, ye shall be judged, and with what measure ye mete, it shall be measured to you again" (Matthew 7:1–3). This reference both conveys some of the central themes of the play in its focus on judgment, hypocrisy, justice, and mercy and indicates various theological issues that inform the play's action. The Sermon on the Mount advocates the code of forgiveness rather than the Old Testament concept of justified retribution, which Isabella demonstrates in her plea for Angelo's life. In addition, the focus on aspects of Christianity indicated by the title increases awareness of its contemporary importance in the play's setting and its characters. For example, from 1558, Vienna was the seat of the Holy Roman Emperor and therefore perhaps linked in a contemporary Protestant English mindset with Catholic extremism in the emperor's suppression of Hungarian Protestantism. This aspect is arguably reflected in the play, where Angelo, whose descriptions as "precise" firmly ally him with Puritanism, is the leading example of religious intolerance. Indeed, in contemporary England, some extreme Puritans did advocate the death penalty for fornication.

The 1604 date of *Measure for Measure* places the play historically in the first year of James I's reign. The play's relation to contemporary politics is supported by the possible occasion of the play's first performance. The earliest recorded performance was at Whitehall on December 26, 1604. This opened the first Christmas celebrations of James's rule. The processional entry of James into London, with pageants involving the acting companies, occurred in March 1604. As well as possible allusions to contemporary events, some critics argue that the Duke potentially embodies certain aspects of James's principles of government set out in his *Basilikon Doron* (1599; reprinted 1603). It certainly deals with areas of interest to the king in the theological and moral dilemmas posed by the play, the issues of slander, and the unseen machinations of power.

The general narrative of *Measure for Measure* is not original to Shakespeare. The story of a chaste young woman propositioned by a person of authority in order to save her brother's life would have been familiar to audience members from various European folktales and more recently from George Whetstone's play *History of Promos and Cassandra* (1578), itself based on a tale in Giraldi Cinthio's *Hecatommithi* (1565). Shakespeare takes the general plot from Whetstone, but he complicates it greatly through setting and character and invents the situation with Mariana to avoid the sexual union of the Isabella and Angelo characters found in the source material.

Early modern ideology concerning sexuality, chastity, and marriage is also key to understanding the text's complexities and dilemmas. The focus in *Measure for Measure* on sexual behavior and status is epitomized in Isabella's chastity. As in early modern England as a whole, her chastity is emphasized, utilized, and ultimately fetishized. Historically, this obsession with controlling female sexual behavior is economic and political: A chaste wife ensures the inheritance of land and wealth for the legitimate male heir, perpetuating patrilineal social structures. However, Isabella's virginity is so rare in the fictional Vienna that it conveys on her a certain influence, as Lucio describes, as "a thing enskied and sainted" (1.4.34).

Isabella's religious conviction also brings into question theological and moral debate regarding individual sin. Isabella believes she will be damned if she sleeps with Angelo, but contemporary and historical writers on sexual morality disagree about the intricacies of blame and guilt in this issue. Some argue that the body and soul are separate, and therefore a nonconsensual sexual act does not result in damnation. However, chastity is also well-defined in the period as being a physical as well as mental state. These arguments are further complicated by the concept that if Isabella is, paradoxically, forced to consent, then whether this constitutes a lack of consent is still highly debatable.

The geographical structure of Vienna in the play echoes that of contemporary London with its suburban "stews" containing brothels, playhouses, taverns, and bear pits. Similarly, the church's punishment of those found guilty of either fornication (including premarital intercourse and adultery) or deserting contracted sexual partners was both public and often corporal. Therefore, the situation in fictional Vienna is arguably uncomfortably close to the truth of contemporary London, albeit presented with increased fervency and extending, logically yet disturbingly, to instances many individuals would have felt excusable. Some Puritans argued at the time that the church courts' punishments were too lenient, and Angelo's probable identification as Puritan offers an imagined outcome of stricter law. A more secular and grassroots interpretation of marital contracts understood at the time would strengthen an audience's reaction to Angelo's law enforcement in relation to Claudio and Juliet. Their mutual promise to marry would arguably have been seen as being as good as binding, and thereby their sexual interaction, if not entirely legitimate (the church still asserted that consummation should be delayed until marriage, publicly officiated), is understandable and easily condoned through ceremony. The same rule applies to Mariana and Angelo, and it is why the Duke (as the friar) can reassure Isabella and the audience that Mariana is committing no offence in sleeping with her forsworn husband.

Date and Text of the Play

The first recorded performance of *Measure for Measure* was on December 26, 1604, as detailed in the Revels Account Book, but the only existing early text is the 1623 Folio. Inconsistencies in this text have led some editors to suggest that it was amended by the playwright Thomas Middleton, perhaps because the "original" Shakespearean playhouse text was lost.

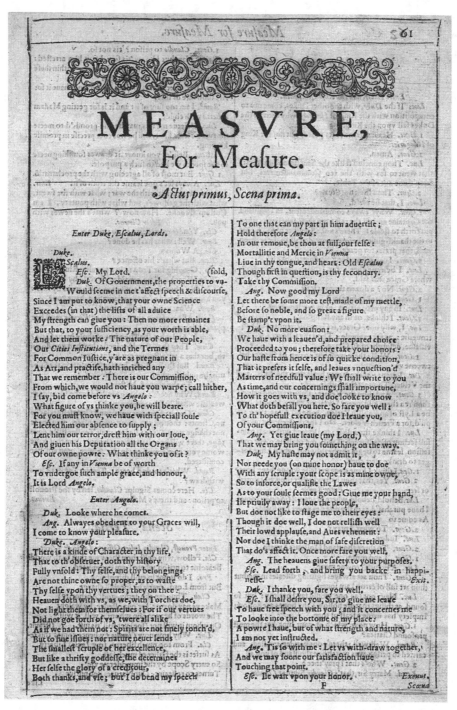

Title page of the First Folio edition of *Measure for Measure*, published in 1623

SYNOPSIS
Brief Synopsis

Measure for Measure is set in Vienna, where the indulgent Duke Vincentio has failed to enforce various laws. The result is a proliferation of brothels and a general lack of sexual morality. The Duke pretends to leave Vienna and nominates the devout Angelo to be his replacement and enforce the law, while remaining behind in disguise to monitor the progress of his experiment. Some of the first victims of the laws are Claudio and Juliet, whose premarital sexual intercourse is evidenced by Juliet's pregnancy. Representatives of the lower classes whose activities and professions are curtailed by the law are the bawd, Mistress Overdone; Pompey, a tapster and pimp; and Lucio, "a fantastic" and friend of Claudio. Scenes involving these characters and the clownish policeman Elbow provide some comic relief. Claudio is sentenced to death unless his sister, Isabella, about to begin her training as a novice nun, can persuade Angelo to pardon her brother. Angelo will, on the condition that Isabella will sleep with him. This, to the disappointment and annoyance of Claudio, she will not do.

The Duke, disguised as a friar, sets in motion a solution. He knows about Mariana, Angelo's one-time fiancée, cast off by him when her fortune was lost. The Duke and Isabella substitute Mariana in Angelo's bed for Isabella. However, Angelo negates his promise and orders Claudio's execution. The Duke substitutes the head of a deceased prisoner for Claudio's but does not tell Isabella of this, instead advising her to make a case against Angelo when the Duke returns. This leads to a climactic scene in which all is revealed: Angelo is exposed and sentenced to death, but he is pardoned after Isabella's intervention and made to marry Mariana. The Duke reveals Claudio, alive and well, and proposes to Isabella. Lucio is punished for his licentiousness and continual slander throughout the play by being forced to marry the prostitute mother of his child before being executed.

Act I, Scene 1

The play opens with the Duke and his adviser Escalus discussing the Duke's absence and naming Angelo, whose virtue is stressed, as his proxy. The proposal is put to Angelo, who is eager to be given such responsibility.

Act I, Scene 2

Lucio and two gentlemen discuss the Duke's trip to Poland, their conversation falling into repartee heavy with sexual puns and images of venereal disease. Mistress Overdone enters to inform the men of Claudio's arrest and sentence, confirmed by Pompey. Claudio and Juliet are marched through the scene, under arrest. Claudio claims in conversation with Lucio that he and Juliet are contracted to be married and are therefore innocent, and he sends Lucio to find Isabella to attempt to find a reprieve.

Act I, Scene 3

The Duke explains his plan to an old friar, admitting he has been lax in enforcing the law in the city. He requests a friar's robe for his disguise.

Act I, Scene 4

Isabella is introduced discussing the rules of the nunnery she intends to join and expressing regret the strictures are not more severe. Lucio enters and informs Isabella of her brother's plight. Isabella is surprised that Claudio cannot simply marry Juliet, and she agrees to try to persuade Angelo to pardon her brother.

Act II, Scene 1

Angelo expresses his desire to enforce the law fully and condemns succumbing to temptation, despite Escalus's advice of leniency in the case of Claudio and his status as a gentleman of good family. The date for Claudio's execution is set for the following day. Police officers enter with Froth and Pompey in custody, and Elbow attempts, through multiple malapropisms, to explain the nature of the arrest to the officials as Angelo leaves. The arrest centers on an insult to Elbow's wife, who it seems mistakenly entered a brothel, and the comic confusion it causes is exploited by Pompey, who uses bawdy slang and deliberate misunderstanding to undermine Elbow. Escalus intervenes and questions the prisoners. Froth is set free, and Pompey briefly defends his role as pimp and asserts the reinforced law is unworkable. Escalus gives him a warning and retires, lamenting Claudio's fate.

Act II, Scene 2

The Provost establishes that Angelo is entirely set in his judgment against Claudio. Isabella, accompanied by Lucio, enters and states her purpose. Angelo flatly denies any leniency, and this seems final to Isabella, who immediately turns to leave. Lucio insists she stay and advises her to show more emotion and warmth in her plea. Throughout the following discussion of Claudio's crime and the morality surrounding it, Isabella is continually urged on by Lucio and, privately, the Provost. Isabella gives a rational argument, stressing the lack of harm from Claudio's offense, and is horrified that his execution is so soon. Angelo admits that he is making an example of Claudio. Isabella asks for pity, for mercy, and accuses Angelo of tyranny until, in an aside, Angelo reveals that he thinks her argument is rational. He tells her he will think it over and instructs her to return the morning after. After Isabella and the other characters leave, Angelo's soliloquy expresses an unexpected stirring of desire for Isabella. He admits to himself that he is attracted to her, and that he finds her virtue more beguiling than overt sexual availability. This is the motivation behind his request that she return in the morning.

Act II, Scene 3

The Duke, disguised as a friar, gains access to the prison in order to counsel and hear the confessions of the prisoners. Juliet admits to full mutual responsibility for her and Claudio's actions, and the Duke states that this means Juliet's sin, presumably as a woman, is greater. Juliet agrees and repents; she is horrified upon learning of Claudio's immediate fate.

Act II, Scene 4

Angelo describes his frustration at his inability to stop thinking about Isabella, even when pray-

Isabella pleads with Angelo in Act II, Scene 4 of *Measure for Measure*. (Illustration by John Thurston; engraving by Allen Robert Branston)

ing. When she enters, however, Angelo is as self-possessed as ever. He states again that her brother must die as punishment, but cryptically implies that Claudio's life could be lengthened. Angelo also introduces a discussion of repentance and of the separation of body and soul, seemingly theoretically proposing to Isabella the question of whether she would save her brother through committing a sexual sin. Isabella seems to misunderstand, and Angelo is compelled to directly ask whether Isabella would give up her chastity to a person in power in order to save her brother. Isabella replies that she would certainly not, and that she would rather die than sin in this way as it would result in damnation. After agreeing on the frailty of humanity in the face of temptation, especially that of women, Angelo expressly declares his "love" for Isabella, understood by both characters, it seems, to mean sexual desire, and declares that he will pardon Claudio if Isabella sleeps with him. Isabella, after pointing out the hypocrisy in this proposal, seizes a chance for the upper hand and threatens to make public Angelo's offer unless he frees Claudio. Angelo counters this with the calm statement that no one, given his own virtuous reputation, will believe her. He explicitly repeats his offer, suggesting that Isabella's refusal would constitute an "unkindness" that will kill Claudio. He gives Isabella until the next day to consider it, then he leaves. Alone, Isabella despairs that Angelo is right and that no one will believe her. She resolves to go and tell Claudio what has happened, believing he will support her decision, and she will help him prepare for death.

Act III, Scene 1

The disguised Duke counsels Claudio in prison. The Duke leaves upon Isabella's entrance, but he and the Provost conceal themselves in order to overhear the conversation between Isabella and Claudio. Isabella presents the result of her audience with Angelo as there being no hope for Claudio until he specifically questions her series of figurative implications that there is a way he could be saved. Isabella first asks Claudio if he is prepared for death, as she is afraid of how he is going to react to her news. Claudio claims, to Isabella's pride, to be ready, and Isabella tells him of Angelo's proposition. At first, Claudio is appalled, and Isabella supportively tells him if she could die in his place, she would. However, as Isabella again tells Claudio he must prepare for death, Claudio starts to think about what dying might actually be like. Fear of the unknown, as well as the horror of the body decomposing, leads him to quickly change his mind, and he pleads with Isabella to save him, saying that such an act to save his life would be a virtue rather than a sin.

Isabella turns on Claudio, disgusted at what she sees as his cowardice and lack of honor. She will not let him speak and accuses him of being as good as a pimp, when they are interrupted by the Duke. He tells Claudio that Angelo's proposition to Isabella

is merely a test of her virtue, a fact known to him as he is Angelo's confessor, and again he advises Claudio to go and prepare for death. Left alone with Isabella, the Duke praises her beauty and virtue in her resolve to refuse Angelo. The Duke then suggests that he can help; he tells Isabella of Mariana, who was engaged to Angelo. Angelo left Mariana when her dowry (and brother) was lost at sea, and he invented evidence of her dishonor to make this abandonment legal. The Duke tells Isabella to accept Angelo's proposition on the conditions that she is with him for a short time only, and that the interaction is conducted in silence and darkness. The Duke will arrange for Mariana (who still loves Angelo) to take Isabella's place, thus saving Claudio, reinstating Mariana, and preserving Isabella. Isabella agrees to this plan and goes off to see Angelo while the Duke sets off to visit Mariana.

Act III, Scene 2

The Duke comes across Pompey with Elbow under arrest again for being a pimp. The Duke condemns this vice and orders Pompey off to prison. The entrance of Lucio gives Pompey the hope of securing bail, but after a facetious exchange, Lucio refuses, and Pompey is led offstage by Elbow and the other officers. Lucio enters into conversation with the "friar" about the whereabouts of the Duke. He speaks approvingly, though almost certainly ironically, of Angelo's strict enforcement of the law, and he suggests Angelo is the immaculately conceived offspring of a mermaid and thereby, unsurprisingly, as cold as a fish. Lucio compares Angelo's attitudes to the lenient Duke's and goes on to inform the protesting friar that the Duke is a lecherous, drunken womanizer. In addition, Lucio claims to know the Duke is an ignorant man, with a secret reason for leaving Vienna. He asks the Duke if he can confirm Claudio's execution, laments the absence of the Duke who would not prosecute such actions, and leaves, reiterating the Duke's lechery. The Duke barely has time to recover from this assault, musing that not even the great can escape slander, when Escalus and other officials enter with Mistress Overdone, on her way to prison. She protests that it is Lucio who has accused her of being a bawd, and we learn in her counteraccusation that he has a child with a prostitute, Kate Keepdown. Escalus orders Lucio to be called before the magistrates and sends Mistress Overdone to the prison. He and the Provost then discuss Claudio's impending execution, and the Duke joins them. He inquires of Escalus as to the character of the absent Duke and is informed of his own good and generous nature. The conversation returns to Claudio and Angelo's refusal to overturn the sentence, despite all the officials' unease. The scene closes with the Duke soliloquizing on justice and on Angelo's hypocrisy, and he reminds the audience of his impending plan.

Act IV, Scene 1

A boy is singing a melancholy song to Mariana when they are interrupted by the Duke's arrival. Mariana leaves while the Duke waits for Isabella, who then arrives with news of her arrangements with Angelo. Mariana reenters, and she and Isabella briefly walk apart as Isabella relates the circumstances and plot. Returning to the Duke, Mariana agrees to the plan if advised to by the friar, who establishes a moral dimension by asserting that Angelo is, theoretically, Mariana's husband, and so there is no sin in the deception.

Act IV, Scene 2

The Provost needs an assistant for the prison executioner, Abhorson, for the execution of Claudio and another prisoner, Barnardine, the next morning. The Provost agrees with Pompey that he will secure his pardon by fulfilling this role. Claudio is called before the Provost to be instructed of his death and returns to his cell. The Duke enters, claiming there is hope for Claudio and inquiring if his pardon has arrived yet, as we are to understand that the substitution of Mariana for Isabella has occurred. There is no pardon as yet, but the Duke confidently says it will come by morning. To the Duke's satisfaction, a messenger from Angelo arrives with a note, but to his horror, the note, read aloud by the Provost, orders the execution of

Claudio first thing in the morning and his head to be sent to Angelo immediately afterward. The note also stipulates that Barnardine is to be executed in the afternoon for murder. The Duke ascertains Barnardine's guilt, his refusal of counsel, and his character as dissolute and constantly drunk. The Duke manages to persuade the Provost to delay Claudio's execution for four days, truthfully saying he is no more guilty than Angelo himself, and to send Barnardine's head to Angelo in the morning instead by showing the Provost the Duke's seal. The Duke then promises that the Duke intends to return in two days, giving the Provost papers confirming this.

Act IV, Scene 3

Pompey muses on how his circle of acquaintance all seem to be present in the prison, then he and Abhorson find it difficult to rouse Barnardine for his early morning execution. The Duke witnesses the scene as Barnardine refuses to be executed when he is hungover and returns to his cell, followed by the executioners. The Provost then enters to inform the Duke that another prisoner, the pirate Ragozine, has died in the night through illness, and that this prisoner bears a much closer resemblance to Claudio. They agree to send Ragozine's head to Angelo. The Duke then reveals that he has written to Angelo, announcing his imminent return and wish to be met at the city walls in order to enter in procession. Isabella enters, and the Duke lets her believe that Angelo has reneged, that Claudio is dead, and that Claudio's head is on its way to Angelo. Isabella is both furious and distraught, and the Duke comforts her by telling her of the return of the Duke on the following day. He then advises her to interrupt the procession with her grievance against Angelo. Lucio enters to repeat his assertions of the Duke's lechery and to confirm that he has indeed fathered a prostitute's child, a fact he has previously denied before the Duke in court.

Act IV, Scene 4

Angelo and Escalus discuss the Duke's return. His letters also order a proclamation that any public complaints can be made at this time. This latter order makes Angelo privately uneasy, but he decides that Isabella would not dare to speak against him.

Act IV, Scene 5

The Duke, as himself, instructs Friar Peter to deliver letters that possibly explain his plan.

Act IV, Scene 6

Isabella and Mariana discuss the Duke's instructions on how to approach the procession. Friar Peter enters with further advice on where, precisely, to do this.

Act V, Scene 1

The Duke "returns" to Vienna and is welcomed by officials. He tells Angelo that he has heard excellent reports of his conduct. Isabella enters requesting justice. Isabella insists the Duke himself hear her complaint, while Angelo attempts to claim that she is mentally unstable due to her brother's lawful punishment. Isabella publicly accuses Angelo of hypocrisy and fornication with her, while the Duke pretends to believe Angelo's accusation of her madness. He states his confidence in Angelo's character and threatens to send Isabella to prison. Isabella cites the mysterious Friar Lodowick (the Duke's disguise) as being able to verify her story, and Lucio complicates matters by slandering the friar and accusing him of speaking out against the absent Duke. Friar Peter also claims to know Friar Lodowick as a holy and honorable man, presently ill, and claims his place as his representative.

Isabella is taken away as the Duke sets up a trial of Angelo over which Angelo presides. Mariana is brought forward, veiled, as first witness, and the Duke questions her, interrupted by jokes from Lucio. Mariana reveals that she took Isabella's place in Angelo's bed, claims her place as Angelo's wife, and removes her veil. Angelo remains composed, claiming the women are both lying. Friar Peter recommends sending the Provost to bring Friar Lodowick, while the Duke excuses himself, leaving the matter of slander in Escalus and Angelo's hands.

Isabella asks the Duke to hear her complaint in Act V, Scene 1 of *Measure for Measure*. (*Illustration by Henry Howard; engraving by John Thompson*)

Isabella returns with the Provost and the Duke back in his friar disguise. Escalus questions Isabella, saying that Mariana's testimony contradicts her own charges against Angelo and the friar, accusing him of setting up the women to slander Angelo. Encouraged by Lucio, Escalus arrests the Duke, and in the ensuing struggle, his true identity is revealed. Angelo immediately confesses, and he and Mariana are married quickly offstage. When they return, the Duke sentences Angelo to death. Mariana begs for his pardon, pleading with Isabella to join her. Isabella does, forgiving Angelo herself. The prisoners are brought onstage, and Claudio is revealed. In a single speech, the Duke presents Claudio, proposes marriage to Isabella, pardons Angelo, and finally turns on Lucio. Lucio's sentence for slander is to be whipped through the city, married to the mother of his child, and hanged. The Duke closes the play by wishing joy upon all the couples, thanking the characters who helped his plan, and restating his proposal to Isabella.

CHARACTER LIST

Isabella   A young gentlewoman ready to enter a nunnery as a novice. Isabella, who has a very strong sense of morality and virtue, is known for being articulate and persuasive.

Vincentio (the Duke) The Duke of Vienna has ruled indulgently for many years, not applying various strict laws controlling the sexual behavior of his subjects. The Duke spends most of the play in disguise as Friar Lodowick in order to witness the progress of his experiment in leaving the city in another's hands.

Angelo The Duke's proxy, left by him to rule in his supposed absence. Angelo is renowned for his virtue, self-discipline, and strict attention to the details of the law. He is also described as being of such great self-control that he is almost inhuman.

Claudio Isabella's brother, engaged to be married to Juliet. It is the premarital sexual intimacy of Claudio and Juliet that results in Claudio's death sentence. Claudio's honor is possibly debatable, given some of the company he keeps and his disappointment in Isabella's refusal to capitulate to Angelo's demands, but overall he is a sympathetic character.

Escalus An old lord and adviser to the Duke and to Angelo, Escalus can be seen as one of the moral centers of the play. His name possibly contains a pun on the scales of justice.

Lucio A friend of Claudio's. Described intriguingly in most copies as a "fantastic," Lucio is a young gentleman of liberal morals, quick wit, and bad company. The epithet *fantastic* could indicate one full of fancies or simply a flamboyant dresser. His relentless facetiousness and sexual obsession drive many of the comic scenes and ultimately get him into trouble.

Provost The officer in charge of the arrest, incarceration, and punishment of criminals; an honorable, moral, and trustworthy man.

Elbow A simpleminded policeman. Elbow is involved in apprehending the play's petty criminals and is hopelessly outwitted by most of them, at least in conversation and confession. His malapropisms provide much of the comic relief.

Mistress Overdone A retired prostitute, now a madam.

Pompey A barman and pimp working for Mistress Overdone, Pompey is also shrewd and a wit, talking his way out of one arrest, stoically imprisoned later.

Froth A rich, foolish gentleman, interested mainly in drinking.

Juliet Claudio's fiancée, pregnant with his child. Juliet takes full responsibility for her part in their supposed crime.

Mariana Angelo's ex-fiancée, cast off by him when the ship carrying her extensive dowry and her brother (and protector) was lost at sea. Angelo invented tales of her infidelity in order to legitimately annul their engagement. Mariana lives a secluded and melancholy existence in a country house. Despite all this, she still loves Angelo.

Friar Peter A friar in the Duke's confidence.

Francisca A nun of the order of Saint Clare's, the order Isabella wishes to join.

Abhorson The prison executioner.

Barnardine A dissolute and drunken prisoner, guilty of murder.

CHARACTER STUDIES
Isabella

Critics examining Isabella often see her as either a paragon of virtue or as totally unsympathetic. Praise of Isabella focuses on her moral virtue, but she is also extensively criticized for being extremist and for her alleged hypocrisy in the "sacrifice" of Mariana's virtue in exchange for her own. However, later modern criticism produces increasingly gendered or psychological readings of Isabella that emphasize her realistic complexity.

Isabella's intelligence, skill in rhetoric, and rationality is related to the audience before we see her; Claudio says she "hath prosperous art / When she will play with reason and discourse, / And well she can persuade." (1.2.165–167). This is demonstrated in Isabella's scenes with Angelo, wherein she combines a plea for mercy with logical argument— "Who is it that hath dies for this offence? / There's many have committed it" (2.2.90–91)—and accusations of tyranny which undermine Angelo's claims of justice and law. Lucio's repeated "That's well said" (2.2.92, 113) and the Provost's hopeful asides support this observation. Isabella's tirade of accusation in the play's final scene also evidences her rhetorical power: "[D]o not banish reason / For inequality, but let your reason serve / To make the truth appear where it seems hid, / And hide the false seems true" (5.1.64–67).

The tendency for many productions to costume the character in a novice's habit even though she has not yet joined the sisterhood functions as a visual signifier of Isabella's beliefs and sexual virtue. Therefore, when we are introduced to Isabella in 1.4, deep in discussion with a nun, we have already made certain suppositions about her character. Her inquiries about the harshness of life in the nunnery—"I speak not as desiring more [privileges] / But rather wishing a more strict restraint / Upon the sisterhood" (1.4.3–5)—can be seen as either commendable eagerness for spiritual improvement through physical hardship or an overzealous interest in discomfort. Any accusations of religious extremism are, however, deflated by her initial response to Claudio's problem: "O, let him marry her" (1.4.49). This is the most logical solution, and it demonstrates a pragmatic approach to problems of everyday life. Isabella's conversation with Lucio presents her as a self-possessed and wary young woman, which is possibly understandable given the society in which she lives. Lucio's relentless emphasis on her virginity, on the sexual state of female characters, is possibly reflected in Isabella herself. Indeed, it can be argued that Isabella's retreat to the nunnery is a way of both keeping herself separated from the sordid world around her and retaining personal autonomy. Isabella's virtuous moral code also leads her to forgive Angelo at the climax of the play, an action admirable in its embodiment of Christian charity.

Isabella's focus on, or obsession with, her own sexual virtue can make her seem curiously detached from the matters at hand in the play and more interested in dealing with the abstraction of issues as "More than our brother is our chastity" (2.4.186). Her initial approach to Angelo is cautious, and she seems content to accept his initial unbending answer, "Oh just but severe law: / I had

Isabella in *Measure for Measure*. This is a print from Charles Heath's 1848 edition of *The Heroines of Shakspeare: Comprising the Principal Female Characters in the Plays of the Great Poet.* (Painting by J. W. Wright; engraving by W. H. Mote)

a brother then" (2.2.42–43), leading Lucio, who compares her plea to a request for a pin, to accuse her of being "too cold" (2.2.46, 57). Similarly, Isabella's resultant conversation with her brother, while focused on the outrage of Angelo's proposition, seems curiously unsympathetic to Claudio. She says, "Oh, were it but my life / I'd throw it down for your deliverance / As frankly as a pin" (3.1.103–105), before bluntly advising Claudio to "Be ready . . . for your death tomorrow" (3.1.106). She seems to lack empathy with his terror, seeing his plea for her cooperation instead as further personal insult: "Oh, you beast! / Oh faithless coward, oh dishonest wretch! / . . . / I'll pray a thousand prayers for thy death / No word to save thee" (3.1.136–147). The prioritization of her own virtue is also seen in her complicity with the exchange of Mariana's virginity for her own, though it should be said that both female characters are reassured by the "friar" that this is legitimate because of the preexisting bond between Mariana and Angelo.

Such detachment and focus possibly has further ramifications, revealed in Isabella's conversation with Angelo. Her defiance of participating in any coerced sexual activity leads her to produce some extraordinary imagery. She says, "were I under the terms of death, / Th'impression of keen whips I'd wear as rubies, / And strip myself to death as to a bed / That longing have been sick for, ere I'd yield / My body up to shame" (2.4.100–104). It is as if, like Angelo, the continual repression of desire manifests subconsciously in fantasies of discipline and violence.

Vincentio (the Duke)

The Duke's character is another point of ambiguity in this play. His omnipresence and directive power can be viewed as evidence of his political and moral power, but also of his duplicitous nature and arrogance. The fact that he leaves his city in the hands of a deputy he suspects will not live up to expectation after failing to uphold the law for many years does not encourage the audience to see him as entirely trustworthy or as a responsible leader. However, it is the Duke who resolves all the play's issues, and his skill as an actor and director of action perhaps elevates him, potentially enabling a reading of the Duke as a dramatic function rather than a psychologically realistic character. Dramatically, his casual meddling in his subjects' affairs also embodies the presence of the state in citizens' personal lives.

The Duke explains his plan to Friar Thomas as being a necessity of his own leniency in enforcing the strict laws of Vienna, the result of which is an inversion of the natural state: "Liberty plucks Justice by the nose, / The baby beats the nurse" (1.3.30–31). His sudden reinforcement of these laws, he says, would be "tyranny" (1.3.37), and so it is left to Angelo. Whether this is responsible leadership or not, it is certain that the Duke is aware of the implications of his decisions. The official characters are entirely loyal to the Duke, which indicates we are to comply with this view and see his machinations as the moral resolutions of Angelo's mistakes. Escalus says that the Duke is "A gentleman of all temperance" (3.2.204). Temperance—a moderate approach in government between justice and mercy, between unrestrained desire and strict restraint—is a vital ethical virtue, which suggests the intention of a positive view of the Duke.

Lucio's opinion of the Duke is, however, rather different. These scenes of slander may be intended as purely comic in Lucio's extravagant lies, yet his accusations of the Duke's lechery, drinking, and stupidity could contain an uncomfortable grain of truth. Lucio says the Duke's lechery is such that "he would mouth with a beggar though she smelt brown bread and garlic" (3.2.155–156). While this is probably in itself wildly untrue, it is a fact that the Duke has been lax in applying laws concerning fornication. That immediately after the conversation with Lucio the Duke seeks reassurance from the loyal Escalus—"of what disposition was the Duke?" (3.2.198)—perhaps indicates he is not above insecurity regarding how he is seen by the people, despite his knowledge that "No might nor greatness in mortality" / Can censure "scape" (3.2.158–159) and therefore also, perhaps, indicates a touch of vanity.

The Duke's disguise as a friar involves hearing the confession of Claudio, Juliet, Mariana, and, he claims, Angelo. This usurpation of church authority is potentially rather suspect, but the conflation of church and state sits more comfortably in considering the Protestant background of the play in the ruler being head of both institutions. The Duke's philosophizing on death with Claudio in 3.1 also conveys relevant gravitas here, though it should also be remembered that he is a consummate actor.

The Duke's most contentious action is letting Isabella believe Claudio has been executed after the theoretical surrendering of her virginity. The Duke's reason for doing this is "To make her heavenly comforts of despair / When it is least expected" (4.3.101–102), which is not a satisfactory explanation. It could be argued that the revelation of Claudio, alive and well at the play's climax, may be used as leverage in the Duke's proposal to Isabella, as he makes clear that he personally saved her brother and delivers him safely back to her immediately before proposing. Isabella's gratitude for this is possibly intended to sway her response. If so, then this action reveals a ruthless side to the Duke and an extensive test of Isabella, yet it certainly complies with his capacity for scheming and his manipulative skill as evidenced through the entire preceding plot.

Angelo

Angelo is a man who badly fails to live up to his own impossible ideals. Angelo's intentions are entirely honorable, if rather severe; to follow and enforce the law that has become, as he puts it, a "scarecrow" (2.1.1). He is confident in his own virtue, as he preaches, "'Tis one thing to be tempted . . . / Another thing to fall" (2.1.17–18), but his latent hypocrisy in being only "outward-sainted" (3.1.88) is self-evident in his treatment of Isabella and in his capacity for deception in his despicable failure to keep to his bargain. Angelo's reputation and capability are evidenced in the Duke's choice of him to be the deputy in his absence. The only external remark on his character in relation to this is Escalus's statement that "If any in Vienna be of worth / To undergo such ample grace and honor / It is Lord Angelo" (1.1.22–24).

However, when the Duke confirms to Friar Thomas that Angelo is "A man of stricture and firm abstinence" (1.3.13), the comment concentrates firmly on Angelo's self-discipline and self-denial rather than any external manifestation of morality or judgment. It is these qualities that elevate Angelo in the play world where discipline and abstinence are lax. Similarly, Lucio describes Angelo's blood as being "snow-broth" (1.4.58) and as "one who never feels / The wanton stings and motions of the sense, / But doth rebate and

blunt his natural edge / With profits of the mind: study and fast" (1.4.58–61). The Duke says Angelo "Stands at a guard with envy, scarce confesses / That his blood flows, or that his appetite / Is more to bread than stone. Hence shall we see, / If power changes purpose, what our seemers be" (1.3.52–55). This revealing statement reiterates both Angelo's unnatural self-control, as also articulated by Lucio, and the Duke's suspicions that Angelo's carefully constructed personal virtue will be tested in his new role. An interesting contextual point is that the Duke describes Angelo as "precise" (1.3.51), which relates his religious intolerance and extremism to a contemporary group of powerful Puritans known as "precisians," who also campaigned for stricter punishments, as mentioned above. This possibly suggests that Angelo's reputed virtue is not to be taken at face value, given contemporary social and theatrical frustration with Puritanical pronouncements.

Lucio, whose perception makes his facetious statements carry more weight than sometimes supposed, describes Angelo as being inhuman, "not made by man and woman after this downright way of creation" (3.2.91–92); and as the offspring of a mermaid or fish—"Some report a sea-maid spawned him, some, that he was begot between two stock-fishes" (3.2.95–96)—who urinates "congealed ice" (3.2.97). Lucio's fantasy of unnatural procreation and perversion both indicates the anomalous existence of Angelo and his beliefs in the fictional Vienna and informs a reading of Angelo's character that sees his excessive control as forcing natural desire to manifest, arguably like Isabella's, in alternative ways.

Angelo's self-denial and repressed desires surface in his reaction to Isabella. He analyses his motivation for desiring Isabella, demonstrating a self-awareness that possibly makes his hypocrisy worse, and he concludes that it is her extreme virtue and righteous rhetoric that attract him to her: "[T]his virtuous maid / Subdues me quite" (2.3.189–190); "She speaks, and 'tis such sense / That my sense breeds with it." (2.2.146–147). Angelo's confusion is evident: "What dost thou or what art thou

Angelo? / Dost thou desire her foully for those things / That make her good?" (2.3.177–179). His desire, however, though he professes at one point to "love" her (2.4.142), is not seen as a positive feeling. As can be seen in the previous quote, he desires Isabella "foully." The same disgust with which he views unregulated sexuality and brothels—"these filthy vices" (2.4.41), which he intends to eradicate—informs his articulation of his own desire. He wants Isabella, but he wants to ruin her purity, suggesting she "Give up your body to such sweet uncleanness" (2.4.53). This combination of prohibition and destruction is what he finds sexually exciting. Mariana, allegedly cast off for economic reasons (suggesting a further hypocritical aspect of Angelo in his greed), is entirely legitimate in terms of sexual availability, but Angelo does not want her.

Lucio

Lucio provides a mouthpiece for the city's lowlife and for the moral ambivalence that runs throughout much of the play. Though he associates freely with Vienna's underclass, his loyalty is not with them. He denies Pompey any assistance or bail, cheerfully saying, "Well then, imprison him: if imprisonment be the due of a bawd, why, 'tis his right. Bawd is he" (3.2.59–60). Lucio's amoral mindset sees no problem in Pompey being punished for being exactly what he is.

Lucio is evidently a libertine, but he believes Isabella's virginity elevates her: "I hold you as a thing enskied and sainted, / By your renouncement an immortal spirit, / And to be talked with in sincerity / As with a saint" (1.4.34–37). It is difficult not to read these lines as ironic, but Lucio's insistence in Isabella's worth and virtue is consistent. He also believes it is a view universally acknowledged, saying that "when maidens sue / Men give like gods, but when they weep and kneel / All their petitions are as freely theirs / As they themselves would owe them" (1.4.80–83). In contrast, he accepts his own lack of moral virtue casually, joking about his probable venereal disease (1.2.36), and he comprehends sexual behavior lightly, describing

Claudio's predicament as being in danger of being "lost at [because of] a game of tick-tack" (1.2.171). Lucio describes the prostitute mother of his unacknowledged child as a "rotten medlar" (4.3.161), and his general attitude toward the sexual economy is deeply ambivalent. His final statement, "Marrying a punk . . . is pressing to death, whipping and hanging!" (5.1.514–515), articulates the contempt with which he holds such women. Lucio's views on the female characters, as virgins or whores, convey a distillation of the play's ideological system. Some critics have found his interaction with female characters to evidence his superficiality, but it is the same ideological division that informs the entire viewpoint of the play world. The value of Isabella's virginity, the contempt with which sexuality is discussed, the commodification of all female characters, and Mariana's confusing status as not "maid, widow . . . wife" (5.1.177)—all function within tenets that divide women into these polarized extremes.

Lucio can be read as a version of Shakespeare's wise fool, in that his trivial speech is also truthful, exposed by a cynicism that sees through the unrealistic ideals of many of the play's "higher" characters. He is also extremely perceptive. Lucio's initial conversation with the disguised Duke, where he says, "It was a mad fantastical trick of him [the Duke] to steal from the state and usurp the beggary he was never born to" (3.2.82–83), has led some critics to suggest that he immediately sees through the Duke's disguise, but this is not supported by Lucio's following suicidal barrage of slander directed at the apparently absent Duke. Similarly, Lucio's characterization of "the old fantastical Duke of dark corners" (4.3.147–148) is at the least dramatic irony; it also draws an intriguing parallel between the "fantastical" Duke with his "mad fantastical trick[s]" (3.2.82) and Lucio, described in the Dramatis Personae as "a fantastic." Lucio's accusation that the Duke himself "had some feeling of the sport" (3.2.104)—that is, the sport of womanizing—and therefore would be more sympathetic than the inhuman-seeming Angelo, is expanded with charges of the Duke's liking of drink and whoring, "your beggar of fifty: and his use was, to put a ducat in her clack-dish . . . He would be drunk too" (3.2.110–112). How far are we to suppose these claims are entirely fabricated? Lucio's evaluation of Angelo's perversity is extremely near to the truth, as is his musing on the unrealistic aim of eradicating lust from human nature, noting that "it is impossible to extirp it quite . . . till eating and drinking be put down" (3.2.90–91). His commentary on the interaction between Isabella and Angelo also reveals and stresses Isabella's initial lack of conviction: "If you should need a pin, / You could not with more tame a tongue desire it" (2.2.46–47). It also reveals the potential perception of her as "too cold" (2.2.46, 57). These insights function to both convey Lucio's perceptive nature and increase the complexity of other characters.

Lucio's illuminating undermining of the leading characters combined with his comedic function and sexual license constitute a reading that potentially sees Lucio as an agent of chaos and resistance. This latter point is dramatized in Lucio's interactions with the disguised Duke, in which Lucio's casual slander serves to undermine how the Duke presumes he is seen in his subjects' eyes, and ultimately in Lucio's containment through marriage and execution. Lucio, like the other "low" characters, exists independently of the moral framework that governs the actions of the characters charged with keeping moral order or attempting to live by that framework. Lucio is unlike the other low characters in his higher class (he is friends with young gentleman Claudio), in his articulate speech, and in his detachment from the economic investment in the existence or destruction of the stews. Lucio represents disorder—amoral, challenging, facetious, disrespectful, and anarchic.

DIFFICULTIES OF THE PLAY

For many readers, the difficulty of *Measure for Measure* derives from its striking ambiguity. Some readers find it difficult to empathize with the characters, especially Isabella. This introduces a further difficulty in the appreciation of the surrounding theological and philosophical issues and debates. Isabella's motivation for denying Angelo's request can seem excessively zealous, even selfish, to a modern, increasingly secular audience. In a similar vein, the Duke's motivation is also questioned. Suspicion of these characters and the uncertainty of whether the play is intended to be comic or not can leave the reader or audience member feeling uneasy and dissatisfied at the conclusion.

Isabella's protection of her chastity may seem extreme to some modern readers, but it is based on a standard contemporary interpretation of sin and damnation. Isabella believes—and we can arguably be certain of her religious conviction because of her intended vocation—that if she sacrifices her virginity and sexual honor to save Claudio's life, then she will be eternally damned to hell for this sin. As she says to Angelo, "I had rather give my body than my soul" (2.4.55), a witty answer that sounds like a capitulation but is not—by giving her body in a sexual sense, Isabella *would* be giving her soul. She repeatedly says she would, however, give her body in death: "were it but my life / I'd throw it down for your deliverance / As frankly as a pin" (3.1.103–105). She is willing to retain her virtue and renounce the physical world for spiritual salvation. Similarly, Isabella claims she would endure physical torture, "ere I'd yield / My body up to shame" (2.4.103–104). On the other hand, if Isabella retains her honor, and Claudio is executed, he will spend eternity in heaven as long as he is fully confessed. Physical death and spiritual death are not of the same importance, with physical existence believed to be short in comparison to the afterlife of the soul. There exists a wealth of philosophical and theological discussion with regard to the specifics of such a situation. The separation of body and soul in sexual dishonor was discussed by Augustine, among others, and no definitive conclusion was ever reached by such thinkers. Shakespeare offers conflicting interpretations of this dilemma in the mouths of his characters, particularly in Isabella and Angelo's discussion in 2.4. Both Claudio and Angelo, neither objectively, attempt to persuade Isabella that committing a sin to save a life is a positive action and that virtue is a spiritual, rather than physical, condition. Claudio argues, "What sin you do to save a brother's life, / Nature dispenses with the deed so far / That it becomes a virtue" (3.1.134–136), and Angelo agrees: "Might there not be a charity in sin / To save this brother's life?" (2.4.63–64). However, in Isabella's interpretation, even a forced sin is a sin, and she sticks firmly to her argument, as a "shamèd life" is "hateful" (3.1.117).

Isabella asks Claudio to prepare for death since she cannot save his life by renouncing her virtue in Act III, Scene 1 of *Measure for Measure*. This is a print from Malcolm C. Salaman's 1916 edition of *Shakespeare in Pictorial Art*. (*Painting by W. Holman Hunt*)

In addition to Isabella's fixed belief system, her later actions in the play and her angry denouncement of her brother limit the empathy of some audience members or readers, even when they appreciate the contextual reasoning behind her unwillingness to sacrifice her virginity. Isabella's complicity with the substitution of Mariana in her place has led to accusations of hypocrisy. While empathy is largely a subjective reaction, and in performance Isabella's powerlessness and naïveté can be stressed by the physical presence of the Duke, who dominates her actions from the third act onward, Isabella's ambiguity does fit perfectly within the play. As such, it is possibly the inconclusive nature of the play as a whole that is the sticking point for readers and audiences. As discussed previously, the play's generic confusion makes it a more "modern" text than many contemporary plays. If an audience expects a straightforward Shakespearean romantic comedy, then they are likely to be disappointed. However, the comedy present in *Measure for Measure* is not atypical of contemporary texts: Crudity, lewdness, mockery, and cruelty are all central ingredients to many contemporary comic dramas. What is different and thereby potentially disturbing or unsatisfactory in this play is how the darker comic elements relate to the romantic elements. Here, the romantic element is largely reduced to sex and tempered with political, philosophical, and theological ideologies. This makes the insertion of the conventional marriages and betrothals in the climactic final scene even more unexpected. Here, too, however, the play's characteristic uncompromisingly multifaceted play world and thematic complexities refuse to be repressed. Aside from Claudio and Juliet, the pairings-off in the finale include an unanswered proposal to a novice nun whose exposure to the outside world has severely tested her convictions and two forced marriages to legitimize sexual actions previously committed, one of which, we are informed, is a sentence worse than death. Such difficulties in the text are paradoxically also its strength, leading to the play's more recent critical popularity and raising a wealth of questions, if not satisfaction, for all observers.

KEY PASSAGES
Act I, Scene 2, 128–158

LUCIO. Why, how now, Claudio? Whence comes this restraint?

CLAUDIO. From too much liberty, my Lucio, liberty.
As surfeit is the father of much fast,
So every scope by the immoderate use
Turns to restraint. Our natures do pursue
Like rats that ravin down their proper bane
A thirsty evil, and when we drink, we die.

LUCIO. If I could speak so wisely under an arrest, I would send for certain of my creditors; and yet, to say the truth, I had as life have the foppery of freedom as the morality of imprisonment. What's thy offence, Claudio?

CLAUDIO. What but to speak of would offend again.

LUCIO. What, is't murder?

CLAUDIO. No.

LUCIO. Lechery?

CLAUDIO. Call it so.

PROVOST. Away, sir, you must go.

CLAUDIO. One word, good friend: Lucio, a word with you.

LUCIO. A hundred, if they'll do you any good. Is lechery so looked after?

CLAUDIO. Thus stands it with me. Upon a true contract
I got possession of Julietta's bed—
You know the lady, she is fast my wife,
Save that we do the denunciation lack
Of outward order. This we came not to
Only for propagation of a dower
Remaining in the coffer of her friends,
From whom we thought it meet to hide our love
Till time had made them for us. But it chances
The stealth of our most mutual entertainment
With character too gross is writ on Juliet.

This scene dramatizes the ramifications of Angelo's enforcement of the law and introduces various characters who shall become victims of it: Mistress Overdone, Lucio, Pompey, Claudio, and Juliet. In the passage quoted above, Claudio explains his arrest to Lucio and in doing so reveals several main points of interest in the play. First, Claudio's description of his own crime both anticipates what the Duke says about the results of allowing the laws to be relaxed—that too much liberty is the cause of unregulated behavior—and conveys how sexual intercourse is viewed within this play. Even though Claudio is referring to the act between himself and the woman he loves and wants to marry, he describes it as akin to "rats that ravin down their proper bane / A thirsty evil"—that is, an image of rats ravenously swallowing poison. In this description, Claudio's desire for Juliet is likened to irrational self-destruction rather than an expression of mutual love and desire. Similarly, his description of the proof of his and Juliet's sexual activity in her pregnancy as the "character too gross is writ on Juliet" is highly ambivalent and hardly encouraging. The licentious world the characters move in is also evident in Lucio's surprised response to Claudio's arrest, "Is lechery so looked after?" Up until this point, it seems, lechery is very much part of the social fabric of everyday life, as evidenced in Lucio's opening conversation with the two gentlemen, joking about venereal disease.

In addition, Claudio's description of his and Juliet's relationship heightens the unjust nature of his punishment and would probably encourage a contemporary audience to feel increased sympathy for their situation. They are, he says, as good as married. Juliet is "fast [his] wife," in that the two are contracted verbally. This was perceived as being a legal bond, lacking only, as Claudio says, "denunciation" "of outward order"—that is, it has not been publicly announced or solemnized by the church. The fact that this affirmation follows Claudio's previous disconcerting description of his and Juliet's sexual activity makes the former even more unexpected. The precise nature of pre-contracted marriage and the sexual morality surrounding it introduced in this scene is reiterated in the case of Mariana and Angelo and the characters' lack of moral quibbles over duping Angelo into sleeping with the virginal Mariana, as well as her claim in the final scene to be Angelo's "wife" even though they are not officially married. The severe demarcations over what is and is not socially acceptable with regard to sexual behavior are blurred here and throughout the play; sexual desire is contained within the social structure of marriage, but exactly what constitutes such marital license is by no means clear-cut. As such, the sexual liberty running rampant in Vienna is demonstrated to be found not just in the stews and brothels and among such individuals as loose young men and prostitutes. It seems to be a problem, or at least an aspect of life, that pervades the social strata.

Act I, Scene 3, 19–54

DUKE. We have strict statutes and most biting laws,
The needful bits and curbs to headstrong weeds,
Which for this fourteen years we have let slip,
Even like an o'er-grown lion in a cave
That goes not out to prey. Now, as fond fathers
Having bound up the threatening twigs of birch
Only to stick it in their children's sight
For terror, not to use—in time the rod
More mocked than feared—so our decrees,
Dead to infliction, to themselves are dead,
And Liberty plucks Justice by the nose,
The baby beats the nurse, and quite athwart
Goes all decorum.

FRIAR. It rested in your grace
To unloose this tied-up justice when you pleased,
And it in you more dreadful would have seemed
Than in Lord Angelo.

DUKE. I do fear, too dreadful.
Sith 'twas my fault to give the people scope,
'Twould be my tyranny to strike and gall them
For what I bid them do: for we bid this be done
When evil deeds have their permissive pass
And not the punishment. Therefore indeed, my father,
I have on Angelo imposed the office,
Who may in th'ambush of my name strike home,
And yet my nature never in the fight
To do in slander. And to behold his sway
I will, as 'twere a brother of your order,
Visit both prince and people. Therefore I prithee
Supply me with the habit, and instruct me
How I may formally in person bear
Like a true friar. More reasons for this action
At our more leisure shall I render you;
Only this one: Lord Angelo is precise,
Stands at guard with envy, scarce confesses
That his blood flows, or that his appetite
Is more to bread than stone. Hence shall we see,
If power change purpose, what our seemers be.

This short scene is crucial in understanding the play, as the Duke explains his reasoning behind his plan to pretend to leave the city so that Angelo can enforce certain laws that he, the Duke, has not over the past years of his rule. In the opening scene of the play, the audience is led to believe, as are the other characters onstage, that the Duke is to undertake a state visit and so leave the governing of Vienna to Angelo and Escalus. It is in this scene, and specifically the passage above, where we learn of the Duke's real intentions. This scene is important because one of the play's central questions is the Duke's motivation in his pretended absence and in his own unwillingness to reinforce the law.

The Duke considers his subjects to be unbroken horses requiring "bits and curbs" and "weeds," in a dual image which implies that the lack of policing subjects' affairs inevitably has led to the current situation, and that individuals cannot be trusted to act within the law if it is not enforced. This possibly relates retrospectively to Claudio's description of his desire as an animalistic, suicidal drive discussed in the preceding key passage, which, unchecked, urges on self-destructive behavior. The image of the horse is from Plato, who compared the aspect of the human soul that feels physical desire to a headstrong horse that needs to be kept under control by the rational part of the soul. The Duke describes the state of Vienna as one of inversion, where "The baby beats the nurse," which conveys the unnatural order of things. Chaotic inversion is a common contemporary image of societies not conforming to the given lawful order, again implicating the necessity of law enforcement. The Duke himself is both a contented lion and a "fond father," both standard regal images, in his 14-year lenience. He offers no real reason for this lenience but asserts that his reason for leaving it to Angelo to reinforce the law is that it would be tyranny to do so himself. He says that his lack of punishment is the same as endorsing illegal behavior: "'Twould be my tyranny to strike and gall them / For what I bid them do: for we bid this be done / When evil deeds have their permissive pass / And not the punishment."

The Duke's intention to mingle among his subjects in the disguise of a monk is also made clear here, in a motif common to folktales and also used by Shakespeare in *Henry V* (1599). The purpose this device usually serves is so the ruler can avert some injustice, as in this case, but also be made familiar with the common people and their lives, problems, and daily trials. This often also includes hearing some opinions of themselves they may not wish to hear, in an exercise in humility and grace under criticism. The Duke is immediately immersed in injustice and deception, and yet he seems to enjoy manipulating events to his, and others', advantage. The disguised Duke also makes the presence of state law in subjects' lives visible onstage. To continue with this concept, it could also be argued that the Duke's resolution to the problems of the plot also suggests both the necessity and the benevolence of the regulatory state laws.

This passage also is the first indication of another purpose of the Duke's plan and of his lack of total trust in Angelo. He states that Angelo is "precise," which allies Angelo with Puritan extremism and thereby suggests to the audience that Angelo is not to be taken at virtuous face value. The Duke also finds Angelo too controlled, he "scarce confesses / That his blood flows," and so either suspects that Angelo potentially has dangerous weaknesses or simply wants to see if power itself will corrupt him, "If power change purpose." This aspect invites tension in the scenes to come between Isabella and Angelo, as the audience wonders what such a man will do. Yet it also possibly reassures the audience that the Duke is in control of the play's action and that nothing too bad will happen to the characters introduced in the preceding scene.

Act II, Scene 2, 163–187

ANGELO. What's this? What's this? Is this her fault, or mine?
The tempter or the tempted, who sins most, ha?
Not she: nor doth she tempt: but it is I
That, lying by the violet in the sun,
Do as the carrion does, not as the flower,
Corrupt with virtuous season. Can it be
That modesty may more betray our sense
Than woman's lightness? Having waste ground enough
Shall we desire to raze the sanctuary
And pitch our evils there? Oh fie, fie, fie,
What dost thou or what art thou, Angelo?
Dost thou desire her foully for those things
That make her good? Oh, let her brother live:
Thieves for their robbery have authority
When judges steal themselves. What, do I love her

That I desire to hear her speak again
And feast upon her eyes? What is't I dream on?
Oh cunning enemy that, to catch a saint,
With saints doth bait thy hook! Most
   dangerous
Is that temptation that doth goad us on
To sin in loving virtue. Never could the
   strumpet
With all her double vigour, art, and nature,
Once stir my temper; but this virtuous maid
Subdues me quite. Ever till now
When men were fond, I smiled, and wondered
   how.

Angelo's soliloquy closes the scene of his first meeting with Isabella, wherein she registers her plea for Claudio's life. Isabella has proved herself an intelligent and pious debater, leading Angelo to instruct her to return the following day for his verdict. The above soliloquy superbly articulates Angelo's confusion at his own desire for Isabella and provides an insightful analysis of the reasons for it.

This soliloquy is vital in the wider scheme of the play for understanding Angelo's character and motivation in his dealings with Isabella: his desire for her; the reason for this desire; and his continued simultaneous disgust for it, which is a potential reason for him not keeping the bargain he makes with Isabella. Angelo immediately places the blame for his stirrings of desire on himself; Isabella has done nothing—"Not she: nor doth she tempt"—to encourage this feeling. As a result, Angelo depicts himself as "carrion" putrefying in the sun instead of flourishing like a healthy plant, and here the beginning of the interesting paradox he feels in his desire can be found. Angelo fully admits his reasons for desiring Isabella, but he is still unable (like most characters in the play) to see this as anything positive. As it is, he uses the aforementioned image of decay and says that he "desire[s] her foully."

The audience is informed that "light" women—that is, women of light morals, or "strumpet[s]"—do not attract Angelo. The sort of woman we must suppose is easy enough to find in Shakespeare's Vienna, who attempts seduction with "double

vigour," leaves him entirely unaffected. Such a statement indicates the reasons why Angelo is considered an anomaly in his society, and yet it also offers some deeper understanding as to his desire for Isabella. If Vienna is indeed the permissive society suggested by the scenes thus far, then perhaps the relentless temptation and visible sexual availability is desensitizing to Angelo. Though he suggests part of his fascination is Isabella's beauty and intelligence—"I desire to hear her speak again / And feast upon her eyes"—the main reason behind this attraction is also, ironically, the aspect of Isabella that would be destroyed if Angelo achieves his desire. He wants her "for those things / That make her good": her modesty, faith, virtue, and virginity, relative rarities in this setting. He compares Isabella to a sanctuary and a saint: a sanctuary that he, inexplicably to himself, wants to destroy, and a saint sent by the "cunning enemy," the devil, to tempt him to sin. It is interesting that Angelo exhibits his extreme vanity in figuring himself as another saint, implicitly drawing a comparison between himself and Isabella, and yet is also entirely aware of his own hypocrisy. As he says, "Oh, let her brother live: / Thieves for their robbery have authority / When judges steal themselves."

Act II, Scene 4, 88–113

ANGELO. Admit no other way to save his
   life—
As I subscribe not that, nor any other,
But in the loss of question—that you, his sister,
Finding yourself desired of such a person
Whose credit with the judge, or own great
   place,
Could fetch your brother from the manacles
Of the all-binding law, and that there were
No earthly mean to save him, but that either
You must lay down the treasures of your body
To this supposed, or else to let him suffer:
What would you do?

ISABELLA. As much for my poor brother for
   myself:
That is, were I under the terms of death,

Th'impression of keen whips I'd wear as rubies,
And strip myself to death as to a bed
That longing have been sick for, ere I'd yield
My body up to shame.

ANGELO. Then must your brother die.

ISABELLA. And 'twere the cheaper way:
Better it were a brother dies at once,
Than that a sister by redeeming him
Should die for ever.

ANGELO. Were you not then as cruel as the
sentence
That you have slandered so?

ISABELLA. Ignomy in ransom and free
pardon
Are of two houses: lawful mercy
Is nothing kin to foul redemption.

This passage occurs during the second meeting of Angelo and Isabella, where he denies her plea for Claudio's life and yet continues the debate concerning justice and mercy. The audience's knowledge of Angelo's desire for Isabella contributes an undercurrent to his questions and responses, which come to a head in this brief passage. Angelo pretends here to be talking entirely theoretically in positing to Isabella the question of what she would do if propositioned by someone in power who could save Claudio's life if she slept with them and the ethics surrounding such a choice. Following this passage, Angelo propositions Isabella directly, as she seems unaware of his many hints.

Angelo's tentativeness is conveyed in his supposition through its punctuation; the hyphens, subordinate clauses, and clarifications appear awkward and stilted as Angelo, through nervousness or excitement, tests his idea on Isabella. Isabella's response is helpful in understanding both her character and her strict moral code, which sees Angelo's suggestion as entirely out of the question. Her initial reply here is interesting in its imagery of whips, stripping, and beds and its focus on her own naked

Angelo offers to free Claudio if Isabella will sleep with him in Act II, Scene 4 of *Measure for Measure*. This is a print from the Boydell Shakespeare Gallery project, which was conceived in 1786 and lasted until 1805. *(Painting by Robert Smirke; engraving by William Charles Wilson)*

body as an expression of the physical martyrdom she would be willing to undergo to achieve spiritual salvation. These images, however, are also arguably sadomasochistic. It has been suggested that Isabella subconsciously expresses her own sexual desire through images of violence and restraint, possibly resulting from her abstinence inducing a redirection of her desire, which also potentially draws parallels between her own self-control and Angelo's deviation from his. This theory suggests that if sexual desire is repressed, then it will manifest in alternative forms.

Isabella's central reasoning for both her theoretical and actual refusal to agree to give up her virginity to save Claudio is simply put here: "Better it were a brother dies at once, / Than that a sister by redeeming him / Should die for ever." As explained in the section on Difficulties of the Play, for Isabella, following Christian beliefs, physical death and spiritual death are hugely differentiated, with the greater emphasis on the latter. For someone with entire faith in this concept, Isabella is right. There is no sense in her sacrificing her immortal soul just so her brother's physical life can be extended for the relatively short time he will be alive. The moral debate that the play instigates is instead the parameters of Isabella's sacrifice—that is, whether it is sinful to commit a sin to save another's life, or if sexual intercourse is forced whether a sin is committed at all, and whether her own faith is this unshakable. This is a huge classical and contemporary philosophical and theoretical question, which yields no definitive answer.

In the passage above, following Isabella's fierce rejection of Angelo's theory, their conversation reverts to a debate on the ethics of Claudio's crime and the respective roles of justice and mercy. Angelo suggests that by letting her brother die when she could prevent it, Isabella is as good as killing him herself, potentially preempting criticism from the audience for her forthcoming decision, which Isabella is more than capable of contesting.

Act V, Scene 1, 168–178

DUKE. First let her show her face, and after speak.

MARIANA. Pardon, my lord, I will not show my face
Until my husband bid me.

DUKE. What, are you married?

MARIANA. No, my lord.

DUKE. Are you a maid?

MARIANA. No, my lord.

DUKE. A widow, then?

MARIANA. Neither, my lord.

DUKE. Why, you are nothing then: neither maid, widow, nor wife?

LUCIO. My lord, she may be a punk, for many of them are neither maid, widow, nor wife.

This brief passage is taken from the long final scene, and it is included as an illustration of the gender politics of the play world, and, by extension, of 17th-century England. Isabella has interrupted the Duke's procession back into Vienna with accusations against Angelo, and Mariana is brought forward as a witness.

Mariana's introduction of her "husband" functions to keep the issue of the ethics surrounding marital contracts at the foreground of the play. This issue, introduced at the beginning of the play in the entrance of Claudio and Juliet, underpins their case, Mariana's lack of sin in sleeping with Angelo, and a general ambiguity in the sexual morality depicted in the play. It is not just prostitutes, pimps, and those who use them who are punished by the draconian laws governing personal sexual behavior, but also individuals nearer to conceptions of respectability and licensed sexuality. Desire is contained within marriage, but a contemporary precontracted couple, sometimes engaged for years for financial or familial reasons, inhabits a rather "grey" area within the related laws. In Mariana's case, the consummation of her and Angelo's contract has made their marriage legally binding, at least in her, the Duke's, and Isabella's opinion, none of which, it should be noted, is without personal investment.

Mariana is not, however, officially married, and so begins the Duke's riddle in his attempt to find out what she "is." If Mariana is not married, a virgin, or a widow, he cannot think of any other socially acceptable "thing" for her to be. Needless to say, all of these are positions that depend on the

Mariana in *Measure for Measure*. This is a print from Charles Heath's 1848 edition of *The Heroines of Shakspeare: Comprising the Principal Female Characters in the Plays of the Great Poet. (Painting by J. W. Wright; engraving by T. Knight)*

DIFFICULT PASSAGES
Act II, Scene 1, 47–82

ELBOW. If it please your honour, I am the poor Duke's constable, and my name is Elbow. I do lean upon justice, sir, and do bring in here, before your good honour, two notorious benefactors.

ANGELO. Benefactors? Well, what benefactors are they? Are they not malefactors?

ELBOW. If it please your honour, I know not well what they are: but precise villains they are, that I am sure of, and void of all profanation in the world that good Christians ought to have.

ESCALUS. This comes off well: here's a wise officer.

ANGELO. Go to. What quality are they of? Elbow is your name? Why dost not speak, Elbow?

POMPEY. He cannot sir: he's out at elbow.

ANGELO. What are you, sir?

ELBOW. He, sir? A tapster, sir, parcel bawd, one that serves a bad woman, whose house, sir, was, as they say, plucked down in the suburbs; and now she professes a hot-house; which I think is a very ill house too.

ESCALUS. How know you that?

ELBOW. My wife, sir, whom I detest before heaven and your honour—

ESCALUS. How? Thy wife?

ELBOW. Ay, sir: whom I thank heaven is an honest woman—

ESCALUS. Dost thou detest her therefore?

woman's relation to men and her resultant sexual state. This sexual economy runs throughout the entire play, and through contemporary society. If sexual activity, at least for women, is only legitimate through marriage, then an unmarried non-virgin has no sphere of existence—that is unless, as Lucio typically, helpfully, suggests, she is a "punk," a prostitute. Here, female sexuality is either contained through marriage or reviled through sexual excess. The Duke's joke reiterates this. When he says, "Why, you are nothing then," there is a pun on "nothing": "Nothing" is common contemporary slang for the female genitalia. In having no "thing" (i.e. no penis), and unable to be labeled, Mariana is indeed, in her society, nothing.

ELBOW. I say, sir, I will detest myself also, as well as she, that this house, if it be not a bawd's house. It is pity of her life, for it is a naughty house.

ESCALUS. How dost thou know that, constable?

ELBOW. Marry, sir, by my wife, who, if she had been a woman cardinally given, might have been accused in fornication, adultery, and all uncleanliness there.

The difficulty of this passage is not that its comedy is dependent on labyrinthine and archaic puns, but in demonstrating how these comic scenes of "low" characters relate to both the play as a whole and the main plot. At hand here are issues of class and language, as Elbow strives to be linguistically respectable and yet succeeds only in being laughable, confusing "benefactors" with "malefactors," "profanation" with, possibly, "profession," and "detest" with "attest." Later in the scene, Pompey offers a parody of overly verbose legal language and literally talks his way out of trouble in direct contrast to the minion of the law's inability to use language convincingly. Issues of rhetoric pervade the play—in Isabella and Angelo's debates, for example—and this passage offers a comic take on the potential inaccuracies of language.

Elbow's wayward language also resonates among wider issues. His description of Pompey and Froth as "precise villains" relates directly to Angelo, who, as has been discussed, is both "precise," or Puritan, and a villain. The confusion of all good Christians having "profanation" and Elbow's wife being suspected of being "cardinally," rather than "carnally," inclined, directly relates to the hypocrisy of Angelo's external virtue and inner corruption, as well as potentially being a wider comment on the corruption of religion.

The concept of the comic scenes informing the wider narrative also applies to the opening of this scene, where Lucio and two gentlemen exchange jokes based on venereal disease and shared experience of the brothels, aspects that feed into the general approach to and description of sexuality and sexual experience in the play. Jokes are made out of situations to be feared, i.e. contracting syphilis, and in the sharing of such jokes, fear is made communal and potentially expelled.

Act V, Scene 1, 342–378

LUCIO. Oh thou damnable fellow, did not I pluck thee by the nose for thy speeches?

DUKE. I protest I love the Duke as I love myself.

ANGELO. Hark how the villain would close now, after his treasonable abuses.

ESCALUS. Such a fellow is not to be talked withal: away with him to prison. Where is the provost? Away with him to prison. Lay bolts enough upon him. Let him speak no more. Away with those giglets too, and with the other confederate companion.

DUKE. Stay, sir, stay a while.

ANGELO. What, resists he? Help him, Lucio!

LUCIO. Come, sir, come, sir, come, sir! Foh, sir! Why, you bald-pated, lying rascal, you must be hooded, must you? Show your knave's visage, with a pox to you! Show your sheep-biting face, and be hanged an hour! Will't not off? *[Pulls off the friar's hood and reveals the Duke]*

DUKE. Thou art the first knave that e'er mad'st a duke!
First, provost, let me bail these gentle three—
[To Lucio] Sneak not away, sir, for the friar and you
Must have a word anon.—Lay hold on him.

LUCIO. This may prove worse than hanging.

DUKE. *[To Escalus]* What you have spoke, I pardon. Sit you down.

We'll borrow place of him. *[To Angelo]* Sir, by
   your leave:
Hast thou or word or wit or impudence
That yet can do thee office? If thou hast,
Rely upon it till my tale be heard,
And hold no longer out.

ANGELO. Oh, my dread lord,
I should be guiltier than my guiltiness
To think I can be undiscernible
When I perceive your grace, like power divine,
Hath looked upon my passes. Then, good
   prince,
No longer session hold upon my shame,
But let my trial be mine own confession:
Immediate sentence then, and sequent death,
Is all the grace I beg.

The difficulty of this passage is the rapidity of
the action, which makes it difficult for the reader
to grasp how the scene brings together most of
the entire play's issues. In condensed form, we
are shown a miscarriage of justice, Angelo's corruption, Lucio's slander, and the Duke's disguise,
while the scene also contains many parallels to the

The Duke reveals himself to Angelo and sentences the
latter to death in Act V, Scene I of *Measure for Measure.*
This is a print from the Boydell Shakespeare Gallery
project, which was conceived in 1786 and lasted until
1805. *(Painting by Thomas Kirk; engraving by Jean Pierre
Simon)*

scene with Elbow and Pompey described above in
the mock trial and accusations against Isabella,
Mariana, and the friar. All is revealed when Lucio
pulls off the friar's hood, and all is resolved.

All modern editions of the play include stage
directions at pertinent points, as above, but this still
leaves open the implications of the stage arrangement. For example, Angelo is isolated in his exposure, a fact often emphasized in stage action that
has him shamefully leave his seat in the makeshift
court. He, Isabella, and Mariana are all isolated
at this point, both physically and emotionally, as
dramatic irony engages the audience and increases
tension. The Duke's judgment—after a play full of
discussions of mercy and justice, retributive judgment, law, order, and personal freedom, and fully
informed by his omniscient knowledge of events—
is awaited. The action following this passage also
condenses the previous action—for example, Isabella's plea of forgiveness for Angelo's life mirrors
that of her plea for Claudio's.

CRITICAL INTRODUCTION
TO THE PLAY

The central dilemma of *Measure for Measure* is not
original to Shakespeare. The chaste young woman
pressured into compromising her sexual honor in
order to liberate a male relative is found in a variety of narratives, folktales, and legends. Similarly,
the solution to the problem is enacted through
the employment of two other established motifs of
folktale, romance, and drama: the disguised ruler
and the bed trick. These relatively simple stock
plot devices are, however, grounded in a vastly
more complicated world, one of post-Reformation
Christianity, philosophy, political theory, and law.
Shakespeare's treatment of the dilemma situates
the problem in a setting that is at once entirely contemporary and removed from early 17th-century
London.

Politics, the State, and the Individual

The condition of Vienna in the play is a result of
the present Duke's negligence in enforcing strict
laws concerning fornication and licentious behavior

through a combination of excessively liberal views, indulgence, and a love for the people. The Duke's relationship with the people is examined throughout the play as he walks among them, directs the details of how the newly enforced law plays out, and hears a variety of opinions about his own rule.

The Duke's plan to leave the enforcement of the law to a man he suspects is not up to it may seem like irresponsible leadership. However, his determination to remain and keep an eye on Angelo possibly suggests the opposite. The role of the leader is raised throughout the play, as the Duke aims to find a middle way between enforcing the laws deemed necessary for the good of the people and the city-state, and his own leniency. The Duke's affection for his subjects is stressed—"I love the people" (1.1.67)—and his modesty, or lack of interest in vanity and public adoration, is described: "[I] do not like to stage me to their eyes: / Though it do well I do not relish well / Their loud applause and aves vehement, / Nor do I think the man of safe discretion / That does affect it" (1.1.68–72). There is possibly a moral judgment here regarding leaders who enjoy or prioritize public displays of appreciation from their subjects, though it has been suggested that the Duke's dislike of crowds and self-display are a supportive reference to the new king, James I. Unlike his predecessor, Elizabeth, who was an expert in self-presentation and displays of power, James preferred a more implicit form of government.

In Act I, Scene 3, the Duke sees himself as both a (lazy) lion and (indulgent) father, whose willingness to leave the people to their own devices is somewhat disastrous. As highlighted in the Key Passages section, there is a common consensus of the inevitability of people indulging in self-destructive behavior if they are not controlled. Claudio's image of the rat ravenously consuming poison to describe his own desire for his fiancée illustrates this, as does his claim that it is "too much liberty" that has led to his arrest (1.2.107). Thereby, the play seems to advocate the *necessity* of the state interfering in what are usually considered private matters and personal choices. The reasons for this advocacy are arguably largely contextual. With no reliable contraception, unregulated sexual activity means an increase in illegitimate births, thus undermining the whole structure of patrilineal inheritance upon which the economic and political systems of western European society are based. Desire is regulated and legitimated through marriage; chastity in women is prioritized; and property, titles, and power pass securely along the familial line. In addition, as the brothels of *Measure for Measure* attest, untreatable sexual diseases are both highly contagious and debilitating, draining charitable resources and increasing the burden on society.

As mentioned previously, the Duke's omnipresence in his friar's disguise problematizes this legal interference in arguably private matters. His embodiment of the state moving among the people—eavesdropping, confessing, advising—is emphasized by his own opening remarks considering the concept of the body of state, "the organs / Of our own power" (1.1.20). His personal surveillance of the other characters—for example, eavesdropping on Claudio and Isabella in 2.4—implies, at least to a modern audience, something intrusive and controlling about the state's regulation of behavior, however much many of the characters in the play seem to believe it necessary. In contrast, as discussed below in "Underworld and Subplot," certain of the lower-class characters do not believe human nature can be controlled through state intervention. As Pompey asks insolently, "Does your worship mean to geld and splay all the youth of the city?" (2.1.197–198).

Some critics argue that the totalitarian and libertine are at odds in this play, suggesting that the solution the text advocates is moderation, the "temperance" we are told by Escalus the Duke possesses ("A gentleman of all temperance" [3.2.204]). The argument is reiterated through Isabella and Angelo's discussions of how, at least according to Isabella, the law should be tempered with mercy— "it is excellent / To have a giant's strength, but it is tyrannous / To use it like a giant" (2.2.110–112). However, typically, the play does not offer an answer so clearly as this. If it is suggested, then the totalitarianism under discussion is that of Angelo's extremism, not the Duke's surveillance. The Duke's machinations and manipulations, while distasteful and disturbing to many viewers, are not criticized in the play. The Duke solves everything; the guilty are punished; the not-so-guilty, disruptive Lucio is also punished; and the Duke closes the final scene, possibly rejected by Isabella, possibly not, but with the status quo restored.

Sexuality

The Vienna of *Measure for Measure* is a city immersed in sex and sexuality. It permeates characters' conscious and subconscious thoughts, manifesting in language strewn with both deliberate and accidental innuendo and imagery, as well as their lives, the sinful "stews" a physical representation of human desire and debauchery. As evidenced in conversation with Escalus in 2.1, Pompey believes both sexes, "the drabs and the knaves" (201), to be driven mainly by sexual appetite. Juliet's stated complicity in her and Claudio's "offenceful act" as "Was mutually committed" (2.3.26–27) supports the concept behind Pompey's crude assertion in offering a token balance to the play's lustful men.

An example of the play's linguistic emphasis on the results of sex and sexuality can be seen in the repeated imagery of pregnancy running throughout the text. The Duke uses the word *pregnant* to convey Escalus's familiarity with the workings of Vienna and Viennese law: "y'are as pregnant in / As art and practice hath enriched any / That we remember" (1.1.11–13). Angelo says, "'Tis very pregnant" to mean "evident," and later, when under pressure, he describes the Duke's "return" with "This deed unshapes me quite, makes me unpregnant" (4.4.18), meaning he lacks ideas or incentive. Mariana's brother's loss of riches, property, and life at sea is described as a miscarriage (3.1.201). In a less figurative sense, we are told that Elbow's wife is "great with child" (2.1.81), and the audience has the visual literal pregnancy of Juliet. The images of pregnancy are supported by a wealth of bawdy punning, largely from the lower-class

characters, and perhaps most strikingly in Isabella's refutation of Angelo's hypothetical offer in highly sexualized language. Indeed, to an extent, Isabella's chief quality in terms of how she is seen by other characters (see "Gender Politics," below) and as part of her governing system of belief, her virginity, is in its very negation of sexuality a constant reminder of the omnipresence of sex in the play.

Measure for Measure is one of Shakespeare's last romantic comedies, plays revolving around love, desire, courtship, and consummation. Usually in these plays, we see how a society regulates and controls the desires of its citizens through rules of courtship and marriage. The laws enacted to "clean up" the city do not just target the disease-ridden brothels and immorality of the individuals running and frequenting them, but also the upper-class characters who, in a more conventional play, are in love and engaged. Premarital sexual intercourse in their situation is condemned in the eyes of the law. It is, however, easy enough to contain—as Isabella says upon hearing of Claudio and Juliet's predicament, "O, let him marry her" (1.4.49). While the climactic multiple betrothals and marriages of *Measure for Measure* structurally suggest that this is also the case in this play, desire is altogether a different force, arguably instigating social destruction instead of cohesion—uncontained, unregulated, and unromanticized. The way all the characters articulate sexual desire is negative and filled with images of disease, infection, and dirt. Imagery of venereal disease runs throughout the discussions of the "low" characters—for example, Lucio and the two gentlemen's pun-filled discourse about "dolours," or diseases, in 1.2: "piled . . . French velvet" (28), "French crown[s]" (41), hollow bones and sciatica (45–48) revolve around perceived symptoms of syphilis. Claudio compares his own desire for the woman he loves to rats drinking poison, and Juliet's visible pregnancy is "too gross" (1.2.136). Angelo describes his desire for Isabella as decaying meat in the sun and the destruction of a sanctuary, and as "filthy vices" (2.4.41), "uncleanness" (2.4.53) which "stains" (2.4.54). In turn, Isabella consciously articulates sinful sex as "abhorred pollution" (2.4.184) and, subconsciously, suggests sexuality based on physical restraint and violence.

However, this manifestation of Isabella's repressed desires reflected in Angelo's own attraction to the concept of defiling something sacred suggests that abstinence is not necessarily the remedy to a sexually licentious society. The way the text almost insists on the institution of marriage in the final scene, despite the complexities this introduces, suggests that is indeed the only way desire can be controlled and regulated.

Gender Politics

There are severe demarcations of gender roles in *Measure for Measure*. Masculinity seems fraught with anxiety; it is the city's male characters—the "gentlemen" jesting about venereal disease and discussing the pitfalls of using prostitutes—who, at least in an immediate sense, suffer more for transgression in the threat of capital punishment. However, it is arguably also male desire that drives the sexual obsession of the play and the plot. The only person countering this view is Juliet, who states, wonderfully, that she is as much to blame for her and Claudio's "crime" as he, though she is immediately told by the Duke/friar that in this case, her crime was worse, "Then was your sin of heavier kind than his" (2.3.27), indicating a latent misogyny.

Being female in Vienna is risky, with the implication (though no examples exist in the play) that the only respectable option is that of married, productive chastity. Isabella's virginity is continually addressed, by herself certainly but constantly by other characters, particularly Lucio. He immediately addresses her as "virgin" (1.4.16) and proclaims that by her "renouncement" of sexuality, he holds her to be "an immortal spirit, / And to be talked with in sincerity / As with a saint" (1.4.35–37). Similarly, the Provost describes Isabella as "a very virtuous maid" (2.2.21), a phrase repeated by Angelo in his soliloquy at the end of the scene. Isabella's virginity is also a great part of the reason behind Angelo's desire. Her perceived purity and virtue both raise her above the norm, and arguably this is partly why she would like to retain her

virginity, but it also becomes a prize, a "treasure" to be won or defiled. As Angelo suggests figuratively, Isabella could "lay down the treasures of your body" (2.4.96). Isabella's choice to enter the nunnery is a way of both retaining her virginity and guarding against attempts upon it. Viewing the play as a whole, it does seem that whenever Isabella has asked a male character for assistance, they have tried to sleep with her, either illegitimately, in the case of Angelo, or legitimately, in the case of the Duke. Isabella's status as a nun would be a way of making her asexual status official and untouchable. In this way, she would manage to keep her autonomy in that she is not subject to any man, and her decision can thereby be seen to be a logical and commendable choice for a young woman in Vienna. The negative counterpoint here is that by entering the nunnery, Isabella also removes herself from society, and therefore her autonomy is rather limited and socially useless.

The process of attaining married respectability is also dangerous, risking giving in to sexual desire, as in the case of Juliet, or relying on another party to confirm that respectability, in the case of Mariana. Claudio and Angelo may face execution, but if bereft of Claudio, Juliet certainly faces a life of pov-

Isabella refuses Angelo's proposition in this 19th-century depiction of Act II, Scene 4 of *Measure for Measure*. *(Painting by August Friedrich Spiess; engraving by W. Schmidt)*

erty, dependence, or dishonor. Similarly, Mariana is left high and dry, dishonored by Angelo's rumors, isolated economically; emotionally, given her continued love for the man who has ruined her chances of a normal life in this society; and physically in her moated grange. As described in the Key Passages section, the short exchange surrounding Mariana's sexual, and thereby social, state in 5.1 expresses the sexual categorization of the entire play. The Duke states that Mariana is "nothing" if, as she says, she is "neither maid or widow or wife."

The only alternative to marriage or the nunnery in this play's society is outright dishonor in prostitution. We never see any prostitutes; we never hear any speak. What is said of them is said by the men who use them. The jovial conversation about the risk of contracting syphilis in 1.2, the refusal of Lucio to acknowledge his child, and his assertion that "Marrying a punk, my lord, is pressing to death, whipping, and hanging!" (5.1.507)—all convey some idea of the social position of prostitutes in the play. The closest character to a prostitute offered onstage is Mistress Overdone, whose name, a pun on over-"doing," signifies her long years as a working prostitute, having been "done" by too many sexual partners. Pompey reiterates that she has "worn your eyes almost out in the service" (1.2.92). The pun is reinforced shortly after Mistress Overdone's entrance, as she asks in reference to Claudio, "Well, what has he done?" and Pompey answers, "A woman" (1.2.72–73). The portrayal of Overdone is not unsympathetic, though evidently her name is a joke at her own expense, and the aging bawd is a stock comic figure, perhaps redressing the balance in the sex industry. This is not a straightforward case of women being exploited by men. As the representative of the prostitute community, Mistress Overdone voices the grievances of, for example, Kate Keepdown, and, together with Pompey, reminds the audience of an industry that trades in male desires and women's bodies.

Underworld and Subplot

There is a pervasive image in *Measure for Measure* of the contrast between the crowd and the clois-

tered individual. For example, Angelo in his study, Isabella in the nunnery, the Duke (who does not like crowds), and Mariana all attempt to remain separate from the heaving masses that make up the city. The laws Angelo reinforces are targeted primarily at the suburbs, the contemporary location of brothels, public houses, bear pits, and theaters, and it is the characters inhabiting this area who constitute both an underclass to the higher, authoritative characters and the subplot to the main play.

Members of the underclass move from the streets to the prison, then back to the streets, indicating that the prosecution of felony here is, in effect, the prosecution of a whole community. As Pompey says in the prison, "I am as well acquainted here as I was in our house of profession" (4.3.1–2). Shakespeare's lower-class characters are sometimes considered as present merely for comedy, but this community provides a commentary to the main narrative of *Measure for Measure*. The laws that Angelo enforces are going to affect these characters most severely through loss of livelihood, homes, and imprisonment as all the houses are to be pulled down "To the ground" (1.2.86). In addition, the morality and self-conscious virtue of characters such as Isabella and Angelo are a world away from the characters lacking options, education, and ideals.

The status of the law among the characters inhabiting the underbelly of Vienna is embodied to an extent in the figure of Elbow, a lowly representative of it. Pompey is an expert in evading the law, humiliating Elbow and talking his way out of arrest in 2.1, changing his profession from pimp to tapster to executioner's assistant in 4.2 in order to stay a step ahead of the law. Pompey asserts that the state's attempts to regulate and criminalize private behavior are pointless, and that human nature cannot be repressed in this way, while Lucio seems to revel in the disruption it causes. Lucio, as explored in the Character Study section, is the most overt disruptive element, full of slander and irreverence. Lucio's slander of the Duke to his face in 3.2, while unwitting, is the most overt representation of a challenge to the state's order and authority. This is possibly the reason behind his extremely harsh punishment. Before his execution, Lucio is to be married to a whore, a fate he sees as being worse than death because of the social position of prostitutes and because he is automatically a cuckold. While this seems incredible given Angelo's reprieve, Lucio's crime of slander and overt mockery of the ruling figure could be seen as not only traitorous but heretical, following the the contemporary belief in the monarch's divine right. The Duke knows that Lucio has to be squashed and silenced, if only to establish and assert his own political authority.

Secular and Sacred Law

The debates between Isabella and Angelo focus on the role of mercy within the law. Angelo, at least initially, sees things very clearly in his determination to follow the law to the letter. He proudly sees this determination as related to his own virtue, perceiving no discrepancy between state law and Christian ideals. What Isabella introduces, and the Duke blows wide open, is the concept of context, of judging cases on individual merit and applying the Christian virtue of mercy to temper strict laws.

The Provost advises deliberation in meting out punishment, as "I have seen / When, after execution, judgement hath / Repented" (2.2.10–12), but he is coldly silenced by Angelo. Escalus, too, argues that the law should be applied keenly but compassionately in the case of Claudio, suggesting that Angelo can perhaps empathize: "Whether you had not sometime in your life / Erred in this point which now you censure him, / And pulled the law upon you" (2.1.14–16). Angelo, however, though admitting that the jury may contain individuals "Guiltier than him they try" (2.1.21), claims (ironically) that he himself is presently virtuous and would expect in the future exactly the same strict application of the law should he fall: "When I that censure him do so offend, / Let mine own judgement pattern out my death / And nothing come in partial" (2.1.29–31).

Isabella and Angelo's debates in 2.2 and 2.4 on the application of mercy to law and the place of Christian forgiveness in secular law implicitly refer back to the play's title in its wider context from the Sermon on the Mount. Angelo's "measure" will indeed be revisited upon his own head, something he advocates in his self-belief. Isabella's plea for mercy and leniency highlights the virtuous power of mercy: "Not the king's crown, nor the deputed sword, / The marshal's truncheon, nor the judge's robe / Become them with one half so good a grace / As mercy does" (2.2.61–64). Her assertion that if Claudio and Angelo's roles were reversed, Claudio would "not have been so stern" (67) recalls the Sermon's advice to judge as oneself would be judged. Isabella also places the responsibility for judgment in God's, not man's, hands—"man, proud man, / Dressed in a little brief authority, / Most ignorant of what he's most assured" (2.2.121–123). The issue of the intersection between secular and Christian law is reflected throughout the play and contributes to the suggestion that extremism in any aspect of life is detrimental.

Substitution and Exchange

One of the leading thematic aspects of *Measure for Measure* is the concept of substitution or exchange. Numerous examples of this permeate the play; the Duke is substituted by Angelo, Angelo intends Isabella's maidenhead to be exchanged for Claudio's head, Mariana is substituted for Isabella in the bed trick, and Ragozine's head is substituted for Claudio's. As the Duke says, "An Angelo for a Claudio, death for death; / Haste still pays haste, and leisure answers leisure; / Like doth quit like, and measure still for measure" (5.1.402–404). This statement neatly returns to the biblical quote of the title, though the Duke, in this guise, ignores the Sermon on the Mount's wider implications of mercy and avoidance of hypocrisy. These aspects are instead played out in Angelo's judgment and reprieve, previously introduced by Isabella in her debates with him, as discussed above.

The system of exchange that permeates the play is one that, perhaps mainly to those lacking autonomy, results in characters becoming objectified and—more specifically, in that they are exchanged for something else—commodified. Commodities of the play world are helpfully listed by Pompey (brown paper, ginger, peach-colored satin, 4.3.4–9); this is a thriving urban commercial world where such items are readily available should one have the money. Correspondingly, images of coining are used figuratively throughout; Angelo says, "Let there be some more test made of my metal / Before so noble and so great a figure / Be stamped upon it" (1.1.48–50), and he later uses the metaphor of printing coins for breeding. It is significant that the stamp and bed used for creating coins is called the "matrix" (womb). Such language conflates images of biological and material production, of stamping images on offspring and "breeding" coins.

The "worth" of individuals is also stressed, most explicitly in relation to female characters. The "value" of Isabella's virtue is discussed above in "Gender Politics," and Mariana's material worth and sexual value are also linked by Angelo. He says "her reputation was disvalued" (5.1.219), aligning Mariana's lost dowry and thus her loss of financial worth with her alleged loss of virtue. Here we can also see the intersection of many of the play's themes in that, taken to its logical conclusion, the trade in people as commodities brings this discussion back to the ultimate commodification implicit in prostitution (see above). This is made clear figuratively by Isabella, who accuses Claudio of prostituting her—"Thy sin's not accidental, but a trade. / Mercy to thee would prove itself a bawd" (3.1.149–150)—that is, of exchanging her body and virtue for his life.

EXTRACTS OF CLASSIC CRITICISM
Samuel Johnson (1709–1784) [Excerpted from the preface to *The Plays of William Shakespeare* (1765), the great critic's landmark edition.]

Of this play the light or comick part is very natural and pleasing, but the grave scenes, if a few passages be excepted, have more labour than elegance. The plot is rather intricate than artful. The time of the action is indefinite; some time, we know not how much, must have elapsed between the recess of the Duke and the imprisonment of Claudio; for he must have learned the story of Mariana in his disguise, or he delegated his power to a man already known to be corrupted.

A. W. Schlegel (1767–1845) [Excerpted from *Lectures on Dramatic Art and Literature* (1808). Schlegel translated the plays of Shakespeare into German and was an important influence on Samuel Taylor Coleridge.]

In *Measure for Measure,* Shakspeare was compelled, by the nature of the subject, to make his poetry more familiar with criminal justice than is usual with him. All kinds of proceedings connected with the subject, all sorts of active or passive persons, pass in review before us . . . But yet, notwithstanding this agitating truthfulness, how tender and mild is the pervading tone of the picture! The piece takes improperly its name from punishment; the true significance of the whole is the triumph of mercy over strict justice; no man being himself so free from errors as to be entitled to deal it out to his equals. The most beautiful embellishment of the composition is the character of Isabella, who, on the point of taking the veil, is yet prevailed upon by sisterly affection to tread again the perplexing ways of the world, while, amid the general corruption, the heavenly purity of her mind is not even stained with one unholy thought: in the humble robes of the novice, she is a very angel of light. When the cold and stern Angelo, heretofore of unblemished reputation, whom the Duke has commissioned, during his pretended absence, to restrain, by a rigid administration of the laws, the excesses of dissolute immorality, is even himself tempted by the virgin charms of Isabella, supplicating for the pardon of her brother Claudio, condemned to death for a youthful indiscretion; when at first, in timid and obscure language, he insinuates, but at last impudently avouches his readiness to grant Claudio's life to the sacrifice of her honor; when Isabella repulses this offer with a noble scorn; in her account of the interview to her brother, when the latter at first applauds her conduct, but at length, overcome by the fear of death, strives to persuade her to consent to dishonor;—in these masterly scenes, Shakspeare has sounded the depths of the human heart. The interest here reposes altogether on the represented action; curiosity contributes nothing to our delight, for the Duke, in the disguise of a Monk, is always present to watch over his dangerous representative, and to avert every evil which could possibly be apprehended; we look to him with confidence for a happy result. The Duke acts the part of the Monk naturally, even to deception; he unites in his person the wisdom of the priest and the prince. Only in his wisdom he is too fond of round-about ways; his vanity is flattered with acting invisibly like an earthly providence; he takes more pleasure in overhearing his subjects than governing them in the customary way of princes. As he ultimately extends a free pardon to all the guilty, we do not see how his original purpose, in committing the execution of the laws to other hands, of restoring their strictness, has in any wise been accomplished. The poet might have had this irony in view, that of the numberless slanders of the Duke, told him by the petulant Lucio, in ignorance of the person whom he is addressing, that at least which regarded his singularities and whims was not wholly without foundation.

Samuel Taylor Coleridge (1772–1834) [Excerpted from *Lectures and Notes on Shakspere and Other English Poets* (1883). Coleridge's 1818 lectures on Shakespeare, first published in 1883, introduced new concepts of dramatic psychology and thereby a dominating consideration of character in the plays. In contrast to Schlegel, Coleridge found nothing to admire in *Measure for Measure*.]

This play, which is Shakspere's throughout, is to me the most painful—say rather, the only painful—part of his genuine works. The comic and tragic parts equally border on the ["odious"],—the one being disgusting, the other horrible; and the pardon and the marriage of Angelo not merely baffles the strong indignant claim of justice—(for cruelty, with lust and damnable baseness, cannot be forgiven, because we cannot conceive them as being morally repented of) but it is likewise degrading to the character of woman.

[Excerpted from "Table Talk," June 24, 1827]:

> "Measure for Measure" is the single exception to the delightfulness of Shakespere's plays. It is a hateful work, although Shaksperian throughout. Our feelings of justice are grossly wounded in Angelo's escape. Isabella herself contrives to be unamiable, and Claudio is detestable.

William Hazlitt (1778–1830) [Excerpted from *Characters of Shakespear's Plays* (1817). Hazlitt was heavily influenced by Coleridge in his early years; he went on to become one of the most important Shakespearean critics of the 19th century.]

This is a play as full of genius as it is of wisdom. Yet there is an original sin in the nature of the subject, which prevents us from taking a cordial interest in it. "The height of moral argument" which the author has maintained in the intervals of passion or blended with the more powerful impulses of nature, is hardly surpassed in any of his plays. But there is a general want of passion; the affections are at a stand; our sympathies are repulsed and defeated in all directions. The only passion which influences the story is that of Angelo; and yet he seems to have a much greater passion for hypocrisy than for his mistress. Neither are we greatly enamoured of Isabella's rigid chastity, though she could not act otherwise than she did. We do not feel the same confidence in the virtue that is "sublimely good" at another's expense, as if it had been put to some less disinterested trial. As to the Duke, who makes a very imposing and mysterious stage-character, he is more absorbed in his own plots and gravity than anxious for the welfare of the state; more tenacious of his own character than attentive to the feelings and apprehensions of others. Claudio is the only person who feels naturally; and yet he is placed in circumstances of distress which almost preclude the wish for his deliverance. Mariana is also in love with Angelo, whom we hate. In this respect, there may be said to be a general system of cross-purposes between the feelings of the different characters and the sympathy of the reader or the audience. This principle of repugnance seems to have reached its height in the character of Master Barnardine, who not only sets at defiance the opinions of others, but has even thrown off all self-regard,—"a man that apprehends death no more dreadfully but as a drunken sleep; careless, reckless, and fearless of what's past, present, or to come." He is a fine antithesis to the morality and the hypocrisy of the other characters of the play. Barnardine is Caliban transported from Prospero's wizard island to the forests of Bohemia or the prisons of Vienna. He is the creature of bad habits as Caliban is of gross instincts . . . We do not understand why the philosophical German critic, Schlegel, should be so severe on those pleasant persons, Lucio, Pompey, and Master Froth, as to call them "wretches." They appear all mighty comfortable in their occupations, and determined to pursue them, "as the flesh and fortune should serve." A very

Isabella condemns Claudio for his cowardice in Act III, Scene I of *Measure for Measure*. This is a print from Malcolm C. Salaman's 1916 edition of *Shakespeare in Pictorial Art. (Painting by William Hamilton)*

good exposure of the want of self-knowledge and contempt for others, which is so common in the world, is put into the mouth of Abhorson, the jailer, when the Provost proposes to associate Pompey with him in his office—"A bawd, sir? Fie upon him, he will discredit our mystery." . . . Shakespear was in one sense the least moral of all writers; for morality (commonly so called) is made up of antipathies; and his talent consisted in sympathy with human nature, in all its shapes, degrees, depressions, and elevations. The object of the pedantic moralist is to find out the bad in everything: his was to show that "there is some soul of goodness in things evil." Even Master Barnardine is not left to the mercy of what others think of him; but when he comes in, speaks for himself, and pleads his own cause, as well as if counsel had been assigned him. In one sense, Shakespear was no moralist at all: in another he was the greatest of all moralists. He was a moralist in the same sense in which nature is one. He taught what he had learnt from her. He showed the greatest knowledge of humanity with the greatest fellow-feeling for it.

One of the most dramatic passages in the present play is the interview between Claudio and his sister, when she comes to inform him of the conditions on which Angelo will spare his life. . . . What adds to the dramatic beauty of this scene and the effect of Claudio's passionate attachment to life is, that it immediately follows the Duke's lecture to him, in the character of the Friar, recommending an absolute indifference to it.

Edward Dowden (1843–1913) [Excerpted from *Shakspere: A Critical Study of His Mind and Art* (1875). This work heavily influenced future approaches to Shakespearean biography.]

When *Measure for Measure* was written Shakspere was evidently bidding farewell to mirth; its significance is grave and earnest; the humorous scenes would be altogether repulsive were it not that they are needed to present without disguise or extenuation the world of moral licence and corruption out of and above which rise the virginal strength and severity and beauty of Isabella. . . . Isabella is the only one of Shakspere's women whose heart and eyes are fixed upon an impersonal ideal, to whom something abstract is more, in the ardour and energy of her youth, than any human personality. Out of this Vienna in which

> Corruption boils and bubbles
> Till it o'errun the stew,

emerges this pure zeal, this rectitude of will, this virgin sanctity. Isabella's saintliness is not of the passive, timorous, or merely meditative kind. It is an active pursuit of holiness through exercise and discipline. She knows nothing of a Manichean hatred of the body; the life runs strongly and gladly in her veins; simply her soul is set upon things belonging to the soul, and uses the body for its own purposes. And that the life of the soul may be invigorated she would bring every unruly thought into captivity, "having in readiness to revenge all disobedience."

☙ ☙ ☙

Isabella does not return to the sisterhood of Saint Clare. Putting aside from her the dress of religion, and the strict conventual rule, she accepts her place as Duchess of Vienna. In this there is no dropping away, through love of pleasure or through supineness, from her ideal; it is entirely meet and right. She has learned that in the world may be found a discipline more strict. More awful than the discipline of the convent; she has learned that the world has need of her; her life is still a consecrated life; the vital energy of her heart can exert and augment itself through glad and faithful wifehood, and through noble station more fully than in seclusion. To preside over this polluted and feculent Vienna is the office and charge of Isabella, "a thing ensky'd and sainted'.

A. C. Swinburne (1837–1909) [Excerpted from *A Study of Shakespeare* (1879). A perceptive and original critic, Swinburne's studies were key in reviving interest in early modern drama.]

The relative disfavour in which the play of *Measure for Measure* has doubtless been at all times generally held is not in my opinion simply explicable on the theory of late years has been so powerfully and plausibly advanced and advocated on the highest poetic or judicial authority in France or in the world, that in the land of many-coloured cant and many-coated hypocrisy the type of Angelo is something too much a prototype or an autotype of the huge national vice of England. This comment is in itself as surely just and true as it is incisive and direct: but it will not cover by any means the whole question. The strong and radical objection distinctly brought forward against this play, and strenuously supported by the wisest and warmest devotee among all the worshippers of Shakespeare, is not exactly this, that the Puritan Angelo is exposed: it is that the Puritan Angelo is unpunished. In the very words of Coleridge, it is that by his pardon and marriage "the strong indignant claim of justice" is "baffled." The expression is absolutely correct and apt: justice is not merely evaded or ignored or even defied: she is both in the older and newer sense of the word directly and deliberately baffled; buffeted, outraged, insulted, struck in the face. We are left hungry and thirsty after having been made to thirst and hunger for some wholesome single grain at least of righteousness and too long retarded retribution: we are tricked out of our dole, defeated of our due, lured and led on to look for some equitable and satisfying upshot, defrauded and derided and sent empty away.

That this play is in its very inmost essence a tragedy, and that no sleight of hand or force of hand could give it even a tolerable show of coherence or consistency when clipped and docked of its proper and rightful end, the mere tone of style prevalent throughout all its better parts to the absolute exclusion of any other would of itself most amply suffice to show. Almost all that is here worthy of Shakespeare at any time is worthy of Shakespeare at his highest: and of this every touch, every line, every incident, every syllable, belongs to pure and simple tragedy. The evasion of a tragic end by the invention and intromission of Mariana has deserved and received high praise for its

ingenuity: but ingenious evasion of a natural and proper end is usually the distinctive quality which denotes a workman of a very much lower school than the school of Shakespeare. In short and in fact, the whole elaborate machinery by which the complete and completely unsatisfactory result of the whole plot is attained is so thoroughly worthy of such a contriver as "the old fantastical duke of dark corners" as to be in a moral sense, if I dare say what I think, very far from thoroughly worthy of the wisest and mightiest mind that ever was informed with the spirit of genius of creative poetry.

Walter Pater (1839–1894) [Excerpted from *Appreciations* (1889). Pater is possibly the most "modern" of the 19th-century critics in his reading of the text in terms of dramatic construction and design rather than character. His approach highlights broader themes of forgiveness and mercy.]

In *Measure for Measure,* as in some other of his plays, Shakespeare has remodelled an earlier and somewhat rough composition to "finer issues," suffering much to remain as it had come from the less skilful hand, and not raising the whole of his work to an equal degree of intensity. Hence perhaps some of that depth and weightiness which make this play so impressive, as with the true seal of experience, like a fragment of life itself, rough and disjointed indeed, but forced to yield in places its profounder meaning. . . . [U]nder his touch certain select portions of it rise far above the level of all but his own best poetry, and working out of it a morality so characteristic that the play might well pass for the central expression of his moral judgements. It remains a comedy, as indeed is congruous with the bland, half-humorous equity which informs the whole composition . . . yet it is hardly less full of what is really tragic in man's existence than if Claudio had indeed "stooped to death." Even the humorous concluding scenes have traits of special grace, retaining in less emphatic passages a stray line or word of power, as it seems, so that we watch to the end for the traces where the nobler hand has glanced along, leaving its vestiges, as if accidentally or wastefully, in the rising of the style.

∛ ∛ ∛

Of Angelo we may feel at first sight inclined to say only *guarda e passa!* or to ask whether he is indeed psychologically possible. In the old story, he figures as an embodiment of pure and unmodified evil . . . But the embodiment of pure evil is no proper subject of art, and Shakespeare, in the spirit of a philosophy which dwells much on the complications of outward circumstance with men's inclinations, turns into a subtle study in casuistry this incident of the austere judge fallen suddenly into utmost corruption by a momentary contact with supreme purity. But the main interest in *Measure for Measure* is not, as in *Promos and Cassandra,* in the relation of Isabella and Angelo, but rather in the relation of Claudio and Isabella.

∛ ∛ ∛

[I]n its ethics it is an epitome of Shakespeare's moral judgments. They are the moral judgments of an observer, of one who sits as a spectator, and knows how the threads in the design before him hold together under the surface: they are the judgments of the humourist also, who follows with a half-amused but always pitiful sympathy, the various ways of human disposition, and sees less distance than ordinary men between what are called respectively great and little things.

MODERN CRITICISM AND CRITICAL CONTROVERSIES

Critical views of *Measure for Measure* evolved throughout the 20th century; it was initially mainly seen as a "problem" comedy and gradually as a more complex and ambiguous work of art. As

Arthur Quiller-Couch and John Dover Wilson wrote in 1922, "What is wrong with this play? Evidently *something* is wrong, since the critics so tangle themselves in apologies and interpretations. Some have taken offence at its bawdry: others . . . would have us enjoy it for its realism . . . judging this tragic-comedy at a squint" (xiii). Critical appreciation of *Measure for Measure*'s ambiguity is evident particularly from the mid-20th century onward. As L. C. Knights observed in 1942, "In *Measure for Measure* the process of clarification is incomplete, and one finds not paradox but genuine ambiguity" (150). Interest in such ambiguity developed throughout the latter half of the century as the text seemed open to engagement with pertinent social issues and theoretical developments such as historicism, cultural materialism, and feminism.

The ambiguity of *Measure for Measure,* however, offers no conclusions as to what the play is "about," which contributes to some critics' dissatisfaction with the play. Some have attempted to solve the problem of the problem play by reading the play as allegorical or as essentially moral. In the 1940s, M. C. Bradbrook and G. Wilson Knight both proposed an allegorical solution, though their signifying systems differed slightly. Bradbrook stated: "Angelo stands for Authority and for Law, usurping the place of the Duke, who is not only the representative of Heavenly Justice but of Humility, whilst Isabel represents both Truth and Mercy" (385). Knight argued that "Isabella stands for sainted purity, Angelo for . . . righteousness, the Duke for a psychologically sound and enlightened ethic" (393). In opposition, critics such as E. M. W. Tillyard and, later, Alexander Leggatt argued against this solution, Tillyard criticizing the play as lacking coherence and Leggatt pointing to the complexity and inconsistency of the characters. Tillyard concluded: "The simple and ineluctable fact is that the tone in the first half of the play is frankly, acutely human and quite hostile to the tone of allegory or symbol. And, however much the tone changes in the second half, nothing in the world can make an allegorical interpretation poetically valid through-out" (129).

Critics of the 20th and 21st centuries have also suggested that *Measure for Measure* is essentially a morality play. Quiller-Couch, Wilson, and Northrop Frye took this view, as to a greater extent did H. B. Charlton, who wrote in 1938: "There is an almost intolerable insistence on meting out reward to the virtuous and punishment to the guilty. . . . It is a sense of the potential richness of humanity rather than despondency" (213), even though he stressed that this despondency is the overwhelming initial, almost nihilistic impression.

Later critics have stressed such nihilism at the expense of any moral indications in the text, seeing its problematic or ambiguous aspects to be

The Duke, disguised as a friar, asks Isabella to deliver a letter to Friar Peter in Act IV, Scene 3 of *Measure for Measure,* in this illustration published by Amies in 1888. *(Illustration by Felix Octavius Darley)*

precisely the point. Kathleen McLuskie asserts: "Moral absolutes are rendered platitudinous by the language and verse, particularly in the Duke's summary [of 3.2] where the jingling rime of the couplet mocks the very morals it asserts" (94).

Earlier criticism found its focus, as in preceding works, in the generic difficulty of the play and in the roles of Isabella and the Duke. Critical reaction to the Duke has been mixed throughout critics' work of the 20th century. Clifford Leech evaluates the mixed reaction as suggesting "an ambivalence in the character, a contradiction between its dramatic function and the human qualities implied by its words and actions . . . his supreme indifference to human feeling is a persistent note as any in the play" (158). Negative criticism of the Duke has focused on his avoidance of responsibility and unworkable law, as stressed by Frye. In a different approach, Tina Krontiris instead highlights the Duke's manipulative directive strategy and omniscience as "one who stages a spectacle for his own benefit—to reaffirm his absolute authority through a display of God-like power."

In contrast, some critics have argued that having faith in the Duke can facilitate an audience's reaction to a play ambiguous in genre. F. R. Leavis states, "His attitude . . . *is* meant to be ours—his total attitude, which is the total attitude of the play" (169). Bertrand Evans agrees that this concept introduces a reassuring objectivity and develops it in an argument that the Duke is conducting a moral lesson for Isabella and Angelo and is in total control for the entire play—a control that, in opposition to other critics, is seen as a positive force: "Working in mysterious ways, he has transformed an erstwhile 'saint' into a creature of human sympathies and forced her to demonstrate them against odds" (218).

When considering Isabella, earlier 20th-century criticism followed that of the 19th century in offering opposing views. Quiller-Couch and Wilson pointed out that that "the critics can make nothing of her or—which is worse—they make two opposite women of her, and praise or blame her accordingly" (xxvii). However, the overlap between the two views is much more evident, with, for example, Charlton continuing to emphasize Isabella's spirituality and moral virtue, yet also writing: "Her belief begins to look like a narrow formal dogmatism, and her turning on her desperate brother appears as a mere cheap triumph in verbal theatricality" (120). In contrast, other thinkers were increasingly one-sided, A. P. Rossiter finding Isabella "unnatural" and Quiller-Couch and Wilson finding "something rancid in her chastity." Simultaneously, an argument for psychological complexity began to gather ground, Leavis asking as early as 1942, "why assume that it must be 'either or'— that she has to be merely the one or else merely the other?" (241).

Later modern criticism has increasingly produced gendered or psychological readings of Isabella that emphasize her more realistic complexity. Rossiter and Frye both emphasize her fear of the world, Frye describing her, perhaps more accurately, as "demoralised." In contrast, Joanne Altieri sees Isabella as more complex in her lack of ability to apply theoretical conditions to real life, "her attitude towards death, as towards her virtue and her brother's plight, is thoroughly theoretical, abstract. Hers is the abstraction of naiveté . . . Hers is a failure of imagination, an inability to see from any but her own narrow perspective."

Recent critical focus on the relevance of contemporary ideologies has brought valuable critical interpretations that relate the play to contemporary cultural factors. For example, Isabella's status as a potential nun and young female in a play focusing on sexual transaction is crucial, and critics point out that throughout the play, Isabella's chastity is emphasized, utilized, and fetishized. The value of Isabella's chastity evidently is rooted in contemporary ideology, as Barbara J. Baines emphasizes: "[F]ornication results in bastardy, and bastardy threatens the social and political privileges of the legitimate male heir within an aristocratic, patrilineal society. . . . In a patriarchal society, men are privileged with authority, yet, somewhat paradoxically, that authority depends upon the chastity of women" (286).

This is one concern of feminist criticism of *Measure for Measure.* Several critics, such as Baines, Jonathan Dollimore, and Marcia Riefer, argue that Isabella's grim determination to retain her virginity and enter the nunnery is a way of escaping the patriarchal values and sexual obsession of the play world. Though Dollimore sees this as positive, Riefer believes Isabella demonstrates "a deeply rooted fear of exploitation," and Baines argues that the chastity required by the nunnery is "a form of freedom, the only form of autonomy left for women in a world where sexuality means submission to men and degradation in that submission" (287); Isabella's cloistered chastity "is deprived of its social, political, and psychological power through isolation and renunciation." Indeed, Riefer goes further, suggesting that as the play progresses, Isabella is steadily reduced from an assertive and articulate character to "a stunned, angry, defensive woman" to, finally, "on her knees before male authority in Act V." Riefer concludes that *Measure for Measure* traces Isabella's gradual loss of autonomy" (169) and cites her lack of response to the Duke's proposal as embodying this loss of self. In contrast, Baines sees Isabella's silence as resistance to patriarchal authority and evidence of her intentions regarding the Duke's offer: "In her silence to the Duke's proposal, Isabella thus adheres to the rules of the sisters of St. Clare: she shows her face but remains silent" (299).

Feminist critics do not concentrate solely on Isabella but on the play's sexual context. As critics such as McLuskie point out, the emphasis on women's sexual status results in a widespread objectification of the female characters: They are made visible, or identified, through this, and thus are expressly figured as the property (or potential property) of men.

Ernest Schanzer's important 1960 investigation into the meaning of the marriage contracts in the play offers some valuable insights into contemporary understanding of marital engagement. It therefore stresses the likelihood of a contemporary audience's sympathy for Claudio and the lessening of the charge of hypocrisy against Isabella if she truly believes that Angelo and Mariana are practically married. Schanzer does, though, differentiate between the agreement of Claudio and Juliet and that of Angelo and Mariana, asserting that "Claudio and Juliet are guilty in the eyes of the Church of two transgressions—of having contracted a secret marriage and of having consummated it." This argument is contested by Margaret Scott, who argues that the law in the play "is fictional law, the like of which has never been enacted in England, nor . . . in Vienna. It seems reasonable to assume, then, that other subsidiary legislation in the play, including that relating to marriage contracts, is also part of the texture of a world which is in some sense self-enclosed . . . it is perhaps. . . futile to inquire the precise form of words used by the betrothed couples before *Measure for Measure* begins." Scott stresses that to differentiate between Claudio and Angelo's crime violates the meaning of the play, avoiding its central irony and coherence.

Historicism also includes Josephine Waters Bennett's earlier reading of the play, which links it inextricably to its possible first performance at Whitehall in 1604 and the play's potential allusions to James I's principles of government. Debora Kuller Shuger's recent study develops this observation to assert that the play is inherently linked with its political time of production, that the combination of state rule and religion in the Duke's disguise constitutes "a sustained meditation on its own political moment—the political moment of James' accession, but also, more significantly, of the Reformation's aftermath" and also supports James I's beliefs of the necessity of a good monarch also being a morally good individual.

Later modern criticism has also developed concepts concerning the play's political implications that are rather less benign than Bennett's. Critics such as Rossiter and Shuger have raised pertinent points about the text's dubious conflation of the public and private in the attempt to control individual private behavior. More radically, the Duke's surveillance is seen by Dollimore in particular as a manifestation of an oppressive state's attempt to control its people, a reading that "interprets low-life transgression as *positively* anarchic, ludic, carnivalesque—a subversion from below of a repressive official ideology of order" (73). Such readings also focus on class and provide understanding of the "low" characters' functions.

Throughout the 20th century, several critics, such as Knight, Frye, and Dollimore, provided increasingly in-depth analyses of Lucio. Knight identifies Lucio as "illuminating" and "terribly dangerous," while Frye and Dollimore develop this to give credence to Lucio's slander, Dollimore claiming: "Unawares and carelessly, Lucio strikes at the heart of the ideological legitimation of power. Along with Barnardine's equally careless refusal of subjection, this is what angers the Duke the most" (83). Later critics such as Brian Gibbons also stress the potentiality of the play's lawless underclass, with Gibbons writing: "Many critics have been troubled by the impression of a disorder, and a latent anarchy, more rooted, defiant, and aggressive than might be thought compatible with . . . comedy" (23).

THE PLAY TODAY

Measure for Measure continues to engage critics, audiences, students, and theater companies, as the issues raised in and explored by the play are as relevant to modern life as to life in Shakespeare's time. Admittedly, the text's religious aspects are often given less in-depth consideration today, the sociopolitical implications proving more relevant to the majority of modern readers. The most recent criticism continues to reevaluate the play's gender politics and sexual aspects, its political arguments and contemporary relevance, in addition to exploring the ambiguity of its characters, particularly that of the Duke. In modern stage productions, *Measure for Measure* has continued to prove to be versatile in terms of the production's interpretation of the play. For example, John Barton's 1970s production advocated sexual liberation, but the play has also been successfully used to criticize opposing totalitarian regimes, capitalism in Brecht's 1951 production and communism in a 1956 Polish production.

In productions up to the 1950s, the text was often cut in order to reduce the ambiguity in the characters of Isabella and the Duke. Such was the case in Peter Brook's seminal 1950 production and Anthony Quayle's in 1956. Removal of compromising or suspect lines resulted in Isabella seeming less extreme or selfish and the Duke nobler and less devious. This practice has lessened in more recent productions. From the 1970s onward, textual fidelity and an interest in psychological depth has resulted in increasingly ironic, and in some cases brutal, productions that tend to emphasize social and political issues. As such, aspects of the play that are open to dramatic interpretation are utilized to enhance the impetus of the production as a whole. The key example here is in the Duke's unanswered proposal, which has become something of a cornerstone in production decisions. Barton's version offered an open-ended interpretation in which Isabella (Estelle Kohler) remained alone on stage, an action that was taken by most reviewers to be a rejection of the offer. In Jonathan Miller's 1974 production, Isabella's refusal was conveyed physically as she turned and walked offstage.

The aforementioned versatility of the play and the continuing relevance of its thematic concerns mean that producers and directors are rather spoiled for choice in their decisions regarding setting and emphasis. Keith Hack's Royal Shakespeare Company (RSC) production at Stratford in 1974 was critically unsuccessful but stressed Vienna's poverty in shabby scenery and jaded actors going through the motions demanded by an overacting, melodramatic Duke, thus exposing the Duke's manipulative machinations and the general poor state of the play world. In contrast, in 1975 Robin Philip's Canadian production was set in 1912 Vienna, making Freud and Freudian theories of sexuality an explicit point of reference. Adrian Noble chose an 18th-century setting that contrasted extravagant foppery with underclass grotesques in his 1983 RSC production. The RSC production of 2003 directed by Sean Holmes was set in 1940s postwar Vienna, which vividly conveyed the struggle of people trying to live after the war and regain some

guidance of morality and order, yet are potentially driven into crime or prostitution purely through socioeconomic reasons.

The Complicite production at London's National Theatre in 2004, directed by Simon McBurney, succeeded in being both sinister and comic, with reviewers "terrified" by David Troughton's "dastardly" and "sadistic" Duke. This ambivalence in presenting the Duke is a continuing central aspect of modern productions. The Folger Theatre's 2006 version directed by Aaron Posner presented the Duke's "disguise" as a large hand puppet of a friar operated by the Duke (Mark Zeisler), literalizing his role as puppet master, manipulator, and director.

The play's relevance for modern audiences, critics, and students is manifested most clearly in the questions concerning political control and personal sexuality. The moral questions concerning the characters' personal decisions, morality, and sexuality are eternally applicable, while the particularly urban setting relates to modern cities' problems with poverty, class inequality, a disadvantaged underclass, the sex trade, and crime and how a state is to approach policing such areas. Contemporary debates on capital punishment, "zero tolerance," and liberal regulatory approaches are very relevant as the play perhaps suggests the dangers of both extreme liberalism and fundamentalism. Arguably, in both the modern United Kingdom and the United States, the government similarly attempts to police citizens' private behavior; the former mayor of New York (1994–2001), Rudolph Giuliani, tried to clean up the city with a program of zero tolerance, and the U.K. government is continually accused of becoming a "nanny state." The 1998 RSC production of *Measure for Measure* directed by Michael Boyd capitalized on this concept and the contemporary preoccupation with the morality of state leaders, with Robert Gore-Langton writing in the *Express* that the play depicts a government that runs a ruinous "back-to-basics" (the ill-fated campaign of John Major's Conservative government, 1990–97) moral crusade. Questions of sleaze and morality still plague current administrations.

The individual and state machinery, maintenance of social order, a moral dilemma, the committing of one crime to compensate for another, a society seemingly obsessed with sex, the right to control one's sexual activity, administrative hypocrisy, corrupt rulers, a wealth of grey areas in the black and white spheres of the law, the desire for justice: All of these issues will continue to be relevant as long as human beings continue to live according to both their desires and social constraints.

FIVE TOPICS FOR DISCUSSION AND WRITING

1. **State and subject:** Can a state be controlled through the control of subjects' private affairs? Is surveillance of subjects morally justifiable? Do the public and private need to be separate? How is the authoritative state represented? Why does the Duke not enforce the laws himself? The disguised ruler among the people is a common contemporary conceit—why do you think the Duke does this? Do you think the Duke's control of the action suggests how the audience is supposed to view both his character and the play? What do the scenes of the common people add to your understanding of this play? How "dangerous" is Lucio?

2. **Chastity and sexuality:** Why does Angelo want Isabella? Is Angelo's reported virtue similar or different to Isabella's? How is Isabella's virginity described and perceived by other characters? Do you think Isabella acts admirably or not? Is she a hypocrite? How would you stage Claudio's reaction to her decision? How are the female characters made "visible" in this play? Read Luce Irigaray's *Speculum of the Other Woman* (1974)—how can you apply the theory therein to this play? In this play, does masculine desire cause the decline of social order? Is sexual desire in general destructive? How would you describe Viennese society? Is it understandable that Isabella wants to be a nun?

3. **Commodification:** Discuss the various ways in which the female characters are commodified in this play. What constitutes a woman's value?

How does the transaction of prostitution contribute to the theme of commodification? Is it significant that we do not see any of the prostitutes endlessly referred to?

4. **Marriage:** Consider how marriage functions within a state in relation to desire and sexuality. Discuss how you would stage Isabella's lack of verbal response to the Duke's climactic proposal. How would the staging of an acceptance or refused alter the reading of the text? Would a contemporary audience consider Claudio and Juliet as good as married? Does the same apply to Angelo and Mariana? Why is enforced marriage to a prostitute (and the mother of his child) considered a worse punishment for Lucio than death? Multiple betrothals are a convention of Shakespearean comedy—is this a comedy? If not, how would you classify this text?

5. *Measure for Measure:* Why is this the title of the play? What are some examples of instances of substitution? Consider the biblical source. How far is this play about retribution and justice? What is the role of mercy? Is it significant that Shakespeare chooses to set the play in Catholic Vienna?

Bibliography

Adelman, Janet. "Bed Tricks: On Marriage as the End of Comedy in *All's Well That Ends Well* and *Measure for Measure*." In *Shakespeare's Personality*, edited by Norman H. Holland, Sidney Horman, and Bernard J. Paris, 151–174. Berkley: University of California Press, 1989.

Altieri, Joanne. "Style and Social Disorder in *Measure for Measure*." *Shakespeare Quarterly* 25 (1974): 6–16.

Baines, Barbara J. "Assaying the Power of Chastity in *Measure for Measure*." *Studies in English Literature* 30 (1990): 281–301.

Bennett, Josephine Waters. Measure for Measure *as Royal Entertainment*. New York: Columbia University Press, 1966.

Bennett, Robert B. *Romance and Reformation: The Erasmian Spirit of Shakespeare's* Measure for Measure. Newark: University of Delaware Press, 2000.

Bloom, Harold, ed. *William Shakespeare's* Measure for Measure. New York: Chelsea House, 1987.

Bradbrook, M. C. "Authority, Truth, and Justice in *Measure for Measure*." *Review of English Studies* 17 (1941): 385–399.

Brown, Carolyn E. "Erotic Religious Flagellation and Shakespeare's *Measure for Measure*." *English Literary Renaissance* 16 (1986): 139–165.

Carrithers, Gale H., Jr., and James D. Hardy, Jr. *"Rex absconditus:* Justice, Presence, and Legitimacy in *Measure for Measure."* In *Renaissance Tropologies: The Cultural Imagination of Early Modern England,* edited by Jeanne Shami, 23–41. Pittsburgh, Pa.: Duquesne University Press, 2008.

Charlton, H. B. *Shakespearian Comedy.* London: Methuen, 1938.

Chedgzoy, Kate. *William Shakespeare: Measure for Measure.* Tavistock, U.K.: Northcote House, 2000.

Crane, Mary Thomas. "Male Pregnancy and Cognitive Permeability in *Measure for Measure*." *Shakespeare Quarterly* 49 (1998): 269–292.

Dawson, Anthony B. *"Measure for Measure,* New Historicism and Theatrical Power." *Shakespeare Quarterly* 39 (1988): 328–341.

Dodd, William. "Power and Performance: *Measure for Measure* in the Public Theatre of 1604–1605." *Shakespeare Studies* 24 (1996): 211–240.

Dollimore, Jonathan. "Transgression and Surveillance in *Measure for Measure*." In *Political Shakespeare: New Essays in Cultural Materialism,* 2nd ed., edited by Jonathan Dollimore and Alan Sinfield, 72–87. Manchester, U.K.: Manchester University Press, 1994.

Evans, Bertrand. *Shakespeare's Comedies.* Oxford, U.K.: Clarendon Press, 1960.

Friedman, Michael D. "'O, let him marry her!': Matrimony and Recompense in *Measure for Measure*." *Shakespeare Quarterly* 46 (1995): 454–464.

Frye, Northrop. *The Myth of Deliverance: Reflections on Shakespeare's Problem Comedies.* Brighton, U.K.: Harvester Press, 1983.

Geckle, George L., comp. *Twentieth Century Interpretations of* Measure for Measure: *A Collection of Critical Essays.* Englewood Cliffs, N.J.: Prentice-Hall, 1970.

Gless, Darryl J. Measure for Measure, *the Law, and the Convent.* Princeton, N.J.: Princeton University Press, 1979.

Gurr, Andrew. *"Measure for Measure*'s Hoods and Masks: The Duke, Isabella, and Liberty." *English Literary Renaissance* 27 (1997): 89–105.

Hawkins, Harriett. *Measure for Measure.* Boston: Twayne, 1987.

Kamaralli, Anna. "Writing about Motive: Isabella, the Duke and Moral Authority." *Shakespeare Survey* 58 (2005): 48–59.

Kirsch, Arthur. "The Integrity of *Measure for Measure*." *Shakespeare Survey* 28 (1975): 89–105.

Knight, G. Wilson. *"Measure for Measure* and the Gospels." In *The Wheel of Fire.* London: Oxford University Press, 1930, 80–106.

Knights, L. C. "The Ambiguity of *Measure for Measure*." In *Measure for Measure: A Casebook,* edited by C. K. Stead, 138–151. London: Macmillan, 1971.

Knoppers, Laura Lunger. "(En)gendering Shame: *Measure for Measure* and the Spectacles of Power." *English Literary Renaissance* 23 (1993): 450–471.

Korda, Natasha. "Singlewomen and the Properties of Poverty in *Measure for Measure*." In *Money and the Age of Shakespeare: Essays in New Economic Criticism,* edited by Linda Woodbridge, 237–250. Basingstoke, U.K.: Palgrave Macmillan, 2003.

Kott, Jan. "Head for Maidenhead, Maidenhead for Head: The Structure of Exchange in *Measure for Measure*." *Theatre Quarterly* 8 (1978): 18–24.

Krontiris, Tina. "The Omniscient 'Auctor': Ideology and Point of View in *Measure for Measure*." *English Studies* 80 (1999): 293–306.

Lascelles, Mary Madge. *Shakespeare's* Measure for Measure. London: Athlone Press, 1953.

Leavis, F. R. "The Greatness of *Measure for Measure*." *Scrutiny* 10 (1942): 234–247.

Leech, Clifford. "The 'Meaning' of *Measure for Measure*." In *Measure for Measure: A Casebook,* edited by C. K. Stead, 152–166. London: Macmillan, 1971.

Leggatt, Alexander. "Substitution in *Measure for Measure*." *Shakespeare Quarterly* 39 (1988): 342–359.

Magedanz, Stacy. "Public Justice and Private Mercy in *Measure for Measure*." *Studies in English Literature 1500–1900* 44 (2004): 317–332.

Maus, Katharine Eisaman. "Sexual Secrecy in *Measure for Measure*." In *Inwardness and Theater in the English Renaissance,* 157–181. Chicago: University of Chicago Press, 1995.

McLuskie, Kathleen. "The Patriarchal Bard: Feminist Criticism and Shakespeare: *King Lear* and *Measure for Measure*." In *Political Shakespeare: New Essays in Cultural Materialism,* 2nd ed., edited by Jonathan Dollimore and Alan Sinfield, 88–108. Manchester, U.K.: Manchester University Press, 1994.

Muir, Kenneth, and Stanley Wells, eds. *Aspects of Shakespeare's "Problem Plays": Articles Reprinted from* Shakespeare Survey. Cambridge: Cambridge University Press, 1982.

Nuttall, A. D. "*Measure for Measure:* The Bed-Trick." *Shakespeare Survey* 28 (1975): 51–56.

Price, Jonathan R. "*Measure for Measure* and the Critics: Towards a New Approach." *Shakespeare Quarterly* 20 (1969): 179–204.

Riefer, Marcia. "'Instruments of Some More Mightier Member': The Constriction of Female Power in *Measure for Measure*." *Shakespeare Quarterly* 35 (1984): 157–169.

Rossiter, A. P. *Angel with Horns and Other Shakespeare Lectures.* London: Longmans, 1961.

Schanzer, Ernest. "The Marriage-Contracts in *Measure for Measure*." *Shakespeare Survey* 13 (1960): 81–89.

———. *The Problem Plays of Shakespeare: A Study of Julius Caesar, Measure for Measure, Antony and Cleopatra.* London: Routledge & Kegan Paul, 1963.

Scott, Margaret. "'Our City's Institutions': Some Further Reflections on the Marriage Contracts in *Measure for Measure*." *ELH: English Literary History* 49 (1982): 790–804. 49 (1982): 790–804.

Shakespeare, William. *Measure for Measure.* Edited by N. W. Bawcutt. Oxford, U.K.: Clarendon Press, 1991.

———. *Measure for Measure.* Edited by Brian Gibbons. Cambridge: Cambridge University Press, 1991.

———. *Measure for Measure.* Edited by J. W. Lever. London: Arden Shakespeare, 2008.

———. *Measure for Measure.* Edited by Arthur Quiller-Couch and John Dover Wilson. Cambridge: Cambridge University Press, 1922.

———. *Measure for Measure.* Edited by Niegel Wood. Buckingham, U.K.: Open University Press, 1996.

Shell, Marc. *The End of Kinship:* Measure for Measure, *Incest, and the Idea of Universal Siblinghood.* Stanford, Calif.: Stanford University Press, 1988.

Shuger, Debora Kuller. *Political Theologies in Shakespeare's England: The Sacred and the State in* Measure for Measure. New York: Palgrave, 2001.

Stead, C. K., ed. *Measure for Measure: A Casebook.* London: Macmillan, 1971.

Stevenson, David Lloyd. *The Achievement of Shakespeare's* Measure for Measure. New York: Cornell University Press, 1966.

Tillyard, E. M. W. *Shakespeare's Problem Plays.* London: Chatto & Windus, 1950.

Watson, Robert N. "False Immortality in *Measure for Measure:* Comic Means, Tragic Ends." *Shakespeare Quarterly* 41 (1990): 411–432.

Wheeler, Richard. *Shakespeare's Development in the Problem Comedies: Turn and Counter-Turn.* Berkeley: University of California Press, 1981.

FILM AND VIDEO PRODUCTIONS

Davis, Desmond, dir. *Measure for Measure.* With Kenneth Colley, Kate Nelligan, and Tim Piggot-Smith. BBC, 1979.

Komar, Bob, dir. *Measure for Measure.* With Josephine Rogers, Daniel Roberts, and Simon Phillips. Press on Features, 2007.

—Sarah Carter

The Merchant of Venice

INTRODUCTION

On one level, *The Merchant of Venice* is as detached from reality as *A Midsummer Night's Dream,* the comedy that Shakespeare wrote immediately before it. A dead father's will requires his daughter to marry the suitor who chooses the correct casket, regardless of her feelings and his suitability. Yet the daughter is won by the very man she loves. A moneylender makes a merry bond with a merchant, calling for the forfeit of a pound of the latter's flesh if he does not repay a loan within three months, and the merchant, despite the reservations of his closest friend and the deep hostility between lender and borrower, signs it. All the merchant's ships miscarry, causing him to forfeit his bond, but a young woman disguises herself as a doctor of law to save him. In the last act, half his ships arrive in port safely.

The Merchant of Venice nonetheless feels a world away from *A Midsummer Night's Dream* and fairyland. Many of Shakespeare's comedies steer uncomfortably close to tragedy: *A Midsummer Night's Dream* rewrites *Romeo and Juliet* in a major key but could easily repeat that tragedy; *Much Ado About Nothing* is *Othello* narrowly averted. *Merchant* sails even closer to tragedy, perhaps even crosses over into it. The anti-Semitism of the play's Christians, if not of the play itself, deprives Shylock of daughter, wealth, and identity. Nonetheless, there is something almost heroic about him. In Philip Larkin's novel *Jill* (1946), John Kemp, on his first night at Oxford, opens one of his roommate's notebooks and reads, "Thus we see that in creating the character of Shylock, Shakespeare's original intention was deflected, and instead of a comic moneylender, he produced a figure of tragic significance." Nor is Shylock the only sufferer. The title character, too, loses what is most dear to him, as Bassanio, for whom Antonio offers his life, leaves him for Portia. Jessica's happiness in her marriage remains questionable at the play's end.

Despite the play's ambiguities, it has enjoyed immense popularity in the classroom and on the stage. It was the first Shakespeare drama to be staged in America (Williamsburg, 1752), Japan, and China. Scholars say that it has generated more commentary than any other Shakespeare work except for *Hamlet*. However one understands the intended genre—the first printing of *Merchant* in 1600 calls it a history, not a comedy—the play transcends a love story with a happy ending to explore questions of prejudice and hatred, friendship and love, mercy and revenge, appearance and reality, and the corrupting power of money. Like all other great works of art, it challenges its audiences to rethink their assumptions, to reexamine their lives, and to hear the still, sad music of humanity playing even within a comedy.

BACKGROUND

Many students reading about *The Merchant of Venice* are interested in the place of Jews in the English society of Shakespeare's time. The truth is that there were very few Jews in England then, but the idea of Jews and Jewishness seemed to have a hold on the Elizabethan imagination. In 1594, Dr. Rodrigo Lopez, a converted Portuguese Jew and physician to Queen Elizabeth, was executed on a trumped-up charge of plotting to poison her and Don Antonio Pérez, pretender to the Portuguese throne. This event was widely publicized and may well have helped prompt Shakespeare to write a Jewish play. Thomas Dekker and Thomas Middleton also wrote plays capitalizing on Lopez's notoriety. After Lopez was convicted, his estate was seized by the government. Elizabeth returned his property to his widow and five children, just as the Venetian duke waives the state's claim to Shylock's wealth in Shakespeare's play. Elizabeth kept only a ring that Lopez had received from the Spanish minister, another possible suggestion for the ring plot in *Merchant*. (For more information on Jews in English society, see the section on Difficulties of the Play. Also, James Shapiro's *Shakespeare and the Jews* [1996] provides a very interesting analysis of this subject).

Scholars have extensively explored the question of literary sources for the play, and some believe that an earlier play must have inspired it. In the case of *The Merchant of Venice,* three candidates for this role present themselves. In *The Schoole of Abuse* (1579) Stephen Gosson mentions the play *The Jew,* performed at the Bull, "representing the greediness of worldly chusers, and bloody mindes of usurers." Without excessive straining, one could apply the first phrase to the unsuccessful suitors who select the gold and silver caskets, the latter to Shylock's attempt on Antonio's life. Philip Henslowe's diary mentions, under the date of August 15, 1594, *The Venesyon Comedy,* and Thomas Dekker wrote a play entitled *The Jew of Venice* (date uncertain). All three of these works are lost, so it is impossible to determine how much Shakespeare drew from them.

Shakespeare also could have found the stories that make up *The Merchant of Venice* in a variety of sources other than those plays. Giovanni Fiorentino's *Il Pecorone* (1378; printed in Italian in 1558, though not yet in English by the 1590s) consists

An illustration for the *Daily Graphic* of the performance of *The Merchant of Venice* for King George of Greece at Windsor on November 15, 1903 *(Illustration by Douglas MacPherson)*

of 50 stories divided into days, in the manner of Giovanni Boccaccio's *Decameron* (ca. 1354). The first tale of the fourth day contains many of the key elements of Shakespeare's drama. In that narrative, Giannetto, left penniless by his father's will, goes to live with his godfather, Ansaldo, the richest merchant in Venice. Ansaldo furnishes Giannetto with a ship and cargo to trade at Alexandria. The young man sails into the harbor of Belmonte, where a beautiful widow offers to marry the man who can satisfy her in bed. If the man fails, his wealth is forfeit to her. Giannetto, though warned of the ill success of many others, resolves to win her. She feasts him and at night takes him into her bedroom, but her servant gives him drugged wine to drink. He sleeps through the night; the next morning, the widow claims his ship and its contents.

Back in Venice, Giannetto claims that he suffered shipwreck. Ansaldo furnishes him with a second vessel and goods. Again Giannetto sails to Belmonte, where he is once more feasted and then drugged, so that he loses his wealth again. Still undeterred, Giannetto goes back to Venice and desires a third ship. To equip this one, Ansaldo must borrow 10,000 ducats from a Jew, who stipulates that if the debt is not repaid by St. John's

Day, the Jew can claim a pound of flesh from the merchant's body. As Giannetto departs, Ansaldo asks him to return even if his enterprise fails: "If I can see you once before I die, I can die willingly." Antonio echoes this sentiment when he declares, "Pray God Bassanio come / To see me pay his debt, and then I care not!" (3.3.35–36).

On this visit, Giannetto is warned by one of the maids not to drink the drugged wine. He satisfies the lady, and they wed. Giannetto then forgets about his godfather until he sees people going to church on St. John's Day. He grows sad, and when his wife asks the cause of his unhappiness, he tells her about the loan. She gives him 100,000 ducats to take to Venice and tells him to bring Ansaldo back to Belmonte with him if he can save the merchant. After Giannetto departs, his wife disguises herself as a lawyer and follows him, as Portia does in Shakespeare's play. As a lawyer, she also serves as judge.

The Jew refuses repayment, insisting on his pound of flesh. He and Giannetto appeal to the disguised judge for a verdict. She offers the Jew the 100,000 ducats, just as Portia at the trial repeatedly tries to get Shylock to accept repayment of his loan. Like Shylock, the Jew refuses. The judge then declares that the Jew is entitled to enforce his bond. As he prepares to carve out Ansaldo's flesh, she adds that if he spills a drop of blood or takes more or less than a pound of flesh, he dies. Portia relies on this same literalism, though she also introduces the law that condemns aliens for plotting against Venetians. The Jew now wants the 100,000 ducats, as Shylock tries to claim repayment once he learns he cannot shed blood. The judge and Portia both state that having refused the money earlier, he cannot claim it now. In *Il Pecorone,* the Jew tears his bond and leaves. He does not suffer the additional punishment inflicted on Shylock.

Giannetto offers the judge the 100,000 ducats he was going to pay the Jew, but she asks only for his wedding ring. Giannetto initially refuses to part with it because his wife will think he gave it to a lover. When the judge persists, he yields, just as Bassanio behaves in the play. The lady then returns

to Belmonte ahead of her husband and Ansaldo. As Giannetto feared, his wife, seeing that he is not wearing his wedding ring, accuses him of giving it to some woman. They argue, and Giannetto begins to weep. She then produces the ring and explains her ruse. Portia does the same. Ansaldo marries the maid who warned Giannetto about the drugged wine, and everyone lives happily.

The lady's bed test for choosing a husband was not well-suited for the Elizabethan stage. Instead, Shakespeare required the suitors to choose the casket that contains Portia's picture. Such a procedure appears in story 32 of the *Gesta Romanorum* (ca. 1300; first printed in English by Wynkyn de Worde, 1510–15). To demonstrate her worthiness to marry the son of the Roman emperor, the daughter of the king of Naples must select from among three vessels. One, of gold, bears the inscription "They that choose me shall find in me that they deserve." Inside are bones. On the second, silver, vessel is carved "They that choose me shall find in me that nature and kind desire." The third vessel, made of lead, carries the motto "They that choose me shall find in me that God hath disposed." Inside this unpromising container are precious stones. The princess chooses the lead vessel and so wins the emperor's son.

Shakespeare used the same metals, though he reversed the inscriptions on the gold and silver caskets and changed the leaden one to read, "Who chooseth me must give and hazard all he hath" (2.7.16), emphasizing the play's theme of hazarding and giving. Shakespeare also altered the contents to pictures and poems. The 1595 edition of the *Gesta Romanorum,* in the English translation by Richard Robinson, states the motto on the leaden vessel was "insculped"; Shakespeare uses that word at 2.7.57, the only appearance of that word in his works.

Another possible source for the debate between Shylock and Portia in the trial scene (4.1) is Alexandre Sylvain's *Epitome de cent histoires* (1581, translated into English as *The Orator* in 1596 by "L. P.," i.e., Lazarus Pyott, a pseudonym for Anthony Munday). As in *Il Pecorone,* a Christian merchant borrows money (900 ducats) from a Jew. If the loan is not repaid in three months, the same period stipulated in *The Merchant of Venice*, the Jew can claim a pound of the merchant's flesh. The merchant defaults, the Jew claims the forfeit, and the judge rules that the Jew must take precisely a pound of flesh or he will die. The Jew protests this ruling as violating the principle of contracts. He grants that taking a pound of flesh is cruel, but worse are imprisonment or enslavement for debt, yet these are common practices. Shylock raises the issue of slavery at 4.1.90–98. Also, Sylvain's Jew maintains that the debtor is obliged to give him the pound of flesh; as creditor, he should not be responsible for taking it. The Christian's reply attacks Jews and asks for mercy but does not counter any of the Jew's arguments. Sylvain does not indicate which side prevails.

The late 13th-century *Cursor Mundi* also addresses such a bond between a Jew and a Christian. Denied his forfeit because he cannot shed any blood, the Jew curses the judges and then is condemned to death, as Shylock is. In *Cursor Mundi*, the Jew saves himself by showing Queen Helena the site of the true cross. The ballad of "Gernutus" again involves a bond between a Christian and Jew calling for the loss of a pound of flesh if the former fails to repay the latter. This poem may predate Shakespeare's play, but it might also be based on that work.

The subplot of Jessica's elopement probably derives from the 14th tale in Masuccio Salernitano's *Il Novellino* (1476; no English translation in the 16th century). Salernitano's name may have suggested Shakespeare's Salerio and Solanio as well. In Masuccio's tale, Giuffredi Saccano falls in love with Carmosina, daughter of a miserly merchant who keeps her imprisoned and treats her worse than a servant. At 2.3.2, Jessica complains, "Our house is hell," and Shylock in 2.5 instructs her not to look out the window at a masque. Saccano pretends to befriend the miser and insinuates a maid, Anna, into the man's house to abet Carmosina's flight, just as Launcelot Gobbo, Shylock's erstwhile servant, assists Lorenzo to secure Jessica. Carmosina

escapes her father's house at night, taking 1,500 ducats with her, as Jessica steals money and jewels from Shylock when she flees with Lorenzo. In this story, the lovers eventually marry and Carmosina's father accepts the match. In Shakespeare's play, Shylock is compelled to make Jessica and Lorenzo his heirs.

Anthony Munday's *Zeleuto or the Fountaine of Fame* (1580) offers another version of the Jessica-Lorenzo story; his includes a trial as well. In this tale, Truculento, a Christian usurer of Verona, loves Rodolfo's sister, Cornelia. Rodolfo's friend Strabino also loves her. Rodolfo borrows money from Truculento and buys a jewel for his friend; Strabino gives the gem to Cornelia's father, who then allows Strabino and Cornelia to marry. Rodolfo marries Brisana, daughter of Truculento, who does not know of Rodolfo's plot. The young lovers have pledged their right eyes as well as their lands to obtain the loan from Truculento, who initially claims that he will never enforce the bond, just as Shylock says he has no desire for Antonio's flesh (1.3.160–168).

Once Truculento learns that he has been deceived, he changes his mind, just as Jessica's flight may prompt Shylock to turn the "merry bond" (1.3.173) into a serious one. The men fail to repay Truculento on time, so he insists on removing their eyes. Like Portia and Nerissa, the women disguise themselves as men and save their husbands by declaring that Truculento's contract does not allow the spilling of blood. Truculento had refused repayment and declared that he did not want their lands. Thwarted in his revenge, he, like Shylock, now asks for the money he earlier rejected but is denied. Shakespeare probably knew this story, since he apparently drew on it for *The Taming of the Shrew* (ca. 1594). In Masuccio's story, Strabino's father, Vincentio, has sent his son to Verona to further his education, just as in Shakespeare's comedy, Lucentio, son of Vincentio, has come to Padua to "institute / a course of learning and ingenious studies" (1.1.8–9).

Christopher Marlowe is Shakespeare's great precursor, and his shade haunts works from *Venus and*

Adonis (1593) to *The Tempest* (1611). Marlowe's *The Jew of Malta* (1592) suggested lines, situations, characters, and themes for Shakespeare's Jewish play. Barabas, Marlowe's title character, is both merchant and moneylender. Shakespeare divided these occupations between Antonio and Shylock, but the men remain two halves of a whole. When Barabas protests the confiscation of his wealth, a fate that also befalls Shylock, a Maltese knight justifies the action with pious protestations. Barabas retorts, "What, bring you Scripture to confirm your wrongs?" (1.2.111). Shakespeare turned this line into Antonio's "The devil can cite Scripture for his purpose" (1.3.98). Barabas continues,

> Why, I esteem the injury far less,
> To take the lives of miserable men
> Than be the causers of their misery

by impoverishing them (1.2.147–149). Both Shylock (4.1.376–377) and Antonio (5.1.286) link life and livelihood.

In *The Jew of Malta*, to retrieve some of her father's money, Barabas's daughter, Abigail, gains entrance to his seized house and tosses down to him money, pearls, and jewels he had concealed there. In *Merchant*, Act II, Scene 6, Shylock's daughter takes money and jewels from his house and tosses them down to her lover. Barabas praises Abigail: "O, my girl, / My gold, my fortune, my felicity, / . . . O girl! O gold! O beauty! O my bliss" (2.1.46–47, 53). According to Solanio, when Shylock learns of his daughter's robbery and flight he laments, "My daughter! O my ducats! O my daughter! / Fled with a Christian! O my Christian ducats!" (2.8.15–16). Abigail of the Bible is the daughter of Jesse, whose name may have suggested Jessica. Both Barabas and Shylock want their daughters to marry a Jew, but both women fall in love with Christians, and both convert to Christianity. Lodowick, Abigail's lover, calls her "gentle" (2.3.317), and Lorenzo applies the same adjective to Jessica (2.4.19), in both cases punning on *gentile*.

Barabas says that in Florence, he learned to "Heave up my shoulders when they call me dog, /

And duck as low as any bare-foot friar" (2.3.23–25). Shylock declares (1.3.109–110) that he has borne Antonio's calling him a dog and his other insults "with a patient shrug / (For suff'rance is the badge of all our tribe)." Barabas buys a skinny rather than a fat slave because he wants one who will not eat much. Shylock complains that Launcelot Gobbo is "a huge feeder" (2.5.46). Barabas's slave Ithamore tells the courtesan Bellamira, "I'll be thy Jason, thou my golden fleece" (4.2.94). Bassanio compares Portia to the Golden Fleece (1.1.169–170), and after he and Gratiano win their ladies' hands, the latter exclaims, "We are the Jasons, we have won the fleece" (3.2.241). Barabas and Shylock dominate their respective plays, and while both are vengeful, they are also wronged. Both plays show the corrupting influence of money, and both reveal the truth of Barabas's accusation against the Christians:

> For I can see no fruits in all their faith,
> But malice, falsehood, and excessive pride,
> Which methinks fits not their profession.
>
> (1.1.114–116)

Murray J. Levith's "Shakespeare's *Merchant* and Marlowe's Other Play" (Mahon and Mahon: 95–106) sees parallels with *Doctor Faustus* (ca. 1588–92) as well. *The Jew of Malta* was revived in 1594 when Dr. Rodrigo Lopez was executed.

The commedia dell'arte could also have furnished hints for *The Merchant of Venice*. Pantaloon is a greedy Venetian householder with a large knife, greedy servants, and an errant daughter. In commedia dell'arte, Graziano is a stock figure, a physician usually in conflict with Pantaloon, as Gratiano sharply attacks Shylock. Like his commedia dell'arte counterpart, Shakespeare's Gratiano is presumptuous and garrulous. Sometimes in commedia dell'arte, the character is cuckolded, as Gratiano fears he has been (5.1.265).

Shakespeare's plays are replete with biblical allusions, none more so than *The Merchant of Venice*. The story that Shylock tells of Laban, Jacob, and the parti-colored sheep comes directly from Genesis 30:25–43. Shylock is well versed in the New Testament as well. He observes that Antonio resembles a publican (1.3.41) and refers to Jesus' driving devils into pigs (Mark 5:1–13; *Merchant* 1.3.33–35). Shylock's exclamation "My deeds upon my head!" (4.1.202) echoes Matthew 27:25, in which the Jews declare, "His blood be on us and on our children." Blind Gobbo's blessing his hairy son (2.2) derives from Isaac's blessing Jacob, again in Genesis. Jessica's claim that she will be saved through her husband (3.5.15–16) recalls 1 Corinthians 7.14. Portia's famous speech about mercy draws on the Sermon on the Mount, Daniel, and Eccelesiasticus. Antonio's statement "I hold the world but as the world" (1.1.77) alludes to Matthew 6:15–20, which is about laying up stores in heaven rather than on Earth. The poem inside the silver casket says that its metal has been tried in the fire seven times (2.9.63), a line based on Psalm 12:6.

Date and Text of the Play

The Stationers' Register, Register C, records the following entry for July 22, 1598, for James Roberts:

> Entred for his copie vnder the handes, of bothe the wardens, a booke of the Marcaunt of Venyce or otherwise called the Iewe of Venyce. Prouided that yt bee not printed by the said Iames Robertes; or anye other whatsoeuer without lycence first had from the Right honorable the lord Chamberlen.

This may have been a blocking entry, intended to prevent piracy. Whatever the entry's intent, it shows that *The Merchant of Venice* had been written by 1598, and the title appears in the list of Shakespeare's comedies in Francis Meres's *Palladis Tamia,* printed a few months later. At 1.1.27, Salerio refers to a ship called the *Andrew.* In his June 1596 raid of Cadiz, the earl of Essex captured two Spanish galleons, the *San Matias* and the *San Andrés,* and brought both ships back to England. The latter vessel was renamed the *Andrew.* These

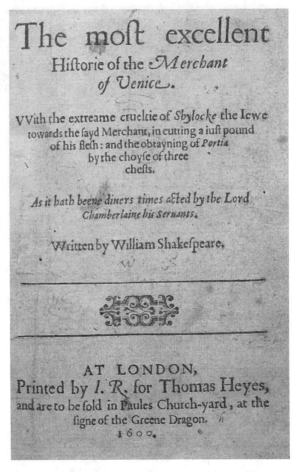

The most excellent Historie of the *Merchant* of *Venice*.

VVith the extreame crueltie of *Shylocke* the Iewe towards the fayd Merchant, in cutting a iuft pound of his fleſh: and the obtayning of *Portia* by the choyſe of three cheſts.

As it hath beene diuers times acted by the Lord Chamberlaine his Seruants.

Written by William Shakeſpeare.

AT LONDON, Printed by *I. R.* for Thomas Heyes, and are to be fold in Paules Church-yard, at the ſigne of the Greene Dragon. 1600.

Title page of the first edition of *The Merchant of Venice,* a quarto published in 1600

references as well as the play's style indicate that Shakespeare composed the work between 1596 and 1598.

On October 28, 1600, Thomas Hayes placed the following entry in the Stationers' Register, Register C: "Entred for his copie vnder the handes of the Wardens & by Consent of mr Robertes. A boke called the boke of the merchant of Venyce." Roberts printed the text for Thomas Hayes (or Heyes), probably using either Shakespeare's foul papers or a scribal transcription of that original. An indication that the foul papers served as copy text is that in the speech prefixes, Shylock is sometimes named

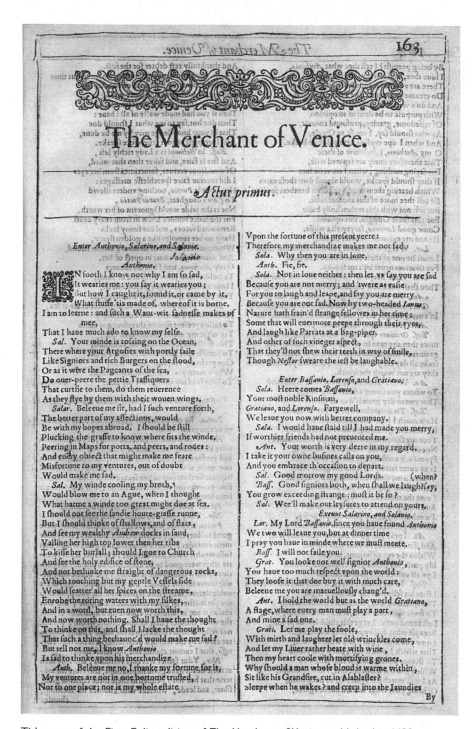

The Merchant of Venice. 163

The Merchant of Venice.

Actus primus.

Enter Anthonio, Salarino, and Salanio.

Anthonio.

IN footh I know not why I am so sad,
It wearies me: you say it wearies you;
But how I caught it, found it, or came by it,
What stuffe 'tis made of, whereof it is borne,
I am to learne: and such a Want-wit sadnesse makes of
    mee,
That I haue much ado to know my selfe.

Sal. Your minde is tossing on the Ocean,
There where your Argosies with portly saile
Like Signiors and rich Burgers on the flood,
Or as it were the Pageants of the sea,
Do ouer-peere the pettie Traffiquers
That curtsie to them, do them reuerence
As they flye by them with their wouen wings.

Salar. Beleeue me sir, had I such venture forth,
The better part of my affections, would
Be with my hopes abroad. I should be still
Plucking the grasse to know where sits the winde,
Peering in Maps for ports, and peers, and rodes:
And euery obiect that might make me feare
Misfortune to my ventures, out of doubt
Would make me sad.

Sal. My winde cooling my broth,
Would blow me to an Ague, when I thought
What harme a winde too great might doe at sea.
I should not see the sandie houre-glasse runne,
But I should thinke of shallows, and of flats,
And see my wealthy *Andrew* docks in sand,
Vailing her high top lower then her ribs
To kisse her buriall; should I goe to Church
And see the holy edifice of stone,
And not bethinke me straight of dangerous rocks,
Which touching but my gentle Vessels side,
Would scatter all her spices on the streame,
Enrobe the roring waters with my silkes,
And in a word, but euen now worth this,
And now worth nothing. Shall I haue the thought
To thinke on this, and shall I lacke the thought
That such a thing bechanc'd would make me sad?
But tell not me, I know *Anthonio*
Is sad to thinke vpon his merchandize.

Anth. Beleeue me no, I thanke my fortune for it,
My ventures are not in one bottome trusted,
Nor to one place; nor is my whole estate

Vpon the fortune of this present yeere:
Therefore my merchandize makes me not sad.

Sola. Why then you are in loue.

Anth. Fie, fie.

Sola. Not in loue neither: then let vs say you are sad
Because you are not merry; and 'twere as easie
For you to laugh and leape, and say you are merry
Because you are not sad. Now by two-headed *Ianus*,
Nature hath fram'd strange fellowes in her time:
Some that will euermore peepe through their eyes,
And laugh like Parrats at a bag-piper.
And other of such vineger aspect,
That they'll not shew their teeth in way of smile,
Though *Nestor* sweare the iest be laughable.

Enter Bassanio, Lorenso, and Gratiano.

Sola. Heere comes *Bassanio*,
Your most noble Kinsman,
Gratiano, and *Lorenso*. Faryewell,
We leaue you now with better company.

Sala. I would haue staid till I had made you merry,
If worthier friends had not preuented me.

Ant. Your worth is very deere in my regard.
I take it your owne busines calls on you,
And you embrace th'occasion to depart.

Sal. Good morrow my good Lords.   (when?

Bass. Good signiors both, when shall we laugh? say,
You grow exceeding strange: must it be so?

Sal. Wee'll make our leysures to attend on yours.

Exeunt Salarino, and Solanio.

Lor. My Lord *Bassanio*, since you haue found *Anthonio*
We two will leaue you, but at dinner time
I pray you haue in minde where we must meete.

Bass. I will not faile you.

Grat. You looke not well signior *Anthonio*,
You haue too much respect vpon the world:
They loose it that doe buy it with much care,
Beleeue me you are maruellously chang'd.

Ant. I hold the world but as the world *Gratiano*,
A stage, where euery man must play a part,
And mine a sad one.

Grati. Let me play the foole,
With mirth and laughter let old wrinckles come,
And let my Liuer rather heate with wine,
Then my heart coole with mortifying grones.
Why should a man whose bloud is warme within,
Sit like his Grandsire, cut in Alablaster?
Sleepe when he wakes? and creep into the Iaundies

By

Title page of the First Folio edition of *The Merchant of Venice,* published in 1623 and sometimes listed as "Iew" (Jew). Launcelot's speech prefixes sometimes use his name and sometimes refer to him as "Clowne." Also, Shakespeare had not yet sorted out Antonio's two friends with the similar names, who at the beginning of Act I are listed as Salaryno and Salanio. Elsewhere, the latter is called Solanio, the former Salerio. In 1619, Thomas Pavier attempted to produce an unauthorized quarto edition of Shakespeare's plays. He printed 10 titles before he was caught and forced to stop; one of these was *The Merchant of Venice,* bearing the false imprint of 1600 and supposedly printed by J. Roberts. This second quarto edition of the play (Q2) was based on the 1600 quarto (Q1). The text that appears in the 1623 First Folio (F1) is also based on Q1. Neither quarto divides the play into acts or scenes. F1 added act divisions. The scene breaks were created by various 18th-century editors.

SYNOPSIS
Brief Synopsis

The play unfolds over a period of three months. In the opening scene, Bassanio appeals to Antonio, a rich Venetian merchant, for a loan that will allow him to woo Portia, a rich heiress who lives in Belmont. If Bassanio gains her hand, he will be able to repay all the money he has previously borrowed from Antonio. Antonio replies that all his money is tied up in his business ventures abroad, but he will allow Bassanio to use his credit to raise the needed money.

The scene then shifts to Belmont, where Portia laments that she cannot choose her husband. Rather, she is bound by her dead father's will to wed the man who correctly guesses which one of three caskets contains her picture. Portia's lady-in-waiting, Nerissa, assures her that because her father was a religious man, the lottery he devised will ensure that Portia marries the man she loves.

Back in Venice, Bassanio and Antonio arrange for a loan of 3,000 ducats for three months from the Jewish moneylender Shylock. Rather than charging interest, Shylock states that as a jest, Antonio should agree to forfeit a pound of flesh if

the loan is not repaid in the time stipulated. Bassanio urges Antonio not to sign such a bond, but Antonio replies that he will easily repay the money a month before it is due.

While the Prince of Morocco prepares to choose a casket at Belmont, in Venice Shylock's servant Launcelot Gobbo resolves to leave his old master and go to serve Bassanio, and Shylock's daughter, Jessica, prepares to elope with the Christian Lorenzo. That evening, disguised as a boy, she flees with her lover, as Bassanio and Gratiano set off for Portia's house. There, Morocco and then the Prince of Arragon choose the wrong casket, the former opting for the golden one, the latter for the silver.

Back in Venice, Shylock laments his daughter's flight and vows revenge on Antonio, whose ships have been reported lost. Unaware of his friend's plight, Bassanio in Belmont tells Portia of his love for her, and she expresses hers for him. He wins her by choosing the correct (lead) casket. Gratiano, who has accompanied Bassanio to Belmont, announces that he has won Nerissa's love as well. Each woman gives her fiancé a ring, which the men vow to keep as long they live. The lovers' celebration is cut short as Salerio arrives with news of Antonio's inability to repay Shylock. The merchant therefore faces death at the hand of his creditor. Portia tells Bassanio to marry her and then hasten to Venice with ample funds to repay Antonio's loan. She says that she and Nerissa will await the men's return.

Once Bassanio and Gratiano leave, Portia and Nerissa disguise themselves as men, Portia as a lawyer, Nerissa as her clerk, and travel to Venice. The women appear in court, where, through a legalistic ruse, Portia saves Antonio's life. Shylock is forced to convert to Christianity, make Lorenzo and Jessica his heirs, and surrender half his wealth to Antonio, who will use it in trust until Shylock's death, when that money, too, will go to Shylock's daughter and son-in-law. In payment for her services, Portia requests only Antonio's gloves and Bassanio's ring. Bassanio at first refuses her, but at Antonio's urging, he yields. Nerissa secures Gratiano's ring as well.

When Portia, Nerissa, Bassanio, Gratiano, and Antonio arrive at Belmont, the women accuse their husbands of giving their rings away to Venetian lovers. The men protest their innocence, but the women seemingly remain incredulous. The wives finally produce the rings, claiming that they received them for sleeping with the lawyer and his clerk. Portia soon relieves the men's anxiety by revealing the truth, and she informs Antonio that three of his ships that were rumored lost have in fact come to harbor safely.

Act I, Scene 1

Antonio, the title character, enters in the midst of a conversation with Salerio and Solanio. Antonio observes that he does not know why he is sad. His two friends suggest that he is concerned about his business affairs. When Antonio rejects that suggestion, Solanio says that the merchant must be in love; Antonio dismisses the idea. Bassanio enters with Lorenzo and Gratiano; Salerio and Solanio depart. Gratiano comments on Antonio's melancholy appearance, which he, too, attributes to financial worries. To Antonio's denial, Gratiano responds that Antonio must then be sad by choice.

Lorenzo and Gratiano leave Antonio and Bassanio alone. The latter declares that he wants to wed Portia, an heiress in Belmont, but to woo her he needs to borrow money, since he squandered his estate as well as whatever Antonio had previously advanced him. He hopes Antonio will again be his creditor. Antonio replies that all his money is tied up in his business ventures abroad, but he will serve as surety for any loan Bassanio raises.

Act I, Scene 2

At Belmont, Portia, like Antonio, complains of her sadness. Portia, however, has a clear reason for her discontent. According to her dead father's will, she cannot choose a husband. Rather, she must wed whoever solves the riddle of the three caskets. One of these—the gold, the silver, or the lead—contains Portia's picture; he who guesses correctly, and only he, may marry her. Those who choose wrongly are sworn never to wed. Nerissa, Portia's attendant, assures her that her father's test will produce the right husband.

Nerissa then asks Portia's opinion of her current suitors. Portia responds with a satiric verbal portrait of each. Nerissa informs her lady that she need not fear having to marry any of them because they have all declined the test. Then Nerissa recalls Bassanio; both she and Portia remember him fondly. As the scene ends, four suitors depart, but a new one, the Prince of Morocco, arrives.

Act I, Scene 3

Bassanio asks Shylock for a loan of 3,000 ducats for three months; Antonio will guarantee repayment. As the merchant approaches, Shylock, in his only soliloquy, declares that he hates Antonio because the merchant is a Christian but even more because by borrowing money without interest, Antonio lessens Shylock's profits. Moreover, Antonio is anti-Semitic and publicly condemns Shylock's dealings.

Antonio states that though he never charges or pays interest, he will make an exception to help Bassanio. Shylock tries to justify his charging interest by citing the story in Genesis of Jacob, Laban, and the parti-colored sheep, but Antonio denies the relevance of that account. Asked again whether he will lend Antonio the money, Shylock recounts Antonio's numerous insults. Antonio remains impenitent. He tells Shylock to lend the money as to an enemy.

Shylock retorts that he wishes to befriend Antonio. Rather than charging interest, he will require only a "merry bond" (1.3.173), stipulating that if Antonio defaults on his loan, Shylock may take a pound of Antonio's flesh from any part of the merchant's body the lender chooses. Bassanio urges Antonio not to sign such a dangerous document, but Antonio reassures his friend that he will be able to repay the money well before it is due.

Act II, Scene 1

At Belmont, the Prince of Morocco urges Portia not to shun him because of his skin color. Portia replies that she does not judge by sight alone. Moreover, she must abide by the result of the casket lottery. Morocco wishes that he could win her through heroic action. She reminds him that there is only one way he can gain her hand; if he fails, he never can marry. He agrees to try his luck after dinner.

Act II, Scene 2

On a street in Venice, Launcelot Gobbo debates whether to leave Shylock's employ. Just as he resolves to seek service with Bassanio, blind Old Gobbo enters and asks the way to Shylock's house. Launcelot gives his father impossible directions and then tells him that the son he seeks is dead, but he reveals the truth at length. Old Gobbo has brought a gift for Shylock; Launcelot asks him to give the present to Bassanio instead. Bassanio appears at that moment, and the two Gobbos confusedly interrupt each other as they try to explain that Launcelot wants to serve him. Bassanio grants their suit. As the two Gobbos leave, Gratiano enters with a request of his own: He wants to accompany Bassanio to Belmont. Bassanio agrees under the condition that Gratiano curb his boisterousness, which Gratiano promises to do.

Act II, Scene 3

Jessica tells Launcelot that she will miss him. She hands him a letter for Lorenzo, with whom she plans to elope that night.

Act II, Scene 4

Lorenzo, Gratiano, Salerio, and Solanio plan a masque to entertain Bassanio and his dinner guests that evening. Launcelot appears and hands Lorenzo Jessica's letter. Lorenzo instructs Launcelot to reassure Jessica of his intention to come to her that night. Launcelot sets off on his errand, and Salerio and Solanio leave to prepare for the night's revelry. Lorenzo tells Gratiano of his plan to elope and gives his friend Jessica's letter to read as they exit.

Act II, Scene 5

In front of his house, Shylock warns Launcelot that his new master, Bassanio, will prove less generous

Shylock (Jacob P. Adler) speaks to Jessica while Launcelot looks on in Act II, Scene 5 of *The Merchant of Venice*. This photograph was published by the Byron Company in 1903.

than Shylock has been. As Shylock talks to his now former servant, he keeps calling for Jessica, who finally appears. He tells his daughter that Bassanio has invited him to dinner; he gives her his keys and orders her to lock up his house. When Launcelot promises Shylock a masque, he warns Jessica not to look out the window at the festivities. Launcelot whispers to Jessica that a Christian worth seeing will pass by. To Shylock's question of Launcelot's message to her, Jessica replies that he merely has said goodbye. When Launcelot leaves, Shylock expresses delight at having rid himself of his servant, who, Shylock says, is lazy and a big feeder. Now Launcelot will cost Bassanio some of his borrowed money. Shylock leaves, again telling Jessica to lock up his house. She bids him farewell and observes that she is about to lose a father, he a daughter.

Act II, Scene 6

In front of Shylock's house, Gratiano and Salerio await Lorenzo. When Lorenzo arrives, he calls to Jessica. Disguised as a boy, she appears on the balcony and asks who is summoning her. Lorenzo identifies himself. Does he love her, she asks. He assures her that he does; she responds by tossing him a casket filled with ducats. She then goes back inside to get more money from her father's store and lock up the house.

Lorenzo intends for Jessica to serve as a torchbearer in the masque to be presented at Bassanio's house, but Antonio arrives to inform the men that Bassanio is leaving for Belmont immediately. The masque, therefore, is canceled.

Act II, Scene 7

At Portia's house, Morocco confronts the three caskets. Twice he reads their inscriptions aloud before selecting the golden one. When he opens it, he finds the picture of a death's head and a poem telling him that he chose foolishly. He leaves, much to Portia's relief.

Act II, Scene 8

Back in Venice, Salerio and Solanio mockingly report Shylock's grief at the loss of his daughter and his money. Solanio comments that Antonio will suffer if he does not repay his loan in time. Salerio replies that a ship has foundered in the English Channel; he hopes this is not one of Antonio's. He then describes Antonio's affectionate parting with Bassanio. The two leave to comfort the merchant.

Act II, Scene 9

At Belmont, the Prince of Arragon is ready to select a casket. He reviews the rules: If he chooses wrongly, he must never reveal which casket he picked, never marry, and depart immediately. He reads the inscriptions aloud and then decides on the silver container. When he unlocks it, he finds a picture of an idiot and a poem calling him a fool. As soon as he departs, a messenger announces the arrival of a Venetian. Nerissa hopes the new suitor is Bassanio.

Act III, Scene 1

On a Venetian street, Solanio and Salerio discuss the loss of one of Antonio's ships. Shylock enters and accuses them of being party to his daughter's elopement. He then declares that Antonio should beware his bond. Salerio asks what good Antonio's flesh will do Shylock, who retorts that it will feed his revenge. He declares that Antonio has repeatedly insulted him and hindered his moneymaking, and only because Shylock is Jewish. He then delivers his famous "Hath not a Jew eyes?" speech (3.1.59–73), concluding that just as Christians avenge themselves on Jews who wrong them, he will avenge himself on Antonio. Tubal enters as Salerio and Solanio leave to join Antonio. Tubal has gone to Genoa in search of Jessica. He has heard about her but has not found her. He alternately reports on Jessica's extravagance, plunging Shylock into lament, and on Antonio's losses, which delight Shylock. Shylock instructs Tubal to hire a sherrif's officer to arrest Antonio for debt as soon as the bond falls due.

Act III, Scene 2

At Belmont, Portia confesses her love for Bassanio and urges him to put off choosing a casket, for if he chooses incorrectly, she will lose the pleasure of his company. Bassanio replies that delay is torture; he wants to learn his fate immediately. Portia orders music to be played, and someone sings a song about infatuation's originating in appearance. Bassanio recognizes that "The world is still deceived with ornament" (3.2.74) and so chooses the lead casket, which contains Portia's image and a poem praising his choice. The scroll instructs him to claim his bride with a kiss.

Bassanio asks Portia whether she truly is his. She responds that she and all she owns belong to him. To symbolize her gift, she gives him a ring. If he loses it or gives it away, she will know that he no longer loves her. He swears that only death can part him from her ring. Nerissa and Gratiano congratulate the happy couple. Then Gratiano asks permission to marry Portia's attendant.

Lorenzo, Jessica, and Salerio enter. Salerio gives Bassanio a letter from Antonio. Alarmed by Bassanio's reaction to the letter, Portia asks about its contents. He informs her of Antonio's bond. According to the letter, all of Antonio's ships have sunk. The loan is now due, and Shylock demands the forfeit. Jessica interjects that her father swore he would prefer Antonio's flesh to repayment of the loan 20 times over. Learning the sum owed, Portia instructs Bassanio to marry her and then hasten to Venice with ample money to cover Antonio's debt.

Act III, Scene 3

Antonio's jailor has allowed him out of prison to plead with Shylock, who remains obdurate. Solanio says that the duke will set aside the bond, but Antonio says that Venice is too dependent on foreign trade to abrogate a contract.

Act III, Scene 4

Lorenzo praises Portia for allowing Bassanio to return to Venice before consummating their marriage and assures her that Antonio merits her sacrifice. Portia replies that Antonio must resemble Bassanio, so she is rescuing one who is like her own soul. She then commits the management of her estate to Lorenzo. She and Nerissa, Portia claims, will go to a nearby monastery to pray. She dispatches her servant Balthazar to Padua to her cousin, Doctor Bellario, who will give him notes and clothes. Balthazar is to bring these to Portia, who will await him at the ferry to Venice. Alone with Nerissa, Portia says that they will disguise themselves as men and join their husbands.

Act III, Scene 5

In Belmont, Launcelot teases Jessica, saying she is damned because she is not a Christian. She replies that she will be saved through Lorenzo. Launcelot then blames her husband for converting her because increasing the number of Christians will raise the price of pork. Lorenzo enters, and Jessica repeats Launcelot's comments. Lorenzo replies that the servant has impregnated a Moor. He instructs Launcelot to bid the servants prepare for dinner. After some verbal sparring, Launcelot

leaves. Jessica praises Portia; Lorenzo praises himself, and the two go off to eat.

Act IV, Scene 1

In a Venetian courtroom, the duke expresses sympathy for Antonio, who says he is prepared to suffer the loss of his flesh. Shylock is summoned. When he appears, the duke tries to cajole him into abandoning his suit. Shylock refuses to relent. Bassanio offers to pay 6,000 ducats, but Shylock insists on the terms of his bond.

The duke now declares that he will adjourn the court unless Bellario, "a learned doctor" (4.1.105), appears to judge the case. At that moment, Salerio reports the arrival of a messenger from Padua. Bassanio tries to comfort Antonio, who again asserts his readiness to die. Disguised as a lawyer's clerk, Nerissa enters and hands the duke a letter. As the duke reads, Shylock sharpens his knife on the sole of his shoe. Gratiano curses Shylock; the moneylender remains impervious to Gratiano's railing.

The duke reads the letter aloud. It states that Bellario is too ill to attend the trial, but he is sending Balthazar (i.e., Portia dressed as a man) in his stead. Balthazar enters and declares that since Antonio's flesh is forfeit legally, Shylock must show mercy. When Shylock bristles at her "must," she responds with her famous "Quality of mercy" speech (4.1.184–202). Shylock, unmoved, rejects Bassanio's offer of twice the sum of the debt.

Portia twice offers Shylock 9,000 ducats, which he still refuses. She then asks Shylock to summon a physician to prevent Antonio's bleeding to death. Shylock replies that the contract does not mention a physician.

Antonio bids farewell to Bassanio, who says that he would sacrifice Portia to save his friend. Portia notes that his wife would not approve of that speech. Gratiano declares that he wishes his own wife were dead so she could intercede for Antonio in heaven. Nerissa retorts that if his wife heard him say so, an argument would ensue.

Shylock demands that Portia pronounce her judgment, and she grants him his pound of flesh.

As he steps forward to claim it, she stops him: If he sheds any blood, his property will be forfeit to the state. He now asks for the 9,000 ducats instead. Bassanio begins to hand over the money, but Portia stops him. Shylock shall have only his bond. If he takes more or less than a pound of flesh, his life is forfeit and his goods will be confiscated. Shylock says he will settle for 3,000 ducats, but Portia maintains that he has publicly refused repayment.

Shylock abandons his suit and prepares to leave the court, but Portia has not finished with him. He is an alien, not a Venetian citizen. If an alien conspires against a Venetian, the plotter's life is forfeit; half his goods will go to the intended victim, and the other half belongs to the state. Shylock is subject to those penalties. The duke immediately pardons his life and offers to limit the state's claim to a fine. Antonio adds that he will keep his half to use during Shylock's lifetime; after Shylock's death, this money will go to Lorenzo and Jessica. Antonio also requires Shylock to convert to Christianity and draft a will leaving his estate to Jessica and Lorenzo. The duke declares that if Shylock refuses, he will be executed. Shylock yields to these terms and leaves.

Portia declines the duke's invitation to dinner and Bassanio's offer of 3,000 ducats as payment. When he insists that she take something for her efforts, she requests Antonio's gloves and Bassanio's wedding ring. Bassanio protests that he promised his wife never to part with it. Portia replies that she has well earned that ring but leaves without it. Antonio pleads with Bassanio to give away the ring, and Bassanio sends Gratiano to catch up with the "lawyer" and hand the ring to "him."

Act IV, Scene 2

Gratiano overtakes Portia and gives her the ring. In an aside to Portia, Nerissa says she will try to get her ring from Gratiano.

Act V, Scene 1

On a moonlit bank in front of Portia's house in Belmont, Lorenzo and Jessica converse. Messengers arrive to report the imminent return of Por-

Bassanio (A. Boucicault) and Gratiano reunite with Portia (M. Elliott) and Nerissa (A. Irish) in Act V, Scene 1 of *The Merchant of Venice.* This photograph was published by the Byron Company in 1903.

tia, Nerissa, and Bassanio, who promptly appear. Gratiano and Nerissa begin to quarrel about his missing ring. Portia sides with Nerissa, saying that Bassanio would never surrender the ring she gave him. Gratiano replies that Basanio gave his ring to the judge who requested it. Portia feigns shock when Bassanio confesses. She declares that she never will sleep with him until he produces that token, and Nerissa says the same thing to Gratiano. When Bassanio pleads with his wife, she insists that he gave the ring to a lover. He maintains that the judge had it. In that case, Portia says, she will be as liberal as he. He gave the judge her ring; she will give him her body. Nerissa maintains that she will sleep with the lawyer's clerk who received her ring.

Bassanio begs forgiveness, and Antonio promises to stand pledge for his friend that he never will break another promise to Portia. Portia hands Antonio a ring to give to Bassanio, who should guard it more carefully than he did the last one. Receiving the token from Antonio, Bassanio recognizes it as the one he gave away. Portia says she recovered it by sleeping with the judge. Nerissa produces her ring, which she claims she got by sleeping with the clerk.

Gratiano is stunned to think that he and Bassanio have been cuckolded, but Portia discloses the ruse. She also informs Antonio that three of his ships have safely reached harbor. Nerissa hands Lorenzo Shylock's will, which bequeaths his estate to the young man and his bride. Portia summons everyone inside, where she will more fully explain the recent events. The play ends with a bawdy pun by Gratiano.

CHARACTER LIST

Antonio   The melancholy merchant of Venice, Antonio is devoted to his friend Bassanio.

Shylock   This rich Jewish moneylender bears a long-standing animosity against Antonio for the latter's harsh treatment of him.

Bassanio   Of noble birth, Bassanio has squandered his fortune and much of Antonio's as well.

Solanio   A friend of Antonio.

Salerio   Another of Antonio's friends.

Lorenzo   A friend of Antonio. He is in love with Jessica.

Gratiano   Irrepressible, bawdy friend to Antonio and Bassanio.

Tubal   Shylock's fellow Jew and confidant.

Launcelot Gobbo   Shylock's servant and then Bassanio's. Launcelot enjoys teasing others.

Old Gobbo   Launcelot's blind father.

The Duke of Venice   A nominally powerful figure who possesses little true authority.

The Prince of Morocco   Moorish suitor of Portia; of noble mien.

The Prince of Arragon   Another of Portia's suitors, overly certain of his own worth.

Portia   Intelligent, independent heiress of Belmont.

Nerissa   Portia's lady-in-waiting.

Jessica   Shylock's daughter, who longs to escape from his control.

CHARACTER STUDIES
Shylock

Various origins have been proposed for Shylock's name. In "Bits of Timber: Some Observations on Shakespearian Names" (Gollancz: 170–178), Israel Gollancz observes that the word *Shylock* resembles Shiloh, the place that once held the tabernacle and then was abandoned, just as Shylock's house is left desolate by Jessica's flight. Gollancz also points out that in pseudo-Josephus's *A Compendious . . . History of the Latter Times of the Jewes* (translated by Peter Morwyng, 1561), Schiloch opposes and is killed by the Roman Antonius. Christopher Spencer's *The Genesis of Shakespeare's Merchant of Venice* (1988) links the name to Shelah, father of Eber, in Genesis 10:24 and 11:12–15. According to the Geneva Bible's gloss at 10:24, Eber is the ancestor of the Hebrews. Perhaps Shakespeare chose the name to describe the character: Shylock is reclusive (shy) and keeps his house locked up (*Merchant* 2.5.53).

Shylock is not the title character, though he is sometimes mistaken as such. Yet as the Stationers Register entry for 1598 indicates, he was receiving equal billing with Antonio early on. Although Shylock appears in only five of the play's 20 scenes, he dominates the work when he appears, and only Portia has more lines than Shylock's 361. Since at least the beginning of the 18th century, critics, actors, and directors have debated the nature of the character, and over the centuries he has been portrayed in a variety of ways ranging from comic villain to tragic hero.

Shylock returns to find his daughter missing in *The Merchant of Venice.* This is a print from Malcolm C. Salaman's 1916 edition of *Shakespeare in Pictorial Art.* *(Painting by Charles A. Buchel)*

The title page of the first quarto refers to "the extreame crueltie of *Shylocke* the Iewe towards the sayd Merchant, in cutting a iust pound of his flesh," indicating that on the Elizabethan stage, he was not viewed sympathetically. It is not clear, however, who created the role. The 19th-century Shakespeare scholar and forger John Payne Collier believed that the Lord Chamberlain's Company's leading actor, Richard Burbage, was the first Shylock and played him in a red wig, just as Judas was outfitted in the medieval mystery plays. To support this contention, Collier forged a ballad stating as much. If Burbage, in fact, played Shylock, he probably would have treated the character seriously, perhaps more in Barabas's vein. If Burbage played Bassanio or Antonio in *Merchant,* however, Thomas Pope or William Kempe might have been the first Shylock, in which case he would have been presented more comically. Pope played Sir Toby Belch in *Twelfth Night,* and Kempe was the leading comic actor of the Lord Chamberlain's Men.

Records of 17th-century performances of *The Merchant of Venice* are virtually nonexistent. Nicholas Rowe's early 18th-century comment, quoted below in the Extracts of Classical Criticism section, about Shylock's being played as a comic villain refers to George Granville's verse adaptation of Shakespeare's play, *The Jew of Venice* (1701), which supplanted the original until Charles Macklin restored it to the stage in 1741. Macklin, who continued to act the part for some 50 years, agreed with Rowe, playing Shylock as a villain. Alexander Pope, who edited Shakespeare's works, supposedly said of Macklin's interpretation, "This is the Jew / That Shakespeare drew." The critic Francis Gentleman praised Macklin's presentation, which corresponded to Gentleman's negative assessment of the character. In 1770, in the periodical *The Dramatic Censor or Critical Companion,* Gentleman described Shylock as "a most disgraceful picture of human nature; he is drawn what we think no man ever was, all shade, not a gleam of light; subtle, selfish, fawning, irascible and tyrannic." Even after Macklin retired, this view of Shylock persisted. According to the introduction to John

Roach's 1804 edition of the play, George Frederick Cooke's Shylock was "such a horrid picture of depraved nature, that we scruple not to pronounce him as original and high-finished a character as we can conceive."

Hence, William Hazlitt was surprised when he saw Edmund Kean in the role in 1817, three years after Kean began playing Shylock. As Hazlitt writes in *Characters of Shakespeare's Plays* (1817),

> When we first went to see Mr. Kean in Shylock we expected to see, what we had been used to see, a decrepid [sic] old man, bent with age and ugly with mental deformity, grinning with deadly malice, and the venom of his heart congealed in the expression of his countenance, sullen, morose, gloomy, inflexible, brooding over one idea, that of his hatred, and fixed on one unalterable purpose, that of his revenge.

He had expected, in other words, the Shylock that Macklin had fashioned. Kean presented a more sympathetic character, consistent with Hazlitt's understanding of the character as expressed in the passage cited below in Extracts of Classical Criticism.

On November 1, 1879, at the Royal Lyceum Theatre, London, Henry Irving appeared in the role for the first time. George C. D. Odell described Irving's as "a very human Shylock." In Joseph Hatton's *Henry Irving's Impressions of America* (1884), Irving presented his understanding of Shakespeare's Jew:

> I look on Shylock as the type of a persecuted race; almost the only gentleman in the play and the most ill-used. He is a merchant, who traded in the Rialto, and Bassanio and Antonio are not ashamed to borrow money of him, nor to carry off his daughter. . . . [T]here is nothing in his language . . . that indicates the snuffling usurer.

Reviews of Irving's performance show that the actor succeeded in conveying his sympathetic reading of the part. The reviewer in *The Theatre* for December 1879 wrote of this Shylock,

He feels and acts as one of a noble but long opposed nation. In point of all intelligence and culture he is far above the Christians with whom he comes in contact, and the fact that as a Jew he is deemed far below them in the social scale, is gall and wormwood to his proud and sensitive spirit.

The *Saturday Review* of November 8, 1879, stated that Irving presented "a picturesque figure with an air of a man feeling the bitterness of oppression, and conscious of his own superiority in all but circumstance to the oppressor." *The Spectator* of that same day found Irving's Shylock to be a character "whom none can despise, who can raise emotion both of pity and of fear, and make us Christians thrill with a retrospective sense of shame."

In *Shakespeare on the Stage* (1911), William Winter surveyed Irving's career in the role. According to Winter,

When Irving first acted *Shylock* he manifested a poetically humanitarian ideal of the part, and he indicated the *Jew* as the venerable Hebrew patriarch, the lonely, grieved widower, and the affectionate, while austere, father. [Shylock was] the *vengeful* representative antagonist of intolerant persecution of the Jewish race and religion, but [Irving] personated a man, originally humane, who had been embittered by cruel injustice, without having actually lost the essential attributes of average humanity.

Winter did not agree with this interpretation and noted that over the years Irving's portrayal changed to become what Winter believed was "the true *Shylock* of Shakespeare—hard, merciless, inexorable, terrible. . . . Irving's *Jew* was a man upon whom,—while his every thought was colored and every purpose directed by social antipathy and religious fanaticism,—social oppression had so wrought as to develop only the most radically evil propensities."

Others shared Winter's reservations about Irving's early sympathetic treatment of Shylock.

Indeed, Irving himself called Shylock "a bloody-minded monster" but added, "You mustn't play him so, if you wish to succeed; you must get some sympathy with him." George Bernard Shaw, who disliked Irving, denied that the actor was presenting Shylock at all. Rather, Shaw claimed, he offered his audiences *The Martyrdom of Irving.* In *The Scenic Art: Notes on Acting and the Drama: 1872–1901* (1949), Henry James, who harbored no love of Jews, dismissed Irving's Shylock as sentimental. James maintained that Irving ignored "the deep-welling malignity, the grotesque horror, the red-hot excitement of the long-baffled, sore-hearted member of a despised trade, who has been all his life at a disadvantage, and who at last finds his hour and catches his opportunity."

Herbert Beerbohm Tree rejected these criticisms, playing Shylock as a devout Jew, a good father, and hostile to those who hate Jews. Tree portrayed passions well, so his Shylock was emotional. Edwin Booth, however, presented Shylock as driven by hatred and greed. In a letter to Shakespeare scholar Horace Howard Furness, Booth wrote, "If we side with [Shylock] in his self-defence [sic], 'tis because we have charity, which he has not; if we pity him under the burthen of his merited punishment 'tis because we are human, which he is not—except in shape, and even that, I think, should indicate the crookedness of his nature." In 1884, Booth told William Winter, "I have searched in vain for the slightest hint of anything resembling dignity or worthiness in the part."

The English producer William Poel founded the Elizabeth Stage Society in 1894 with the aim of staging plays as they had been performed in Shakespeare's time. In *Shakespeare in the Theatre* (1913), playing on the title page of Q1, Poel complained that under the influence of Hazlitt, Irving, and their ilk, *The Merchant of Venice* had become "The tragical history of the Jew of Venice, with the extreme injustice of Portia towards the said Jew in denying him the right to cut a just pound of the Merchant's flesh, together with the obtaining of the rich heiress by the prodigal Bassanio." In 1898, Poel staged *The Merchant of Venice* with Shylock in a red beard and false nose, as Poel believed he had been acted in the 1590s. This interpretation influenced Edgar Elmer Stoll, in an article excerpted below, to argue that Shakespeare's Shylock is a comic villain. Stoll argued that pathos, modern ideas about "justice and social responsibility," and irony are irrelevant to an understanding of the character. Stopford Brooke argued in 1905 that Shylock is "mean, mercenary, ungenerous, ignoble in thought and deed, consumed with evil passions" *(On Ten Plays of Shakespeare)*. The literary scholar Walter Raleigh rejected this view. In *Shakespeare* (1907), he described Shylock as

> This gaunt, tragic figure, whose love of his race is as deep as life; who pleads the cause of a common humanity against the cruelties of prejudice; whose very hatred has in it something of the nobility of patriotic passion, whose heart is stirred with tender memories even in the midst of his lament over the stolen ducats; who, in the end, is dismissed, unprotesting, to insult and oblivion. (175)

Still, the actors Arthur Bourchier (1905), Oscar Asche (1915), and Louis Bouwmester (1919) focused on Shylock's vengefulness. In 1932, Randall Ayrton, under the direction of Theodore Komisarjevsky at Stratford-upon-Avon, played Shylock as a comic villain. According to the London *Times* of December 7, 1935, Mark Dignam played Shylock as "A dirty, down-at heel moneylender in a bowler hat several sizes too big for him [who] has no shred of dignity left, and whether bewailing the loss of his ducats and his daughter or pleading the cause of a common humanity he is never more than a grotesque little man in a temper." Three years later, John Gielgud's Shylock (Queen's Theatre) was similarly unsympathetic. According to Audrey Williamson in *Theatre of Two Decades* (1951), Gielgud portrayed Shylock as "a dingy, rancorous, fawning creature of the ghetto, greatly redolent of the slum and the usurer's attic."

Although dignified and tragic Shylocks had appeared on the 19th-century stage, the Holocaust compelled much stronger reexamination of the role in a more sympathetic vein. Peter O'Toole in the 1950s, Laurence Olivier in 1970 under the direction of Jonathan Miller at the National Theatre, and Dustin Hofmann as directed by Sir Peter Hall in 1989 at the Phoenix Theatre returned to Irving's vision of the role. In Arnold Wesker's 1976 adaptation *The Merchant,* Shylock is generous with his money, supports the arts, and helps Jewish refugees fleeing the Inquisition. He proposes the merry bond without malice, and he insists on enforcing it later to prevent gentiles from violating contracts with Jews. When he loses his case, he is relieved.

Just as every reader, viewer, and actor imagines a unique Hamlet, so every student of *The Merchant of Venice* must decide how to regard Shylock. Perhaps more than any other character Shakespeare created, Shylock serves as a mirror to show each age and each individual "his form and pressure" (*Hamlet,* 3.1.24). As Shlomo Bickel observed in "The Argument about Shylock":

> We can't make up our minds what to do with Shylock. We feel the moral grandeur of the Shylock figure, but we are afraid to accept it completely. We admire his challenging aggressiveness, but we shrink from its logical consequences. We are repelled by the subterfuge with which Portia obtains her verdict, but we applaud her, so that we should not ourselves be accused of Shylockism. (255)

So we are prepared to deny Shylock. Yet we know that he is putting forward in our name such a justified and fundamental historic grievance and complaint that it must not be left unsaid.

Portia

When Bassanio first mentions Portia's name, he remarks that she is "nothing undervalu'd / To Cato's daughter, Brutus' Portia" (1.1.165–166). Shakespeare could have found her name in Plutarch's *Lives,* on which he had already drawn for Theseus's loves in *A Midsummer Night's Dream* (ca. 1595), and that would serve as his primary source for *Julius Caesar* (1599). Portia's great-great-grandfather, Cato the Elder, denounced usurers as murderers. Her name suggests port, or harbor; in *Il Pecorone*, Belmonte has a harbor. *Port* also means door, perhaps an allusion to Jesus' statement in John 10:9, "I am the dore." *Portion* is a close analogue to her name, and her father has left her a large one.

Appearing in nine scenes and speaking 578 lines, Portia's is the largest role in the play. In Shakespeare's sources, her analogous characters appear as clever heroines, but in Shakespeare's treatment, she is enigmatic. Her description of her suitors in 1.2 is either witty or catty and xenophobic, depending on one's interpretation. When she learns of the arrival of the Moorish Prince of Morocco, she remarks, "If he have the condition of a saint and the complexion of a devil, I had rather he should shrive me than wive me" (1.2.129–131). At 2.1.20–22, she assures Morocco that she regards him as no worse than any other of her suitors, but that statement would provide cold comfort to him if he had heard her strictures on his rivals. After he chooses incorrectly and departs, Portia says, "A gentle riddance. Draw the curtains, go. / Let all of his complexion choose me so" (2.7.78–79). The lines can be played as sour grapes. Perhaps Portia has been impressed with the dignity Shakespeare confers upon the prince and wishes that he had won her hand. Still, the simple sense of her speeches indicates that she does not seem to see Morocco's visage in his mind as Desdemona sees Othello's (*Othello* 1.3.252).

Critics divide over how much help Portia gives Bassanio in the choosing of the caskets. Portia tells Bassanio that she could teach him to choose the right casket but adds that she would thereby violate the terms of her father's will, which she will not do. Yet she continues, "so may you miss me, / But if you do, you'll make me wish a sin, / That I had been forsworn" (3.2.12–14). In *Il Pecorone*, the heiress's maid reveals the secret of how to win the lady. The song that is sung while Bassanio ponders his choices in 3.2 may assist him. The first three lines end with "bred," "head," and "nourishéd"

Portia in Act I, Scene 2 of *The Merchant of Venice*. This is a print from Charles Heath's 1848 edition of *The Heroines of Shakspeare: Comprising the Principal Female Characters in the Plays of the Great Poet*. (Painting by J. W. Wright; engraving by J. Brown)

(ll. 63–65), which rhyme with "lead." The theme of the piece is the danger of judging by appearances, a warning against the deceptive show of the gold and silver containers. The stage direction does not indicate who sings this piece. Does Portia? Does Nerissa here play the role of her counterpart in *Il Pecorone*? Perhaps the song does not serve as a clue but rather innocently fills the time of Bassanio's choice. When Morocco and Arragon select, they read the inscriptions; a third iteration is unnecessary. Still, as soon as the song ends, Bassanio's reflection indicates that he has understood the song's message: "So may the outward shows be least themselves—/ The world is still deceiv'd with ornament" (3.2.73–74).

In 1876, J. Weiss was the first to suggest that Portia cheats by helping Bassanio. Among modern critics sharing that view are S. F. Johnson in "How Many Ways Portia Informs Bassanio's Choice" (1996), Michael Zuckert in "The New Medea: On Portia's Comic Triumph in *The Merchant of Venice*" (1996), and Samuel Ajzenstat in "Contract in *The Merchant of Venice*" (1997). Taking the opposite view are C. L. Barber in *Shakespeare's Festive Comedy* (1959), Robert Hapgood in his 1967 article "Portia and *The Merchant of Venice:* The Gentle Bond," and Corinne S. Abate in "Nerissa Teaches Me What to Believe: Portia's Wifely Empowerment in *The Merchant of Venice*" (in Mahon and Mahon: 283–304).

When Portia first appears, she suffers from melancholy because she cannot control her marital destiny. She wants power, and as the play proceeds, she increasingly exercises it. Hence, she may well seek to circumvent her father's will to secure the man she loves. In the first flush of excitement at Bassanio's success, she reverts to the ideal of the Elizabethan woman, surrendering herself and her possessions to her soon-to-be husband. At the end of that speech, however, she gives Bassanio a ring. In the Book of Common Prayer of 1559, the husband is supposed to give the ring to his wife. Portia is thus already asserting control again. Bassanio's next speech acknowledges her power, as he compares himself to a crowd overwhelmed by the speech of a prince. His use of that word for Portia indicates not only her authority but also her masculinity.

When Lorenzo, Jessica, and Salerio arrive shortly afterward, Bassanio, as lord now of Portia's estate, bids them welcome. Then he turns to Portia for assent: "By your leave, / I bid my very friends and countrymen, / Sweet Portia, welcome" (3.2.222–224). By the end of that scene, Portia is issuing all the orders: "Pay him six thousand . . . / First go with me to church . . . / bring your true friend along. . . . / Come away! / . . . Bid your friends welcome, show a merry cheer— / . . . dispatch all business and be gone." (3.2.299–323).

When Portia returns to Belmont from the trial, her statement to Bassanio that "Myself, and what is mine, to you and yours / Is now converted" (3.2.166–167) is forgotten. In her first line, she reclaims her property: "That light we see is burning in my hall" (5.1.89). She instructs Nerissa, "Give order to my servants" (5.1.119). Through the ruse of the rings, she once more binds Bassanio to her, and she makes Antonio her debtor with her news of the safe harboring of three of his ships.

Portia's behavior at the trial invites varying interpretations. The trial scene is the longest in the play. Why does she toy so long with Shylock and Antonio? Is she improvising, trying to buy time until she finds a way to rescue the merchant? Does she want to enjoy being the center of attention for as long as possible? Is she provoking Shylock to make his evil evident? Is she testing Shylock? Sinead Cusack, who played Portia in 1981 under the direction of John Barton, offers a provocative answer to these questions. According to Cusack, Portia

doesn't go into the courtroom to save Antonio (that's easy) but to save Shylock, to redeem him—she is passionate to do that. She gives him opportunity after opportunity to relent and to exercise his humanity. . . . It is only when he shows himself totally ruthless and intractable (refusing even to allow a surgeon to stand by) that she offers him more justice than he deserves.

Nonetheless, Portia seems hypocritical. After praising the quality of mercy, she shows none to Shylock. The requirement that he convert does not come from her, but her judgment renders his life and fortune forfeit to the state.

Just as the Holocaust altered the interpretation of Shylock, so feminism has changed the understanding of Portia, who challenged the convention of the passive woman. William Hazlitt in 1817 found her unappealing, and nearly a century later George Brandes observed, "In spite of Portia's womanly self-surrender in love, there is something independent, almost masculine, in her character. She has the orphan heiress's habit and power of looking after herself, directing others, and acting on her own responsibility without seeking advice or taking account of convention" (in *William Shakespeare: A Critical Study* [1902]).

In defending Portia, 19th-century women argued for her femininity. The actress Fanny Kemble preferred her to any other Shakespeare heroine. Kemble described Portia as "so generous, affectionate, wise, so arch and full of fun, and such a true lady . . . her speech to Bassanio, after his successful choice of the casket, the most lovely, tender, modest, dignified piece of true womanly feeling that was ever expressed by woman." Helen Faucit played her as an ideal Victorian woman. Anna Brownell Jameson's defense of Portia appears in the section with Extracts of Classical Criticism. In *Shakespeare's Garden of Girls* (1885), Mrs. M. G. Elliott similarly stresses Portia's intelligence but also her adherence to standards of female propriety:

> Portia has been called the most wonderful of all Shakespeare's feminine creatures, for in her he has made clear that the possession of the highest intellectual endowments is compatible in a woman with the age and susceptibilities for tender and romantic love. . . . When her heart has recovered from the wild throbs of rapture . . . it beats again with the grave and sweet pulsation that is natural to it, as a spirit of inference and a capacity for calm logical deduction, united to a playful flow of wit is natural to her intellect (181).

Ellen Terry played Portia to Henry Irving's Shylock. The Shakespeare scholar F. J. Furnivall described her character as "A lady gracious and graceful, handsome, witty, loving and wise." Terry was amorous, humorous, noble, but also assertive, a "new woman" who uses her wits to get what she wants.

Twentieth-century actresses have been less hesitant to stress Portia's forceful nature. The *Tribune* of April 23, 1965, described Shakespeare's Portia as interpreted by Janet Suzman as anticipating a George Bernard Shaw heroine: someone intelligent and strong-minded as well as sexy. Milton Shulman's review in the *Evening Standard* for April 17, 1965, concurred, claiming that Suzman upstaged the men. In 1987, Deborah Findlay, in the role for the Royal Shakespeare Company under the direction of Bill Alexander, struck Nerissa and shuddered when Morocco touched her. Findlay claimed that "Portia is never mean. . . . She is as loving, as intelligent, as witty, as brave, as compassionate, as everything as you can make her." Such was not, however, the impression her acting made on Michael Coveney of the *Financial Times* (April 30, 1987). He thought that Findlay exposed the character's true nastiness, "a stuck-up daddy's girl, . . . whose pious application of the law as the disguised Balthazar is even more insufferable than the banality and smut she articulates elsewhere. I salute Ms. Findlay in rendering Portia as nasty as she ought to be but so rarely is." Nichola McAuliffe, who played the part in a 1994 production at the West Yorkshire Playhouse under the direction of Jude Kelly, described her Portia as arrogant as well as efficient.

Because Portia and Shylock are antagonists, a sympathetic interpretation of the one will render the other less attractive. Henry Irving complained that "The Duke and Portia preach to Shylock of mercy, but when the day goes against him they do not practice what they preach." Ellen Terry privately objected to Portia's ensnaring Shylock but portrayed her on stage as a heroine. In the 21st century, actresses in the role need not worry about being too assertive or intelligent, traits that Shakespeare gave his Portia. But can Portia be lovable or admirable at the same time?

Antonio

Although Antonio is the title character, he appears in only six of the play's 20 scenes and has fewer lines (188) than Portia, Shylock, or Bassanio. A melancholy man, he is passive and colorless; he does nothing throughout the play beyond agreeing to serve as surety for Bassanio's loan. Shakespeare may have named this character after St. Antonio

(1389–1459), archbishop of Florence, who opposed usury in his *Summa Theologica*. While it is unlikely that Shakespeare would have read that work, it is cited by various 16th-century English authors writing on the subject of lending at interest. Among these writers is Thomas Wilson, whose *A Discourse upon Usury* (1572) Shakespeare may have read. Antonio's is a common enough name, though. Shakespeare uses it in *Two Gentlemen of Verona* (ca. 1593), *Much Ado About Nothing* (1598), *Twelfth Night* (1602), and *The Tempest* (1611).

Charles Boyce in *Critical Companion to William Shakespeare* (2005) offers a traditional reading of the character: "Antonio represents the ideal of selfless generosity that *[The Merchant of Venice]* advocates. . . . Antonio's extravagant willingness to risk his money—and his life—stands in opposition to Shylock's calculating greed" (20–21). He regards himself as a good Christian, refusing to take interest, rescuing borrowers from Shylock's demand for interest, and offering himself as a Christlike sacrifice in 4.1.

His actions, however, belie such an interpretation of his character. In the Bible, 1 John 3:15 proclaims, "Whosoever hateth his brother is a manslayer," a verse that applies to Antonio as well as to Shylock. Antonio hates Shylock, an animosity that Shylock attributes to anti-Semitism (3.1.58). Even if Antonio's disdain is occasioned by Shylock's actions rather than his Judaism, that attitude marks the merchant as unchristian. Upon first seeing Antonio in the play, Shylock remarks, "How like a fawning publican he looks!" (1.3.41). This line may link Shylock to the scribes and Pharisees whom Jesus condemns for rejecting the lowly. The reflection may, however, also recall Jesus' warning in his Sermon on the Mount: "[I]f ye love them, which love you, what reward shall you have? Do not the Publicanes even the same?" (Matthew 5:46). The requirement that Shylock must convert comes from Antonio; and while the duke restores much of the state's half of Shylock's wealth, Antonio does not. Moreover, he requires that Shylock bequeath his wealth to "the gentleman / That lately stole his daughter" (4.1.387–388). It is dif-ficult to determine which is crueler, the pun on "gentile man" or the reminder of Lorenzo's taking Jessica.

Antonio's standing surety for Bassanio may not be as disinterested as it appears, either. Early in 1.1 Antonio tells Salerio and Solanio that his sadness does not result from fears about money. "My ventures are not in one bottom trusted, / Nor to one place; nor is my whole estate / Upon the fortune of this present year" (1.1.42–44). Barely a hundred lines later, after Bassanio asks for a loan, Antonio replies, "Thou know'st that all my fortunes are at sea" (1.1.177). He therefore instructs Bassanio to

Antonio pleads with Shylock in Act III, Scene 3 of *The Merchant of Venice*. This is a print from the Boydell Shakespeare Gallery project, which was conceived in 1786 and lasted until 1805. *(Painting by Richard Westall; engraving by James Parker)*

borrow money, and Antonio will guarantee the loan. Perhaps Shakespeare forgot to remove the inconsistency, but perhaps the contradiction shows Antonio's desire to heighten Bassanio's indebtedness to him.

Thomas Wilson refers to "an usurie of the mynde," a phrase that applies to Antonio's behavior toward Bassanio. When Bassanio promises to hasten his return from Belmont, Antonio replies, "Do not so, / Slubber not business for my sake" (2.8.38–39), sounding much like a Jewish mother. Similarly guilt-inducing, Antonio's letter announcing the forfeiture of the bond asks to see Bassanio once more before the merchant's death. "Notwithstanding," he adds, "use your pleasure; if your love do not persuade you to come, let not my letter." In 4.1 Antonio is not just resigned but eager to die for Bassanio, urging the young man to tell Portia how Antonio suffered. "And when the tale is told, bid her be judge / Whether Bassanio had not once a love" (4.1.276–277). Antonio's request to Bassanio, "Grieve not that I am fall'n to this for you" (4.1.266) echoes the opening lines of Sonnet 71: "No longer mourn for me when I am dead / than you shall hear the surly sullen bell / Give warning to the world that I am fled / From this vile world with vildest worms to dwell." Just as the speaker's instruction in the sonnet to "remember not / The hand that writ" these lines (ll. 5–6) forces the reader into remembrance, so Antonio's words compel grieving. The Antonio-Bassanio relationship resembles that of the speaker and fair youth of Shakespeare's Sonnets 1–126, as the older man tries to maintain the younger man's love.

Eve Sedgwick coined the term *homosocial* in *Between Men: English Literature and Male Homosocial Desire* (1985). Renaissance life and literature offer many examples of strong male friendships that do not cross over into homosexuality. But some do. Antonio in *Twelfth Night* clearly loves Sebastian enough to risk his life to be with him. In *Merchant*, when Salerio suggests that Antonio's melancholy springs from being in love, Antonio does not deny the statement; rather, he brushes it aside with a "Fie, fie!" (1.1.47). Salerio's description of Antonio's parting with Bassanio in 2.8 smacks of something more than friendship:

> And even there, his eye being big with tears,
> Turning his face, he put his hand behind him,
> And with affection wondrous sensible
> He wrung Bassanio's hand, and so they parted.

Solanio replies, "I think he [Antonio] only loves the world for him [Bassanio]." Clifford Williams's 1965 Royal Shakespeare Company production of the play was the first in England to show an openly homosexual Antonio, an interpretation often repeated since. Shakespeare altered the Antonio-Bassanio relationship that he found in his source, where they are kinsmen rather than friends, and whereas the source awards Nerissa to Antonio's counterpart, Shakespeare weds her to Gratiano. Antonio is the only character who goes to bed alone at the end of Act V. Thus, selfish love, not disinterested friendship, may underlie Antonio's actions.

Bassanio

On May 17, 1597, Emilia Lanier visited the astrologer-doctor Simon Forman to learn whether she would ever achieve a title. Forman recorded that she was the daughter of Baptista Bassano, one of the queen's musicians. Elizabeth's father, Henry VIII, had brought the Bassano family from Venice to serve in the "king's noise"—that is, to provide music for the royal household. The Bassanos were not only Venetian but also of Jewish extraction. Emilia told Forman that she had long been the mistress of Lord Hunsdon, the Lord Chamberlain who had served as patron of Shakespeare's company. The historian A. L. Rowse argued that Emilia Lanier was the musical Dark Lady of Shakespeare's sonnets. While that view has found little support, Shakespeare would have known of the Venetian Bassanos, from whom Bassanio probably takes his name.

With 339 lines, Bassanio has the third-longest part in the work. He may be viewed as the romantic hero who wins the heroine through his perception (or her connivance, or both), yet like many of Shakespeare's other romantic heroes, he is flawed. In St. John Ervine's *The Lady of Belmont* (published 1923, staged 1927), 10 years have elapsed since the events depicted in *The Merchant of Venice*. Bassanio has run through most of Portia's money and has tired of her; he is preparing to have an affair with Jessica, who no longer loves Lorenzo. Ervine captures the spendthrift insouciance of Bassanio, whose counterpart in *Il Pecorone* loses two ships in pursuit of a widow.

In *Merchant,* Bassanio's pecuniary difficulties stem from living beyond his income:

> 'Tis not unknown to you, Antonio,
> How much I have disabled my estate,
> By something showing a more swelling port
> Than my faint means would grant
>   continuance.
>
>   (1.1.122–125)

This carelessness dates from an early age. He recounts losing arrows in his youth by not watching their flight and then shooting another in the same direction in the hope of recovering both, which "oft" he did (1.1.140–144)—oft, but not always.

Bassanio comes to Antonio for another loan, having squandered the money he has previously received from the merchant. He intends to use this money to impress Portia, win her hand, thereby gain her fortune, and so "get clear of all the debts I owe" (1.1.134). He refers to himself as a Jason seeking Portia's "golden fleece" (1.1.170). When Bassanio prepares to select a casket, Portia describes him as Hercules rescuing the Trojan princess Hesione. Hercules undertook this task not for love of the lady but for the promised reward of her father's horses. In *Shakespeare and His Comedies,* John Russell Brown observes that "From the beginning Bassanio's quest has been described in commercial terms; indeed, he might have equal claim with Antonio and Shylock for the title of 'The Merchant of Venice.' . . . His quest to Belmont is a business venture" (65). After marrying Portia, Bassanio does not abandon his spendthrift ways. He keeps trying to give Shylock Portia's money even after Shylock has refused it, and after Portia saves her money by outwitting Shylock at the trial, Bassanio tries to give 3,000 ducats to her in her disguise as a doctor of law.

Bassanio's carelessness also manifests itself in his disregard for promises. At the trial, he urges the duke to annul Shylock's contract (4.1.214–217). He regards his oath to Portia as similarly breakable when convenient. Though he has promised never to part with Portia's ring, she secures it from him, and he later defends his violation of his promise (5.1.209–222). Ellen Terry summed him up as "a bit of a loafer, a well-dressed handsome youth of good birth who lives on his charm."

Gratiano

John Florio's Italian-English dictionary *A Worlde of Wordes* (1598) defines *Gratiano* as "a gull, a fool or clownish fellow in a play or comedy." He embraces this stock commedia dell'arte role in *Merchant,* declaring, "Let me play the fool" (1.1.79). Bassanio declares that Gratiano "speaks an infinite deal of nothing, more than any man in Venice. His reasons are as two grains of wheat hid in two bushels of chaff" (1.1.114–116). Gratiano's indiscreet behavior makes Bassanio reluctant to allow him to join the expedition to Belmont, though Gratiano's pledge to behave soberly persuades his friend to relent.

For much of 3.2, in which Bassanio wins Portia, Gratiano remains silent. Once his friend wins his lady, though, Gratiano announces his similar success with Nerissa and resumes his former behavior. He suggests a wager as to who will have the first son, and he caps his proposal with a bawdy pun. At the trial, his virulent hatred of Shylock exceeds that of Antonio and Bassanio. He repeatedly mocks the moneylender and declares that he would show no mercy to him. Just as Bassanio violates his oath to Portia regarding the ring, Gratiano breaks his to Nerissa, and with less cause. Bassanio has been persuaded by Antonio; Gratiano yields his ring to the lawyer's clerk on his own.

Back at Belmont, when he is confronted by his perfidy, he lacks Bassanio's grace to feel ashamed of his action. Rather, he dismisses Nerissa's love token as "paltry" (5.1.147). His overly free language earns him Portia's rebuke, "Speak not so grossly" (5.1.266). Yet his bawdry continues: He concludes the play with another sexually charged pun.

Jessica

As noted above in the "Source" discussion, Jessica's name may derive from Jesse and so may obliquely allude to Abigail of Christopher Marlowe's *The Jew of Malta*. In the Bible, Abigail is Jesse's daughter, as Jessica may be the literary daughter of Abigail. The name Iscah appears in Genesis 11:29; it derives from the Hebrew word for spy or one who looks out. Shylock orders Jessica not to look out the window when the masquers appear. Launcelot, however, informs her, "Mistress, look out at window for all this—/ There will come a Christian by, / Will be worth a Jewess' eye" (2.5.40–43). Jessica appears in seven scenes but speaks only 82 lines.

Jessica takes control of her destiny. Whereas Portia accepts her father's posthumous command to marry whoever chooses the correct casket, Jessica defies Shylock to wed a gentile. She even plans her elopement. Lorenzo tells Gratiano,

> She hath directed
> How I shall take her from her father's house,
> What gold and jewels she is furnish'd with,
> What page's suit she hath in readiness.
>
> (2.4.29–32)

Like Portia, Jessica assumes a man's disguise, and she speaks in the imperative, instructing Lorenzo to catch the casket she is throwing to him. Shakespeare's use of that word again links her to Portia. Later, in 2.6, she orders the men to hasten to the masque.

Even as she abandons and robs her father, Jessica carefully locks his house, thus showing that she still cares for him. She also recognizes that her flight will pain him, commenting that as a result of her elopement, "I have a father, you a daugh-

Jessica in *The Merchant of Venice*. This is a print from Charles Heath's 1848 edition of *The Heroines of Shakspeare: Comprising the Principal Female Characters in the Plays of the Great Poet*. (Painting by J. W. Wright; engraving by W. H. Mote)

ter, lost" (2.5.57). Yet among the jewels she takes is a turquoise ring that was her mother's first gift to Shylock and that he treasures for its sentimental value. In Genoa, she callously exchanges this ring for a monkey. Since the monkey never appears with her or is alluded to again, presumably she subsequently gave it away as well. She thus unites Portia's forcefulness with Bassanio's careless, spendthrift ways.

Whether her marriage to Lorenzo brings Jessica happiness remains unclear. When she and her husband come to Belmont with Salerio, Bassanio greets the two (gentile) men but does not mention Jessica. Seventeen lines after she enters, Gratiano instructs Nerissa to "cheer yon stranger" (3.2.237), thereby suggesting that Jessica is being neglected and appears unhappy. In her only speech in that scene, she confirms Salerio's picture of Shylock's vengefulness, indicating a desire to fit in with Antonio's friends.

Her effort seems unsuccessful. Placing her estate under the management of Lorenzo while she supposedly goes to pray for her husband, Portia does not mention Jessica. Launcelot jokes with Jessica about her Judaism, telling her she is damned. In the conversation between Jessica and Lorenzo at the beginning of Act V, they allude to various pairs of lovers, all of whose relationships ended unhappily. Jessica's last speech here, and practically her last in the play, may be teasing, but it may be serious. She remarks,

> In such a night
> Did young Lorenzo swear he lov'd her well,
> Stealing her soul with many vows of faith,
> And ne'er a true one.
>
> (5.1.17–20)

Her final line is no more reassuring of her happiness: "I am never merry when I hear sweet music" (5.1.69). For Jessica, the rest of the play of over 200 lines is silence. She hears that in his will Shylock has left his fortune to her and her husband. Lorenzo rejoices, but she says nothing. In some productions, she remains outside when the others enter Portia's house, indicating her exclusion from the gentile community she has tried to join.

DIFFICULTIES OF THE PLAY
Anti-Semitism

The central concern that students and scholars of *The Merchant of Venice* have grappled with for more than three centuries is anti-Semitism. England became the first country in Europe to expel its Jews when, in 1290, Edward I decided that he preferred banishing them to repaying them the money he owed. Jews would not legally return to the country until the 1650s, although Jewish refugees from the Iberian Peninsula settled in England. From 1581, Joachim

Ganz, a Bohemian mining engineer, lived openly as a Jew in England for at least 17 years. Nathan Judah Menda practiced Judaism in the country for at least six years before converting in 1578. In 1592, Jewish services were conducted at the London home of Solomon Cormano and Ferdinand Alvares. Four years later, in the year that Shakespeare probably wrote *The Merchant of Venice,* the widow of Richard May, one of Alvares's partners, sued him and his business associates. The trial record states that Alvares and Bernard Leavis sailed to Portugal on business and there had been fined by the Inquisition because of their religion. In *A Social and Religious History of the Jews,* 2nd ed. (1973), Salo Wittmayer Baron records that the court, "beinge moved with the losses and troubles which the poore straungers indured persuaded Mrs. May beinge present to deale charitably with Alvares in regarde thereof" (15:127). The Duke's address to Shylock in the trial scene seems to echo this decision:

> Shylock, the world thinks, and I think so
>   too, . . .
> Thou wilt not only loose the forfeiture,
> But touched with humane gentleness and love,
> Forgive a moi'ty of the principal,
> Glancing an eye of pity on his [Antonio's]
>   losses,
> That have of late so huddled on his back.
>
> (4.1.17–28)

As the Alvares trial indicates, Elizabethan England was not necessarily hostile to Jews. In the early 17th century, Isaac Casaubon invited the Italian Jew Jacob Barnet to assist him in the study of Jewish texts. When authorities in Oxford arrested Barnet and planned to convert him by force, Casaubon appealed to King James, who ordered Barnet's release, though the king also expelled Barnet from the country.

In literature, as well, Jews could be portrayed sympathetically. In Robert Wilson's *Three Ladies of London* (1584), the Christian merchant Mercadore pursues Lady Lucre. When he is sued by his Jewish creditor Gerontus, Mercadore takes advantage

Such favorable portrayals of Jews were, however, in the minority. Robert Wilson's *The Three Ladies of London* (1584) presents the character Usury as Jewish. Abraham in Robert Greene's *Selimus* (1594) is a poisoner. Thomas Nashe's *The Unfortunate Traveller* (1594) presents the Roman Jews Zadoch and Zachary as vicious. John Donne's "A Sermon Preached at Saint Dunstan's upon New Year's Day, 1624, claimed that Jews anointed their dead with the blood of Christians.

Shakespeare was writing in a milieu that was neither ignorant of nor necessarily hostile to Jews. His audiences would not necessarily expect Shylock to be villainous. In other plays, Shakespeare sympathizes with the outsider, portraying Othello as noble, for example. In *Sir Thomas More,* the section in Shakespeare's handwriting criticizes the antialien rioters and pleads for sympathy for the foreigners. His favorable treatment of Catholics in his work has also been noted (especially by those arguing that he was Catholic himself).

Still, critics remain divided over *The Merchant of Venice*'s attitude toward Jews. Salo Wittmayer Baron maintains that "the great poet disliked Jews, not only as men of different faith but as aliens" (15:134). Harold Bloom writes in *Shakespeare: The Invention of the Human* (1998): "One would have to be blind, deaf, and dumb not to recognize that Shakespeare's grand, equivocal comedy *The Merchant of Venice* is . . . a profoundly anti-Semitic work" (171). E. E. Stoll, in a 1911 article, and Derek Cohen (1988) also maintain that the play is anti-Semitic.

Others disagree. This camp includes George Lyman Kittredge (1945), Margaret Webster (1955), James Shapiro, and Jay Halio. In 1959, Tyrone Guthrie directed *The Merchant of Venice* on the Habimah stage in Israel. He, too, rejected the view that the play endorses anti-Semitism. John Barton in *Playing Shakespeare* (1984) claims that Shylock behaves as a bad Jew in seeking Antonio's life, but the play does not attack Jews or Judaism. Reviewing Jude Kelly's 1994 West Yorkshire Playhouse presentation of the play with Gary Waldhorn as Shylock, John Peter declared in the *Times*

The Duke reads Bellario's letter in Act IV, Scene I of *The Merchant of Venice*. This illustration was designed for a 1918 edition of Charles and Mary Lamb's *Tales from Shakespeare*. (Illustration by Louis Rhead)

of a Turkish law that exempts converts to Islam from repaying debts to infidels. Rather than be the cause of Mercadore's apostasy, Gerontus forgives him his debt. The judge remarks, "Jews seek to excel in Christianity and Christians in Jewishness." The year 1594 saw Rodrigo Lopez's execution and the revival of *The Jew of Malta*, as well as a revival of John Heywood's *An Enterlude of the Vertuous and Godly Queene Hester,* originally composed ca. 1522–27. In 1597, Joseph Wyburne of Cambridge University staged *Machiavellus,* in which the evil Machiavel figure opposes the Jew, who outwits the villain and gets the girl. The Jew thus appears as a typical romantic hero.

(London) for March 20, 1994: "I cannot believe that anyone who understands this production could think this an anti-Semitic play: it emerges, rather, as one of painful, hard-earned humanity." That same year, Peter Sellars staged the work with African Americans as Jews, Latinos playing the Venetians, and Asian Americans taking the roles of Portia and Nerissa to demonstrate that the play dealt with racism of any kind.

When Portia enters the courtroom, she asks, "Which is the merchant here? and which the Jew?" (4.1.174). Her question implies that Shakespeare intends for Shylock and Antonio to resemble each other, that there is no obvious distinction between Jews and Christians. Antonio and Shylock at times echo each other. Agreeing to Shylock's terms for a loan, Antonio says, "Content, in faith" (1.3.152). Accepting Antonio's demands at the end of the trial, Shylock declares, "I am content" (4.1.394). Discussing the taking of interest, Antonio says, "I never use it" (1.3.70). Shylock then launches into the story of Jacob's ewes, perhaps prompted by Antonio's homophone. Threatened with the loss of his wealth, Shylock laments, "[Y]ou take my life / When you do take the means whereby I live" (4.1.376–377). After Portia informs Antonio that three of his ships have safely reached harbor, he tells her, "Sweet lady, you have given me life and living" (5.1.286).

Antonio hates Shylock because the money-lender is Jewish; Shylock hates Antonio because the merchant is Christian. Both men lend money to Bassanio. Though Shylock usually charges interest, in the case of Bassanio, he lends as Antonio would, gratis. Shylock refuses pleas for mercy from the Duke and Portia. When Portia asks Antonio, "What mercy can you render him [Shylock] . . . ?" (4.1.378), the demand for Shylock's conversion and insistence on keeping half of Shylock's wealth demonstrate that Antonio is no more compassionate than his antagonist. Both men are condemned to death, but each escapes that fate. Shylock laments the loss of his stones, by which he means jewels, but his statement is understood more grossly by the boys of Venice (2.8.24). Antonio refers to himself as "a tainted wether of the flock" (4.1.114), a wether being a castrated ram.

Both men lose that which they most love: Shylock his daughter, his money, and his religion, while Antonio must surrender Bassanio to Portia. The men's losses are linked in 2.8, as Salerio and Solanio first discuss Jessica's flight with Shylock's money and then describe Antonio's parting with Bassanio. Shakespeare probably did not know that in Dante's fourth circle of hell, hoarders like Shylock collide with wasters, and that in canto 11 of the *Inferno*, Dante placed usurers and Sodomites together in hell's seventh circle. He recognized, however, that beneath the seeming differences of skin color or religion, "one touch of nature makes the whole world kin" (*Troilus and Cressida*, 3.3.175). Following this logic, one could easily claim that Shakespeare made his moneylender Jewish not to demonize members of that faith but to show the common humanity, and inhumanity, of all.

Time

A lesser problem with *The Merchant of Venice* is its treatment of time. Shakespeare could be cavalier about chronology. Though *A Midsummer Night's Dream* opens with the statement that Theseus and Hippolyta will wed four days hence, the play occupies only three days. From the arrival of Desdemona, Cassio, and Othello at Cyprus to Desdemona's death, some 36 hours elapse, hardly long enough for even the randiest teenager to have "the act of shame a thousand times committed" (*Othello*, 5.2.211–212).

In *Merchant*, Shylock and Antonio sign their bond between 1.3 and 2.1. The contract allows Antonio three months in which to repay his loan. In 1.3, Bassanio invites Shylock to dine with him that day. Shylock initially refuses, but in 2.5 he changes his mind. During his absence, Jessica and Lorenzo elope, and that same night, Bassanio and Gratiano sail for Belmont. The journey must require less than a day, since at the end of 3.2, Bassanio promises to go back to Venice, save Antonio, and return without sleeping. Arriving at Belmont in 2.9, Bassanio refuses to delay even "a day or two"

(3.2.1) before choosing among the caskets. Yet no sooner has he won Portia than Salerio arrives with Antonio's letter announcing that his bond is forfeit. Tubal, too, has had time to travel to Genoa to seek Jessica and learn of her extravagances as well as Antonio's losses. In 3.1, Shylock instructs Tubal to engage an officer two weeks before the bond falls due, which it does in 3.2.

While a careful reading exposes these chronological inconsistencies, Shakespeare understood that they vanish in performance. Audiences do not recognize the impossibility of Desdemona's infidelity or the early occurrence of the new moon in *A Midsummer Night's Dream*. Theatrical time bears no relationship to real time, so three months can elapse in Venice even as Bassanio contemplates the caskets in Belmont.

KEY PASSAGES
Act III, Scene 1, 61–76

SHYLOCK. Hath not a Jew eyes? Hath not
a Jew hands, organs, dimensions, senses,
affections, passions, fed with the same food,
hurt with the same weapons, subject to the
same diseases, heal'd by the same means,
warm'd and cool'd by the same winter and
summer, as a Christian is? If you prick us,
do we not bleed? If you tickle us, do we not
laugh? If you poison us, do we not die? And
if you wrong us, shall we not revenge? If
we are like you in the rest, we will resemble
you in that. If a Jew wrong a Christian,
what is his humility? Revenge. If a Christian
wrong a Jew, what should his sufferance be
by Christian example? Why, revenge. The
villainy you teach me, I will execute, and it
shall go hard but I will better the instruction.

Salerio and Solanio have been mocking Shylock on the loss of his daughter and his money. The subject then turns to Antonio's losses; Shylock says that the merchant should "look to his bond" (3.1.47 and 3.1.50). Salerio replies that Shylock surely would not claim his pound of flesh. After all, "What's that good for?" Shylock replies, "To bait fish withal" (3.1.52–53). He proceeds to list the indignities that Antonio has heaped upon him for the sole reason that Shylock is Jewish. Shylock then delivers his well-known plea, which emphasizes the common humanity of all.

These lines have been much admired. William Hazlitt wrote, "In this single speech he [Shylock] was worth a wilderness of monkeys that have aped humanity" (188). Victor Hugo claimed that

This sublime imprecation is the most eloquent plea that the human voice has ever dared to utter for a despised race. Whatsoever be the dénoûment, it is hereby justified. Let Shylock be as implacable as he may, assuredly he will no more than equal his instruction. Even granting that he obtains it, a pound of Antonio's flesh will never outweigh, in the scales of reprisal, the millions of corpses heaped in the Christian shambles by a butchery of thirteen centuries.

For Salerio and Solanio, Shylock serves as a figure of fun. Antonio reduces him to less than human by repeatedly applying animal imagery to him. In the trial scene, Portia exposes Shylock's true status in Christian Venice, that of an alien. In the real 16th-century Venice, Jews were forced to live in a ghetto, which was locked each night. They had to pay special taxes to live in the city, and at least twice in the century, Jewish books were confiscated there and burned. Yet Venice was considered tolerant toward Jews.

Here Shylock speaks out against such "toleration." He reminds his mockers, and Shakespeare reminds the world, of the physical and emotional price of prejudice. In this speech, he offers a proleptic response to Portia's plea for mercy: What mercy do Christians show? For 1,600 years, Christians have ignored the Sermon on the Mount with its injunction to turn the other cheek. They have not left vengeance to God. Why, then, should Salerio and Solanio expect Shylock to behave differently? Shylock uses his assertion of common humanity to justify inhumane behavior, but in doing so he emphasizes not only his own flaw but also the failure of Christian society to abide by its professions. His speech exemplifies the truth that W. H. Auden (in his poem "September 1, 1939") observed all schoolchildren learn: "Those to whom evil is done / Do evil in return."

Act III, Scene 2, 72–107

BASSANIO. So may the outward shows be
  least themselves.
The world is still deceived with ornament.
In law, what plea so tainted and corrupt
But, being seasoned with a gracious voice,
Obscures the show of evil? In religion,
What damnèd error but some sober brow
Will bless it and approve it with a text,
Hiding the grossness with fair ornament?
There is no vice so simple but assumes
Some mark of virtue on his outward parts.
How many cowards, whose hearts are all as
  false
As stairs of sand, wear yet upon their chins
The beards of Hercules and frowning Mars,
Who inward searched have livers white as milk?
And these assume but valour's excrement
To render them redoubted! Look on beauty
And you shall see 'tis purchased by the weight,
Which therein works a miracle in nature,
Making them lightest that wear most of it.
So are those crisped, snaky, golden locks
Which make such wanton gambols with the
  wind
Upon supposed fairness, often known
To be the dowry of a second head,
That skull that bred them in the sepulchre.
Thus ornament is but the guilèd shore
To a most dangerous sea, the beauteous scarf
Veiling an Indian beauty; in a word,
The seeming truth which cunning times put on
To entrap the wisest. Therefore then, thou
  gaudy gold,
Hard food for Midas, I will none of thee;
Nor none of thee, thou pale and common
  drudge
'Tween man and man; but thou, thou meager
  lead,

Which rather threaten'st than dost promise
  aught,
Thy paleness moves me more than eloquence,
And here choose I. Joy be the consequence!

Having just heard the song "Tell me where is fancy bred" (3.2.63–72), which warns against judging by appearance, Bassanio contemplates the three caskets. He articulates a key theme in literature in general and Shakespeare in particular: the danger of judging by appearances. Although Shakespeare wrote in the midst of the English Renaissance, of

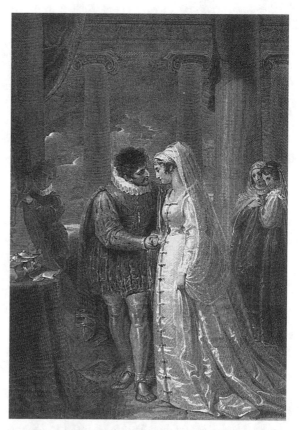

Bassanio wins Portia's hand in marriage by choosing the right casket in Act III, Scene 2 of *The Merchant of Venice.* This is a print from the Boydell Shakespeare Gallery project, which was conceived in 1786 and lasted until 1805. *(Painting by Richard Westall; engraving by Samuel Noble)*

which he is the chiefest ornament, he did not share the belief in empiricism of Francis Bacon and other advocates of the new science. Repeatedly, Shakespeare's plays reveal the fallacy of "ocular proof" (*Othello*, 3.3.360). The senses, especially sight, may be easily deceived.

Bassanio offers examples of such trickery, beginning with legal pleading. He thus anticipates the outcome of Shylock's trial, wherein the moneylender will suffer under the guise of mercy. The speech next considers religious hypocrisy, another key element in this play, which highlights the cruelty of supposedly good Christians. The third category, seeming military prowess, refers to cowards who wear the beards of Hercules but are "stayers of sand," to adopt the reading in Q1, Q2, and F1—that is, as easily overcome as a wall made of sand. Portia has likened Bassanio himself to Hercules (3.2.55). Though he promises to keep Portia's ring until death, he will prove a stayer of sand, surrendering it at Antonio's bidding. Finally, he refers to the deceit of borrowed beauty's "crisped snaky golden locks" (3.2.92). The line recalls Bassanio's earlier reference to Portia's "sunny locks" (1.1.169) and his likening her to the golden fleece. Yet whatever ironic suggestions underlie Bassanio's speech, his reasoning leads him to the correct casket.

Act IV, Scene 1, 186–202

PORTIA. The quality of mercy is not strained.
It droppeth as the gentle rain from heaven
Upon the place beneath. It is twice blest:
It blesseth him that gives and him that takes.
'Tis mightiest in the mightiest. It becomes
The thronèd monarch better than his crown.
His scepter shows the force of temporal power,
The attribute to awe and majesty,
Wherein doth sit the dread and fear of kings;
But mercy is above this sceptred sway.
It is enthroned in the hearts of kings,
It is an attribute to God himself,
And earthly power doth then show likest God's
When mercy seasons justice. Therefore, Jew,
Though justice be thy plea, consider this:
That in the course of justice none of us

Should see salvation. We do pray for mercy,
And that same prayer doth teach us all to
  render
The deeds of mercy.

In the trial scene, Antonio acknowledges the bond giving Shylock a pound of flesh. Portia remarks that in that case, Shylock "must . . . be merciful" (4.1.182). Ever the literalist, Shylock understands her "must" as requirement, and he retorts, "On what compulsion must I" (4.1.183). Portia then launches into one of the best-known speeches in Shakespeare's canon. Her lines derive their central message and imagery from Ecclesiasticus 35:20: "Mercy is seasonable in the time of affliction, as clouds of rain in the time of drought." Portia also echoes the Lord's Prayer and Ecclesiasticus, chapter 18. Her appeal thus unites the Old and New Testaments, once more linking Jew and Christian.

Mercy, she maintains, is not subject to compulsion. Portia launches into a paean to this virtue and warns her audience that with what measure they meet, it shall be measured to them again. She offers Shylock an opportunity to repent of his homicidal scheme, to renounce the vengeance on which he is bent and yield to the better angel of his nature. Much as audiences admire Portia's paean to mercy, it falls on deaf ears. Shylock refuses to relinquish his claim to Antonio's flesh, and when Portia's own literalism saves Antonio, he, too, grants his antagonist no mercy. As Shylock had observed earlier in the play, "If a Jew wrong a Christian, what is his humility? Revenge" (3.1.68–69). The wielder of the loftiest language ever penned recognized the limits of words, no matter how beautiful or how true, to alter people's behavior.

DIFFICULT PASSAGES
Act V, Scene 1, 54–65

LORENZO. How sweet the moonlight sleeps
  upon this bank!
Here will we sit, and let the sounds of music
Creep in our ears. Soft stillness and the night
Become the touches of sweet harmony.

Sit, Jessica. Look how the floor of heaven
Is thick inlaid with patens of bright gold.
There's not the smallest orb which thou
  behold'st
But in his motion like an angel sings,
Still quiring to the young-ey'd cherubins;
Such harmony is in immortal souls,
But whilst this muddy vesture of decay
Doth grossly close it in, we cannot hear it.

Many students regard the last act of *The Merchant of Venice* as incongruous. The idyllic setting can seem excessively sweet after the wrenching events in the previous act. Here, Lorenzo and Jessica sit on a moonlit bank in Belmont awaiting the return of Portia, Nerissa, Bassanio, and Gratiano. Offstage, music plays. Lorenzo's ode to heavenly harmony derives from Pythagorus's ideas about the music of the spheres and music as cathartic, healing. Plato had recorded these views in his strange *Timaeus;* Shakespeare probably encountered them in some Neoplatonic work.

The Greek word *harmonia* refers to an octave composed of the sun, moon, the five planets then known (Mercury, Venus, Mars, Jupiter, Saturn), and the heaven of the fixed stars. This macrocosmic harmony is mirrored in the individual soul. Were it not for the body, Pythagorus's "muddy vesture of decay" (*Merchant,* 5.1.64), the soul's music would match that of the cosmos. Music pierces the physical barrier of flesh to link soul and universe. A soul that does not respond to music is flawed. According to Plato's *Republic,* sirens sit on the planets; Christianity replaced them with angels.

Although *Merchant* contains only one song, the idea of musical harmony pervades the work. The text of Ralph Vaughan Williams's *Serenade to Music* (1938) consists of lines from 5.1, beginning with Lorenzo's speech cited here. Lorenzo goes on to declare, "The man that hath no music in himself, / Nor is not moved with concord of sweet sounds, / Is fit for treasons, stratagems, and spoils; / . . . Let no such man be trusted" (5.1.83–88; these lines, too, appear in *Serenade to Music*). Shylock's soul is out of tune. He commands Jessica to "stop [his] house's ears" (2.5.34) against the music of the masque. At 4.1.49–50 he speaks of those who cannot contain their urine when they hear a bagpipe. This attitude toward music may provide yet another link between Antonio and Shylock, because at the end of 2.6, the merchant arrives to curtail Gratiano's preparations for the night's revelry: "No masque tonight" (2.6.64), he declares.

Lorenzo and Jessica share a private moment on the bank in front of Portia's house in Act V, Scene 1 of *The Merchant of Venice*. This is a print from the Boydell Shakespeare Gallery project, which was conceived in 1786 and lasted until 1805. (*Painting by William Hodges; engraving by John Browne*)

CRITICAL INTRODUCTION
TO THE PLAY
Money and Contracts

A central concern of *The Merchant of Venice* is the power of money. Michael Kahn, who directed a 1999 production of the play in Washington, D.C., reflected that *Merchant* examines "What happens to a society or what goes on in a society when money becomes tremendously important and people begin to be equal with commodities?" (Riggio: 22). Peter Sellars, who directed the 1994 Los Angeles Festival production of *Merchant,* maintains, "This play is about what happens when market values overtake a society completely. Shakespeare titles his play about racism and about the moral, spiritual and romantic collapse of people *The Merchant of Venice* because it's about what happens when making a climate that's good for business is our only concern" (qtd. in Billington: T6).

In the play's opening lines, Salerio and Solanio declare that if they had ventures abroad, they would be able to think of nothing else. A church would recall not the teaching to lay up stores in heaven but rather the dangers that rocks pose to earthly treasures entrusted to ships. When Bassanio asks Antonio for a loan, the merchant replies, "My purse, my person, my extremest means, / Lie all unlock'd to your occasions" (1.1.138–139), linking his wealth to his person in both sound and sense. As noted above, both Shylock and Antonio equate life and living. At the trial, Shylock speaks of slaves, humans as commodity. Flesh serves as collateral for the loan Bassanio seeks.

Bassanio wants money to pursue Portia. The first thing we learn about her is that she is "richly left" (1.1.161), and Bassanio says he wants to marry her to "get clear of all the debts I owe" (1.1.134). In speaking of his hopes of winning her, Bassanio uses the mercantile terms *thrift* and *fortunate* (1.1.175, 176). In the world of the play, which anatomizes early modern capitalism, money is the measure of all things. When Bassanio explains to Shylock the terms of the loan that Antonio will guarantee, the moneylender observes, "Antonio is a good man" (1.3.12). Shylock is not assessing Antonio's moral qualities; rather, he means that Antonio is good for the money.

Jessica "gilds" herself with her father's ducats (2.6.55–56) to render herself more desirable to Lorenzo. Portia wishes she were "ten thousand times more rich" that she might "stand high in [Bassanio's] account" (3.2.154–155). Portia's speech in which she gives herself to Bassanio (3.2.149–174) is filled with words of commerce rather than of love and focuses on the transfer of property. Gratiano refers to the union of Portia and Bassanio as "The bargain of your faith" (3.2.193). Even children become merchandise. Solanio reports Shylock's lament, "My daughter! O my ducats! O my daughter!" (2.8.15). Gratiano proposes to wager a thousand ducats on whether he or Bassanio will sire a son first.

Every relationship in the play depends on money. Antonio gives Bassanio money. Bassanio pursues Portia for her wealth, which she bestows on him. Antonio seeks out Shylock for money. Jessica gives money to Lorenzo. Portia restores money to Antonio through her news about his ships, and she assumes that her wealth can save Antonio from the terms of his bond. Granted, the animosity between Shylock and Antonio derives in part from religion. Shylock declares, "I hate him for he is a Christian" (1.3.42), and when he accuses Antonio of calling him "misbeliever" (1.3.111), Antonio does not deny the charge. At his trial, the merchant states that nothing is harder than Shylock's "Jewish heart" (4.1.80). On both sides, though, money engenders even more hatred. Shylock states that Antonio's interest-free loans anger him more than the merchant's Christianity (1.3.43–45), and Antonio recognizes his lending practices as the cause of Shylock's seeking his life (3.3.21–24). Antonio, in turn, condemns Shylock for taking interest. By forcing the moneylender to convert to Christianity, Antonio ensures that Shylock will no longer be able to charge interest on loans.

Yet only Shylock refuses money; only he recognizes that some things have no price. He laments the loss of his turquoise not because of its monetary value but because it was the first gift he received from his wife. To Jessica, her mother's ring is a commodity like any other. She exchanges it for a monkey, which she then apparently disposes of, since the play says no more about it. Shylock rejects a threefold profit on his loan to Antonio because he values his oath and his revenge above ducats. Henry Irving was right to call him the only gentleman in the play, for he is the only person who cannot be bought.

Bonds

In a world in which money is the measure of all things, relationships become contractual. Shylock requires a bond, though he calls it a "merry" one, before he will lend money to Antonio. Portia's suitors must bind themselves never to marry and to leave Belmont immediately if they choose the wrong casket. Portia is bound by the terms of her father's will to marry the person who chooses correctly. Portia and Nerissa require their husbands never to remove these tokens of love that the men receive from their wives. Having acquired slaves through legal purchase, Venetians may treat them as they wish. Shylock must sign a contract to fulfill the terms imposed upon him by the Venetian court at the end of the trial.

Both Antonio and Portia stress the importance of contracts in a capitalist society. When Solanio tells Antonio that the Duke will not enforce the merchant's agreement with Shylock, Antonio replies,

> The Duke cannot deny the course of law;
> For the commodity that strangers have
> With us in Venice, if it be denied,
> Will much impeach the justice of the state.
>
> (3.2.26–29)

To Bassanio's appeal that the Duke nonetheless breach Antonio's contract to save the merchant's life, Portia replies,

> It must not be, there is no power in Venice
> Can alter a decree established.
> 'Twill be recorded for a precedent,
> And many an error by the same example
> Will rush into the state. It cannot be.
>
> (4.1.218–222)

While legal contracts must be honored, even at the cost of a person's life or liberty, the bonds of love and humanity no longer operate in this capitalist world. Launcelot Gobbo and Jessica recognize that in abandoning Shylock, they are violating the bonds of loyalty of master and servant, daughter and father. Bassanio and Gratiano give away their rings despite their promise not to do so. They do not feel bound by their pledges of love. The Christians in the play reject any ties of humanity to Shylock, who reciprocates their animosity.

Friendship versus Love

A common concern of Renaissance literature is the conflict between love and friendship. In theory, friendship is the more powerful force. The biblical David's love for Jonathan surpasses the love of women. Achilles returns to the fighting at Troy to avenge his dead friend Patroclus. Cicero's *De Amicitia* emphasizes the greater power of same-sex friendship, as does Plato's *Symposium*. Shakespeare's plays expose the fallacy of this doctrine. To assist her beloved Demetrius, Helena betrays her friend Hermia in *A Midsummer Night's Dream*. Proteus betrays his friend Valentine in *The Two Gentlemen of Verona* to try to gain Valentine's Silvia. Benedict challenges his friend Claudio to a duel to show his love for Beatrice *(Much Ado About Nothing)*.

Merchant pits the friendship of Antonio and Bassanio against the love of Bassanio and Portia. Antonio repeatedly tries to enforce his claim on Bassanio. As soon as Bassanio has won Portia's hand, Antonio's letter arrives to summon him away from her. At the trial, Antonio instructs Bassanio,

> Commend me to your honorable wife,
> Tell her the process of Antonio's end,
> Say how I lov'd you, speak me fair in death;
> And when the tale is told, bid her be judge
> Whether Bassanio had not once a love.
>
> (4.1.273–277)

Antonio thus insists that his love is greater than Portia's. Bassanio agrees. He replies that he values Antonio's life above Portia's, that he would sacrifice her life to save his. Having saved Antonio's life, Portia tests Bassanio by demanding his wedding ring as payment. Initially he refuses, but Antonio urges Bassanio to prize friendship above love: "Let his [the lawyer's] deservings and my love withal / be valued 'gainst your wive's commandment" (4.1.450–451). Yielding to Antonio's desire, Bassanio once more chooses Antonio over Portia.

At the end of the play, Portia and love defeat Antonio and friendship. Antonio tries one more time to intervene in the marriage by volunteering to stand surety for his friend yet again. Por-

Bassanio advises Antonio not to enter into an agreement with Shylock (Jacob P. Adler) in Act I, Scene 3 of *The Merchant of Venice*. This photograph was published by the Byron Company in 1903.

tia rebuffs that effort. She makes Antonio return Bassanio's wedding ring and instruct her husband to guard it better in future. Antonio thereby relinquishes his claims on his friend and acknowledges the more powerful demands of marriage. In many productions, when Portia and Bassanio go offstage, Antonio remains alone to mourn the loss of his friend.

Structure

The Merchant of Venice employs a conventional five-act structure. In the first act, exposition, Shakespeare introduces all the major characters and many of the play's central conflicts: Antonio's bond with Shylock, Portia's bond with her dead father, Portia's love of Bassanio, Antonio's friendship with Bassanio that conflicts with Bassanio's love for Portia. The alternation of locations that Shakespeare employs here sets the pattern that he will follow in succeeding acts. The opening scene unfolds in Venice and presents the city's Christians. Scene 2 moves to Belmont, where the audience encounters Portia and Nerissa. In Scene 3, back in Venice, Antonio and Shylock meet and agree on their "merry bond."

The situations established in the opening act then grow more complicated in Act II, the development. Suitors appear to try to win Portia's hand. Antonio's ships are lost, depriving him of the means to repay his loan, and Jessica's elopement further enrages Shylock against the merchant and his fellow Christians. The act begins in Belmont (2.1), then moves to Venice. Although the next five scenes (2.2–2.6) are all set there, the action is continuous and unfolds in front of Shylock's house. All five scenes as 18th-century editors conceived them might be viewed as a single long one. Scenes 7–9 again alternate between the two venues of Belmont (2.7, 2.9) and Venice (2.8).

In Act III, resolutions begin but other problems arise. The wooing of Portia reaches a happy culmination when Bassanio chooses the correct casket (3.2). Antonio's fortunes, however, continue to decline. No sooner has Bassanio succeeded than news arrives of Antonio's imminent death. While the problem of Portia's bond is resolved, another conflict begins when Portia gives Bassanio a ring and binds him never to part with it. The first and third scenes in this act unfold in Venice, the second, fourth, and fifth in Belmont. These two Belmont scenes might, like 2.2–2.6, be viewed as but one.

In Act IV, set entirely in Venice, the Antonio-Shylock conflict ends with the defeat of the latter. While Antonio's life is spared, though, he remains impoverished. Bassanio rewarding the judge with Portia's ring and Gratiano giving his ring to the lawyer's clerk create a new crisis to be resolved in the fifth act, set at Belmont. Without this new problem, the final act would have little function, and indeed, many 19th-century productions ended the play with Shylock's defeat.

Each of the first four acts ends with a looming crisis. At the end of Act I, Antonio signs the bond with Shylock. Act II ends with news of Bassanio's arrival at Belmont. Act III concludes with Antonio's impending trial. Bassanio and Gratiano give away their rings at the end of Act IV. The final act resolves the ring plot and restores Antonio's lost wealth. The play's comic arc is encapsulated in the opening and closing speeches. In the first lines of the work, Antonio discusses his melancholy. Gratiano ends *The Merchant of Venice* with a bawdy joke.

In addition to juxtaposing events in Venice and Belmont, adjoining scenes parallel each other. In Act I, Scene 1, Antonio speaks of his melancholy, for which he claims he can find no cause. In Scene 2, Portia is sad because she cannot wed as she wishes. Perhaps, then, Antonio's unhappiness also springs from thwarted love. In Scene 3, Antonio agrees to Shylock's bond; in Act II, Scene 1, Morocco binds himself to the terms required of those who wish to choose among the caskets. Morocco's attempt ends badly, foreshadowing the peril Antonio will endure because of his contract. In Scene 2, Launcelot abandons Shylock; in Scene 3, Jessica prepares to do so, too. In another contrast, Shylock's house grows emptier with the desertion of Launcelot and Jessica, while Portia's house becomes more crowded as Launcelot, Jessica, and various other Venetians move in. This population shift mirrors the characters' shifting fortunes. Shylock, who controls the action early in the play, is defeated by Portia, who controls the action at the play's conclusion.

In "Portia, the Law, and the Tripartite Structure of *The Merchant of Venice* (Wheeler: 163–194), Alice Benston discusses the importance of the number 3 in this work. The play revolves around three trials, that of the caskets (resolved in Act III), Antonio's bond (concluded in Act IV), and the rings (which ends happily in Act V). Benston also notes the three caskets, three suitors, three rings (Rachel's, Portia's, Nerissa's), and three couples (Lorenzo-Jessica, Bassanio-Portia, Gratiano-Nerissa). Antonio borrows 3,000 ducats for three months. He has six argosies abroad; three safely reach harbor. Shylock and Antonio meet three times. The tripartite structure even influences individual speeches. Justifying his insistence on his bond, Shylock likens his hatred for Antonio to an aversion to a pig, a cat, or a bagpipe. Antonio responds by comparing Shylock's hard heart to a wolf, mountain pines vexed by the wind, or any hard substance. In giving herself to Bassanio, Portia describes herself as "Happy . . . happier

. . . Happiest" (3.2.160–163). She surrenders her "house, . . . servants," and herself (3.2.170).

In "The Counterfeit Order of *The Merchant of Venice*" (54–69), Leonard Tennenhouse remarks on the play's triadic relationships. Thus, Jessica must choose between her loyalty to her father and her love for Lorenzo. Launcelot is torn between his duty to Shylock and his desire to serve Bassanio. Bassanio is beloved of Antonio and Portia and must decide between them. Portia can be faithful to her dead father or teach Bassanio how to choose the right casket. Bassanio and Gratiano can keep their rings and their faith to their wives or give up the tokens to the judge and his clerk.

Style and Imagery

As noted in the thematic discussion of money, mercantile language pervades the play. Caroline F. E. Spurgeon, in her groundbreaking study *Shakespeare's Imagery and What It Tells Us* (1935), discusses several other linguistic patterns. She notes the importance of music, which appears most prominently when Bassanio wins Portia and at the beginning of Act V after Portia has saved Antonio. The play contains lovely word-pictures of nature, as when Lorenzo describes the star-filled night sky as "thick inlaid with patens of bright gold" (5.1.59). Patens are metal plates used to hold communion wafers. This is one of the play's many religious and biblical references. According to Spurgeon, Bassanio uses the most images, and Portia follows closely behind. Gratiano is a distant third.

Other image patterns concern food and animals. The Christians apply animal terms to Shylock, who in turn speaks of rats (1.3.23, 4.1.44), "a gaping pig" (4.1.47, 54), "a harmless necessary cat" (4.1.55). This identity of language between Christians and Jew provides another demonstration of their lack of difference. The word *choose* and its variants occur some 44 times in the play. Portia's suitors must choose among the caskets, but other characters also face choices: Antonio chooses to sign Shylock's bond, while Shylock chooses to enforce it; Bassanio and Gratiano choose to part with their rings. Words connected with risk also recur: Antonio risks his ships and his life; Portia's suitors risk their future matrimonial prospects; Portia faces the risk that a man she does not love will select the right casket.

Shylock employs the rhetorical device of antimetabole, whereby a word changes its meaning. When Shylock says, "Antonio is a good man" (1.3.12), Bassanio understands the word in its moral sense, but Shylock means that the merchant can repay the loan. A few lines later, Bassanio states that Shylock may "Be assur'd" that Antonio has sufficient money. Again, Shylock reinterprets the phrase: "I will be assur'd I may; and that I may be assur'd, I will bethink me" (1.3.28–30).

Shylock also is a literalist, eschewing metaphor. When he lapses into figurative language, he quickly retreats. Pondering Antonio's commercial ventures, Shylock reflects, "There be land-rats and water-rats, water-thieves and land-thieves, I mean pirates" (1.3.22–24). Later he tells Jessica to "stop my house's ears, I mean my casements" (2.5.34) against the music of the masque. At the trial, Portia uses antimetabole and literalism to defeat Shylock by reinterpreting the contract.

Other traits of Shylock's speech are repetition and parallel construction. At the beginning of 1.3, Shylock repeatedly echoes Bassanio. Speaking of Antonio in 3.1, he tells Salerio and Solanio, "He was wont to call me usurer, let him look to his bond. He was wont to lend money for a Christian cur'sy, let him look to his bond" (ll. 47–50). To Tubal, he says, "Why, there, there, there, there! . . . What, what, what? ill luck, ill luck?" (3.1.83–99). John Gross observes: "These speech habits bear an obvious relation to Shylock's business habits—to the world of ledgers, double-entry book-keeping, profit and loss" (66). These iterations also suggest a person reluctant to let go of anything, even words. Shylock also frequently uses "my," as in 2.5: "my keys," "my girl," "my house," "my rest," "my doors" (2.5.13–29). This language shows that he clings to his possessions.

Shakespeare employs puns to show the slipperiness of language and hence the risk of relying, as Shylock does, on literalism. A common pun in the play is "gentle/gentile," which also highlights Christian anti-Semitism: The Christians assume that only a gentile can be gentle. When Shylock offers his "merry bond," which will allow Antonio to borrow money without interest, Antonio remarks, "Hie, thee, gentle Jew, / The Hebrew will turn Christian, he grows kind" (1.3.177–178).

Kind is another word with double meaning. It signifies consideration (kindness) but also identity, likeness, being of the same kind. For Antonio, if Shylock is considerate, he must be abandoning his Judaism to become a Christian. Portia plays on the word *will* when she observes that her dead father's (written) will curbs hers, i.e., her desires (1.2.24–25). The play ends with a bawdy pun about Nerissa's ring (5.1.307). These instances of wordplay provide humor, but they also reveal character and have thematic significance.

EXTRACTS OF CLASSICAL CRITICISM
Nicholas Rowe (1674–1718) [Excerpted from "Some Account of the Life, &c. of Mr. William Shakespear," in *The Works of Mr. William Shakespear* (1709). Here, Rowe, one of Shakespeare's earliest editors and biographers, addresses issues about the play's genre, realism, and lyricism that critics continue to discuss.]

[T]ho' we have seen *[The Merchant of Venice]* Receiv'd and Acted as a Comedy, and the Part of the *Jew* perform'd by an Excellent Comedian [Thomas Doggett], yet I cannot but think it was design'd Tragically by the Author. There appears in it such a deadly Spirit of Revenge, such a savage Fierceness and Fellness, and such a bloody designation of Cruelty and Mischief, as cannot agree either with the Stile or Characters of Comedy. The Play it self, take it all together, seems to me to be one of the most finish'd of any of *Shakespear*'s. The Tale indeed, in that Part relating to the Caskets, and the extravagant and unusual kind of Bond given by *Antonio*, is a little too much remov'd from the Rules of Probability: But taking the Fact for granted, we must allow it to be very beautifully written. There is something in the Friendship of *Antonio* to *Bassanio* very Great, Generous and Tender. The whole fourth Act, supposing, as I said, the Fact to be probable, is extremely Fine. But there are two Passages that deserve particular Notice. The first is, what *Portia* says in praise of Mercy . . .; and the other on the Power of Musick.

William Hazlitt (1778–1830) [Excerpted from *Characters of Shakespeare's Plays* (1817). The famous essayist Hazlitt was one of the most important Shakespearean critics of the 19th century. His defense of Shylock and criticism of the Christians in the play, especially Portia, remain influential.]

[The Merchant of Venice] is a play that in spite of the change of manners and of prejudices still holds undisputed possession of the stage. . . . In proportion as Shylock has ceased to be a popular bugbear, "baited with the rabble's curse," he becomes a half favourite with the philosophical part of the audience, who are disposed to think that Jewish revenge is at least as good as Christian injuries. Shylock is a *good hater;* "a man no less sinned against than sinning." If he carries his revenge too far, yet he has strong grounds for "the lodged hate he bears Anthonio," which he explains with equal force of eloquence and reason. . . . There is a strong, quick, and deep sense of justice mixed up with the gall and bitterness of his resentment. . . . The desire for revenge is almost inseparable from the sense of wrong; and we can hardly help sympathizing with the proud spirit, hid beneath his "Jewish gabardine," stung to madness by repeated undeserved provocations, and labouring to throw off the load of obloquy and oppression heaped upon him and all his tribe by one desperate act of "lawful" revenge, till the ferociousness of the means by which he is to execute his purpose,

Shylock (Arthur Bourchier) sharpens his knife as the Duke reads Bellario's letter in Act IV, Scene 1 of *The Merchant of Venice.* This is an illustration of a 1905 production at the Garrick Theatre. *(Illustration by Max Cowper)*

and the pertinacity with which he adheres to it, turn us against him; but even at the last, when disappointed of the sanguinary revenge with which he had glutted his hopes, and exposed to beggary and contempt by the letter of the law on which he had insisted with so little remorse, we pity him, and think him hardly dealt with by his judges. In all his answers and retorts upon his adversaries, he has the best not only of the argument but of the question, reasoning on their own principles and practice. . . .

The whole of the trial scene, both before and after the entrance of Portia, is a masterpiece of dramatic skill. The legal acuteness, the passionate declamations, the sound maxims of jurisprudence, the wit and irony interspersed in it, the fluctuations of hope and fear in the different persons, and the completeness and suddenness of the catastrophe, cannot be surpassed. Shylock, who is his own counsel, defends himself well, and is triumphant on all the general topics that are urged against him, and only fails through a legal flaw. . . .

Portia is not a very great favourite with us, neither are we in love with her maid, Nerissa. Portia has a certain degree of affectation and pedantry about her, which is very unusual in Shakespeare's women, but which perhaps was a proper qualification for the office of a "civil doctor," which she undertakes and executes so successfully.

Anna Brownell Jameson (1794–1860)

[Excerpted from *Characteristics of Women* (1832). A critic of literature and art, Jameson wrote particularly for women, though her Shakespearean criticism has had an especially broad appeal. Her works were widely read in the 19th and early 20th centuries, but then fell out of favor. Jameson here defends Portia and offers a persuasive explanation of her behavior in the trial scene, which some critics regard as unnecessarily prolonging Antonio's suffering.]

Portia is endued with her own share of those delightful qualities, which Shakespeare has lavished on many of his female characters; but besides the dignity, the sweetness, and tenderness which should distinguish her sex generally, she is individualized by qualities peculiar to herself; by her high mental powers, her enthusiasm of temperament, her decision of purpose, and her buoyancy of spirit. These are innate; she has other distinguishing qualities more external, and which are the result of the circumstances in which she is placed. Thus she is the heiress of a princely name and countless wealth; a train of obedient pleasures have ever waited round her; and from infancy she has breathed an atmosphere redolent of perfume and blandishment. Accordingly there is a commanding grace, a high-bred, airy elegance, a spirit of magnificence in all that she does and says, as one to whom splendour had been familiar from her very birth. . . . She is full of penetrative wisdom, and genuine tenderness, and lively wit; but as she has never known want, or grief, or fear, or disappointment, her wisdom is without a touch of the somber or the sad; her affections are all mixed up with faith, hope, and joy; and her wit has not a particle of malevolence or causticity. . . .

But all the finest parts of Portia's character are brought to bear in the trial scene. There she shines forth all her divine self. Her intellectual powers, her elevated sense of religion, her high honourable principles, her best feelings as a woman, are all displayed. She maintains at first a calm self-command, as one sure of carrying her point in the end; yet the painful heart-thrilling uncertainty in which she keeps the whole court, until suspense verges upon agony, is not contrived for effect merely; it is necessary and inevitable. . . . Thus all the speeches addressed to Shylock in the first instance, are either direct or indirect experiments on his temper and feelings. . . . She begins by an appeal to his mercy, . . . but in vain. . . . She next attacks his avarice. . . . All that she says afterwards—her strong expressions which are calculated to strike a shuddering horror through the nerves—the reflection she interposes—her delays and circumlocution to give time for any latent feelings of commiseration to display itself—all, all are premeditated and tend in the same manner to the object she has in view. . . .

At length the crisis arrives, for patience and womanhood can endure no longer; and when Shylock, carrying his savage bent "to

the last hour of act," springs on his victim—
"A sentence! Come, prepare!" then the
smothered scorn, indignation, and disgust,
burst forth with an impetuosity which interferes with the judicial solemnity she had at
first affected. . . .

But she afterwards recovers her propriety,
and triumphs with a cooler scorn and a more
self-possessed exultation.

Heinrich Heine (1797–1856) [Excerpted from
Shakespeare's Mädchen und Frauen (1839); translated as *Shakespeare's Maidens and Women* (1891).
Like others of his fellow romantics, Heine cham-
pions Shylock. His argument that the play is not
anti-Semitic has found echoes in much subsequent
criticism. Heine also raises questions of genre and
wonders whether Shylock outgrew Shakespeare's
initial intent; these issues have also engaged later
students of the work.]

When I saw this piece played in Drury Lane
there stood behind me in the box a pale British beauty who, at the end of the fourth act,
wept passionately and many times cried out,
"The poor man is wronged!" It was a countenance of noblest Grecian cut, and the eyes
were large and black. I have never been able
to forget them, those great black eyes which
wept for Shylock!

When I think of those tears I must include
the *Merchant of Venice* among the tragedies,
although the frame of the work is a composition of laughing masks and sunny faces,
satyr forms and amorets, as though the poet
meant to make a comedy. Shakespeare perhaps intended originally to please the mob,
to represent a thoroughgoing wehr-wolf, a
hated fabulous being who yearns for blood,
and pays for it with daughter and with ducats, and is over and above laughed to scorn.
But the genius of the poet, the spirit of the
wide world which ruled in him, was ever
stronger than his own will, and so it came to

pass that he in Shylock, despite the glaring
grotesqueness, expressed the justification of
an unfortunate sect which was oppressed by
providence, from inscrutable motives, with
the hatred of the lower and higher class, and
which did not always return this hate with
love.

But what do I say? The genius of Shakespeare rises still higher over the petty strife
of two religious sects, and his drama shows
us neither Jews nor Christians, but oppressors and oppressed, and the madly agonized
cries of exultation of the latter when they can
repay their arrears of injuries with interest.
There is not in this play the least trace of difference in religion, and Shakespeare sets forth
in Shylock a man whom nature bade hate his
enemies, just as he in Antonio and his friends
by no means expresses the disciples of that
divine doctrine which commands us to love
our enemies. . . .

Truly Shakespeare would have written a
satire against Christianity if he had made it
consist of those characters who are the enemies of Shylock, but who are hardly worthy
to unlace his shoes. The bankrupt Antonio
is a weak creature without energy, without
strength of hatred, and as little of love, a
melancholy worm-heart whose flesh is really
worth nothing save "to bait fish withal."
He does not repay the swindled Jew the
three thousand ducats. Nor does Bassanio
repay him—this man is, as an English critic
calls him, a real fortune-hunter; he borrows
money to make a display so as to win a rich
wife and a fat bridal portion. . . .

As for Lorenzo, he is the accomplice of a
most infamous theft, and according to the
laws of Prussia he would have been branded,
set in the pillory, and condemned to fifteen
years' imprisonment, notwithstanding his
susceptibility to the beauties of nature, land-
scapes by moonlight, and music. As for the
other noble Venetians who appear as allies of
Antonio, they do not seem to have any spe-

cial antipathy to money, and when their poor friend is in difficulties they have nothing for him but words or minted air. . . . Much as we must hate Shylock we can hardly take it amiss of him that he despises this folk a little, as he well may do. . . .

In fact, with the exception of Portia, Shylock is the most respectable person in the whole piece. He loves money, he does not conceal it—he cries it aloud in the public market-place. But there is one thing which he esteems above money, it is satisfaction for his injured feelings—the just retribution for unspeakable insults; and though the borrowed sum be offered him tenfold he refuses it, and he does not regret the three thousand, or ten times three thousand, ducats if he can buy a pound of the flesh of the heart of his enemy.

Elmer Edgar Stoll (1874–1959) [Excerpted from "Shylock" (1911). Dissenting from the critical and dramatic orthodoxy of his day, Stoll argues that Hazlitt and his followers misinterpret the play by failing to recognize its historical context. Stoll presents a wealth of 16th- and 17th-century evidence along with textual support to argue that Shylock is intended as a comic villain, not a tragic hero. The contemporary critic Harold Bloom concurs with Stoll's reading of the play as anti-Semitic.]

Shylock's griefs excite no commiseration; indeed, as they press upon him they are barbed with gibes and jeers. . . . We know that the poet is not with Shylock, for on that head, in this play as in every other, the impartial, inscrutable poet leaves little or nothing to suggestion or surmise. As is his custom elsewhere, by the comments of the good characters, by the method pursued in the disposition of the scenes, and by the downright avowals of soliloquy, he constantly sets us right.

Shylock asks Jessica to lock up the house as Launcelot looks on in Act II, Scene 5 of *The Merchant of Venice*. This is a print from the Boydell Shakespeare Gallery project, which was conceived in 1786 and lasted until 1805. *(Painting by Robert Smirke; engraving by Jean Pierre Simon)*

As for the first of these artifices, all the characters who come in contact with Shylock except Tubal, among them being those of his own house—his servant and his daughter—have a word or two to say on the subject of his character, and never a good one. And in the same breath they spend on Bassanio and Antonio, his enemies, nothing but words of praise. Praise or blame, moreover, is, after Shakespeare's fashion, usually in the nick of time to guide the hearer's judgment. . . . As for the second artifice, the ordering of the scenes is such as to enforce this contrast.

First impressions are momentous, every playwright knows (and no one better than Shakespeare himself), particularly for the purpose of ridicule. Launcelot and Jessica, in separate scenes, are introduced before Shylock reaches home, that, hearing their story, we may side with them, and, when the old curmudgeon appears, may be moved to laughter as he complains of Launcelot's gormandizing, sleeping, and rending apparel out, and as he is made game of by the young conspirators to his face. . . . And as for the third artifice, that a sleepy audience may not make the mistake of the cautious critic and take the villain for the hero, Shakespeare is at pains to label the villain by an aside at the moment the hero appears on the boards:

> I hate him for he is a Christian,
> But more for that in low simplicity
> He lends out money gratis, and brings
>   down
> The rate of usance here with us in Venice.

Those are his motives, confessed repeatedly, and either one brands him as a villain more unmistakably in that day, as we shall see, than in ours. . . . As with Shakespeare's villains generally, Aaron, Iago, or Richard III, only what they say concerning their purposes aside or to their confidants can be relied upon. . . .

Only twice does Shakespeare seem to follow Shylock's pleadings and reasonings with any sympathy—"Hath a dog money?" in the first scene in which he appears, and "Hath not a Jew eyes?" in the third act—but a bit too much has been made of this: Either plea ends in such fashion as to alienate the audience. To Shylock's reproaches the admirable Antonio, . . . praised and honored by every one but Shylock, retorts, secure in his virtue, that he is just as like to spit on him and spurn him again. And Shylock's celebrated justification of his race runs headlong into a justi-fication of his villainy:—"The villainy which you teach me I will execute, and it shall go hard but I will better the instruction." "Hath not a Jew eyes?" and he proceeds to show that your Jew is no less than a man, and as such has a right, not to respect or compassion as the critics of a century have had it, but to revenge. Neither large nor lofty are his claims. Quite as vigorously and, in that day, with as much reason, the detestable and abominable Aaron defends his race and color [*Titus Andronicus*, 4.2.98–103], and Edmund, the dignity of bastards [*King Lear*, 1.2.1–22]. The worst of his villains Shakespeare allows to plead their cause: their confidences in soliloquy, if not, as here, slight touches in the plea itself, sufficiently counter-act any too favorable impression. This, on the face of it, is a plea for indulging in revenge with all its rigors; not a word is put in for the nobler side of Jewish character; and in lend-ing Shylock his eloquence Shakespeare is but giving the devil his due.

By all the devices of Shakespeare's drama-turgy, then, Shylock is proclaimed, as by the triple repetition of a crier, to be the villain, a comic villain, though, or butt. Nor does the poet let pass any of the prejudices of that day which would heighten this impression. A miser, a money-lender, a Jew—all three had from time immemorial been objects of popular detestation and ridicule, whether in life or on the stage. The union of them in one person is the rule in Shakespeare's day, both in plays and in "character"-writing: to the popular imagination a moneylender was a sordid miser with a hooked nose. . . .

As we have done with many another mon-ster in history, literature, or holy writ, we have tamed and domesticated the "dog Jew" and drawn his "fangs." "He will speak soft words unto us," he no longer grins or bites. But Shakespeare and the Elizabethans, as we have seen, shuddered at him and laughed at him, and except at popular performances, where racial antipathy is rather to be allayed than fomented, so should we, as much as in us lies, today. Thus we shall come into sympathy with the manifest intention of the poet, with the acting of the part on the Elizabethan stage, with the conception of the money-lending Jew in the contemporary drama, character-writing, and ballad, and with the lively prejudices of the time.

MODERN CRITICISM AND CRITICAL CONTROVERSIES

The major controversy regarding the play is its portrayal of Shylock, which many critics have regarded as anti-Semitic, though many others have just as vehemently denied the accusation. Harold Bloom in his introduction to *The Merchant of Venice* (2008) calls the play "pragmatically anti-Semitic," adding "Shylock remains vital and vitalizing, a great imagining. And yet his image has done great harm in the world." On the other hand, Kennth Gross rejects this interpretation, calling the play and Shylock among Shakespeare's greatest achievements. In his 2006 book *Shylock is Shakespeare,* Gross claims that Shylock is an image of Shakespeare himself: "Shylock provides us a mirror of Shakespeare's sense of himself as a human author." He further writes, "There is much in the text that leads one to call it antisemitic, yet by itself that is too simple. . . . What continues to compel us in Shylock depends on things that cannot be made sense of strictly in terms of his Jewish identity." See the section on Difficulties of the Play for more discussion of the matter.

Marxist Criticism

With its emphasis on money and commerce, *The Merchant of Venice* invites Marxist criticism. Kiernan Ryan in "Re-reading *The Merchant of Venice*" (Coyle: 36–44) argues that the play attacks capitalism in Elizabethan England. Shakespeare shows "the ruthless priority of money values over human values, of the rights of property over the elementary rights of men and women" (39–40). Shylock's

demand for a pound of flesh reifies the ruthlessness of mercantile society. As he observes at 4.1.90–101, the Venetians have no qualms about buying human flesh; they purchase slaves just as they would a dog or a mule or any other commodity.

Writing from the same Marxist perspective, Walter Cohen in "*The Merchant of Venice* and the Possibilities of Historical Criticism" (Coyle: 45–72) arrives at the opposite conclusion, that the play endorses capitalism. He argues that the public theater, itself a commercial enterprise, served to reconcile audiences to the new order. Shylock as usurer is defeated at the end of Act IV, but his vision of the force of contracts remains valid. Moreover, Antonio, the representative of mercantile values, joins the aristocratic assembly at Belmont in a fusion of commerce and landed wealth, feudalism and capitalism.

For John Drakakis, another Marxist critic, Shylock is the evil that capitalism refuses to admit about itself. In "Historical Difference and Venetian Patriarchy" (Wood: 23–53), he argues that Shylock is demonized because Venice does not want to recognize the real basis of its wealth. By forcing Shylock to convert, to become not an alien but a Venetian, the Christians render his wealth socially acceptable.

Feminist Criticism

Feminist criticism, too, has found much to discuss in *The Merchant,* largely because of Portia's strength. Karen Newman's 1987 article "Portia's Ring: Unruly Women and Structure of Exchange in *The Merchant of Venice* argues that Portia challenges the traditional view of gender roles. Newman states that in giving Bassanio a ring, Portia surrenders herself and her property to her husband. Later, however, Portia retrieves the ring, and she confers so much more on Bassanio than he can repay that the conventional marriage roles are subverted. Thus, Portia controls the relationship. For Lynda E. Boose, in "The Comic Contract and Portia's Golden Ring" (1988), Portia most deserves the play's title. Boose claims that Portia is Shakespeare's first fully developed powerful comic heroine. Though she may seem generous, Portia actually accumulates power that she uses to control the men in the play.

Julie Hankey concurs that Portia's behavior questions traditional male and female roles. In "Victorian Portias: Shakespeare's Borderline Heroine" (1994), Hankey writes that Portia's "rational, unemotional composure, her methodical manner of speech and argument, her independence, not only of mind but of actions—encroached on traditionally male ground" (432). Such forcefulness could alienate Victorian male critics and compel women writers and actresses to defend Portia's femininity. Nonetheless, she—like Rosalind in *As You Like It* and Viola in *Twelfth Night*—refutes the male stereotype of the weak, emotional, incapable female.

New Historicism

James Shapiro's *Shakespeare and the Jews* (1996), an expansion of the 1992 Parkes Lecture of the same title that Shapiro delivered at the University of Southampton, exemplifies the New Historicist approach to the play. His book provides much background on Shylock's attempt to claim a pound of Antonio's flesh. Shapiro examines the long tradition of blood libel against Jews going back to 1144. For him, the play highlights anxieties that Elizabethans felt about Jews and that persisted for centuries afterwards.

Kim F. Hall's 1992 article "Guess Who's Coming to Dinner?: Colonisation and Miscegenation in *The Merchant of Venice*" looks at another Elizabethan concern: interracial marriages. Again approaching this matter from a New Historicist perspective, Hall observes that in 1596, Elizabeth twice ordered the expulsion of blacks from her realm. In *Merchant*, Portia escapes having to marry Morocco, but in 3.5, Lorenzo criticizes Launcelot for impregnating a Moor (who nowhere appears in the play and is mentioned only in this scene). Hall notes that commerce crosses borders, and commercial exchanges can lead to social and sexual interchange as well. Thus, *The Merchant*'s economic concerns embody other fears as well.

THE PLAY TODAY

In *A Midsummer Night's Dream*, Bottom the weaver comments, "There are things in this comedy of Pyramus and Thisbe that will never please" (3.2.9–10). The same may be said for *The Merchant of Venice*. The argument over whether the play is anti-Semitic will probably never be resolved to anyone's satisfaction. Shylock suffers more than any of his prototypes in Shakespeare's sources even as Shakespeare makes him more human than any of the literary models on which he drew. Antonio seems Christlike in his willingness to give his life for his friend, yet his treatment of Shylock rejects Christ's teachings. Other characters also continue to pose problems for current critics. In rejecting the subservient role patriarchy would impose upon her, Portia perhaps becomes too controlling. For a romantic hero, Bassanio shows too much interest in Portia's assets and too little regard for his oath to her.

Nonetheless, despite its controversial nature, the play continues to be popular among students, perhaps because it is one of the most dramatic of Shakespeare's comedies and perhaps because of its controversial nature, which leads theater companies and critics to take it on again and again. There have been many recent film and theatrical productions. In the 2004 film adaption, Al Pacino played Shylock and Jeremy Irons played Antonio. Pacino later played Shylock in New York City's Shakespeare in the Park production in 2010, which subsequently moved to Broadway. Henry Goodman and F. Murray Abraham have also played Shylock in recent productions.

Samuel Johnson wrote that Shakespeare's plays depict "the real state of sublunary nature." No one in *The Merchant of Venice* is a paragon of virtue; every character has certain redeeming qualities mingled with his or her flaws. Hence, as John Wilders writes in his introduction to *Shakespeare: The Merchant of Venice: A Casebook* (1969), the play "defies any simple schematic interpretation and refuses to come to heel at the command of producer or literary critic" (21). Every interpretation on the stage or page omits elements of the work that it attempts to clarify. Directors and scholars will continue to seek the heart of the play's mystery. They will thereby enhance the understanding of the work even as they fail to encompass it completely.

FIVE TOPICS FOR DISCUSSION AND WRITING

1. **Anti-Semitism:** Is the play anti-Semitic? Does the play condemn anti-Semitism? Examine Shylock's speeches closely. Are we meant to hate him or sympathize with him? If both, does one of these tendencies predominate over the others?
2. **Genre:** *The Merchant of Venice* ends happily for everyone but Shylock. Is it therefore a comedy? Or does the defeat of Shylock make it more a tragedy?
3. **Shylock:** Shylock is clearly in some respects a villain, though many actors have successfully portrayed him as the hero of the play. Which is truer to the play's meaning? If Shylock is a villain, is he a comic one or a tragic one?
4. **Feminism:** Is Portia a feminist? Is she a victim of patriarchy? Are Jessica and Nerissa victims of patriarchy? Are the women freer when they don men's attire?
5. **Capitalism:** What does the play say about the role of money in early modern England? Does money taint relationships in the play? Are some characters more concerned with money than others. Does this make them nobler?

Bibliography

Adelman, Janet. *Blood Relations: Christian and Jew in The Merchant of Venice.* Chicago: University of Chicago Press, 2008.

Ajzenstat, Samuel. "Contract in *The Merchant of Venice.*" *Philosophy and Literature* 21, no. 2 (1997): 262–278.

Barber, C. L. *Shakespeare's Festive Comedy: A Study of Dramatic Form and Its Relation to Social Custom.* Princeton, N.J.: Princeton University Press, 1959.

Barnet, Sylvan, ed. *Twentieth Century Interpretations of* The Merchant of Venice. Englewood Cliffs, N.J.: Prentice-Hall, 1970.

Baron, Salo Wittmayer. *A Social and Religious History of the Jews.* Volume 15: *Resettlement and Exploration.* New York: Columbia University Press, 1973.

Bickel, Shlom. "The Argument About Shylock." In *Great Yiddish Writers of the Twentieth Century,* translated and edited by Joseph Leftwich, 255. Northvale, N.J.: J. Aronson, 1987.

Billington, Michael. "Love and loot in LA," *Guardian,* 19 November 1994. T4.

Bloom, Harold. *The Merchant of Venice.* Bloom's Shakespeare through the Ages. New York: Chelsea House, 2008.

———. *Shakespeare: The Invention of the Human.* New York: Riverhead, 1998.

Boose, Lynda E. "The Comic Contract and Portia's Golden Ring." *Shakespeare Studies* 20 (1988): 241–254.

Boyce, Charles. *Critical Companion to William Shakespeare.* New York: Facts On File, 2005.

Brooke, Stopford. *On Ten Plays of Shakespeare.* London: Constable, 1905.

Brown, John Russell. *Shakespeare and His Comedies.* 2d ed. London: Methuen, 1962.

Bullough, Geoffrey, ed. *Early Comedies, Poems, Romeo and Juliet.* Vol. 1 of *Narrative and Dramatic Sources of Shakespeare.* New York: Columbia University Press, 1961.

Bulman, James C. *The Merchant of Venice.* Shakespeare in Performance. Manchester, U.K.: Manchester University Press, 1991.

Burckhardt, Sigurd. "*The Merchant of Venice:* The Gentle Bond." *ELH: English Literary History* 29 (1962): 239–262.

Cerasano, S. P., ed. *A Routledge Literary Sourcebook on William Shakespeare's The Merchant of Venice.* New York: Routledge, 2004.

Champion, Larry S. *The Evolution of Shakespeare's Comedy: A Study in Dramatic Perspective.* Cambridge, Mass.: Harvard University Press, 1970.

Coyle, Martin, ed. *New Casebooks: The Merchant of Venice.* New York: St. Martin's Press, 1998.

Danson, Lawrence. *The Harmonies of The Merchant of Venice.* New Haven, Conn.: Yale University Press, 1978.

Elliott, Mrs. M. G. *Shakespeare's Garden of Girls*. London: Remington, 1885.

Garber, Marjorie. *Shakespeare After All*. New York: Pantheon, 2004.

Geary, Keith. "The Nature of Portia's Victory: Turning to Men in *The Merchant of Venice*. *Shakespeare Quarterly* 37 (1986): 55–68.

Gollancz, Israel. *A Book of Homage to Shakespeare*. Oxford: Oxford University Press, 1916.

Grebanier, Bernard. *The Truth about Shylock*. New York: Random House, 1962.

Gross, John. *Shylock: A Legend and Its Legacy*. New York: Simon and Schuster, 1992.

Gross, Kenneth. *Shylock Is Shakespeare*. Chicago: University of Chicago Press, 2006.

Halio, Jay L. *Understanding* The Merchant of Venice: *A Student Casebook to Issues, Sources, and Historical Documents*. Westport, Conn.: Greenwood Press, 2000.

Hall, Kim F. "Guess Who's Coming to Dinner? Colonisation and Miscegenation in *The Merchant of Venice*." *Renaissance Drama* 23 (1992): 87–111.

Hankey, Julie. "Victorian Portias: Shakespeare's Borderline Heroine." *Shakespeare Quarterly* 45 (1994): 426–448.

Hapgood, Robert. "Portia and *The Merchant of Venice:* The Gentle Bond." *Modern Language Quarterly* 28, no. 1 (1967): 19–32.

Hazlitt, William. *Characters of Shakespeare's Plays*. London: C. H. Reynell, 1817.

Holderness, Graham. *William Shakespeare: The Merchant of Venice*. Penguin Critical Studies. Harmondsworth, U.K.: Penguin, 1993.

Holmer, Joan Ozark. *The Merchant of Venice: Choice, Hazard and Consequence*. New York: St. Martin's Press, 1995.

James, Henry. *The Scenic Act: Notes on Acting and Drama: 1872–1901*. London: Rupert Hart-Davis, 1949.

Johnson, S. F. "How Many Ways Portia Informs Bassanio's Choice." In *Shakespeare's Universe: Renaissance Ideas and Convention*, edited by John J. Mucciolo, 144–147. Aldershot, U.K.: Scolar Press, 1996.

Krieger, Elliot. *A Marxist Study of Shakespeare's Comedies*. London: Macmillan, 1979.

Leggatt, Alexander. *Shakespeare's Comedy of Love*. London: Methuen, 1974.

Lelyveld, Toby. *Shylock on the Stage*. Cleveland, Ohio: Press of Western Reserve University, 1960.

Lyon, John. *The Merchant of Venice*. Twayne's New Critical Introductions to Shakespeare. Boston: Twayne Publishers, 1988.

Mahon, John W., and Ellen Macleod Mahon, eds. *The Merchant of Venice: New Critical Essays*. New York: Routledge, 2002.

McLean, Susan. "Prodigal Sons and Daughters: Transgression and Forgiveness in *The Merchant of Venice*." *Papers on Language and Literature* 32 (1996): 45–63.

Newman, Karen. "Portia's Ring: Unruly Women and Structure of Exchange in *The Merchant of Venice*." *Shakespeare Quarterly* 38 (1987): 19–33.

Moody, A. D. *Shakespeare: The Merchant of Venice*. London: Edward Arnold, 1964.

Overton, Bill. *The Merchant of Venice: Text and Performance*. Atlantic Highlands, N.J.: Humanities Press, 1987.

Poel, William. *Shakespeare in the Theatre*. London and Toronto: Sidgwick & Jackson, 1913.

Raleigh, Walter. *Shakespeare*. London: Macmillan, 1907.

Riggio, Milla Cozart, ed. *Teaching Shakespeare through Performance*. New York: Modern Language Association, 1999.

Shakespeare, William. *The Merchant of Venice*. Edited by John Russell Brown. London: Methuen, 1955.

———. *The Merchant of Venice*. Edited by M. M. Mahood. Cambridge: Cambridge University Press, 2003.

Shapiro, James. *Shakespeare and the Jews*. New York: Columbia University Press, 1996.

Silverman, Rita. *Sufferance Is the Badge of All Our Tribe: A Study of Shylock in* The Merchant of Venice. Lanham, Md.: University Press of America, 1981.

Sokol, B. J. "Prejudice and the Law in *The Merchant of Venice*." *Shakespeare Survey* 51 (1998): 159–174.

Spencer, Christopher. *The Genesis of Shakespeare's Merchant of Venice*. Lewiston, N.Y.: Edwin Mellen Press, 1988.

Spurgeon, Caroline F. E. *Shakespeare's Imagery and What It Tells Us*. Cambridge: Cambridge University Press, 1935.

Stoll, Elmer Edgar. "Shylock." *Journal of English and Germanic Philology* 10 (1911): 236–279.

Tennenhouse, Leonard. "The Counterfeit Order of *The Merchant of Venice*." In *Representing Shakespeare: New Psychoanalytic Essays,* edited by Murray M. Schwartz and Coppélia Kahn, 54–69. Baltimore, Md.: Johns Hopkins University Press, 1980.

Tillyard, E. M. W. *Shakespeare's Early Comedies.* London: Chatto & Windus, 1965.

Westlund, Joseph. *Shakespeare's Reparative Comedy: A Psychoanalytic View of the Middle Plays.* Chicago: University of Chicago Press, 1984.

Wheeler, Thomas, ed. *The Merchant of Venice: Critical Essays.* New York: Garland, 1991.

Wilders, John, ed. *The Merchant of Venice: A Casebook.* London: Macmillan, 1969.

Wilson, John Dover. *Shakespeare's Happy Comedies.* Evanston, Ill.: Northwestern University Press, 1962.

Winter, William. *Shakespeare on the Stage.* London: Unwin, 1911.

Wood, Nigel, ed. *The Merchant of Venice.* Buckingham, U.K.: Open University Press, 1996.

Yaffe, Martin D. *Shylock and the Jewish Question.* Baltimore, Md.: Johns Hopkins University Press, 1997.

Zuckert, Michael. "The New Medea: On Portia's Comic Triumph in *The Merchant of Venice*." In *Shakespeare's Political Pageant: Essays in Literature and Politics,* edited by Joseph Alulis and Vickie Sullivan, 3–36. Lanham, Md.: Rowman and Littlefield, 1996.

FILM AND VIDEO PRODUCTIONS

Douglas, Morse, dir. *The Merchant of Venice.* With Tom Yarrow (Shylock), Ed Martineau (Bassanio), Patrick Werner (Antonio), Lizzy Carter (Portia), and Stephanie Bain (Jessica). Films for the Humanities and Sciences, 2009.

Gold, Jack, dir. *The Merchant of Venice.* With Warren Mitchell (Shylock), John Franklyn-Robbins (Antonio), and Gemma Jones (Portia). BBC, 1980.

Hal, Burton, dir. *The Merchant of Venice.* With Michael Hordern (Shylock), Denis Quilley (Bassanio), Rachel Gurney (Portia), and Veronica Wells (Jessica). BBC, 1955.

Horrox, Alan, dir. *The Merchant of Venice.* With Bob Peck (Shylock), Benjamin Whitrow (Antonio), and Haydn Gwynne (Portia). Channel 4, 1996.

Hunt, Chris, and Trevor Nunn, dirs. *The Merchant of Venice.* With David Bamber (Antonio), Derbhle Crotty (Portia), and Henry Goodman (Shylock). BBC and PBS, 2001.

Radford, Michael, dir. *The Merchant of Venice.* With Al Pacino (Shylock), Joseph Fiennes (Bassanio), Jeremy Irons (Antonio), Lynn Collins (Portia), and Zuleikha Robinson (Jessica). Sony Pictures, 2004.

Sichel, John, dir. *The Merchant of Venice.* With Laurence Olivier (Shylock), Joan Plowright (Portia), Jeremy Brett (Bassanio), and Louise Purnell (Jessica). Associated Television, 1973.

———, dir. *The Merchant of Venice.* With Antony Holland (Shylock), Alan Gray (Bassanio), and Trish Grange (Portia). West Coast Actors Company, 1976.

Welles, Orson, dir. *The Merchant of Venice.* With Orson Welles (Shylock), Charles Gray (Antonio), and Irina Maleeva (Jessica). 1969.

—Joseph Rosenblum

The Merry Wives of Windsor

INTRODUCTION

There is perhaps no play that demonstrates Shakespeare's emerging popularity, as well as his ongoing desire to please his fan base, more vividly than *The Merry Wives of Windsor*. The play was written some time after *Henry IV, Part 1,* and perhaps after that play's sequel, *Henry IV, Part 2*. Those plays had been more than simply a chronicle of kings and lords. In them, Shakespeare had introduced his most popular character to date, Sir John Falstaff (originally Oldcastle, but the name was changed to appease a censor), a fat knight who lived at the Boar's Head Tavern in Eastcheap and kept company with the Prince of Wales. Shakespeare appears to have composed this comedy just to give audiences what they most wanted—more Falstaff. It is therefore not surprising that this play has not always been a favorite of literary scholars. Many today consider it one of Shakespeare's weakest comedies; others, however, continue to find this elaboration of Falstaff's character irresistible.

The play moves Falstaff from his familiar setting of the Boar's Head to Windsor, where he is living at the Garter Inn, well beyond his means. As with previous plays, Falstaff is planning devious schemes in order to procure cash. Rather than resort to holding up carriages, as he had done in earlier plays, on this occasion he hopes to seduce two women, both wives of wealthy citizens. Unmoved by Falstaff's amorous gestures, the two wives subject him to a series of pranks. In this respect, the play essentially becomes a vehicle for luring the lecherous knight into comic situations, then laughing at his expense. This portrayal of Falstaff as comic gull seems to depart from Shakespeare's earlier depictions of the character as a mendacious yet caring knight, who has something to teach the young Prince of Wales despite his own clear flaws. Critics routinely notice that the Falstaff of *Merry Wives* is "an altogether different comic from the ready and resourceful, the irrepressible Sir John of *Henry IV*" (Bennett: 429). And indeed, it is very possible that Falstaff of *Merry Wives* was played by somebody other than the comedian Will Kemp, the star in Shakespeare's dramatic troupe who had made Falstaff such a hit to begin with. The changes in Falstaff's character may, in fact, represent changes in the playing conditions that the playwright had available to him.

In *Merry Wives,* Shakespeare was experimenting in several other ways as well, and one could argue that he was using the play as an opportunity to test out new approaches to his craft. It is his only comic play that uses a distinctly local setting. While Shakespeare had made his name staging chronicles of pre-Tudor English histories, no other play focused so closely on what might be regarded as domestic English town life. In this respect, Shakespeare puts a spin on a very popular style of plays known as city comedy, which mocked the fashions and customs of contemporary urban life. Unlike most city comedies, however, which set their scenes in the overcrowded and rapidly changing city of London, Shakespeare set his play in the nearby town of Windsor, where the royal family kept its castle, the connections between court and town life could be made to seem more real, and the local values could be made to seem more traditional. Perhaps it was because he wanted to portray "ordinary" citizens of England that the playwright departed from his traditional writing style of blank verse. Unlike any other Shakespeare play, *Merry Wives* was written almost entirely in prose. This technique gives the play a very distinct flavor among Shakespeare's plays—though given its overall storyline, one is hard-pressed to call the play more true to life.

Finally, while other Shakespeare comedies end with betrothals and weddings, no other comedy so thoroughly explores the trials and vagaries of *marriage*. The Pages and the Fords, the two married couples of this play, have in both cases been together for a long time. It is evident that their marriages were not hatched out of the typical conventions of romantic comedy—or if they were, those illusions had been shattered long ago. Indeed, the couples are intimate, though with each we observe the husband and wife finding ways to sneak behind the other's back. It is up to audiences to puzzle out how the intimacies between the spouses square up with their ongoing process of mutual deception. Altogether, it is rare ground for Shakespeare. When he returns to the subject of marriage in the plays that follow—*Hamlet, Othello, Macbeth, Troilus and Cressida, Cymbeline, The Winter's Tale*—it is with significantly more sinister tones.

With its reputation as one of Shakespeare's instances of "pure comedy," *The Merry Wives of Windsor* has entertained audiences and inspired artists from its earliest performances to the present day. Perhaps its very comic and mercurial elements, which have made the play such a hit for theatergoers, are what make the script such a challenge for scholars and critics. If we look at the play's history in print, which begins in 1602—roughly when Shakespeare began composing *Hamlet*—we find a version of it that raises many of the most basic questions about what it means to look at Shakespeare's plays in printed form.

Falstaff greets Mistress Ford and Mistress Page in *The Merry Wives of Windsor*. This is an illustration of a 19th-century production at Her Majesty's Theatre. *(Illustration by Samat)*

No meaningful interpretation of the play can take place without at least some understanding of what these questions are or why they are important. Likewise, just as scholars continue to ask questions about the makeup of the text, so too do critics question what the play is about. Are we meant to find serious undertones behind all the zany comedy? Does Shakespeare mean to seriously explore themes such as the relations between men and women, husbands and wives, parents and daughters, town and country, royalty and citizens? If we do look at the play with these relationships in mind, what do we discover?

BACKGROUND
Sources and Allusions

In comparison with Shakespeare's histories, as well as many of his comedies and tragedies, *Merry Wives* is not an especially "source-heavy" play. Giorgio Melchiori, the editor for Arden Shakespeare (Third Series) observes that "source-hunters have been asking for a long time where Shakespeare could have found the major situations on which to construct the main plot of his play" (in Shakespeare 2000: 13), and this statement is itself a telling sign of Shakespeare's departure from his conventional playwriting technique, which often reveals these sorts of documents. Nevertheless, there are clear signs that Shakespeare's script was based on adaptations, albeit heavily modified ones, of other sources.

While Shakespeare may have drawn the Fenton-Page scenario from traditional story lines, scholars are more confident that the Falstaff-Ford scenario was drawn from a collection of stories, *Il Pecerone,* by Ser Giovanni Fiorentino (published in Italian in 1558). This conclusion is inferential: Shakespeare had adapted another story from this collection as the basis for his comedy *The Merchant of Venice,* probably written a year or so before the composition of *Merry Wives,* and it is plausible that he would have returned to this collection (though it had not been translated into English) as the basis for another comedy. The scenarios are not identical, and they play out to very different ends. In the Italian story, the would-be seducer is a student who is unaware that the woman he pursues is the wife of his professor; in addition, he is successful in his erotic conquests, a feat that humiliates the teacher and possibly the student as well. When transformed by Shakespeare, the threats of seduction essentially disappear—Falstaff is many things, but he is no young heartthrob—and the jealous husband is made to look like a fool for even suspecting his wife in the first place. Such changes may be a factor of transposition from novella, where events can be described without our having to witness them, to the stage, where actual seduction might seem more difficult to accept. It may also have been a sign that Shakespeare wanted to explore different ends from the one his assumed source had to offer.

One of Shakespeare's main sources for this play was not a text so much as an event. The numerous references to Windsor Castle, to Queen Elizabeth (the Fairy Queen), and to the Order of the Garter collectively suggest that the play was composed with this courtly community in mind.

At several points in the play, characters make obvious references to the late Christopher Marlowe, the poet and playwright who had been a chief rival of Shakespeare's during the early 1590s. As Evans awaits the arrival of Caius, he sings lines from Marlowe's famous poem "Come live with me and be my love," though he confuses the verses

with imagery taken from Psalm 137. The mistake is fitting for a parson, much more so than the song, which he sings while waiting to fight in a duel. Later, as the characters cozen the Host of the Garter, Bardolph describes a team of runaway horses who "threw me off from behind one of them, in a slough of mire, and set spurs and away, like three German devils, three Doctor Faustuses" (4.5). The remark is an obvious reference to a famous scene in Marlowe's play, in which a horse courser is tossed from his horse into a mud puddle. Indeed, Pistol's reference to "Mephistopholus" comes as early as Act I, Scene 1, while the stag's horns that Falstaff dons for the final scene may have recalled a similar visual joke that appeared in Marlowe's play, all the more obviously if audiences were meant to pick up on all the other references. The most plausible explanation for these allusions is that Marlowe's black-magic play was still extremely popular with audiences (and, in fact, a print version of the play first appeared in 1604). Topical allusions to popular plays would have been expected.

In Act IV, Mistress Page tells the legend of Herne the Hunter, a magical figure who haunts Windsor Forest. The story has all the signs of being based in local folk tradition, though no source for it has been identified. Its afterlife has proven richer. A notice of "Herne's Oak" can be found in a "Plan of the Town and Castle of Windsor and Little Park" (1742). We have some accounts that a tree was indeed identified, even set up as a landmark, which members from the Antiquarian Society would show to tourists as a relic of Shakespeare's actual surroundings. During the 19th century, a poem bearing the title "An Ode upon Herne's Oak being cut down in the spring of 1796" made the rounds.

Legendary Origins and Early Performances

According to legend, Shakespeare dashed the play off quickly at the behest of Queen Elizabeth, who loved Falstaff in *Henry IV, Part 1* and wanted to see a play showing him in love. While this story cannot be confirmed, it has been repeated so often, and by so many critics, that it has become a sort of legend, exercising vast influence over criticism of the play. Its origin is as follows.

In 1702, a playwright named John Dennis published a heavily revised version of Shakespeare's play under the title *The Comical Gallant: Or The Amours of Sir John Falstaffe*. In his preface, Dennis introduced the notion that Shakespeare had originally written his play in 14 days, a claim that accounted for the many "Errours" in the plot, which Dennis would correct. Dennis's significant rewriting of Shakespeare was in keeping with the common practice of the time, but his play was a failure all the same. Despite its embarrassingly short run, the basic notion that Shakespeare wrote the play survived.

A few years later, in 1709, Nicholas Rowe's edited collection of Shakespeare's plays appeared. In the preface, he writes:

> Queen Elizabeth had several of his Plays Acted before her, and without doubt gave him many gracious Marks of her Favour. . . . She was so well pleas'd with that admirable Character of Falstaff, in the two Parts of Henry the Fourth, that she commanded him to continue it for one Play more, and to shew him in Love. Thus is said to be the Occasion of his writing *The Merry Wives of Windsor*.

Neither Rowe's nor Dennis's accounts have any basis in any other textual evidence found by scholars. Indeed, Dennis appears to have invented his story in order to justify his own improvements on the play. All the same, the accounts became the cornerstones for subsequent discussions. For one thing, the legend is appealing. It is pleasant to make believe that the queen herself had a role in Shakespeare's inspiration, and that the world of the theater was in harmonious relation with the royal government. Just as important, the suggestion of a rush job, or a play written to please royal fancy, was an especially useful way to frame debates about the play's aesthetic strengths and defects. It may not matter, for instance, whether Harold Goddard took the legend as fact, so much as whether it put him in a position to write, "Shakespeare does appear to have 'tossed off' this sparkling farce-comedy, his one play of purely contemporary life and of almost pure prose, and, along with *The Comedy of Errors*, his most inconsequential and merely theatrical one" (I.182).

Modern critics are largely (but not completely) in agreement that the first performance of the play corresponded with the Garter Induction Ceremony of April 23, 1597. Critics had suspected for a long time that Shakespeare wrote the play for a specific occasion; in 1931, Leslie Hotson developed the hypothesis that the play originally was written as a royal entertainment for a feast held at Westminster Palace on April 23, 1597, for the purpose of celebrating the induction of five new knights (including George Carey, Lord Hunsdon, and the patron for Shakespeare's company) into the Order of the Garter. The argument gained momentum in 1962, when critic William Green published a book-length study, *Shakespeare and the Merry Wives of Windsor*. The argument accounts for certain features in the play, including the name of the inn (the Garter) and the elaborate ceremony of the last scene, which makes references to the Order of the Garter as well as to the Fairy Queen—a clear allusion to Queen Elizabeth. In addition, some of the topical references, such as the horse-stealing episode, can be accounted for by referring to the Garter induction. The argument leaves intact the notion that Shakespeare wrote the play initially to suit occasional purposes, and it does have internal evidence to lend support.

Date and Text of the Play

The play is thought have been written around 1597, certainly after *Henry IV, Part 1* and perhaps just after *Henry IV, Part 2*. The earliest printed edition of the play appeared in 1602, in quarto format. The full title read: *A Most pleasant and excellent conceited Comedie, of Syr* Iohn *Falstaffe, and the merrie Wiues of Windsor*. The title thus put the focus of attention more directly onto the lecherous knight; the wives were treated as appendages

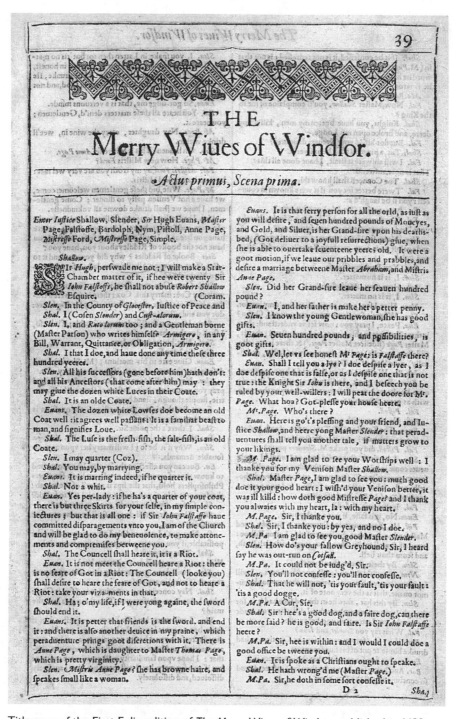

Title page of the First Folio edition of *The Merry Wives of Windsor*, published in 1623

to Falstaff's exploits. Further comments point out additional parts of the play, "Entermixed with sundrie variable and pleasing humors, of Syr Hugh the Welch Knight, Iustice Shallow, and his wise Cousin M. Slender. With the swaggering vaine of Auncient Pistoll, and Corporall Nym." Potential buyers would presumably find plenty of material to enjoy. The name *William Shakespeare* figures prominently in the center of the page; directly beneath it, we learn that the play had already enjoyed considerable popularity, performed in at least two locations: "before her Maiestie, and else-where."

In the 1623 First Folio edition of Shakespeare's works, the play appears third in the section of comedies, preceded by *The Tempest* and *The Two Gentlemen of Verona*. The title has been shortened to *The Merry Wiues of Windsor*. The divisions between acts and scenes, as most readers recognize them today, are established in this version. The names of the characters do not appear, but this is typical for the plays of the First Folio. As an interesting curiosity, probably no more than a coincidence, of the four comedies that do include the names of characters, two are the plays that precede it, while the third is *Measure for Measure*, the play that immediately follows.

There are significant differences between the two versions of the play, and each version has its difficulties. The quarto publication does not include several scenes, including the Latin lesson (4.1), and the first four scenes of Act V. Scenes 4 and 5 of Act III are transposed. Among the remaining scenes, the dialogue is significantly shorter, and altogether the quarto edition runs roughly 60 percent the length of the folio play.

There also are apparent differences in setting. We find none of the local references to Windsor, to the court, or to the Garter ceremony, all of which figure prominently in the later edition. As Leah Marcus suggests, however, the quarto does make several pointed gibes at well-known historical figures, thus maintaining a sense of local topicality.

A major difference in the final scene raises a fundamental challenge to the way we interpret the play. The quarto includes the following stage direction:

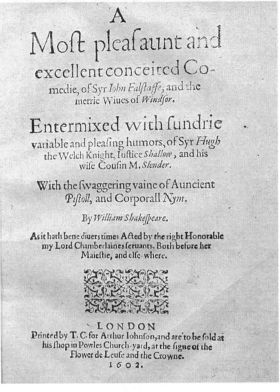

Title page of the first quarto edition of *The Merry Wives of Windsor,* published in 1602

Here they pinch him, and sing about him, & the Doctor comes one way & steales away a boy in read. And Slender another way he takes a boy in green: And Fenton steales misteris Anne, being in white. And a noyse of hunting is made within: and all the Fairies runne away. Falstaffe pulles of his bucks head, and rises up. And enter M. Page, M. Ford, and their wiues, M. Shallow, Sir Hugh.

In addition to pulling off his horns for himself, Falstaff makes mention of the king when he addresses the characters:

Horne the hunter quoth you: am I a ghost? Sblood the Fairies hath made a ghost of me: What hunting at this time at night? Ile lay my

life the mad Prince of Wales Is stealing his
fathers Deare. How now, who haue we here,
what is all Wiindsor stirring? Are you there?

Falstaff makes no such mention of the Prince of
Wales in the later version of the play, and there is
nothing to indicate that Falstaff has had any personal relation with the king whatsoever. Two questions appear as a result of these differences: How
much influence do the wives have over Falstaff's
final punishment, and what connection does the
Falstaff of this play have with the Falstaff(s) found
in the history plays?

Beyond that, we might ask: What do these two
versions of the play represent, and what is their relation to each other? These two questions have been
ongoing concerns for editors. The 1602 edition has
earned the dubious designation as one of the "Bad
Quartos," essentially a version of the play that was
not Shakespeare's own. W. W. Greg describes it in
scathing language, and he says that merely looking
at it "shows that there is everywhere gross corruption, constant mutilation, meaningless inversion
and clumsy transposition" (qtd. in Irace 115).
Greg also suggested that the quarto represented a
memorial reconstruction, or a script that was put
together, from memory, by one of the actors, perhaps for a traveling performance, where the ensem-
ble did not have access to a script. Many subsequent
editors have accepted, in principle, Greg's hypothesis that the early edition was copied down from
memory.

However, in the Arden Shakespeare edition of
the play, Giorgio Melchiori argues that the quarto
edition makes for a more effective performance
on stage, though typically its language represents
more of a paraphrase than a faithful rendition of
what Shakespeare may originally have written. As
he argues:

> It is safe to conclude that the Quarto is a
> reported text, a memorial reconstruction of
> an authorial acting version. It is authoritative
> in that it throws light on how Shakespeare
> could restructure his own work for the

common stage, and it may offer guidance to
directors for 'streamlining' the play's action
for modern audiences, provided they don't
assume that its language is Shakespeare's.
(Shakespeare 2000: 42)

Fittingly, Melchiori's edition prints two versions of
the play, one based on the First Folio and the other a
facsimile reprint of the 1602 quarto. Unfortunately,
the facsmile image is rotated 90 degrees and reduced
to fit the page; but even with these possible setbacks,
readers of Melchiori's edition do have an opportunity to see what original book purchasers might have
seen when the play originally appeared in print.

SYNOPSIS
Brief Synopsis

Shallow, in Windsor to sue Falstaff, confers with
his young relative Slender and the local parson, the
Welshman Evans. Slender mentions his inclination
to marry, and Evans suggests Anne Page. Shallow
suggests that they call on her father, George Page,
whom Falstaff is also visiting.

At Page's home, Falstaff admits to Shallow's
accusations against him. Evans insists that he shall
form a committee to settle these disputes.

Falstaff tells Pistol and Nym that he will seduce
both Mistress Ford and Mistress Page. He asks
his followers to deliver letters to them. When they
spurn the task, he dismisses them, giving the letters
to his page. Pistol and Nym decide to avenge their
dismissal by telling Ford and Page of Falstaff's
intentions.

Evans sends Slender's servant, Simple, to the
house of Dr. Caius with a letter for his house-
keeper, Mistress Quickly, asking her to encourage
Anne Page to marry Slender. Caius returns and
rages against Evans for sending Simple, for he—
Caius—intends to marry Anne Page. Caius writes a
letter challenging Evans to a duel and sends Simple
back with it. After Caius leaves, Fenton appears and
is assured by Quickly that his courtship of Anne is
going well.

Mistress Page and Mistress Ford read Falstaff's
love letters and plot revenge against him.

Pistol and Nym tell Ford and Page that Falstaff is pursuing their wives. After Pistol and Nym leave, the tavern's Host and Shallow enter on their way to oversee the duel between Caius and Evans. Ford bribes the Host to introduce him to Falstaff as "Brook."

Quickly delivers messages from the wives to Falstaff. When she leaves, Ford, disguised as Brook, arrives. Falstaff tells "Brook" of his appointment with Mistress Ford for that very morning. Ford vows revenge.

When Evans and Dr. Caius meet to duel, the Host proposes that they be friends again. Ford invites the group to his house. Page remarks that he favors Slender as a son-in-law, while his wife prefers Caius. He rejects Fenton as a suitor.

The wives instruct two Servants to be ready to carry away a big basket of laundry and dump it in the river. Falstaff arrives and woos Mistress Ford; Mistress Page appears and announces that an angry Ford is approaching, seeking his wife's lover. Falstaff leaps from his hiding place into the laundry basket, which the two Servants carry out as Ford enters to search the house.

Anne asks Fenton to continue to try to befriend her father. Anne's parents arrive and announce their approval of Slender's suit and disparage Fenton's presence.

Quickly brings Falstaff an apologetic message from Mistress Ford, who extends another invitation for that morning. Ford arrives, again disguised as Brook. Falstaff tells "Brook" of his new opportunity.

Falstaff calls on Mistress Ford, and once again Mistress Page arrives and tells of Ford's angry approach. The wives disguise Falstaff as the old woman of Brainford, a witch whom Ford particularly despises. Ford arrives and drives the "old woman" from the house, beating "her" mercilessly.

The Pages and Fords concoct a plot against Falstaff. They will arrange to have the knight meet the women in the woods at midnight, disguised as a mythological creature, Herne the Hunter. When he arrives at the rendezvous, he will be accosted by a group of children disguised as fairies and elves,

led by Anne. As they lay their plans, Ford muses to himself that he will spirit Anne away with Slender and have them married. Mistress Ford plots similarly with Dr. Caius in mind.

Quickly brings a message to Falstaff from the two wives. Fenton bribes the Host to help him. The Host agrees to arrange for a minister to marry the couple that night.

Falstaff, disguised as Herne, arrives at the rendezvous. Evans and the children, all disguised, come out and torment Falstaff. Slender and Caius arrive, and each steals away with a different fairy; Page, Ford, and the wives come forward and reveal their hoax to Falstaff. Fenton and Anne return and explain that they have married. The Pages make the best of it and accept Fenton as their son-in-law. Falstaff is invited to join the others in a festive celebration at the Ford household.

Act I, Scene 1

The scene opens on a street in Windsor, near Page's house, late morning. Justice Shallow and Slender (Abraham) are pressing Sir Hugh Evans to hear their complaint against Sir John Falstaff. Parson Evans, in turn, implores them to settle the manner like friends and in a God-fearing manner; in the meantime, he suggests to Slender to pursue Page's daughter Anne in marriage. Anne has already received an inheritance of 700 pounds from her grandfather, and she stands to gain a pretty penny more from her father. Slender is intrigued, but their complaints against Falstaff resurface when they arrive at Page's door. They have barely begun to broach the subject when Falstaff emerges from within, accompanied by Nym (also rendered as Nim), Bardolph, and Pistol. It is only then that we learn, from Shallow, that Falstaff has beaten his men, killed his deer, and broken open his lodge. As for Slender, he had been drinking with Falstaff's entourage, and he has discovered that one of them has picked his pocket. Evans introduces three umpires to settle their disputes: himself, Page, and the Host of the Garter Inn. After this, the quarrel with Falstaff is never raised again, and Slender pledges from this time forward only to drink with honest gentlemen. It is at this point when Mistresses Page and Ford arrive accompanied by Anne. Anne announces that dinner is on the table, and the characters assemble within. Slender remains, wishing he had with him a good book of poems to make up for his lack of witty repartee. Anne returns to bring him in, and they chat. Slender boasts of having wrestled the famous stage bear, Sackerson, some 20 times in his life. Pages emerges, entreats Slender to dine within, and the characters retire.

Act I, Scene 2

Evans emerges from the house with Simple, Slender's servant. Evans gives Simple a letter and instructs him to find Mistress Quickly and inform her to solicit Page on behalf of Slender, for Mistress Anne.

Act I, Scene 3

The location shifts to the Garter Inn. Falstaff, accompanied by Bardolph, Pistol, and Nym, observes that his expenses have been running to about 10 pounds per week. The Host employs Bardolph on an errand. When he leaves, Falstaff

Falstaff shows Pistol and Nym his letters to Mistress Ford and Mistress Page in Act I, Scene 3 of *The Merry Wives of Windsor*. This is a plate from *Retzsch's Outlines to Shakespeare: The Merry Wives of Windsor*, published in 1844. *(Illustration by Moritz Retzsch)*

announces a scheme to make love to Mistress Ford. He has observed her in passing, and he believes she has made leering eyes at him. He also believes she is in control of her husband's purse, a fancy which inspires him to pursue Page's Wife in identical fashion. Pistol and Nym give encouragement, but when Falstaff sets off with his two letters (accompanied by his page, Robin), they plot revenge. Nym says he will inform Ford about Falstaff's plans; Pistol offers to do the same with Page.

Act I, Scene 4

The location shifts to Caius's house. Mistress Quickly brings Simple within, and she sends off John Rugby to keep an eye out for the master. Simple discusses his business with Quickly, who is familiar with Slender, but while she is unimpressed, she leads Simple along. Rugby returns and announces Caius's return, and Quickly forces Simple to hide in the closet (making an allusion to Caius's jealous streak). Caius enters, attends to personal matters, and discovers Simple in the closet. Simple explains that he has been sent by Parson Evans to woo Anne on Slender's behalf. Caius excuses himself, then returns in an uproar with a written challenge to a duel against Evans—for he himself is in love with Anne and will not tolerate competition. No sooner does Caius depart than Anne's third suitor, Fenton, arrives. Fenton discusses his love for Anne with Quickly. She assures him that she loves him, but after he leaves, Quickly confesses that Anne loves him not. However, she does concede that he is an honest gentleman.

Act II, Scene 1

The location is not specified, but presumably we are on a street between Page's and Ford's house. A day has passed, and it is mid-morning. Mistress Page enters, reading aloud Falstaff's travesty of a love letter. She is visibly put off: She had never received this sort of courtship in her youth, and she is in no state to receive it at this point in her life—least of all from a "Flemish drunkard" whose "guts are made of puddings." She has barely announced her plans to avenge herself when Mistress Ford runs into her. She, too, has received a love letter from Falstaff, in identical language. Only the names have been changed. Mistress Page speculates that Falstaff keeps thousands of them lying around. Mistress Page invites Mistress Ford to join her in revenge. Mistress Ford agrees, but she also shows concern that the letter might fuel her husband's jealousy. They withdraw and observe as Ford and Page arrive with Pistol and Nym, who warn Ford and Page, respectively, that Falstaff means to make off with their wives. The wives and husbands exchange greetings, and Mistress Page invites her husband to dinner. Mistress Quickly appears and asks to have a word or two concerning Mistress Anne. All retire, save Ford and Page, who discuss the warnings they have just heard. Page dismisses them—they are soldiers out of work, liable to turn rogue in such fashion—but Ford admonishes that a man may be too confident.

The Host appears, followed by Shallow, who announces the duel between Caius and Evans. Ford and the Host talk aside. Ford offers a large tankard of burnt sack to introduce him, in disguise and under the name Brook, to Falstaff. The scene ends with Ford alone, criticizing Page for his security and explaining his plan to use his disguise to sound out Falstaff and test his wife in turn.

Act II, Scene 2

The location shifts to the Garter Inn; the time overlaps with that of the previous scene. Falstaff is on the verge of dismissing Pistol from his service for his refusal to deliver a letter. At the last moment, Pistol relents. (Significantly, in the early version of the play, Falstaff dismisses Pistol anyway.) Mistress Quickly is announced. Evidently, she has been made aware of the wives' plan, and she has been brought on as the hook. She lays it on thick with Falstaff: Mistress Ford, who has received hundreds of such requests before, and from earls and pensioned knights at that, is taken with Falstaff's little note. She urges Falstaff to call on her that morning, between 10 and 11, when her husband is sure to be away. Mistress Page also has been taken with her note, and while her husband keeps

close watch on her, she yearns for a time when the two can meet in secret.

Falstaff wonders if the two wives have not found out the other, but Quickly assures him they have not. No sooner does she leave than Ford approaches, disguised as Brook. Like Quickly before him, he flatters Falstaff's romantic prowess. He even offers Falstaff a bag of money in order to make overtures to Ford's wife. Falstaff is confused, but Brook explains that he has been rebuffed by Mistress Ford in the past; if he can only catch her in the act, he can hold the information over her. A visibly elated Falstaff admits that in fact he is on his way to Ford's house that very morning to enjoy his wife. Brook advises Falstaff to beware of Ford, but Falstaff disdains the warning.

As with the previous scene, Ford is left alone on stage. All of his suspicions have been confirmed. Page has been too secure in his trust, and his wife has been plotting against him. He plans to catch her, punish Falstaff in revenge, and laugh at Page. He is clearly agitated leaving the stage, repeating the word *cuckold* on his way off.

Act II, Scene 3

In a field just outside town, Caius is waiting with Rugby. He has been waiting for hours, but Hugh has failed to show for his duel. He tries to force Rugby to allow him a practice round, but he is interrupted by the Host, Page, Shallow, and Slender. The Host praises Caius for his bravado, but his idiomatic phrases repeatedly leave Caius at sea. After sending Page, Shallow, and Slender on an errand—off to Frogmore, on the other side of Windsor, to visit with Evans—the Host promises to lead Caius to Anne Page, in an effort to assuage his anger. The Host, playing off Caius's poor skills in English, promises to be the doctor's adversary, and Caius happily agrees.

Act III, Scene 1

In Frogmore, Evans is with Simple, waiting for Caius. He appears to be carrying a Bible in one hand, rapier in the other. He is full of melancholies, and he is ready to fight. As he waits, he fantasizes about the damage he will bring to his opponent, mixing in snatches from Marlowe's famous poem "The Passionate Shepherd to His Love" and lines from Psalm 137. Page arrives with Shallow and Slender. By this point, Slender is lovesick, repeating the line "Ah, sweet Anne Page" as a refrain. Caius and the Host of the Garter follow shortly after. Evans and Caius prepare to fight, though in an aside Evans mentions to Caius that he will find a more peaceful way to make amends. The Host takes both their hands in a gesture of peace. After he leaves, Evans resumes his talk of friendship, adding revenge against the Host. Caius agrees, feeling that the Host has not lived up to his promise to bring him to Anne.

Act III, Scene 2

Mistress Page is on her way to see Mistress Ford, accompanied by Robin. She runs into Ford. They exchange banter, in which Page intimates that they would indeed remarry if Ford and Page were deceased. Ford cannot believe that Robin is with Mistress Page, and in a third monologue he promises to discover Falstaff and expose Page for a dupe. At this point, the Host of the Garter appears, accompanied by Shallow, Page, Slender, Caius, Evans, and Rugby. Page is discussing Anne's betrothal. There is a conflict: Page prefers Slender, while Mistress Page has expressed her preference for Caius. The Host inquires about Fenton, who is sprightly and youthful, but Page rejects him for being too wild. He observes that Fenton had kept company with the Prince—presumably Hal, later Henry V—and Poins (another character from the *Henry IV* plays). Page will not give consent to Fenton. As everybody retires to dinner, Ford prepares to catch Falstaff.

Act III, Scene 3

Mistress Ford and Mistress Page make final preparations for Falstaff's arrival. Mistress Ford places a long basket in the room, and they instruct two servants (John and Roger) that on her command, they are to take the basket, without a word, and pour out the contents at Datchet Mead (a meadow by the Thames at Windsor Park).

Falstaff arrives and makes overtures to Mistress Ford. She leads him on, manipulating him to aver that he loves her and that he hates Mistress Page. At this point, Mistress Page returns, and Falstaff hides behind the arras. Mistress Page warns Mistress Ford that her husband is returning home, overcome with jealousy. Mistress Ford confesses that she does indeed have a man in the house, and she does not know what to do with him. They consider the laundry basket, but it is too small. At this point, Falstaff steps out and crams himself into the basket. The servants are called, and they are in the process of hauling the basket out when Ford arrives with Page, Caius, and Evans. They search the house, only to discover that Ford's jealousies are unfounded. Mistress Ford cannot decide whose deception she is more pleased with, Falstaff's or her husband's. The two wives agree that there will be plenty of opportunity for more pranks. Ford has staked a dinner on finding Falstaff in the room, and he offers to pay. As the scene ends, Evans reminds Caius of their plans for revenge against the Host, to be carried out on the morrow.

Act III, Scene 4

Fenton is alone with Anne. He laments that Anne's father has rejected him as a suitor for being too wild and for viewing Anne as a monetary prize. Fenton confesses that he had originally wooed her for her dowry, but that upon getting to know her as a person, he loves her more than jewels can offer. Anne urges him to continue to seek permission from her father. At this point, Page arrives with Shallow, Slender, and Mistress Quickly. Page is angry with Fenton and tries to chase him off. Quickly catches him, and they share a private word.

Shallow begins to woo Anne on Slender's behalf. Anne urges Slender to speak for himself, to which Slender replies in startling nonchalance. Anne is deeply concerned that her father will marry her off to a fortune of some 300,000 pounds, but at the cost of a miserable life with Slender. Page returns with his wife, and Fenton approaches her. As they talk, Mistress Page finally agrees to sound her daughter and to take Anne's will into consideration. Fenton gives Quickly a ring to deliver to Anne. Quickly ends the scene with a monologue in which she confesses to giving encouragement to all three suitors. She has promised them all, and she will be as good as her word—though she is leaning to Fenton. She is off on another errand to Sir John Falstaff.

This is the first scene of the play to include long passages of verse dialogue. The wooing between Fenton and Anne is entirely in verse.

Act III, Scene 5

Falstaff enters, soaked from having been dumped into the river. As he shakes himself off, Mistress Quickly returns with a second invitation from Mistress Ford. Falstaff has had enough Ford, having been thrown into a ford and having his belly full of a ford, but Quickly is persistent, and she ultimately convinces Falstaff to try his hand again. Ford will be out bird hunting, and Falstaff plans to visit the house between 8 and 9 o'clock. Falstaff is alone, and he waits for Brook. Ford appears, disguised as Brook, and Falstaff recounts the entire episode to his coconspirator. While his disappointment rings loud throughout the passage, he assures Brook that he is on his way back to the Ford house that morning. Falstaff hurries off while Ford contemplates the information he has just learned about Falstaff's hiding place. Ford will try again, promising this time to search impossible places.

Act IV, Scene 1

This brief interlude was not included in the quarto version. Mistress Page is on her way to the Ford house. Before leaving, she observes that her son has the day off from school. Parson Evans is present, and she requests him to run through Latin lessons with her son (who just happens to be named William). Evans and William take turns stumbling through the lessons, Evans's strong Welsh dialect giving shape to his pronunciation. It is a wild send-up of the learning process, in which pedantic scholars and country boys grapple with an "official."

Act IV, Scene 2

Falstaff has returned to Mistress Ford. They have barely established that Ford is off birding when Mistress Page arrives, warning of Ford's jealousy. Again, Falstaff hides himself, then reappears. He refuses to climb back into the laundry basket, and he considers other escape routes. Through the back door, up the chimney, out the window, all prove impossible—men with pistols are guarding the house. In a pinch, they agree to disguise Falstaff as the old woman of Brentford. Falstaff agrees, unaware that Ford despises the old woman, whom he suspects to be a witch. The wives laugh over their own good fortune, but they acknowledge their virtue. As Mistress Page puts it, "Wives may be merry and yet honest too."

Ford returns with Page, Shallow, Caius, and Evans. John and Robert are hauling the laundry basket again, hoping that no more fat knights are hiding within. Ford spots them, and he runs straight for it, emptying the contents entirely onto the floor. Ford is surprised not to find Falstaff, and Page suggests that Ford's troubles are in his brain.

Thinking Falstaff to be the old Woman of Brentford, Ford beats him for being a witch in Act IV, Scene 2 of *The Merry Wives of Windsor*. This is a plate from *Retzsch's Outlines to Shakespeare: The Merry Wives of Windsor*, published in 1844. *(Illustration by Moritz Retzsch)*

At this point, Mistress Page emerges with Falstaff in disguise. Ford accuses her for being a fortune teller, and he beats Falstaff out of the house. Among the search party, only Evans notices that the old woman has a beard—possibly anticipating Macbeth's encounter with the weird sisters?

The wives decide that their husbands have had enough; Ford will have his suspicions scraped out of his brains, and he needs to be publicly shamed. But the pranks are not over as concerns Falstaff. Already they plan their next assault.

Act IV, Scene 3

In this brief scene, Bardolph requests three horses from the Host of the Garter Inn for some Germans; the Host agrees, but promises to make them pay for their request. This brief scene introduces a minor subplot, with marginal connection to the rest of the play. Thematically, it maintains the basic conceit of the deceiver deceived. The horse-stealing episode is believed to have been a topical reference, probably a snipe at a German duke who pressed for admittance into the Order of the Garter, only to be absent for the induction ceremony.

Act IV, Scene 4

The wives reveal to their husbands (with Evans looking on) both Falstaff's letters and their own deceptions. Ford is chastened and asks for pardon. He and Page wish to continue to punish Falstaff, and the wives introduce their final plot. In Windsor Forest, there lurks one Herne the Hunter; this legendary figure is known to scare the local citizens, inclined to superstitions. Falstaff has agreed to disguise himself as Herne the Hunter, with great horns on his head, and to meet the wives at midnight. Upon a signal, a troupe of children, disguised as fairies, will pinch Falstaff and burn his flesh with candles until he admits his wrongdoings; thereupon, he will be mocked on the way home to Windsor. Evans realizes that this prank will require some rehearsal among the children, and he rushes off to prepare them for their roles. Meanwhile, Page privately remarks that during the ceremony, Slender will sneak off with his daughter Anne,

allowing them to marry in secret. Moments later, Mistress Page announces a similar scheme involving Caius. Slender is an idiot, and Caius happens to be wealthy.

Act IV, Scene 5

The deception of the Host continues. Simple comes to the Garter and asks for Falstaff. Their conversation runs as follows: He wonders if Falstaff happened to have been in the company of a woman recently; Falstaff, recognizing that he refers to the old woman of Brentford, affirms it to be true. Does the old woman know about a chain that Nym has stolen from Slender? Falstaff believes Nym has, in fact, beguiled the chain from its owner. And does the woman happen to know if Slender is going to have Anne in marriage or not? Falstaff replies that indeed he will or not. At this point, Bardolph enters the inn and informs the Host that his horses are fled. He is followed by Evans, and then by Caius, who informs the Host there had never been a German duke in Windsor after all. Finally, Mistress Quickly enters, and she informs him that Mistress Ford has been beaten black and blue. Falstaff recounts to her how he had been mistaken for the old witch of Brentford and beaten all the colors of the rainbow. Quickly has more letters for him, which she will present to him in his quarters.

In the course of this scene, Bardolph compares the Host's horses to the famous horses of Dr. Faustus. The remark continues a series of references to Christopher Marlowe's poems and plays, which appear throughout this play.

Act IV, Scene 6

Fenton is talking with the Host. The Host is distraught, but Fenton offers to restore his lost fortunes with an additional hundred pounds. He describes to the Host the jest that awaits Falstaff between 12 and 1 o'clock. Part of the plan involves Anne making a presentation of the Fairy Queen and her retinue of attendants. During this performance, Anne has promised each of her parents to sneak off with their respective marriage prospects. She has promised Slender that she will wear a disguise of white. To Caius, she has agreed to wear a disguise of green, with ribbons. Fenton is to deceive them both and sneak off with Anne; meanwhile, the Host is to arrange for the vicar to meet them at church, so they can marry in secret. The Host is happy to comply.

Act V, Scene 1

Falstaff has received the invitation, and he is convinced that his third attempt will be lucky. Mistress Quickly promises to procure him a set of horns for his escapade. Ford returns in disguise as Brook. Falstaff again recounts how he had been disguised as a woman and beaten by Ford, but that he intends to have another try.

Act V, Scene 2

It is evening, and Page, Slender, and Shallow are on their way to Windsor Forest. They are making final arrangements to sneak off with Anne. Slender has devised the code words *Mum* and *Budget,* though Shallow believes the white costume ought to be signal enough.

Act V, Scene 3

Mistresses Page and Ford, accompanied by Caius, are on their way to Windsor Forest. They, too, are making final arrangements; Anne will be disguised in green. Mistress Page realizes that her husband will chafe at her deception, but she believes that protecting her daughter from a miserable marriage is worth the cost of her husband's chiding.

Act V, Scene 4

Evans runs across a field, leading the children to their hiding places.

Act V, Scene 5

At midnight in Windsor Forest, Falstaff appears with horns on his head. He is rhapsodic, recounting scenes from Ovid's *Metamorphoses.* Mistress Ford appears, followed shortly by Mistress Page, and Falstaff's excitement grows accordingly. At a signal, music is sounded. Evans appears in disguise as a Welsh fairy. In accompaniment are the

Fenton leaves with the real Anne in Act V, Scene 5 of *The Merry Wives of Windsor.* This is a plate from *Retzsch's Outlines to Shakespeare: The Merry Wives of Windsor,* published in 1844. *(Illustration by Moritz Retzsch)*

children, disguised as fairies, as well as Mistress Quickly, disguised as the Fairy Queen. (In an earlier scene, Evans had suggested putting Anne Page in the role, but she plays a different part here.) They sing songs of praise to the Fairy Queen and her chief virtue—chastity. Falstaff is frightened and tries not to attract notice. Needless to say, the fairies notice him anyway, and they pinch him and burn him with their tapers.

During the course of their mockery, Slender and Caius make off with boys, whom they mistake for Anne; Fenton locates the real Anne, and they depart. Mistresses Ford and Page, along with their husbands, all emerge from hiding and tease Falstaff. Ford is especially enthusiastic, going so far as to demand in return the 20 pounds that he had given to Falstaff earlier on. According to Ford, Falstaff had cozened him out of the money. Ford also hints that Falstaff has been cuckolded—it is not clear how well Ford comprehends the nature of his remarks.

Falstaff realizes that the Mistresses Ford and Page have made an ass of him, but true to his character, he pretends that he had a hunch of what was happening to him all along. Ford apologizes to his wife for mistrusting her and promises never to mistrust her until the Welshman learns to speak proper English. The other characters join in mocking Evans for his Welsh dialect. At this point, Caius and Slender return, angry to discover that they have been deceived. As the citizens wonder where Anne could be, she returns with Fenton. In a solemn speech, Fenton states that her offence was holy. Husband and wife each discover that they have been deceived, but Page is quick to accept the circumstances with happiness. The citizens return home, where they will continue to laugh at the good sport. Ford makes a final allusion to his disguise, and he intimates that on this night, Brook himself will enjoy his wife's embraces.

CHARACTER LIST

Sir John Falstaff Famous for his exploits in Shakespeare's *Henry IV* plays, Sir John Falstaff is the main character in the play. A knight and former friend of Prince Henry, Falstaff spends most of his time drinking in taverns, scheming for cash, and boasting about his narrow escapes from dangerous situations. As he pursues Mistresses Page and Ford, the two wives of the play, he finds himself the butt of several practical jokes.

Bard, Pistol, Nym Members of Falstaff's retinue, these three figures find themselves cashiered from Falstaff's service. For revenge, they inform Page and Ford about Falstaff's designs on their wives. Like Falstaff, these are recurring characters.

Robin Servant to Falstaff, known as "Boy" in other plays.

Mistress Margaret Page One of the two wives alluded to in the title, Mistress Page subjects Falstaff to several jests, a fitting response to his improbable advances. In the meantime, she schemes to have Caius to marry her daughter Anne in secret. This is as much to block her husband's plans as to provide for her daughter's security. Her plans are foiled by the play's conclusion.

George Page Husband to Mistress Page and father to Anne Page. He is interested in securing a profitable marriage for his daughter. Much

like his wife, he arranges for Abraham Slender to sneak her off to a secret wedding ceremony. His plans are foiled, though, and by the end of the play, he is made to accept another for his son-in-law.

William Son of the Pages, a young boy who studies Latin at school.

Mistress Alice Ford The other of the two wives, Mistress Ford conspires with Mistress Page to ridicule Falstaff several times over. In addition, she performs two pranks on her husband in response to his jealous behavior.

Frank Ford Husband of Mistress Ford. He is the only character who suspects his wife could seriously entertain Falstaff's amorous advances. Overcome by suspicion, he disguises himself as Brook and spies on his wife. Little does he know how much the wives are on to his jealousies; like Falstaff, he becomes the victim of their practical jokes. By the end of the play, he is made to confront his follies directly.

John and Robert Ford's servants. They carry out the laundry basket holding Falstaff. Their complaints about his weight are mentioned a few scenes later.

Mistress Quickly Like Falstaff, a recurring character from the *Henry IV* plays. She keeps house for the irascible Dr. Caius, and she serves as a go-between for the wives, luring Falstaff into temptation.

Sir Hugh Evans A Welsh parson of a somewhat choleric disposition, Evans first fights, then joins up with Caius in a plan to retaliate against the Host for a perceived slight. As a schoolteacher, he leads the children into the woods at night, to perform a crucial part in the final jest.

Robert Shallow A justice of the peace up from the country, Shallow is a marriage broker for his cousin Slender.

Abraham Slender Cousin to Justice Shallow, Slender is out for love, particularly when love comes with an enormous dowry. Undeterred by his awkward attempts to woo Anne, he finally makes a secret arrangement to marry her in secret. Predictably, his plans fail.

Simple   Servant to Slender.

Dr. Caius   An irascible French physician, Caius is prone to quarreling, dueling, and taking revenge on the Host of the Garter. Caius is a suitor to Anne Page, and he makes a secret arrangement to carry her off in disguise. True to character, he is outraged to discover he has made off with a boy instead.

Fenton   A young gentleman in love with Anne. In his younger days, he kept company with the wild Prince Hal, but he has since grown honest. He proves this by running off with Anne and marrying her in secret.

Host of the Garter Inn   An innkeeper, the Host eventually piques the Doctor and Parson and is cozened out of his finest horses. He offers assistance to Fenton in his scheme to marry Anne.

John Rugby   Caius's servant.

CHARACTER STUDIES
Sir John Falstaff

Falstaff is the play's central character, and it is impossible to overestimate his importance. He is essentially the reason for the play's very existence, as suggested by the original title, *Sir John Falstaff and the Merry Wives of Windsor*. And while the revised title shifts our attention to the wives themselves, Falstaff still dominates the play.

The play never explains how Falstaff has gone from the Boar's Head tavern in Eastcheap to the Garter Inn of Windsor, nor does it mention what has happened between himself and his beloved Prince Hal. Is this part of his exile from the king's company (the event that takes place at the end of *Henry IV, Part 2*)? Is he living on a pension? Suffice to say, he is living beyond his means, and his current living conditions provide opportunity for several comic situations. The legend states that the play was meant to show Falstaff in love, but the action hardly bears this out. More accurately, Falstaff is in debt. His pursuit of the citizens' wives is clearly an opportunity to relieve the husbands of their money and to maintain his own lavish expenses. He could not have selected a less appropriate audience to listen to his amorous discourse. The wives know it,

and they recall that they never were treated to it when they were of the right age. It does not help that Falstaff sends out identical copies of the same love letter, with only their names penciled in to distinguish them.

Falstaff is the dupe for three major pranks, each one building from the last. Indeed, there is a certain pattern suggested by the times of day when each occurs. The first takes place between 10 and 11 in the morning, the second between 8 and 9 A.M., and the third earlier still, at midnight. On each occasion, Falstaff is all too willing to place himself into awkward situations, generally at the wives' requests. He follows every suggestion by Mistresses Ford and Page, no matter how ludicrous. These include hiding in Ford's laundry basket and disguising himself as the old woman of Brentford, then later as the legendary creature known as Herne the Hunter. Falstaff also contributes to his own mockery through his spoken parts. He has several conversations with Ford, disguised as Brook. It is hilarious when Falstaff unwittingly describes to Ford, in lurid detail, the ways in which he plans to enjoy Ford's wife; it is even funnier when Ford shows up to ruin his plans. Falstaff also has several monologues, which address the audience directly. Routinely given to exaggeration, his accounts of the pranks that befall him are often funnier than the pranks themselves. Indeed, by the end of the play, he suggests that he had known all along that the fairies pinching him were actually children in disguise. Viewers may wonder whether, in fact, Falstaff willingly participates in the jokes, even at his own expense.

Falstaff is a combination of linguistic exuberance and intense physical comedy. Throughout the play, his body is the subject of comic discourse. Various characters, including Falstaff himself, describe his flesh as greasy and buttery, while his insides are compared to puddings. The two laundrymen complain loudly at the prospect of carrying Falstaff out with the basket a second time. The costumes certainly contribute to physical comedy. His disguise as Herne the Hunter is especially complex. The costume involves a set of stag's horns. Visually, this might suggest that it is not Ford but Falstaff himself who plays the cuckold. It is an odd visual wrinkle, made even odder when Falstaff finally admits that he has been made an ass. But in a sense, it does not matter whether all the jokes fit together so much as that they can be made at all. Exuberance is the order of the day, even at the potential cost of continuity.

Mistress Margaret Page

Of the two wives, Mistress Page appears to enjoy the greater liberty. Her husband harbors none of the suspicions that Ford keeps for his own wife. She even has a moment alone with Ford, and she playfully remarks that yes, indeed, the wives will

Mistress Page in Act II, Scene I of *The Merry Wives of Windsor*. This is a print from Charles Heath's 1848 edition of *The Heroines of Shakspeare: Comprising the Principal Female Characters in the Plays of the Great Poet*. (*Painting by J. W. Wright; engraving by W. H. Egleton*)

remarry when their husbands die. Her fortunate conditions may perhaps best be summed up in the memorable line "Wives may be merry and yet honest too." But the Pages' marriage is hardly a marriage of mutual trust. To the contrary, while Mistress Ford is concerned with disabusing her husband's suspicions, Mistress Page is engaged in mutual deception with her husband. She prefers Caius as a suitor to her daughter Anne, and she bluntly views the arrangement as a profitable business transaction. In doing so, she actively dissents from her husband, and by scheming for Caius, she actively seeks to foil her husband's own plots. While she acknowledges that her husband will chide her, from her perspective his reprimands will be tolerable. It is a calculated risk, though we may wonder just how she came to reckon that Page's anger would not cross over into harsher forms of discipline (or simply dissolve into rage). Backing Caius also puts her at odds with her daughter. With that in mind, it is worth pointing out that Mistress Page is not necessarily intimate with Anne; she shares as much stage time with her son William. While she listens to Anne's concerns about a miserable marriage to an unworthy suitor, she does not heed them. In the end, she is deceived as fully as her husband, and they can recognize their mutual faults. But we wonder how Mistress Page could have preferred pecuniary rewards over her daughter's happiness in the first place. Suffice to say, the episode draws our attention to conflicting, perhaps incompatible, values about the purpose of marriage, one that views it as a means to economic advancement, and one that views it as an exchange of intimacies. It is not clear that Mistress Page herself is resolved about which value she prefers.

Mistress Quickly

After Falstaff and Mistress Page, Mistress Quickly has the largest speaking part in the play. She is a go-between for the wives, presumably because of her familiarity with Falstaff (from earlier plays). She also is a go-between for the suitors, and because of her ease of access, she ends up in several awkward situations. She receives Slender's servant Simple in

Caius's own house, and while an intensely comical situation follows when Caius shows up and discovers Simple hiding in the closet, one wonders at Quickly's seeming carelessness. Later on, she remarks that she will try to satisfy all three of Anne's suitors, since she has promised all three of them, and she means to be as good as her word(!). Fenton is a favorite, but not by much. Again, it is a comical remark, but in a play that explicitly affirms the virtues of chastity, Quickly's strategy of helping everyone gain access to Anne has disturbing connotations.

There are two interesting questions of continuity that pertain to Mistress Quickly. Early in the play, Pistol pursues her as his "prize." The issue is not developed—indeed, it only occurs in the First Folio, and it appears to be a late addition—but it explains Quickly's marriage to Pistol in *Henry V.* Meanwhile, she plays the role of the Fairy Queen during the play's final scene, even though the part originally had been recommended for Anne. It is a daring gesture, though there is no sign that Queen Elizabeth gave any thought to being represented on stage by an alehouse lady.

Mistress Alice Ford

Although Mistress Page's speaking part is considerably larger (by nearly a hundred lines in the folio), Mistress Ford is arguably more central to the play's main plotline. The Falstaff scenes occur at the Fords' house, and many of her personal effects become stage properties. In addition, thanks to her husband's jealousy, Mistress Ford holds a larger concern in the jests. She herself cannot decide whose deception gratifies her more, Falstaff's or her husband's. In many respects, Ford's suspicions complicate her status in the play, and they hint at themes that Shakespeare gives much darker treatment in nearly all his other play.

While Mistress Ford seems to choreograph the pranks that take place in her house, she is not fully in control of her husband. Mistress Page makes casual conversation with Ford when Mistress Ford is not around; her remarks would have been disastrous had she made them to Othello, Leontes, or

Mistress Ford in Act II, Scene 1 of *The Merry Wives of Windsor.* This is a print from Charles Heath's 1848 edition of *The Heroines of Shakspeare: Comprising the Principal Female Characters in the Plays of the Great Poet. (Painting by Edward Corbould; engraving by F. Holl)*

even Claudio. For the purposes of this play, Shakespeare seems keen on exploring the ways in which women can use public mockery and shaming rituals in order to protect their honest reputations. Mistress Ford clearly enjoys her creativity and her role in enforcing communal standards. But we should not forget that for all her games and jests, a certain vulnerability underlies her activities. In essence, her pranks are meant not only to humiliate Falstaff but to protect herself from the suspicions of a husband who is not exactly a model of clear, calm thinking.

Pistol, Nym, and Bardolph

Falstaff's retinue. The three characters had been in his service, and they retain their ranks—Pistol is an ancient (like Iago in *Othello*), while Nym and Bardolph are corporals. Falstaff is at the point of turning them out. Nym and Pistol actively seek revenge on Falstaff, and they are the ones who reveal Falstaff's schemes to the husbands. Page dismisses them as "very rogues, now they be out of service." In doing so, he calls attention to the frankly rough circumstances that out-of-work soldiers would have found themselves in. This was a major concern during Shakespeare's lifetime. Queen Elizabeth had published several statutes that addressed strategies for handling disbanded militias and the crime problems that grew out of them. Shakespeare himself developed the topic in his corresponding plays. Depending on whether *Merry Wives* preceded or followed *Henry V,* audiences would either recall or find out what punishments would await Bardolph and Nym. As for Pistol, a lifetime of thieving awaits him.

Frank Ford

Ford and Falstaff are clear rivals with each other, not only as characters but as performers. While Falstaff is famous for his comic monologues, Ford has three of his own, which makes him a close second. And while Falstaff's disguise as Herne the Hunter is the iconic symbol for the play, Ford's disguise as Brook dominates much of the early action, and it has been the subject of extensive critical discussion. (In part, this is based on the name Brook, which appears to be a reference to the family that had raised the objections to Falstaff; Lord Cobham's family name was Brook, and perhaps Shakespeare was slighting him again.) Clearly, Mistress Ford is just as gratified to see her husband deceived as her would-be lover. Indeed, Ford carries so much opportunity for comic performance that scholars have wondered who took his part, and who took Falstaff's?

George Page

Husband to Mistress Page, and a comparatively minor part. Page is a foil to Ford, and while Ford repeatedly hopes to expose him for a gull, in the end it is Page who has the last laugh. His preference for Slender as a son-in-law suggests startlingly poor judgment on his part; even his wife gives con-

sideration to her daughter's financial advantages. That said, Page is quick not only to forgive but to embrace and bless his daughter's marriage at the end of the play. Indeed, Page's reconciliation to Anne's marriage is so rapid that we may go so far as to call it rushed. The play ends so quickly that we are not given time to wonder about whether Anne's disobedience or secret marriage will have a favorable outcome or not.

Anne Page

The Pages' daughter has the smallest speaking part among all the characters, including Slender's errand boy, Simple. We may surmise that the part was written for one of the less-experienced boy

Anne Page in Act I, Scene I of *The Merry Wives of Windsor.* This is a print from Charles Heath's 1848 edition of *The Heroines of Shakspeare: Comprising the Principal Female Characters in the Plays of the Great Poet. (Painting by J. W. Wright; engraving by W. H. Mote)*

actors, and that her character depends on visual cues that only stage performances can produce. That said, she is the ongoing subject of attention, being young, presumably attractive, and undoubtedly wealthy. She also enjoys a certain independence of mind. Of the three suitors, only Fenton strikes her as an acceptable match, and even in his case, she seems to make up her mind about him only about midway through the play. Her primary concern is to prevent herself being subjected to an unhappy marriage, and she is not afraid to take matters into her own hands. She meets alone with Fenton, against both her parents' wishes, and she agrees to sneak off and marry in secret. It is a bold move, one that perhaps anticipates a character like Desdemona, who also disobeys her father's wishes in order to marry in secret.

Host of the Garter Inn

The play's most topical references revolve around the Garter Inn, presumably a reference to the Garter Ceremony that occasioned the play. The Host also is involved in an obscure episode, in which he lends out a team of horses to three Germans. The Host loses his horses in the process, and Caius and Evans laugh at his expense. The entire episode may have its origins in a local incident, during which a German duke pressed for admittance to the Order of the Garter, only to be truant during the induction ceremony. Of course, audiences did not need to know about the incident in order to appreciate the basic notion of a deceptive host who is, in turn, victimized by the people he had previously deceived.

Abraham Slender

Slender is an object lesson in bad courtship. His interest in Anne begins with her inheritance, 700 pounds, with more to come. His first encounter with Anne is a disaster. Lacking words of his own to express fond affections, he wishes for a book of poems to help him find something clever. Is it telling that he just happens to name the most famous and most clichéd books available? While he boasts to Anne of having wrestled the famous show

bear Sackerson, his bravado quickly dissipates. In later scenes, Anne grows tired of listening to go-betweens court her on Slender's behalf, and she is even more tired when Slender steps in for himself. In his most famous scene of the play, he is more or less a tagalong to the other citizens. His words of refrain, "Oh sweet Anne Page," draw attention to him for his profound lack of eloquence. Mistress Page refers to him as an idiot. Harsh words, perhaps, but then again, who can blame her? Slender's name implies something about his stature.

Fenton

It is surprising that in a play featuring Falstaff and his retinue, only Fenton's name should be given explicit mention in association with the wild Prince Hal of the *Henry IV* plays. Even if we accept the claim that Fenton's name had been changed from Peto (a character in *Henry IV, Part 1*) for the purposes of this play, we have to note that only for Fenton does his conduct with Hal make a difference to this play's action. Page mentions Fenton's past as the main reason for objecting to him as a suitable match for Anne, and Fenton himself refers to it when he makes his own case to her. In defending himself, he claims to have reformed his ways, and it is possible that Fenton's reformation could be compared with the one that Hal undergoes at the end of *Henry IV, Part 2* and continues in *Henry V.* Whether he compares favorably or not is a subject for dispute. There are signs that Fenton is meant to be held apart from the other characters. His speeches are predominantly in verse, unlike the prose that makes up the rest of the script. He also has a solemn air about him, an impression that comes forward in his final speech of the play, when he invokes truth and holiness to justify marrying Anne in secret.

Shallow

A justice of the peace, Shallow allegedly hails from the county of Gloucester, although this seems to have no bearing on his jurisprudence in Windsor. (This detail is left out of the quarto edition, though it appears in the First Folio.) The play begins with

Shallow, who seeks redress for a grievance against Falstaff, but this plotline disappears more or less as soon as Falstaff appears onstage.

Sir Hugh Evans

The Welsh parson appears initially as a peacemaker, then as a combatant against Caius. Further in the play, Evans and Caius join together to trick the Host of the Garter out of a team of horses, ostensibly an act of revenge. Evans is among the more explicitly affected by his "humors." As he prepares to battle Caius, he describes himself as being "full of the cholers," as well as the "melancholies." His preparation for the duel makes for one of the play's most memorable visual jokes. Conventionally portrayed with a Bible in one hand and a rapier in the other, he comes across as a figure unprepared for either profession.

Evans's language receives considerable attention throughout the play. Welsh dialect was allegedly a specialty for Robert Armin, a comic actor who had joined the Lord Chamberlain's Men in 1599, and Evans's dialect is several times made the subject of ridicule. His pronunciations of Latin phrases such as *Hing Hang Hog,* make him an easy target. Curiously, Evans quotes lines from Marlowe's famous lyric poem "The Passionate Shepherd to his Love," mixing the lines up with passages from the Psalms; it is possible that his pronunciation of the lines contributed to the episode's humor. Even Ford links his restored trust in his wife to Evans's poor dialect, when he promises never to mistrust her again until Evans will be able to woo her in "good English."

Dr. Caius

A French physician and resident of Windsor, employer of Mistress Quickly. The name Caius was known as a marker of commonality, and in many respects, the doctor is merely a caricature of an angry doctor. Like Evans, Caius is afflicted with the melancholies and the cholers, and his character seems limited to picking fights and mispronouncing English words—often with scatological implications. As a suitor for Anne, Caius is insanely jealous of any rivals, but significantly, his anger over hearing about Slender's mutual interest ultimately leads him to challenge Evans to a duel. This pairs Caius with Evans in explicit ways. They are both explicitly defined by their "humors" as well as their sharp dialects. Meanwhile, as a suitor to Anne, Caius is placed in direct competition with Fenton, whose solemnity contrasts strongly with Caius's out of control passions.

William

The Pages' boy, who struggles through his Latin lesson with Parson Evans. A mediocre instructor is paired up with a bored pupil, as the two struggle through a lesson that has no bearing on their immediate or long-term concerns. He appears only for one scene, and even that scene is cut from the earlier quarto edition. Indeed, he is not central to the play's action; rather, he provides an opportunity for comic interlude. The name William is suggestive, however. Is it possible that he is the playwright's namesake, an example of what the playwright himself had gone through while still a boy in the Midlands—before he left for London and became successful?

DIFFICULTIES OF THE PLAY

Although highly accessible in many respects, *Merry Wives* has its fair share of difficulties for students. While many of the principal characters are already familiar to readers from the *Henry IV* plays, in this new setting they become characters of a different type. The connections between the Falstaff of Eastcheap and Falstaff of Windsor are puzzling enough to challenge even the most sophisticated critics. Furthermore, the play has many stylistic features unusual to Shakespeare's method. The contemporary setting and the substitution of prose for poetry may be the most obvious, though others may escape students' attention and require a more formal introduction. Examples include Shakespeare's playful take on the convention of "humors," as well as his frequent allusions to contemporary courtly ceremonies. The play is farcical in tone, and as in many good farces, its story line grows surprisingly elaborate. Meanwhile, it relies heavily on a brand of comedy that can strain modern readers' imaginations. Jokes fill the play, but a joke without the proper context runs the risk of falling flat; thus, it may require some effort to appreciate its comic effects.

Character

Many of Shakespeare's popular plays gave rise to sequels, and the history plays were written in a serial form, but only *Merry Wives* can be described as a clear case of a "spin-off." The success of the *Henry IV* plays, in particular of Falstaff and his retinue, called for an entirely new play in which these characters could be enjoyed in their own right. Their roles have been amplified, their purpose as characters modified. But most radically, Shakespeare has transported them (incompletely) from 14th-century London to late-16th-century Windsor, and the journey evidently has taken a toll on their memories. From our perspective, understanding the characters depends on some familiarity with their earlier stage career, even as the new play stands apart as a story unto itself. This ambiguous condition can create obstacles, according to the level of familiarity that students bring to the play. In some respects, the effect may be more jarring for well-versed readers than for those who feel that they are dropping in on a story already well underway. Reading *Merry Wives* after the *Henry IV* plays may raise questions about continuity. It may call for certain explanations—for instance, of how Falstaff and Mistress Quickly can seem like total strangers when they had been so close before, while at the same time Fenton can make reference to the "wild prince." Meanwhile, the play may raise discussions about what Shakespeare might have believed about continuity, what it meant for his stagecraft, and why he saw fit to disregard it from time to time.

Language

Unlike Shakespeare's other plays, *Merry Wives* is written almost entirely in prose. This can be a mixed blessing for students, who may be surprised to discover that reading prose presents as many challenges as reading verse, and often for precisely the same reasons. Shakespeare makes extensive use of wordplay, including puns, and complex imagery. Falstaff is especially guilty of these excesses, as exemplified by such phrases as "a gemini of baboons" (a pair of identical twins?) and "red-lattice-phrases" (alehouse talk), and by his question, "Have I lived to be carried in a basket like a barrow of butcher's offal?" (3.5), which yokes together the worlds of laundry and the meat trade mainly through alliteration. Falstaff often piles images on one another for the mere sake of amplification, such as in the following sentences (taken from a longer speech): "But mark the sequel, Master Brook. I suffered the pangs of three several deaths: first, an intolerable fright to be detected with a jealous rotten bell-wether; next, to be compassed like a good Bilbo in the circumference of a peck, hilt to point, heel to head; and then, to be stopped in like a strong distillation with stinking clothes that fretted in their own grease. Think of that, a man of my kidney, think of that—that am as subject to heat as butter—a man of continual dissolution of thaw: it was a miracle to scape suffocation" (3.5). The plain-sense meaning here may be clear enough, especially as we have already witnessed the mishap that Falstaff is now describing from his own perspective. But the point of the passage is to give us insight into Falstaff's mind—not necessarily his fears and sufferings, but his tendency to translate his experiences into an excess of verbiage. For Falstaff, the point of speaking is never simply to explain or clarify. It is to dazzle, if not overwhelm his listeners with novel phrases and sounds.

On a different but related level, Shakespeare draws attention to variations in speech patterns. Some are regional: The Welshman Evans and the Frenchman Caius speak with noticeable accents. Others are more social: Alehouse talk is meant to be distinguished from the language of the citizens. This presents two problems: How exactly do these different accents *sound,* and more important, what are audiences supposed to make of it? While Shakespeare clearly celebrates the diversity of language, with its abundance of variation, students may be surprised to discover him capable of mocking certain idioms for their eccentricities. If Shakespeare meant for his original audiences to laugh, it can be a matter of debate whether those same rules should continue to apply. These questions should invite discussion.

There are several scenes where characters themselves seem unfamiliar with the words they use. On a few occasions, they are made to feel aware of their alienation. The Host of the Garter offers a clear illustration when he addresses Caius near the end of Act II. The Host deliberately uses unfamiliar terms such as *mockwater,* or *clapper-caw,* which call for definitions on stage. Perhaps Shakespeare knew his audiences did not know these terms either, but it is Caius who finally comes to suspect the Host of making a "sot" of him. In other words, throughout the play, we find passages where characters find themselves in comical situations as a direct result of their less than total command of their own language. At one point, Evans comes to the rescue for Slender by offering the following support: "[H]is meaning is good" (1.1). But as readers, we are invited to think more deeply about the effects that such deficiencies may actually have on day-to-day experience.

Humor

Although the play is undoubtedly comical, some of the humor is either too topical or too local to be readily accessible to modern readers, and some seems unusually "low-brow." Indeed, the playwright's penchant for slapstick, visual puns, and other performance-related devices has never enjoyed as much esteem as his linguistic skills. Such critical preferences may or may not be justified—since Shakespeare clearly relied on physical humor throughout his career—but in the end, physical comedy simply does not read as well as it performs on stage. On paper, a crucial dimension of the play's comedy remains virtually inaccessible. Indeed, while Shakespeare's genius as a writer is not in question, such passages are a vivid reminder just how much his success in his lifetime owed to those performers who brought his words to life.

KEY PASSAGES
Act I, Scene 1, 113–144

FALSTAFF. Now, Master Shallow, you'll complain of me to the King?

SHALLOW. Knight, you have beaten my men, killed my deer and broke open my lodge.

FALSTAFF. But not kissed your keeper's daughter!

SHALLOW. Tut, a pin! This shall be answered.

FALSTAFF. I will answer it straight: I have done all this. That is now answered.

SHALLOW. The Council shall know this.

FALSTAFF. 'Twere better for you if it were known in the counsel: you'll be laughed at.

EVANS. *Pauca verba,* Sir John good worts.

FALSTAFF. Good worts? Good cabbage!— Slender, I broke your head: what matter have you against me?

SLENDER. Marry, sir, I have matter in my head against you, and against your cony-catching rascals, Bardolph, Nym and Pistol. Thay carried me to the tavern and made me drunk, and afterward picked my pocket.

BARDOLPH. You Banbury cheese!

SLENDER. Ay, it is no matter

PISTOL. How now, Mephistophilus?

SLENDER. Ay, it is no matter.

NYM. Slice, I say! Pauca, pauca, slice, that's my humour.

SLENDER. Where's Simple, my man? Can you tell, cousin?

EVANS. Peace, I pray you! Now let us understand: there is three umpires in this matter, as I understand. That is, Master Page, *fidilicet* Master Page; and there is myself, *fidilicet* myself; and the three party is, lastly and finally, mine host of the Garter.

As the play opens, Shallow and Slender both raise complaints against Falstaff, but they disappear almost as soon as they confront the knight directly. The entire episode seems to have been designed for the exclusive purpose of bringing Falstaff and his retinue on stage, after which Shallow never brings up these specific grievances again. Despite the passage's incidental quality, it is rich in language, references, and themes that will be essential to the rest of the play. Already we see Falstaff's irreverence in the face of criminal charges, mixed with a bit of physical intimidation (Pistol and Bardolph). The first of several references to Christopher Marlowe's *Dr. Faustus* appears here, when Pistol ironically addresses Slender as "Mephistophilus"—that is, the devil Mephistopheles. Some of the mannerisms that distinguish speech patterns among different characters are present here as well. Nym offers a foretaste of what will become a catchphrase of his, while Evans's Welsh dialect and his wordiness are clear.

The accusation that Falstaff has killed Shallow's deer brings to mind a famous legendary anecdote. In his biographical sketch of William Shakespeare's early years, Nicholas Rowe alludes to an episode in which the young man is caught stealing deer out of a park owned by Sir Thomas Lucy. Ostensibly, his discovery was what forced him to leave his business and family in Warwickshire, move to London, and ultimately become a playwright, for which he is remembered today. Rowe's account is clearly false, and it seems to be based on the above passage, which he himself recounts in another portion of his essay. It is yet one more piece among the larger process of transforming Shakespeare from man into legend.

Act II, Scene 1, 1–32
Enter Mistress Page, *reading of a letter.*

MISTRESS PAGE. What, have I scaped love-letters in the holiday-time of my beauty, and am I now a subject for them? Let me see:

[reads.] Ask me no reason why I love you, for, though Love use Reason for his precisian, he admits him not for his counsellor. You are not young, no more am I: go to, then, there's sympathy; you are merry, so am I: ha, ha, then there's more sympathy: you love sack, and so do I: would you desire better sympathy? Let it suffice thee, Mistress Page, at the least if the love of soldier can suffice, that I love thee. I will not say "pity me"—'tis not a soldier-like phrase— but I say "love me."
By me, thine own true knight, by day or night,
Or any kind of light, with all his might,
For thee to fight. John Falstaff.

What a Herod of Jewry is this? O wicked, wicked world! One that is well-nigh worn to pieces with age, to show himself a young gallant? What an unweighted behaviour hath this Flemish drunkard picked—with the devil's name!—out of my conversation, that he dares in this manner assay me? Why, he hath not been thrice in my company! What should I say to him? I was then frugal of my mirth—heaven forgive me!—Why, I'll exhibit a bill in the parliament for the putting down of men. How shall I revenged on him? For revenged I will be, as sure as his guts are made of puddings.

Mistress Page's indignation over Falstaff's letter is clear. She resents the idea that her previous conversations with Falstaff—they exchange about half a dozen words in the first scene—could have been interpreted as an encouraging sign. She

Mistress Ford and Mistress Page compare their love letters from Falstaff in Act II, Scene 1 of *The Merry Wives of Windsor*. This is a print from the Boydell Shakespeare Gallery project, which was conceived in 1786 and lasted until 1805. *(Painting by Rev. William Peters; engraving by Robert Thew)*

apparently is under no illusions about her beauty, and we may wonder if she resents being addressed as such, and for such transparent reasons. Falstaff's attempts at romance are abysmal, and it is not long before he betrays his true affections for inexpensive wine. Mistress Page's sharp tone here gives way to a more tempered perspective as she enjoys her revenge.

Act III, Scene 1, 1–25

EVANS. I pray you now, good Master Slender's serving-man, and friend Simple by your name, which way have you looked for Master Caius, that calls himself Doctor of Physic?

SIMPLE. Marry, sir, the Petty-ward, the Park-ward, every way: Old Windsor way, and every way but the town way.

EVANS. I most fehemently desire you, you will also look that way.

SIMPLE. I will, sir.

EVANS. Jeshu pless my soul, how full of cholers I am, and trempling of mind. I shall be glad if he have deceived me. How melancholies I am. I will knog his urinals about his knave's costard when I have good opportunities for the 'ork. Pless my soul!
(sings) To shallow rivers, to whose falls
Melodious birds sing madrigals—
There will we make or peds of roses
And a thousand fragrant posies.
To shallow—
Mercy on me, I have a great dispositions to cry.
(sings) Melodious birds sing madrigals—
Whenas I sat in Pablyon—
And a thousand vagram posies . . .

Evans's idiosyncrasies are especially prominent, and such will be the case with other characters as the scene unfolds. Onstage, he typically is portrayed with a Bible in one hand, rapier in the other. His anger is overly dramatic, and of course his boasts about what he will do to Caius never come to pass. The lines of poetry were written by Christopher Marlowe, a poet and playwright who was famously killed in a duel—this may be part of his reason for recalling them at this point. As might be expected from a parson, his memory fails him and he substitutes lines from Psalm 137 for the actual poem.

Act III, Scene 2, 30–50

FORD. Hath Page any brains? Hath he any eyes? Hath he any thinking? Sure they sleep, he hath no use of them. Why, this boy will carry a letter twenty mile, as easy as a cannon will shoot point-blank twelve score. He pieces out his wife's inclination, he gives her folly motion and advantage. And now she's going to my wife, and Falstaff's boy with her. A man may hear this shower sing in the wind: and Falstaff's boy with her! Good plots they are laid, and our revolted wives share damnation together. Well, I will take him, then torture my wife, pluck the borrowed veil of modesty from the so-seeming Mistress Page, divulge Page himself for a secure and willful Actaeon, and to these violent proceedings all my neighbours shall cry aim. *[Clock strikes.]* The clock gives me my cue, and my assurance bids me search: there I shall find Falstaff. I shall be rather praised for this than mocked, for it is as positive as the earth is firm that Falstaff is there. I will go.

Ford has been listening to Falstaff, who relishes plans to visit his wife later that morning. His disguise has put him in a position to hear things that he would not otherwise have been privy to hearing. He is convinced that his wife is committing adultery, and, strangely, this leads him to think he has an advantage over Page, who is far more trusting of his own wife. His suspicions have been confirmed, though he is still largely unaware of his ignorance. His condition is an object lesson in the dangers of having access to information without the proper context.

In his disguise, Ford bears a resemblance to a popular stage character known as a meddling officer. Shakespeare has several examples of such figures in his plays, including *Henry V* and *Measure for Measure;* like Shakespeare does in this play, Ben Jonson famously ridiculed the convention with his clumsy Justice Overdo in *Bartholomew Fair.*

There are surprising political overtones in Ford's suspicions of infidelity. When he is alone, he accuses his wife of devising "plots," and in confronting her, he announces that "there is a conspiracy against me!" Needless to say, his espionage leads him nowhere, other than to his own embarrassment for mistrusting his wife in the first place. It is not clear what, if anything, Shakespeare wanted to establish through such language, other than the utter hollowness behind the fear that our closest intimates are perpetually plotting against us.

Act III, Scene 5, 96–133

FALSTAFF. Nay, you shall hear, Master Brook, what I have suffered o bring this woman to evil for your good. Being thus crammed in the basket, a couple of Ford's knaves, his hinds, were called forth by their mistress, to carry me in the name of foul clothes to Datchet Lane. They took me on their shoulders, met the jealous knave their master in the door, who asked them once or twice what they had in their basket. I quaked for fear lest the lunatic knave would have searched it; but Fate, ordaining he should be a cuckold, held his hand. Well, on went he for a search, and away went I for foul clothes. But mark the sequel, Master Brook. I suffered the pangs of three several deaths: first, an intolerable fright to be detected with a jealous rotten bell-weather; next, to be compassed like a good bilbo in the circumference of a peck, hilt to point, heel to head; and then, to be stopped in like a strong distillation with stinking clothes that fretted in their own grease. Think of that, a man of my kidney, think of that—that am as subject to heat as butter—a man of continual dissolution and thaw: it was a miracle to scape suffocation. And in the height of this bath—when I was more than half stewed in grease, like a Dutch dish—to be thrown into the Thames and cooled, glowing hot, in that surge like a horseshoe—think of that—hissing hot—think of that, Master Brook.

FORD. In good sadness, sir, I am sorry that for my sake you have suffered all this. My suit, then, is desperate: you'll undertake her no more?

FALSTAFF. Master Brook, I will be thrown into Etna, as I have been into Thames, ere

I will leave her thus. Her husband is this morning gone a-birding; I have received from her another embassy of meeting: 'twixt eight and nine is the hour, Master Brook.

This is one of several encounters between Falstaff and Ford, disguised as Brook, in which Falstaff unwittingly gives away all the information he means to hide. Falstaff's language is especially noteworthy for its hyperbole, its rapid wit, and its several comparisons of his body to foods (the greasier the better). If we did not know better, we would think Falstaff enjoyed his sufferings, inasmuch recounting them gave him the opportunity to entertain.

In his disguise, Ford is relatively quiet, but this does not mean that he is totally restrained. Much depends on the way the characters are positioned on stage, and the number of times that Falstaff turns his back on Brook, as he loses himself in his tale of misfortunes.

Act V, Scene 5, 59–80

QUICKLY. About, about!
Search Windsor Castle, elves, within and out.
Strew good luck, oafs, on every sacred room,
That it may stand till the perpetual doom
In state as wholesome as in state 'tis fit,
Worthy the owner and the owner it.
The several chairs of Order look you scour
With juice of balm and every precious flower;
Each fair instalment, coat and several crest,
With loyal blazon, evermore be blest.
And nightly, meadow-fairies, look you sing,
Like to the Garter compass, in a ring.
Th'expressure that it bears, green let it be,
More fertile-fresh than all the field to see;
And *Honi soit qui mal y pense* write
In em'rald tufts, flowers purple, green and white,
Like sapphire, pearl and rich embroidery,
Buckled below fair knighthood's bending knee:
Fairies use flowers for their charactery.
Away, disperse. But till 'tis one o'clock,
Our dance of custom round about the oak
Of Herne the hunter let us not forget.

The Fairy Queen's ceremonious instructions to the fairies make explicit reference to Windsor Castle, to the Order of the Garter and its motto— shame unto anybody who thinks ill of this. The entire passage explicitly honors the Order of the Garter, though it is not certain whether the lines were intended for the knights themselves or, instead, for London citizens who might have had a curious interest in the affairs of court.

Mistress Quickly's appearance as the Queen of the Fairies surprises everybody. Earlier, Mistress Page had explicitly mentioned that her daughter Anne would play this role; though it turns out that Anne plays a part of a very different nature, sneaking off with Fenton. But the idea of Quickly, a tavern keeper, representing the Fairy Queen suggests a breach of decorum; the idea that Quickly could speak lines upholding the virtue of chastity may have raised an eyebrow. Some critics have wondered how Queen Elizabeth might have responded to this spectacle, though of course there is no sign that she ever did.

Act V, Scene 5, 226–260

PAGE. My heart misgives me: here comes Master Fenton.
Enter FENTON *and* ANNE PAGE
How now, Master Fenton!

ANNE. Pardon, good father! good my mother, pardon!

PAGE. Now, mistress, how chance you went not with Master Slender?

MISTRESS PAGE. Why went you not with master doctor, maid?

FENTON. You do amaze her: hear the truth of it.
You would have married her most shamefully,
Where there was no proportion held in love.
The truth is, she and I, long since contracted,
Are now so sure that nothing can dissolve us.
The offence is holy that she hath committed;

And this deceit loses the name of craft,
Of disobedience, or unduteous title,
Since therein she doth evitate and shun
A thousand irreligious cursed hours,
Which forced marriage would have brought
  upon her.

FORD. Stand not amazed, here is no remedy.
In love the heavens themselves do guide the
  state:
Money buys lands, and wives are sold by fate.

FALSTAFF. I am glad, though you have ta'en
  a special stand to strike at me, that your arrow
  hath glanced.

PAGE. Well, what remedy? Fenton, God give
  thee joy!
What cannot be eschewed must be embraced.

FALSTAFF. When night-dogs run, all sorts of
  deer are chased.

MISTRESS PAGE. Well, I will muse no
  further. Master Fenton,
Heaven give you many, many merry days!
Good husband, let us every one go home,
And laugh this sport o'er by a country fire;
Sir John and all.

FORD. Let it be so. Sir John,
To Master Brook you yet shall hold your word
For he tonight shall lie with Mistress Ford.

The play's final conflict is resolved, to a mostly happy conclusion. Fenton's language is especially solemn here, as he indicates that whatever offence Anne has committed is holier even than honoring her father and her mother. Fenton speaks not only in defense of his own deceptions but in admonishment against the miseries of enforced marriage. According to him, Anne's marriage would have had a tragic outcome had she married one of her two wealthy but unlovable suitors. (It was a common theme for plays, so audiences might not have needed Fenton to spell out what those miseries would have been.) Significantly, Anne has nothing of her own to add here, and Page offers his blessing to Fenton alone—adding explicitly that his blessing is largely a factor of having his hand forced.

These minor lapses admitted, we are left with the impression that no serious harm has occurred, and that there will be no Malvolio left to nurse grudges at the play's end. The characters are eager to return to their homes and to enjoy collectively the adventures they have just been through. Mistress Page's invitation upholds an ideal of a harmonious community, held together by its relatively small size, shared interests, and good spirits.

DIFFICULT PASSAGES
Act III, Scene 4, 1–21

FENTON. I see I cannot get thy father's love,
Therefore no more turn me to him, sweet Nan.

ANNE. Alas, how then?

FENTON. Why, thou must be thyself.
He doth object I am too great of birth,
And that, my state being galled with my
  expense,
I seek to heal it only by his wealth.
Besides these, other bars he lays before me:
My riots past, my wild societies—
And tells me 'tis a thing impossible
I should love thee, but as a property.

ANNE. Maybe he tells you true.

FENTON. No, God so speed me in my time
  to come!
Albeit I will confess thy father's wealth
Was the first motive that I wooed thee, Anne,
Yet, wooing thee, I found thee of more value
Than stamps in gold or sums in sealed bags.
And 'tis the very riches of thyself
That now I aim at.

ANNE. Gentle Master Fenton,
Yet seek my father's love, still seek it, sir.

Fenton confesses his love to Anne in Act III, Scene 4 of *The Merry Wives of Windsor*. This is a plate from *Retzsch's Outlines to Shakespeare: The Merry Wives of Windsor*, published in 1844. *(Illustration by Moritz Retzsch)*

If opportunity and humblest suit
Cannot attain it, why then—hark you hither—

Fenton's courtship with Anne raises many difficult points, as this scene suggests. Here, for the first time in the play, characters are speaking in verse. Presumably, this is a sign of Fenton's status, which he alludes to in mentioning the time he has spent with Prince Hal. The verse gives Fenton's language a more solemn overtone, even if the content is of a more scandalous nature. He admits to a wild lifestyle, all the more troubling in that it involved the future king of England. He admits that he originally pursued Anne for her wealth, and his confession of loving her personal richness is ambiguous. Does he mean that he has discovered that there is more to love than the pursuit of wealth alone, or is it that she herself is a treasure of greater value than all her personal effects combined?

Anne's speaking part is shorter, though no less important. Her response to Fenton shows signs of consideration to her parents, and at the very least she has entertained the possibility that her father's misgivings are grounded. Of course, performance might help establish whether Anne is playing coy, or whether she also entertains doubts about her suitor's intentions.

CRITICAL INTRODUCTION TO THE PLAY
Humors

As the 1602 title page indicates, the play's main story line is intermixed with "sundrie variable and pleasing humors, of Syr Hugh, the Welch Knight, Iustice Shallow, and his wise Cousin M. Slender." The word *humor* or *humors* appears over two dozen times throughout the 1623 script, and Corporal Nym repeats the line "that's the humor of it" as a sort of trademark phrase. No other play by Shakespeare comes close to this frequent use of the word. In this respect, *Merry Wives* stands out as Shakespeare's most distinct "humor play."

What was a humor—or humors? Why was the term important in the first place, and why would Shakespeare have been interested in it? In fact, we find the word all over the place, in medical handbooks and sermons, essays and plays. Like most words that have their home in several disciplines, *humor* (the British spelling is *humour*) had several meanings, most of which would have been important to writers who were themselves interested in creating characters. In a physiological sense, the humors referred to the four basic substances of blood, phlegm, bile (choler), and black bile (melancholy). All animal organisms were thought to be composed of these substances, each of which played a role in the body's normal physical activities. Not all bodies had them in equal amounts, however, and if one particular humor was present in abundance, it could determine a person's overall demeanor. (We still hold on to this basic idea in our everyday language, such as when, for instance, we describe somebody as "sanguine" or "phlegmatic.")

If one humor dominated in excess, disorders might follow. This basic concept gave rise to an extraordinary amount of writing. There were volumes of treatises on the humors, or on specific humors—such as melancholy—in Shakespeare's lifetime alone. In fact, there was not a single known disorder that could not be accounted for by some imbalance of the humors. But whatever its value was as a physiological system, in popular usage the humors were an extremely imprecise way to characterize any sense of disorder. Shakespeare includes examples of such usage through characters like Evans, who declares at points that he is full of the "cholers" and the "melancholies." Certainly Evans has picked up the term somewhere, and it may be enough to use these words in order to give himself the sense that he is ready to take part in the duel; but as he awaits the arrival of Caius he does not exactly come across as someone who really knows what he is talking about.

In a slightly related sense, the word *humor* could refer to the notion of an individual, even an egoistical outlook on life. The literary scholar Hiram Haydn discusses the word as follows:

> In short, "humour" later comes to take
> on the special coinage of "style," "whim,"
> "fancy," or "idiosyncrasy"—usually with a
> foppish implication. But as [Ben] Jonson first
> uses it, it refers to the pursuit of one's own
> inclinations—those dictated by "selfe love, and
> affection." (385)

In this sense, humors referred to idiosyncrasies, which defined characters as individuals but often defined individuals as though they *were* these idiosyncrasies. Accordingly, a person who acted according to his humor did not have to have a particular reason. It was enough that it was pleasing, or at any rate that it seemed pleasing. The Elizabethan stage was filled with examples of characters who labored under particular illusions, and who placed their individual inclinations ahead of everything else. But no playwright captured the idea as precisely or as successfully as Ben Jonson (1572–1637). Originally an actor in Shakespeare's playing company, Jonson had established himself by the end of the 1590s as a promising playwright, thanks in large part to his comedy *Every Man in His Humour,* as well as its follow-up, *Every Man Out of His Humour.* It is apparent that Shakespeare's *Merry Wives* was written with Jonson's success in mind, though it is by no means clear whether Shakespeare

was sympathizing, merely cashing in on a popular trend, or sending up the popular comedies that his chief rival was renowned for.

Jesting as Social Discipline (Skimmington Rituals)

Whether celebrating it for its crowd-pleasing qualities or dismissing it as somehow inferior to Shakespeare's talents as a poet, many critics have repeatedly remarked that *Merry Wives* is "pure comedy." It is easy for audiences to become caught up in the farcical aspects of the story line. Even when Falstaff exaggerates the accounts of his suffering, he takes the jokes in good sport. Ford repents his jealousies the instant the wives admit to their conduct. Rather than scold his wife for deceiving him, he asks forgiveness for mistrusting her in the first place. The Pages deceive each other one and all, but the effects come to little harm. Page never chides his wife, as she had anticipated, and he accepts his daughter's marriage at the play's end. Critics do point out that he acknowledges Fenton only; none of his remarks are directed at Anne. That may be true, but it is a favorable marriage all the same.

At the end of the play, audiences hear Mistress Page invite everyone to "go home, / And laugh this sport o'er by a country fire, / Sir John and all." Perhaps it is easy to forget, at this point, that Mistress Page had originally vowed revenge against Falstaff, or that she had used the word *revenge* three times in Act II. (Even the ghost of Hamlet's father stops at two.) Perhaps it is Windsor's good fortune that there is no character among them like Malvolio, who does not take practical jokes in good stride, and whose vows for revenge darken the happy ending of *Twelfth Night.* In these respects, perhaps the best way to characterize the comedy of *Merry Wives* is with the well-known phrase "tragedy averted."

In fact, there are serious aspects behind the behavior that lead to the wives' deceptions in the first place. Falstaff may make for captivating theatrical performances, but he is a menacing character all the same. As a knight, presumably he lives on a pension, but all the same he lives beyond his means. Since there is no thought of working, he resorts to more devious methods for monetary gain. He initially views his romantic overtures in this light. What impresses him most about the wives is their control over their husbands' fortunes. (Even his good humor becomes part of the con—a pickpocket who entertains us is still a pickpocket.) Ford is not much better, driven as he is to suspicion. It is true that he listens to Falstaff gloat in anticipation, but does he really fail to notice about Falstaff what everybody else can spot in an instant? His jealousy is hardly a private matter. To the contrary, he is accompanied by several peers when he drops in on his wife, hoping to catch her in the act of deceiving him. Not only has he made his jealousy the subject of public discourse, but he has made wagers—against his wife! We can only wonder what had gone on before, which leads Ford to concede, "Well, I promised you a dinner." For that matter, we can only wonder what might be running through Mistress Ford's mind as she listens to her husband announce it.

There is a serious side to the wives' pranks as well. Indeed, we may call their jokes "practical" in the sense that they perform the important social function of regulating social conduct. Many readers have observed that the pranks they play on Falstaff are, in fact, derived from a public ceremony known as Skimmington rituals. According to many critics, who develop their research from the historian David Underdown and the cultural anthropologist Natalie Zemon Davis, a Skimmington ritual was a sort of informal disciplinary tool, found mainly in smaller communities and used to regulate various infractions. Often, these infractions had to do with private, domestic disorders that had taken on public dimensions. Unruly wives (scolds) might be disciplined by being forced to wear a bridle, and dunked in the water (cf. Falstaff in the laundry basket). Obstreperous husbands, perhaps those who could not hold their liquor, might be placed in women's clothing and paraded about the town (cf. Falstaff in disguise as the old woman of Brentford.) Deceived husbands might also be forced to wear antlers on their heads, the traditional sign of

Mistress Page and Mistress Ford urge Falstaff to run away from the Fairy Queen and her fairies, who would punish him for his lack of chastity, in Act V, Scene 5 of *The Merry Wives of Windsor*. This is a print from the Boydell Shakespeare Gallery project, which was conceived in 1786 and lasted until 1805. *(Painting by Robert Smirke; engraving by W. Sharpe)*

the cuckold (cf. Falstaff in disguise as Herne the Hunter.) Often, the men who participated in Skimmington rituals would wear women's clothing, in part to enhance the theatrical nature of their public ritual as well as to emphasize a "topsy-turvy" state of affairs.

Windsor and Its Inhabitants

While *Merry Wives* presumably was performed in London, the title page reminds us that the play is set in the nearby town of Windsor. In this respect, it bears a resemblance to the very popular city comedies, which set their stories in contemporary London and made contemporary London fashions the main source for their comic material. As a city, London was growing, and its metropolitan look was changing with tremendous speed. By contrast, Shakespeare's Windsor seems to be interested in a smaller, less urbanized population. All the same, he clearly is interested in the life of his native England.

Shakespeare had written chronicles of English history before, but in all of his other plays, he went out of his way to set them in far-flung locales. By contrast, *Merry Wives* has a distinctly local setting. At times, this setting becomes fairly precise. For a play that presumably was written for performance on a bare stage, the script makes its share of references to specific locations and towns. Frogmore, Datchet Mead, and Windsor Forest are all named as places the characters visit. From a literary standpoint, this creates the effect of a recognizable, even familiar environment. We almost feel we can go to the very spot from which Falstaff was tossed into the river. From a thematic standpoint, such precision suggests that the location for the story matters almost as much as the story itself. It calls attention to the basic question of how our local environments, such as the town we dwell in, give shape to the way we form our beliefs and conduct our affairs.

Not everybody in the play is native to Windsor. Falstaff and his retinue, including Mistress Quickly, had been famous inhabitants of Eastcheap. Justice Shallow hails from Gloucester. Two characters, the Welsh Evans and the French Doctor Caius, are non-English. The sense of foreignness registers a number of ways but most obviously in the way characters use—or misuse—the language they speak. The play repeatedly calls attention to the English that characters speak and the effects that this language has on the others' ears. As Melchiori points out, "In no other Shakespearean play does the word 'English' with reference to the language and its misuse appear so frequently" (7–8).

To be sure, English was not then a standardized, let alone a homogenous language. There was tremendous and rapid population growth in London—with people moving in from all parts of England and beyond. We can only speculate the effect that this migration had on local language, but it is not hard to imagine that residents routinely came into contact with different dialects, and that this occasionally made for difficult communication. Shakespeare had been exploring the use of varying dialects and intriguing speech patterns in his history plays, most famously in *Henry V.* It was not unusual for him to put characters of different languages on the stage together, in order to call attention to their mutual estrangement. In *Merry Wives,* he seems to limit his focus to the two foreign characters. Their respective pronunciations are distinct and, occasionally, the source of gross humor, such as when Caius refers to himself as the "turd," rather than the "third" on a list he had been enumerating. There is an intriguing moment early on when Evans corrects one of Slender's errors: "The 'ort is, according to our meaning, 'resolutely'—his meaning is good" (1.1.236–237). (Editors, take note!) And at the conclusion of the play, the mocking of Falstaff gives way to the mocking of Evans for his peculiar speech problems, with Ford promising never to mistrust his wife again until Evans can learn to woo her in "good English." It is a testament to Shakespeare's own linguistic talents that he could not only create but was deeply aware of the richness of the language that surrounded him, and that he had an equally strong sense of the social consequences when people must come to terms with such diversity.

Marriage—and Love

Other plays certainly have wedding ceremonies, and other plays certainly have married couples (often among royalty or high-ranking military figures), but again, as the play's very title reminds us, this play is about merry *wives.* No other play by Shakespeare focuses so much on characters whose social statuses are defined through their marriages. Watching this play, we witness the goings-on of husbands and wives. We observe the domestic chores—after all, a laundry basket is more than just a convenient place to stuff a lecherous knight.

We also catch a glimpse of the intimacies, as well as the games of mutual deception, that make up their marital relations. Indeed, when Mistress Page deceives her husband in preferring Caius over Slender, she seems to know exactly what to expect from her husband as a consequence. She carries out her scheme with a sense that she knows her way around her husband's mind reasonably well.

At the heart of the story is the question of Anne's marriage, and answering it involves deciding whether marriage constitutes an economic transaction or a union based on love. Slender is clear about which comes first: Anne is wealthy. Mistress

Anne Page asks Slender and Simple to come in for dinner in Act I, Scene 1 of *The Merry Wives of Windsor*. This is a print from the Boydell Shakespeare Gallery project, which was conceived in 1786 and lasted until 1805. (*Painting by Robert Smirke; engraving by Jean Pierre Simon*)

Page is blunt in declaring her reasons for preferring Caius, namely that he is "well moneyed." While she has nothing but scorn for Slender, her interest in Caius is nearly identical with Slender's interest in her daughter. Both characters share a mindset that regards Anne as property, the gateway to financial comfort. Perhaps it is this mindset that first gives Falstaff the inspiration to treat a blatantly insincere courtship as an avenue for financial gain.

Only Fenton seems to break from this model, as he prefers Anne for her intrinsic qualities over her fortunes. But his account of it is lame, while Anne's choice for Fenton seems largely negative. She does *not* want to endure the presumed miseries of enforced marriage. On the whole, we may be meant to see that there is a clear difference between marrying purely for money and marrying for love, but we may feel hard-pressed to say exactly what that difference consists of. Fenton does very well for himself anyway, while Anne presumably gains in social status, if nothing else. In the end, the play cautiously affirms the rights of children to decide their marriage partners for themselves, as well as the power of true love to deflect the scheming designs of parents who view marriage as an extension of their economic concerns. Alternately, we could say that the discourse of love is a screening device that allows for a smooth, though by no means seamless, alliance between members of court and merchants whose wealth gives them considerable power of their own.

Spying and Hunting

When Pistol initially warns Ford that Falstaff is scheming for his wife, the informer admonishes, "Prevent, or go thou like sir Actaeon he, / With Ringwood at his heels" (2.1.18–19). During the next act, Ford is convinced that it is Page who ultimately will be discovered as the play's real "Actaeon." These references to the classical figure are complex. According to legend—one could find this anywhere, but Ovid's *Metamorphoses* remains the best place to start—the famous hunter once caught the goddess Diana while she was bathing. As punishment for spying on the goddess, and for seeing something not meant for his eyes, he was transformed into a stag and killed by his own dogs. In a moment of tragic irony, the very act of hunting turned the hunter into the hunted. By Shakespeare's lifetime, the name Actaeon had taken on the additional association with cuckoldry, horns being the traditional symbol for the cuckold. Shakespeare takes up this imagery throughout his plays, but he gives it surprising twists. Ford repeatedly tries to spy on his wife, but in fact he never does become a stag. That dubious honor is reserved for Falstaff, who is punished for trying to violate the wives' chastity. (We recall that Diana herself was the goddess of chastity, and a hunter as well.) In wearing the antlers, Falstaff effectively represents the stag that Actaeon had become. Meanwhile, he is subject to torments. The children pinch him and burn him with candles, while the entire town gathers around to mock him. Surely, the punishment is a far cry from what happened to Actaeon, who was eaten by his own dogs, but it should be clear enough that Falstaff's punishment is a lighthearted reenactment of the classical legend.

Nor does Ford become a cuckold, though it is not entirely clear that he fully grasps the point. At the play's end, he teases Falstaff (who is wearing horns), "who's the cuckold now," which is not quite the right thing to say. The vague sense that he still retains unworthy thoughts grows in the last lines of the play, when Ford makes yet one more public joke at his wife's expense: "To Master Brook you yet shall hold your word, / For he tonight shall lie with Mistress Ford." Of course we know that Brook is Ford, but why would Ford decide on this moment to imagine himself in the role of his alter ego as a way for expressing his reconciled trust with his wife? Yes, he is making a joke, but it just happens to be a joke that allows Ford to perpetuate a mindset in which he can imagine his wife in bed with another person, a person Ford can describe from the third-person point of view.

Falstaff as Icon

More than a character in a play, or even a series of plays, Falstaff enjoys celebrity status in his own right. He has been inspirational for creative artists of several fields, including painters, composers, and filmmakers. Several operas featuring Falstaff have been composed, beginning in the 18th century and continuing through the 20th. Among the better known (and more accessible), we have the following operas: the extremely successful *Falstaff,* by the great court composer Antonio Salieri (1799); *Die lustigen Weiber von Windsor,* composed by Otto Nicolai (1849); and *Falstaff—a Symphonic Study in C Minor,* a symphonic poem created by the great romantic English composer Edward Elgar (1913).

Of all the operatic adaptations, special mention may perhaps be reserved for Giuseppi Verdi's *Falstaff.* Composed in 1893, with a libretto supplied by Arrigo Boito, the opera combines scenes from *Merry Wives* as well as the two parts of *Henry IV.* The scenography is deliberately light, and it was meant to be viewed as a foil to Verdi's other famous adaptation from Shakespeare, his *Otello* of 1887. (The same singer performed the parts of Iago and Falstaff in the operas' respective premieres).

The pastiche method of storytelling resurfaces in the great 1965 film *Chimes at Midnight* (aka *Falstaff*), directed by Orson Welles. Welles's script contains passages from several additional plays, including *Richard II* and *Henry V.* Notable performances include those of Sir John Gielgud as King Henry IV and Orson Welles as the knight himself. While Welles's screenplay does include passages from *Merry Wives,* overall the film is far more memorable for its scenes from *Henry IV.* These include Gielgud's mesmerizing performance of the king as he rebukes his wayward son and Falstaff's response to the Battle of Shrewsbury, a powerful combination of bewilderment and all too much wisdom. As people fight around him, Falstaff wanders across the battlefield, as though too heartbroken to join in the destruction.

EXTRACTS OF CLASSICAL CRITICISM

The most famous critical responses to *The Merry Wives of Windsor* remain the two produced by John Dennis and Nicholas Rowe in the early 18th century. Dennis, in an adaption under the title *The Comical Gallant: or the Amours of Sir John Falstaffe* (1702), wrote that Shakespeare's "comedy was written at [the queen's] command, and by her direction, and she was so eager to see it Acted, that she commanded it to be finished in fourteen days." Rowe's comment is below.

Nicholas Rowe (1674–1718) [From *Some Account of the Life of Mr. William Shakespear* (1709). Rowe was an actor and dramatist, and in 1715, he was appointed poet laureate of England. His edition of Shakespeare's works is said to mark the beginning of the modern Shakespeare text. What follow is his version of the influential Queen Elizabeth anecdote.]

> Queen Elizabeth had several of his Plays Acted before her, and without doubt gave him many gracious Marks of her Favour. . . . She was so well pleas'd with that admirable Character of *Falstaff,* in the two Parts of *Henry the Fourth,* that she commanded him to continue it for one Play more, and to shew him in Love. This is said to be the Occasion of his writing *The Merry Wives of Windsor.*

[Rowe also gives his opinion of the play and of Falstaff's character. He provides a double-sided assessment: On the one hand, carrying on a tradition recognized by Dryden and continued through the 20th century, he recognizes that the play is extremely well crafted and one of the only examples of what one critic called "pure comedy." On the other hand, he gives the sense that this "sparkling farce comedy" was "tossed off," in Harold Goddard's words (182)—and that the play suffered for being written on commission.]

> *The Merry Wives of Windsor, The Comedy of Errors,* and *The Taming of the Shrew,* are all pure Comedy; the rest, however they are call'd have something of both

Kinds . . . *Falstaff* is allow'd by every body to be a Master-piece; the Character is always well-sustain'd, tho' drawn out into the length of three Plays; and even the Account of his Death, given by his Old Landlady Mrs. *Quickly,* in the first Act of *Henry V,* tho' it be extremely Natural, is yet as diverting as any Part of his Life. . . . Amongst other Extravagences, in *The Merry Wives of Windsor,* he has made him a Dear-stealer [sic], that he might at the same time remember his *Warwickshire* Prosecutor, under the Name of Justice *Shallow;* he has given him very near the same Coat of Arms which *Dugdale,* in his Antiquities of that Couty, describes for a Family there, and makes the *Welsh* Parson descant very pleasantly upon 'em. That whole Play is admirable; the Humours are various and well oppos'd; the main Design, which is to cure *Ford* of his unreasonable Jealousie, is extremely well conducted. *Falstaff's Billet-doux,* and Master Slender's "Ah! Sweet Ann Page!" are very good Expressions of Love in their Way. (27–28)

August Wilhelm von Schlegel (1767–1845) [Excerpted from *A Course of Lectures on Dramatic Art and Literature* (1815). Schlegel's translation of Shakespeare (1797–1810) is a masterpiece of German literature and did much to popularize Shakespeare on the Continent. Furthermore, his literary criticism influenced Samuel Taylor Coleridge and his fellow English romantics. Schlegel here repeats the Queen Elizabeth legend and then gives his own low opinion of the play.]

This piece is said to have been composed by Shakespeare, in compliance with the request of Queen Elizabeth, who admired the character of Falstaff, and wished to see him exhibited once more, and in love. In love, properly speaking, Falstaff could not be; but for other purposes he could pretend to be so, and at all events imagine that he was the object of love. . . . That Falstaff should fall so repeatedly into the snare gives us a less favorable opinion of his shrewdness than the foregoing pieces had led us to form; still it will not be thought improbably, if once we admit the probability of the first infatuation on which the whole piece is founded, namely, that he can believe himself qualified to inspire a passion.

Of all Shakespeare's pieces, this approaches the nearest to the species of pure Comedy: it is exclusively confined to the English manners of the day, and to the domestic relations; the characters are almost all comic, and the dialogue, with the exception of a couple of short love scenes, is written in prose.

William Hazlitt (1778–1830) [From *Lectures on the Literature of the Age of Elizabeth; and Characters of Shakespeare's Plays* (1870). The famous essayist Hazlitt was one of the most important Shakespearean critics of the 19th century. He published *Characters of Shakespeare's Plays* in 1817 and *Lectures Chiefly on the Dramatic Literature of the Age of Elizabeth* in 1820; the two works were first published together in a single volume in 1870. Some scholars say Hazlitt singlehandedly reduced the play's esteem among criticism from the romantic period forward. His essays on Shakespeare's characters elevated Falstaff to monumental status, but his interest in Falstaff's powers of imagination and self-possession prevented him from accepting the fat knight in an ostensibly inferior role as a comic dupe in a physical comedy. As a result, he finds the role in *Merry Wives* to be of generally inferior quality.]

We could have been contented if Shakespeare had not been "commanded to show the knight in love."

Mistress Page and Mistress Ford hide Falstaff in a basket in Act III, Scene 3 of *The Merry Wives of Windsor*. This is a print from the Boydell Shakespeare Gallery project, which was conceived in 1786 and lasted until 1805. *(Painting by Rev. William Peters; engraving by Jean Pierre Simon)*

Falstaff in the *Merry Wives of Windsor* is not the man he was in the two parts of *Henry IV*. His wit and eloquence have left him. Instead of making a butt of others, he is made a butt of by them. Neither is there a single particle of love in him to excuse his follies: he is merely a designing, bare-faced knave, and an unsuccessful one. . . . Nym, Bardolph, and Pistol, are but the shadows of what they were and Justice Shallow himself has little of his consequence left. But his cousin, Slender, makes up for the deficiency. He is a very potent piece of imbecility.

MODERN CRITICISM AND CRITICAL CONTROVERSIES

Critics have always elevated Falstaff to a position of prominence, making him among the most significant of all Shakespeare's literary creations, and modern critics are no exception. Within that tradition, however, many critics, even today, base their evaluation of Falstaff exclusively on the history plays: *Henry IV, Part 1* and *Part 2;* and *Henry V,* in which Falstaff's death is recorded. In 1774, Maurice Morgann wrote *An Essay on the Dramatic Character of Sir John Falstaff* (published in 1777), but in focusing on Falstaff's military exploits, he neglects *Merry Wives* altogether. This essay has been credited for introducing detailed studies of individual characters. The great 20th-century critic William Empson observes:

The question whether Falstaff is a coward may be said to have started the whole snowball of modern Shakespeare criticism; it was the chief topic of Morgann's essay nearly two hundred years ago, the first time a psychological paradox was dug out of a Shakespeare text. (38)

Like Morgann before him, Empson never mentions a word about *Merry Wives,* neither in the essay on Falstaff from which this remark is taken, nor in his famous critical study *Some Versions of Pastoral* (1935). The critic C. L. Barber is indifferent to *Merry Wives,* though his remarkable book *Shakespeare's Festive Comedy* (1959) includes an important chapter on the *Henry IV* plays. His indifference regarding the one Falstaff play actually classified as a comedy is remarkable.

Not all critics share this scorn for the play. In *Shakespeare: A Survey* (1925), E. K. Chambers ridicules critics who ignore the comedy, writing:

After all, is there anything in this theory of a true Falstaff of *Henry the Fourth* and a mock Falstaff of *The Merry Wives* beyond an ingenious paradox born of that supersubtlety which is the special bane of those who are called, at this late hour, to add yet another stone to the monumental cairn

of Shakespearean analysis—Gigadibses, compelled eternally to—
Believe they see two points in Hamlet's soul
Unseized by the Germans yet?

(167–168)

(The lines of verse are taken from Robert Browning's poem "Bishop Brougham's Apology.").

Chambers goes so far as to prefer the comedy to the history plays, asserting:

The play is a good one, even more so on the stage than in the closet; and, after all, Shakespeare wrote for the stage, which gave him bread and butter and New Place at Stratford. In particular, it is markedly better than either part of *Henry the Fourth,* wherein, indeed, Shakespeare probably reaches his low-water mark as a dramatic artist. There is insufficient motive to fill the great space of blank canvas that stretches between *Richard the Second* and *Henry the Fifth;* and even the Falstaff scenes, amazing revelation of Elizabethan London though they are, can hardly galvanize the tedious Lancastrian chronicle into life. (169)

Two major 20th-century critical developments regarding the play were concerned with situating it in as precise a historical context as possible, and with analyzing it according to mythological types. Of the first, Leslie Hotson published the most significant study. His book *Shakespeare Versus Shallow* (1931) is a tremendous example of investigative historical criticism; of the nearly 400 pages, almost two-thirds consist of reprinted documents, ranging from letters to court testimonies to receipts for fines. Hotson's analytical section reads like a mystery, as the following passage suggests:

For what occasion in 1596–1597, we may now ask, was the *Merry Wives* ordered to be prepared in such post-haste? Let us look to the play for a suggestion. Although Shallow is a Gloucestershire justice, and Falstaff a denizen of London, we see them both brought by the author to Windsor. Now Windsor was, of course, the headquarters of the Order of the Garter and the scene of the brilliant ceremonies of installing the new Knight of the Garter. In the course of the play Doctor Caius is represented as hastening to *la grande affaire* at Court; and in the last scene of the play a graceful and appropriate compliment is paid to Queen Elizabeth in her quality as Sovereign of the Order. These indications lead us to suspect, with Sir Edmund Chambers and other scholars, that the play was written for some Feast of the Order of the Garter. The natural question, for which particular Feast? has however received no satisfactory answer; and I think I can now point to the very occasion which satisfies all the conditions. (112–113)

As his authoritative title suggests, one of Shakespeare's objectives was not only to celebrate the induction of Lord Hunsdon but to use some of his more ridiculous characters to settle old scores with individuals who had threatened the playing company's livelihood. Prominent among Shakespeare's enemies at the time was a justice by the name of William Gardiner, and it was a long-standing

Disguised as fairies, Mistress Quickly and the children burn Falstaff with tapers in Act V, Scene 5 of *The Merry Wives of Windsor.* This is a print from the Boydell Shakespeare Gallery project, which was conceived in 1786 and lasted until 1805. *(Painting by Robert Smirke; engraving by Isaac Taylor)*

quarrel between the writer and the man of law, which gave rise to Justice Shallow. It is an important discovery, at least as Hotson reckons, and he makes much of it in his conclusion:

> More important, however, than the fresh light on the external life of Shakespeare, more significant than the alteration in the dates of his plays, is the ocular demonstration now given us of his dramatic use of some of the life he knew: unique evidence of his use of persons, to quote Ben Jonson, ". . . such as Comedy would choose / When she would show an image of the times. . . ." When we consider the true history of Justice Gardiner, and the local world's opinion of him, the figure of Justice Shallow appears as a new triumph of the dramatist. Shakespeare is here revealed for the first time as a master of personal satire, taking with devastating humour a satisfactory revenge for himself, his associates of the theatre, and Gardiner's victims in Southwark. A few months after the production of the *Merry Wives,* exit Gardiner from the Elizabethan scene into a well-merited oblivion, carrying with him the bitter sting of the contemporary caricature. (130–131)

Hotson does concede that the play loses none of its pleasant qualities for our not having been aware of its meticulously designed send-ups of local figures.

The great critic Northrop Frye drew attention to the ritualistic dimensions that can be found in the play, especially its conclusion, in his classic book *Anatomy of Criticism.* Interested more broadly in an archetypal approach to literature, Frye made the following brief observation about *Merry Wives* as a comic reenactment of an ancient ritual:

> The green world charges the comedies with the symbolism of the victory of summer over winter, as is explicit in *Love's Labor's Lost,* where the comic contest takes the form of the medieval debate on winter and spring at the end. In *The Merry Wives* there is an elaborate ritual of the

defeat of winter known to folklorists as "carrying out Death," of which Falstaff is the victim; and Falstaff must have felt that, after being thrown into the water, dressed up as a witch and beaten out of a house with curses, and finally supplied with a beast's head and singed with candles, he had done about all that could reasonably be asked of any fertility spirit. (183)

Frye's book inaugurated a tradition of folklorist criticism, and for a time many interpretations of *Merry Wives* pursued the theme accordingly.

As a play with plenty of room for caricature, physical comedy, and even plenty of lowbrow humor, does *Merry Wives* amount to anything but a light farce, or does it address more serious issues in a meaningful way? This has become a key question for many contemporary critics. T. W. Craik has raised the stakes in his introduction to the Oxford Shakespeare edition, wherein he denies the play has any claims to addressing serious problems. Countering virtually all forms of social criticism is one fell swoop, he observes, and "No director has tried to center the play upon social conflict, though some have gestured towards it in their programme notes and interviews. Feminist criticism has had little to say, and that little not illuminating, about the women's roles in the play and in the society that the play depicts" (Shakespeare 1990: 42).

Craik's remarks are based largely on the history of the play in performance, where indeed the reasons for gathering together and sitting on uncomfortable (and expensive) seats may finally have more to do with amusement than with ruminating on the "social issues of the day." The above remark also speaks to his own dissatisfaction with feminist criticism, which is not the same as saying that no such criticism exists—or, *pace* Craik, that it is unhelpful across the board. One of the more compelling instances appears in Leah Marcus's discussion of the play's handling of Skimmington rituals, in her book *Unediting the Renaissance.* Granted, Marcus's book did not appear until 1996, some six years after Craik's introduction was published, and her interpretation of the play is as deeply steeped in textual analysis as anybody's could be. (As a book, it is perhaps not for first-time readers of Shakespeare.) That said, Marcus offers a compelling viewpoint on the cultural ideologies that the play upholds and those it seems to reject.

Scholars also are deeply divided on whether the play was meant to be satire of a topical nature. For that matter, there is still controversy on whether it was meant to be topical praise. Modern critics are largely in agreement that the first performance of the play corresponded with the Garter Induction Ceremony of April 23, 1597. Baron Hunsdon's induction ceremony certainly was a major event, and it seems probable that Shakespeare—along with the rest of Lord Chamberlain's Men—would have made up part of the 300 or so who waited on him in attendance. The dance of the fairies includes explicit references to Windsor Castle and to the Order of the Garter, including its motto "Honi soit qui mal y pense"; and the story's many plotlines that lead nowhere, such as the horse-stealing episode, contain references that suggest that Shakespeare may have been familiar with topical events. But consensus does not amount to fact. As at least one editor has suggested, even if the dating were correct, we would still have no idea what the first audiences would have seen, much less what they would have thought of it.

We also know that the play was performed in multiple locations and at multiple points in time, and there is every reason to believe that the script was modified substantially to reflect those conditions. In that respect, Barbara Freedman challenges the very notion that the play was written specifically for an occasional purpose. While topical references abound, she describes the strength of the play, reflected in its rich early stage history, as follows: "The ability of *Merry Wives* to withstand alteration and censorship, to append itself to the vogue of humors comedy and to the Henriad alike, to capitalize on local events and to rewrite them suggests that its topicality functions less as a liability than as a survival strategy" (210). At any rate, it is clear that the play's appeal to modern audiences has little to do with anything that was taking place at Windsor Castle or its environs during the late 1590s. Even in a contextual analysis as sophisti-

cated as T. W. Craik's historical introduction to the play, the editor acknowledges that the first thing to come to audiences' minds when recalling the play is the moment when Falstaff is placed into the buck-basket and tossed into the river.

Several aspects of the play suggest that Shakespeare meant to dramatically represent a harmonious union between the town and the royal court. Indeed, the play may originally have owed much of its popularity to its ability to unite the two social strata in harmonious, even loving fashion. Given the early signs of performances at multiple venues, though, and given the appearance of deliberate revisions to the scripts, the question emerges whether the play was designed to perform to diverse audiences with different cultural values. Leah Marcus observes cautiously that the First Folio suggests a more "courtly ethos" with a sophisticated literary sensibility, whereas the shorter script bears signs of a traveling script, designed for audiences who would have had less interest in the court—or in Windsor, for that matter (since all the specific references to the town are missing). With these differences in mind, we may continue to probe just what sort of relation takes hold between the royal court and the wealthy citizens who are not directly connected with it, but who clearly live under its reach.

Finally, an interesting take on the legend that the play was written quickly at the behest of Queen Elizabeth appears in Jonathan Bate's study (2008) of Shakespeare's posthumous reputation. Bate is less interested in the factual value of these early accounts than in the effect such accounts produce in establishing Shakespeare's reputation as a genius playwright. In that vein, Bate comments:

> The anecdote retains its point whether or
> not the commission came from the Queen:
> Shakespeare is imagined to have the gift of
> dashing off a new play in less than a fortnight,
> while Falstaff is made into a larger-than-life
> character who bursts the bounds of the play
> in which he originally appeared. He generates
> not only a second part of *Henry IV,* but also

The Merry Wives. We cannot have enough of Falstaff, so what better than a play which shows him in love? One of the first things we want to know about our heroes is who they fell in love with. (36)

THE PLAY TODAY

The play continues to be a popular subject for contemporary critics. Indeed, from a survey of criticism published over the last 20 years, which includes articles or book chapters by Rosemary Kegl (1994), Jonathan Hall (1998), Richard Helgerson (1998), Leo Salingar (2001), Pamela Allen Brown (2003), and Regina Buccola (2003), one could not fail to notice the predominating contemporary concerns over such topics as class conflict, gender relations, homoeroticism (faintly suggested by the play's brief references to transvestism and marriage in the final scene), popular culture, and the nature of ethnocentrism as expressed through language.

Students' experiences with the play in a course on Shakespeare might be shaped in significantly different ways, depending on the textbook that the instructor adopts. In her introduction to the play for *The Riverside Shakespeare* edition, Anne Barton focuses on the play's origin and early performances, its relation to the other Falstaff plays, its possible sources, and its structure as a comedy. Her comments about character focus largely on Falstaff, whom she characterizes as "a larger-than-life, mythic figure" (322). While she comments on several other characters, she is noticeably brief about the wives themselves; instead, her discussion tends more broadly toward "the citizens of Windsor" (323).

By contrast, Walter Cohen overwhelmingly emphasizes the play's sociological themes in his introductory essay for the *Norton Shakespeare.* Indeed, his essay begins with a critical statement by Friedrich Engels, which reads: "The first act of the *Merry Wives* alone contains more life and reality than all German literature." Cohen himself addresses a number of topics in the pages that follow, including the sense of "middle-class community," the complex relations between social rank and financial standing, the connections between "gender relations and sexuality" and "emerging middle-class norms," and a "cheerfully casual ethnocentrism," represented through the several ethnic jokes scattered throughout the play's dialogue. It is a full seven pages into his introduction before he mentions that the main plot revolves around Falstaff.

Critical controversies aside, *Merry Wives* remains popular in performance worldwide, especially if one counts Verdi's *Falstaff* (which borrows heavily from *Merry Wives*) as an adaptation. Audiences appear to be drawn to the play for essentially the same reason that some critics have held it at a distance—namely, that the play strives to please without making too many additional demands for reflection. As E. K. Chambers observes, "such farce you may define, if you will, as acted *fabliau*. And of acted *fabliau, The Merry Wives* is the best English specimen, just as Chaucer's *Miller's Tale* and *Reeve's Tale* are the best English specimens of *fabliau* in narrative" (170). Indeed, the play's success in performance may have an indirect effect among contemporary critics. Current attention to differences among the early scripts easily connects to questions about how the play might originally have been performed, and even to how the play as we know it today was shaped by its performance among different settings and circumstances.

The play's popularity onstage has not carried over to the screen. The BBC has produced two full-length versions, one directed by Julian Amyes in 1952 and another directed by David Hugh Jones in 1982. The latter was produced for the BBC's Television Shakespeare, which adapted the complete plays of Shakespeare for television audiences. Another version, directed by Jack Manning, was produced for television in 1970 and released as a film in 1983. It, too, was ostensibly designed for a complete series of Shakespeare plays adapted for television. To date, no Hollywood studio has taken it on as a production.

FIVE TOPICS FOR DISCUSSION AND WRITING

1. **Marriages:** Are the Pages happily married? What about the Fords? What role does deception play in determining the conditions of their married life? Does the marriage between Anne

and Fenton look like a successful match? Does the marriage benefit one character more than the other, or are both fortunate?

2. **Court, town, and country:** How are royal figures represented on stage, both in appearance and through descriptions? What sorts of interaction take place between the royal castle and the inhabitants of Windsor? What values do the members of the gentry uphold? How do they compare with the values of the rest of the citizens? What are the qualities that make Windsor a happy town?

3. **Falstaff and Windsor:** What is Falstaff's position in Windsor, and how does his public role correspond with the other residents of Windsor? Is he a "useful" member of his society, and does it matter? Do the people of Windsor "deserve" Falstaff? Does his status as a knight make a difference in the way he acts or in the ways he is treated? Are there aspects of his conduct that would strike us as unpleasant, were they not explicitly presented in the form of comical farce? What are the ways to interpret his final punishment at the play's conclusion? Why does his punishment make for a happy ending?

4. **Individualism versus community values:** Is there such a thing as a set of "community values" operating among the characters in this play? Which characters strike us for their independence of mind, and which ones come across as eccentrics? What types of behavior, if any, distinguish these two groups from each other?

5. **Disguises and power:** Several characters take on disguises and false personas during various points of the play. What are these disguises and what purposes do they serve (what ends are they meant to achieve)? What are the effects of wearing disguises, as they come across in this play? Which characters appear to benefit as a result of their false appearances? By contrast, which ones seem to lose whatever power they may have held?

Bibliography

Barber, C. L. *Shakespeare's Festive Comedy: A Study of Dramatic Form and its Relation to Social Custom.* Princeton, N.J.: Princeton University Press, 1959.

Bate, Jonathan. *The Genius of Shakespeare.* 10th anniversary ed. Oxford and New York: Oxford University Press, 2008.

———. *The Romantics on Shakespeare.* London: Penguin Books, 1992.

Bennett, A. L. "The Sources of Shakespeare's *Merry Wives.*" *Renaissance Quarterly* 23 (1970): 429–433.

Brown, Pamela Allen. *Better a Shrew Than a Sheep: Women, Drama, and the Culture of Jest in Early Modern England.* Ithaca, N.Y.: Cornell University Press, 2003.

Buccola, Regina M. "Shakespeare's Fairy Dance with Religio-Political Controversy in *The Merry Wives of Windsor.*" In *Shakespeare and the Culture of Christianity in Early Modern England,* edited by Dennis Taylor and David Beauregard, 159–179. New York: Fordham University Press, 2003.

Chambers, E. K. *Shakespeare: A Survey.* 1925. Reprint, New York: Hill and Wang, 1958.

Davis, Natalie Zemon. *Society and Culture in Early Modern France.* Stanford, Calif.: Stanford University Press, 1975.

Empson, William. *Essays on Shakespeare.* Cambridge: Cambridge University Press, 1986.

Freedman, Barbara. "Shakespearean Chronology, Ideological Complicity, and Floating Texts: Something is Rotten in Windsor." *Shakespeare Quarterly* 45 (1994): 190–210.

Frye, Northrop. *Anatomy of Criticism.* Princeton, N.J.: Princeton University Press, 1971.

Goddard, Harold C. *The Meaning of Shakespeare.* 2 vols. Chicago: University of Chicago Press, 1951.

Green, William. *Shakespeare's Merry Wives of Windsor.* Princeton, N.J.: Princeton University Press, 1962.

Gurr, Andrew. "Intertextuality at Windsor." *Shakespeare Quarterly* 38 (1987): 189–200.

Hall, Jonathan. "The Evacuations of Falstaff (*The Merry Wives of Windsor*)." In *Shakespeare and Carnival: After Bakhtin,* edited by Ronald Knowles, 123–151. New York: St. Martin's Press, 1998.

Haydn, Hiram. *The Counter-Renaissance.* New York: Grove Press, 1950.

Hazlitt, William. *Characters of Shakespeare's Plays.* London: R. Hunter, 1817.

———. *Lectures Chiefly on the Dramatic Literature of the Age of Elizabeth.* London: Stodart and Steuart, 1820.

Helgerson, Richard. "Language Lessons: Linguistic Colonialism, Linguistic Postcolonialism, and the Early Modern English Nation." *Yale Journal of Criticism* 11 (1998): 289–299.

Hotson, Leslie. *Shakespeare Versus Shallow.* Boston: Little, Brown, and Company, 1931.

Irace, Kathleen O. *Reforming the 'Bad' Quartos: Performance and Provenance of Six Shakespearean First Editions.* Cranbury, N.J.: Associated University Presses, 1994.

Johnson, Gerald D. "*The Merry Wives of Windsor*, Q1: Provincial Touring and Adapted Texts." *Shakespeare Quarterly* 38 (1987): 154–165.

Kegl, Rosemary. "'The Adoption of Abominable Terms': Middle Classes, Merry Wives, and the Insults That Shape Windsor." In *The Rhetoric of Concealment: Figuring Gender and Class in Renaissance Literature.* Ithaca, N.Y.: Cornell University Press, 1994, 77–125.

Marcus, Leah. *Unediting the Renaissance: Shakespeare, Marlowe, Milton.* London and New York: Routledge, 1996.

Shakespeare, William. *The Merry Wives of Windsor.* Oxford Shakespeare. Edited by T. W. Craik. Oxford and New York: Oxford University Press, 1990.

———. *The Merry Wives of Windsor.* Arden Shakespeare. Edited by Giorgio Melchiori. London: Thomson Learning, 1999.

———. *The Merry Wives of Windsor.* Edited by Sir Arthur Quiller-Couch and John Dover Wilson. Cambridge: Cambridge University Press, 1964.

———. *Mr. William Shakespeare's Comedies, Histories, & Tragedies: A Facsimile of the First Folio, 1623.* New York and London: Routledge, 1998.

———. *The Norton Shakespeare.* Edited by Stephen Greenblatt, Walter Cohen, Jean E. Howard, and Katharine Eisaman Maus. New York and London: W. W. Norton and Company, 1997.

———. *The Riverside Shakespeare.* Edited by G. Blakemore Evans. Boston: Houghton Mifflin, 1974.

Morgann, Maurice. *An Essay on the Dramatic Character of Sir John Falstaff.* London: T. Davies, 1777.

Roberts, Jeanne Addison. *Shakespeare's English Comedy: The Merry Wives of Windsor in Context.* Lincoln and London: University of Nebraska Press, 1979.

Rowe, Nicholas. *Some Account of the Life of Mr. William Shakespear.* London: Nicholas Rowe, 1709.

Salingar, Leo. "The Englishness of *The Merry Wives of Windsor.*" *Cahiers élisabéthans* 59 (2001): 9–25.

Underdown, David, *Revel, Riot and Rebellion: Popular Politics and Culture in England 1603–1660.* Oxford and New York: Oxford University Press, 1985.

FILM AND VIDEO PRODUCTIONS

Amyes, Julian, dir. *The Merry Wives of Windsor.* With Robert Atkins, Mary Kerridge, and Elizabeth Regan. BBC, 1952.

Jones, David Hugh, dir. *The Merry Wives of Windsor.* With Richard Griffiths, Prunella Scales, and Judy Davis. BBC Worldwide, 1982.

Manning, Jake, dir. *The Merry Wives of Windsor.* With Leon Charles and Gloria Grahame. Kultur Video, 1983.

Meth, Agnes, and Claus Viller, dirs. *Falstaff.* Opera (Salieri). With John del Carlo, Teresa Ringholz, and Richard Croft. Conducted by Arnold Ostman. Schwetzinger Festspiele, 1995.

Verdi, Giuseppe. *Falstaff.* Opera. With Giuseppe Taddei, Fedora Barbieri, Rosana Carteri, Anna Moffo, and Luigi Alva. Conducted by Tulio Seraffin. Radiotelevisione italiana (RAI), 1956.

Welles, Orson, dir. *Chimes at Midnight.* With Jeanne Moreau, John Gielgud, and Margaret Rutherford. Continental Film, 1965.

OPERA RECORDINGS

Verdi, Giuseppe. *Falstaff.* With Giuseppe Taddei, Raina Kabaivanska. Conducted by Herbert von Karajan. Sony, 1982.

———. *Falstaff.* With Gabriel Bacquier, Max-Rene Cosotti, Karen Armstrong, Vienna Opera Philharmonic. Conducted by Georg Solti. Deutsche Grammophone, 2005.

—Adam H. Kitzes

A Midsummer Night's Dream

INTRODUCTION

At the end of their inspiring introduction to the recent Royal Shakespeare Company edition, Jonathan Bate and Eric Rasmussen argue that *A Midsummer Night's Dream* "should be everybody's introduction to Shakespeare, preferably well before the age of eleven" (Shakespeare: xv). Their advice is well founded. There is no better play for introducing young readers to the dazzling brilliance of Shakespeare's artistry. The play is filled with whimsical and charming elements, such as fairies, magic, mischief, and a foolish artisan who wears a donkey's head for part of the play. It also has the added appeal of being among the most reader-friendly of Shakespeare's works in terms of the relative simplicity of its language. The jokes (and there are many) and key moments of plot are conveyed in accessible language, and they remain funny, even to modern audiences. For example, when Bottom's head has been transformed into that of a donkey (or *ass*), he tells the fairy Mustardseed, "I must to the barber's, monsieur, for methinks I am marvellous hairy about the face; and I am such a tender ass, if my hair do but tickle me, I must scratch" (4.1.26–29). The insults the two women hurl at each other once Hermia discovers that her man, Lysander, has fallen in love with Helena, and Helena believes the the other three are playing a trick on her, provide another case in point:

> HERMIA. You juggler! You canker-blossom!
> You thief of love! What have you come by night
> And stolen my love's heart from him?

> HELENA. Fine, i'faith!
> Have you no modesty, no maiden shame,
> No touch of bashfulness? . . .
> Fie, fie! you counterfeit, you puppet you!

> HERMIA. Puppet! . . .
> Now I perceive that she hath made compare
> Between our statures; she hath urg'd her
> height.
> . . . . .
> How low am I, thou painted maypole? speak;
> How low am I? I am not yet so low
> But that my nails can reach unto thy eyes.
>   (3.2.282–298)

Such a scene is as comically accomplished as any thing Shakespeare ever wrote, yet the humor is strikingly accessible.

However, even if we missed Bate and Rasmussen's ideal reading age by four, six, 10, or even 60 years, there is no need to be embarrassed. Nor is there danger of finding the play less rewarding. It is easier to read than *Romeo and Juliet* (the play with which many students in the United States begin their studies of Shakespeare), but the language is still Shakespeare's, complex and brilliant, holding dizzying and inexhaustible pleasures that resist obsolescence from age or time.

The play dramatizes something quite familiar: the painfully arbitrary nature of love. Four lovers and would-be lovers face incredible obstacles to love and pursue happiness in ways that often pit are the cause of much disorder in the human world. While he is trying to forge happiness with one hand, he is set on humiliating or injuring his queen with the other by making her fall in love with a monster. The attempts they make (and those the fairies make on their behalf) to remedy their love only deepen their confusion.

Although the situation in *A Midsummer Night's Dream* sounds painful, its dramatization in the play tends to have the opposite effect. Part of the play's appeal is that while it shows the pain of being in love, it allows the audience to experience this phenomenon as pleasure rather than as the agony it most often is and even appears to be for much of the play. What is painful in life is shown here as ridiculous. The audience feels comforted in the assurance that things will work out for the lovers in the play, despite the chaos and threat to safety. While the controlling spirit Puck may hold "mortals" in contempt as "fools," he seems bound by the proverb that "Jack shall have Jill / Nought shall go ill" (3.2.461–462). Plus, although mortals may be fools, Bottom's story line shows how love can dignify folly, translating the most asinine laborer into the consort of the fairy queen. However, as shown in the case of Titania, Shakespeare is also keenly aware of the complement, that love can make the most regal fairy queen, a "spirit of no common rate" (3.1.157), into an ass. If Bottom and Titania represent opposite ends on the social scale, the four lovers fall somewhere in the middle. In these ways, the forces of love's chance are given, to use Theseus's words from late in the play, "a local habitation and a name" (5.1.17).

Oberon and Titania look down on the four lovers in this 19th-century depiction of *A Midsummer Night's Dream*. (Painting by Johann Heinrich Ramberg; engraving by Josef Axmann)

them against one another. Hermia and Lysander love each other, but Hermia's father, Egeus, insists on pain of death or forced celibacy that she marry Demetrius. Meanwhile, Helena pines for Demetrius, who once loved her but now pursues Hermia. When Oberon, the king of the fairies, and his minion Puck attempt to intervene, their good intentions merely make matters worse. Oberon, however, is a poor ambassador for love's harmony. His spat with his fairy queen, Titania, and the jealousy that results from believing she favors Theseus

A Midsummer Night's Dream succeeds because it is able to impart the feel of fairy magic long past the age where we no longer believe such magic exists. The play puts onstage for us the paradox of the imagination, examining particularly its functions in theater and love. On one hand, it insists on the absolute necessity of the imagination in both venues. Without imagination to "transpose" what is "base and vile" . . . to "form and dignity" (1.1.233), we would have neither love nor theater. At the same time, the imagination is unavoidably the cause of problems in both these capacities. Even in the best situations, the imagination will err and cause problems, and human love and theater are almost never considered under the best circumstances. So while the play urges and demands that viewers endorse the imagination as supreme, it also notes the hefty price for doing so.

BACKGROUND

As far as scholars have been able to discover, there is no one source for the main plots of this play. Instead, Shakespeare drew on a number of sources for the principal figures and some of the actions. His work is impressive for its indebtedness to so many authors and its creative use of sources. Because Shakespeare mainly drew from characters rather than plot, it makes more sense to organize first by character groups and then by sources Shakespeare adapts.

Theseus and Hippolyta

For his depiction of the Athenian duke and his consort, Shakespeare drew from two main sources: Geoffrey Chaucer's romance "The Knight's Tale" (the opening story from *The Canterbury Tales*) and Plutarch's portrait of Theseus in *The Lives of the Noble Grecians and Romans,* translated by Sir Thomas North (1579). As in Shakespeare's play, in "The Knight's Tale," Theseus is duke of Athens and is married to "Ypolita" (Hippolyta), an Amazonian queen whom he had conquered. Chaucer's story also begins by mentioning their wedding feast and a "tempest at their hoom-coming." As in Shakespeare, Chaucer's Theseus adjudicates a knotty lovers' dispute, in this case between two brothers, Palamon and Arcite, who have fallen in love with the same woman. However, as in Shakespeare, larger metaphysical forces put the outcome beyond his jurisdiction.

Although the plots of the two works differ significantly, thematically they are similar. Chaucer's tale and Shakespeare's play both dramatize the irresistible supremacy of love as well as the inevitability of love's folly. Chaucer writes: "Love is a gretter lawe by my pan / Than may be yeve [given]

to any erthely man." That love's law is greater than man's seems to be the lesson that Theseus learns by the end of Shakespeare's play when he overrules Egeus's desire to have the Athenian's "law upon [Lysander's] head" (4.1.152).

Plutarch's influence is less direct. From this depiction of Theseus, Shakespeare gets the Athenian duke's reputation as a rake and deserter of women, a reputation that Oberon accuses Titania of abetting:

> Didst not thou lead him through the
>   glimmering night
> From Perigouna, whom he ravished;
> And make him with fair Aegles break his faith,
> With Ariadne and Antiopa?
>
> (2.1.77–79)

The play brings this reputation forward as part of the duke's background, but Theseus does not live up to it in the play's action. Although the characterization is not simple, Shakespeare focuses on presenting Theseus as a rational and principled ruler who is leaving behind his former womanizing.

Bottom and the Rude Mechanicals

In formulating Bottom's translation into an ass, Shakespeare certainly must have known of Apuleius's famous romance *The Golden Ass* (translated into English in 1566), in which a similar transformation takes place (Brooks: lxi). Reginald Scot's *The Discoverie of Witchcraft* (1584), a puritanical attack on the folk superstition from which Shakespeare could have gotten part of his fairy lore, also contains recipes for turning one into a half-beast or at least creating the illusion of putting a horse's head on a man. Shakespeare might have found inspiration for his story of the mechanicals in Anthony Munday's 16th-century play *John a Kent and John a Cumber*. In his introduction to the Arden Shakespeare edition of *A Midsummer Night's Dream*, Harold F. Brooks reports that Munday's play contains "a crew of clowns [i.e. rustics] who organize buffoonish entertainment in honour of their territorial overlord, on the occasion of a double wedding" (lxv). In Shakespeare's play, these "hempen homespuns" perform "Pyramus and Thisbe," which is based on a story in the classical Roman poet Ovid's *Metamorphoses,* but Shakespeare could have drawn on a number of other extant versions.

Oberon, Titania, Puck, and the Fairies

Oberon's name could have come from the 13th-century French epic *Huon of Bourdeaux,* in which Oberon is a diminutive fairy, or from a lost play of that same title performed by the Earl of Sussex's Men. An Oberon also appears in book 2 of Edmund Spenser's *The Faerie Queene* (1590) and in Robert Green's history play *James IV* (ca. 1591). Titania's name appears in Ovid's *Metamorphoses* as an alternate name for the witch Circe and for the virgin goddess Diana, two very different figures. Titania as queen of the fairies has properties of each.

Direct sources for Shakespeare's other fairies are harder to trace. To create his fairies, Shakespeare could have drawn on his own considerable knowledge of oral tradition and folklore. Most of the characteristics of fairies' activities were well known; the most notable innovation in Shakespeare's depiction is their diminutive size. But other aspects of the fairies are familiar and derivative. In the play, although Titania's acquisition of the changeling boy is the result of a loving relationship with the boy's mother, it is also a reminder of the dangers fairies presented. The theory of changelings held that an exceptional child was one whom fairies had exchanged for a healthy child they had spirited away. The principal fairy, Puck, or Robin Goodfellow, draws on a different and common aspect of folklore—the fairy as mischievous and shape-shifting trickster. The Puck/Robin Goodfellow conflation in Shakespeare's character points to two divergent personalities. Puck's sweeping at the end of the play adapts the tradition of the helpful fairy, who performed housework for women who showed proper reverence to fairies. By contrast, trickster fairies punished *sluts,* which at the time were young women who were simply untidy and did not keep a good house.

The Four Lovers

The specific plot of the four lovers is in many ways Shakespeare's invention, although similar plots were common in his time. Romantic love plots featuring rivalries among lovers and misunderstanding would have been familiar to the audience from other plays, even those by Shakespeare.

Date and Text of the Play

A Midsummer Night's Dream first appeared in publication in a quarto edition in 1600. Most consider this version of the play to have been used by Shakespeare's company. It was first staged several years earlier, probably in 1595. In his 1598 work *Palladis Tamia,* Francis Meres mentions the work as one of six comedies that rival those of the classical Roman dramatist Plautus, who was highly influential in Shakespeare's early comedies. Most editors agree that the play could not have been composed before 1594 because it seems to allude to an event reported in a publication that could not have been printed before October that year. According to the report, a lion was to draw a carriage at a feast at the court of King James of Scotland, but as this was thought to be too terrifying for the women present, a man from North Africa substituted; this seems reflected in Bottom's fear in Act III that a lion would terrify the ladies.

Many scholars believe also that the play was originally an occasional piece, composed to celebrate the wedding of nobles at which Queen Elizabeth might have been in attendance. The evidence for such claims lies generally in the play's subject and theme of marriage and specifically in some standard elements of other celebratory dramatic forms, such as the bergomask the artisans perform near the end of the play. Scholars and editors also believe that the long mythological explanation that Oberon gives for the aphrodisiac properties of "love-in-idleness" is a compliment that is being paid to Queen Elizabeth (2.1). Even if *Midsummer* was written with this celebratory intent, the play, like most of Shakespeare's plays, exceeds the expectations of the genre, offering a dramatization

A
Midsommer nights dreame.

As it hath beene sundry times pub-
lickely acted, by the Right honourable, the Lord Chamberlaine his
seruants.

Written by William Shakespeare.

¶ Imprinted at London, for *Thomas Fisher*, and are to
be soulde at his shoppe, at the Signe of the White Hart,
in *Fleetestreete.* 1600.

Title page of the first quarto of *A Midsummer Night's Dream*, published in 1600

of love much more complex and less flattering than the purely happy one expected on such occasions.

With the exception of Hymen's unexpected appearance at the end of *As You Like It*, *Midsummer* is the only Shakespeare comedy up to this point to use magic as a way of complicating and resolving the plot. In other comedies, "magic," to the extent that it exists, is a product of the human heart, wit, craft, or just dumb luck. In fact, in *The Taming of the Shrew*, a play probably written around the same time, the audience could well doubt the claim that the love accomplished between couples is a "miracle." It would be at the end of his career, in *The Tempest*, before Shakespeare would once again employ magic in a play with a happy ending, and

in that play happiness is achieved as much through giving magic up as it is through using it to other ends. In most Shakespeare comedies, humans are left on their own to effect a happy ending.

If Shakespeare did write the play in 1595, it is a significant advancement in his use of comic material. Although he was writing accomplished comedy before *Midsummer*, with this play he seems to have ceased his dependence on the Roman playwright Plautus. It seamlessly weaves together four different plots into a single fabric and is able to connect them throughout on the level of theme and experience. What is more, unlike earlier plays, including *The Taming of the Shrew*, this play does not depend on a comprehensive source for any of its plotlines. Rather, it mines native and classical traditions and sources to create entirely new plots.

SYNOPSIS
Act I, Scene 1

At the opening of the play, Theseus (the duke of Athens) and Hippolyta (his conquered Amazonian warrior bride) are discussing their forthcoming nuptials. Theseus bemoans the four days separating him from his desires, while Hippolyta reassures him that four days will quickly steep themselves in night. Right after Theseus orders his servant to "stir up the Athenian youth to merriment" (1.1.14), Egeus enters with complaints against his daughter Hermia for defying his command for her to marry Demetrius and against Lysander for having "bewitched" her with all manner of "love tokens" (1.1.27–29). Egeus demands that Hermia comply or face death, the punishment under the law for such disobedience. Hermia boldly defends herself by wishing her father would see with her eyes, and she patiently submits to whatever punishment the duke determines. Theseus tells her that she must either marry Demetrius or become a nun, and he gives her until his wedding day to decide.

Once alone with Hermia, Lysander tries to console her by recounting the vexations all lovers inevitably undergo, and he suggests the two of them elope to an aunt who lives seven leagues from Athens (and therefore outside of Theseus's

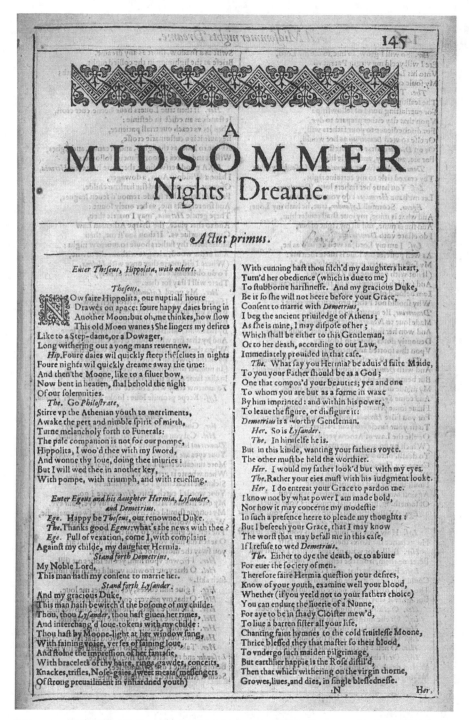

Title page of the First Folio edition of *A Midsummer Night's Dream*, published in 1623

jurisdiction). They agree to meet in the woods on the following evening to escape from Athens.

Demetrius's former love, Helena, appears, bewailing her inability to make Demetrius love her; she asks Hermia to teach her the art of making Demetrius fall in love. Hermia comforts Helena by telling her that her elopement with Lysander will disqualify her as an object of Demetrius's affection. Once alone, Helena considers further the mysterious nature of love, which blindly selects among equals and dignifies undeserving objects. Still, she chooses to tell Demetrius of Hermia and Lysander's plan in order to win whatever scraps of thanks he might throw her way.

Act I, Scene 2

A crew of artisans, including Bottom (a weaver), Flute (a bellows mender), Snout (a tinker), and Starveling (a tailor), meet to learn from Peter Quince (a carpenter and self-styled director) their assigned roles in "The most lamentable comedy and cruel death of Pyramus and Thisbe," an interlude they hope to perform for the wedding of Theseus and Hippolyta. (The story in this play, familiar to the educated portion of the audience, presents two characters, kept apart by parents and able to communicate only through a wall. They agree to elope. But at the meeting place, a lion frightens Thisbe before Pyramus arrives and, with his already bloody maw, soils the handkerchief Thisbe has dropped. When Pyramus arrives, he spots the bloody handkerchief and, believing Thisbe dead, kills himself. Thisbe arrives shortly thereafter and follows her love to the grave.)

Quince assigns the lead male role to Bottom, who accepts the lover's part with relish but then confesses his preference to play the tyrant; he gives a demonstration of his ability to portray "Ercles" (Hercules). As Quince assigns the roles of Thisbe and Lion, Bottom interposes his desire to play each role and boasts of his abilities to do it. Quince discourages Bottom through flattery by claiming that his lion would frighten the ladies so much that they would be executed and that only a sweet-faced and proper "gentleman" like Bottom can play Pyramus.

They decide to hold their rehearsal in the woods a mile from the castle and at night so as to avoid being "dogged with company" and having their "devices known" (1.2.105–106).

Act II, Scene 1

The spritely spirit Puck (or Robin Goodfellow) meets a fairy servant of Titania, the fairy queen, who explains his job of putting dew on flowers. Puck warns the fairy to keep the queen from Oberon (a fairy king figure), who is angry with her for keeping a changeling from him (a changeling is a mortal child stolen by fairies). The fairy correctly identifies his interlocutor as Robin Goodfellow, a "shrewd and knavish sprite" responsible for minor mishaps in the world such as butter failing to churn or beer to form froth (2.1.33). Puck eagerly admits his role and relates more detailed examples of his knavery.

Both spirits scamper as Oberon and Titania enter and fall out, initially not over the boy but over the larger underlying issue of their jealousies of the affections each thinks the other holds for mortals, including Theseus and Hippolyta. Titania then explains how their jealous imaginations have been causing all manner of ills for humans, including flood, famine, disease, and destructively unseasonable weather. Oberon tells Titania that the remedy lies entirely with her willingness to give up the changeling boy. Titania replies with the story of her affectionate relationship with the child's mother, who was a votaress of hers and died during childbirth. Titania's loyalty to the mother makes her loath to part with the boy.

After Titania's brusque departure, Oberon vows to make her suffer for the injury she has given him. He sends Puck to find the juice of a flower, love-in-idleness, which he will apply to her eyes so that when she awakens, she will fall in love with a fierce beast. While Puck is away, Helena enters in pursuit of Demetrius, who spurns her love in the most unmistakable and belittling terms. She, in turn, continues to pursue him, happy to have any kind of attention, even violence and insults. After they depart, Oberon decides to assist Helena. He tells

Puck to anoint the eyes of the disdainful young man, whom, Oberon says, Puck will know by the Athenian garments that he wears.

Act II, Scene 2

The scene opens with Titania calling on her fairies to dance a roundel and sing a fairy song. Titania also sets the fairies to work on their nightly offices, which include killing cankers in rosebuds and making coats for elves. The lullaby sung by the attending fairies chiefly works as a charm to ward off wild beasts (snakes and spiders) and other spells that could harm their queen. After Titania falls asleep, Oberon enters and squeezes the love flower's juice in her eyes in the hope that she will awaken while a wild beast is near.

A fairy (Elizabeth Parkina) sings Titania to sleep in Act II, Scene 2 of *A Midsummer Night's Dream.* This is an illustration of a 1905 production at the Royal Adelphi Theatre. *(Illustration by Charles Mills Sheldon)*

Lost and tired, Lysander enters with Hermia and suggests they stop for the night. Lysander tries to get Hermia to sleep by him, but she gently reproves him for the sake of modesty. Having no luck locating Demetrius, Puck arrives and is pleased to discover a youth in Athenian dress, whom he mistakes for the intended target of his love potion. Puck finds further support for his mistake in the distance between the two lovers, stating that the young woman, "durst not lie / Near this lack-love, this kill-courtesy" (2.2.76–77).

After Puck's departure, Helena comes in pursuit of Demetrius, who continues to scorn her self-abasing advances. Out of breath, Helena is no longer able to chase Demetrius and pauses to bemoan what she perceives as her own monstrosity, which is responsible for driving her love away. Spotting Lysander asleep, Helena awakens him, then must contend with his fervent declarations of love. When Helena expresses disbelief and reminds him of Hermia, Lysander claims his love for Hermia was the result of youthful caprice, and now that he has become an adult, his reason convinces him that Helena is "the worthier maid" (2.2.116). Convinced that Lysander is viciously mocking her, Helena flees. Lysander follows her after renouncing Hermia as a "surfeit" and a "heresy" (2.2.141).

Hermia awakes, frightened by a nightmare in which a serpent ate her heart while Lysander, smiling, looked on. At this point, she discovers Lysander missing and vows to find immediately either him or her death.

Act III, Scene 1

Bottom, Quince, and the other artisans gather to rehearse "Pyramus and Thisbe" in the same grove of hawthorn where Titania slumbers. Bottom worries about two things in the comedy "that will never please" (3.1.10): (1) that Pyramus must draw his sword and kill himself, and (2) that the lion will frighten the ladies in the audience. To address the first problem, Bottom proposes that they write a prologue informing the audience that Pyramus is "not Pryamus but Bottom the weaver" (3.1.21). To alleviate the ladies' fear, he suggests having

Snout identify Snug, the actor playing the lion, by name and having Snug leave his face visible to the audience. Furthermore, he recommends that Snug entreat the ladies not to have fear of him and, in case that is not enough, to "tell them plainly he is Snug the joiner" (3.1.47).

Quince identifies two physical challenges to presenting the play. Given that the two characters meet at night, he wonders how to get moonlight onstage. He also does not know how to get a wall onstage. They decide to have one of them represent moonshine by carrying a bush and lantern, two accoutrements in the classic representation of the man in the moon. They also decide that one of them will "signify wall" by covering himself with plaster and loam and remaining on stage while the lovers meet (3.1.71).

They begin rehearsing, and while Bottom is offstage awaiting his cue, Puck affixes the head of an ass (a donkey) to him. When he enters, only slightly off cue, he sets his fellow artisans in a panic. Believing that he is being made the butt of a joke, Bottom resolves to sing to show them he is not afraid. His rustic song of a cuckoo's call awakens Titania, who calls his song angelic and falls in love with his "shape" and "fair virtue's force" (3.1.142–143). When Bottom tries to leave, Titania uses her power to detain him and calls forth her fairies to bring him favors. The scene ends with Bottom meeting and offering comments on Cobweb, Peaseblossom, Mote, and Mustardseed, the fairies Titania has ordered to serve him.

Act III, Scene 2

Oberon awaits Puck, who, upon arriving, informs his lord that his mistress is in love with a monster. He relates the story of how he stumbled on the "rude mechanicals" rehearsing a play and fixed an "ass's noll" to Bottom's head (3.2.17). Pleased with this turn of events, Oberon then inquires about his plan to make Demetrius fall in love with Helena. As Puck begins to tell him, Demetrius enters pursuing Hermia, who is accusing him of killing Lysander in his sleep because she cannot imagine how her true love would have forsaken her. Demetrius claims that while he would like to give Lysander's carcass to his hounds, he neither killed him nor believes him to be dead. Overcome with fatigue, Demetrius is unable to pursue and falls asleep.

Oberon upbraids Puck for turning a true lover false. Although Puck believes that his mistake is fate, he willingly complies with Oberon's wish that he find Lysander and bring him to reverse the spell. While Oberon anoints Demetrius's eyes so that the correct Athenian youth will love Helena, Puck leads Lysander and Helena to Demetrius. Once there, Puck suggests that they stand aside and watch their "fond pageant" unfold, observing, "Lord, what fools these mortals be" (3.2.114–115). When they arrive, Lysander and Helena are still engaged in the same argument, in which she scorns his love as mockery. Demetrius wakes and falls in love immediately with Helena, but she responds with disbelief, thinking that he is in league with Lysander to mock her.

Following the sound of Lysander's voice, Hermia enters, still ignorant of what could have drawn her true love from her side. Lysander once again professes his love for Helena, who accuses Hermia of being part of their conspiracy to gull her. Once Hermia becomes aware that Lysander's hate for her is sincere, she accuses Helena of having stolen her man's love by trickery. Helena defends herself, but by returning the insult, she sets off a passionate row that nearly ends in violence. In trying to defend Hermia, the men themselves decide to have it out offstage. Helena follows with Hermia close behind.

Annoyed at Puck's negligence, Oberon orders him to thwart their attempts at violence by leading them in confusion, to put them under a sleeping spell, and to crush an antidote into Lysander's eyes so that his love for Hermia will return and love for Helena feel like a dream. Puck observes the need for haste, given that dawn is near, which beckons all ghosts and damned souls back to the grave. Oberon reminds him that they "are spirits of another sort" and may operate by day. Nevertheless, he tells Puck to proceed with haste. By imitating the voices of the two men, he leads them individually back to the same place and makes them fall asleep. Once the ladies follow and themselves fall asleep, Puck provides the remedy to Lysander.

Act IV, Scene 1

Titania lavishes affection on Bottom, who characteristically asks for favors appropriate to his new identity as an ass. After they fall asleep, Oberon releases Titania from the spell because he finds her affection repugnant and pities her and also because in her doting, she agreed to give him the changeling boy. While Bottom continues to sleep, Puck removes his donkey head, allowing him once more to see the world through his "own fool's eyes" (4.1.89). Oberon and Titania depart after having danced by the sleepers (which include the four lovers).

Having observed the rites of May, Theseus and Hippolyta arrive on the scene about to start a hunt, and they discuss the lovely discordant music of his hounds. They almost stumble upon the four lovers. Theseus recalls that this is the day that Hermia was to render her decision, and he awakens them with the sound of his horns. Upon awakening, Lysander explains how Hermia and he planned to elope and escape Athenian law, at which point Egeus interrupts and demands Lysander's death for robbing Demetrius and him of their right of consent. Demetrius replies by recounting the story of how his love for Hermia "melted as the snow" and all his faith is now fixed upon Helena (4.1.163). Theseus overrules Egeus and commands that the lovers be married along with Hippolyta and him. The four lovers are still having trouble distinguishing dream from reality, but they eventually shake off the cobwebs and follow Theseus.

At this point, Bottom awakens, thinking that it is his cue to enter the play he was rehearsing when Puck transformed him. In soliloquy, he tries to take in what has happened to him. He claims that his dream (he never says what it concerned) is "past the wit of man" to understand and would make a fool of any who tried to expound it (4.1.204). He decides to have Peter Quince write a ballad of his dream that he will sing at the play, or perhaps at

the death of Thisbe (we assume; Bottom only says "her" death).

Act IV, Scene 2

Back in Athens, the rude mechanicals worry over the fate of Bottom, who they are sure has been transported to the fairy realm, and over their play, which cannot commence without Pyramus. To their great rejoicing, Bottom appears, and he has information that their play is a finalist for the duke's wedding. He tells them to preserve their sweet breath (by abstaining from onions) so that their comedy will be sweet.

Act V, Scene 1

Having heard the stories of the lovers' plight, Hippolyta and Theseus debate the truthfulness of their claims. Theseus dismisses their tale as the flight of lover's fancy. According to Theseus, lovers are like lunatics and poets in the way that they are ruled by the imagination. Hippolyta argues that the consistency of all four lovers' stories points to something more than mere imagination. Once the other newlyweds arrive, Theseus requests a list of entertainment from the Master of the Revels, named Philostrate. He chooses the rude mechanicals' "A tedious brief scene of young Pyramus and his love Thisbe" over other, less fitting, candidates and over and against the objections of Philostrate. Hippolyta worries about the pain of seeing actors in over their heads, but Theseus instructs her that there is more virtue in appreciating the intention of their labor than in the performance of it.

The mechanicals perform their play in the humorously inept way the play has led the audience to expect. They mispunctuate lines, deliver heavy-handed and clumsy verses, and interrupt themselves. Their newlywed audience responds with lightly derisive commentary throughout. When Pyramus and Thisbe have killed themselves, Bottom offers the audience a choice between a bergomask (a rustic dance) and an epilogue. Theseus prefers the dance, saying the play needs no excuse because the death of the characters pays all debts.

After the dance, Theseus sends all to bed, reminding them that it is "almost fairy time," and announces that their celebrations are to continue for a fortnight (5.1.371). After they depart, Puck enters carrying a broom to offer a charm against natural and supernatural harm and to "sweep the dust behind the door" (5.1.397). Oberon and Titania next perform a dance and song, the latter of which serves as a blessing on the offspring of all the couples to protect them from birth defects. He and the other spirits depart to bless the other chambers of the house.

Left alone, Puck offers the epilogue, speaking as both character and actor and instructing the audience that if they have taken offence at the play, they can improve it by considering the performance a dream. He also promises that if the audience pardons them and restrains from hissing at them, the actors or characters will "mend," in the first place by improving or, in the second, by compensating them with blessings. In the end, he calls for the audience to applaud if they want to be considered his friends, in return for which he will bless them . . . or at least not harm them.

CHARACTER LIST

Theseus   The duke of Athens, who has violently wooed Hippolyta. All three of the play's main story lines involve him. The punishment he proposes to Hermia in her dispute with her father is the cause of her attempt to elope with Lysander. The quarrel between Oberon and Titania in part causes his jealousy over her affection for Theseus. The rude mechanicals rehearse their play in the hope of performing at his nuptial celebration.

Hippolyta   Amazonian warrior who marries Theseus. She typically uses a no-nonsense approach that punctures the absurdities of the Athenians, low and high.

Egeus   Hermia's father, who demands his daughter obey his command that she marry Demetrius instead of Lysander on pain of death. When Demetrius no longer wants to marry Hermia late in the play, there is no indication that Egeus

has changed his mind. His desire for Lysander's death is overruled by Theseus.

Hermia   Bravely defies her father for the love of Lysander, who later forsakes her when Puck mistakenly pours love potion in his eyes so that he falls in love with Helena. Her distress over his rejection provides a number of the play's most comic moments.

Lysander   Hermia's chosen love, who concocts the plan to elope that takes them into the Athens woods where they encounter Puck's accidental mischief. He innocently deserts Hermia in favor of Helena before Puck undoes his mistake.

Demetrius   The husband Egeus has chosen for his daughter, Hermia, but whom she does not love in return. On information from his former love, Helena, he pursues Hermia into the Athenian wood in the hope of stopping her elopement with Lysander. Under the influence of Puck's love potion, he, too, falls in love with Helena, so the object of their rivalry fully switches from Hermia to Helena.

Helena   Demetrius's devoted admirer and Hermia's longtime friend. She willingly betrays her friend in the hope of getting Demetrius's affection. However, once Demetrius and Lysander both fall for her, she is unable to trust them, believing they are in league to humiliate her.

Peter Quince   A carpenter who is directing a crew of less-than-gifted artisans in a production of "The most lamentable comedy and cruel tragedy of Pyramus and Thisbe."

Bottom (Nick Bottom)   A weaver who overestimates his talents and enthusiastically pursues every part in Quince's play. As a punishment or joke, Puck fixes the head of an ass (donkey) to him and puts him in position so that the waking Titania will fall in love with him. Bottom's speech upon waking is one of the most rich and complex moments in the play.

Flute, Snug, Snout, and Starveling   The rest of the "rude mechanicals." Flute plays Thisbe; Snug plays Lion; Snout plays Wall; Starveling plays Moonshine.

Puck (Robin Goodfellow) Fairy servant to Oberon. Although, by folk tradition, Puck is the cause behind all manner of life's mishaps, in the play his mischief is accidental. However, he still exults in the folly of mortals.

Fairy Unnamed servant to Titania, whom Puck warns to stay away from Oberon's revels.

Oberon King of the fairies, who vies with Titania because he is jealous of her affection for Theseus and covetous of a changeling boy in her possession. In retaliation, he puts her under a spell that causes her to fall in love with a transformed Bottom.

Titania Fairy queen, who is jealous of Oberon's affection for Hippolyta and committed to keeping the boy who was given to her by a votaress of her order who died in childbirth.

Peaseblossom, Cobweb, Mote, and Mustardseed Diminutive fairies attending Titania. Their special role is to serve Bottom once their queen falls in love with him.

Philostrate Master of the Revels at Theseus and Hippolyta's wedding celebration. He is disdainful of the mechanicals and their play and attempts to dissuade Theseus from watching it.

CHARACTER STUDIES

As in many Shakespeare's comedies, characters in *A Midsummer Night's Dream* appear to display a degree of simplicity, especially compared to those in Shakespeare's tragedies and histories, where soliloquies indicate characters' internal thoughts and complicated personalities. Still, characters in this play are also complex in their own way: They act in unexpected ways, show knowledge and maturity that belies their otherwise obvious folly, and hint that there might be more to them than meets the eye.

Hippolyta

The Amazonian Queen of Athens speaks only around 23 lines and has no direct influence on any of the plots. In fact, although Theseus promises to marry her "with pomp, with triumph, and with revelry," we have no way of knowing whether she has any choice in marrying the Athenian

duke (who confesses that he "wooed [her] with [his] sword, and won her love doing injuries" [1.1.16–19]). However, having few lines and lacking control over the action have no necessary bearing on the centrality of a character. One need look no further than Gertrude in *Hamlet:* Though she speaks little, she is central to action over which she has little control, and she possesses a degree of inscrutability surpassed only by Hamlet.

Like Gertrude, Hippolyta's few words open up large possibilities, especially in light of the moments where they occur. Her response to Theseus's exaggerated sense of time's delay at the opening of the play is one such moment. In the opening, Theseus is bemoaning how slowly the time is passing that separates this moment from their wedding and the satisfaction of his desires:

> Four happy days bring in
> Another moon; but, oh, methinks, how slow
> This old moon wanes! She lingers my desires,
> Like to a stepdame or a dowager
> Long withering out a young man's revenue.
> (1.1.2–6)

To which Hippolyta's response offers another view of the same moon and time:

> Four Days will quickly steep themselves in
> night
> Four nights will quickly dream away the time;
> And then the moon, like to a silver bow
> New bent in heaven, shall behold the night
> Of our solemnities (1.1.7–11).

In many ways, Hippolyta is being kind, soothing her lord's desire by gently correcting his notion of time. Her no-nonsense approach provides a potent antidote to Theseus's exaggerated sense of time's delay and foreshadows the larger thematic preoccupation the play shows with love's effect on the imagination. In fact, her down-to-earth thinking often distinguishes her from Athenians.

However, while it is probable that Hippolyta is tenderly adjusting Theseus's perception of time, the imaginative effects of desire on perception might affect her to the same degree, if in the opposite way. In other words, Hippolyta may think time is passing more quickly because she is less than keen on the idea of marrying the man who obtained her love by force and injury. It is possible that she might not have been converted to his way of thinking about his love and is less than thrilled with the idea of marrying him. In this case, time's haste might result from her unwillingness to marry her conqueror.

Admittedly, such a reading might seem less than compelling and would certainly dampen the play's comic tone. But the altercation that follows between Egeus and Lysander and Hermia centers on the role of choice in marriage and the consequences of disobedience. Hippolyta's response to this episode is equally telling. Although Shakespeare does not give her lines, he clearly indicates her response. After pronouncing sentence, Theseus turns to her, saying, "What cheer, my love" (1.1.122). Her disapproval might be general distaste for an Athenian custom that subjugates young women to their fathers' will and threatens death for their disagreement, or it may be the depression of having witnessed a scenario of forced marriage that hits too close to home. In the end, reasoning only takes us so far until it degenerates into conjecture. But what we can see is that Shakespeare has created the impression in a few words that there is much more to her than meets the eye.

Hippolyta's mixture of good sense and inscrutability characterizes all of her dialogue. She calls the *Pyramus and Thisbe* the "silliest stuff that I ever heard" (5.1.211). When Theseus tries to lecture her on the nature of plays, which are always silly unless "imagination amend them," Hippolyta replies, "It must be your imagination then, and not theirs" (5.1.213–214). Yet, despite her claim, she seems to be the only one who borders on having a real emotional response to the play-within-the-play. As Pyramus calls on the Furies and Fates to end his life, Hippolyta finds sympathy for him, even against her will: "Beshrew my heart, but I pity the man" (2.2.54). The question of why Hippolyta

moves from ridiculing to having genuine feelings for someone is not easy to answer. But it might have something to do with witnessing a violent ending to a story similar to the real-life one that had upset her earlier.

Lysander/Hermia/Helena/Demetrius

Of the four lovers, no one character is more prominent than the others. However, taken together, the four lovers share enough traits to warrant discussing them as a character in and of themselves. The play itself justifies this collective consideration. In many ways, it takes pains to show how little differentiated each one is from the others. In his defense of his suitability as Hermia's chosen lover, Lysander stresses the similarity between his rival and his self to Egeus: "I am, my lord, as well derived as he, / As well possessed" (1.1.99–100). Helena, too, when struggling to understand the nature of love, asserts a similar identity between herself and Hermia: "How happy some o're other some can be! / Through Athens I am thought as fair as she" (1.1.226–227). In essence, Helena is asking why, all things being equal, Demetrius should prefer Hermia to herself. Given their lack of clear differentiation, it is little wonder, first, that Puck can so easily mistake Lysander for his rival, or, second, that the lovers can change affection so easily. The stock-comedic qualities of these characters also make them easy targets for the love folly the play represents.

However, despite the shallowness suggested by the characters' lack of differentiation, the play still manages to confer complexity upon them. This complexity resides primarily in the difference between their levels of awareness of what love is and the actions they carry out as the subjects of human desire. At the beginning of the play, Hermia passionately offers a mature insight into the nature of her predicament. When confronted with the ultimatum from her father, Hermia tells Theseus, "I would my father looked but with my eyes" (1.1.56). She is also composed in her own willingness to accept whatever punishment may befall her rather than marry against her will:

I know not by what power I am made bold
Nor how it may concern my modesty
In such a presence to plead my thoughts
But I beseech Your Grace that I may know
The worst that may befall me in this case
If I refuse to wed Demetrius (1.1.59–64).

Hermia's resigned stoicism and apparent willingness to "abjure forever the society of men" make her violently passionate response to having lost Lysander more surprising and poignant (1.1.65). Once Hermia grasps the gravity of her situation, she reviles her competitor for Lysander's affection, "How low am I, thou painted maypole? Speak! / How low am I? I am not yet so low / But that my nails can reach unto thine eyes" (3.2).

Lysander shows a similar disparity between his mature thought and irrational action. His speech on the transitory nature of love appears to show stoicism and resignation to their plight. Even in the midst of his pain, he offers himself and Hermia consolation in the general truth that

Puck sends Lysander and Hermia to sleep in Act III, Scene 2 of *A Midsummer Night's Dream.* This illustration was designed for a 1918 edition of Charles and Mary Lamb's *Tales from Shakespeare. (Illustration by Louis Rhead)*

even in the best cases, love is "Swift as a shadow, short as any dream, / Brief as lightning in the collied night" (1.1.144–145). Hermia clearly follows his point when she concludes that they must show "patience." However, Lysander's character appears more complex because of the actions that follow. Lysander, surprisingly, uses love's general frailty as a foundation for arguing that they elope, an action that directly contradicts his ideas that love is brief and that they have little control over it.

Like the others, Helena's complexity grows out of the same distinction between awareness and actions. In fact, Helena's assessment of love as an act of the imagination challenges even Oberon's for accuracy and is even more remarkable because its apparently detached objectivity is offered from someone in the throes of unrequited passion. In her soliloquy in Act I, she recognizes that love by definition improves the quality of the object it beholds: "Things base and vile holding no quantity, love can transpose to form and dignity" (1.1.232–233). Still more remarkable is her ability to apply such an assessment not only to Demetrius's love for Hermia but also to her own love for him. (For a more detailed analysis of this speech, see the section on Key Passages.) Given the detached self-awareness that she shows here, it is even more surprising that in the very same speech, she determines to betray her lifelong friend Hermia for the uncertain scraps of thanks Demetrius might be willing to toss her way: "and for this intelligence, if I have thanks, it is a dear expense" (1.1.248–249). That thanks turns out to be little, indeed. When we see them in the woods, Demetrius contemptuously insults her while she debases herself, urging him, "Use me as your spaniel, spurn me, strike me, / Neglect me lose me" (2.1.205–206). She, like Hermia, has moved from stoic resignation to passionate absorption in her own plight.

Given that the lovers seem unable to apply any love wisdom they might have obtained, it should be of little surprise that at the end of the play, it is doubtful that they have learned anything from their experience. Their collective awakening on the morning after their escapades shows promise of a kind of awe in the presence of the greater power of love's magical transformations. Hermia observes the world with "a parted eye, where everything seems double" (4.1.185–186). Helena seems aware of the precarious possession that we have over those who love us, commenting that Demetrius has been found "like a jewel, [her] own and not [her] own" (4.2.186–187). Yet their criticisms of the play-within-the-play show their inability to grasp their love folly in a more unflattering way. Through their mockery, they show themselves singularly incapable of seeing their own exaggerated passion and foolish behavior when it is reflected before them.

Bottom

Among the most endearing characters in this or any other Shakespearean play is Nick Bottom, who showcases Shakespeare's ability to create a character who is unmistakably foolish but still manages to deserve sympathy and even affection. Whereas the lovers' folly is lessened to some degree by their awareness of it, Bottom is completely unaware of the image he casts. When he first appears, he eagerly volunteers for every part based on his misplaced confidence in his abilities. Yet Bottom never shows that he realizes he cannot be Pyramus, Thisbe, and Lion, all at once. He shows a similar misunderstanding of the nature of theater when he believes that the audience will not understand that Thisbe is not dead unless he tells them so in a prologue or that the ladies in the audience will be frightened out of their wits unless half of the actor's face is visible in Snout's lion costume. Therefore, when Puck translates Bottom into an ass, he merely makes literal what before was powerfully figurative. The difference between Bottom pre- and post-transformation is only in kind, not really in degree.

Although he may be overconfident in his own abilities, Bottom always operates out of a sense of enthusiasm and generosity that makes him as attractive as he is foolish. Thus, the play compensates for the folly to which it subjects him by making him beloved by the queen of the fairies. It also accords him accidental and even real wisdom. When he tells Titania that he sees "little reason" (3.1.146) that she should love him, he adds parenthetically an idea that is key to understanding the folly of others in the play more than his own: "And yet, to say the truth, reason and love keep little company together nowadays" (3.1.146–147). The rustic song with which he awakens Titania shows a similar wisdom. In the song, he acknowledges that all men who hear the song of the cuckoo (which implies that they are cuckolds, or men whose wives have been unfaithful to them) must deny that they have heard it: "The finch, the sparrow, and the lark / The plainsong cuckoo gray, / Whose note fully many a man doth mark, / And dares not answer nay—" (3.1.133–136). Yet, even in the act of wisdom, he performs his folly. His word of denial, *nay*, through which he shows his wisdom doubles as the braying of his ass's noll. In this way, Bottom also dramatizes what was clear in the four Athenian lovers—that no wisdom gained in love is ever of any use.

The play encourages the audience's affection for Bottom by making him the beloved of the queen of the fairies. Such affection makes this the clearest instance of the power of love to "transpose" the "base and vile" into "form and dignity." Yet the specific form of his translation makes us doubt whether love has the power to transform at all. In the same way that his change into the ass-headed beast simply recreates a more intensified form of what he already is, Bottom's good fortune seems to have little effect on his character. Blessed with Titania's love and with infinite possibilities attending him, Bottom can think of no greater wants than oats for food, the rustic "tongs and bones" for music, and a good face-scratch for pleasure. At no point while with Titania does he ever seem to grasp the magnitude of his being loved by the fairy queen. In essence, though he is loved by Titania, he is stubbornly an ass. At the same time, the humble nature of his requests is as redeeming as it is unflattering. One could hardly imagine Bottom lording his power over Titania in the same way that Demetrius does Helena when he tells her,

You do impeach your modesty too much
To leave the city and commit yourself
Into the hands of one who loves you not,
To trust the opportunity of night
And the ill counsel of a desert place
With the rich worth of your virginity.

(2.1.214–219)

Titania's behavior is also a fitting reminder that for every one ennobled by love, there are scores for whom love amplifies folly.

Bottom's ambiguous status as a sympathetic fool follows him until the end of the play. When he awakens from the spell and is returned to his old foolish self, his speech on "Bottom's dream" is at once both deep (bottomless) and foolish. (For an extended treatment of this speech, see the discussion in the section on Key Passages). And in his foolish rendition of Pyramus, one has to wonder whether it is something close to pathos in his character that prompts Hippolyta to pity him against her will: "Beshrew my heart, but I pity the man" (5.2.295).

Theseus

Some of Shakespeare's audience would have known Theseus from his frequent appearances in classical mythology. Those who recognized him from Plutarch, either in Thomas North's translation or in the original Latin, would have been familiar with how the heroism of his youth eventually degenerated into a string of sexual betrayals. Plutarch's portrait of him mainly recounts his numerous sexual exploits in which he was abandoning one love or trying to acquire another by force. Oberon alludes to Theseus's reputation as a blackguard when he accuses Titania of having helped him escape from Ariadne. Hippolyta has been both a military and sexual conquest. Some viewers might also have been aware of the tragedy of his and Hippolyta's son, Hippolytus, whom Theseus's second wife, Phaedra, betrayed by making her husband believe that she had been raped by her stepson. Such knowledge would have added an ironic touch to Oberon's blessing that the offspring of the newly married couples "ever shall be fortunate" (5.1.413).

However, in the play, this reputation either is background or is quickly moving into it, as Theseus's fidelity to Hippolyta suggests. The primary role that he plays is reformed lover and Athenian governor, not sexual predator. How the play is characterizing him as a governor is a bit of an enigma. In the opening, he shows a commitment to Athenian law over the desires of the young lovers. The only criticism the play offers of his position is Hippolyta's silence.

In the latter parts of the play, Theseus's complexity emerges more fully. He notably stands out for his ultrarational disbelief of the lovers' story of their adventures in the woods outside Athens. In his speech to Hippolyta, he equates lovers with lunatics and poets inasmuch as all of them confuse imagination and reality. On one level, the play fully supports this rational view of love as a function of the frenzied imagination; Helena specifically backs him up on this point. However, on another level, the play completely contradicts his view. The lovers have not been imagining things, even if their reality has been turned into a dream. Hippolyta's choices of the words *strange and admirable* more closely match the nature of what has occurred. Their experience is something that seems incredible but cannot merely be dismissed as fancy.

Puck (Robin Goodfellow)

Any character sketch of the figure must include both names because they point to different sides of his personality. Puck is the devilish trickster that he describes himself as being to the anonymous fairy before the quarrel between Oberon and Titania. But Robin Goodfellow was also a helpful fairy who would assist with housework by night. His sweeping the dust at the end of the play shows this side of his identity in action. Both sides of the Robin Goodfellow/Puck division are dramatized in *Midsummer*. Puck is the lover of mischief who causes harm when he administers the love juice to the wrong Athenian youth. Yet it must be remembered that, at least under Oberon's rule, Puck has been trying to restore order. Still, he exults in his mistake and the consequences

James Lewis as Bottom in a late 19th-century production of *A Midsummer Night's Dream* (Photographed by Napoleon Sarony)

that follow, asking Oberon, "Shall we their fond pageant see / Lord, what fools these mortals be" (3.2.114–115). His insult is particularly unjust because he seems to have forgotten that the folly of the "fond pageant" is in part his own creation. Puck's epilogue also brings out these contrary impulses in his personality because it offers friendship but reminds the audience of his potential to be a trickster.

DIFFICULTIES OF THE PLAY

On a surface level, *A Midsummer Night's Dream* offers fewer difficulties than most of Shakespeare's plays. The language is accessible, and even though there is a large number of characters, they are organized into four distinct groups, so they are easy to keep in order. The most challenging parts of the play are the analytical difficulties it puts forth. These difficulties largely concern two qualities: character and atmosphere. How is the audience to take, for example, Theseus as a lover and ruler in the opening scenes or as a commentator on love, the imagination, theater, and lunacy later in the play? He certainly rules with a sense of fairness; his interpretation of the law is more liberal than that of Egeus. But the play does not unequivocally display his heroism or rectitude. Hippolyta's sullen silence suggests she dissents from his ruling. The same question might be asked of Oberon and his affairs with his consort. He acts as if he is entitled to the changeling boy currently with Titania. But do our sympathies lie with him or with Titania?

The fairies, especially Puck, are also at the center of these problems. They involve themselves on an intimate level with the affairs of mortals and, for the most part, are genially disposed toward them. But they operate with a pronounced contempt for the mortal characters even as they are pushing them toward harmony.

Another longstanding difficulty is whether characters have undergone a real transformation. The play certainly opens up the possibility of transformation. When the four lovers awaken from their night in the Athenian forest, their affections have been thoroughly scrambled but have emerged back in a more desirable order. Theseus likewise seems to recognize the irresistible power of love and willingly subjugates Athenian law to a larger sense of justice. Bottom, too, has seemingly undergone a life-changing experience that put him frighteningly close to the fairy world but has returned him unscathed.

However, the play seems to cast doubt on the validity of the transformations it presents. If the lovers' transformation has enlightened them, they show no sign of it having done so. Before their sojourn into the woods, the four lovers operate with a certain sense of self-possession, of surety in themselves. Even the scorned Helena was sure of her own beauty and of Demetrius's error in loving Hermia. Their mocking contempt for the rude mechanicals' play suggests that their narrow escape from misfortune has not taught them pity or humility. They do not recognize that the fates of Pyramus and Thisbe could have been their own. As for Theseus, although his forgiveness of the lovers shows that he respects a higher form of justice, he dismisses the story of its effects that the lovers relate. Of all the candidates for transformation, Bottom is the only one who undergoes it and does so in the most literal of senses. He is also given the most to say about his experience and what it means. Yet Bottom is perhaps the least convincing in his transformed act. He is no more convincing as Pyramus than he is at making people think he has undergone real change. Any transformation, whether theatrical or real, seems just a truer form of the self he already is.

KEY PASSAGES
Act I, Scene 1, 128–149

LYSANDER. How now, my love, why is your
  cheek so pale?
How chance the roses there do fade so fast?

HERMIA. Belike for want of rain, which I
  could well
Beteem them from the tempest of my eyes.

LYSANDER. Ay me! For aught that I could
  ever read,
Could ever hear by tale or history,
The course of true love never did run smooth;
But either it was different in blood—

HERMIA. Oh, cross! Too high to be
  enthralled to low.

LYSANDER. Or else misgrafted in respect of
  years—

HERMIA. Oh, spite! Too old to be engaged
  to young.

LYSANDER. Or else it stood upon the choice
  of friends—

HERMIA. Oh, hell, to choose love by
  another's eyes!

LYSANDER. Or if there were a sympathy in
  choice,
War, death or sickness did lay siege to it,
Making it momentary as a sound,
Swift as a shadow, short as any dream,
Brief as lightning in the collied night
That in a spleen unfolds both heaven and
  earth.
And ere a man hath power to say "Behold!"
The jaws of darkness do devour it up.
So quick bright things come to confusion.

This exchange takes place right after the trial scene in which Theseus has given Hermia until his nuptials with Hippolyta to decide whether she will comply with her father's wish that she marry Demetrius or "abjure forever the society of men." Here Lysander is attempting to console her by appealing to the general failure and transient nature of love. The failure holds true whether there is sympathy in love or not. If the affection between the two is mutual, a number of external pressures still make it "brief as lightning in the collied night." Hermia, by contrast, is more agitated in her antiphonal responses, specifically when Lysander reminds her of a situation like theirs where marriage depends "upon the choice of friends"—a state she has compared to "hell." However, as soon as Hermia resigns herself to let their "destiny" teach them "patience," Lysander reveals that he has been playing with a stacked deck. All along, he has planned to elope and have their marriage subsidized by his rich aunt who lives outside Theseus's jurisdiction. Lysander shows that his experience of love is no more rational and dignified than Hermia's or anyone else's when problems with love occur for which he does not have a backup plan. When he suddenly falls for Helena, Lysander abandons any pretense to the kind of stoicism he professes here and is ready to fight Demetrius to the death for her sake.

Act I, Scene 1, 226–245

HELENA. How happy some o'erother some
  can be!
Through Athens I am thought as fair as she.
But what of that? Demetrius thinks not so;
He will not know what all but he doth know.
And as he errs, doting on Hermia's eyes,
So I, admiring of his qualities.
Things base and vile holding no quantity,
Love can transpose to form and dignity.
Love looks not with the eyes but with the
  mind,
And therefore is winged Cupid painted blind.
Nor hath Love's mind of any judgment taste;
Wings and no eyes figure unheedy haste.
And therefore is Love said to be a child,
Because in choice he is so oft beguiled.
As waggish boys in game themselves forswear,
So the boy Love is perjured everywhere.
For, ere Demetrius look'd on Hermia's eyne,
He hail'd down oaths that he was only mine;
And when this hail some heat from Hermia felt,
So he dissolv'd and show'rs of oaths did melt.

Helena offers these observations in a soliloquy at the end of the scene. They bring the issues that have underscored the action to this point into focus in a more explicit sense, namely the mysterious nature of desire and the role of the imagination in it. Helena begins by linking Demetruis's preference for Hermia over her with the inexplicable nature of desire, wondering how he can prefer the other given that their beauty is equal. Her point is essentially the same as the one Lysander makes to Egeus about his preference for Demetrius as a suitor to his daughter: "I am my lord as well deriv'd as he, / As well possess'd." Helena's observation about their comparative states already contains her analysis. This analysis resides in the term she chooses as a point of comparison, the word *happy.* As it does now, the word then could mean a state of contentment, but the stronger connotation in

Shakespeare's day was that of being "fortunate" or having been randomly selected by chance. In other words, Helena is arguing that happiness in love is mere chance.

Her follow-up observation is equally interesting for its word choice, given what she has said about the arbitrary nature of desire. According to Helena, the problem with Demetrius is that he does not "know" what everyone except him knows. Helena progresses from the word *thought,* which more accurately matches the nature of perception to *know.* However, the distinction between belief and knowledge inherent in the shift is appropriate for the nature of love that Helena is analyzing, for while love may indeed be an act of perception, it is experienced with all the force of knowledge.

This contrary nature of love is more pronounced in the next point Helena makes. She concludes that Demetrius "errs" when he prefers Hermia, but this conclusion here forces her to acknowledge that she herself errs when she admires "his qualities." In other words, to enter into love is to enter into a perpetual state of error in which one overestimates the value of the object of affection. Thus, Helena says, "Things base and vile, holding no quality, / Love can transpose to form and dignity." The play will later dramatize both her point and the logical limit of love's capacity to improve its object when Titania, the queen of the fairies, dotes on Bottom, who has been "translated" from a bungling weaver into an ass. The question of love's transformational capacity is one of the play's central questions.

Helena concludes that the motivating force behind love's power to transform is the imagination. "Love," she claims, "looks not with the eye but with the mind." Helena clearly does not intend *mind* to mean reason; rather, she is talking about the mind's eye. The process she has described throughout suggests that love has neither "taste" nor "judgment." Love is never based on an accurate measure of object and perception. And this lack of judgment or taste is what allows the mind's eye of imagination to shift from Helena to Hermia.

Helena's analysis of love ends with a further thought about the conventional representation of

Cupid as a blind boy. Cupid is blind, inasmuch as he misjudges, and he is waggish, inasmuch as all boys perjure themselves as a joke.

Act II, Scene 1, 122–138

TITANIA. Set your heart at rest.
The fairy land buys not the child of me.
His mother was a vot'ress of my order;
And in the spiced Indian air, by night,
Full often hath she gossip'd by my side,
And sat with me on Neptune's yellow sands,
Marking th'embarked traders on the flood;
When we have laughed to see the sails conceive
And grow big-bellied with the wanton wind;

Titania in *A Midsummer Night's Dream*. This is a print from Charles Heath's 1848 edition of *The Heroines of Shakspeare: Comprising the Principal Female Characters in the Plays of the Great Poet. (Painting by K. Meadows; engraving by B. Eyles)*

Which she, with pretty and with swimming gait
Following (her womb then rich with my young
   squire)
Would imitate, and sail upon the land
To fetch me trifles, and return again,
As from a voyage, rich with merchandise.
But she, being mortal, of that boy did die,
And for her sake do I rear up her boy;
And for her sake I will not part with him.

In this exceptionally lyrical passage, Titania defends her decision to keep the changeling boy by citing the relationship she had with the boy's mother. This amicable relationship between divinity and mortal stands in marked contrast to the discord she has just reported between these two types of beings that has resulted from her argument with Oberon. The love between the two also offers an idealized portrait of female friendship. Helena appeals to a similar amicability in an equally lyrical passage:

We, Hermia, like two artificial gods,
Have with our needles created both one flower,
Both on one sampler, sitting on one cushion,
Both warbling of one song, both in one key,
As if our hands, out sides, voices and minds
Had been incorporate.

(3.2)

While this passage offers an equally beautiful portrayal of human harmony, Helena is delivering it at a moment of pronounced discord between her and her former friend. The relationship between mortals and supernatural creatures is also under constant strain. Although the passage depicts a harmonious relationship between natural and supernatural, it also underscores the disparity between the two in the death of the votaress. This fate points to a more realistic version of the physical dangers that love presents.

Act IV, Scene 1, 203–222

BOTTOM. When my cue comes, call me, and I will answer. My next is "Most fair Pyramus."

Heigh-ho! Peter Quince! . . . I have had a most rare vision. I have had a dream, past the wit of man to say what dream it was. Man is but an ass if he go about to expound this dream. Methought I was—there is no man can tell what. Methought I was—and methought I had—but man is but a patched fool if he will offer to say what methought I had. The eye of man hath not heard, the ear of man hath not seen, man's hand is not able to taste, his tongue to conceive, nor his heart to report what my dream was. I will get Peter Quince to write a ballad of this dream. It shall be called "Bottom's dream," because it hath no bottom; and I will sing it in the latter end of a play, before the Duke. Peradventure, to make it more gracious, I shall sing it at her death.

Bottom speaks this soliloquy after Puck and Oberon return him and Titania to their previous states. As Oberon has ordained, Bottom's experience has been rendered a dream, and the whole speech appears to be Bottom's clumsy attempt to plumb the depths (the "bottom") of his experience. In the speech, Bottom appears at the point of apprehending what has occurred with Titania. But every time he approaches awareness, he suddenly breaks off and comments on the impossibility of drawing conclusions. His garbled version of St. Paul's "No eye hath seen" (1 Cor. 2:9) both emphasizes the magnitude of his experience and shows his inability to comprehend it.

In a way, Bottom's posttransformation state resembles his pretransformation one. From the beginning of the play, Bottom has been characterized by an utter incognizance of his stupidity. He never reveals to the audience whether he has actually learned something new and, if so, what kind of knowledge he has gained. Instead, he procrastinates on revealing his experience, saying only that he will translate the dream into a ballad—into art. This dream, he claims, will describe not just the dream but also the problem of understanding the dream because, as he says, "Bottom's dream . . . hath no bottom" (4.2). What exactly this dream translated into art looks like is never revealed to us directly because "Bottom's dream" is never sung. But, in essence, the song of the fairy love and metamorphosis and its confusion is being sung to the audience all along. But instead of appearing under "Bottom's dream," it appears under the more familiar title of *A Midsummer Night's Dream*, which, like the rude mechanical's dream, has no bottom.

Bottom's soliloquy involves the audience in a more direct way by recreating the same struggle to establish reality and orient itself that Bottom himself is having. It does this through the unfinished statements that the audience is asked to complete. Struggling to apprehend the supernatural experience that recedes even as he tries to grab hold of it, Bottom claims, "Methought I was—and methought I had." Although the passage tempts readers into completing the idea, they may not do so without falling into the trap that Bottom is inadvertently creating. He stipulates that "man is but a patched fool if he will offer to say what methought I had." The question that Bottom does not answer is whether what he thought he had was an ass's head or the love of Titania. No matter which the audience picks, the act of picking itself turns the audience into patched fools. As for Bottom, the more closely the audience examines the speech, the less certain it is of sense and certainty. Thus, the speech recreates the experience of the fairy world for the audience, who are likewise put in touch with knowledge from which it is held at a distance.

Act V, Scene 1, 1–22

HIPPOLYTA. 'Tis strange, my Theseus, that these lovers speak of.

THESEUS. More strange than true. I never
  may believe
These antique fables, nor these fairy toys.
Lovers and madmen have such seething brains,
Such shaping fantasies, that apprehend
More than cool reason ever comprehends.
The lunatic, the lover, and the poet
Are of imagination all compact:

One sees more devils than vast hell can hold;
That is the madman: the lover, all as frantic,
Sees Helen's beauty in a brow of Egypt:
The poet's eye, in a fine frenzy rolling,
Doth glance from heaven to earth, from earth
   to heaven;
And as imagination bodies forth
The forms of things unknown, the poet's pen
Turns them to shapes, and gives to airy
   nothing
A local habitation and a name.
Such tricks hath strong imagination,
That if it would but apprehend some joy,
It comprehends some bringer of that joy:
Or, in the night, imagining some fear,
How easy is a bush suppos'd a bear!

Theseus offers this extensive explanation of why
he cannot believe the stories of the lovers' transformation in the Athenian woods. Here he claims
that lovers' old stories ("antique fables") and talk
of fairy tricks ("fairy toys") are the product of an
overexcited imagination ("seething brain") that likens them first to madmen and then to poets. Like
Helena earlier in the play, Theseus acknowledges
that the lover dignifies the object of his affection,
here by imputing more beauty than the object
deserves: "[T]he lover . . . sees Helen's beauty in
a brow of Egypt" (i.e., dark eyebrows). The poet's
imagination, in a similar vein, looks from heaven to
earth and creates something out of nothing. The
general function of the imagination is to impute a
personified origin ("a bringer of that joy") to powerful human feelings—fear or joy.

In this way, Theseus is cataloging the cognitive processes characters have been carrying out all
along, and the play has been inciting its audience
to carry them out as well. In fact, Theseus's speech
consolidates thematic elements that have been
occurring separately throughout the play. What
characterizes all their brains is the tendency for the
imagination to confer a real existence on something
that is not otherwise there. Theseus first suggests
this overt distinction more subtly in his choice of
verbs, where he moves from reason that compre-

hends to fantasies that apprehend. The verbs *apprehend* and *comprehend* are nearly synonymous, both
having to do with the way the mind understands
the world. However, *apprehend*, as it does today,
carries with it a greater level of emotional engagement and mental creativity than *comprehend*.

In typical fashion, the play both supports and
denies Theseus's claim. On one level, such a demys-
tifying view of love provides a fitting rebuttal to
Egeus's overimaginative view of Lysander and Hermia at the play's beginning, but on another, the
play directly contradicts his ungenerous assessment of love. Hippolyta's follow-up seems to more
closely capture the issue of love's origins and transforming power as they are represented in the play.
Love is, in the end, more than "fancy's images."
The better words for them she provides are *strange
and admirable*.

Act V, Scene 1, 430–445

PUCK [as epilogue]. If we shadows have
   offended,
Think but this and all is mended,
That you have but slumber'd here
While these visions did appear.
And this weak and idle theme,
No more yielding but a dream,
Gentles do no reprehend:
If you pardon, we will mend.
And, as I am an honest Puck,
If we have unearned luck
Now to scape the serpent's tongue,
We will make amends ere long;
Else the Puck a liar call.
So, goodnight unto you all.
Give me your hands, if we be friends,
And Robin shall restore amends.

Puck's epilogue is typical of the form in that a
personage (usually a central character) from the play
addresses the audience directly while still in character or in the nebulous space in-between actor and
character. As in Quince's prologue to "Pyramus and
Thisbe," the purpose of the epilogue is to apologize for shortcomings and elicit a favorable response

from the audience. Puck's apology is significant because it does address issues not only of the play's quality but also of its substance. The fear is that that the "shadows" might have "offended" the audience. In Shakespeare's day, *offend* was a wide-sweeping verb that meant "to come up short" or "transgress" and could be applied to a number of different kinds of failings—moral, religious, and professional. The conventions of the epilogue suggest the latter of these. Puck, however, might be referring to the very existence of himself and his ilk as the source of offense. Puritans opposed beliefs in fairies as immoral, and it is easy to imagine that their very presence on stage might have been a source of moral offense. Still, it is not completely clear who has done the offending. Puck's reference to himself and his crew as "shadows" initially suggests that he is talking about the spirits of the night. The word *shadow* is a near-synonym for fairies and other specters who tread the night's forests. Puck employs the term in this way when he refers to Oberon as "King of shadows" (3.3). However, once again, the conventions urge the audience to think more generally of shadows as other characters in the play or perhaps the actors who animate them. The play more directly draws this parallel between the fairies and actors during the play-within-the-play, when Theseus tells Hippolyta "the best [of plays] are but shadows." The ambiguity here is telling, given the dual nature of the theatrical event. Characters have an existence like a specter inasmuch as they exist for a short time and disappear out of mortal sight.

Puck's advice to consider what one has seen to be a dream reflects the play's thematic preoccupation. This ability to convert reality into a dream is the special function of the fairies. Oberon and Puck produce such a conversion for the four lovers and for Bottom. Once her enchantment for Bottom has been broken, Titania observes, "My Oberon! What visions have I seen! Methought I was enamored of an ass" (4.1). One thing the play has asked the audience to call into question is just how persuasive a dream happens to be. In the play, what is understood to be a dream turns out to have had a significant influence on reality.

Puck holds the flowers whose juice will force Titania to fall in love with a beast in Act II, Scene I of *A Midsummer Night's Dream*. This is a print from the Boydell Shakespeare Gallery project, which was conceived in 1786 and lasted until 1805. *(Painting by Joshua Reynolds; engraving by Luigi Schiavonetti)*

The sincerity of Puck's apology is also ambiguous. On one level, Puck's speech shows the deference for and dependence on the audience that is expected in an epilogue. He refers to them as "gentles" and begs the unearned luck in escaping the "serpent's tongue," which refers to the hiss of the audience, a sign of disapproval, like a "boo" today. However, the folk traditions from which Shakespeare borrowed give this line an additional, and more literal, dimension that aggravates their vulnerability. As has been clear throughout the play, the fairies in it are all of an extraordinarily diminutive size, to which an actual serpent's tongue could pose a real threat. The fairies' lullaby to Titania contains a charm against just such a danger: "You spotted snakes with double-tongue, / Thorny-hedgehogs, be not seen; Newts and blind worms do no wrong, / Come not near our fairy-queen" (3.1).

Although Puck represents himself and his crew as vulnerable, his posture is not entirely repentant. He stakes his promise to "mend" in exchange for "pardon" on his honesty: "And as I am an honest Puck;" "Else the Puck a liar call." Although Puck does nothing to forfeit this respect, his very nature and reputation as a trickster should cast doubt on such promises. In other words, he may be an honest Puck, but Pucks are not known for honesty. His request for the audience's applause is similarly equivocal. The way he requests applause plays on the phrase to request a handshake in token of friendship, greeting, or bargain: "Give me your hands if we be friends." Such a request harkens back to the pact he suggested before—"If you pardon, we shall mend"—a contract he reiterates here: "And Robin shall restore amends." Puck's offer, though implied, has a darker corollary, for one must consider what might result if they do not applaud—if they are not Puck's friends. In Shakespeare's day, those in the audience who were familiar with fairy lore would have known the potentially terrible end awaiting those who were not friends of the fairies or Robin Goodfellow.

DIFFICULT PASSAGES
Act III, Scene 2, 378–395

PUCK. My fairy lord, this must be done with
     haste,
For night's swift dragons cut the clouds full
     fast,
And yonder shines Aurora's harbinger,
At whose approach ghosts, wand'ring here and
     there,
Troop home to churchyards. Damned spirits
     all,
That in crossways and floods have burial,
Already to their wormy beds are gone.
For fear lest day should look their shames upon,
They willfully themselves exile from light
And must for aye consort with black-browed
     night.

OBERON. But we are spirits of another sort.
I with the Morning's love have oft made sport,
And, like a forester, the groves may tread
Even till the eastern gate all fiery red,
Opening on Neptune with fair blessed beams,
Turns into yellow gold his salt green streams.
But not withstanding, haste, make no delay.
We may effect this business yet ere day.

This exchange occurs after Puck and Oberon have witnessed the scene of chaos among the four Athenian lovers and have devised the means to restore order. It is one of several instances in the play wherein characters speak in lyrical passages that are supplementary to the main action. Here, Puck is explaining at some length his need to hasten the resolution before dawn appears. For Puck, the end of night marks the return of ghosts and other "damned spirits" who are "exiles from light" to their "wormy beds." Although Oberon distinguishes the two of them as "spirits of another sort," this clarification occurs only after the audience has entertained the possibility (if not the likelihood) that the two of them are damned spirits. Although this supplement may not add to the action, it certainly addresses important issues that have been at the heart of the play, namely the relationship between the natural and supernatural realms that is the source of the lovers' confusion and eventual happiness. The contrary roles the fairies play in human happiness add to this ambiguity. Shakespeare's audience would have known of the evil possibilities the fairies present. In the folklore of Shakespeare's day, fairies were certainly part of the fears of the night, although they often were credited with good deeds as well.

The contrast between the spirits of light and darkness heralds the end of night and the end of confusion. Although fairies have the potential to cause both harm and good to mortals, here the act is decidedly favorable. It is worth noting, however, that the good the fairies pursue not only causes and aggravates chaos, but also that Puck resolves the issues by pursuing the chaos to its utmost degree. Mimicking the taunts that Lysander and Demetrius make to each other, he leads both of them into the wood and darkness, even as a means of clarification.

Act III, Scene 1, 128–138

BOTTOM. The ousel cock, so black of hue,
With orange-tawny bill
The throstle with his note so true,
The wren with little quill

TITANIA. What angel wakes me from my
flowery bed?

BOTTOM. The finch the sparrow, and the
lark,
The plain-song cuckoo gray,
Whose note full many a man doth mark,
And dares not answer nay.
For indeed, who would set his wit to so foolish
a bird?
Who would give the bird the lie, though he cry
"cuckoo" never so.

After Puck has transformed him into an ass, Bottom accidently awakens Titania with this charmingly rustic song. Although easily overlooked, the song encapsulates the dual nature of Bottom, who always displays his asslike nature, even when he utters wisdom. This apparently innocent list of birds culminates in a familiar and tired joke about the cuckold, which is the name given to men whose wives are unfaithful to them. His point is that although many will hear the song of the cuckoo, which identifies them as cuckolds, all who hear must by necessity deny their cuckold status. Whatever degree of wisdom such an observation holds, the better joke is on as much as through Bottom, who ends the song by emitting a sound that befits his new role. Although "nay" is more properly the whinny of a horse, it also suggests an ass's braying. The point of his joke is that those who deny their status as cuckolds reveal their nature as fools. Ironically, the figure who gets caught up in this trap is Oberon, whose desire to have his consort Titania fall in love with "some vile thing" threatens

Titania (Roxy Barton) falls in love with Bottom (Oscar Asche) in Act III, Scene 1 of *A Midsummer Night's Dream*. This is an illustration of a 1905 production at the Royal Adelphi Theatre. *(Illustration by A. M. Faulkner)*

to make him a cuckold. Oberon discovers that he is jealous of the punishment he inflicts upon her:

Her dotage now do I begin to pity;
For, meeting her of late behind the wood,
Seeking sweet favors for this hateful fool,
I did upbraid her and fall out with her:
For she his hairy temples then had rounded,
With coronet of fresh and fragrant flowers.

(4.1)

Although Oberon claims that he is undoing the spell out of pity for Titania, the details of the disdain he feels for her case suggest jealousy as much as pity. It is difficult to tell whether what bothers him most is the indignity of her situation or the affection she lavishes on someone other than him.

Act V, Scene 1, 108–117

PETER QUINCE [as prologue to "Pyramus and Thisbe"].
If we offend, it is with our good will.
That you should think, we come not to offend,
But with good will. To show our simple skill,
That is the true beginning of our end.
Consider then, we come but in despite.
We do not come, as minding to content you,
Our true intent is. All for your delight,
We are not here. That you should here repent
  you,
The actors are at hand; and by their show,
You shall know all that you are like to know.

Peter Quince speaks this passage as the prologue to "Pyramus and Thisbe." By convention, prologues apologize for the show the actors perform and attempt to propitiate the audience. Although Peter Quince's heart might be in the right place, his punctuation is not. In fact, the punctuation is so out of place that it creates the opposite message from the one it intended. Quince consciously offends and does so deliberately. Below is a conjectural revision of the punctuation so that the passage comes closer to making sense.

If we offend, it is with our good will
That you should think we come not to offend
But with good will to show our simple skill.
That is the true beginning of our end.
Consider then, we come. But in despite
We do not come. As, minding to content you,
Our true intent is all for your delight.
We are not here that you should here repent
  you.
The actors are at hand; and by their show,
You shall know all that you are like to know.

Although the insult in Quince's speech is comical, there is something about the overt affront to the audience that seem appropriate to Shakespeare's comedy in general, which often implicates the audience in the folly it depicts, and particularly to the moment at hand, in which a drama is being performed before an audience that does not appreciate the irony of the situation it is in. In Quince's lamentable comedy, a dignified act of love has been rendered ridiculous. But to a large extent, this situation mirrors that of the larger theatrical audience of *Midsummer,* which has witnessed a serious matter turned in a comic direction. By the same token, the play's lovers have played out their affairs with no more dignity and éclat than the mechanicals have theirs and seem equally oblivious to their folly.

CRITICAL INTRODUCTION TO THE PLAY

The famous critic Maynard Mack once cannily observed, "*A Midsummmer Night's Dream* has qualities that prompt one to regard it as a loving and perhaps even fully conscious study of what the imagination can and cannot do" (278). The functions of the imagination turn out to be central to understanding the key issues in the play—namely, love, theater, and the possibility of transformation in both. *Midsummer* explicitly links both love and theater to the imagination in Theseus's speech on the "lunatic, lover, and the poet" (5.1), but it so strongly relates the two throughout the play that this thematic link really does not need his clarification. To grasp the play more fully, we might add to Mack's language of ability the language of necessity. While the play is about what the imagination *can* and *cannot* do, it is also about what the imagination *must* do. *Midsummer* repeatedly shows the functional necessity of the imagination in life and, especially, in theater. Without the imagination, love could not exist; neither could theater. Yet, at the same time, the play makes this necessity complex by making the very quality without which love and theater could not exist the source of problems in it. So while *Midsummer* is "loving" in the way it explores the imagination, it is in equal parts reverent and scornful in the way it represents something we cannot avoid as foolish.

The very title of the play is an invitation to imagine. Although the play may be about a midsummer night's "dream," as opposed to "imagination," a dream is the sleeping complement to the wakeful state of the imagination. The nearness of these two states emerges clearly in 5.1, when Theseus easily transforms the "dream and fruitless vision" into which Oberon renders the lovers experience into the product of the imagination. The question that emerges from the title is whether the dream in the play more properly belongs to the mortal characters, who perforce translate their encounters with the supernatural into a dream; or to the audience, who, by witnessing a play, view something like a dream, a vision over which they have no control and over which they must exercise a dreamlike faculty of the imagination in order to experience it at all. The function of the imagination is all the more pronounced given that the audience is witnessing this nighttime spectacle in the day.

The term *midsummer* only intensifies the workings of the imagination. Proverbially, midsummer refers to a time when the moon's effect on human behavior was at its peak. By the same token, the title is an invitation to dismiss the play as mere imagination. Not only is the play, as Puck says, "no more yielding but a dream" (5.1), it also is a dream of a particular kind, one formed in midsummer, under the influence of "lunacy." Therefore, the title covers both its content and the contradictory attitudes the audience might have toward that content.

"Imagination" as a way of understanding the play works so well because it befits the mysterious nature of love that is central to it. At many points in *Midsummer,* the characters' actions raise perplexing questions about the nature of love: "What is love?" "Where does it come from?" "What can be done about it?" The court scene at the play's opening shows characters trying to deal with these questions and mysteries. When his daughter, Hermia, prefers Lysander over Demetrius, the man he insists she marry, Egeus attributes her stubborn preference and disobedience to quasi- if not full-blown magic. He accuses Lysander of having "bewitch'd the bosom of [his] child." Yet, when he lists the more specific forms of Lysander's magic, the extraordinary means he has supposedly used suddenly sound much more pedestrian:

> Thou, thou, Lysander, thou hast given her
> *rhymes,*
> And interchang'd *love-tokens* with my child:
> Thou hast by moonlight at her window sung
> With feigning voice *verses of feigning love,*
> And stol'n the impression of her fantasy
> With *bracelets of thy hair, rings, gauds, conceits,*
> *Knacks, trifles, nosegays, sweetmeats*
> (messengers
> Of strong prevailment in unharden'd youth);
> With cunning hast thou filched my daughter's
> heart.
>
> (1.1; italic added)

In the abstract, rhymes, love tokens, songs, hair, rings, gauds, conceits, knacks, trifles, sweetmeats, and so on are less-than-compelling evidence of witchcraft. In fact, some of the charms that Egeus lists work against his argument by their pronounced lack of value, in particular gauds and trifles. The audience is here being asked to react to Egeus's accusation with the same skepticism that Othello displays to his onstage audience when Desdemona's father believes that the only way his fair Venetian daughter could have fallen in love with a swarthy African moor is if he bewitched her. In his own defense, Othello sarcastically points to the story of the "dangers [he] had passed" as evidence for the "drugs," "charms," "conjurations," and "mighty magic" (*Othello* 1.3) that he supposedly used to beguile Desdemona. As with Othello, such items as Egeus mentions could only have such an effect if they indeed are enchanted.

To a certain extent, Egeus anticipates this objection when he qualifies the list of charms as "strong prevailment in unharden'd youth" (1.1.35). In other words, such items only become enchanted under the right conditions, and these conditions exist in the way the imagination of the lover meets the object of love. To the person in love, rhymes become spells, gauds become charms, trifles (idle stories) become the strongest magic there is. Egeus's mistake is placing the blame on the object rather than the beholder. The items Egeus mentions neither have nor take on these properties until one is disposed to be in love; the properties do not dwell or cannot be placed in the objects by one wishing to make another love him. However, Egeus is not alone in his mistake inasmuch as other characters will make the same one over and over again.

One item from Egeus's list that brings the relationship between object and imagination to the fore is "conceits." *Conceit* had a very different meaning in Shakespeare's time from what it does today, existing now mainly in its adjective form of *conceited,* meaning "egotistical." In Shakespeare's time, the word had more diverse and far-reaching applications. In general, *conceit* meant "idea" or "concept," a use that survives in the literary use of the term as "extended metaphor" or in the literary term *metaphysical conceit.* Egeus's use of the term is concrete, referring to a "fancy article" that one might give a lover *(Oxford English Dictionary).* In the more usual abstract sense, however, *conceit* refers not just to an idea but also to a fanciful notion or whim—or, more important, to the imagination itself. Shakespeare and Egeus seem to be bringing together the concrete and abstract uses; the point of Egeus's whole argument is that by giving Hermia conceits (shining objects), Lysander has sparked her imagination. Conceits can inspire conceit and therefore lead to love.

In many ways, Egeus's mistaken belief that Lysander has power over love merely projects his own desire to control his daughter's affection and have her marry the man he has chosen. However, the play strongly suggests in the opening scenes that love is beyond control. In fact, it goes much further and suggests that love and control are incompatible. At the opening, Theseus is essentially admitting this incompatibility to Hippolyta when he confesses, "I woo'd thee with my sword, / And won thy love doing thee injuries" (1.1.18–19). Love is not only beyond others' control; it is beyond self-control. Hermia implies both conditions when she

objects, "I would my father looked with my eyes." Theseus may counter, "Rather you must with his judgment look," but Bottom's observation on discovering that Titania loves him calls into questions the role of judgment in love and more closely captures love's working than Theseus's statement. However, judgment has little to do with love. Unable to grasp Titania's love for him, Bottom tells the fairy queen, "Methinks, mistress, you should have little reason for that. And yet, to say the truth, reason and love keep little company together nowadays" (3.1.145–148). In her early soliloquy, Helena echoes Bottom's assessment of love's irrationality when she struggles to determine how Demetrius's affection strayed from her to Hermia. Given that her beauty equals Hermia's, Helena can only conclude, "Love looks not with the eyes but with the mind." By "mind" here, Helena does not mean reason but imagination—the mind's eye. Her idea of looking with the imagination means that love is constantly an error, one that applies not only to Demetrius's love for Hermia but also to her love for Demetrius (see the section on Key Passages for a more extensive analysis of this soliloquy). After the lovers return from their transformative night in the woods, Theseus seems to have learned this point when he overrules Egeus's command that Lysander be put to death for trying to defy Athenian law. Later in the play, Theseus will more directly assert that love is subject solely to the imagination.

Although love's mystery causes pain for those who wish to control the love in third parties, its pain is much more severe for those directly involved in it, especially the lover. In a long exchange once they are alone on stage, Lysander and Helena catalog the forces that work against love's success. Lysander observes, "The course of true love never did run smooth" (1.1.134). It either tries to yoke those unequal in years or "stands upon the choice of friends." Even under the most promising circumstances, when there is "sympathy in choice," love is "[s]wift as a shadow, short as any dream / Quick as lightning in the collied night." However, although Lysander may fully acknowledge the futility of controlling love, his actions point him in an opposite direction. His experience of love as out of one's control seems to amplify the desire to control it. What makes love painful is precisely that it lies beyond the control of those who experience it.

Since it is evident that the characters' belief in love's magical provenance has been wrought out of desperation, the audience or reader is forced into a change in perspective when it turns out that magic does indeed exist in the play and behind it much human day-to-day activity, including love. The job of the unnamed fairy who serves Titania is to hang a "pearl in every cowslip's ear" (2.1.15). Puck is responsible for the minor accidents of life—but-

ter not churning, beer refusing to barm, widows falling from their stools. In other words, the play dramatizes and makes real what the play has previously suggested is the product of the imagination of those who desperately seek a refuge from love's pain. By making the imagination real, the play provides a telling instance of the way, as Theseus claims, the "poet's pen . . . gives to airy nothing / a local habitation and a name" (5.1.15–17).

The belief in love's magical provenance is the common resort of those who are frustrated with its inexplicable workings. Later in the play, when trying to understand how Lysander has suddenly

Titania and her fairies stand over a transformed Bottom in a 1796 depiction of Act IV, Scene 1 of *A Midsummer Night's Dream*. This is a print from the Boydell Shakespeare Gallery project, which was conceived in 1786 and lasted until 1805. *(Painting by Henry Fuseli; engraving by John Peter Simon)*

transferred his affection from her to Helena, Hermia accuses her rival of being a "juggler," a "canker-blossom," and a "thief of love," and she grants her the same magical properties that Egeus attributes to Lysander: "What, have you come by night / And stol'n my love's heart from him?" (3.2.283–284). Her metaphor closely matches the reality of what has occurred. By aligning reality with a mythological explanation that was previously ridiculed, the play demands that readers be of two minds about the prospects of the imagination, making them reject it as false even as it shows it to be true.

The play creates other ambivalences, even within this same structure of the imagination. Although Oberon and Puck clearly have the ability to control and even create love, that same love lies outside of their control. The fairies and their magic potions are able to produce real love, but the love they create is more powerful than the means of creation. Their attempts to set the world in order cause more chaos than they resolve. Plus, no matter what the extent their control over others' love happens to be, we should not overlook their inability to regulate their own affairs. The same jealousies and strife in love that humans experience also beset Oberon and Titania, whose fight over a changeling boy is a symptom of a greater relationship problem. Their problems expand into the world of humans, where they are responsible for significant hardships. Moreover, the problems in their love originate in the same place as those of humans: the imagination. Titania calls Oberon's suspicion that she favors Theseus and has favored him all along, "the forgeries of jealousy" (2.1.81). Like the word *conceit* in Egeus's accusation, the word *forgeries* suggests a relationship between the abstract and concrete, between the imagination and the real, that is vital to the play. A forgery can be something real made in a forge and something concocted in the mind. Both these ideas are relevant here because, as she explains, their imaginative accusations have real effects on the world of mortals. Jealousy, it turns out, is the negative function of love's imagination. Where the positive force of love envisions the love's object as better than it is,

jealousy activates the negative, creating, as it does, monsters of molehills, bears where bushes should be. And so it does with Oberon and Titania: Their jealousies cause a host of natural disasters that roil the natural world and hurt people.

It is a fairly safe bet for Shakespeare to assume that his audience members would understand and would probably have themselves experienced the problems of the imagination that attend love. However, *A Midsummer Night's Dream* ensures that the audience experiences the problem of imagination in a more direct way by creating and thematizing a parallel experience they cannot possibly avoid, that of the theater. The mysteries of love and the problems of the imagination are central to the plots of the four lovers and Theseus and Hippolyta, as well as Oberon and Titania. Yet the artisan players are not experiencing the problems of love directly. Instead, they are dramatizing the problems in a literal way for a different audience in "the most lamentable comedy and most cruel death of Pyramus and Thisbe" (1.2). Or, rather, they are attempting to dramatize them in the most inept way imaginable. However, their problems with dramatizing the problems of love end up being the problems of the imagination, particularly the ways the theater demands that we use it. When the artisans meet by moonlight to rehearse their play, Bottom worries that Pyramus's death and the lion's will frighten the audience too much. They solve these problems in the most unimaginative of ways—by penning a prologue that tells the audience: "Pyramus is not killed indeed," and by having Snug, who is playing the Lion, reveal his face and address the "Fair ladies" of the audience directly (3.1.19). Later in the scene, Quince worries about more practical problems of building a wall onstage and representing moonlight in an indoor venue. They address these problems in ways that seem ridiculous by having "some man or other present wall" and another dress as the conventional representation of the man in the moon, who carries a lantern and a bush of thorns in order to, as Quince blunders, "disfigure or to present the person of moonshine" (3.1.61). The problems that the mechanicals are having all involve mistaken ideas about how the imagination of the audience is engaged in the theatrical event. They think the audience will have either too much imagination, and so not be able to distinguish fiction from the real world, or too little, and therefore not be able to suspend their disbelief to think the moon is shining on the characters. In both cases, the imagination is calibrated incorrectly.

However, while the rude mechanicals under- and overestimate the audience, they are not entirely mistaken. Every theatrical event requires using the imagination to convert actors into characters, for example, and in an important sense, every use of the imagination must by definition be a distortion of what the audience sees. Using the imagination correctly means entering a state of always getting facts wrong. *A Midsummer Night's Dream* provides a pointed instance of how this principle works. To understand it, we can start by considering the title and setting of the play. Almost all of the play takes place not only at night but under the light of the moon. However, the audience seeing the play in James Burbage's Theatre (which was later rebuilt as the Globe) would have been witnessing the play in the open air and the broad light of day. If the audience finds itself laughing at the mechanicals for worrying over how to get moonlight into Theseus's chamber, they are laughing at a problem that they have already resolved by using their imagination to compensate for what is not there.

However, the question the play implicitly poses is this: Is the artisans' belief that they need to reproduce reality in order to be convincing any less ridiculous than the audience's belief that they are watching events at night when the sun is shining? In this way, our experience of the theater and particularly of *Midsummer* validates Quince's blunder in his call for someone "to disfigure or to present the person of moonshine"; every figuration on stage is a disfiguration of what is being represented because the actor and character can never be the same. The artisans get theater wrong in all the wrong places to demonstrate how theater requires the audience to get it wrong in the right ways.

The point the rude mechanicals demonstrate about theater is very similar to the one theater has been illustrating about love. As Helena says in soliloquy, love as a function of the imagination means that that being in love is constantly getting it wrong. We "err" and dignify things otherwise "base and vile." There is a right way to do it, but the right way may be distinguished from the wrong only inasmuch as one leads to happiness whereas the other leads to sorrow. As a matter of fact, the problems and confusion in the play issue from characters whose mistakes about love lead to unhappiness instead of joy. Titania claims that Oberon has too much imagination in thinking that she favors Theseus. Egeus, too, imputes too much power to Lysander in thinking that he used magic to woo his daughter. If we can believe Helena, Demetrius suffers from a flaw in his imagination, an inability to make the right kind of error in loving her instead of Hermia. Given the inability to formulate a consistent plan to deal with love, characters can only be thankful when it works out the way they wish.

The latter part of the play reinforces the roles of the imagination in theater and in love (as well as connections between them) by elevating them from implicit themes to topics of discussion. These connections occur plainly in two minor quarrels Theseus has with his new bride in the final act. In the first of these, Theseus disputes the lovers' account of the sylvan transformations that brought them into harmonious coupling. In his famous speech beginning "The lunatic, the lover, and the poet," Theseus derides the lovers' stories of their transformation as samples of "antique fables" and "fairy toys," and he likens the lovers themselves to lunatics and poets (5.1). What links them all together is a "strong imagination" that, in the case of a lover, must always invent a cause or impetus for love: "Such tricks hath strong imagination / That if it would but apprehend some joy, / It comprehends some bringer of that joy." Theseus is trying in the end to make the point that both poetry and love are born of the imagination, a quality that likens them to "the lunatic." (See Key Passages for a more complete discussion of this speech.) Not coincidentally, a "lunatic" is one who suffers from lunacy, which derives from the belief that madness is the result of the moon's astrological influence, which is more pronounced in midsummer.

In a similar way, the role of the imagination in theater, implicit in the artisans' rehearsal scenes, becomes explicit in their bungled and inexpert performance at the end of the play. Although Theseus and the two male lovers find "sport" in the mechanicals' "intent," the more literal-minded Hippolyta is unable to pretend their performance is tolerable and interjects, "This is the silliest stuff that ever I heard." Theseus responds by comparing the performance to the experience of theater in general: "The best of these kinds are but shadows; and the worst no worse, if imagination amend them." His point is that even the best theater is insubstantial and therefore easily dismissed. Only by extending grace in the form of the imagination can the audience credit any performance. In this way, theater works like love, which, by definition improves what it perceives. Although Theseus may be correct on a theoretical level, on a practical one, there is still a difference between good theater and bad. In the same way that Titania's love for Bottom challenges the limit of the imagination to dignify the object of love, the performance of "Pyramus and Thisbe" pushes the limit of this general principle of theater. Hippolyta has this point in mind when she counters with, "It must be your imagination then, and not theirs." And even though Theseus argues in favor of indulging the play, he remains aloof from the action of it, tearing apart the spectacle he claims his imagination will "amend."

While the rude mechanicals' play may expose the limits of the imagination when faced with a too-stark reality, *A Midsummer Night's Dream* on the whole complicates the distinction between the two. The play sets up the division between real experience and the imagination only to break it down. Characters attribute real human emotions to "fairy toys" and to witchcraft—both offshoots of the imagination—and to the imagination itself. Yet it is hard to find a reality that has not been altered by the imagination (in a way that brings characters and audience together). The moon's treatment at the opening of the play is an example of this inability to find a reality uncolored by the imagination. Theseus perceives the waning moon as drawing out his desire to consummate his love with Hippolyta. Her apparently gentle correction, however, no more establishes a moon free from human perception than his observation. Her remarks on how "quickly" the four nights will pass reveal the same perceptual coloration taken in the opposite direction. Additionally, her comments on the moon redirect questions from moon to motives, where they open up the possibility that her perception of time's swiftness comes from her dread of marrying the man who wooed her with his sword. The question of the moon's reality only deepens in the move from character to audience, for in "reality" there is no moon—no moon, that is, without the aid of the audience's imagination. The play reminds the viewer of the moon's literal absence by way of farce when the rude mechanicals worry about how to bring moonshine onstage in their own production.

In a further twist of irony, the play's reality, which was already a form of the imagination, is turned back into a dream when the lovers awake from their experience. But the lovers do not experience their reality as a dream, a condition for which Theseus mocks them by attributing the story of their night's adventure to an overworked imagination. Moreover, the reality of the lovers was never stable to begin with. Demetrius's love for Helena may be fixed and real, but it is the product of fairy intervention rather than internal motivation. Furthermore, the lovers fail to recognize themselves in the imaginative version of themselves that is presented on stage as Pyramus and Thisbe. Like Bottom's dream, the reality of the lovers is always beyond their grasp. These contradictions and ironies point up the way the separate realms of imagination and reality are tightly bound up with each other.

The interplay of imagination and reality provides a fitting way to understand theater. Of all forms of art, theater is the most palpable: It is the only art form that takes real human bodies and recasts them in imaginary ways. In order to participate in theater, real bodies, with their own identities, must be turned into a dream so that the imagination can be experienced as reality. Therefore, the relationship between the audience and the stage is precisely analogous to that of the mortals and fairies. They come into close proximity and even contact with each other, but the chasm between the two can never be crossed.

EXTRACTS OF CLASSIC CRITICISM

Edmund Malone (1741–1812) [From "An attempt to Ascertain the Order in Which the Plays attributed to Shakespeare Were Written" (1778). Here, Malone exhibits preferences typical of neoclassicism—namely, a concern with propriety. In arguing that the play is an early comedy, Malone complains that Theseus does nothing to match the dignity of his station, and that the action follows the fortunes of four insignificant and indistinguishable lovers.]

The poetry of this piece, glowing with all the warmth of a youthful and lively imagination, the many scenes which it contains of almost continual rhyme, the poverty of the fable, and want of discrimination among the higher personages, dispose me to believe that it was one of our authour's earliest attempts in comedy.

It seems to have been written, while the ridiculous competitions, prevalent among the histrionick tribe, were strongly impressed by novelty on his mind. He would naturally copy those manners first, with which he was first acquainted. The ambition of a theatrical candidate for applause he has happily ridiculed in *Bottom* the weaver. But among the more dignified persons of the drama we look in vain for any traits of character. The manners of Hippolyta, *the Amazon,* are undistinguished from those of other females. Theseus, the associate of Hercules, is not engaged in any adventure worthy of his rank and reputation, nor is he in reality an agent throughout the play. Like K. Henry VIII he goes out a Maying. He meets the lovers in perplexity, and makes no effort to promote their happiness; but when super-

natural accidents have reconciled them, he joins their company, and concludes his day's entertainment by uttering some miserable puns at an interlude represented by a troop of clowns. Over the fairy part of the drama he cannot be supposed to have any influence. This part of the fable, indeed, (at least as much of it as relates to the quarrels of Oberon and Titania,) was not of our author's invention.— Through the whole piece, the more exalted characters are subservient to the interests of those beneath them. We laugh with Bottom and his fellows, but is a single passion agitated by the faint and childish solicitudes of Hermia and Demetrius, of Helena and Lysander, those shadows of each other? That a drama, of which the principal personages are thus insignificant, and the fable the meager and uninteresting, was one of our authour's earliest compositions, does not, therefore, seem a very improbable conjecture; nor are the beauties with which it is embellished inconsistent with the supposition; for the genius of Shakspeare, even in its minority, could embroider the coarsest materials with the brightest and most lasting colours.

❦ ❦ ❦

Oberon and *Titania* had been introduced in a dramatick entertainment exhibited before Queen Elizabeth in 1591, when she was at Elvetham in Hampshire; as appears from *A Description of the Queene's Entertainment in Profess at Lord Hartford's &c.* printed in quarto in 1591. Her majesty, after having been pestered a whole afternoon with speeches in verse from the three Graces, Sylvanus, Wood Nymphs, & c. is at length addressed by the Fairy Queen, who presents her majesty with a chaplet, "Given me by Auberon [Oberon] the fairie king."

William Hazlitt (1778–1830) [From *Lectures on the Literature of the Age of Elizabeth; and Characters of Shakespeare's Plays* (1870). The famous essayist Hazlitt was one of the most important Shakespearean critics of the 19th century. He published *Characters of Shakespeare's Plays* in 1817 and *Lectures Chiefly on the Dramatic Literature of the Age of Elizabeth* in 1820; the two works were first published together in a single volume in 1870. Hazlitt often exhibited the romantics' appreciation for the loftiness of poetry over the grittiness of human life and exalting of Shakespeare as a poet of nature. His observations on the incompatibility of poetry and the stage were to prove influential on some forms of early and mid-20th-century criticism, which preferred studying the text of Shakespeare's texts to the performance of them. When he argues at the end of his discussion here that the stage cannot do justice to the imagination, he seems unaware that Theseus addresses this very issue in the play, where he says that the imagination is what must mend the failure of theater to live up to it.]

Bottom the Weaver is a character that has not had justice done him. He is the most romantic of mechanics. And what a list of companions he has—Quince the Carpenter, Snug the Joiner, Flute the Bellows-mender, Snout the Tinker, Starveling the Tailor; and then again, what a group of fairy attendants, Puck, Peaseblossom, Cobweb, Moth, and Mustardseed! It has been observed that Shakespeare's characters are constructed upon deep physiological principles; and there is something in the play which looks very like it. Bottom the Weaver, who takes the lead of "This crew of patches, rude mechanicals / That work for bread upon the Athenian stalls," follows a sedentary trade, and he is accordingly represented as conceited, serious, and fantastical. He is ready to undertake anything and everything, as if it was as much a matter of course as the motion of his loom and shuttle. He is for playing the tyrant, the lover, the lady, the lion. "He will roar that it shall do any man's heart good to hear him"; and this being objected to as improper, he still has resource in his good opinion of himself and "will roar you an 'twere any nightingale." Snug the Joiner is the moral man of the piece who proceeds by measurement and discretion in all things. You see him with his rule and compasses in his hand. "Have you the lion's part written? Pray you, if it be, give it me, for I am slow of study." Starveling the Tailor keeps the peace, and objects to the lion and the drawn sword. "I believe we must leave the killing out when all's done." Starveling, however, does not start the objections himself, but seconds them when made by others, as if he had not spirit to express his fears without encouragement. It is too much to suppose all this is intentional: but it very luckily falls out so. Nature includes all that is implied in the most subtle analytical distinctions; and the same distinctions will be found in Shakespeare. Bottom, who is not only chief actor, but stage-manager for the occasion, has a device to obviate the danger of frightening the ladies: "Write me a prologue, and let the prologue seem to say that Pyramus is not killed indeed; and for better assurance, tell them that I, Pyramus, am not Pyramus, but Bottom the Weaver: this will put them out of fear." Bottom seems to have understood the subject of dramatic illusion at least as well as any modern essayist. If our holiday mechanic rules to roast among his fellows, he is no less at home in his new characters of an ass, "with amiable cheeks, and fair large ears." He instinctively acquires a most learned taste, and grows fastidious in the choice of dried pease and bottled hay. He is quite familiar with his new attendants, and assigns them their parts with all due gravity. "Monsieur Cobweb, good Monsieur, get your weapon in your hand, and kill me a red-hipt humble-bee on the top of a thisle, and good Monsieur, bring me the honey-bag." What an exact knowledge is here shewn of natural history!

Puck and one of the four lovers in Act IV, Scene I of *A Midsummer Night's Dream,* in this illustration published by Gebbie & Husson Company

Puck, or Robin Goodfellow, is the leader of the fairy band. He is the Ariel of the *Midsummer Night's Dream;* and yet as unlike as can be to the Ariel in *The Tempest.* . . . Puck is a mad-cap sprite, full of wantonness and mischief, who laughs at those whom he misleads—"Lord, what fools these mortals be!" . . . Puck is borne along on his fairy errand like the light and glittering gossamer before the breeze. He is, indeed, a most Epicurean little gentleman, dealing in quaint devices, and faring in dainty delights. Prospero and his world of spirits are a set of moralists: but with Oberon and his fairies we are launched at once into the empire of butterflies. How beautifully is this race of beings contrasted with the men and women actors in the scene, by a single epithet which Titania gives to the latter, "the human mortals!" It is astonishing that Shakespeare should be considered, not only by foreigners, but by many of our own critics, as a gloomy and heavy writer, who painted nothing but "gorgons and hydras, and chimeras dire." His subtlety exceeds that of all other dramatic writers, insomuch that a celebrated person of the present day said that he regarded him rather as a metaphysician than a poet. His delicacy and sportive gaiety are infinite. In the *Midsummer Night's Dream* alone, we should imagine, there is more sweetness and beauty of description than in the whole range of French poetry put together. . . .

It has been suggested to us, that the *Midsummer Night's Dream* would do admirably to get up as a Christmas after-piece; and our prompter proposed that Mr. Kean should play the part of Bottom, as worthy of his great talents. He might, in the discharge of his duty, offer to play the lady like any of our actresses that he please, the lover or the tyrant like any of our actors that he pleased, and the lion like "the most fearful wild-fowl living." The carpenter, the tailor, and joiner, it was thought would hit the galleries. The young ladies in love would interest the side-boxes: and Robin Goodfellow and his companions excite a lively fellow-feeling in the children from the school. There would be two courts, an empire within an empire, the Athenians and the Fairy King and Queen, with their attendants, and with all their finery. What an opportunity for processions, for the sound of trumpets and glittering of spears! What a fluttering of urchins' painted wings; what a delightful profusion of gauze clouds and airy spirits floating on them!

Alas, the experiment has been tried, and has failed; not through the fault of Mr. Kean, who did not play the part of Bottom, nor of Mr. Liston, who did, and who played it well, but from the nature of things. The

Midsummer Night's Dream, when acted, is converted from a delightful fiction into a dull pantomime. All that is finest in the play is lost in the representation. The spectacle was grand; but the spirit was evaporated, the genius fled.—Poetry and the stage do not agree well together. The attempt to reconcile them in this instance fails not only of effect, but of decorum. The *ideal* can have no place upon the stage, which is a picture without perspective: every thing there is in the foreground. That which was merely an airy shape, a dream, a passing thought, immediately becomes an unmanageable reality. Where all is left to the imagination (as is the case of reading) every circumstance, near or remote, has an equal chance of being kept in mind, and tells according to the mixed impression of all that has been suggested. But the imagination cannot sufficiently qualify the action impression of the senses. Any offense given to the eye is not to be got rid by explanation. Thus Bottom's head in the play is a fantastic illusion produced by magic spells: on the stage, it is an ass's head, and nothing more; certainly a very strange costume for a gentleman to appear in. Fancy cannot be embodied any more than a simile can be painted: and it is as idle to attempt it as to personate *Wall* or *Moonshine.* Fairies are not incredible, but fairies six feet high are so. Monsters are not shocking, if they are seen at a proper distance. When ghosts appear at mid-day, when apparitions stalk along Cheapside, then may the Midsummer Night's Dream be represented without injury at Covent-Garden or at Drury-lane. The boards of a theatre and the regions of fancy are not the same thing.

MODERN CRITICISM AND CRITICAL CONTROVERSIES

What distinguishes this play from Shakespeare's others is that it seems unusually lighthearted and happy, though maintaining the usual Shakespearean complexity and brilliance. Its richness is in

evidence in the many lively debates among critics, who continue to discover new ways that the play is surprising, relevant, and delightful.

One question that spans all modern criticism is that of how seriously we are to take the play, or rather, which parts of the play or characters we should take seriously. The play itself anticipates this question in part in Theseus's dismissal of the lovers' story of their transformations in the woods and the debate about how characters should regard the rude mechanicals' play. One place where what we might call the serious study of the ridiculous gets carried out first is in K. M. Briggs's study *The Anatomy of Puck* (1959). Briggs investigates folklore and other beliefs about fairies held by Shakespeare's contemporaries. This investigation, coincidentally, stems from the question of how serious beliefs in fairies were during Shakespeare's day and recounts how religious officials seriously undertook the task of discrediting stories of fairies' existence. Briggs's work not only recounts the history of 16th- and 17th-century attitudes toward fairies, it also traces the literary origins of the supernatural figures in *Midsummer.*

A larger question of seriousness has to do with the tone of the play. Is the depiction of love in the play genial or menacing? Admittedly, both possibilities exist, but the question is whether one or the other predominates. Believing that the *Midsummer's* principal influence is the court masque, Enid Welsford suggests that this genre happily imbues the play with a joyful "blending of tones" and "harmony of colors" (331). G. Wilson Knight believes that the prevailing mood is a tempest of the kind depicted by Titania's speech on the "forgeries of jealousy" (144). Dorothea Kehler likens the play to *Macbeth* in the way "darkness and fear permeate the play" (18). It may be "darkness shot through with light," but darkness still rules.

One of the most extreme early statements about the play's tone and mood comes from Jan Kott's *Shakespeare Our Contemporary* (1964). For Kott, the play is filled with bestial eroticism and cruel humor, a far cry from the romanticized Arcadian dream of the Athenian forest and its temporary denizens that critics often put forth. Kott claims that whatever human harmony there is in the play comes only after the lovers "pass through animal eroticism," with some, such as Bottom and Titania, passing "in a quite literal, even visual sense" (225). Although Kott's attempt to discover, as his title suggests, that a modern cruelty and Brechtian aesthetic in this play and other of Shakespeare's plays was not widely influential on other critics at the time, few today would deny that the play houses these tendencies, at least in potential form,

In the mid-20th century, scholars known as New Critics focused primarily on artistic patterns that confer a sense of unity and wholeness on the play. R. W. Dent's "Imagination in *A Midsummer Night's Dream*" (1964) both describes and exemplifies this method. He begins his essay by observing how, "For many years, editors and critics have customarily praised *A Midsummer Night's Dream* for its artistic fusion of seemingly disparate elements" (115). As his title suggest, Dent believes the play's "most pervasive unifying element is the partially contrasting role of imagination in love and in art" (115).

Closely related to the formalism of New Critics such as Dent are the metadramatic studies of scholars such as James Calderwood. *Midsummer,* as much as any other Shakespeare play, invites critics to contemplate what the play seems to say about its own medium. Metadramatic critics tend to make the unity of the plays even tighter, not only in that the play is unified in theme, but that the theme is, in the end, about drama. For Calderwood, Oberon is "kind of an interior dramatist" (130), responsible for Theseus overruling Egeus and bringing harmony out of discord. The lovers' identities, blurred and lost in the forest, recall actors' unstable identities; indeed, the artisans' play fails because the artisans cannot "lose their identities even imaginatively in fictional roles (132)" (qtd. in Kehler: 32).

C. L. Barber's "May Games and Metamorphoses on a Midsummer Night" (1959) concedes a certain frivolity to the play, but frivolity of this type has a very serious and necessary social function. Barber suggests that *A Midsummer Night's Dream* repro-duces the effect of holiday festivities and games, particularly those associated with Maying, a fertility festival practiced in spring and at other occasions during the summer. Like that pattern in the play, May Day festivities "'move from town to the grove' and back again" (119). This anthropologically based approach is part of his larger thesis that *Shakespeare's Festive Comedies,* as his work is titled, structurally resemble social games and festivities that allow "clarification through release." By this phrase, Barber points to the way holiday customs' temporary descent into social disorder have a salutary effect by which society is refreshed and the social order is maintained. Barber claims that the fairies that romantic critics said were part of Shakespeare's youth are "serious in a very different way, as embodiments of the May-game experience of eros in men and women and trees and flowers" (124). According to Barber, the entire play is a dramatization of "May-game action" that "brings out underlying magical meanings of the ritual while keeping always a sense of what it is humanly, as an experience" (132).

The dominant forms of criticism from the 1980s forward have been from schools notable for taking altogether new aspects of the play seriously, aspects that were rarely considered before. In fact, there seems to be no feature of the play that is not potentially subject to study for its political design and effect. Feminist critics have rightly challenged the patriarchal bias that blinds readers not just to the injuries that Theseus has caused Hippolyta but also to those that Oberon causes Titania. In "*A Midsummer Night's Dream:* 'Jack Shall Have Jill; Nought Shall Go Ill'" (1998), Shirley Nelson Garner takes an idea that is similar to Barber's, that the comedy renews the social order, but she sees this renewal as oppressive to women rather than reassuring—not salutary but sickening. She says that "the renewal at the end of the play affirms patriarchal order and hierarchy, insisting that the power of women must be circumscribed, and that it recognizes the tenuousness of heterosexuality as well" (127). The other result of this renewal is "the disruption of female bonds with each other" (127).

In this way, Garner shifts the focus from order and harmony to those who are victims of that harmony.

In his 1982 essay "Exchanging Visions: Reading *A Midsummer Night's Dream,*" David Marshall shows how the concerns of feminist critics are consonant with larger challenges to conventional ways of reading. Marshall addresses problematic questions about the play that have often been overlooked in the assumption that the play is recommending the order it sets forth. Marshall recounts a number of issues in the play that critics have overlooked because of a bias toward the male characters. His strongest example is Hippolyta's silence, which, he asserts, we must learn to hear—"we must recognize that she does not speak" (550). As the cases of Hermia at the beginning and Titania later in the play reveal, the central problem is, according to Marshall, "fitting one's fancy to someone else's will" (552). Marshall tries to show how this desire and practice, it turns out, are shared both by critics and characters in the play.

Also in the 1980s, the anthropologically influenced studies of C. L. Barber were to give way to a more politicized form of cultural studies called New Historicism or cultural materialism. New Historicism is predicated on the idea that literary texts both reflect and define the historical period in which they held currency and that culture will find its way into literature, often in indirect ways. According to New Historicism, this history is always political and consists of tensions and power struggles within cultures. One of the most well-known and influential New Historicist arguments is Louis Montrose's "Shaping Fantasies: Figurations of Gender and Power in Elizabeth Culture" (1983). Building on the long-accepted tradition that the play is an occasion piece performed at a wedding that Queen Elizabeth attended, Montrose argues that "whether or not [she] was physically present at the first performance of *A Midsummer Night's Dream,* her pervasive cultural presence was a condition of the play's imaginative possibility" (480). Montrose is mainly concerned with how the play negotiates having a female ruler with a sex/gender system that subordinates women. In Eliza-

Oberon undoes the spell on Titania and Bottom in Act IV, Scene I of *A Midsummer Night's Dream.* This is a print from the Boydell Shakespeare Gallery project, which was conceived in 1786 and lasted until 1805. *(Painting by Henry Fuseli; engraving by Jean Pierre Simon)*

beth culture, this cognitive dissonance produced fantasies of subordination and control in which subjects both desired to serve and command the queen. Such contrary impulses emerge in the play in the person of Titania, who manipulates and commands Bottom but is herself "manipulated by Oberon" (65). Montrose therefore asserts: "A fantasy of male dependency upon woman is expressed and contained within a fantasy of male control over woman; the social reality of the player's dependency upon a Queen is inscribed within the imaginative reality of the dramatist's control over a Queen" (65). Montrose's work is typical of New Historicism in which the connection of the historical issue is symbolically represented and inflected through the story of the text. In other words, *A Midsummer Night's Dream* is not about Queen Elizabeth directly, but it symbolically captures currents of social energy that were in play at the time.

THE PLAY TODAY

One of the many competing explanations for why *Macbeth* is referred to as "the Scottish play" is the perhaps apocryphal story that the tragedy's universal popularity meant that a theater company would drag it out only when it was teetering on bankruptcy. But if any Shakespeare play in a world that is increasingly removed from his language merits the title of universal crowd-pleaser, it would have to be *A Midsummer Night's Dream*. In the world of theater, *Midsummer* gave us perhaps the most influential and innovative production of Shakespeare ever staged, Peter Brook's 1968 version of the play for the Royal Shakespeare Company. In his *New York Times* review of the Broadway version, Clive Barnes called Brook's staging "without any equivocation whatsoever the greatest production of Shakespeare" he had ever seen. The gushing praise for the Brook production is based on an appreciation for his having found a theatrical medium that matched the play's imaginative possibilities. Brook rejected any attempt to represent the Athenian court or woods and instead substituted a three-sided white box that formed the location for either or both. Such a setting gave director, actor, and audience veritable carte blanche for playing out the possibilities of the imagination that are at the heart of *Midsummer*. Against this dazzling white background, Brook presented a world of colorful characters who juggled and performed other acrobatic tricks. Particularly important for Brook's production was having all characters from noble to artisans robed in the same way; thus, the production combined striking visual contrast with characters who risked dissolving into undifferentiated space.

Given the imaginative possibilities of *A Midsummer Night's Dream*, it is little wonder that it

Still photograph from the 1935 film version of *A Midsummer Night's Dream,* with Mickey Rooney (right) as Puck

is one of the earliest plays to be put on film. In 1935, the German film director William Dieterle joined force with the German theater director Max Reinhardt to produce a star-studded film version of the play in the United States. James Cagney played Bottom, while Mickey Rooney played a childlike Puck. Given the play's popularity onstage, it is somewhat surprising that there is no modern film version that has enjoyed the success or stature of productions such as Kenneth Branagh's *Much Ado About Nothing* or *Henry V.* This is not to say that there is no good film version of the play. Michael Hoffman's 1999 version is certainly entertaining and worth watching. Set in Tuscany, the film offers a visual experience of bounty that is equal to the play's imaginative one. The critic Samuel Crowl has accurately noted this film's resemblance to 1930s Hollywood and debt to Reinhardt's film. Like Branagh does for his plays, Hoffman fills his screen with recognizable stars, including Michelle Pfeiffer, Kevin Kline, and Calista Flockhart, an actor from one of the trendier television shows of the day. In Hoffman's hands, the play clearly becomes "Bottom's dream." Hoffman invents a backstory of a shrewish wife who chides Bottom's theatrical aspirations, and he presents Bottom as the victim of wine-pouring street urchins whose abuse works contrapuntally to the blandishments of actual urchins such as Peasblossom and Mustardseed later in the play. Helping promote Bottom's centrality is the casting of Kline, an actor who is every bit as equal to the part as Bottom envisions himself to be of all the parts he would play. Even Pyramus's speech, which is supposed to showcase bad theater, comes off, in Crowl's fine account, as "a great tenor pouring forth his soul through an inadequate lyric" (181).

Since the play both promotes a childlike imagination that can see the world as better than it is and operates on childish fears that never fully leave us as adults, the move made obvious in the title of Christine Edzard's film *The Children's Midsummer Night's Dream* (2001) seems to fit the play. The play takes literally the idea that love is a child by having schoolchildren ages eight through 12 from schools in South London act the roles. Among the many things such casting accomplishes, one is the pointed disparity between the emotions that characters experience and their ability to control those emotions. In the play, the love characters feel is beyond what any character can easily manage, so the gap between the emotions that these actors portray in the film and their readiness for those emotions dovetails surprisingly well with the play.

One major feature of the criticism written in the 1980s and '90s was a discernible turn from issues of aesthetics to issues of politics, particularly as they concern power, class, and gender. Recently, critics have begun reevaluating the political turn and entertaining questions that they had previously rejected. One such article from 2008 is Hugh Grady's "Shakespeare and Impure Aesthetics: The Case of *A Midsummer Night's Dream.*" In it, Grady attempts to show how the aesthetic and the social are not exclusive, particularly by expanding the definition of the aesthetic so it no longer means an artwork that is "purely beautiful or the organically unified"—it is also "disunified, constituted by internal clashes and by the insubordination of repressed materials" (274). Based on this expanded concept of "impure aesthetics," Grady breaks down the traditional definition between the aesthetic and the social. Particularly, he argues that *Midsummer* sets up ideals that are impure, fractious, and dissentious and therefore are aestheticized utopian ideals. Such aesthetic moves run counter to the traditional ideas of the aesthetic as harmonious and unified. Certainly, one article does not encapsulate the variety of criticism on *Midsummer* that is being published, but that variety is the point. Scholars are finding that the play opens up endless possibilities for investigation but resists being fully contained within or exhausted by any approach.

The more scholars acknowledge the complexity of the work, the closer they come to capturing the multiplicity of pleasures the play presents. These pleasures are available to readers and viewers whether they are familiar with Shakespeare scholarship or not. While the work of scholars helps us better understand many of the play's points of interest, nonspecialists still enjoy them. All that is required is openness to the imaginative possibilities the play holds.

FIVE TOPICS FOR DISCUSSION AND WRITING

1. **Sympathies and silences:** To what extent does the play invite readers or viewers to sympathize with the plights (if we should call them that) of Titania? Of Hippolyta? To a lesser extent, of Hermia and Helena? Of Bottom? Hippolyta is a captive fiancée who often disagrees with Theseus, first, perhaps, about his adjudication of Egeus's complaint and later about the lovers and the play. After she is cursed into falling in love with Bottom, why does Titania give up the changeling boy without a struggle or without saying a word? Do Thisbe's plight and performance warrant discussion in relation to those of the others? Helena and Hermia, respectively, get the man each wanted. If they are sympathetic, what might be the function of such sympathy in the play?

2. **Tone and atmosphere:** What kind of tone does the play's language and action set? For example, how seriously does the play suggest Egeus's threat to be? Does it give assurances that everything will turn out well? As a point of comparison, you might consider *Romeo and Juliet*, which shares a plot of perceived parental opposition, and things do not turn out well for the lovers. Even though things work out for the lovers in *Midsummer*, does the play's tone remain happy and joyous to the end? Readers might consider Act V. Has the tone changed, or is it more of the same? Another way to approach the question of tone is to ask what parts of the play viewers should take seriously and what parts or issues in it should be dismissed as farce.

3. **The imagination:** How often and where does the imagination come up in the play? How important is it to understanding the way characters act? Theseus's soliloquy in Act V addresses the centrality of the imagination as a link among lunatics, lovers, and poets. What are his observations, and to what extent does the play validate them? In what ways does the play complicate his ideas about the nature of love or art? What are the possibilities and limits of the imagination as the play is dramatizing them?

4. **Natural and supernatural:** How does the play represent natural and supernatural realms and the relationships among them? What are the fairies in terms of identity function or character? How do they resemble or differ from human characters in meaningful ways? How are humans distinguishable from the fairies in the play? Analyze the points of contact between the two realms. How does the contact occur? How does it affect either or both realms after they take place? In other words, does the fairy world leave a lasting impression on mortals? And, if so, what kind of impression does it leave?

5. **Art and Artisans:** What is the function of the rude mechanicals in the play? What issues do they bring into focus? How do their character and existence relate them to other figures or groups of figures in the play? What does the play they perform (the content and inept form) and how it is performed (its context, delivery, and reception) suggest about the nature of art and love, especially in relation to other representations of these phenomena in the play?

Bibliography

Barber, C. L. "May Games and Metamorphoses on a Midsummer Night." In *Shakespeare's Festive Comedy.* Princeton, N.J.: Princeton University Press, 1959, 119–162.

Barnes, Clive. "Peter Brook's *A Midsummer Night's Dream*," *New York Times,* 21 January 1971. Available online. URL: http://nyti.ms/ev8TrY. Accessed June 6, 2010.

Bevington, David. "'But we are spirits of another sort': The Dark Side of Love and Magic in *A Midsummer Night's Dream*." *Medieval and Renaissance Studies* 7 (Summer 1975): 80–92.

Booth, Stephen, "A Discourse on the Witty Partition of *A Midsummer Night's Dream*." In *Inside Shakespeare: Essays on the Blackfriars Stage,* edited by Paul

Menzer. 216–222. Selinsgrove, Pa.: Susquehanna University Press, 2006.

Briggs, K. M. *The Anatomy of Puck.* London: Routledge, 1959.

Brooks, Harold F. Introduction to *A Midsummer Night's Dream,* edited by Harold F. Brooks, xxi–cxliii. The Arden Shakespeare. London: Methuen, 1979.

Calderwood, James L. "*A Midsummer Night's Dream:* Art's Illusory Sacrifice." In *Shakespearean Metadrama: The Argument of the Play in* Titus Andronicus, Love's Labour's Lost, Romeo and Juliet, A Midsummer Night's Dream, *and* Richard II. Minneapolis: University of Minnesota Press, 1971, 120–148.

Chambers, E. K. *"A Midsummer Night's Dream."* In *Shakespeare: A Survey.* 1925. Reprint, London: Sidgwick and Jackson, 1958, 77–87.

Crowl, Samuel. "Shakespeare and Hollywood Revisited: The Dreams of Noble and Hoffman." In *Shakespeare at the Cineplex: The Kenneth Branagh Era.* Athens: Ohio University Press, 2003, 170–186.

Dent, R. W. "Imagination in *A Midsummer Night's Dream." Shakespeare Quarterly* 15, no. 2 (1964): 115–129. Reprinted in *A Midsummer Night's Dream: Critical Essays,* edited by Dorothea Kehler, 3–76. New York: Garland, 1998.

Dobson, Michael. "Shakespeare as a Joke: The English Comic Tradition, *A Midsummer Night's Dream* and Amateur Performance." *Shakespeare Survey* 56 (2003): 117–125.

Garner, Shirley Nelson, *"A Midsummer Night's Dream:* 'Jack Shall Have Jill; Nought Shall Go Ill.'" In A Midsummer Night's Dream: *Critical Essays,* edited by Dorothea Kehler, 127–143. New York: Garland, 1998.

Grady, Hugh, "Shakespeare and Impure Aesthetics: The Case of A Midsummer Night's Dream." *Shakespeare Quarterly* 59, no. 3 (2008): 272–302.

Joughin, John J. "Bottom's Secret . . ." In *Spiritual Shakespeares,* edited by Ewan Fernie, 130–156. London: Routledge, 2005.

Kehler, Dorothea. "*A Midsummer Night's Dream:* A Bibliographic Survey of the Criticism." In A Midsummer Night's Dream: *Critical Essays,* edited by Dorothea Kehler, 3–76. New York: Garland, 1998.

Knight, G. Wilson. "The Romantic Comedies." *The Shakespearian Tempest.* Oxford University Press, 1932, 75–168.

Kott, Jan. "Titania and the Ass's Head." In *Shakespeare Our Contemporary,* translated by Boleslaw Taborski, 213–236. 1964. Reprint, New York: W.W. Norton, 1974.

Leinwand, Theodore B. "I Believe We Must Leave the Killing Out": Deference and Accommodation in *A Midsummer Night's Dream. Renaissance Papers* (1986): 11–30.

Mack, Maynard. "Engagement and Detachment in Shakespeare's Plays." In *Essays on Shakespeare and Elizabethan Drama in Honor of Hardin Craig,* edited by Richard Hosley, 275–296. Columbia: University of Missouri Press, 1962.

MacOwan, Michael. "The Sad Case of Professor Kott." *Drama* 88 (Spring 1968): 30–37.

Malone, Edmund. "An Attempt to Ascertain the Order in Which the Plays Attributed to Shakespeare Were Written: *A Midsummer Night's Dream."* In *The Plays and Poems of Shakespeare According to the Improved Text of Edmund Malone.* vol. 2, edited by A. J. Valpy, 333–340. London: Bohn, 1853.

Marshall, David. "Exchanging Visions: Reading *A Midsummer Night's Dream." ELH: English Literary History* 49 (1982): 543–575.

McDonald, Marcia. "Bottom's Space: Historicizing Comic Theory and Practice in *A Midsummer Nights Dream."* In *Acting Funny: Comic Theory and Practice in Shakespeare's Plays,* edited by Frances Teague, 85–108. Rutherford: Fairleigh Dickinson University Press, 1994.

Montrose, Louis Adrian. "Shaping Fantasies: Figurations of Gender and Power in Elizabethan Culture." *Representations* 1, no. 2 (1983): 61–94.

Nevo, Ruth. "Fancy's Images." In *Comic Transformations in Shakespeare.* London: Methuen, 1980, 96–114.

Parker, Patricia. "Peter Quince: Love Potions, Carpenter's Coigns and Athenian Weddings." *Shakespeare Survey* 56 (2003): 39–54.

Reimer, A. P. "Emblems of Art." *Antic Fables: Patterns of Evasion in Shakespeare's Comedies.* New York: St. Martins, 1980.

Shakespeare, William. *A Midsummer Night's Dream.* Edited by Jonathan Bate and Eric Rasmussen. The Royal Shakespeare Company Shakespeare. New York: Modern Library, 2008.

Stansbury, Joan. "Characterization of the Four Lovers in *A Midsummer Night's Dream.*" *Shakespeare Survey* 35 (1982): 57–63.

Taylor, Michael. "The Darker Purpose of *A Midsummer Night's Dream.*" *Studies in English Literature: 1500–1900* 9 (1969): 259–273.

Watts, Cedric. "Fundamental Editing: In *A Midsummer Night's Dream,* Does Bottom Mean 'Bum'? And How About 'Arse' and 'Ass'?" *Anglistica Pisana* 3, no. 1 (2006): 215–222.

Welsford, Enid. "The Masque Transmuted." *The Court Masque: A Study in the Relationship between Poetry and the Revels.* Cambridge University Press, 1927, 324–349.

FILM AND VIDEO PRODUCTIONS

Edzard. Christine, dir. *The Children's Midsummer Night's Dream.* With Jamie Peachey, John Heyfron, and Danny Bishop. Sands Films, 2001.

Hall, Peter, dir. *A Midsummer Night's Dream.* With Paul Rogers, Ian Holm, Diana Rigg, Helen Mirren, Ian Richardson, Judi Dench, and Sebastian Shaw. Royal Shakespeare Company, 1968.

Hoffman, Michael, dir. *A Midsummer Night's Dream.* With Kevin Kline, Rupert Everett, Michelle Pfeiffer, Stanley Tucci, Sophie Marceau, Christian Bale, Dominic West, and Calista Flockhart. Regency Enterprises, 1999.

Moshinsky, Elijah, dir. *A Midsummer Night's Dream.* With Helen Mirren, Peter McEnery, Robert Lindsay, Geoffrey Palmer, and Brian Glover. BBC Television, 1981.

Reinhardt, Max, and William Dieterle, dir. *A Midsummer Night's Dream.* With James Cagney, Dick Powell, and Ian Hunter. Warner Brothers, 1935.

—James Wells

Much Ado About Nothing

INTRODUCTION

The comedy *Much Ado About Nothing* remains popular today for a number of reasons, among them its sparkling wit and wordplay; its explorations of relationships between men and women, gender and society, and "outsiders" and society; and the questions it raises about marriage as a social institution. The play is timeless in its themes and as contemporary as an episode of *Sex and the City,* which itself might be viewed as a current-day reworking of many of the themes found in *Much Ado,* and whose title could serve as an alternate title for the play.

Shakespeare does not provide easy answers to the questions he raises; rather, he presents complex and multifaceted characters caught up in events that they can only partially control, if that. In other words, his characters exist much as we do. The men and women of the play have to sort out personal issues, issues of their own identity, problems with their relationships with members of their own sex, and problems with their relationships with members of the opposite sex. Feminists and theorists on gay and lesbian studies have found much to discuss here; indeed, the play's sexual politics are fertile ground for analysis and discussion of current ideas of gender and sexual roles.

Much Ado shows us that we are often victims of the plots, schemes, and tricks of others who seek to get us to act in certain ways. Certainly, such trickery is no less common in our generation than it was

in Shakespeare's; indeed, in this world of Facebook, Twitter, Myspace, and other forms of social networking, the opportunities for manipulation, game playing, and peer pressure might be even greater.

Similarly, the play delves deeply into the issues of appearance and reality. It asks such basic—and important—questions as "What is real?" "What is true?" "How do I know the truth?" Characters in the play come near disaster and suffer numerous problems, often being unable to distinguish truth from falsehood or appearance from reality. Situations and scenes are contrived. Characters are "set up." Events are staged. People don disguises and masks to hide their true feelings or, sometimes, to allow themselves to express their true feelings. Characters learn that what they see and hear is not always true or real. In our modern, image-driven, multimedia environment, questions as to what is true, what is real, and what is authentic remain all-important. *Much Ado* is a play that helps us think more carefully and deeply about such questions.

While *Much Ado* offers a wealth of interesting and, yes, entertaining explorations of gender and relationships, it also offers important insights into the nature of society. The Messina of the play is a society administered by a governor. The play commences just after the successful conclusion of a military campaign, as a group of mostly young nobles come to the city fresh from the fight. The play's action navigates a path between the states of peace and war, military power and the rule of law, civil and military society. The forces at work are strong enough to tear the society apart, but in the end, these forces are reconciled, at least temporarily, by the social convention of marriage, a force that brings people together. In our own age of far-flung wars, political polarization, and conflict between socioeconomic groups, the play's lessons remain entirely relevant.

Much Ado also has much to offer regarding the role and effects of the "outsider." In the character of Don John, we have a classic example of the angry outsider, a person dispossessed by the nature of his illegitimate birth from a respected place in society. He is angry, antisocial, and vengeful, and he provides the worrisome dark side to the comedy's light side of romance and marriage. *Much Ado* poses questions on how society creates its Don Johns and how it should deal with them.

In contrast to Don John, there is the constable Dogberry. This bumbling, comic figure should, by the usual social and economic standards of society, also be an outsider. Yet, rather than seethe with resentment as Don John does, Dogberry has evidently taken his lowly position in the social hierarchy and turned it to his advantage. He is a self-made man, representative of a new civil order in which industry, merit, and self-confidence provide the path to status. Don John, on the other hand, may be seen as a man "unmade" by his weakness of character and failure to find a meaningful role in society. One may—and does—laugh at Dogberry's fumbling and mangling of the language, yet he is one character who actually speaks meaningfully of the events of the day. It must also be kept in mind that it is Dogberry and his companions who discover the plot hatched by Don John, rather than any of the more educated and privileged nobles. Again, the play provides us with food for thought on how individuals and groups can make a place for themselves in society.

BACKGROUND

The play's far-off setting of Messina, located off the "toe" of the Italian "boot," on the coast of the island of Sicily, would have suggested to Shakespeare's audience a remote, fantastic, and romantic place. One might argue, however, that the distant

Ursula and Hero speak of Beatrice's flaws and Benedick's love while Beatrice listens from her hiding place in Act III, Scene 1 of *Much Ado About Nothing*. This illustration was designed for a 1918 edition of Charles and Mary Lamb's *Tales from Shakespeare*. *(Illustration by Louis Rhead)*

location allowed Shakespeare to explore certain themes that might otherwise have been more difficult to portray were the play set at home. While set in a distant land, the play does draw on realities of English, Italian, and Spanish history and aspects of English life, especially courtly life. Thus, some background on these matters is helpful.

First, while Messina might have served to represent a distant other world for Shakespeare's audience, it was a real place. Messina's history was one of occupation by succeeding conquerors. At the time of Shakespeare, the city was under the control of the Spanish and was substantial and important. The fact of Spanish rule is reflected in the name of some of the play's characters, most notably Don Pedro and Don John. It is useful to keep in mind that Protestant England under Elizabeth I viewed Catholic Spain with deep suspicion and even antagonism. After all, the English had fought off the Spanish Armada in 1588, probably only about a decade before the play's initial performance, which was probably in 1598–99. The portrayal of Don Pedro and, even more so, Don John as schemers and tricksters, whether for good or ill, would probably have resonated with the English audience.

But though Messina was occupied by Spain, it was an Italian city. Although Shakespeare almost certainly never visited Italy, many of his plays—*The Two Gentlemen of Verona, Romeo and Juliet, The Taming of the Shrew,* and others—are set there. Shakespeare's interest in and involvement with Italy is substantial. *Much Ado* reflects many of the attitudes and views, often contradictory, that Shakespeare and the English held about Italy. For Shakespeare, it was a land of strong, even violent, passions. We can see this in the outbursts of Leonato, first against Hero when it is alleged she is unfaithful, then against Don Pedro and Claudio when it is found that they have mistakenly slandered Hero.

Because of Italy's reputation for strong sexual passions and illicit liaisons, it seems more natural to charge inappropriate conduct against Hero. At the same time, Italy also had a tradition of courtly and idealized love, exemplified in Dante's love for Beatrice and Petrarch's love for Laura. It is this tradition that underlies the nature of the romance between Hero and Claudio before Don John attempts to sabotage it. It might be argued that the relationship between Beatrice and Benedick is fascinating just because it walks a fine line between both traditions, the passionate and the courtly.

The literary sources Shakespeare drew on for the play were Italian as well. Canto 5 of Ludovico Ariosto's *Orlando Furioso* (1591), which Shakespeare probably read in a translation by Sir John Haring-

ton, probably provided him with the story of the marriage between Hero and Claudio and Don John's plot to prevent it. It is believed that Matteo Bandello's *La Prima Parte de le Nouelle* (1554) gave Shakespeare the idea of setting the play in Messina, while Baldassare Castiglione's *The Courtier* (1588), perhaps in Sir Thomas Hoby's translation, offered a source for the romance between Beatrice and Benedick.

Thus, while Messina was indeed a far-away place, the locale generated certain assumptions and attitudes on the part of its initial English audience, and it had already become somewhat familiar, at least to the well-educated members of the audience, through earlier stories by Italian authors.

The play was written, produced, and first published under the reign of Queen Elizabeth (1558–1603), at a time when English cultural life and national feeling was at a new height. The victory over the Spanish Armada helped inspire these feelings, giving the English a sense of independence and identity, aided by their mastery of the seas. This maritime strength also brought about increases in trade, which then led to a greater interaction with foreign cultures and foreign citizens. In addition, the turn to Protestantism, begun by Elizabeth's father, King Henry VIII, and continued under Elizabeth, marked for many citizens a new freedom from the domination of the pope and the Roman Catholic Church (although some English remained devout, if covert, Catholics). Against this background, *Much Ado,* set in Italy and shaded with Spanish influence, might be said to occupy a space between fascination and opposition in the view of its English audience.

Finally, the play itself contains another form of theatrical entertainment within it: the masque, which had been popular in England and preferred in royal circles. Masques were a sort of costume play, or ball, built around a theme, often from mythology or literature. Perhaps the most famous literary work built around the form of a masque is Milton's *Comus* (1634). The members of the royal circle would each dress up in a chosen role, and the masques would continue through the evening, often with much partying and merrymaking. These performances gave the nobility a chance to show off, literally and figuratively, in ways that they could not do in their normal routine. They also provided a chance for romantic dalliances; it was reported that Henry VIII wooed Anne Boleyn during a masque. In *Much Ado,* the masque gives Don Pedro a chance to woo Hero for Claudio. This scene would have looked very familiar to some members of the audience. Shakespeare's use of the masque might also indicate that in the language of Beatrice and Benedick and Hero and Claudio, he may have been reflecting what he heard at actual masques in which he participated. Certainly, the play offers a kind of highly bred yet bold language that would not have been alien to a courtly masque.

Date and Text of the Play

Most authorities date the play to the winter of 1598–99. Shakespeare was then becoming well known as a playwright. During this same period, he wrote *A Midsummer Night's Dream, The Merchant of Venice, As You Like It,* and *Twelfth Night.* The play was probably first performed by the acting troupe the Lord Chamberlain's Men at The Theatre, just prior to that playhouse being dismantled and rebuilt later as the now legendary Globe. The Theatre was an outdoor, open-air amphitheatre, just outside the jurisdiction of the City of London, with three gallery levels and a roofed stage area. It is important to keep in mind that all the actors, or "players," as they were called, at this time were men. Since women were not permitted to perform onstage during Elizabethan times, their roles— Hero, Beatrice and others—were played by boys. Although the actors were male, both men and women formed the audience, which typically was drawn from all London society but was predominately of the lower social and economic classes.

The play was first published in 1600 in a quarto edition and later included in the 1623 First Folio collection of Shakespeare's plays. The title page of the quarto states that *Much Ado About Nothing* "hath been sundrie times publikely acted by the Right Honourable, the Lord Chamberlaine his seruants."

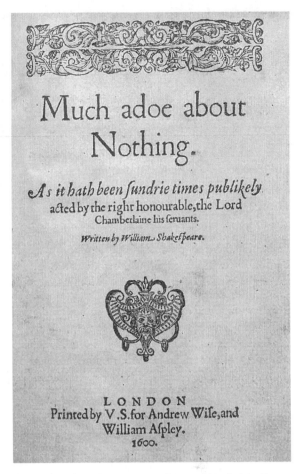

Title page of the first quarto edition of *Much Ado About Nothing,* published in 1600

The only surviving records for early performances are the payments made by the Lord Chamberlain to John Heminge in May 1613 for presenting several plays, including *Much Ado About Nothing,* for Princess Elizabeth (daughter of James I) and Frederick V (Elector Palatine of the Rhine), who were married that year. The performance of this play would seem to be a fitting wedding present.

SYNOPSIS
Brief Synopsis

A messenger arrives in Messina to spread the news that the recent military conflict between Don

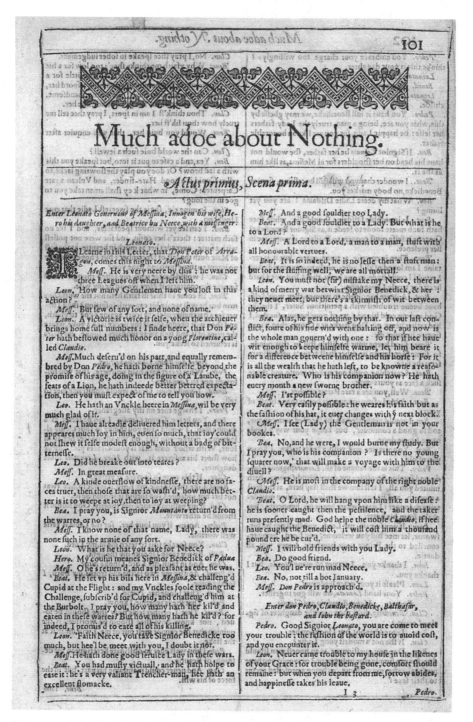

Title page of the First Folio edition of *Much Ado About Nothing,* published in 1623

Pedro, Prince of Aragon, and his half brother, Don John, is resolved, with Don Pedro claiming victory. This success comes as good news to Leonato, the governor of Messina, and the members of his household, including Beatrice. Don Pedro arrives, accompanied by Benedick, Claudio, and his brother, Don John. Benedick and Beatrice exchange humorous insults, each of them asserting an extreme aversion to love, particularly for the other. Once alone, Claudio confesses to Benedick that he has fallen in love with Leonato's daughter, Hero, and wishes to marry her. Benedick reveals Claudio's desire to Don Pedro, who offers to court Hero while pretending to be Claudio at the masque scheduled for that evening. Once assured of Hero's response, he will approach her father on Claudio's behalf.

Don John privately complains to his attendant Conrade of his bitter melancholy and asserts that he wishes to spread discontent.

Don Pedro and his courtiers arrive for the festivities, and all the participants put on masks. Benedick and Beatrice, in disguise, trade insults. Don John tells Claudio that he has heard the prince courting Hero. After Claudio leaves embittered, Benedick berates Don Pedro for betraying Claudio. The prince assures Benedick that he means well by their friend. When Claudio and Beatrice appear, Don Pedro tells Claudio that he has arranged his marriage to Hero. After Beatrice leaves, the prince reveals his plan to trick Benedick and Beatrice into falling in love with each other.

Borachio proposes a scheme to the villain Don John: he, Borachio, will recruit Hero's waiting-woman, Margaret, to disguise herself as Hero and admit him into Hero's window that night. If Don John can get Claudio and Don Pedro to witness this charade, they will believe that Hero has a lover, and Claudio will repudiate her.

In the garden, Benedick reflects on the seductiveness of love. When Don Pedro, Claudio, and Leonato appear, he hides himself in an arbor. They see him and, following Don Pedro's plan, speak loudly about Beatrice's passionate love for him. When they leave, Benedick declares that he will

marry Beatrice. Beatrice appears to summon him to dinner, and Benedick comically imagines that he hears double meanings in her words that prove her love.

When Beatrice eavesdrops on Hero and Margaret talking in the garden, she hears them speak loudly of Benedick's passion for her. They profess reluctance to tell Beatrice this news, fearing her mockery. Beatrice decides that she will return Benedick's love.

Don John appears and tells Claudio and Don Pedro of Hero's infidelity, offering to prove the truth of his accusation that night.

The rustic Constable Dogberry assembles the Watchmen for their nightly patrol. Conrade and Borachio appear. Borachio describes the success of his plan to deceive Claudio and tells of Claudio's determination to disgrace Hero at the wedding. The Watchmen arrest the two men.

During the marriage ceremony, Claudio rejects Hero, asserting that he has witnessed her rendezvous with a lover. Although Leonato initially rages cruelly at Hero and supports Claudio, he finally recovers his faith in his daughter when Friar Francis, Beatrice, and Benedick assert their faith in Hero. The Friar suggests they pretend that Hero has died. Then, if Hero is not exonerated, she can at least be secretly transferred to a nunnery. Beatrice and Benedick reveal their feelings for each other. Beatrice demands that Benedick prove his love by challenging Claudio to a duel in support of Hero.

Don John has fled from Messina. After Dogberry fails at interrogating Conrade and Borachio, the sexton questions the Watchmen, who tell of Don John's plot. The Sexton orders the prisoners bound and taken to Leonato, and he goes to report what he has learned.

Benedick challenges Claudio to a duel. Dogberry arrives with his prisoners, and Borachio confesses all. Claudio begs for Leonato's forgiveness, promising to perform any penance. Leonato states that he must publicly mourn Hero and then marry Hero's cousin.

Claudio prepares to marry the veiled cousin, who reveals herself to be Hero. Benedick and

Beatrice cannot bring themselves to admit their love for each other. Claudio produces a love poem that Benedick has written about Beatrice, and Hero presents a similar lyric by Beatrice about Benedick. Exposed, Beatrice and Benedick agree to be married. As plans are made for a double wedding, word comes that Don John has been apprehended.

Act I, Scene 1

The play opens with a messenger arriving in Messina (Sicily). The messenger meets Messina's governor, Leonato; Leonato's daughter, Hero; and Leonato's niece, Beatrice, and he tells them of the successful military campaign waged by Don Pedro, prince of Arragon. He also reports that Don Pedro is on his way to Messina that evening with his entourage to rest and celebrate the victorious campaign. We learn that Claudio, a young lord of Florence, and Benedick, a young lord of Padua, have done valiant military service with Don Pedro. From Beatrice's questions and comments, we also learn that there is a "merry war" between her and Benedick.

Don Pedro, Claudio, Benedick, Balthasar (Don Pedro's attendant), and John the Bastard (illegitimate brother of Don Pedro) now enter and greet Leonato and his family. Beatrice and Benedick engage in witty mockery of each other. After the others leave, Claudio tells Benedick that he has fallen for Hero and wants to make her his wife. Don Pedro now comes to find Claudio and Benedick, and Claudio reveals his love for Hero to Don Pedro. Benedick asserts that he himself will not be like Claudio; he will not fall in love. Don Pedro tells Claudio that he will disguise himself as Claudio in order to woo and win Hero for Claudio, and once he has done so, will obtain Leonato's approval for the marriage.

Act I, Scene 2

Leonato and his brother Antonio, an old man, are in a conversation. Antonio tells Leonato that he has overheard Don Pedro and Claudio speaking of Hero. Antonio mistakenly believes he hears Don Pedro reveal his love for Hero and that Don Pedro intends to tell Hero of his love at a dance that night, after which he will inform Leonato of his love. Leonato tells Antonio he will inform Hero so that she might be prepared.

Act I, Scene 3

John the Bastard and his companion Conrade are in a conversation. John reveals that he does what he wants, seeks no one else's regard, and, in his own words, is "a plain dealing villain." John seeks some way to express his discontent. Borachio, another follower of John, enters the scene and tells John of Don Pedro's plan to woo Hero on behalf of Claudio. John sees an opportunity to vent his displeasure and thwart Claudio.

Act II, Scene 1

Leonato, Antonio, Hero, Beatrice and a "kinsman" (not identified) are at dinner. They first talk of John, who Hero notes has a "very melancholy disposition." Beatrice criticizes Benedick and husbands and marriage generally. Don Pedro, Claudio, Benedick, John, and Borachio enter the scene as revelers wearing masks. Don Pedro induces Hero to a private conversation. Beatrice and Benedick engage in witty criticisms of each other. The revelers all leave, except for John, Borachio, and Claudio, who is still wearing a mask. John, pretending to mistake Claudio for Benedick, tells him that his brother, Don Pedro, loves Hero and intends to marry her this night. John and Borachio then leave, leaving Claudio alone. Claudio believes what he has heard from John, so he thinks Don Pedro and Hero have betrayed him. Benedick then enters and realizes that Claudio is upset and unhappy; Claudio leaves. Benedick is himself unhappy because of the critical wit that Beatrice used on him at the masked party.

Don Pedro now enters. Benedick tells Don Pedro how Beatrice's words have hurt him. Claudio returns with Beatrice, Leonato, and Hero. Since Benedick cannot endure more criticism from Beatrice, he leaves. Don Pedro tells Beatrice she has lost Benedick's heart, and Beatrice responds that "once before he won it of me with false dice." Claudio, still believing John's false accusation, treats

Don Pedro coldly. Don Pedro now tells Claudio that he has wooed and won Hero for him and has obtained the consent of Leonato, Hero's father. Claudio, now overjoyed, agrees to marry Hero. Don Pedro asks Beatrice if she will marry him, but Beatrice declines and leaves. Claudio sets the wedding for the next day. In the meantime, Don Pedro decides to find a way to bring Beatrice and Benedick to fall in love with each other. Claudio and Hero agree to help.

Act II, Scene 2

John and Borachio meet. John has found out that Claudio is to marry Hero; he seeks a way to thwart the marriage and bring discredit on his brother, Don Pedro, who has arranged it. Borachio tells John to tell Don Pedro and Claudio that Hero only pretends to be a maiden, and when they seek proof, to bring them near the outside of Hero's window that night. Borachio, who is having an affair with Hero's attendant, Margaret, will arrange for Hero to be absent and for Margaret, dressed in Hero's clothes, to come to the bedroom window, where Borachio will call her Hero and Margaret will call him Claudio. John agrees to the plan.

Act II, Scene 3

Benedick contemplates the change in behavior of the soon-to-be married Claudio, who once thought only of war and now thinks only of love. Benedick moves off to the side, and Don Pedro, Leonato, and Claudio enter. They intend to carry out Don Pedro's scheme to get Benedick to fall in love with Beatrice. Balthasar enters and sings a song about men as deceivers of women. Don Pedro launches his scheme by talking with the others about how much Beatrice loves Benedick but is afraid to let him know that, knowing that Benedick overhears what they are saying. They "bait the hook" in order to get Benedick to "bite." Don Pedro, Claudio, and Leonato leave. Benedick comes forward and acknowledges he has acted badly toward Beatrice and intends to show his love to her. Beatrice then enters to invite Benedick to dinner; she rudely rebuffs his overture.

Act III, Scene 1

Hero, Margaret, and another attendant, Ursula, enter and plan their scheme to get Beatrice to love Benedick. Hero has Margaret tell Beatrice that Hero and Ursula are talking about her in the garden, and Margaret must arrange for Beatrice to hide in the bower in order to overhear what they are saying. They hope Beatrice will "devour the treacherous bait." With Beatrice listening from the bower, Hero and Ursula discuss Beatrice's pride, wounding wit, and inability to show affection. They praise Benedick and talk about his love for Beatrice. Hero and Ursula leave. Beatrice comes forward, admits her faults, and intends to show her love for Benedick.

Ursula and Hero speak of Beatrice's flaws and Benedick's love while Beatrice listens from her hiding place in Act III, Scene I of *Much Ado About Nothing*. This is a print from the Boydell Shakespeare Gallery project, which was conceived in 1786 and lasted until 1805. *(Painting by William Peters; engraving by Jean Pierre Simon)*

Act III, Scene 2

Don Pedro, Claudio, Benedick, and Leonato engage in conversation and make fun of Benedick's love sickness. Benedick and Leonato leave, and John enters. He tells Don Pedro and Claudio that Hero has been "disloyal." John induces them to come to Hero's bedroom window that night to see for themselves. Claudio vows that if he sees anything improper, he will "shame" Hero at the wedding altar the next day, and Don Pedro agrees to do likewise.

Act III, Scene 3

Dogberry, the constable, Verges, a petty constable, and the Watchmen discuss how they will keep the peace that night. They overhear Borachio tell Conrade of the plot he has executed with John against Claudio and Don Pedro. Borachio recounts how he wooed Margaret, dressed as Hero, from her bedroom window, while John placed Don Pedro and Claudio in the orchard at a distance. Borachio recounts that Don Pedro and Claudio believe what they saw, and that Claudio went away "enrag'd," vowing to "shame" Hero before the congregation at the wedding altar. The Watchmen arrest Borachio and Conrade.

Act III, Scene 4

Hero, Margaret, and Ursula get ready for the wedding. Ursula is sent to get Beatrice, who then joins them. Beatrice, Margaret, and Hero exchange witticisms on the relations of men and women. Ursula reenters and notifies Hero that Don Pedro, Claudio, Benedick, John, and other townsfolk have come to bring Hero to the church for the wedding.

Act III, Scene 5

Dogberry and Verges meet Leonato and attempt to tell him of the treacherous plot they have uncovered, but their account is so convoluted and confused that Leonato tells them to examine the witnesses and come back to him tomorrow. Leonato hurries off to attend the wedding.

Act IV, Scene 1

The Friar, Don Pedro, John, Leonato, Claudio, Benedick, Hero, and Beatrice, with attendants, are at the altar for Hero and Claudio's wedding. When the Friar ask if there are any impediments to marriage, Claudio responds by accusing Hero of being false and wicked, charging she is not a maiden but rather "an approved wanton." Hero maintains her maidenly innocence. Don Pedro recounts what he and Claudio saw during the night outside Hero's window. Claudio again charges Hero with "impiety and impious purity." Don Pedro, John, and Claudio leave, while Hero faints at the altar. Leonato, believing the accusations, berates his daughter. Beatrice, Benedick, and the Friar are stunned by the turn of events. The Friar believes there must be some misunderstanding, and Beatrice sees the villainous hand of John in these events. The Friar suggests that a rumor be put out that Hero has died and that she should be taken away and hidden until the situation can be better understood and her true worth acknowledged. This is agreed upon by all.

Beatrice and Benedick are left alone. Benedick openly avows his love for Beatrice. Beatrice challenges Benedick to prove his love by killing Claudio for his treatment of Hero. Benedick at first refuses, then finally agrees to do so.

Act IV, Scene 2

Dogberry, Verges, the Town Clerk, and the Watchmen, with Borachio and Conrade, enter the prison. They have learned of the whole plot. The church sexton informs them that John has fled town. They decide to bring Borachio and Conrade to Leonato's house.

Act V, Scene 1

Leonato tells his brother Antonio of his unendurable anguish. Don Pedro and Claudio enter. They tell Leonato and Antonio that they are soon leaving Messina. Leonato and Antonio begin to berate Don Pedro and Claudio for what they have done; they soon work themselves into a fighting

Dogberry condemns the villain Borachio "into everlasting redemption" in Act IV, Scene 2 of *Much Ado About Nothing.* This is a print from the Boydell Shakespeare Gallery project, which was conceived in 1786 and lasted until 1805. *(Painted by Robert Smirke; engraving by John Ogborne)*

fever against Don Pedro and Claudio. Don Pedro and Claudio forbear from fighting Leonato and Antonio. Don Pedro maintains that although he is sorry for Hero's death, he believes that the charges against her were true and proven. Leonato and Antonio leave. Benedick enters and, finding Don Pedro and Claudio, berates Claudio and challenges him to a duel. Don Pedro and Claudio mock Beatrice's relationship with Benedick and ask Benedick when they shall see him married. Benedick tells Don Pedro that John has fled from Messina and that he and Claudio have killed the innocent Hero. He then leaves, still seeking to duel with Claudio. Don Pedro and Claudio realize Benedick is in earnest.

Dogberry, Verges, and the Watchmen enter with Conrade and Borachio, who are under arrest. Dogberry reports how Borachio has made a false report and slandered Hero. Borachio discloses the whole of the plot hatched by John and himself. Borachio observes that what supposedly wise and educated men like Don Pedro and Claudio could not see, ignorant Watchmen were able to find out. Don Pedro is stricken by the revelation. Claudio now sees Hero in the light in which he first loved her. Leonato and Antonio return with the sexton and confront Borachio. Leonato charges Don Pedro and Claudio with his daughter's death. Claudio maintains he has sinned only in mistaking. He is willing to accept Leonato's punishment. Leonato commands that Don Pedro and Claudio inform the people of Messina of Hero's innocence. Leonato directs Claudio to sing a song at Hero's grave and to hang an epitaph on it. Leonato tells Claudio that his brother has a daughter nearly identical to Hero, and Claudio will take this daughter as his wife tomorrow. Leonato asks for Margaret to be brought to him for questioning; Borachio claims that Margaret did not know the plot. Claudio goes to mourn Hero.

Act V, Scene 2

Benedick meets Margaret and asks her help in calling Beatrice to him. Margaret and Benedick exchange double entendres and witticisms about men and women. Margaret leaves and Beatrice enters. Beatrice demands to know what happened between Benedick and Claudio. Benedick tells Beatrice he has challenged Claudio to a duel. Benedick asks Beatrice what she loves most about him. Beatrice tells Benedick that he has so many bad aspects that it is hard for any good ones to stand out. Beatrice asks Benedick the same question. Benedick tells Beatrice that he loves her against his will, which causes him to suffer. Benedick concludes that he and Beatrice know each other too well to love each other. Benedick asks how Hero is doing; Beatrice tells him she is very ill. Ursula enters and tells Beatrice and Benedick that it has been found out that Hero has been falsely accused, Don Pedro and Claudio tricked, and John, who is responsible for all of it, has fled town. They go to Leonato's house to hear the news.

Act V, Scene 3

Enter Claudio, Don Pedro, and attendants bearing lighted torches at Leonato's family tomb in the cemetery. Claudio, as he promised to Leonato, reads out an epitaph for Hero, recounting how Hero was slandered and died in shame but lives in memory for her true virtue. A song is sung. Daylight begins to break. The villains have done their worst; now a new day begins.

Act V, Scene 4

Enter Leonato, Benedick, Margaret, Ursula, Antonio, the Friar, and Hero. Leonato recounts that Don Pedro and Claudio have realized they were wrong in their accusations against Hero. Leonato notes that Margaret, after questioning, seemed unaware of the larger purpose of John's plot and participated against her will. Antonio is glad everything has worked out well, and Benedick is also relieved, as he will not have to duel Claudio. Leonato sends Hero and her attendants to another chamber and tells them to come back, masked, when he calls for them. Benedick tells Leonato and the Friar that he, too, hopes to be married this day. Antonio leaves.

Don Pedro and Claudio now enter, thinking Claudio is to marry Leonato's "niece," as Leonato has made Claudio promise. Antonio reenters with Hero, Beatrice, Margaret, and Ursula, all in masks. Claudio agrees to marry the woman Leonato has selected for him, and he takes her hand. Hero takes off her mask and agrees to marry Claudio, who is amazed. As the Friar explains, the old Hero "died" while slander shamed her, but she has been reborn now that she has been vindicated. Benedick asks for Beatrice, and Beatrice unmasks. Benedick asks her if she loves him. Beatrice tells him that she loves him "no more than reason." Beatrice asks Benedick the same question and receives the same answer. They each exclaim that what others had told them must have been wrong, for each was led to believe that the other loved them. Claudio produces a paper in which Benedick declares his love for Beatrice, and Hero produces another paper stolen from Beatrice's pocket in which Beatrice declares her love for Benedick. Benedick tells Beatrice he will take her out of pity, while Beatrice tells Benedick she will take him to save his life. Benedick tells Beatrice he "will stop your mouth" and kisses her.

Benedick declares wisecracks and jokes will not stop him from marrying, as he is intent on doing so. Benedick and Claudio assert their friendship again. Benedick calls for a dance before the marriage. Benedick notes that Don Pedro looks sad and advises him to get a wife. A messenger arrives with news that John has been caught and is being brought back to Messina under armed guard. Benedick says he will think up suitable punishments for John, but for now, it is time to dance, and the pipers strike up a tune.

CHARACTER LIST

Don Pedro Prince of Arragon, who has led a group of other noblemen to war and is returning victorious with only minor losses. An "alpha male," he takes control of Claudio's wooing of Hero, is tricked by his half brother John's plot, and, despite his authority, is lonely and without a mate at the end of the play.

Don John The "bastard," i.e., the illegitimate brother of Don Pedro. Perhaps because of his illegitimate status, or due to his own personality, he is a man of few words, goes his own way, respects no one, and seeks to do harm where possible, in order to thwart the happiness of others. He considers himself a "plain-dealing villain" and implements a plot that nearly destroys the happiness of the other characters.

Claudio A straightforward young lord of Florence who has acquitted himself well in the war as part of Don Pedro's entourage. His thoughts turn to love, not war, when he falls in love with Hero; however, he is quick to believe John's slander about her and shames her publicly, although they are quickly reconciled when the truth becomes known.

Benedick A witty and humorous young lord of Padua, brother in arms to Claudio. Benedick is caught in a "love-hate" relationship with the equally witty and humorous Beatrice, who, after much mocking and some rebuffs, agrees to marry him.

Leonato Governor of Messina, the site of the play's action, father to the lady Hero, and uncle to Beatrice. Like most fathers, he is proud and protective of his daughter and distraught when Hero is nearly ruined by John's plot.

Antonio Leonato's brother, he exhibits some of the signs of a somewhat senile older man—for example, foolishly challenging Don Pedro and Claudio to fight as a result of their treatment of Hero.

Hero Daughter to Leonato, she is lovely, mild, and willing to follow the wishes of her father, suitor, and society. She agrees to marry Claudio, even after he publicly and falsely accuses her of shameful conduct.

Beatrice Niece to Leonato, she is spirited, witty, humorous, and independent, and she follows her own wishes in matters of personal happiness. She is engaged in a war of words with Benedick, which we realize masks deeper feelings for him.

Balthasar An attendant to Don Pedro who, although often called upon to sing to the other characters, is not a very skillful singer.

Borachio An attendant to Don John, he furthers his employer's malicious intentions by devising the plot that will trick Don Pedro and Claudio into believing that Hero is not virtuous, using his illicit relationship with Hero's attendant, Margaret, to accomplish the trickery.

Conrade Another attendant to Don John, a reflection of his master, who encourages his misanthropy and mischief making.

Margaret An attendant to Hero, Margaret is witty and humorous. She is complicit in her lover Borachio's plot against Hero, although unaware of its deeper purposes.

Ursula Another attendant to Hero, Ursula mirrors her mistress's personality.

Dogberry A constable and a self-made man, with a propensity for using the wrong word at the right time, to unintentionally humorous effect. Although something of a bumbler, he and his colleagues manage to uncover the plot hatched by John and Borachio, and they bring the truth to light, which better-educated and higher-ranking characters fail to do.

Verges Chief officer under the constable, he shares Dogberry's bumbling and humorous ways but helps bring Borachio and John to justice.

Friar Was to marry Hero and Claudio; he comes up with a stratagem to hide Hero until the truth of Claudio's accusations can be determined.

CHARACTER STUDIES

The central characters in *Much Ado About Nothing,* Claudio and Benedick, and Hero and Beatrice, form a contrasting quartet that offers multiple perspectives on personal relationships, love, and marriage.

Claudio

We first meet Claudio on his return from the war as part of Don Pedro's entourage. The messenger describes Claudio as "the right noble Claudio" (1.1.84–85). When he first sees Hero, he falls in love with her. However, he is a romantic with a very conventional streak in him. Claudio first comments on Hero's modesty (1.1.165), a point that will be central in the play's plot. Benedick, put off by Claudio's interest in Hero, asks him, "Would you buy her, that you inquire after her?" Claudio responds, "Can the world buy such a jewel?" (1.1.179–181). The sense of a commercial transaction thus pervades the relationship between Claudio and Hero at an early stage. This aspect is further emphasized when Claudio asks Don Pedro if Leonato has any son, indirectly asking about any inheritance problem that might arise. Don Pedro assures Claudio that Hero is Leonato's "only heir" (1.1.203–204). The conventional and commercial underpinnings of the relationship are thus assured.

Claudio's personal weaknesses become apparent as his wooing of Hero progresses, and John's plot affects the relationship. First, there is Claudio's passivity and willingness to be led by others. Most lovers prefer to do their own wooing and winning, but Claudio readily acquiesces when Don Pedro decides to woo Hero himself, win her for Claudio, and obtain Leonato's permission for the marriage. Don Pedro tells Claudio he will assume Claudio's identity in disguise, "And tell fair Hero, I am

Claudio / And in her bosom I'll unclasp my heart / And take her hearing prisoner with the force / And strong encounter of my amorous tales" (1.1.321–328). Claudio goes along with the ploy.

This ploy leads to a revelation of Claudio's other major failings: gullibility and jealousy. In a prelude to his much more elaborate and serious trick, John takes advantage of the masked ball at which Don Pedro woos Hero to tell Claudio, whom he pretends to mistake for Benedick, that Don Pedro actually woos Hero for himself, not Claudio. Claudio promptly falls for the lie and believes Don Pedro has betrayed him. He complains, "Friendship is constant in all other things / Save in the office and affairs of love" (2.1.175–176). Claudio resolves to "trust no agent," believes "beauty is a witch" (2.2.175), and finishes by absolving himself of his relationship with Hero, stating, "Farewell therefore Hero!" (2.1.182). Not for the last time will he throw aside his relationship with the one he supposedly loves on a flimsy lie. We might add to the list of Claudio's failings a lack of faith or trust in those he considers a friend or beloved.

Having fallen for one of John's trick, he soon falls for another. Claudio's initial jealousy is assuaged when Don Pedro does, in fact, obtain Hero's hand in marriage for him. Claudio reminds us of the commercial nature of the relationship when he tells Hero, "I give away myself for you, and dote upon the exchange" (2.1.308–309). That momentary happiness is soon squelched when Don Pedro and Claudio take the bait that John offers in the form of his false accusation that Hero is unfaithful and unchaste. When John brings them to a bower near Hero's chamber to witness Margaret, dressed as Hero, entertain the overtures of a disguised Borachio, they promptly believe what they see. As recounted by Borachio, who has arranged the whole ploy, Claudio goes away "enrag'd," promising that he will meet Hero at the wedding altar, and there, "shame her with what he saw o'er night, and send her home again without a husband" (3.3.159–163). At the wedding altar, Claudio follows through on his threat, berating Hero as an "approved wanton" (4.1.44). Claudio

refutes the insinuation that he himself might have had a premarital relationship with Hero by describing his love as that of "a brother to his sister, show'd / Bashful sincerity and comely love" (4.1.53–54), surely a somewhat odd way to describe his feelings toward his intended wife.

When Claudio learns that he has been tricked by John, he follows Leonato's direction that he hang an epitaph on Hero's grave and marry Leonato's niece (in fact, Hero in disguise). Despite not knowing the proposed niece, Claudio humbly agrees to marry her, demonstrating perhaps that for Claudio, marriage is not so much an expression of individual love and commitment as a necessary social arrangement. Claudio attempts to excuse his actions by claiming "yet sinn'd I not / But in mistaking" (5.1.273–274) suggesting that he has not learned much about himself.

Hero
Hero seems the appropriate female counterpart to Claudio. Like Claudio, she is accepting, passive, and conventional. At the masked ball at which Don Pedro undertakes to woo Hero on Claudio's behalf, Don Pedro asks her if she will walk with him; she responds, "So you walk softly, and look sweetly, and say nothing" (2.1.88–89), which might be said to sum up Hero herself nicely. As Don Pedro tells Claudio, "Here, Claudio, I have woo'd in thy name, and fair Hero is won" (2.2.298–299). It is not clear whether Hero finds out this imposture; if she does, it does not seem to have hindered her acceptance of the marriage, nor is she resentful of the imposture. It is also apparent that winning Hero's hand was neither extraordinarily difficult nor prolonged.

Hero shows more of her character when she implements Don Pedro's ploy to get Beatrice to believe that Benedick loves her, even as Claudio assists Don Pedro in tricking Benedick into believing that Beatrice loves him. Thus, both Hero and Claudio are capable of their own little tricks, albeit in a good cause. During her ploy against Beatrice, Hero criticizes her cousin Beatrice, commenting she is too proud, values her wit too much, is incapable of showing affection, and is too self-centered. From this, one can reasonably assume that Hero strives to embody the opposite qualities, which in fact she does. She is less concerned about shining in society, demonstrates affection, and embraces society's norms and expectations.

When she is shamed publicly at the altar by Claudio, Hero faints dead away. In fact, she has suffered a sort of social death, for being disgraced publicly is equivalent to death for Hero. During her period of public shame, she is immured. She is only reborn when she is brought back to the altar and marries Claudio. She returns to the altar under the disguise of being her father's niece, and only reveals herself when Claudio states his willingness to marry her, at which time she tells the amazed Claudio, "One Hero died defil'd, but I do live / And surely as I live, I am a maid" (5.4.53–54). What Hero does not say, however, is equally significant as what she does say: no recriminations, no blame, no anger toward Claudio, who has treated her so harshly and so publicly. She accepts what happens without complaint, she accepts marriage, and she accepts Claudio.

Benedick

Benedick is a young lord of Padua who has joined Don Pedro and Claudio in the recent military campaign and their stopover in Messina. Beatrice asks the messenger who brings notice of the imminent arrival of Don Pedro, Claudio, and Benedick to Messina of Benedick's well-being, indicating her interest in, and concern for, Benedick, but she does so in her usual mocking way. Beatrice calls Benedick "Signior Mountanto," *mountanto* being a term from fencing describing an upward thrust, perhaps either her sense of Benedick being "stuck up" or a sexual double entendre, both of which might fit this young bachelor. The messenger describes Benedick as "pleasant as ever he was" (1.1.37–38), an early indication of Benedick's essential character. In the exchange between the messenger and Beatrice, the messenger extols Benedick's virtue as a "good soldier" and "stuff'd with all honorable virtues" (1.1.53–57), while Beatrice mocks him for his capacity for food and for

George Alexander as Benedick in a late 19th-century production of *Much Ado About Nothing,* in this photograph published by Virtue & Company *(Photographed by J. & L. Caswall Smith)*

being full of himself. Leonato informs us: "There is a kind of merry war betwixt Signior Benedick and her; they never meet but there's a skirmish of wit between them" (1.1.61–64). This "skirmish of wit" serves to reveal the good and bad traits in both characters.

Let us first take Benedick's view of himself, then the views of the other characters, and finally how these views come together to achieve true insight. According to Benedick, "it is certain I am lov'd of all ladies" with the exception of Beatrice, but equally certain in his own eyes, "truly I love none" (1.1.125–127). Benedick takes a rather dismissive attitude toward women; for example, in response to Claudio's query, he criticizes Hero as "too low for a high praise, too brown for a fair praise, and too little for a great praise" (1.1.171–173). Benedick boasts of himself as a confirmed bachelor. He tells Claudio, "I will not do them [women] the wrong to mistrust any, I will do myself the right to trust none. . . . I will live a bachelor" (1.1.243–246). In so saying, expressing his distrust of women, Benedick reveals himself to be something of a misogynist as well. Certainly he speaks with the egoistic assurance of the young nobleman and bachelor.

While Claudio changes quickly from warrior to lover, Benedick is resistant. He is surprised to see the change in Claudio, and he reflects on whether such a change can occur to himself. He swears that love "shall never make me such a fool" (2.3.26). Benedick believes himself armored against the attractions of women: "One woman is fair, yet I am well; another is wise, yet I am well; another virtuous, yet I am well; but till all graces be in one woman, one woman shall not come into my grace" (2.3.26–30). Like many bachelors, Benedick seeks the perfect woman, enumerating the traits he is looking for: rich, wise, virtuous, mild, noble, well-spoken, an "excellent musician," and "nice hair" (although he is broad-minded enough not to be concerned about the color) (2.3.30–35). The lengthy and somewhat ill-assorted list suggests his expectations are unrealistic and immature.

Let us turn to the view of others. Early in the play, Beatrice charges Benedick with fickleness and faithlessness: "He wears his faith but as the fashion of his hat: it ever changes with the next block" [that is, changes with the fashion] (1.1.75–77). Later, Beatrice hints again at Benedick's faithlessness when she tells Don Pedro, "Once before he won it [her heart] of me with false dice" (2.1.280–282), suggesting that Benedick failed to honor or return the love Beatrice had once offered him. But Beatrice has even harder words, calling Benedick "the Prince's jester, a very dull fool; . . . None but libertines delight in him; . . . he both pleases men and angers them, and then they laugh at him and beat him" (2.1.137–142). So, while Benedick is appreciated for his pleasant company, he is not respected. Don Pedro, while recogniz-

ing Benedick's shortcomings, also recognizes his virtues, describing Benedick as being "of a noble strain, of approv'd valor, and confirmed honesty" and "not the unhopefullest husband that I know" (2.1.377–380).

Don Pedro plans a trick to bring Benedick and Beatrice together. With the help of Claudio and Leonato, he arranges for Benedick to overhear their comments; they discuss Beatrice's supposed concealed love for Benedick and Benedick's faults. They pretend to be reluctant to tell Benedick of this love because of his manner of dealing with such things: He would scorn it and treat it contemptuously. Don Pedro says, "I love Benedick well, and I could wish he would modestly examine himself, to see how much he is unworthy so good a lady" (2.3.206–209). Benedick does just that and acknowledges that "happy are they that hear their detractions, and can put them to mending" (2.3.279–280). He realizes his attitude toward women has been immature, in that "I did never think to marry" (2.3.228), but that attitude has now changed, and he observes, "A man loves the meat in his youth, that he cannot endure in his age" (2.3.238–240). Although he realizes he will be mocked, as he had once boasted he would die a bachelor, Benedick accepts that "the world must be populated" (2.3.242). He resolves to court Beatrice; he will have to prove his love and faith to her. In the end, having won Beatrice's hand, Benedick tells the assembled friends, "I do purpose to marry." He has traveled from confirmed bachelor to husband, from fickle to faithful, from youth to maturity.

Beatrice

As Benedick can be seen as a foil to Claudio, one may see Beatrice as a foil to Hero. Whereas Hero quietly accepts marriage, Beatrice, like Benedick, is loath to join in that union. Leonato warns her that "thou wilt never get thee a husband, if thou be so shrewd of thy tongue" (2.1.18–19). Beatrice is indifferent to this possibility. Like Benedick, Beatrice sets impossible demands: "He that hath a beard is more than a youth, and he that hath no

Beatrice in Act I, Scene I of *Much Ado About Nothing*. This is a print from Charles Heath's 1848 edition of *The Heroines of Shakspeare: Comprising the Principal Female Characters in the Plays of the Great Poet*. (Painting by J. W. Wright; engraving by W. H. Mote)

beard is less than a man, and he that is more than a youth is not for me, and he that is less than a man, I am not for him" (2.1.36–39). Beatrice draws the crucial distinction between herself and her cousin Hero: "Yes, faith, it is my cousin's duty to make cur'sy and say, 'Father, as it pleases you.' But yet for all that, cousin, let him be a handsome fellow, or else make another cur'sy and say, 'Father, as it please me'" (2.1.52–56). For Beatrice, her choice of husband must please herself alone.

Beatrice has a wonderful and often quite funny wit. But Benedick levels the most pointed criticism of Beatrice when, following her verbal mauling of him at the masked ball, he exclaims, "She speaks poniards [i.e., daggers], and every word stabs"

(2.1.247–248). This criticism is echoed by Hero when she implements the ploy designed by Don Pedro to make Beatrice believe that Benedick is deeply in love with her. With Beatrice overhearing, Hero observes that Beatrice does not realize "How much an ill word may empoison liking" (3.1.85–86). Hero also criticizes Beatrice for her self-regard: "But nature never fram'd a woman's heart, / Of prouder stuff than that of Beatrice, / Disdain and scorn ride sparkling in her eyes, / Misprising what they look on, and her wit, / Values itself so highly that to her, / All matter else seems weak. She cannot love, / Nor take no shape nor project of affection, / She is so self-endeared" (3.1.49–56). In essence, Hero is saying that Beatrice is so wrapped up in herself that she cannot sympathize with another. In this, she is, ironically, much like Benedick, whose egoistical view of women prevents him from forming a true relationship.

Beatrice acknowledges the validity of Hero's criticism: "Stand I condemn'd for pride and scorn so much? / Contempt, farewell, and maiden pride, adieu! / No glory lives behind the back of such" (3.1.108–110). Believing what she has heard of Benedick's love for her, she intends to return his love, "Taming my wild heart to thy loving hand" (3.1.112). As the trick on Benedick succeeds in having him abandon his bachelorhood, so the trick on Beatrice moves her to abandon her "maiden pride."

That reference to "wild heart" is no mere exaggeration, for Beatrice is something of a "maiden warrior." When she asks how many Benedick has killed in the recent war, she comments, "I promis'd to eat all of his killing" (1.1.45), certainly a stark and bloodthirsty image. Of course, she is engaged in a "merry war" (1.1.52–54) between herself and Benedick, in which verbal daggers are the weapons of choice. An even starker reminder of her valiant, even warlike, spirit can be found after Claudio has publicly disgraced Hero. When Benedick asserts his love for her, she tells him to prove it by avenging Hero. Her command to Benedick is stark: "Kill Claudio" (4.1.289). When Benedick hesitates, Beatrice laments, "O God, that I were a man! I would eat his heart in the market place" (4.1.306–307).

In the end, John's plot is discovered, and Don Pedro's tricks have brought Beatrice and Benedick together. But even at the verge of the altar, Beatrice has not completely surrendered her spirit. She accepts Benedick but in qualified terms: "I would not deny you, but by this good day, I yield upon great persuasion, and partly to save your life, for I was told you were in a consumption" (5.4.94–97). The verbal sparring is stopped when Benedick kisses her. It is the peace that follows war.

DIFFICULTIES OF THE PLAY

Compared to many of Shakespeare's plays, *Much Ado About Nothing* is not particularly difficult to understand. Unlike the history plays, it does not assume knowledge of historical events and characters, for the Messina of the play is faraway and unreal, a romantic Shangri-la of sorts. The actions there seem to happen almost out of time. Messina is perhaps an urban counterpart to the enchanted forests of *A Midsummer Night's Dream*.

But the play does present numerous analogies and conceits that draw upon long-obsolete activities or elaborate wordplay. One example of this is found at the very beginning of the play, when Beatrice mocks Benedick's military accomplishments by comparing them to a child's activities:

> He set up his bills here in Messina, and
> challeng'd Cupid at the flight, and my uncle's
> fool, reading the challenge, subscrib'd for
> Cupid, and challeng'd him at the burbolt.
>
> (1.1.39–42)

This witticism is not only long and complicated, but presents difficulty in its use of obsolete terms such as *set up his bills here* and *challeng'd him at the burbolt*. Yet by a bit of effort, and the aid of a good footnoted edition, most students can catch on to the cleverness of the language, so that, in this instance, one understands Beatrice is mocking Benedick by comparing his boasted military exploits to one who challenges a child at a game of shooting arrows. (*Burbolt* probably means "bird-bolt," an arrow used to hunt birds.)

Similarly, the malapropisms and linguistic confusion of Constable Dogberry might cause some students confusion, but no more than Dogberry causes the play's other characters, who eventually figure out that Dogberry often means the reverse of what he says.

Since many of the characters in the play are prone to conceits and witticisms, especially Beatrice and Benedick, most students will need to work out the language using available textual aids. Yet it is likely that once the style of the language becomes familiar, most readers will quickly pick up on its meaning—and pleasures. Furthermore, good live or video performances of the play go a long way toward making the language more easily understood and enjoyed through the visual mannerisms and vocal articulation of the actors. Indeed, for those having difficulties reading the play, watching a live performance first is highly recommended. The 1993 film starring Emma Thompson as Beatrice, Kenneth Branagh as Benedick, Denzel Washington as Don Pedro, and Keanu Reeves as Don John proved quite popular and is another reminder that Shakespeare is hardly outmoded for our times.

Some readers might also have some difficulties with the mores implicit in the play, such as the public designation of Don John as Don Pedro's "bastard" brother, or, perhaps, the seemingly socially acceptable public shaming of Hero at the altar by Claudio. These attitudes certainly seem unpleasant to us today, and yet the contemporary social and psychological reasons for them are certainly easily understandable and perhaps even familiar.

KEY PASSAGES
Act I, Scene 1, 230–249

CLAUDIO. That I love her, I feel.

DON PEDRO. That she is worthy, I know.

BENEDICK. That I neither feel how she
  should be lov'd, nor know how she should be
  worthy, is the opinion that fire cannot melt
  out of me; I will die in it at the stake.

DON PEDRO. Thou ever was an obstinate heretic in the despite of beauty.

CLAUDIO. And never could maintain his part but in the force of the will.

BENEDICK. That a woman conceiv'd me, I thank her; that she brought me up, I likewise give her most humble thanks; but that I will have a recheat winded in my forehead, or hang my bugle in an invisible baldrick, all women shall pardon me. Because I will not do them the wrong to mistrust any, I will do myself the right to trust none; and the fine is (for which I may go the finer), I will live a bachelor.

Don Pedro, Claudio, and Benedick explain how they view Hero, whom Claudio has said he loves. Claudio declares, "That I love her, I feel." Don Pedro asserts, "That she is worthy, I know." And Benedick avers, "That I neither feel how she should be lov'd, nor know how she should be worthy, is the opinion that fire cannot melt out of me." While the exchange is typically played for laughs, it still embodies three ways of looking at love that will figure significantly in the play. For Claudio, love is about feeling—one might even say an excess of feeling. The problem is that his idea of love lacks a cognitive function; that is, feelings can be fleeting and variable and need something more enduring to rely on. Don Pedro, on the other hand, asserts his knowledge of Hero's worthiness, yet it is this same "knowing" that later proves fallible and betrays Don Pedro (and Claudio) when they are tricked by Don John into believing that Hero is unfaithful. Knowing without feeling can never be the basis for an enduring commitment. Finally, Benedick neither knows nor feels and is substantially indifferent to the issue; he represents the uninformed opinion of the general public. As the plots of *Much Ado* play out, we come to understand that feeling, knowledge, and public regard are all factors that influence and shape personal and social relationships. Benedick's lines at the end of the scene

suggest typical male ways of looking at women: as mother ("woman conceiv'd me"); as mother or nurse ("brought me up"); as wife (though he would remain a bachelor); and as a sexual cheat or adulteress, who will make him a cuckold (put horns on his head). These various perceptions of "Woman" fuel the gender conflicts between the play's characters.

Act II, Scene 1, 392–400

DON PEDRO. And Benedick is not the unhopefullest husband that I know. Thus far can I praise him; he is of a noble strain, of approv'd valor, and confirmed honesty. I will teach you [Hero, Claudio] how to humor your cousin [Beatrice] that she fall in love with Benedick, and I with your two helps, will so practice on Benedick that he shall fall in love with Beatrice.

Don Pedro figures strongly in a pair of tricks designed to bring Benedick and Beatrice together; he essentially produces, casts, and directs these little plays within the larger play. In Act II, Scene 3, using Claudio and Leonato, Don Pedro sets a scene in which Benedick is tricked into overhearing the others talk of Beatrice's intense but concealed love for Benedick (then considered just a neat trick by Don Pedro and the others, but later confirmed as true). Beatrice is also tricked (in Act III, Scene 1), in a similar manner to Benedick, when Hero and her attendants arrange for Beatrice to overhear them talk of Benedick's hidden love for Beatrice. In both of the tricks played on Benedick and Beatrice, the ultimate goal is benevolent: to bring together frustrated lovers despite themselves. The tricks also have another effect: They become vehicles for Benedick and Beatrice to learn more about themselves by putting them in positions in which they can hear what others say and think about them, and thus bring about a reform of character.

But playing the trickster can be dangerous too. Don John malevolently tricks Don Pedro and Claudio into thinking that Hero is a wanton. Whereas Don Pedro's tricks are designed to bring people together, John's are designed to separate and alienate people. Whereas Pedro's tricks help reveal character, John's help create false characterization. Don Pedro's tricks are in the service of love, Don John's in the service of hate. And yet, in the end, even John's tricks ultimately reveal truth and character, bring people together, and result in more loving relationships, even though that was the opposite of what was intended.

Act II, Scene 1, 174–189

CLAUDIO. Thus answer I in the name of Benedick,
But hear these ill news with the ears of Claudio.
'Tis certain so; the Prince [Don Pedro] woos for himself.
Friendship is constant in all other things
Save in the office and affairs of love;
Therefore all hearts in love use their own tongues.
Let every eye negotiate for itself,
And trust no agent; for beauty is a witch
Against whose charms faith melteth into your blood.
This is an accident of hourly proof,
Which I mistrusted not. Farewell therefore Hero!

Don John has cleverly made Claudio, whom he pretends to believe is Benedick, believe that Don Pedro is enamored of Hero and intends to marry her that night. Claudio falls for the trap, believing that Don Pedro, who took it upon himself to act as an ambassador of love to Hero for Claudio, has tricked him and taken Hero for himself. The poison of jealousy corrodes the bonds of friendship between Claudio and Don Pedro ("Friendship is constant in all things, / Save in the office and affairs of love"). Female beauty is a "witch" (suggesting yet another possible role for a woman), against whom men have no defense. For Claudio, female sensuality is a force of great power, to be feared and mistrusted. Claudio cites the eyes (to see), the tongue (to speak), and occasion ("hourly proof") as the bases for belief, yet it is through all

these means that he is betrayed into a false position toward Hero and his former friends, Don Pedro and Benedick. Claudio "mistrusted not," although in this case it is trust, albeit in the wrong person, that nearly turns the play's events to tragedy. Claudio is caught in a web of perceptions because he is unable to ground his affections in love and trust. He is forever seeking, as Othello once did, "ocular proof" of the loyalty and fidelity of others. He is thus easily misled.

Act IV, Scene 1, 29–42

CLAUDIO. Sweet Prince, you learn me noble thankfulness,
There Leonato, take her back again,
Give not this rotten orange to your friend,
She's but the sign and semblance of her honor.
Behold like a maid she blushes here!
O, what authority and show of truth
Can cunning sin cover itself withal!
Comes not that blood as modest evidence
To witness simple virtue? Would you not swear,
All you that see her, that she were a maid,
By these exterior shows? But she is none;
She knows the heat of a luxurious bed;
Her blush is guiltiness, not modesty.

This is one of the central scenes of the the play: Claudio's rejection of Hero at the altar. As we know by this point in the play, Claudio, duped by Don John and Borachio into believing that Hero is unfaithful, has vowed to publicly shame and reject her. Don Pedro, the Prince, and Leonato, Hero's father, have presented Hero to Claudio at the altar. There is a deep irony in the phrase "noble thankfulness," suggesting at once both an admirable form and level of gratitude, but also a criticism of the sort of royal tricks and stratagems that the aristocracy may play on those beneath them, for Claudio believes that Don Pedro is implicated in Hero's supposed lewdness. Class and conflict are intertwined. The "orange" is a fruit known for its juiciness and sweetness, but to Claudio, insofar as it is "rotten," it is now bitter. The use of this fruit

Hero faints on her wedding day after Claudio and Don Pedro accuse her of being false, in Act IV, Scene I of *Much Ado About Nothing.* This is a print from the Boydell Shakespeare Gallery project, which was conceived in 1786 and lasted until 1805. *(Painting by William Hamilton; engraving by Jean Pierre Simon)*

also suggests another play on words: as oranges are typically squeezed to extract their juice, so would a wanton woman be subject to the squeezes of illicit lovers who sought her pleasures. The color of the orange may also suggest the blushes of the bride to be. And finally, we recall that Beatrice describes Don Pedro, whom Claudio is led to believe has amorous intentions toward Hero, as, "civil as an orange, and something of that jealous complexion" (2.1.293–295).

Claudio sounds some of the play's main themes when he charges Hero with being "but the sign and semblance of her honor"—that is, she only appears to be the virtuous, which is to say virginal, bride but, in reality, is a lewd and lascivious woman. Appearance and reality, as we have seen, is a dominant motif. The characters play tricks on each other in sport and in deadly earnest. One might say that the question that perplexes each of the characters in the play could be summed up as: Is what we see what we get? In Claudio's deceived eyes, Hero is "like a maid," which is to say not a maid at all. Like a maid (and like an orange), she blushes, but Claudio sees that blush as evidence of her guilty con-science. Hero's appearance, undisguised to us who know how Claudio has been deceived, is for Claudio but "exterior shows," false appearances. He is offered a maid but believes her to be a whore who lies in "luxurious bed" with her lovers. This theme of appearance and reality is inextricably bound up with woman's virtue. For Claudio, his very sense of himself as a man is tied to Hero's virtue. Like another famous lover, Othello, Claudio is blinded by his fears and jealousies. In the case of Othello, Desdemona really dies as a result of her lover's jealousy; here, Hero dies "only" a symbolic death from Claudio's actions.

Act IV, Scene 1, 212–245

FRIAR. Marry, this well carried shall on her
  behalf
Change slander to remorse; that is some good:
But not for that dream I on this strange
  course,
But on this travail look for greater birth.
She dying, as it must so be maintain'd,
Upon the instant that she was accused,
Shall be lamented, pitied and excused
Of every hearer: for it so falls out
That what we have we prize not to the worth
Whiles we enjoy it, but being lack'd and lost,
Why, then we rack the value, then we find
The virtue that possession would not show us
Whiles it was ours. So will it fare with Claudio:
When he shall hear she died upon his words,
The idea of her life shall sweetly creep
Into his study of imagination,
And every lovely organ of her life
Shall come apparell'd in more precious habit,
More moving-delicate and full of life,
Into the eye and prospect of his soul,
Than when she lived indeed; then shall he
  mourn,
If ever love had interest in his liver,
And wish he had not so accused her,
No, though he thought his accusation true.
Let this be so, and doubt not but success
Will fashion the event in better shape
Than I can lay it down in likelihood.

But if all aim but this be levell'd false,
The supposition of the lady's death
Will quench the wonder of her infamy:
And if it sort not well, you may conceal her,
As best befits her wounded reputation,
In some reclusive and religious life,
Out of all eyes, tongues, minds and injuries.

One should include the Friar's words of wisdom—or at least "real politics"—in any discussion of the play. The Friar reminds us that death tends to minimize the faults, failures, and vices, real or supposed, of the deceased. People are reluctant to speak ill of the dead. Thus, in the mind of the public, Hero's reputation will benefit, or at least not appear as dark as it did on her wedding day. As the Friar realizes, time will also allow the truth to come out. If the truth is as bad as it appears, Hero could find some "reclusive" life, out of the public eye. If the truth would serve to redeem Hero, time will allow it to emerge from the confusion of the moment, which is indeed what happens. Finally, the Friar also reminds us that we tend not to appreciate what we have; when we no longer have it, then we realize what we have lost. Hero will be more greatly appreciated once the situation rights itself.

Act V, Scene 4, 101–110

BENEDICK. I'll tell thee what, Prince, a college of wit-crackers cannot flout me out of my humour. Dost thou think I care for a satire or an epigram? No, if a man will be beaten with brains, a' shall wear nothing handsome about him. In brief, since I do purpose to marry, I will think nothing to any purpose that the world can say against it, and therefore never flout at me for what I have said against it. For man is a giddy thing, and this is my conclusion.

The final scene of *Much Ado,* like most of Shakespeare's comedies, ends in marriage and a coming together of the community in joy. Hero and Claudio are reconciled; now Beatrice and Benedick must join together. In this passage, Benedick dismisses jests about his former jeers at marriage and his intention to remain a bachelor: "In brief, since I do purpose to marry, I will think nothing to any purpose that the world can say against it, and therefore never flout at me for what I have said against it, for man is a giddy thing, and this is my conclusion." The "bottom line"—that "Man is a giddy thing"—provides the play's ultimate moral. People are not entirely rational creatures. We may say one thing now and another later, as our passions sway us. The play of emotions cannot be subject to a strict logic. It does not matter what jokes or criticisms are made at our expense. We are driven by our feelings, and the impulse to join with another cannot be withstood. This seems a satisfactory conclusion for this comedy. One last detail—John's punishment—is held for another day. In the meantime, there is dancing and marriage.

DIFFICULT PASSAGES
Act 1, Scene 1, 318–330

DON PEDRO: What need the bridge much
  broader than the flood?
The fairest grant is the necessity.
Look what will serve is fit; 'tis once, thou
  lovest,
And I will fit thee with the remedy.
I know we shall have revelling tonight;
I will assume thy part in some disguise,
And tell fair Hero I am Claudio,
And in her bosom I'll unclasp my heart,
And take her hearing prisoner with the force
And strong encounter of my amorous tale;
Then after to her father will I break,
And the conclusion is, she shall be thine.
In practice let us put it presently.

Claudio has previously confessed his love for Hero to Don Pedro, but here he acknowledges that he is reluctant to pass his suit too strongly or too quickly to Hero, "But lest my liking might too sudden seem, / I would have salv'd it with a longer treatise" . . . (314–315)—that is, he wants to take his time in broaching the subject to her. Don Pedro dismisses Claudio's caution, commenting, "What need the bridge much broader than the flood?" Don Pedro's advice is to do what it takes to achieve the object—in this case, Hero—and to do it quickly and forcefully. There is no need to practice such caution as Claudio's in this situation.

The oddity of this behavior, however well-intended, will later be exploited by Don John, who convinces Claudio that Don Pedro is wooing Hero for himself. One can hardly blame Claudio for believing Don John. Don Pedro's language in the passage quoted above is certainly heated, and a suggestive lustiness is evident: "her bosom," "take her hearing prisoner," and "strong encounter of my amorous tale" (the last phrase quite likely a bawdy play on words). Don Pedro almost seems to be ravishing Hero in his very language. If nothing else, the scene illustrates a certain weakness and passivity in Claudio's character; he is too easily acted upon by other men. This flaw will be amply illustrated in the rest of the play. It may be that Claudio is intimidated by aristocratic privilege and prerogative, and he is reluctant to cross Don Pedro. In any case, one feels the urge to yell at Claudio to "be a man!"

Act IV, Scene 4, 53–65

CLAUDIO. Which is the lady I must seize upon?

ANTONIO. This same is she, and I do give you her.

CLAUDIO. Why then she's mine. Sweet, let me see your face.

LEONATO. No, that you shall not till you take her hand,
Before this friar, and swear to marry her.

CLAUDIO. Give me your hand before this holy friar—
I am your husband if you like of me.

HERO [*unmasking*]. And when I liv'd, I was your other wife.

And when you lov'd, you were my other husband.

CLAUDIO. Another Hero!

HERO. Nothing certainer:
One Hero died defiled, but I do live,
And surely as I live, I am a maid.

Leonato has obtained a promise from Claudio, as a sort of penance for his actions toward Hero, that Claudio will marry, sight unseen, the "niece" of Leonato. In Act V, Scene 4, the second marriage ceremony takes place—or, one could say, the interrupted marriage ceremony is resumed. Leonato asks Claudio, "Are you yet determined / To-day to marry with my brother's daughter?"—to which Claudio, now certainly less exacting than he was previously, responds, "I'll hold my mind were she an Ethiope." The reference to Ethiopia is undoubtedly intended to suggest a person from the farthest and most unknown corners of Earth, yet it also injects an element of race into the affair; that is, Claudio would marry "even" a black woman to keep his promise. The issue, insinuated but not pursued, is worth noting as it adds to the complex of gender and social themes in which the play is immersed.

Soon the women—Hero, Beatrice, Margaret, and Ursula—enter, masked. Claudio asks, "Which is the lady I must seize upon?" (5.4.52), which can certainly be played for laughs, but which continues the use of terms of military force in matters of male-female relationships (recall Don Pedro's language when he discusses wooing Hero). The masked Hero is moved forward, and Claudio accepts her: "Why then she's mine" (5.4.54). He asks to see her face but is denied until he is willing to swear to marry her, which he does, saying, "Give me your hand . . . I am your husband if you like of me" (5.4.58–59). Hero then unmasks, saying: "And when I liv'd, I was your other wife / And when you lov'd, you were my other husband" (5.4.60–62). This is a complex construction of their previous relationship, and its meaning is not quite easily captured in full. In essence, however, Hero seems to be

Hero in Act V, Scene 4, of *Much Ado About Nothing*.
This is a print from Charles Heath's 1848 edition of
*The Heroines of Shakspeare: Comprising the Principal
Female Characters in the Plays of the Great Poet.*
(Painting by J. W. Wright; engraving by W. H. Mote)

character as a virgin and virtuous woman was being
slandered by Don John, Don Pedro, Pedro, Claudio, and others in town, she could not live in society; she was "dead to the world," so to speak. It is
only with her vindication that she can again live
among her friends, family, and neighbors. Clearly,
the passage suggests that a woman's virtue is para-
mount to her social standing.

CRITICAL INTRODUCTION
TO THE PLAY

Much Ado About Nothing can be seen as a series of
pairings that are not so much opposites as comple-
mentary elements: war and peace, single life and
marriage, appearance and reality, society and class,
insiders and outsiders. Let us take each of these
pairings in turn.

Battle of Wits

The play opens with the messenger bringing news
to Messina of the arrival of Don Pedro, prince of
Arragon, and his entourage: his bastard brother,
Don John; Benedick, a young lord of Padua; and
Claudio, a young lord of Florence. All are returning victorious from a recent military campaign; one
notes that this is a multinational group of soldiers,
and they are all a long way from home. This can be
a ticklish situation, for the conversion to peacetime
can be difficult for young warriors, yet it must be
made. Coming to meet the warriors is Leonato,
the governor of Messina, with his daughter, Hero,
and niece, Beatrice. The implicit touchiness of the
situation is indicated in Don Pedro's question rendered as a statement in the Folio to Leonato, when
he asks, "Good Signior Leonato, you are come
to meet your trouble?," to which Leonato replies,
"Never came trouble to my house in the likeness
of your Grace" (1.1.96–100). The warriors must be
welcomed and accommodated.

Not all the warriors are foreign: There is already
a warrior among the Messinans, in the person of
Beatrice, who insults and taunts Benedick with her
wit. She mocks his accomplishments as a warrior,
comparing his actions to those of childish games,
and makes fun of his capacity to eat. As Leonato

saying that when Claudio previously loved her, she
was his wife and he her husband, despite the fact
that the wedding did not take place; the commitment between them was their bond. When Claudio
broke that bond, he ended their "marriage."

The reappearance of Hero amazes Claudio;
he exclaims, "Another Hero!" It's clear he does
not quite know what is going on. Hero tells him,
"Nothing certainer / One Hero died defil'd but I
do live / And surely as I live I am a maid." Don
Pedro also seems amazed, exclaiming, "The former
Hero! The Hero that is dead!" (5.4.65). It is the
Friar who draws the moral: "She died, my lord, but
while her slanders liv'd" (5.4.66–67). What Hero
and the Friar both mean to say is that while Hero's

points out, "There is a kind of merry war betwixt Signior Benedick and her; they never meet but there's a skirmish of wit between them" (1.1.61–63). Beatrice is capable of an even tougher talk. When Claudio has publicly shamed Hero, Beatrice is livid and seeks retribution. She recognizes her lack of physical strength to punish the slanderers: "Oh that I were a man! . . . I would eat his heart in the marketplace" (4.1.306–307). Instead, she issues a pungent command to Benedick, which makes even that young warrior quail: "Kill Claudio" (4.1.289). This is a comedy with a deep streak of violence.

War is often inextricably bound up with love. When the young Claudio falls in love with the beautiful and virtuous (if passive) Hero, he tells Don Pedro, "I look'd upon her with a soldier's eye, / That lik'd, but had a rougher task in hand / Thank to drive liking to the name of love" (1.1.298–300). Don Pedro decides to woo Hero on behalf of Claudio. He tells Claudio, "I will assume thy part in some disguise, / And tell fair Hero I am Claudio, / And in her bosom I'll unclasp my heart, / And take her hearing prisoner with the force / And strong encounter of my amorous tale" (1.1.321–325). The language of war is mixed with the language of love.

The smitten Claudio is an initial disappointment to his comrade in arms, Benedick, who wonders at the change in Claudio, from warrior to erstwhile lover. Benedick recalls: "I have known when there was no music with him but the drum and the fife, and now he had rather hear the tabor and the pipe. I have known when he would have walk'd ten mile afoot to see a good armor, and now will lie ten nights awake carving the fashion of a new doublet; he was wont to speak plain and to the purpose (like an honest man and a soldier), and now is he turn'd ortography—his words are a very fantastical banquet" (2.3.12–21).

Although turned lover, Claudio still feels embroiled in the twists and turns of war when he is duped by Don Pedro's bastard brother, Don John, into believing that Don Pedro has tricked Claudio and woo'd Hero for himself, not Claudio. Claudio

bemoans this supposed treachery: "Friendship is constant in all other things / Save in the office and affairs of love . . . trust no agent" (2.1.175–180). In other words, as the ancient adage has it, all is fair in love and war.

Indeed, the use of tricks, ploys, and stratagems throughout the play are a form of warfare in themselves. Don John tricks Claudio into believing Don Pedro is attempting to win Hero for himself. Don John and his attendant, Borachio, trick Claudio and Don Pedro into believing that Hero is unfaithful. Don Pedro and Claudio trick Benedick into believing that Beatrice is madly, secretly in love with him. Hero and her attendants Ursula and Margaret (Margaret herself also a part of Borachio's and Don John's scheme), at the direction of Don Pedro, trick Beatrice into thinking that Benedick is madly and secretly in love with her. The Friar tricks the populace (including Claudio and Don Pedro) into thinking Hero is dead, to gain time to find out the truth of the charges against Hero's virtue. This is war; sometimes no one is hurt (the tricks against Beatrice and Benedick); sometimes it is nearly fatal (the nearly deadly trick against Hero). The point of all these stratagems is to gain an advantage over the other party—that is, to achieve victory on the battleground of love.

Single or Married

The questions of bachelorhood and the marital (close enough to remind us of *martial*) state are extensions of the themes of war and peace, in that they evoke the power struggle between men and women, and more particularly, husbands and wives—that "merry war" in the case of Beatrice and Benedick, and the not-so-merry war in the case of Hero and Claudio. Benedick and Beatrice are the prime espousers of the perceived benefits of the single life. For Benedick, it seems the chief objection to becoming a husband is the threat of being cuckolded—that is, of having an unfaithful wife who will embarrass and shame her unknowing husband. The play is filled with allusions to husbands wearing the "horns" of the cuckold. Benedick is also very much concerned with losing his freedom, of being beholden to a wife. When he learns that Claudio is thinking of marrying Hero, he tells Claudio, "In faith, hath not the world one man but he will wear his cap with suspicion? . . . Go to, i'faith, and thou wilt needs thrust thy neck into a yoke, wear the print of it, and sigh away Sundays" (1.1.198–202). The cap is a reference to the possibility of a cheating wife putting the horns on her husband; alternately, the wife may impose a yoke (like that placed on an ox [a horned animal]) that will subordinate her husband and leave a lasting mark on his manhood and freedom.

Benedick lacks trust in women. In another passage, he fears having a "recheat winded in my forehead" (1.1.240–241)—that is, horns of the cuckold placed on his forehead. When Don Pedro and Claudio tease him about the possibility that his confirmed bachelorhood might give way to marriage, Benedick again asserts that he will not wear the yoke of the "savage bull," and were he to consent to marry, he tells his companions to "pluck off the bull's horns and set them in my forehead" (1.1.261–264). What does Benedick want? Not one who is only fair or wise or virtuous, but one who incorporates all these virtues, as well as some others, including rich, fair, mild, noble, well-spoken, and "an excellent musician," although her hair "shall be of what color it please" (2.2.26–35). It seems that Benedict is looking for a mythical creature: the perfect woman. Shortly after this internal accounting by Benedick, he will be tricked by Don Pedro and Claudio into believing that Beatrice is madly in love with him; this contrived revelation will lead him to change his thinking and wish to marry Beatrice.

For her part, Beatrice, unlike the mild Hero, also resists the married state. Leonato and his brother Antonio chide Beatrice for her resistance to marriage. Leonato tells her, "By my troth, niece, thou wilt never get thee a husband, if thou be so shrewd of thy tongue" (2.1.18–19)—that is, if she continues to talk to Benedick and other men in such a sharp and wounding manner, she will never marry. That possibility does not bother Beatrice. Echoing Benedick's fears that he would be cuckolded, Bea-

trice comments that "God sends a curst cow short horns—but to a cow too curst he sends none" (2.1.22–24). In other words, if God sent her a husband, he would send her a cuckold, for she may cuckold her unwanted husband. Beatrice's qualifications for a husband again echo Benedick's impossible qualifications for a wife: "He that had a beard is more than a youth, and he that had no beard is less than a man; and he that is more than a youth is not for me, and he that is less than a man, I am not for him" (2.1.36–39). When Antonio tells Hero, standing nearby, that she should be ruled by her father, Leonato, Beatrice responds that such compliance suits her cousin Hero, who will always say, "As it pleases you," but for herself it is "Father, as it please me"—a crucial assertion of her individual

Julia Marlowe as Beatrice and Edward Hugh Sothern as Benedick in a 1904 production of *Much Ado About Nothing*

right to choose whom she will (2.1.50–56). What Beatrice wants is the freedom to choose, to fit herself with a husband and not be fitted.

In the end, through the benevolent schemes of Don Pedro, Beatrice and Benedick do pledge their love to each other. As we learn, they had both secretly yearned for the other; the trick merely served to "break the ice" and allow each to express that love. Each chose whom they had wished for. In the final scene, Benedick must confront his previous comments about marriage. He recognizes the contrast between what he said then against marriage and what he says now for marriage to Beatrice: "In brief since I do purpose to marry, I will think nothing to any purpose that the world can say against it, and therefore never flout at me for what I have said against it; for man is a giddy thing, and this is my conclusion" (5.4.105–109). Indeed, Benedick turns into a proponent of marriage: When he notices that Don Pedro, who has schemed to mate others, has himself ended up without a mate, he tells him, "Prince, thou art sad, get thee a wife" (5.4.122). The play suggests that there is a natural, if not entirely rational, order to these things that will overcome mere individual attitudes.

Appearance and Reality

Much Ado About Nothing asks us to think about the difference between appearance and reality and how misunderstanding that difference can lead to serious problems. As noted, the play is filled with tricks and schemes, which are, in effect, plays within plays, each with its own director, actors, scripts, and audiences. From this perspective, Don Pedro might be said to be a master playwright. First, he organizes the wooing of Hero, using the masked ball (a type of play in itself) to adopt the disguise of the actual suitor, Claudio, to win the love of Hero and the consent of her father, Leonato. Although the end result is successful, the goal was accomplished by false appearances—that of Don Pedro in disguise, rather than the real suitor, Claudio—in the context of a masked ball, in which confusion of appearance and reality is a necessary part of the event.

Having now successfully accomplished the goal of winning Hero for Claudio, Don Pedro organizes two ploys that are intended to bring about a love match between Beatrice and Benedick. Using Hero and her attendants Ursula and Margaret to trick Beatrice, and using Claudio and Leonato to trick Benedick—in both cases by representing that each was madly in love with the other—Don Pedro again gains his ends by a false representation of reality (at least as these individuals knew it when his ploys were carried out). Beatrice and Benedick watch and listen to these little plays within the play from the sideline, forming an audience within the larger audience of those watching the play itself. They have been "set up" to participate in these "scenes," so that Don Pedro's goal is achieved. This goal might be benevolent, but the action is nevertheless a manipulation of appearance and reality.

In the scheme to trick Benedick, the attendant Balthasar is asked to sing a song. the lyrics of which warn the "ladies" that "Men were deceivers ever," and "The fraud of men was ever so" (2.3.62–74)—certainly a warning to players and audience alike that appearances are often deceptive. When, in carrying out the scheme, Claudio urges the others to "Bait the hook well, this fish will bite" (2.3.108–109), he suggests that the manipulation of appearances can often be a strategy to get others to do what the trickster(s) want. This may not necessarily be something bad. In the case of Benedick, the trick allows the others to speak candidly of Benedick's faults. Benedick is actually grateful to overhear his faults enumerated, in a way that allows him to listen without being directly confronted: "I am censur'd: . . . happy are they that hear their detractions, and can put them to mending" (2.3.224–230). Similarly, the ploy used with Beatrice allows Hero and the other ladies to document Beatrice's faults. Hero offers a stiff critique of Beatrice's pride and wounding wit. Beatrice, overhearing what the "actors" say, is able to confront her own behavior privately. She recognizes the truth of what has been said and resolves to reform: "What fire is in my ears? . . . Stand I condemn'd for pride and scorn so much? Contempt, farewell, and maid-enly pride, adieu!"

In the cases of Beatrice and Benedick, the ploy or "play" leads to constructive and positive outcomes, both individually and in relation to others. But the manipulation of appearance and reality can have other outcomes as well. Don Pedro is a master playwright in his own way, but so is his illegitimate and hateful brother, Don John. While Don Pedro's initial foray into "play acting" is to don a disguise at the masked ball to win Hero for Claudio, Don John's is to turn that scene upon itself by telling Claudio falsely that Don Pedro is actually wooing Hero for himself, not Claudio. Perhaps due to the inherent deceit of Don Pedro's "plot," Claudio is quick to believe Don John. Disconsolate, he comes to believe that one should "trust no agent" (2.1.179). Claudio is duped by multiple manipulations of appearance, so that he comes to the wrong conclusion. It is only when Don Pedro delivers Hero to him that Claudio believes Don Pedro did not trick him.

Perhaps emboldened by his initial success in duping Claudio, Don John is more than eager to set in motion a plot hatched by his attendant, Borachio, to make Hero appear to be a wanton, unfaithful woman. It is Borachio who thus "produces" and "directs" this malevolent play within a play. Borachio's plan is to have Don John bring Don Pedro and Claudio near, but not too near, Hero's bedchamber window to watch, just as Don Pedro arranged to have Beatrice and Benedick brought near to overhear what was said about them, so that the "hook" might be properly baited. In the same fashion, Borachio and Don John intend to bait a hook with poisonous bait intended to wreck Claudio's impending marriage to Hero. Borachio plots to have his illicit girlfriend, Margaret, Hero's attendant, dress as Hero and, while Hero is gone from her room, come to the window to exchange lovers' talk with a disguised Borachio. As Borachio tells Don John, in a key line in the play, "and there shall be such seeming truth of Hero's disloyalty, that jealousy shall be call'd assurance, and all the preparation overthrown" (2.3.47–50). "Seeming truth"

is the difficult, intangible, crucial question that is at the heart of this play.

The success of Borachio's plot is recounted later in a conversation between Borachio and another of Don John's attendants, Conrade. Borachio tells how, by careful manipulation of the scene, Don Pedro and Claudio were tricked—that is, "took the bait." It was partly by Don John's "oaths" and "partly by the dark night, which did deceive them, but chiefly by my villainy, which did confirm any slander that Don John had made, away went Claudio enrag'd" (3.3.156–159). Whereas exposure, revelation, and reformation were the outcomes of the "plots" against Benedick and Beatrice, here the outcome is misrepresentation, deceit, and misunderstanding. Whereas Don Pedro's plot led to bringing lovers together, this plot leads to lovers being parted and Claudio publicly shaming Hero at the altar, where he rejects her.

The crucial and painful scene at the altar returns to the themes of appearance and reality. When Claudio accuses Hero of being but the "sign and semblance of her honor" (4.1.33), he accuses her of false appearances and dishonesty. When he boasts of his own pure love for her, Hero responds, "And seem'd I ever otherwise to you?" (4.1.55), arguing thus for the reality and honesty of her appearance. Duped by Don John, Claudio rejects her response: "Out on thee seeming!" (4.1.56). The duped Claudio has fallen into a dangerous confusion of appearance and reality. So has Don Pedro, who supports Claudio's charges, recounting how they stood near Hero's window and "did see her, did hear her" (in fact, the disguised Margaret) talk to "a ruffian" (the disguised Borachio) and admit the "vile encounters they have had" (4.1.88–93). The Friar officiating at the wedding recognizes this, observing, "There is some strange misprision in the princes [Don Pedro and Claudio]" (4.1.184–185)—that is, a misperception, a false seeing and understanding. The Friar himself becomes a play director when he instructs that a false report be issued that Hero, who has fainted dead away at the altar, is in fact dead, in order to gain time to find out what is behind these charges made by Claudio and Don Pedro. Here is yet another ruse or ploy, which depends like the others on trickery, but this time to do good.

Don John's plot finally is discovered when the bumbling, malapropism-prone constable Dogberry and other members of the night watch overhear Borachio and Conrade talking about the plot and obtain full confessions. Borachio admits to Don Pedro, "I have deceiv'd even your very eyes: what your wisdoms could not discover, these shallow fools have brought to light" (5.1.232–234). Borachio and Don John obtained such complete control of plot and scene that they "deceiv'd even your very eyes," a fundamental manipulation and distortion of appearance and reality. This is a very telling comment on the complexities of appearance and reality.

The playmaking is not yet complete. Now it is Leonato's turn to play the director. All having learned of Don John's plot, and thus Hero's innocence, Leonato directs Claudio to go to Leonato's family tomb in the cemetery and hang an epitaph on the purported tomb of Hero, whom Claudio still believes is dead. Again, there is an element of deceit. Leonato continues the ruse designed by the Friar, so that Claudio can do proper penance for his actions. This is scene setting for ritual purposes. The ruse is continued when Leonato obtains Claudio's agreement to marry another niece of Leonato's, sight unseen, as proper restitution for his false charges against Hero. At the altar, a masked Hero reveals herself, saying, "One Hero died defil'd, but I do live, / And surely as I live, I am a maid" (5.4.63–64). This final ritual playacting, ironically involving yet another ruse and more masking, finally resolves Don John's distortions. Don Pedro's tricks on Beatrice and Benedick are also resolved when the lovers unmask their own feelings and agree to marry. In a comedy, all the problems of appearance and reality are resolved, but the deeper lesson of the play is that life is more complex than that, leading sometimes to comedy, sometimes to tragedy.

Insiders and Outsiders in Society

Beneath the more obvious themes of war, love, marriage, and the difference between appearance and reality, the play examines deeper issues regarding the arrangement of society. Our first impression of the society of Messina is that of noblemen and women, princes and lords, coming together in celebration of military victory and peace. As we have noted, this is a touchy and difficult transition, with violence and treachery lurking not far below the surface. A closer look also reveals some social chasms. None of the lords are from the play's locale, Messina, located at the far tip of the Italian peninsula, in a corner of Sicily. They are a diverse and far-flung group. Mostly, they are away from their native lands. On the other hand, the head of the local government of Messina, while clearly a member of the governing class, is not among the nobility but a civil governor, a member of what might be construed as a civil servant class. While he is apparently familiar with some of these lords, there is enough of a gap to induce Don Pedro to note, "Good Signior Leonato, you are come to meet your trouble" (1.1.96–97). While the statement is not meant to offend, it raises a tremor of social discord.

Leonato's own house is in a state of imbalance. He has a daughter, Hero, but not a wife, and his daughter does not have a mother. Leonato has a brother, Antonio, and a niece, Beatrice, although Beatrice is not Antonio's daughter. Beatrice's relationship to Leonato is not quite made clear. He has no apparent authority over Beatrice; as we have seen, his efforts to "fit her" with a husband are unavailing. When Leonato is confronted by Don Pedro and Claudio's false accusations regarding Hero, he and his brother Antonio work themselves up into a fighting frenzy, which is treated dismissively by Don Pedro and Claudio; these two old men are no match for lords just returned from real war. Leonato's political and domestic households may be said to lack effectiveness and coherence; there is an inherent imbalance at play.

Don Pedro's own family is riven by dissension and social conflict in the person of Don John, described as his "bastard brother"—that is, his illegitimate brother. As a bastard, Don John would traditionally be deprived of the royal standing and social respect automatically given his legitimate brother. The very label of "bastard" serves to seal off Don John from his place in society. He is afflicted with a "sadness without limit" (1.3.4). Don John observes of himself: "I cannot hide what I am: I must be sad when I have cause and smile at no man's jests, eat when I have stomach and wait for no man's leisure, sleep when I am drowsy and tend on no man's business, l laugh when I am merry and claw no man in his humor" (1.3.13–18). This argument for a supreme individualism, or even iconoclasm, reveals a man deeply alienated from society. He is a classic outsider and, as such, a danger to society. He underscores this potential harm early in the play when he describes himself as a "plain-dealing villain" (1.3.32). When he hears that Claudio is to have Hero, it angers him, as it seems to further displace him from what he thinks is his rightful place in society: "This young start-up hath all the glory of my overthrow" (1.1.66–67). When Borachio tells him that he can prevent Claudio's marriage to Hero, Don John is gratified: "Any bar, any cross, any impediment will be med'cinable to me. I am sick in displeasure to him and whatsoever comes athwart his affections ranges evenly with mine" (2.2.4–8). Don John poses the classic danger of the alienated outsider: In the play, he attempt to wreck a marriage. In a later age, he might be the shooter who inflicts random violence on innocent victims. The question he poses is: How does one reach this type of outsider and bring him into a more constructive engagement with society?

While Don John is the most notable of the social outsiders, he is not the only one. There is a sort of underclass that operates beneath the veneer of the social high life in which the lords and ladies are engaged. Don John's attendants, described in the dramatis personae as "followers" of Don John, are rather rootless, placeless individuals who seem to feel allegiance to no one person or group. Borachio hatches the scheme against Hero that Don John avidly joins in, but why Borachio does so is not clear. Obviously, he wants to please his master, but this scheme is too awful to be justi-

Dogberry and the watch in Act IV, Scene 2 of *Much Ado About Nothing. (Illustration by Frederick Barnard; engraving by Joseph Swain)*

fied solely by that reason. It is possible that this very lack of place motivates, or at least permits, Borachio to launch such a vicious trick. Similarly, Conrade feels no compunction upon hearing the scheme. Not as audacious as Borachio, he is sufficiently amoral to allow evil to happen. A sense of the social order's larger fragility is implied in the fact that Borachio is having an illicit affair with Margaret, Hero's maid, who is instrumental in assisting the scheme by posing as Hero. Although later partially cleared for her role in the scheme, her actions leave a question mark on the fabric of this society and an implication of other unsavory and shadowy elements.

Perhaps the most interesting member of the underclass is Dogberry, the constable. A comic figure for his bumbling and his mangling of the language, he is still a socially important figure. He boasts of himself: "I am a wise fellow, and which is more, an officer and which is more, a householder, . . . and one that hath two gowns, and everything handsome about him" (4.2). In other words, he is a self-made man, a member of the rising civil class, risen on his own. Indeed, as constable, he underpins the administration of Governor Leonato. It is useful to think of Dogberry as the counterpart to Don John: the latter an outsider who works his way down and out of the social order, the former an outsider who is working his way up and into the social order. Borachio indirectly validates Dogberry when he comments to Don Pedro, probably ruefully: "What your wisdom could not discover, these shallow fools [Dogberry and the members of the watch] have brought to life" (5.1.232–234). Unencumbered by the pretenses, masks, and stratagems of court life, Dogberry is a new sort of man making a place for himself in a new sort of society.

EXTRACTS OF CLASSIC CRITICISM

William Richardson (1743–1814) [Excerpted from "On Shakespeare's Imitation of Female Characters (addressed to a friend)" (1797). Richardson was a well-known professor at Glasgow University who published several books on Shakespeare. Here, he notes the "vivacity and wit of Beatrice" (350) and observes, "She does not defend herself, or make her attacks with grave, argumentative, and persuasive elocution: but, endowed with the powers of wit, she employs them in raillery, banter, and repartee." He argues that her "dissimulation" may be found in both men and women "who are actuated by serious principles; but who are rendered timid, either from some conscious imbecility; or who become suspicious by an early, too early an observation of designing persons" (353). This is an interesting observation on Richardson's part, as it suggests that Beatrice resorts to raillery because of her concerns about the actions of "designing persons" around her—and Messina is filled with such persons.]

But if the gentle, unsuspecting, and artless simplicity of Miranda *[The Tempest]*; if the good sense and affecting eloquence of Isabella *[Measure for Measure]*, should not induce you to acquit the poet, you will yield, perhaps, to the vivacity and wit of Beatrice.—No less amiable and affectionate than Miranda and Isabella, she expresses resentment, because she feels commiseration for the sufferings of her friend.

Is he not approved in the height a villain, that hath slandered, scorned, and dishonoured my kinswoman?

Like Isabella, too, she is distinguished by intellectual ability; but of a different kind. She does not defend herself, or make her attacks with grave, argumentative, and persuasive elocution: but, endowed with the powers of wit, she employs them in raillery, banter, and repartee.

Ben. What, my dear Lady Disdain! are you yet living?

Beat. Is it possible Disdain should die, while she hath such meet food to feed upon, as signor Benedict?—The count is neither sad, nor sick, nor merry, nor well; but civil count, civil as an orange, and something of that jealous complexion.

Her smartness, however, proceeds from wit rather than from humour. She does not attempt, or is not so successful in ludicrous description, as in lively sayings.

Beat. My cousin tells him in his ear, that he is in her heart.

Claud. And so she does, cousin.

Beat. Good lord for alliance! thus goes every one to the world, but I, and I am sun-burned; I may sit in the corner, and cry heigh-ho for a husband.

Pe. Lady Beatrice, I will get you one.

Beat. I would rather have one of your father's getting.

Another distinction, not unconnected with the preceding, is, that though lively, she is nevertheless serious, and though witty, grave.

Possessed of talents for wit, she seems to employ them for the purposes of defence, or disguise. She conceals the real and thoughtful seriousness of her disposition by a shew of vivacity. Howsoever she may speak of them, she treats her own concerns, and those of her friends, with grave consideration. A compliment, and the enticement of a playful allusion, almost betrays her into an actual confession.

Ped. In faith, lady, you have a merry heart.

Beat. Yea, my lord, I thank it, poor fool, it keeps on the windy side of care.

She is desirous of being reputed very sprightly and disdainful: but it is not of the qualities which we chiefly possess that we are usually most ostentatious. Congreve wished to be thought a fine gentleman; Swift would be a politician; and Milton a divine. What Beatrice, who is really amiable, would have herself thought to be, appears in the following passage, where Hero, pretending not to know she was present, describes her in her own hearing.

Nature never fram'd a woman's heart
Of prouder stuff than that of Beatrice.
Disdain and scorn ride sparkling in her
    eyes,
Misprizing what they look on, &c.

Ada Rehan as Beatrice in an 1896 production of *Much Ado About Nothing*

Tender, affectionate, and ingenuous; yet conscious of more weakness than Miranda, or not like her educated in a desert island, she is aware of mankind, affects to be mirthful when she is most in earnest, and employs her wit when she is most afraid.—Nor is such dissimulation, if it may be so termed, to be accounted peculiarly characteristical of female manners. It may be discovered in men of probity and tenderness, and who are actuated by serious principles; but who are rendered timid, either from some conscious imbecility; or who become suspicious by an early, too early an observation of designing persons. If such men are endowed with so much liveliness of invention, as, in the society to which they belong, to be reckoned witty or humorous, they often employ this talent as an engine of defence. Without it, they would perhaps fly from society, like the melancholy Jacques *[As You Like It],* who wished to have, but did not possess a very distinguished, though some, portion of such ability. Thus, while they seem to annoy, they only wish to prevent: their mock encounter is a real combat: while they seem for ever in the field, they conceive themselves always besieged: though perfectly serious, they never appear in earnest: and though they affect to set all men at defiance; and though they are not without understanding, yet they tremble for the censure and are tortured with the sneer of a fool. Let them come to the school of Shakespeare. He will give *them*, as he gives many others an useful lesson. He will shew them an exemplary and natural reformation or exertion. Beatrice is not to be ridiculed out of an honourable purpose; nor to forfeit, for fear of a witless joke, a connection with a person who is "of a noble strain, of approved valour, and confirmed honesty."

Samuel   Johnson (1709–1784) [Excerpted from *The Plays of William Shakespeare* (1765). The great English dictionary maker and critic Samuel Johnson, in his "Preface to Shakespeare," offers fine insights into Shakespeare's dramatic methods that can usefully be applied to *Much Ado*. It is certainly true in *Much Ado* that Shakespeare has "excited laughter and sorrow" in one play.]

Shakespeare's plays are not in the rigorous and critical sense either tragedies or comedies, but compositions of a distinct kind; exhibiting the real state of sublunary nature, which partakes of good and evil, joy and sorrow, mingled with endless variety of proportion and innumerable modes of combination; and expressing the course of the world, in which the loss of one is the gain of another; in which, at the same time, the reveller is hasting to his wine, and the mourner burying his friend; in which the malignity of one is sometimes defeated by the frolick of another; and many mischiefs and many benefits are done and hindered without design.

Out of this chaos of mingled purposes and casualties the ancient poets, according to the laws which custom had prescribed, selected some the crimes of men, and some their absurdities; some the momentous vicissitudes of life, and some the lighter occurrences; some the terrours of distress, and some the gayeties of prosperity. Thus rose the two modes of imitation, known by the names of tragedy and comedy, compositions intended to promote different ends by contrary means, and considered as so little allied, that I do not recollect among the Greeks or Romans a single writer who attempted both.

Shakespeare has united the powers of exciting laughter and sorrow not only in one mind, but in one composition. Almost all his plays are divided between serious and ludicrous characters, and, in the successive evolutions of the design, sometimes produce seriousness and sorrow, and sometimes levity and laughter.

Samuel   Taylor   Coleridge (1772–1834) [Excerpted from *Shakspeare, with Introductory Remarks on Poetry, the Drama, and the Stage* (1818). Coleridge, best known for poems such as "The Rime of the Ancient Mariner," was also an inventive critic. Like later critics of Shakespeare, Coleridge here observes that a central element of Shakespeare's drama is his application of the "understanding or prudence, wit, fancy, imagination, judgment" to "the objects on which these are to be employed," certainly themes that resonate in *Much Ado*.]

Let me, then, once more submit this question to minds emancipated alike from national, or party, or sectarian prejudice:—Are the plays of Shakespeare works of rude uncultivated genius, in which the splendour of the parts compensates, if aught can compensate, for the barbarous shapelessness and irregularity of the whole?—Or is the form equally admirable with the matter, and the judgment of the great poet, not less deserving our wonder than his genius?—Or, again, to repeat the question in other words:—Is Shakespeare a great dramatic poet on account only of those beauties and excellences which he possesses in common with the ancients, but with diminished claims to our love and honour to the full extent of his differences from them?—(63)

I greatly dislike beauties and selections in general ; but as proof positive of his unrivalled excellence, I should like to try Shakespeare by this criterion. Make out your amplest catalogue of all the human faculties, as reason or the moral law, the will, the feeling of the coincidence of the two . . . called the conscience, the understanding or prudence, wit, fancy, imagination, judgment,—and then of the objects on which these are to be employed, as the beauties; the terrors, and the seeming caprices of nature, the realities and the capabilities, that is, the actual and the ideal, of the human mind, conceived as an individual or as a social being, as in innocence or in guilt, in a play-paradise, or in a war-field of temptation;—and then compare with Shakespeare under each of these heads all or any of the writers in prose and verse that have ever lived ! Who, that is competent to judge, doubts the result?

William Hazlitt (1778–1830) [Excerpted from *Characters of Shakespear's Plays* (1817). Hazlitt, another romantic critic, is arguably one of the most important Shakespearean critics of the 19th century. Here he offers a view that we might find contrarian today. It is Hero who is the principal attraction of the play to Hazlitt, leaving "an indelible impression on the mind by her beauty, her tenderness, and the hard trial of her love." Hazlitt captures something important about the play when he observes that it captures folly and feeling in a way that brings us back to our common humanity.]

MUCH ADO ABOUT NOTHING

This admirable comedy used to be frequently acted till of late years. Mr. Garrick's Benedick was one of his most celebrated characters; and Mrs. Jordan, we have understood, played Beatrice very delightfully. The serious part is still the most prominent here, as in other instances that we have noticed. Hero is the principal figure in the piece, and leaves an indelible impression on the mind by her beauty, her tenderness, and the hard trial of her love. The passage in which Claudio first makes a confession of his affection towards her conveys as pleasing an image of the entrance of love into a youthful bosom as can well be imagined.

> Oh, my lord,
> When you went onward with this ended action,
> I look'd upon her with a soldier's eye,
> That lik'd, but had a rougher task in hand
> Than to drive liking to the name of love;
> But now I am return'd, and that war-thoughts
> Have left their places vacant; in their rooms
> Come thronging soft and delicate desires,
> All prompting me how fair young Hero is,
> Saying, I lik'd her ere I went to wars.

In the scene at the altar, when Claudio, urged on by the villain Don John, brings the charge of incontinence against her, and as it were divorces her in the very marriage-ceremony, her appeals to her own conscious innocence and honour are made with the most affecting simplicity.

> Claudio. No, Leonato,
> I never tempted her with word too large,
> But, as a brother to his sister, show'd

Bashful sincerity, and comely love.

Hero. And seem'd I ever otherwise to
  you?

Claudio. Out on thy seeming, I will
  write against it:

You seem to me as Dian in her orb,

As chaste as is the bud ere it be blown;

But you are more intemperate in your
  blood

Than Veilus, or those pamper'd animals

That rage in savage sensuality.

Hero. Is my lord well, that he doth speak
  so wide?

Leonato. Are these things spoken, or do
  I but dream?

John. Sir, they are spoken, and these
  things are true.

Benedick. This looks not like a nuptial.

Hero. True! O God!

The justification of Hero in the end, and
her restoration to the confidence and arms of
her lover, is brought about by one of those
temporary consignments to the grave of
which Shakespeare seems to have been fond.
He has perhaps explained the theory of this
predilection in the following lines:

Friar. She dying, as it must be so
  maintain'd,

Upon the instant that she was accus'd,

Shall be lamented, pity'd, and excus'd,

Of every hearer: for it so falls out,

That what we have we prize not to the
  worth,

While we enjoy it; but being lack'd and
  lost,

Why then we rack the value; then we
  find

The virtue, that possession would not
  show us

Whilst it was ours.—So will it fare with
  Claudio;

When he shall hear she dy'd upon his
  words,

The idea of her love shall sweetly creep

Into his study of imagination;

And every lovely organ of her life

Shall come apparel'd in more precious
  habit,

More moving, delicate, and full of life,

Into the eye and prospect of his soul,

Than when she liv'd indeed.

The principal comic characters in MUCH
ADO ABOUT NOTHING, Benedick and
Beatrice, are both essences in their kind. His
character as a woman-hater is admirably supported, and his conversion to matrimony is no
less happily effected by the pretended story of
Beatrice's love for him. It is hard to say which
of the two scenes is the best, that of the trick
which is thus practised on Benedick, or that
in which Beatrice is prevailed on to take pity
on him by overhearing her cousin and her
maid declare (which they do on purpose) that
he is dying of love for her. There is something
delightfully picturesque in the manner in
which Beatrice is described as coming to hear
the plot which is contrived against herself:

For look where Beatrice, like a lapwing,
  runs "Close by the ground, to hear our
  conference."

In consequence of what she hears (not
a word of which is true) she exclaims when
these good-natured informants are gone:

What fire is in mine ears? Can this be
  true?

Stand I condemn'd for pride and scorn
  so much?

Contempt, farewell! and maiden pride
  adieu!

No glory lives behind the back of such.

And, Benedick, love on, I will requite
  thee;

Taming my wild heart to thy loving
  hand;

If thou dost love, my kindness shall
  incite thee
To bind our loves up in an holy band:
For others say thou dost deserve; and I
Believe it better than reportingly.

And Benedick, on his part, is equally sincere in his repentance with equal reason, after
he has heard the grey-beard, Leonato, and
his friend, 'Monsieur Love', discourse of the
desperate state of his supposed inamorata.

This can be no trick; the conference was
sadly borne.—They have the truth of
this from Hero. They seem to pity the
lady; it seems her affections have the full
bent. Love me! why, it must be requited.
I hear how I am censur'd: they say, I
will bear myself proudly, if I perceive the
love come from her; they say too, that
she will rather die than give any sign of
affection.—I did never think to marry;
I must not seem proud:—happy are they
that hear their detractions, and can put
them to mending. They say, the lady is
fair; 'tis a truth, I can bear them witness:
and virtuous;—'tis so, I cannot reprove
it; and wise—but for loving me;—by my
troth it is no addition to her wit;—nor
no great argument of her folly, for I will
be horribly in love with her.—I may
chance to have some odd quirks and
remnants of wit broken on me, because
I have rail'd so long against marriage:
but doth not the appetite alter? A man
loves the meat in his youth, that he
cannot endure in his age.—Shall quips,
and sentences, and these paper bullets
of the brain, awe a man from the career
of his humour? No: the world must be
peopled. When I said, I would die a
bachelor, I did not think I should live till
I were marry'd.—Here comes Beatrice;
by this day, she's a fair lady: I do spy
some marks of love in her.

Beatrice (Winifred Emery) tells Benedick (Herbert
Beerbohm) to prove his love for her by killing Claudio
in Act IV, Scene 1 of *Much Ado About Nothing*. This is
an illustration of a 1905 production at His Majesty's
Theatre. *(Illustration by Max Cowper)*

The beauty of all this arises from the characters of the persons so entrapped. Benedick
is a professed and staunch enemy to marriage,
and gives very plausible reasons for the faith
that is in him. And as to Beatrice, she per-
secutes him all day with her jests (so that he
could hardly think of being troubled with
them at night), she not only turns him but
all other things into jest, and is proof against
everything serious.

Hero. Disdain and scorn ride sparkling
  in her eyes,
Misprising what they look on; and her wit
Values itself so highly, that to her

All matter else seems weak: she cannot
  love,
Nor take no shape nor project of
  affection,
She is so self-endeared.
Ursula. Sure, I think so;
And therefore, certainly, it were not
  good
She knew his love, lest she make sport
  at it.
Hero. Why, you speak truth: I never yet
  saw man,
How wise, how noble, young, how rarely
  featur'd,
But she would spell him backward: if
  fair-fac'd,
She'd swear the gentleman should be her
  sister;
If black, why, nature, drawing of an
  antick,
Made a foul blot: if tall, a lance
  ill-headed;
If low, an agate very vilely cut:
If speaking, why, a vane blown with all
  winds;
If silent, why, a block moved with none.
So turns she every man the wrong side
  out;
And never gives to truth and virtue that
Which simpleness and merit purchaseth.

These were happy materials for Shakespeare to work on, and he has made a happy use of them. Perhaps that middle point of comedy was never more nicely hit in which the ludicrous blends with the tender, and our follies, turning round against themselves in support of our affections, retain nothing but their humanity.

Dogberry and Verges in this play are inimitable specimens of quaint blundering and misprisions of meaning; and are a standing record of that formal gravity of pretension and total want of common understanding, which Shakespeare no doubt copied from real life, and which in the course of two hundred years appear to have ascended from the lowest to the highest offices in the state.

Anna Jameson (1794–1860) [Excerpted from *Shakespeare's Heroines: Characteristics of Women, Moral, Poetical & Historical* (1833). An important early female critic of Shakespeare, Jameson found much to admire in Beatrice.]

Shakespeare has exhibited in Beatrice a spirited and faithful portrait of the fine lady of his own time. The deportment, language, manners, and allusions are those of a particular class in a particular age; but the individual and dramatic character which forms the ground-work is strongly discriminated, and being taken from general nature, belongs to every age. In Beatrice, high intellect and high animal spirits meet, and excite each other like fire and air. In her wit (which is brilliant without being imaginative) there is a touch of insolence, not unfrequent in women when the wit predominates over reflection and imagination. In her temper, too, there is a slight infusion of the termagant; and her satirical humour plays with such an unrespective levity over all subjects alike, that it required a profound knowledge of women to bring such a character within the pale of our sympathy. But Beatrice, though wilful, is not wayward; she is volatile, not unfeeling. She has not only an exuberance of wit and gaiety, but of heart, and soul, and energy of spirit; and is no more like the fine ladies of modern comedy,—whose wit consists in a temporary allusion or a play upon words, and whose petulance is displayed in a toss of the head, a flirt of the fan, or a flourish of the pocket-handkerchief,—than one of our modern dandies is like Sir Philip Sidney.

In Beatrice, Shakespeare has contrived that the poetry of the character shall not only soften, but heighten its comic effect. We are not only inclined to forgive Beatrice all her scornful airs, all her biting jests, all her assumption of superiority; but they amuse and delight us the more, when we find her, with all the headlong simplicity of a child, falling at once into the snare laid for her affections; when we see her, who thought a man of God's making not good enough for her, who disdained to be o'ermastered by a "piece of valiant dust," stooping like the rest of her sex, vailing her proud spirit, and taming her wild heart to the loving hand of him whom she had scorned, flouted, and misused, "past the endurance of a block." And we are yet more completely won by her generous enthusiastic attachment to her cousin. When the father of Hero believes the tale of her guilt; when Claudio, her lover, without remorse or a lingering doubt, consigns her to shame; when the Friar remains silent, and the generous Benedick himself knows not what to say, Beatrice, confident in her affections, and guided only by the impulses of her own feminine heart, sees through the inconsistency, the impossibility of the charge, and exclaims, without a moment's hesitation: "O, on my soul, my cousin is belied!"

George Bernard Shaw (1856–1950)
[Excerpted from a review of a performance that took place at the Saint James Theatre, London, on February 16, 1898. The great playwright George Bernard Shaw was frequently critical of Shakespeare. Here Shaw exhibits some strong strains of Victorian prudery in panning the play. In Shaw's view, Benedick is a barroom figure who would not be welcome in any "suburban imitation of polite society," and Beatrice is no better. Shaw does concede that "the mood is charming and the music of the words expresses the mood."]

Much Ado is perhaps the most dangerous actor-manager trap in the whole Shakespearean repertory. It is not a safe play like *The Merchant of Venice* or *As You Like It*, nor a serious play like *Hamlet*. Its success depends on the way it is handled in performance; and that, again, depends on the actor-manager being enough of a critic to discriminate ruthlessly between the pretension of the author and his achievement.

The main pretension in *Much Ado* is that Benedick and Beatrice are exquisitely witty and amusing persons. They are, of course, nothing of the sort. Benedick's pleasantries might pass at a sing-song in a public-house parlor; but a gentleman rash enough to venture on them in even the very mildest £52-a-year suburban imitation of polite society today would assuredly never be invited again. From his first joke, "Were you in doubt, Sir, that you asked her?" to his last, "There is not staff more reverend than one tipped with horn," he is not a wit, but a blackguard.

He is not Shakespeare's only failure in that genre. It took the bard a long time to grow out of the provincial conceit that made him so fond of exhibiting his accomplishments as a master of gallant badinage. The very thought of Biron, Mercutio, Gratiano, and Benedick must, I hope, have covered him with shame in his later years. Even Hamlet's airy compliments to Ophelia before the court would make a cabman blush. But at least Shakespeare did not value himself on Hamlet's indecent jests as he evidently did on those of the four merry gentlemen of the earlier plays. When he at last got conviction of sin, and saw this sort of levity in its proper light, he made masterly amends by presenting the blackguard as a blackguard in the person of Lucio in *Measure for Measure*.

Lucio, as a character study, is worth forty Benedicks and Birons. His obscenity is not only inoffensive, but irresistibly entertaining, because it is drawn with perfect skill, offered at its true value, and given its proper interest without any complicity of the author in its lewdness. Lucio is much more of a gentleman than Benedick, because he keeps his coarse sallies for coarse people. Meeting one woman, he says humbly: "Gentle and fair: your brother kindly greets you. Not to be weary with you, he's in prison." Meeting another, he hails her sparkingly with: "How now? Which of your hips has the more profound sciatica?" The one woman is a lay sister, the other a prostitute. Benedick or Mercutio would have cracked their low jokes on the lay sister, and been held up a gentlemen of rare wit and excellent discourse for it. Whenever they approach a woman or an old man you shiver with apprehension as to what brutality they will come out with.

Precisely the same thing in the tenderer degree of her sex is true of Beatrice. In her

Beatrice talks to Benedick in this 19th-century depiction of Act II, Scene 3 of *Much Ado About Nothing. (Painting by Max Adamo; engraving by Tobias Bauer)*

character of professed wit she has only one subject and that is the subject which a really witty woman never jests about, because it is too serious a matter to a woman to be made light of without indelicacy. Beatrice jests about it for the sake of the indelicacy. There is only one thing worse than the Elizabethan merry gentleman, and that is the Elizabethan "merry lady."

Why is it, then, that we still want to see Benedick and Beatrice, and that our most eminent actors and actresses still want to play them? Before I answer that very simple question let me ask another, Why is it that Da Ponte's "dramma giocosa," entitled "Don Giovanni," a loathsome story of a coarse, witless, worthless libertine, who kills an old man in a duel and is finally dragged down through a trapdoor to hell by his twaddling ghost, is still, after more than a century, as "immortal" as Much Ado? Simply because Mozart clothed it with wonderful music, which turned the worthless words and thoughts of Da Ponte into a magical human drama of moods and transitions of feeling.

That is what happened in a smaller way with *Much Ado*. Shakespeare shows himself in it a commonplace librettist, working on a stolen plot, but a great musician. No matter how poor, coarse, cheap, and obvious the thought may be, the mood is charming, and the music of the words expresses the mood. Paraphrase the encounters of Benedick and Beatrice in the style of a blue-book, carefully preserving every idea they present, and it will become apparent to the most infatuated Shakespearean that they contain at best nothing out of the common in thought or wit, and at worst a good deal of vulgar naughtiness. Paraphrase Goethe, Wagner, or Ibsen in the same way, and you will find original observation, subtle thought, wide comprehension, far-reaching intuition, and serious psychological study in them.

Give Shakespeare a fairer chance in the comparison by paraphrasing even his best and maturest work, and you will get nothing more than the platitudes of proverbial philosophy, with a very occasional curiosity in the shape of a rudiment or some modern idea not followed up. Not until the Shakespearean music is added by replacing the paraphrase with the original lines does the enchantment begin. Then you are in another world at once. When a flower girl tells a coster to hold his jaw, for nobody is listening to him, and he retorts, "Oh, you're there, are you, you beauty?" they reproduce the wit of Beatrice and Benedick exactly. But put it this way: "I wonder that you will still be talking, Signor Benedick; nobody marks you." "What! My dear Lady Disdain, are you yet living?" You are miles away from costerland at once.

When I tell you that Benedick and the coster are equally poor in thought, Beatrice and the flower girl equally vulgar in repartee, you reply that I might as well tell you that a nightingale's love is no higher than a cat's. Which is exactly what I do tell you, though the nightingale is the better musician. You will admit, perhaps, that the love of the worst human singer in the world is accompanied by a higher degree of intellectual consciousness than that of the most ravishingly melodious nightingale. Well, in just the same way there are plenty of quite second-rate writers who are abler thinkers and wits than William, though they are unable to weave his magic into the expression of their thoughts.

It is not easy to knock this into the public head, because comparatively few of Shakespeare's admirers are at all conscious that they are listening to music as they hear his phrases turn and his lines fall so fascinatingly and memorably; while we all, no matter how stupid we are, can understand his jokes and platitudes, and are flattered when we are told of the subtlety of the wit we have relished and the profundity of the thought we have fathomed. Englishmen are especially susceptible to this sort of flattery, because intellectual subtlety is not their strong point. In dealing with them you must make them believe that you are appealing to their brains when you are really appealing to their senses and feelings.

With Frenchmen, the case is reversed; you must make them believe that you are appealing to their senses and feelings when you are really appealing to their brains. The Englishman, slave to every sentimental ideal and dupe of every sensuous art, will have it that his great national poet is a thinker. The Frenchman, enslaved and duped only by systems of calculation, insists on his hero being a sentimentalist and artist. That is why Shakespeare is esteemed a mastermind in England and wondered at as a clumsy barbarian in France.

MODERN CRITICISM AND CRITICAL CONTROVERSIES

Like all of Shakespeare's work, *Much Ado About Nothing* continues to find readers in each new generation, and with new readers, there are new points of view and new controversies. Modern criticism of the last few decades has tended to look at the play from sociological, psychological, feminist, and gay and lesbian perspectives.

Frank Kermode observes that *Much Ado About Nothing* is a different kind of comedy from Shakespeare's other comedies, "in that it is dependent on a well-maintained flow of witty and varied talk" (99). Kermode writes, "More than other comedies of the period, *Much Ado About Nothing* anticipates the witty dueling of Restoration comedy, perhaps by developing an older Elizabethan style, the courtly comedy of John Lyly, which had been out of fashion for a while" (99). He also notes that the witty exchanges of the play may "reflect more closely the character of aristocratic conversation in the later years of [Queen] Elizabeth, as Shakespeare might have heard it in Southampton circles" (100).

In "The Success of *Much Ado About Nothing*" (1959), Graham Storey finds that Benedick's statement in the play's final scene, "For man is a giddy thing, and this is my conclusion," is "surely the play's 'cause' or ruling theme" (20). This "giddiness" leads to the "inconstancy, mental intoxication, elation to thoughtfulness" resulting in "deception, self-deception, miscomprehension" (21). In Storey's view, the shaming of Hero at the wedding altar is "a repulsive scene" (19).

Francis Fergusson, in "Ritual and Insight" (1957), takes a somewhat similar line, finding that the several narrative lines of the play are joined under the "more general vision of man as laughable" (54). For Fergusson, the play is filled with ritual and "ceremonious occasions" (56), such as the wedding and cemetery scenes, that establish a sense of general truth.

Marjorie Garber also focuses on ritual in the play. In *Coming of Age in Shakespeare* (1981), a title purposely intended to evoke anthropologist Margaret Mead's famous book *Coming of Age in Samoa*, Garber finds a "submerged" analogy with the story of Orpheus and Eurydice, "another situation in which the dead bride can be retrieved from the underworld only by her husband's faith" (227). Claudio goes through various rituals, such as hanging an epitaph on Hero's "tomb," in order to enact this ritual rebirth.

John Crick takes a more sociological view of the play. In "Messina" (1969), Crick finds that the play provides "the precise delineation of an aristocratic and metropolitan society" (33). One aspect of this society is the flippant use of language: Words can and do harm. Hero is too "nebulous," while Claudio embodies "the worst aspects of Messina society . . . shallowness, complacency, and inhumanity" (36). In such an artificial and shallow society, true evil is possible.

In "Crime and Cover-up in Messina" (1985), Richard A. Levin also casts a critical eye on Messina and its society. The play "consists largely of upper-class conversation among friends and relatives who are at leisure to enjoy one another's company" (72). Yet, "Beneath a thin veneer of civility, Messina is an anxious and insecure world," where, Levin notes, citing *Othello*, "the men hold their honors in a wary distance" (113), which easily sparks conflict.

Robert Grams Hunter, in "Forgiving Claudio" (1965), calls the play a "comedy of forgiveness" (60). Hunter argues: "Romantic love is celebrated as a source of happiness for the man and woman who love each other, and as the socially acceptable form of the force upon which the continued existence of society depends—sexual desire" (60). In the play, "Man's love fails, and women must charitably forgive the failure" (60).

Whereas Hunter sees a "comedy of forgiveness," Walter N. King sees the play as a "comedy of manners." In "Much Ado About Something" (1964), King argues: "Central to *Much Ado,* as to all great comedies of manners, is the critical inspection of a leisure-class world grown morbidly flabby by thoughtless acceptance of an inherited social code" (145).

David Horowitz, in "Imagining the Real," takes his theme from a play on the words of the title, finding that the key term of the play is *noting,* which is a "special kind of perception" (39). In Horowitz's view, the issue of perception leads to larger questions of appearance and reality and the "tenuous and always complex" relationship between them, and "because of this uncertainty at the center of experience, reality is in a large sense what men make of it" (43–44). In Horowitz's view, a true relationship between lovers like Beatrice and Benedick achieves a "substantiality and permanence that no dream can have" (52).

Carl Dennis also deals with issues of perception. In "Wit and Wisdom in *Much Ado About Nothing*" (1973), he argues that the play "works on a distinction between the two modes of perception: the mode of 'wit,' which relies on prudential reasoning and a practical evaluation of sensory evidence, the mode of belief, which rejects reason and on reliance on the senses for intuitive modes of understanding" (223). In Dennis's view, the protagonists move from one mode of perception to another, and their success "is determined by their willingness to lay down their wits and approach the world through faith, through irrational belief" (223).

In "Love, Appearance and Reality: Much Ado About Something" (1968), Barabara Lewalski believes the play "presents Messina as a place of manifold confusions of appearance and reality, or constant mistakes, play-actings, pretences and misapprehensions, and proposes that the state of true love provides an ambiance from which a heightened knowledge of reality can be obtained" (235).

Karen Newman, in "Mistaking in *Much Ado*" (1985), finds that the two plots (Beatrice/Benedick, Hero/Claudio) "are linked by this common theme of credulity and self-deception" (123). Newman addresses the concerns of critics that the play mixes comic and tragic elements in an uneasy arrangement; instead, she finds that Shakespeare uses "deliberative strategies common to tragic characterization within the dramatic boundaries of his romantic comedies" so that "we perceive his comic characters as complex and lifelike" (132).

Ruth Nevo, in "Better Than Reportingly" (1980), sees the play as embodying numerous interlocking dualities: "courtly love conventions and natural passion, affection and spontaneity, romance and realism, . . . style and substance, saying and believing, simulation and dissimulation" (5). These dualities allow for the "reversals, exchanges and chaotic repositionings of those contraries during the dynamic progress of the plots" (5). As for the two couples who are central to the play, Nevo finds that "Beatrice and Benedick's unorthodox views on marriage are a parody of normal conventions and so confirm Hero and Claudio in their soberer ways" (5).

In "*Much Ado About Nothing:* The Temptation to Isolate" (1984), Joseph Westlund sees the play raising the central issue of "control" (63). In Westlund's view, "Messina is at once a world with too much control and too little—the worst of all possibilities since it causes confusion and anger, as well as the feeling of being manipulated" (64). Where Beatrice and Benedick experience "outer control—the tricks played on them—as self-control"—that is, they work through the tricks to gain their own

ends—Hero and Claudio "are subjected to outer controls which they experience as impositions: they feel pushed about" (64). In this same manner, Don John's efforts are an attempt at freedom from control.

The famous poet W. H. Auden was one of those critics who found that the "subplot overwhelms and overshadows the main plot" (113). In his *Lectures on Shakespeare* (1946–47), Auden argues that the main plot, based on romantic traditions, is "boring," and that the play "shows some carelessness" in its construction (113). Auden believes that the "relation of pretense to reality is a major concern of the play" (113). Auden also observes that the play hovers between the light comedy foreground and the dark, malicious background represented by Don John.

Carol Thomas Neely, in "Broken Nuptials in Shakespeare's Comedies: *Much Ado About* Nothing" (1985), picks up on critics' uncertainty as to the gravitational center of the play, observing that whereas most critics find the Hero/Claudio plot to be central, they are attracted to the Beatrice/Benedick subplot and "concur that the subplot is rhetorically richer, dramatically more interesting and psychologically more complex" (105). The dramatic problem of the play is understanding the relationship between the two plots. In Neely's view, the Hero/Claudio plot explores the "anxieties and risks underlying the conventions of romantic love [that] are expressed and contained by the broken nuptials" (106), while the Beatrice/Benedick plot uses motifs, such as trickery, mockery, and parody, found in festive comedy (107). Drawing on modern feminist thinking, Neely finds that "The two plots are played out against a backdrop of patriarchal authority" (107), where men employ aggressive sexual manners and demonstrate fear of women's sexual power, while women fear male domination and employ "cuckoldry" as their own form of power.

Valerie Traub also employs a feminist critical perspective in her *Desire and Anxiety: Circulations of Sexuality in Shakespearean Drama* (1992). Traub relates the plot of *Much Ado* to those of *A Win-*

ter's Tale and, particularly, *Othello*. Traub argues that "the fraught courtship of Claudio and Hero is replicated in Othello's marriage to Desdemona" (41), and Claudio, like Othello, "first idealizes the object of his affection" before symbolically slaying her at the altar (41). Comparing Hero to other Shakespearean heroines, Desdemona and Ophelia, Newman observes, "Hero is divided into virgin and whore" in the eyes of Claudio (41). In turn, "The flip side of Claudio's romantic idealism is his misogyny," which stems from "a fear of female erotic power" (42). Traub argues that chastity is the defining issue in Shakespeare's treatment of women's role, a veritable matter of life and death.

Thomas J. Scheff takes a sociological perspective on the gender issue in "Gender Wars: Emotions in *Much Ado About Nothing*" (1993). Scheff argues: "Although *Much Ado* is certainly a comedy, it displays the usual Shakespearean dark underside with considerable prominence: physical and emotional violence between men, and between men and women" (151). He applies sociological theory to argue the connections between romance, shame, and anger. The play suggests "that love between a man and a woman involves unending tension and conflict, much like the distrust, deception and outright warfare between nations" (149).

Adam Piette draws on sociological theories on the self and society in "Performance, Subjectivity and Slander in *Hamlet* and *Much Ado About Nothing*" (2001). Piette's point of departure is the work of the American sociologist Erving Goffman, particularly *The Presentation of Self in Everyday Life* (1959), in which Goffman "argued for the theatricality of the self, relocating the source of the generation of identity in social interaction rather than in inner psychobiology" (3). Drawing from Goffman, Piette argues that "what we took to be the source of our sense of real being, our own nodular psychobiological self, is a contrivance, a confidence trick, a mere performance of false figures of the self. The only valid source of the real is in social situations themselves proven to be thoroughly and incontrovertibly staged" (6). Noting the numerous instances of "staged" per-

formances in *Much Ado* (particularly the scenes in which Beatrice and Benedick are tricked into thinking each is loved by the other), Piette finds that the identity of the self is both performative (making others think what we want them to think of ourselves) and subject to the performances of others (others making us think what they want us to think of ourselves).

Douglas E. Green draws on queer theory in his view of the play and focuses on its presentation in current cinema, particularly the Kenneth Branagh version, in "Shakespeare, Branagh, and the 'Queer Traitor': Close Encounters in the Shakespearean Classroom" (2002). Green writes, "The whole of Shakespeare's *Much Ado* certainly emphasizes the reluctance of (young aristocratic) men to shift their primary interests away from each other and their masculine pursuits toward marriageable women," and he notes that this "homosociality" feeds the misogynistic tendencies of the men in the play (198).

Celestino Deleyto also finds relevance in Branagh's cinematic version of *Much Ado About Nothing*. In "Men in Leather: Kenneth Branagh's *Much Ado About Nothing* and Romantic Comedy" (1997), Deleyto argues that Branagh's adaptations of *Much Ado* follows in the tradition of Hollywood romantic comedy. In Deleyto's view, the movie presentation of the play "hinges on Beatrice, the female protagonist, as the main point of identification for the audience" (92). Deleyto also finds that Branagh's treatment of the play allows him "to deal at length with the threat that homoerotic desire may pose to heterosexual romances" (92). Prospects of marriage in the play do not lead to harmony; rather, "the immediate prospect of socialization through heterosexual monogamy seems to bring to the surface all the sexual tensions that have remained muted during the war" (93). The men in the play "are only half-heartedly reconciled to an immediate future of stable monogamy, because such a prospect will entail the abandonment of the company of men and the intense state of male bonding favored by the war" (93).

As these selected critical works demonstrate, there are many ways to think about and discuss Shakespeare generally and *Much Ado About Nothing* specifically. Each provides a new slant on the play. As each new generation evolves its own interests and concerns, new modes of writing about the play will continue to develop.

THE PLAY TODAY

Much Ado About Nothing continues to engage and fascinate audiences. Concepts of male and female and the nature of the relationship between genders have changed over the centuries, yet the play continues to spark new insights and challenges to our assumptions. *Much Ado* endures because it is wonderfully open and multifaceted. Critics from the most conventional to the most radical have found material in the play with which to develop new critiques and propose new answers.

Today, we are seeing new forms of critical discourse, such as feminist, postfeminist, queer theory, various forms of psychoanalytical theory, New Historicism studies, and other forms of critical thinking applied to *Much Ado*. These and other modes of contemporary criticism have found rich veins of raw material to mine in the play. The reason surely is that the play works with elements basic to the human condition: friendship, love, marriage, and men and women. It also deals with the nature of social interaction and how the personal can become the political—that is, how breakdowns in human relationships can lead to breakdowns in the social fabric. Don John's personal animosities nearly produce bloody discord in the state; only personal reconciliation and marriage restore the peace of the state. Indeed, in its portrayal of "outsiders," one finds a theme that continues to resonate today. The "question" of Don John remains a question we still ask today of those outsiders who seek to take their revenge on society in sometimes terrible ways.

But beyond all this, it must be said that the play has endured because it contains a veritable cascade of witty language, as well as interesting characters. Some recent examples of new approaches to Shake-speare will serve to illustrate that *Much Ado* continues to find new audiences and provide new ways of looking at the world. Tom Provenzano, in *"Much Ado About Nothing:* Mariachi Style" (2000), offers a review of a production of *Much Ado,* by Bert Rosario and Tony Plana, at the East Los Angeles Theater on August 10, 1999. Provenzano observes:

> This *Much Ado* transforms Italy into a 19th century fantasy in which Mexicans and Anglos live in peace and harmony. The Mexican Wars and Gold Rush are over and California has been admitted to the Union, but rich, landed "ranchero" gentry like Leonato still control much of the land. When white soldiers Claudio and Benedick return triumphantly from battle, they are greeted jubilantly by Leo and his daughter, Hero, and niece, Beatrice. Love and joy abound with masques and frivolity as the cultures blend happily. Unfortunately, a betrothal between Mexican Hero and Anglo Claudio strikes a chord within the cruel Don John. (178)

Such an adaptation takes the play into new cultural territories and attracts new audiences far beyond those who first saw the play 600 years earlier and a continent away.

Similarly, Ruru Li, in "Negotiating Intercultural Spaces: *Much Ado About Nothing* and *Romeo and Juliet* on the Chinese Stage" (2005), describes the cultural negotiations that have to take place in staging Shakespeare in a culture where social expectations may differ widely. As Li reports, "*Much Ado* was adapted to suit the conventions of a regional type of traditional type of traditional Chinese operatic theatre" (40). The producers of the performance adapted to cultural realities: "The adaptation sets the story in a remote area on the Chinese border; a liminal space where many ways of life unacceptable in mainstream China become conceivable" (42). One might have said the same of far-off Messina for its initial English audience.

Finally, *Much Ado* has enjoyed not only frequent theater productions in recent years but also an important film production in Kenneth Branagh's 1998 version. Samuel Crowl, in *Shakespeare at the Cineplex: The Kenneth Branagh Era* (2003), argues that Branagh's productions of Shakespeare have managed to "erase the fault lines separating popular and elite forms of entertainment" (13). *Much Ado* seems very suited to such a fusion of "popular and elite" entertainment.

FIVE TOPICS FOR DISCUSSION AND WRITING

1. **Infidelity:** The play has numerous references to unfaithfulness by both men and women. Men fear having the cuckold's horns placed on them. Women fear being charged as a wanton. What do these attitudes tell us about the society of Messina in the play? And what does the play offer in contrast as an example of faithfulness?

2. **Food:** Food and eating are recurrent motifs in the play. For example, in the first scene, Beatrice mocks Benedick's capacity for food and eating, calling him a "very valiant trencherman." Later in the play, Beatrice, angry at Claudio for shaming Hero, says, "I would eat his heart in the market-place." What are some other examples of food and eating? What do these tell us about the play's characters and the action?

3. **Hero's shaming:** Perhaps the play's crucial scene is the public shaming of Hero at the altar. Does the play condone this sort of public accusation? If the accusations had been true, would this public shaming have been justified in the eyes of the other characters? Why or why not? Has this type of public shaming been exhibited across cultures? Which ones, and why?

4. **Nothing and triviality:** What does the "Nothing" in the play's title refer to?

5. **Hero and Beatrice:** The two main female characters, Hero and Beatrice, seem to exemplify two different attitudes toward marriage. Are these the differences between male and female approaches? Does the play seem to support one attitude more than the other? Which approach to marriage seems to be the ideal, based on evidence within the play?

Bibliography

Auden, W. H. *Lectures on Shakespeare*. Edited by Arthur Kirsch. Princeton, N.J.: Princeton University Press, 2000.

Best, Michael. "Shakespeare's Life and Times." Internet Shakespeare Editions. Available online. URL: http://ise.uvic.ca/Library/SLT/. Accessed April 24, 2009.

Coleridge, Samuel Taylor. *Notes and Lectures upon Shakespeare and Some of the Old Poets and Dramatists with Other Literary Remains*. Vol. 1. Edited by H. N. Coleridge. London: Pickering, 1849.

Crick, John. "Messina" [editor's title]. In *Twentieth Century Interpretations of* Much Ado About Nothing: *A Collection of Critical Essays,* edited by Walter R. Davis, 33–38. Englewood Cliffs, N.J.: Prentice-Hall, 1969.

Crowl, Samuel. *Shakespeare at the Cineplex: The Kenneth Branagh Era*. Athens: Ohio University Press, 2003.

Deleyto, Celestino. "Men in Leather: Kenneth Branagh's *Much Ado About Nothing* and Romantic Comedy." *Cinema Journal* 36, no. 3 (Spring 1997): 91–105.

Dennis , Carl. "Wit and Wisdom in *Much Ado About Nothing*." *Studies in English Literature, 1500–1900* 13, no. 2 (Spring 1973): 223–237.

Fergusson, Francis. "Ritual and Insight" [editor's title]. In *The Human Image in Dramatic Literature*. Garden City, N.Y.: Anchor Doubleday, 1957. Reprinted in *Twentieth Century Interpretations of* Much Ado About Nothing: *A Collection of Critical Essays,* edited by Walter R. Davis, 54–59. Englewood Cliffs, N.J.: Prentice-Hall, 1969.

Garber, Marjorie. *Coming of Age in Shakespeare*. London: Methuen, 1981.

Green, Douglas E. "Shakespeare, Branagh, and the 'Queer Traitor': Close Encounters in the Shakespearean Classroom." In *The Reel Shakespeare: Alternative Cinema and Theory,* edited by Lisa S. Starks and Courtney Lehmann, 191–208. Madison, N.J.: Fairleigh Dickinson University Press, 2002.

Hazlitt, William. *Characters of Shakespear's Plays.* London: C. H. Reynell, 1817. Available online. URL: http://www.library.utoronto.ca/utel/criticism/hazlittw_

charsp/charsp_ch27.html. Accessed March 25, 2009.

Horowitz, David. "Imagining the Real." In *Shakespeare: An Existential View.* New York: Hill and Wang, 1965. Reprinted in *Twentieth Century Interpretations of* Much Ado About Nothing: *A Collection of Critical Essays,* edited by Walter R. Davis, 39–53. Englewood Cliffs, N.J.: Prentice-Hall, 1969.

Hunter, Robert Grams. "Forgiving Claudio" [editor's title]. In *Shakespeare and the Comedy of Forgiveness.* New York: Columbia University Press, 1965, 93, 98–105. Reprinted in *Twentieth Century Interpretations of Much Ado About Nothing: A Collection of Critical Essays,* edited by Walter R. Davis, 60–66. Englewood Cliffs, N.J.: Prentice-Hall, 1969.

Jameson, Anna Murphy. *Shakespeare's Heroines: Characteristics of Women, Moral, Political and Historical.* Edited by Cheri L. Hoeckley. Peterborough, Ont.: Broadview Press, 2005.

Johnson, Samuel. *Preface to his Edition of Shakespear's Plays.* London: Tonson, 1765.

Kermode, Frank. *The Age of Shakespeare* New York: Modern Library, 2004.

King, Walter N. "Much Ado About Something." *Shakespeare Quarterly* 15, no. 3 (Summer 1964): 143–155.

Levin, Richard A. "Crime and Cover-up in Messina." In *Love and Society in Shakespearean Comedy: A Study of Dramatic Form and Content.* Newark: University of Delaware Press, 1985. Reprinted in *William Shakespeare's* "Much Ado About Nothing," edited by Harold Bloom, 71–104. New York: Chelsea House, 1988.

Lewalski, B. K. "Love, Appearance and Reality: Much Ado About Something." *Studies in English Literature, 1500–1900* 8, no. 2 (Spring 1968): 235–251.

Li, Ruru. "Negotiating Intercultural Spaces: *Much Ado About Nothing* on the Chinese Stage." In *World-Wide Shakespeares: Local Appropriations in Film and Performance,* edited by Sonia Massai, 40–54. London: Routledge, 2005.

Neely, Carol Thomas. "Broken Nuptials in Shakespeare's Comedies: *Much Ado About* Nothing." In

Broken Nuptials in Shakespeare's Plays. New Haven, Conn.: Yale University Press, 1985. Reprinted in *William Shakespeare's* Much Ado About Nothing, edited by Harold Bloom, 105–122. New York: Chelsea House, 1988.

Nevo, Ruth. "Better Than Reportingly." In *Comic Transformations in Shakespeare.* London: Methuen, 1980. Reprinted in *William Shakespeare's* Much Ado About Nothing, edited by Harold Bloom, 5–19. New York: Chelsea House, 1988.

Newman, Karen. "Mistaking in *Much Ado.*" In *Rhetoric of Comic Character: Dramatic Convention in Classical Renaissance Comedy.* London: Methuen, 1985. Reprinted in *William Shakespeare's* "Much Ado About Nothing," edited by Harold Bloom, 123–132. New York: Chelsea House, 1988.

Piette, Adam. "Performance, Subjectivity and Slander in *Hamlet* and *Much Ado About Nothing.*" *Early Modern Literary Studies* 7, no. 2 (September, 2001): 4.1–29.

Provenzano, Tom. "*Much Ado About Nothing:* Mariachi Style." *Theatre Journal* 52, no. 1 (2000): 118–119.

Richardson, William. *Essays on Some of Shakespeare's Dramatic Characters to which is added an Essay on the Faults of Shakespeare.* 5th ed. London: J. Murray and S. Highley, 1797, 338–363.

Scheff, Thomas J. "Gender Wars: Emotions in *Much Ado About Nothing.*" *Sociological Perspectives* 36, no. 2 (Summer 1993): 149–166.

Storey, Graham. "The Success of *Much Ado About Nothing.*" In *More Talking of Shakespeare,* edited by John Garrett, 128–143. London: Longmans, 1959. Reprinted in *Twentieth Century Interpretations of Much Ado About Nothing: A Collection of Critical Essays,* edited by Walter R. Davis, 18–32. Englewood Cliffs, N.J.: Prentice-Hall, 1969.

Traub, Valerie. *Desire and Anxiety: Circulations of Sexuality in Shakespearean Drama.* London: Routledge, 1992.

Westlund, Joseph. "*Much Ado About Nothing:* The Temptation to Isolate." In *Shakespeare's Reparative Comedies: A Psychoanalytic View of the Middle Plays.* Chicago: University of Chicago Press, 1984. Reprinted in *William Shakespeare's* "Much Ado

About Nothing," edited by Harold Bloom, 63–70. New York: Chelsea House, 1988.

FILM AND VIDEO PRODUCTIONS:

Branagh, Kenneth, dir. *Much Ado About Nothing.* With Richard Briers, Kate Beckinsale, Emma Thompson, Denzel Washington, Keanu Reeves, and Kenneth Branagh. BBC, Renaissance Films, 1993.

Burge, Stuart, dir. *Much Ado About Nothing.* With Lee Montague, Cherie Lunghi, Katherine Levy, Jon Finch, Robert Lindsay, and Robert Reynolds. BBC, 1984.

Havinga, Nick, dir. *Much Ado About Nothing.* With Sam Waterston, Kathleen Widdoes, Bernard Hughes, April Shawnham, and Glenn Walken. New York Shakespeare Festival, 1973.

—Anthony G. Medici

Othello

INTRODUCTION

In an age when interracial marriage is still contro-versial, when prejudice against Muslims is on the rise in Europe and the United States, and when themes of jealousy and murder are ubiquitous in popular films, *Othello* may be Shakespeare's most relevant and accessible tragedy. As a Moor (Mor-rocan or North African) in Venice, Othello faces prejudice based on his dark skin, foreign origin, and Muslim background. He is a self-made man who manages to overcome prejudice to rise to the rank of general and marry a beauty from an exclusive Venetian family. His unlikely achievement could be seen as a prototype for the immigrants who, despite racism and xenophobia, achieve the American Dream.

Other characters in the play also seem more than usually relevant from a 21st-century perspec-tive. Emilia may be seen as a role model for women when she defies her husband, Iago, to stand up for her mistress, Desdemona. In turn, Desdemona, Othello's wife, might also be seen as a proto-feminist in daring to rebel against her father when she elopes with Othello, the man she loves. She also acts bravely when she advocates for Lieuten-ant Cassio, whom she feels Othello has wrongfully demoted, rather than staying out of military affairs as a traditional wife might have done.

This play shows Shakespeare's amazing under-standing of the psychology of prejudice, jealousy, insecurity, sociopathy, and revenge. Iago is some-what comparable to a serial killer depicted in mod-ern films. He is a sociopath who happily causes the violent deaths of Desdemona, Othello, Emilia, and Roderigo. Shakespeare manages to keep Iago from being the cardboard villain he might have been in the hands of a less skillful playwright. Instead, Iago is a fascinatingly opaque character, whose resent-ment of Othello for having promoted Cassio over him and whose professed jealousy of Othello for having supposedly slept with his wife seem inad-equate motives for his complex plot. His sexual jealousy in particular seems completely unjusti-fied. Today's readers can, however, somewhat sym-pathize with Iago's complaints against Othello as his employer. Iago argues that seniority, not birth or education, should have the greatest weight in promotion decisions. He could be compared to a battle-worn, working-class sergeant in today's American army, complaining about the privileges of young officers with no military experience, just a college education and an affluent family back-ground. As frighteningly Machiavellian as Iago is, some of his class resentment against Othello and Cassio should be familiar to a 21st-century audience.

BACKGROUND

Shakespeare seems to have based the story of *Othello* on a 1566 short story by the Italian writer Giambattista Giraldi, who was known as Cinthio. Cinthio's story differs from Shakespeare's play in several ways. Unlike Shakespeare, Cinthio portrays Othello "as a brutal and seedy murderer," and

Othello (Hubert Carter) and Desdemona (Tita Brand) embrace in *Othello*. This is a photograph of a 1905 production at the Lyric Theatre.

Desdemona and Emilia are much less developed characters in Cinthio than in Shakespeare (Hadfield: 8). In addition, Cinthio explains Iago's cruel plot as resulting from his frustration over having been rejected by Desdemona—a motive absent from Shakespeare's play (Greenblatt, *Will in the World:* 325).

Andrew Hadfield observes that by inventing the tragic hero Othello, Shakespeare departs from his own stereotypical depiction of a Moorish character as evil in *Titus Andronicus* (ca. 1594), as well as rebelling against the popular depictions of Moors and Turks as monstrous brutes in Christo-

pher Marlowe's *Tamburlaine* in 1587 and Robert Greene's *Selimus* in 1594 (7). Hadfield contends that with *Othello*, Shakespeare "deliberately produces a work that challenges the stereotypes of cruel Moors and Turks who had appeared on the English stage" (8).

The Elizabethans defined tragedy as being about the fall of highly placed people such as kings (Barnet: vi). Othello is not a king, but he is a powerful general who eventually rules Cyprus for Venice and defends the island from Turkish invaders. Sylvan Barnet observes that in some Elizabethan tragedies, the protagonist causes his fall through vice and crime, but in others, he is a victim of chance misfortune (vi). Seeing *Othello* as rooted in the old-fashioned morality plays, such as *Everyman*, that were still popular in Shakespeare's time, Bernard Spivack argues that in terms of Christian allegory, Othello is torn between his good angel Desdemona and his bad angel Iago in a struggle for his soul, which traditionally might be called a "Psychomachia" (56). Spivack contends that Iago's motivation seems inadequate because he is a hybrid between the allegorical, gleeful vice figure from the old-fashioned Psychomachia and morality plays and the new, more realistic villain figure that became popular during Shakespeare's time (35, 443). Spivack finds similar hybrid villains in other Shakespeare plays such as *Titus Andronicus* and *Richard III*, as well as in those of his contemporaries, Marlowe's *The Jew of Malta* and Middleton's *The Spanish Tragedy* (34).

Critics have debated whether Othello contributes to his downfall through such traits as insecurity (due to his ethnicity and age); gullibility; a military man's inexperience with women; and even his nobility, which incites Iago's envy. However, starting with leading 19th- and early 20th-century critics such as Samuel Taylor Coleridge and A. C. Bradley, most critics have seen Othello as the victim of Iago's evil plot; consequently, modern audiences sympathize with Othello for being deceived and maddened by Iago into killing Othello's own beloved, innocent wife, and then himself.

Nevertheless, Michael D. Bristol points out that early audiences, as part of a society in which racism was normal, might have considered Othello to be "comically monstrous" for marrying a white woman and leading a white army (79). "Racism in this early, prototypical form entails a specific physical repugnance for the skin colour and other typical features of the black Africans," Bristol explains (79). He argues that early audiences might have interpreted Shakespeare's play not as a tragedy but as a kind of charivari—a ritual expressing disapproval of an "unnatural" marriage—in which Iago humiliates and destroys Othello and Desdemona because of their interracial marriage. Frank Kermode likewise observes that *Othello* contains a charivari, but only in the first act, when Iago and Roderigo taunt Brabantio with racial slurs about his daughter and her new husband, causing Brabantio to try to get the Venetian Senate to disrupt Desdemona's wedding night (167).

Venice was at the frontier of Europe, close to the much-feared Ottoman Empire of the Turks; the early 17th-century audience of *Othello* would have seen that Cyprus, as Venice's outpost against the Turks, was crucial to Venice's—and hence, Europe's—safety (Hadfield: 10). In 1599, the English feared that the Spanish were about to launch another giant armada of ships against them, as they had attempted to do in 1588, when storms sunk the Spanish fleet; James Shapiro argues that the widely differing rumors about the size of the Turkish fleet about to invade Cyprus that are recounted in the Venetian Senate during the first act of *Othello* echo the hysteria of 1599 and add suspense to Shakespeare's play (175–177).

Andrew Hadfield thinks that in *Othello*, Shakespeare may be commenting critically on Queen Elizabeth's banishment of English "blackamoors" in 1596 and 1601 by implicitly contrasting the more racially diverse and tolerant city of Venice with the racially homogenous London of his audience (11–12).

Social conditions of the time may explain certain other motivations in the play. Shakespeare's tragedies generally end with the survivors attempting to create a just system that would replace the horrors that destroyed the dead protagonists. According to Stephen Greenblatt, state torture was accepted by Elizabethans; therefore, the promise by the survivors that Iago is to be tortured for his crimes after the play ends may actually have been intended to restore order, though of course the damage done by Iago cannot be repaired (Greenblatt, *Will*: 180). Finally, Renaissance Venice was famous for its beautiful courtesans; the stereotype of Venetian women as loose might have helped English audiences understand why Othello believes his Ensign when Iago accuses Desdemona of adultery, according to Andrew Hadfield (9).

Date and Text of the Play

No complete, handwritten manuscripts by Shakespeare survive, which makes it difficult for scholars to decide which printed version of a play is most authentic. *Othello* is especially controversial in this regard. Although *Othello* was probably composed in 1604, it was not printed until 1622, in a quarto (Q) version of the play unaccompanied by other plays. However, in 1623, *Othello* was printed as part of a collection of Shakespeare's plays called the First Folio (F). The Q version of *Othello* is shorter by about 160 lines than the F version, but about 12 lines are missing from F that appear in Q. Also, many profane oaths that are in Q are not in F, probably due to censorship. Critics have debated whether Q or F was composed earlier, without coming to a consensus. F is generally preferred today, though editors often include oaths and some lines from Q that seem to correct missing lines in F.

SYNOPSIS
Brief Synopsis

Roderigo, who has been courting Desdemona, is distressed to learn that she has eloped with Othello, a Moorish general in the service of Venice. Iago, a subordinate of Othello, tells Roderigo that he, too, hates the Moor. Iago and Roderigo informs Desdemona's father, Brabantio, of the elopement.

THE TRAGEDIE OF
Othello, the Moore of Venice.

Actus Primus.   Scœna Prima.

Enter Rodorigo, and Iago.

Rodorigo.

Euer tell me, I take it much vnkindly
That thou (*Iago*) who haft had my purfe,
As if § ftrings were thine, fhould'ft know of this.
Ia. But you'l not heare me. If euer I did dream
Of fuch a matter, abhorre me.
  Rodo. Thou told'ft me,
Thou did'ft hold him in thy hate.
  Iago. Defpife me
If I do not. Three Great-ones of the Cittie,
(In perfonall fuite to make me his Lieutenant)
Off-capt to him : and by the faith of man
I know my price, I am worth no worfe a place.
But he (as louing his owne pride, and purpofes)
Euades them, with a bumbaft Circumftance,
Horribly ftufft with Epithites of warre,
Non-fuites my Mediators. For certes, faies he,
I haue already chofe my Officer. And what was he ?
For-footh, a great Arithmatician,
One *Michaell Caffio*, a *Florentine*,
(A Fellow almoft damn'd in a faire Wife)
That neuer fet a Squadron in the Field,
Nor the deuifion of a Battaile knowes
More then a Spinfter. Vnleffe the Bookifh Theoricke :
Wherein the Tongued Confuls can propofe
As Mafterly as he. Meere pratle (without practife)
Is all his Souldierfhip. But he (Sir) had th'election;
And I (of whom his eies had feene the proofe
At Rhodes, at Ciprus, and on others grounds
Chriften'd, and Heathen) muft be be-leed, and calm'd
By Debitor, and Creditor. This Counter-cafter,
He (in good time) muft his Lieutenant be,
And I (bleffe the marke) his Moorefhips Auntient.
  Rod. By heauen, I rather would haue bin his hangman.
  Iago. Why, there's no remedie.
'Tis the curffe of Seruice;
Preferment goes by Letter, and affection,
And not by old gradation, where each fecond
Stood Heire to th'firft. Now Sir, be iudge your felfe,
Whether I in any iuft terme am Affin'd
To loue the *Moore* ?
  Rod. I would not follow him then.
  Iago. O Sir content you.
I follow him, to ferue my turne vpon him.
We cannot all be Mafters, nor all Mafters
Cannot be truely follow'd. You fhall marke
Many a dutious and knee-crooking knaue;
That (doting on his owne obfequious bondage)
Weares out his time, much like his Mafters Affe,
For naught but Prouender, & when he's old Cafheer'd.
Whip me fuch honeft knaues. Others there are
Who trym'd in Formes, and vifages of Dutie,
Keepe yet their hearts attending on themfelues,
And throwing but fhowes of Seruice on their Lords
Doe well thriue by them.
And when they haue lin'd their Coates
Doe themfelues Homage.
Thefe Fellowes haue fome foule,
And fuch a one do I profeffe my felfe. For (Sir)
It is as fure as you are *Rodorigo*,
Were I the Moore, I would not be *Iago* :
In following him, I follow but my felfe:
Heauen is my Iudge, not I for loue and dutie,
But feeming fo, for my peculiar end :
For when my outward Action doth demonftrate
The natiue act, and figure of my heart
In Complement externe, 'tis not long after
But I will weare my heart vpon my fleeue
For Dawes to pecke at ; I am not what I am.
  Rod. What a fall Fortune do's the Thicks-lips owe
If he can carry't thus ?
  Iago. Call vp her Father :
Rowfe him, make after him, poyfon his delight,
Proclaime him in the Streets. Incenfe her kinfmen,
And though he in a fertile Clymate dwell,
Plague him with Flies: though that his Ioy be Ioy,
Yet throw fuch changes of vexation on't,
As it may loofe fome colour.
  Rodo. Heere is her Fathers houfe, Ile call aloud.
  Iago. Doe, with like timerous accent, and dire yell,
As when (by Night and Negligence) the Fire
Is fpied in populus Cities.
  Rodo. What hoa, *Brabantio*, Siginor *Brabantio*, hoa.
  Iago. Awake: what hoa, *Brabantio* : Theeues, Theeues.
Looke to your houfe, your daughter, and your Bags,
Theeues, Theeues.
  Bra. Aboue. What is the reafon of this terrible
Summons ? What is the matter there ?
  Rodo. Signior is all your Familie within ?
  Iago. Are your Doores lock'd ?
  Bra. Why ? Wherefore ask you this ?
  Iago. Sir, y'are rob'd, for fhame put on your Gowne,
                                                                Your

Title page of the First Folio edition of *Othello*, published in 1623

THE
Tragœdy of Othello,

The Moore of Venice.

As it hath beene diuerse times acted at the
Globe, and at the Black-Friers, by
his Maiesties Seruants.

Written by VVilliam Shakespeare.

LONDON,
Printed by *N. O.* for *Thomas Walkley,* and are to be sold at his
shop, at the Eagle and Child, in Brittans Burse.
1 6 2 2.

Title page of the first quarto edition of *Othello,* published
in 1622

The Duke has summoned Othello to a council of war. Brabantio accompanies him there
and, before the Duke, accuses Othello of having
bewitched his daughter. Othello replies that Desdemona married him of her own free will. After
Brabantio concedes, Othello is ordered to leave for
Cyprus, which is threatened by an imminent Turkish attack. Desdemona is permitted to follow him
on a different ship.

In Cyprus, a storm destroys the Turkish fleet.
Iago arrives in Cyprus first with his wife, Emilia,
Desdemona, and Roderigo. Iago tells Roderigo
that Desdemona is in love with Cassio, Othello's
lieutenant, and proposes that Roderigo pick a fight
with him that night.

Despite Cassio's insistence that a little wine
will make him very drunk, Iago convinces him
to drink. When Cassio, drunk, goes to take his
guard post, Iago sends Roderigo to provoke him.
Roderigo shortly reappears with an angry Cassio
behind him. Confused, Cassio starts a fight with
Montano, the Venetian governor. Afterwards,
Iago slyly places the blame on Cassio, and Othello
immediately demotes Cassio. Iago later convinces
Cassio that his only hope of recovering his position
is to get Desdemona to present his case to Othello.
Iago's plot against Othello is developing.

Cassio meets privately with Desdemona, who
assures him she will plead his case. Cassio withdraws as Othello and Iago approach. Iago pretends
to find the situation suspicious. Desdemona asks
Othello to take Cassio back, and he agrees. When
she leaves, Iago inflames Othello with the idea of a
sexual affair between Cassio and Desdemona. He
suggests that if Othello delays Cassio's reappoint-
ment, he can test Desdemona's fidelity.

Iago's wife, Emilia, Desdemona's servant, gives
him one of Desdemona's handkerchiefs. When
Othello returns, Iago asserts that Cassio has Desdemona's handkerchief. Othello swears vengeance.

Othello then demands his handkerchief from
Desdemona, who denies that it is lost. She tries
to change the subject back to Cassio, and Othello
leaves in a rage.

Iago tells Othello that Cassio has admitted to
sleeping with Desdemona and that if Othello eavesdrops on the meeting he has arranged with Cassio,
the general will hear Cassio speak of his affair with
Desdemona. Cassio returns, and Iago speaks to
him of Bianca, Cassio's lover. Othello, crying out in
asides, believes Cassio is speaking of Desdemona.

Desdemona appears with Lodovico, who brings
a message from Venice recalling Othello and placing Cassio in command of Cyprus. Othello hits
Desdemona and orders her away.

Iago sets Roderigo up to ambush Cassio, hoping that Roderigo and Cassio will kill each other.
Cassio appears and Roderigo attacks him, but he
is wounded by Cassio. Iago then wounds Cassio
from behind and flees. Othello sees the wounded

Cassio crying for help and exults in the sight. Iago returns, pretends to be enraged at the assault on Cassio, and kills Roderigo.

Othello approaches at the bed of the sleeping Desdemona. She wakes, and he tells her to prepare for death. She pleads for mercy, but Othello smothers her. Emilia appears, and Othello proclaims that he has murdered Desdemona because she was unfaithful. Emilia denies it and calls for help. Montano, Gratiano, and Iago appear. Othello speaks of Desdemona's handkerchief, and Emilia reveals the truth. Iago kills her and flees. Montano chases him. When Iago is brought back, Othello attacks him and wounds him before being disarmed himself. Othello stabs himself with a hidden weapon and dies.

Act I, Scene 1

The play opens in a street in Venice at night. The gentleman Roderigo and the soldier Iago discuss the promotion of Michael Cassio to lieutenant for Othello, a Venetian general who is also a Moor. Iago claims that Cassio's promotion is unfair, since Iago served in many battles under Othello, whereas Cassio is young and inexperienced. Iago complains that Cassio's promotion results from his gentle birth, not from merit. Iago's resents that his rank is "ancient" (an ensign, or junior officer who is also a standard bearer). To get revenge on Othello for promoting Cassio over Iago, Iago and Roderigo taunt Brabantio, Desdemona's father, who is also a senator of Venice. Yelling up at Brabantio, who appears at his house's second-story window, Iago and Roderigo make racist jokes about Desdemona having eloped with Othello despite his dark complexion, foreign extraction, Muslim background, and lack of youth.

Act I, Scene 2

On a street in Venice, Iago tells Othello that Brabantio is seeking him, claiming he abducted his daughter. Cassio and the Duke's officers appear, telling Othello that the Duke and Senate have summoned him about a possible military problem in Cyprus. Then Brabantio, Roderigo, and their officers arrive. Brabantio uses racial epithets to insult Othello while trying to arrest and take him to prison for seducing Desdemona. Othello explains that he is on the way to see the Duke in council.

Act I, Scene 3

In the Duke's council chamber, the senators discuss the Turks' impending invasion of Cyprus. When Othello arrives, they tell him he must go to Cyprus to fight the Turks. Brabantio interrupts the planning of war with his complaints against Othello for eloping with Desdemona. Brabantio argues that only witchcraft could have made his daughter betray him to leave with a man who is from neither her class, generation, nor race. Othello calmly explains that he got to know Desdemona when he was Brabantio's dinner guest on several occasions. She fell in love with Othello when he told stories about his military exploits and rescue from slavery. Desdemona concurs with Othello's version of their courtship, stressing her love for him and the obedience she owes him as well as her father. Believing Othello and Desdemona's story, the Duke suggests that Brabantio should accept her marriage to Othello. The Duke and senators order Othello

Othello and Desdemona plead with the Duke and Brabantio, Desdemona's father, in Act I, Scene III of *Othello*, in this illustration published by the Photogravure & Color Company in the late 19th century.

to Cyprus. Desdemona says she would like to go, too. Othello tells the council that he will have her travel there with his trustworthy junior officer, Ensign Iago.

After Othello and Desdemona leave, Roderigo privately tells Iago that he is considering suicide since his hopes of marrying Desdemona are lost. Iago encourages Roderigo to use his money to gain Desdemona's favors as surely she will tire of her ugly husband soon. Feeling hopeful again, Roderigo exits. Iago's soliloquy reveals that he hates Othello for possibly having slept with Iago's wife and that he plans to gain Cassio's lieutenancy and destroy Othello's happiness through spreading innuendos about an improper intimacy that is supposedly occurring between Desdemona and Cassio.

Act II, Scene 1

At Cyprus, Montano, who is the island's governor, discusses the storm with two gentlemen. They hear from Venetian messengers that the gale has driven the Turks' ships away from shore, causing them to give up their plans to invade Cyprus. Cassio enters, stating his concern about Othello's fate in the storm. Desdemona, Iago, Roderigo, and Emilia (Iago's wife) then arrive, their ship having safely moored. Iago jokes with Desdemona about women's nature; Iago's banter may suggest to the audience, who knows his plots, that he is a misogynist. Othello and his attendants arrive.

In the background of Othello and Desdemona's joyous reunion, Iago plots against them through asides to the audience. After the newlyweds depart along with their attendants, Iago says to Roderigo that he saw Desdemona flirting with Cassio. Nevertheless, Roderigo is not convinced by Iago's arguments that Desdemona desires Cassio. But when Iago orders Roderigo to prepare to attack Cassio that evening, Roderigo agrees to do so, apparently convinced that eliminating Cassio will bring him closer to sleeping with Desdemona. In his second soliloquy after Roderigo departs, Iago states that he desires Desdemona, and he repeats his assertion that Othello once slept with Emilia. Iago then glories in the prospect of being rewarded by Othello

for manipulating the general into feeling painfully jealous of Cassio.

Act II, Scene 2

In a street in Cyprus, Othello's herald announces that a celebration will be held all evening throughout the town in honor of the destruction of the Turkish fleet at sea and of Othello and Desdemona's wedding.

Act II, Scene 3

In the citadel (or fort) of Cyprus, Othello warns Cassio not to drink too much during the celebration and to make sure the guards do not get drunk. After Othello and Desdemona depart, Iago arrives. He convinces Cassio to get drunk with other soldiers, though Cassio protests that he does not hold his liquor as well as most men do. Iago tells Montano that Cassio is an alcoholic.

When Roderigo enters, Iago tells him to pursue Cassio. Roderigo and Cassio fight with swords; when Montano attempts to intervene, Cassio fights with Montano. Othello and his attendants arrive, finding Montano gravely wounded by Cassio. When Othello asks Iago what happened, Iago

Othello enters to find Montano gravely wounded by Cassio in Act II, Scene 3 of *Othello*. This is a plate from *Retzsch's Outlines to Shakespeare: Othello*, published in 1842. *(Illustration by Moritz Retzsch)*

seems to minimize Cassio's fault, again convincing Othello of Iago's honesty. Othello demotes Cassio for having gotten drunk and injuring Montano. Desdemona and her attendants enter, then depart with Othello.

Cassio tells Iago how humiliated he is at having damaged his honor through drunken fighting. Iago urges Cassio to ask Desdemona to intercede with Othello in an attempt to restore him to his position as lieutenant. Trusting Iago as much as Othello does, Cassio agrees, then leaves.

Roderigo enters, complaining that his bruises at Cassio's hands and Roderigo's lavish spending have brought him no closer to Desdemona. After Roderigo leaves, Iago's brief soliloquy describes his plan to get Emilia to convince Desdemona that she should intercede with Othello to restore Cassio to his position; Iago also says he will contrive to place Othello where he can watch Cassio pleading with Desdemona.

Act III, Scene 1

In a street in Cyprus outside Othello's house during the following morning, Cassio hires musicians, who play. A clown insults their playing. Cassio pays the clown to ask Emilia if Desdemona is up and willing to see him. Iago arrives and promises Cassio that he will keep Othello out of the way when Cassio speaks with Desdemona. Emilia enters. She tells Cassio that Desdemona has already pleaded for him with Othello. Othello replied that Montano is an important man, so it would be unsafe to restore Cassio to his lieutenancy, even though Othello feels great affection for him.

Act III, Scene 2

At the citadel of Cyprus, Othello hands Iago some letters to the Senate in Venice. He then tells Iago to join him on top of the fort after the letters to the pilot have been delivered. Othello exits with his officers to walk to the fortifications.

Act III, Scene 3

At the citadel, Desdemona promises Cassio that she will plead his case with Othello. Emilia says that Cassio's disgrace pains Iago. They see Iago and Othello coming from a distance, and Cassio quickly leaves. Iago plants suspicion of Cassio and Desdemona in Othello by reacting to Cassio's departure with dismay. Playfully yet persistently, Desdemona begs Othello to restore Cassio to his position, ignoring Othello's increasing irritation. After she and Emilia depart, Iago fosters Othello's jealousy and despair by arguing, like Brabantio, that it was against Desdemona's nature to fall in love with a man so different from her in race, nationality, beauty, and age; hence, it makes sense that she would turn to the young, handsome Cassio now while lying to Othello as she once did to her father. Iago persuades Othello that if Desdemona continues to be Cassio's advocate, that will be proof of her disloyalty to her husband.

In a brief soliloquy after Iago leaves, Othello expresses his newfound loathing for Desdemona in misogynistic terms. When she returns, Othello tells her he has a headache. Trying to soothe him, she accidentally drops the handkerchief from Othello's mother that he once gave her as a love token. When Desdemona and Othello depart, Emilia picks up the handkerchief, handing it to Iago when he enters, for he had asked her to obtain it for him.

Soon after Emilia leaves, Othello returns, transformed by rage from the calm leader seen in Acts I and II. Furious about Desdemona's purported lechery, he demands that Iago prove his assertions about Desdemona and Cassio, or Othello will kill him. Iago tells Othello that he heard Cassio speak of Desdemona in his sleep; he tried to kiss Iago, calling him Desdemona. Iago then tells the shocked Othello that he saw Cassio wipe his beard with Desdemona's handkerchief that had belonged to Othello's mother. Believing Iago's lies, Othello vows to get his revenge on Desdemona and Cassio. Iago swears to aid Othello in this. Othello orders Iago to have Cassio murdered within three days and says he will think of a way to kill Desdemona. The scene ends with Othello foolishly calling his deceiver, Iago, his "lieutenant" in their plot of vengeance.

Act III, Scene 4

In a street, Desdemona, accompanied by Emilia, asks the Clown to find Cassio and tell him that she has sued with Othello for Cassio to be forgiven. When Othello appears, Desdemona again asks him to return Cassio to his lieutenancy. Othello asks his wife where his dead mother's handkerchief is. He tells Desdemona that his mother had told him that if his wife ever lost that handkerchief, it would be an ill omen. When Othello asks her about the handkerchief, Desdemona lies, claiming she has not lost it. After Othello exits, Emilia repeats her contention that he is behaving like a jealous man. Iago then brings in Cassio, who again importunes Desdemona to plead for him.

After Desdemona and Emilia leave, Bianca, a townswoman who is in love with Cassio, enters. Cassio hands her Desdemona's handkerchief, saying he found it in his room and does not know to whom it belongs. He asks Bianca to copy its design onto another handkerchief. Bianca is irritated by his request, as she thinks another of Cassio's lovers left the handkerchief in his room.

Act IV, Scene 1

In a street, Iago tells Othello about Desdemona's supposed adultery with Cassio. Othello has a seizure. Cassio enters, and Iago tells him that Othello had another fit yesterday.

With Othello hiding at a distance, Iago jokingly questions Cassio about the passionate Bianca, whom Iago believes is a prostitute. Not being able to hear much of what Cassio and Iago say, Othello thinks Cassio is speaking slightingly of Desdemona rather than of Bianca, as Iago intends. Bianca enters, throwing Desdemona's handkerchief on the floor and asserting jealously that it must belong to another lover of Cassio's.

After Bianca storms out and then Cassio leaves, Iago and Othello discuss what has just transpired. Othello takes the encounters between Iago and Cassio, and then Cassio and Bianca, as definitive proof that Cassio and Desdemona are having an affair. Othello says he will not talk to Desdemona about his suspicions, as she might use her beauty to

fool him again. He asks Iago to get him poison to use on Desdemona; Iago responds that strangling Desdemona in the marriage bed she has defiled would be a more fitting end for her.

A nobleman, Lodovico—who is Desdemona's cousin—arrives from Venice and enters the room, along with Desdemona and their attendants. Lodovico gives Othello a letter from the Duke and senators of Venice, which commands Othello to return home, appointing Cassio governor of Cyprus. Desdemona tells Lodovico that Othello and Cassio have fallen out but that she has been trying to heal their breach and would be glad to have Cassio made governor of Cyprus, whereupon Othello strikes her. She departs, and later, Othello does, too. Lodovico tells Iago that he is shocked at the change in Othello, and he asks Iago if Othello is going mad.

Act IV, Scene 2

Othello questions Emilia about whether Desdemona is chaste. Emilia defends her. After Emilia exits, Othello says he thinks Emilia is Desdemona's bawd. Emilia reenters, accompanied by Desdemona. Othello begins to taunt them both with their supposed lewdness. Emilia departs. Desdemona defends her chastity against Othello's insults. Emilia and then Iago enter, comforting Desdemona. Desdemona speculates that someone has been slandering her virtue in Othello's hearing. Emilia tells Iago that probably someone had slandered her also in the past when he accused her of having slept with Othello.

After Emilia and Desdemona depart, Roderigo enters. He complains to Iago that his money is almost gone and that all the jewels he gave Iago to pass on to Desdemona have not made Roderigo into her lover. He asks Iago to get Roderigo's jewels back so he can return to Venice. Iago convinces Roderigo that if he murders Cassio that night, he will finally gain access to Desdemona.

Act IV, Scene 3

Othello, Desdemona, Lodovico, and their attendants enter a room in the citadel. Othello proposes that he and Lodovico go for a walk, and he orders Desdemona to go to bed.

Emilia and Desdemona converse while Emilia is preparing her mistress for bed. Desdemona sings a sad song called "Willow" that she learned from her mother about a woman named Barbary whose lover forsakes her when he goes mad. Desdemona says she does not believe wives could stand to be unchaste and that she would not sell her virtue to give her husband power over the whole world. Emilia says she would and adds that when wives do fall, it is the fault of their husbands for mistreating their wives.

Act V, Scene 1

On a dark street at night, Roderigo wounds Cassio. Othello enters, overhearing Cassio's groans, and applauds Iago, whom he assumes attacked Cassio. Lodovico and Gratiano, another Venetian nobleman, enter, followed by Iago, who is carrying a light. Iago stabs Roderigo, as though punishing him for attacking Cassio.

Bianca enters and, seeing Cassio wounded in the leg, commences a loud lament. Iago pretends to discover Roderigo's body, protesting that his friend

Iago stabs Roderigo after the latter wounds Cassio in Act V, Scene I of *Othello*. This is a plate from *Retzsch's Outlines to Shakespeare: Othello,* published in 1842. *(Illustration by Moritz Retzsch)*

has been murdered. Some attendants carry Cassio away. Iago accuses Bianca of being a prostitute and of being involved in the attacks on Roderigo and Cassio; Bianca denies both of Iago's accusations. Emilia enters and joins Iago in accusing Bianca.

Act V, Scene 2

Carrying a light, Othello enters Desdemona's bedroom and delivers a soliloquy about murdering her as though snuffing out a candle that cannot be relit. She awakens. He tells Desdemona to confess any sins to God before he kills her. Othello accuses her of giving his mother's handkerchief to Cassio. She denies it and asks him to summon Cassio to find out the truth. Othello replies that Iago has had Cassio killed, then he smothers Desdemona.

Emilia calls to Othello through the bedroom door. He lets her in, drawing the curtains around Desdemona's bed to conceal her body. Emilia says that Cassio has murdered Roderigo; Othello protests that it is the other way around. Desdemona speaks, blaming herself for her death while protesting her innocence; then she dies. Othello at first denies the murder, but then he confesses to Emilia that he has killed Desdemona. To Emilia's amazement, Othello tells her that Iago is the one who found out that Desdemona was having an affair with Cassio. Emilia cries out that Othello is a fool and that she will make his crime known.

Iago, Montano, Gratiano, and others enter. Emilia asks Iago to explain his accusations of Desdemona; he protests that he told Othello only what he believed to be true of her. Emilia calls Iago a liar and screams out that her mistress has been murdered. Othello protests that he saw Cassio holding the handkerchief Othello had given Desdemona. Disobeying Iago's order that she be quiet, Emilia explains that Iago had asked her to steal Desdemona's handkerchief and give it to him. Othello runs at Iago but is disarmed by Montano. Iago stabs Emilia with his sword, then flees. The others follow Iago out, leaving Othello and Emilia, who laments while she dies.

Othello expresses his guilt and sorrow over murdering Desdemona because of Iago's lies. Gratiano returns, remarking that it is a good thing Brabantio died from grief over Desdemona's elopement before he learned his daughter had been murdered. Then Lodovico, Cassio, Montano, and Iago, now a prisoner, arrive. Othello wounds Iago before he is again disarmed. Iago refuses to answer the others' questions about his motives. Gratiano says Iago will confess when they torture him. Cassio and the others recap what they have learned about Iago's plot. Lodovico tells Othello that they must arrest him and return him to Venice for trial; Cassio will serve in Othello's place as governor of Cyprus.

Othello speaks of himself as being not jealous by nature, but as having been deceived. Othello reminds the others of the time when he had once killed a Turk who had beaten a Venetian and insulted Venice; then he stabs himself in the same style, falls across Desdemona's body, and dies. Lodovico's speech concludes the play as he reminds Cassio to torture Iago and states that Gratiano will inherit Othello's fortune.

CHARACTER LIST

Othello A middle-aged, dark-skinned Moor who has managed, through his brave and brilliant military exploits, to become a respected Venetian general in a racist, xenophobic Renaissance society. Othello falls in love with Desdemona, the young daughter of a Venetian senator, and elopes with her. Sent by the Venetian Duke to Cyprus to defend Venetian interests against invading Turks, Othello starts to lose his sanity and have epileptic seizures when his junior officer, Iago, poisons him with lies about his wife being unchaste. Suffering from jealousy, Othello strangles Desdemona, then finds out that she was in fact chaste. Remorseful, he wounds Iago and kills himself.

Iago An ensign, or junior officer, who resents that Othello promoted young Cassio over him, despite Iago's seniority. Iago manipulates Othello, Cassio, Desdemona, Roderigo, and Emilia to cause the play's initial tragedy, Desdemona's murder, which leads to its closing tragedy, Othello's suicide. Angry because his wife, Emilia, is more loyal to Desdemona than to him, Iago murders her, too, as well as killing Roderigo after getting him to give Iago all of his money to buy Desdemona's favors. When arrested at the play's end, Iago refuses to explain why he plotted to destroy Othello, Desdemona, and Cassio.

Desdemona Othello's wife and daughter of the Venetian senator Brabantio. She is a traditionally virtuous lady in being chaste, kind, and loyal to her husband. However, she is also somewhat rebellious, since she dared to defy Brabantio in eloping with a Moor, and since she persistently argues with Othello that Cassio should be restored to his lieutenancy in Cyprus, even when Othello tries to quiet her.

Cassio Othello's young, newly promoted lieutenant whom Iago tricks into getting drunk at Cyprus. While drunk, Cassio fights Roderigo and accidentally wounds Montano. Othello demotes Cassio as a result. Cassio asks Desdemona to be his advocate to Othello, not realizing that Iago has told Othello that Cassio is her lover. After Cassio finds Desdemona's handkerchief in his room (where Iago planted it), he unintentionally convinces Othello of his perfidy when the latter sees Cassio's mistress, Bianca, throw Desdemona's handkerchief on the floor in a jealous rage. On Othello's orders, Iago tells Roderigo to kill Cassio, but he merely wounds Cassio. At the end of the play, Cassio becomes governor of Cyprus when Othello is arrested (and then kills himself.)

Emilia Wife of Iago and maid to Desdemona, she tries to be loyal to both her husband and her mistress. At Iago's request, she steals Desdemona's handkerchief and gives it to Iago. But when Emilia discovers that Iago's slanders regarding Desdemona have led Othello to strangle her, Emilia stands by her mistress against her husband and Othello, so Iago murders her.

Bianca Mistress to Cassio, whom Iago labels a prostitute; she denies Iago's insult. After Cassio asks Bianca to make a copy of Desdemona's handkerchief, which he found in his room (where Iago put it), Bianca goes into a jealous rage that Othello misinterprets. Later, Iago blames the attacks on Cassio and Roderigo—which Iago in fact caused—on Bianca, since her intimate relations with Cassio make her a suspicious character.

Roderigo Infatuated with Desdemona and rejected as her suitor by Brabantio, Roderigo, a young gentleman of Venice, is fooled by Iago into thinking that by following Desdemona to Cyprus and giving her rich gifts, he will become her lover. In fact, Iago pockets Roderigo's gifts to Desdemona. Iago manipulates Roderigo into fighting Cassio twice: The first time, Montano tries to stop their fight and is badly wounded; the second time, Roderigo injures Cassio, and then Iago murders Roderigo since he has no further use for him as Roderigo's funds have all been spent.

Brabantio Desdemona's father, a senator of Venice who had befriended Othello before the play started but turns against him after Othello elopes with Desdemona. Brabantio spews racist slurs at Othello, accusing him of having bewitched his daughter, and he accuses his daughter of being untrustworthy. Disappointed in his daughter's marriage, Brabantio dies soon after Othello and Desdemona leave Venice for Cyprus.

Duke of Venice The Duke approves Othello and Desdemona's reasons for getting married out of love, despite Brabantio's protests against the elopement. He and the senators send Othello to Cyprus as general of the Venetian army to fight against the Turks.

Montano, governor of Cyprus Soon after Othello arrives in Cyprus, Cassio injures Montano when Montano tries to stop the drunken Cassio from fighting with Roderigo.

Lodovico A Venetian nobleman who comes to Cyprus and is shocked when he sees Othello strike Desdemona for no apparent reason. He helps arrest Iago and gives the last speech in the play, chastising Iago and ordering Cassio to torture him.

Gratiano A Venetian nobleman who comes to Cyprus and is horrified to discover that Othello has murdered Desdemona. After Othello's suicide, Gratiano will be his heir.

Clown Serves as a messenger for Cassio and, later, Desdemona; he makes witty comments.

CHARACTER STUDIES
Othello

Othello is a Moor and former slave who has managed to overcome racism through his military heroism, becoming a general for Venice. He is known for his sound judgment and valor. At the beginning of the play, Othello tells the Duke and senators of Venice about his friendship with Senator Brabantio, whose young daughter, Desdemona, fell in love with the middle-aged Othello when

Russian tenor Arnold Azrikan in the 1945 Sverdlovsk State Academic Opera and Ballet Theater production of Verdi's *Otello*, based on Shakespeare's *Othello*

she heard his stories of the hardships he faced in battle. As stalwart as Othello has been in standing up against prejudice to become a general, he is so once again in eloping with a white aristocrat, Desdemona. Perhaps because the Duke and Senate need Othello's services, this time to fight the Turks in Cyprus, they accept his love marriage to Desdemona. Our sympathy stays with Othello in Cyprus as he deteriorates into a jealous husband, poisoned by Iago's lies about Desdemona having an affair with Othello's lieutenant, Cassio.

Iago plays on Othello's understandable insecurity as an outsider in persuading him to believe Iago's lies. After all, how likely is it that an aging, dark-skinned foreigner could permanently engage the affection of a lovely, young aristocrat of Venice? Othello knows how surprising his own military promotion has been, due to his merit on the battlefield; why should he be just as fortunate in his personal life as he has been in the public realm? Certainly, Cassio, as a young, handsome Venetian of Desdemona's high class, is the kind of man Othello might have expected her to fall for. Even Desdemona's father, Brabantio, could not believe she had fallen in love with Othello; perhaps Brabantio was right, Iago suggests, and Othello agrees. Throughout the play, characters repeatedly call Othello "the Moor," making it impossible for him to forget that they see him as an outsider in terms of his race, religion, and ethnicity; even Desdemona calls him "the Moor," so why should Othello doubt that the prejudice against Moors that her father and society taught her might gradually reemerge to estrange her from him?

As well as activating Othello's self-doubts, Iago arouses Othello's misogynistic tendencies to get him to distrust Desdemona. As a military officer, Othello has spent most of his adult life among men, not women, and has trusted his fellow soldiers with his very life. It would be his habit to trust Iago, since he has served worthily with Othello in many battles. Iago uses the bond between military comrades to turn Desdemona and Cassio into enemies in Othello's mind; he also manipulates Othello into believing degrading stereotypes about Vene-

tian women, which Desdemona's supposed infidelity merely confirms. As a Moor, Othello comes from a culture that the English of Shakespeare's time stereotyped as being misogynistic. Perhaps when Othello refers to killing a Turk when he commits suicide, he is referring to that stereotype of misogyny. In killing himself, he executes the woman-hating aspect of himself, which he seems to associate with so-called infidels and which led him to believe Iago's slanders about Desdemona. Another stereotype the English held about Muslims was that they kill those who are thought to be unchaste: Othello, though a convert to Christianity, confirms this stereotype in planning to strangle Desdemona without asking her to defend herself against Iago's charges; similarly, he orders Iago to have Othello's friend Cassio killed without asking for his side of the story first. When Othello strikes Desdemona in front of the Venetian noblemen who are visiting Cyprus, he also confirms European stereotypes of barbarous Moors abusing their wives.

Othello's dignified joy early in the play changes into despair and rage under Iago's tormenting lies. The onset of his epileptic seizures seems to symbolize his loss of control over his emotions once Iago poisons his mind against his wife and lieutenant; it as though his fits embody how Othello is twisted and paralyzed by anger and grief. Because he suffers so profoundly, the audience's sympathy remains with him despite his foolish, hasty condemnation of his wife and lieutenant. When he is about to smother Desdemona, he invites her to pray, confessing her sins; this suggests Othello the murderer is not completely heartless. His wounding of Iago after he learns how his ensign has deceived him also adds to the audience's empathy with Othello, as does his suicide as a kind of self-execution for murdering his loving wife.

Iago
Iago claims to Roderigo that his hatred of Othello is based on the general having unfairly promoted Cassio to lieutenant when Iago was the one who merited the post, since he had seniority. Iago points out that Cassio is young and untried and

was promoted because of his family connections, education, and handsome appearance. Iago also thinks, or claims to think, that Othello may have slept with his wife, Emilia, though there seems to be no evidence for this. Though understandable, the motives that Iago admits seem inadequate to explain his destruction of Othello, Desdemona, Roderigo, and Emilia. At the end of the play, after he has been arrested, he refuses to answer questions about why he plotted to wreck so many people's lives; perhaps he does not know why, or perhaps he simply will not give his enemies the satisfaction of an explanation.

Envy could be a major reason for Iago's plotting. His belief that Othello slept with Emilia may not come only from gossip, as Emilia thinks, but from his jealousy of Othello as a powerful, respected man whom Emilia and other women would be likely to find more attractive than he is. Iago may also envy Othello his beautiful wife as well as Othello and Desdemona's happiness and goodness, since he lacks both, and Cassio and Desdemona's high birth and inherited wealth, which he also lacks. When Iago taunts Brabantio with disgusting racist slurs against Othello during the play's first scene, Iago is probably voicing his own prejudices; if so, he might well think it unjust that a Moor has gained power, wealth, and even a high marriage when Iago has not, though he is a Venetian.

Another motive for Iago's plot might be sadism. His soliloquies express his joy at deceiving, manipulating, and harming others. Instead of Othello being the ruling general or governor that his titles suggest, Iago usurps his place as the puppet master pulling the strings that determine characters' behavior. As an apparent sociopath, the conscienceless Iago finds dangerous Machiavellian activity amusing and stimulating.

In addition, some modern critics believe that Iago is attracted to Othello in a homoerotic way that motivates Iago's cruelty toward him. Othello will not promote him to lieutenant, which would have given Iago a socially acceptable way to be close to Othello. Since Iago's possible homoerotic desires are socially unacceptable in the world of the play, he may have developed a hatred of Othello to hide his secret love for the other man from himself. In other words, he may destroy Othello to keep his passion for him from threatening Iago's reputation as a man who only fancies women. From this vantage point, Iago's destruction of Desdemona and Emilia punishes them for being false love objects dictated by a heterosexual world. Likewise, he sees Cassio not only as a rival for the position of lieutenant but for Othello's friendship and love. By destroying Othello's loyalty to Desdemona and Cassio, Iago achieves a kind of intimacy with his general as they avenge Othello's supposed disgrace. Their vows of loyalty to one another in Act III, Scene 3 supplant Othello's recent marriage vows and Iago's old ones.

Whether or not Iago has homosexual desires toward Othello, he certainly enjoys degrading women. Iago slanders Desdemona to Brabantio in the play's first scene; in the first scene of the second act, he insults womanhood in jest with Desdemona and Emilia, but he does so in earnest with Roderigo in the third scene of the first act and with Othello in 3.3. Iago also tries to blame Cassio's mistress, Bianca, for his own plot to kill Cassio and his murder of Roderigo. Iago uses the language of misogyny to make Bianca look as guilty as he can; contending that she is a harlot, he suggests she may also be a thief and an accomplice to murder. When Iago murders Emilia, it is under the pretext that she has been disloyal to him in revealing his crimes against Desdemona and Othello. One gets the sense from early in the play, however, that he never felt any love for Emilia or loyalty toward her. Iago's apparently unpremeditated murder of Emilia occurs in his full knowledge of Emilia's virtue and of what he is doing. Hence, it contrasts with Othello's passionate, mistaken, if premeditated, murder of Desdemona, which at first glance seems to be Iago's model.

Like Edmund's malicious, clever machinations in *King Lear,* Iago's actions invite critical reflection. Both men are bitter, ambitious, and not only ruthless but malignant beyond what is usually encountered in life.

Desdemona

Though Desdemona fits her era's notion of feminine virtue in being chaste, kind, and innocent, she is a rebel in disobeying her father by eloping with a Moor. In doing that, she shows her ability to look beyond the physical; Othello is neither young, nor handsome, nor of high birth, nor of her complexion. According to Othello, Desdemona fell in love with his stories of survived hardships, which made her wish she had been born such a man as he; this reason shows her to be a rebel against gender expectations, yet again. Not only is she assertive in choosing her own husband, which would have been unusual for a rich Venetian aristocrat during the Renaissance, but Desdemona is assertive with Othello in persisting to champion Cassio because

Desdemona in *Othello*. This is a print from Charles Heath's 1848 edition of *The Heroines of Shakspeare: Comprising the Principal Female Characters in the Plays of the Great Poet. (Painting by A. Egg; engraving by B. Eyles)*

she believes he has been demoted unfairly. Perhaps it is her loving idealism that makes it hard for her to see that Othello is capable of misconstruing her advocacy of Cassio: When Emilia accuses Othello of behaving jealously, Desdemona denies it as long as she can.

When she and Emilia discuss wives who commit adultery to enrich or aggrandize their husbands, Desdemona cannot believe that such women could exist, which again implies that she is both idealistic and naive, befitting her youth. Emilia reasons with her, but stubborn Desdemona cannot be convinced, much as her father could not shake her from her attachment to Othello, nor could Othello shake her loyalty to Cassio. When, before he smothers her, she tells Othello the truth that she had misplaced his mother's handkerchief, he does not believe her, misinterpreting her panic as prevarication. Like Othello and the other characters, her faith in Iago's honesty opens her to his attacks; Desdemona's nature is nothing if not trusting, even more so than her husband's. When she is dying, she refuses to blame Othello, again suggesting her steadfastness.

Still, from a contemporary perspective, Desdemona's refusal to condemn Othello might seem like that of an abused wife whose adherence to denial is part of what destroys her. It might also be compared to Cordelia's generous forgiveness of her father in *King Lear:* Unconditional love forgives all, suggesting Christ. In her boundless love and trust, Desdemona contrasts with Iago, who loves and trusts no one.

It is ironic that the rebelliousness that enabled her to elope with Othello is what Iago uses to explain her supposed deviation from the chastity expected of a wife. Othello falls easily into the misogynistic thinking that enabled Brabantio to warn his son-in-law against his daughter's supposed deceitfulness.

Emilia

As Iago's wife and Desdemona's maid, Emilia must choose to whom her loyalty most belongs. When she gives Desdemona's handkerchief to Iago at his request, Emilia's loyalty is to him. Later, however, when she realizes that Iago plotted to have Othello murder his wife, Emilia courageously fights to uphold her employer against her husband. She disobeys not only her master, Othello, but Iago in telling the shocking truth about her husband to Othello and the other characters. Even after Iago stabs her, she continues to speak. Her steadfastness and rebelliousness echo Desdemona's in a more dramatic fashion.

Emilia serves as Desdemona's foil, too, in being older and less naive, and in lacking beauty, wealth, and high birth. Being the wife of Iago, Emilia does not, of course, have the glowing view of marriage that the newlywed Desdemona does. In contrast with idealistic Desdemona, Emilia argues pragmatically that wives might commit adultery if their husbands were rewarded for it, adding that she would do so if the reward were great enough. Yet at the end of the play, Emilia does not act pragmatically to save her own life by obeying Iago; instead, she serves as a model, brave servant, similar to Kent in *King Lear*.

Cassio

Cassio serves as a foil to both Othello and Iago. The lieutenant is good-looking, young, well-educated, and well-born, and he has inherited wealth; both Othello and Iago lack these traits. Iago envies him and transplants his envy onto Othello. He feeds Othello's jealousy by suggesting that Desdemona prefers Cassio because of those inborn advantages that Othello, the man who rose from nothing, can never possess; ironically, Desdemona does not care for such inborn traits like Cassio's, only for those that Othello has gained through a difficult life of achievement in battle.

Like Othello at the start of the play and unlike Iago throughout the play, Cassio sees his future with optimism and trusts others. It is Cassio's trusting nature that makes him vulnerable to Iago when Iago persuades him to get drunk in spite of Othello's warnings. Cassio then fights Roderigo when the latter challenges him and severely wounds the governor of Cyprus, Montano, when he tries to intercede. Instead of regretting the actual dam-

Othello (Johnston Forbes-Robertson) demotes Cassio (Ben Webster) for injuring Montano in Act II, Scene 3 of *Othello*. This is an illustration of a 1902 production at the Lyric Theatre. *(Illustration by Charles A. Buchel)*

age he did to Montano, though, Cassio regrets the damage he has done to his own reputation, which makes him seem rather shallow. Consistent with such apparent shallowness, Cassio foolishly takes Iago's advice to request Desdemona as an advocate with Othello to get his lieutenancy back after he has lost it because he injured Montano. If Cassio were truly sorry for injuring Montano, perhaps he would not have so quickly tried to get Desdemona to intercede for him.

In contrast with Iago, Cassio respects Desdemona for her high birth, reproving the ensign's view of her as an object of lust. However, Cassio himself treats his lover, Bianca, a lower-class woman who may be a prostitute, with the disrespect Iago shows to women of every class.

Ironically, Cassio's high birth and other fortuitous inherited traits bring him back to power at the end of the play, when he replaces the disgraced Othello, the self-made hero, as governor of Cyprus.

DIFFICULTIES OF THE PLAY

The play addresses the theme of racism, but in a complicated way that can be difficult for us to grasp today. The title of the play states that Othello is a Moor, and he is referred to as "the Moor" many times during the play, even by Desdemona. Is "Moor" a derogative label for Othello? Moors were Muslims from North Africa who had conquered much of Spain and who originally spoke Arabic rather than Spanish. In 1492, the Spanish forced the final Moorish ruler from Granada. In Shakespeare's time, the term *Moor* held a variety of meanings. It might refer to a dark-skinned person from anywhere, even the New World, or it could specifically mean a Muslim; also, the group includes "white, tawny and black Moors," writes Michael Neill (46). Neill adds that a Moor might be seen as a heathen enemy of Christianity or as a potential ally with England against Catholic Spain (47).

In 1525, the Spanish king forced Moors to convert to Christianity, leave Spain, or become slaves. Jews were in a similar position under pressure of torture and execution by the Spanish Inquisition. In the 16th century, Christians suspected converted Moors and Jews of being infidels because forced conversions were not necessarily believed to be sincere (Hecht 127). In fact, many Moors and Jews continued to practice their traditional religions in private while publicly conforming to Catholicism. Anthony Hecht argues that the Elizabethan audience of *Othello* would have suspected that Othello's Christianity was merely a pose; in addition, the audience would not have been surprised when Othello murders his Christian wife, as it confirms their negative stereotypes of Moors (128–129).

A particular difficulty of the play is that students sometimes say that in depicting Othello as easy to fool, Shakespeare affirms racist views of dark-skinned people as stupid and gullible. However, Iago also deceives all the other major characters—Cassio, Desdemona, Emilia, and Roderigo; Othello is no more gullible than the rest. Harold C. Goddard notes that Othello is at times criticized for being deceived by Iago when they spy on Bianca and Cassio, and Othello mistakenly thinks the two are speaking of Desdemona; however, Goddard points out that Othello had just had "an epileptic fit and is in no condition to exercise his critical faculty" (93).

Finally, students may also be surprised that multiple versions of Shakespeare's plays exist, and they may wonder how to figure out which version is the best one. Denise Walen's 2007 article about the First Folio (1623) versus the quarto (1622) versions of 4.3 in *Othello* offers an excellent example of the performance and textual history that has long preoccupied Shakespeare critics. Walen contends that the longer Folio (F) version of *Othello* was performed before the shorter quarto (Q) version. Walen notes that in the Globe Theatre, where *Othello* was initially produced, no intermissions occurred; hence, 4.3 served an important function of slowing the action and inserting pathos when Desdemona sang her "Willow" song at the end of the fourth act. But when *Othello* began to be performed at the small, indoor Blackfriars Theatre some years later, musical interludes were inserted after each act. Hence, there was no longer a need for the slowdown function of 4.3 or for the novelty of having Desdemona sing; instead, a cliffhanger was desirable at the end of each act so the audience would return to their seats after the intermission. As a result, 4.3 was abbreviated in Q, with the unfortunate result that Desdemona and Emilia became flatter characters. Until the 1930s, performing short versions of 4.3 continued, and often the scene was omitted entirely, including Emilia's speech about husbands prompting their wives to fall. Walen observes: "The history of this scene in performance shows an unnerving disposition to still the female voice, which makes it all the more remarkable that Shakespeare wrote the scene at all" (508).

KEY PASSAGES
Act I, Scene 1, 8–42

IAGO. Three great ones of the city
In personal suit to make me his lieutenant,
Oft-capped to him; and by the faith of man,
I know my price; I am worth of no worse a
  place.
But he, as loving his own pride and purposes,
Evades them with a bombast circumstance,
Horribly stuffed with epithets of war;
Nonsuits my mediators. For, "Certes," says he,
"I have already chose my officer." And what
  was he?
Forsooth, a great arithmetician,
One Michael Cassio, a Florentine,
(A fellow almost damned in a fair wife)
That never set a squadron in the field
Nor the division of a battle knows
More than a spinster; unless the bookish
  theoric,
Wherein the tongued consuls can propose
As masterly as he. Mere prattle without practice
Is all his soldiership. But he, sir, had th'
  election;
And I, of whom his eyes had seen the proof
At Rhodes, at Cyprus, and on other grounds
Christian and heathen, must be belee'd and
  calmed
By debitor and creditor. This counter-caster,
He, in good time, must his lieutenant be,
And I—God bless the mark!—his Moorship's
  ancient.

RODERIGO. By heaven, I rather would have
  been his hangman.

IAGO. Why, there's no remedy; 'tis the curse
  of service:
Preferment goes by letter and affection,
And not by the old gradation, where each
  second
Stood heir to th' first. Now, sir, be judge
  yourself,
Whether I in any just term am affined
To love the Moor.

RODERIGO. I would not follow him then.

IAGO. O, sir, content you.
I follow him to serve my turn upon him.

The play opens with Iago explaining to his friend, Roderigo, why he hates Othello. Iago had employed important men to be his advocates with Othello for promoting Iago to lieutenant. But Othello had already chosen Michael Cassio for his lieutenant, and he planned to name Iago his ancient, or ensign, a junior rank. Iago feels Cassio's promotion over him is unfair because it violates the tradition of seniority in the military, "where each second stood heir to the first." Cassio has never served in battle, unlike Iago, whose soldierly feats Othello has witnessed. According to Iago, Cassio has merely had a theoretical education, which Iago scoffs at by calling Cassio an "arithmetician." Like American anti-intellectuals who scoff at ivory-tower eggheads, Iago thinks education is much less valuable to a lieutenant than the actual battle experience he himself has endured. Iago believes that Cassio has been promoted due to "preferment and affection," because he is good-looking (a pretty boy deserving of "a fair wife"), well-born (his "preferment" championed by other well-born folks, presumably), and Othello's friend ("affection").

Act I, Scene 3, 60–171

BRABANTIO. She is abused, stol'n from me,
  and corrupted
By spells and medicines bought of
  mountebanks;
For nature so prepost'rously to err,
Being not deficient, blind, or lame of sense,
Sans witchcraft could not. . . .

OTHELLO. Her father loved me; oft
  invited me;
Still questioned me the story of my life
From year to year, the battle, sieges, fortune
That I have passed.
I ran it through, even from my boyish days

To th' very moment that he bade me tell it.
Wherein I spoke of most disastrous chances,
Of moving accidents by flood and field,
Of hairbreadth scapes i' th' imminent deadly
  breach,
Of being taken by the insolent foe
And sold to slavery, of my redemption thence
And portance in my travel's history,
Wherein of anters vast and deserts idle,
Rough quarries, rocks, and hills whose heads
  touch heaven,
It was my hint to speak. Such was my process.
And of the Cannibals that each other eat,
The Anthropophagi, and men whose heads
Grew beneath their shoulders. These things to
  hear
Would Desdemona seriously incline;
But still the house affairs would draw her
  thence;
Which ever as she could with haste dispatch,
She'd come again, and with a greedy ear,
Devour up my discourse. Which I observing,
Took once a pliant hour, and found good means
To draw from her a prayer of earnest heart
That I would all my pilgrimage dilate,
Whereof by parcels she had something heard,
But not intensively. I did consent,
And often did beguile her of her tears
When I did speak of some distressful stroke
That my youth suffered. My story being done,
She gave me for my pains a world of kisses.
She swore in faith 'twas strange, 'twas passing
  strange;
'Twas pitiful, 'twas wonderfully pitiful.
She wished she had not heard it; yet she wished
That heaven had made her such a man. She
  thanked me,
And bade me, if I had a friend that loved her,
I should but teach him how to tell my story,
And that should woo her. Upon this hint I
  spake.
She loved me for the dangers I had passed,
And I loved her that she did pity them.
This only is the witchcraft I have used.
Here comes the lady. Let her witness it.

DUKE. I think this tale would win my
  daughter too.

In front of the senators and the Duke of Venice, Desdemona's father, Brabantio, complains that Othello has bewitched his daughter into eloping with him. Brabantio uses the logic of prejudice—that it is unnatural for a girl to choose a husband who does not match her in class, race, nationality, religion, looks, or age; hence, Othello must have used magic to make Desdmona fall for him.

Othello starts by informing the senators and the Duke that he had been Brabantio's frequent dinner guest until Desdemona fell in love with him; for Brabantio, like some people even today, prejudice can be overcome when it comes to establishing friendships, but when marriage is proposed, the walls of prejudice are reerected. Othello explains that "the witchcraft I have used" on Desdemona was describing the dramatic story of his life as a soldier, when he survived many battles and a period of enslavement. Desdemona "loved me for the dangers I had passed, / And I loved her that she did pity them." When Desde-

Othello wins Desdemona's heart by telling her of his adventures, as described in Act I, Scene 3 of *Othello*, in this print published by Virtue & Company in the 19th century. *(Painting by Charles West Cope; engraving by Thomas Vernon)*

mona wishes "that heaven had made her such a man," she rises above the barriers of gender and racial prejudice to empathize with Othello. Her wish to have been born a man also recalls the cross-dressing heroines of Shakespeare's comedies such as *Twelfth Night* and *The Merchant of Venice,* who take on the active role of men when they don masculine clothes.

When the Duke of Venice says his daughter might also have fallen in love with Othello were she in Desdemona's place, established authority blesses their elopement. Like Desdemona, the Duke has set aside the barriers of prejudice to which Desdemona's father holds, siding with the newlywed couple over Senator Brabantio.

Act II, Scene 3, 342–368

IAGO. And what's he then that says I play the
  villain,
When this advice is free I give, and honest.
Probal to my thinking, and indeed the course
To win the Moor again? For 'tis most easy
Th' inclining Desdemona to subdue
In any honest suit; she's framed as fruitful
As the free elements. And then for her
To win the Moor—were't to renounce his
  baptism,
All seals and symbols of redeemed sin—
His soul is so enfettered to her love
That she may make, unmake, do what she list,
Even as her appetite shall play the god
With his weak function. How am I then a
  villain
To counsel Cassio to this parallel course,
Directly to his good? Divinity of hell!
When devils will the blackest sins put on,
They do suggest at first with heavenly shows,
As I do now. For whiles this honest fool
Plies Desdemona to repair his fortune,
And she for him pleads strongly to the Moor,
I'll pour this pestilence into his ear;
That she repeals him for her body's lust;
And by how much she strives to do him good,
She will undo her credit with the Moor.
So will I turn her virtue into pitch.

And out of her own goodness make the net
That will enmesh them all. How now,
  Roderigo?

Iago's soliloquy describes his plot to ruin Desdemona and his rationalization of it as helping Cassio get his job as lieutenant back. Iago's rationalization comes across as tongue in cheek, for surely he knows that by telling Othello that Cassio is Desdemona's lover, Iago will doom Cassio in Othello's eyes. Iago's awareness that he is playing "the villain" suggests his metaliterary dimension as a kind of hidden playwright manipulating the play's plot; he finds great amusement in this role as puppet master of the tragedy, as when he proclaims "Divinity of hell!" Like Dr. Faustus in Christopher Marlowe's Renaissance play of that name, Iago is a disturbingly happy, humorous sadist. Here he also anticipates the joy in malignity seen in Milton's Satan in *Paradise Lost,* for whom Iago serves as a prototype.

He explains his strategy thus: "When devils will the blackest sins put on, / They do suggest at first with heavenly shows, / As I do now." Iago pretends to be honest, loyal, and trustworthy so that Othello and the other characters will believe his lies. Sadly, his pretense works, as many mention his honesty throughout the play.

When Iago says, "Even as her appetite shall play the god / With his weak function," he implies that the aging Othello might be nearly impotent, with Desdemona's desire for him working like divine magic to revive his potency. As usual, Iago degrades their marvelous love into a matter of mere, disgusting lust.

"So will I turn her virtue into pitch." As when Iago spoke of "blackest sins," he again stereotypes sin as dark in using the word *pitch.* His racist references play off Othello's dark complexion. Iago will make pale Desdemona seem as dark as her husband, spiritually speaking. Othello, despite being non-white, is noble and good, until Iago makes him confirm the prejudice that equates dark colors with evil.

"And out of her own goodness make the net / That will enmesh them all." Iago summarizes his strategy of making Othello believe in a topsy-turvy, degraded world in which Desdemona's kind wish to help their friend Cassio is actually advocacy of her lover's interests. Iago compliments Desdemona upon being "framed as fruitful / As the free elements"; however, because she is a free and generous spirit, it is ironically easy for Iago to mislead Othello about her actions, for Desdemona deviates from tradition, not only when she elopes with a Moor but when she interferes in military matters by suing for Cassio to get his lieutenancy back. Iago will twist both of Desdemona's rebellions against gender expectations to convince Othello that she has also violated the chastity expected of a wife.

Act III, Scene 3, 165–233

IAGO. O, beware, my lord, of jealousy!
It is the green-eyed monster, which doth mock
The meat it feeds on. That cuckold lives in bliss
Who, certain of his fate, loves not his wronger;
But O, what damned minutes tells he o'er
Who dotes, yet doubts—suspects, yet fondly
    loves!

OTHELLO. O misery.

IAGO. Poor and content is rich, and rich
    enough;
But riches fineless is as poor as winter
To him that ever fears he shall be poor.
Good God the souls of all my tribe defend
From jealousy!

OTHELLO. Why? Why is this?
Think'st thou I'd make a life of jealousy,
To follow still the changes of the moon
With fresh suspicions? No! To be once in
    doubt
Is to be resolved. Exchange me for a goat
When I shall turn the business of my soul
To such exsufflicate and blown surmises,
Matching the inference. 'Tis not to make me
    jealous

To say my wife is fair, feeds well, loves
    company,
Is free of speech, sings, plays, and dances;
Where virtue is, these are more virtuous.
Nor from mine own weak merits will I draw
The smallest fear or doubt of her revolt,
For she had eyes, and chose me. No, Iago,
I'll see before I doubt; when I doubt, prove;
And on the proof there is no more but this;
Away at once with love or jealousy!

IAGO. . . . In Venice they do let heaven see
    the pranks
They dare not show their husbands; their best
    conscience
Is not to leave't undone, but kept unknown.

OTHELLO. Dost thou say so?

IAGO. She did deceive her father, marrying
    you;
And when she seemed to shake and fear your
    looks,
She loved them most.

OTHELLO. And so she did. . . .

IAGO. . . . My lord, I see y' are moved.

OTHELLO. No, not much moved.
I do not think but Desdemona's honest.

IAGO. Long live she so. And long live you to
    think so.

OTHELLO. And yet, how nature erring from
    itself—

IAGO. Ay, there's the point, as (to be bold
    with you)
Not to affect many proposed matches
Of her own clime, complexion, and degree,
Whereto we see in all things nature tends—
Foh! One may smell in such a will most rank,
Foul disproportions, thoughts unnatural.

Desdemona and Emilia speak with Cassio while Othello and a scheming Iago look on in Act III, Scene 3 of *Othello*. This is a plate from *Retzsch's Outlines to Shakespeare: Othello*, published in 1842. *(Illustration by Moritz Retzsch)*

Iago begins by hinting to Othello that jealousy could turn him into a monster but overtly warns him about continuing to love his wife while suffering a cuckold's doubts. With the decisiveness that makes him an excellent commander in battle, Othello responds, "To be once in doubt / Is to be resolved." Ironically, quick decision making causes Othello's undoing as a husband, though it presumably brought him fame as a general.

Iago plays on Othello's prejudice against upper-class Venetian women when he says, "In Venice they do let heaven see the pranks/ They dare not show their husbands; their best conscience/ Is not to leave't undone, but kept unknown." Since he was raised as a Moor and lived among soldiers, Othello's knowledge of women would presumably be quite limited, so it is not surprising that he believes Iago's slanders about them. Iago then reminds Othello of Brabantio's warning that since Desdemona had lied to her father, she might also lie to her husband: "She did deceive her father, marrying you; / And when she seemed to shake and fear your looks, / She loved them most." Iago convinces Othello that he cannot read her feelings and character from her behavior, since in the past

he had been misled when shy Desdemona seemed to fear him when she first knew him. Once Iago has destroyed his trust in his wife, Othello begins to see her as just another lying, rapacious Venetian lady.

Echoing Brabantio in 1.3.60–64, Othello speaks the language of prejudice: "And yet, how nature erring from itself—." Here Othello implies that Desdemona's attraction to him was unnatural since he is not of her race, class, generation, or religion. Iago amplifies Othello's doubts with "Ay, there's the point, as (to be bold with you) / Not to affect many proposed matches / Of her own clime, complexion, and degree, / Whereto we see in all things nature tends— / Foh! One may smell in such a will most rank, / Foul disproportions, thoughts unnatural." Iago twists Desdemona's beautiful liberation from prejudice when she fell in love with Othello into a foul indictment of her as a degenerate. He implies that since Desdemona has proven herself subject to "Foul disproportions, thoughts unnatural," it is not difficult to imagine her going further along the road of depravity by having an affair with a man of "her own clime, complexion, and degree," Cassio. Sadly, Iago has turned Othello, who has often been a victim of prejudice, into its perpetrator against his loving, chaste wife.

Act IV, Scene 3, 61–97

DESDEMONA. . . . Dost though in
   conscience think, tell me, Emilia,
That there be women do abuse their husbands
   in such gross kind?

EMILIA. There be some such, no question.

DESDEMONA. Wouldst thou do such a deed
   for all the world?

EMILIA. Why, would not you?

DESDEMONA. No, by this heavenly light!

EMILIA. Nor I neither by this heavenly light.

I might do't as well i' th' dark. . . .
But I do think it their husbands' faults
If wives do fall. Say that they do slack their
 duties
And pour our treasures into foreign laps;
Or else break out in peevish jealousies,
Throwing restraint upon us, or say they
 strike us,
Or scant our former having in despite—
Why, we have galls—and though we have some
 grace,
Yet have we some revenge. Let husbands know,
Their wives have sense like them. They see,
 and smell,
And have their palettes for both sweet and
 sour,
As husbands have. . . .

In the first lines of this passage, newlywed Desdemona proves her virtuousness and naïveté in
being unable to believe that women actually do
commit adultery. Emilia, her maid, who has been
married to Iago for an unspecified period, takes a
more realistic view. When Desdemona denies that
she would commit adultery, even if it meant gaining the whole world as a reward, Emilia again is a
foil in saying she would do so.

Then Emilia goes on to blame husbands for
their wives committing adultery. She explains
that husbands may neglect their wives for other
women, irritate their wives with groundless jealousy, hit them, hinder their freedoms, or reduce
their allowances. Any of these cruel actions is
likely to make a wife want to revenge herself upon
her husband by making him into a cuckold. In
other words, Emilia states, women are the same
as men, with similar minds and desires, and husbands who do not realize this may someday regret
it. The bitterness behind Emilia's words makes
sense given that she is enduring marriage to Iago.
Her protofeminism is implied when she states that
"wives have sense like" their husbands. Emilia's
well-reasoned explanation of why wives commit
adultery is much more credible than Iago's misogynistic views stated in Act III, Scene 3, at around

line 200, "In Venice they do let heaven see the
pranks / They dare not show their husbands;
their best conscience / Is not to leave't undone,
but kept unknown."

Act V, Scene 2, 122–140

DESDEMONA. A guiltless death I die.

EMILIA. O, who has done this deed?

DESDEMONA. Nobody—I myself. Farewell.
Commend me to my kind lord. O, farewell.
[*She dies.*]

OTHELLO. Why, how should she be
 murd'red?

EMILIA. Alas, who knows?

OTHELLO. You heard her say herself, it was
 not I.

EMILIA. She said so. I must needs report the
 truth.

OTHELLO. She's like a liar gone to burning
 hell!
'Twas I that killed her.

EMILIA. O, the more angel she,
And you the blacker devil!

OTHELLO. She turned to folly, and she was
 a whore.

EMILIA. Thou dost belie her, and thou art a
 devil.

OTHELLO. She was false as water.

EMILIA. Thou art rash as fire to say
That she was false. O, she was heavenly true!

OTHELLO. Cassio did top her. Ask thy
 husband else.

O, I were damned beneath all depth in hell
But that I did proceed upon just grounds
To this extremity. Thy husband knew it all.

EMILIA. My husband?

After Othello smothers Desdemona, she returns to consciousness to speak to Emilia, who has just entered the bedroom. In response to Emilia's question about who killed her, though, Desdemona lies, protecting Othello by pretending that he is still "kind" to her. She is a loving, loyal wife to the end. At first, Othello pretends he does not know

Emilia condemns Othello after the murder of Desdemona in Act V, Scene 2 of *Othello*. This illustration was designed for a 1918 edition of Charles and Mary Lamb's *Tales from Shakespeare*. *(Illustration by Louis Rhead)*

who killed Desdemona, but then angrily confesses that he did so. Furious, Emilia retorts with racist stereotypes, calling Othello "the blacker devil" who contrasts with Desdemona, who "was heavenly true." Othello explains that it was appropriate that he executed Desdemona because she was "a whore" who slept with Cassio. Emilia's question shows she is shocked when Othello tells her that not only he but Iago believed Desdemona had erred. Now Emilia must decide whether to remain Iago's loyal wife or shift her loyalty to his victim, Desdemona.

DIFFICULT PASSAGES
Act V, Scene 2, 1–22

OTHELLO. It is the cause, it is the cause, my
  soul.
Let me not name it to you, you chaste stars.
It is the cause. Yet I'll not shed her blood,
Nor scar that whiter skin of hers than snow,
And smooth as monumental alabaster.
Yet she must die, else she'll betray more men.
Put out the light, and then put out the light.
If I quench thee, thou flaming minister,
I can again thy former light restore,
Should I repent me; but once put out thy light,
Though cunning'st pattern of excelling nature,
I know not where is that Promethean heat
That can thy light relume. When I have
  plucked the rose,
I cannot give it vital growth again;
It needs must wither. I'll smell thee on the
  tree.
[*He kisses her.*]
O balmy breath, that dost almost persuade
Justice to break her sword. One more, one
  more!
Be thus when thou art dead, and I will kill
  thee,
And love thee after. One more, and that's the
  last!
So sweet was ne'er so fatal. I must weep,
But they are cruel tears. This sorrow's
  heavenly;
It strikes where it doth love. She wakes.

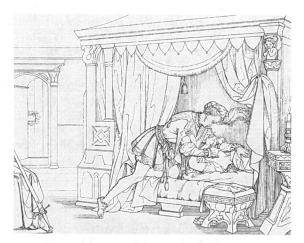

Othello smothers Desdemona in Act V, Scene 2 of *Othello*. This is a plate from *Retzsch's Outlines to Shakespeare: Othello*, published in 1842. *(Illustration by Moritz Retzsch)*

Watching Desdemona sleep before strangling her, Othello ponders her beauty in this soliloquy. The "it" of the first line has no stated referent. "It" appears to be something corrupt, since Othello does not want to "name it" to the "chaste stars"—Desdemona's supposed adultery, perhaps? Or Othello's prejudice against women, which Iago has stoked? Or Othello's self-doubt as an outsider that makes him distrust Desdemona's loyalty? Or Othello's pride as one who surmounted incredible odds to become a general, which makes Desdemona's supposed betrayal an intolerable humiliation? Or Othello's raging jealousy? Or all of these factors?

When Othello says he must kill Desdemona "else she'll betray more men," he paints himself as a savior of his gender. His statement shows how Iago has been successful in shifting Othello's loyalties away from his wife and back toward the male soldiers Othello has long served with.

Out of respect for Desdemona's beauty, Othello will use the relatively nonviolent means of smothering to kill her. This allows him to compare snuffing a candle to strangling his wife. A candle can be lit again after having been snuffed, but murder is permanent, even if the murderer regrets it after the fact.

Othello then compares Desdemona to a rose that, once plucked from the tree, can grow no more. He kisses her repeatedly, weeping at the violence he is about to inflict upon her. Othello betrays some necrophiliac tendencies when he wishes that Desdemona might remain asleep while he kisses her after her death; perhaps he is implying that he feels that he can only love her when she is insensible to the point of death, since he does not trust her when she is awake. His saying "So sweet was ne'er so fatal" makes it seem as though he thinks her kiss is poisonous, when he is actually the one who is about to kill her. Perhaps he feels that his love for her is a disease that threatens his very life, which he must defend himself against by killing its source, his wife. (Ironically, the poison that is corrupting him actually comes from Iago's lies about his wife.) He continues to rationalize his intent to murder Desdemona with, "This sorrow's heavenly; / It strikes where it doth love." Seeing himself in grandiose terms as a champion of virtue in killing the wife he loves, Othello thinks his pain over the murder is god-given, "heavenly."

Act V, Scene 2, 338–361

OTHELLO. Soft you, a word or two before
  you go.
I have done the state some service, and they
  know't.
No more of that. I pray you, in your letters,
When you shall these unlucky deeds relate,
Speak of me as I am. Nothing extenuate,
Nor set down aught in malice. Then must you
  speak
Of one that loved not wisely, but too well;
Of one not easily jealous, but, being wrought,
Perplexed in the extreme; of one whose hand,
Like the base Indian, threw a pearl away
Richer than all his tribe; of one whose subdued
  eyes,
Albeit unused to the melting mood,
Drops tears as fast as the Arabian trees
Their med'cinable gum. Set you down this.

And say besides that in Aleppo once,
Where a malignant and a turbaned Turk
Beat a Venetian and traduced the state,
I took by th' throat the circumcised dog
And smote him—thus. [*He stabs himself.*]

LODOVICO. O bloody period!

GRATIANO. All that is spoke is marred.

OTHELLO. I kissed thee ere I killed thee. No
  way but this,
Killing myself, to die upon a kiss.
[*He falls over Desdemona, and dies.*]

CASSIO: This did I fear, but thought he had
  no weapon;
For he was great of heart.

In Othello's final speech after he has been arrested for murdering Desdemona, he faces the crime he has committed like a hero and does not blame Iago for it: "Nothing extenuate," he admonishes his listeners. He claims that he was not "easily jealous, but, being wrought, / Perplexed in the extreme." "Perplexed in the extreme" alludes to his epilepsy, madness, and violence against his wife. He refers to himself as a false Christian, like Judas, and to Desdemona as a Christ figure with "Like the base Indian, threw a pearl away / Richer than all his tribe." The word *tribe,* so primitive in its connotations to Europeans, suggests that he may see his vengefulness against Desdemona for perceived adultery as coming from his foreign background. He carries this conceit further when he stabs himself after recalling an incident when he executed a Turk for beating "a Venetian" and slandering "the state." Sadly, the hero who had become an insider in Venice—a general, Christian convert, and the governor of Cyprus—executes himself as the Muslim outsider he was born as, a barbarian who violates Venetians.

Gratiano finds Othello's speech less credible because it ends with suicide, but Cassio sees it as a result of Othello being "great of heart." As Othello

dies, falling over Desdemona in a disturbing echo of their living union in their marriage bed, he recalls their last kiss.

CRITICAL INTRODUCTION TO THE PLAY

Among the tragedies of Shakespeare *Othello* is supreme in one quality: beauty. Much of its poetry, in imagery, perfection of phrase, and steadiness of rhythm, soaring yet firm, enchants the sensuous imagination. . . . The play has a rare intellectual beauty, satisfying the desire of the imagination for order and harmony between the parts and the whole. Finally, the play has intense moral beauty . . . in its presentation in . . . Desdemona of a love which does not alter.—Gardner, "The Noble Moor": 169

Helen Gardner observes above that *Othello* is beautiful not only in its language but also in its structure and in the fidelity of Desdemona to Othello despite his mistreatment of her.

Themes

Themes of *Othello* include not only fidelity but the following:

love—marital, romantic, possessive (like Othello's and Brabantio's love for Desdemona, and Bianca's for Cassio), or selfless (like Desdemona's love for Othello and Emilia's for Desdemona);

jealousy—sexual for Othello, while for Iago it is jealousy of Cassio's military promotion and the beauty of his life, of Othello's good fortune, and of Desdemona's virtue;

friendship—false or perverted friendship between men like Iago and Othello, Iago and Roderigo, and Othello and Cassio, and true friendship between employer and servant as seen with Desdemona and Emilia;

unjust revenge—Iago's on Othello, Emilia, and Cassio, and Othello's on Desdemona;

loyalty—Desdemona's to Othello and Emilia's to Desdemona;

Othello (Paul Robeson) speaks with Desdemona (Uta Hagen) in this 1943 Theatre Guild production of *Othello*.

stereotyping—Brabantio, Iago, and Roderigo stereotype Othello based on racism, religious prejudice, and xenophobia, while Iago and Othello stereotype Desdemona, Emilia, and Bianca based on misogyny;

courage—Othello's on the battlefield, Othello and Desdemona's when eloping, Iago's to plot and lie, and Emilia's when opposing Iago and Othello to tell the truth about Desdemona's innocence;

idealism—Othello and Desdemona display idealism when daring to elope, as does Desdemona when championing Cassio and Emilia when doing the same for the deceased Desdemona; and

the exotic and travel—these are seen via setting the first act in Venice and the rest of the play in Cyprus and through starring a Moor who is featured in the title and who exoticizes himself in his speech before committing suicide at the end of the play.

Other themes include the following:

class—Iago resents Cassio for class reasons, and Othello marries up into the aristocracy, while Othello and Iago form an alliance of outcasts in race and class against the well-born Cassio and Desdemona; yet the servant Emilia is arguably the hero of the play when she stands up for her upper-class mistress to Iago and Othello;

interracial relationships—Othello is dark-skinned and Desdemona is white in a period when such a marriage would be rare and controversial;

age—Othello is middle-aged, whereas Desdemona and Cassio are young, making Othello feel less attractive than Cassio and worried about his virility;

sadism—Iago's plot is so evil that the motives he confesses cannot fully account for it, and he seems to take great joy in hurting and manipulating the other characters;

lust—Iago and Roderigo take a lustful view of women rather than a romantic view, and so does Cassio with Bianca;

a daughter's rebellion against her father—as in *The Merchant of Venice, A Midsummer Night's Dream,* and other Shakespeare plays, a woman chooses her husband against her father's wishes, angering him;

murder—Othello of Desdemona, and Iago of Emilia and Roderigo;

suicide—Othello's, as a form of self-execution or punishment;

torture—after the play's end, Iago will be tortured, but Iago has tortured Othello mentally since Act II;

madness—Othello goes mad due to jealousy, and perhaps Iago does in sociopathy, and so does Barbary in "Willow," the song Desdemona sings about a woman whose lover betrays her;

wife abuse—Othello strikes, taunts, and eventually strangles Desdemona, but she remains loyal to him, while Emilia's bitterness toward Iago suggests he might have abused her before he murdered her when she rebelled against him;

homosocial desire—possibly that is a motive for Iago's obsession with Othello, which Iago denies;

bonds among soldiers—Othello trusts Iago because they served together in battle;

deceit—Iago is repeatedly called "honest" by many characters, but he is not, and he convinces Othello that Desdemona's seeming unfaithfulness is real, when it is not;

reputation, rivalry, and status—Iago, Cassio, and Othello are preoccupied with status and reputation, and bitterness about these helps motivate Iago's plot and Othello's mistaken revenge against Desdemona and Cassio for supposedly disgracing him;

social mobility—Othello has managed to become a general despite the prejudices against Moors that he faces, and he manages to convince the Venetian Senate that his elopement with a white aristocrat is appropriate, while Iago is frustrated because he has failed at becoming socially mobile, as Othello has done.

Some other themes include:

voyeurism—Iago convinces Othello to spy on Cassio meeting Desdemona and Cassio meeting Bianca, from which meetings Othello draws misleading conclusions, while throughout the play the audience uncomfortably watches encounters between characters that are too private and disturbing for public viewing, especially Othello's murder of Desdemona and his subsequent suicide;

self-doubt—it may be Othello's tragic flaw, since it makes him believe Iago's lies about Desdemona, for a lifetime of facing prejudices based on Othello's race, ethnicity, and religion has made Othello feel unworthy of his young, wealthy, well-born Venetian wife;

trust—Othello, Emilia, Cassio, Roderigo, and Desdemona mistakenly trust Iago, while Othello mistakenly distrusts Desdemona, and she trusts him so much that she attempts to vindicate him for murdering her;

judgment—legal judgment is given by the Venetian Senate when it permits Othello and Desdemona's elopement, while Othello in Cyprus judges Cassio as deserving demotion until Othello is arrested for strangling Desdemona and executes himself as a kind of sentence for murder—nevertheless, personal judgment is the trait Othello lacks in believing Iago's lies rather than trusting his wife;

necrophilia—when Othello kisses Desdemona's corpse, the body of the beautiful woman is fetishized, as it will be centuries later in Edgar Allan Poe's stories and Pre-Raphaelite painting;

witchcraft—Brabantio accuses Othello of bewitching Desdemona, and her name contains the word *demon*, as hinted when Othello later accuses her of being a devil, then executes her as though she were a witch or siren who endangers men;

monstrosity—due to racism, Brabantio mistakenly regards interracial marriage as monstrous, while Iago's plot to ruin Othello, Desdemona, and Cassio is actually monstrous, as is Othello's murder of Desdemona; imagery of bestiality throughout the play expresses the theme of monstrosity.

Structure

Written in five acts, *Othello* is set in Venice during the first act and in Cyprus, an outpost of Venice, during the remaining acts. The first, second, and fourth acts are composed of three scenes in each act; the third act is composed of four scenes; and the final act is composed of two scenes.

The first act occurs during a single evening. Othello and Desdemona are presumably consummating their elopement during the first two scenes, when Iago and Roderigo conspire and then go to Desdemona's father's house to taunt him over his daughter's elopement with Othello. (Not all critics think Othello and Desdemona ever consummate their marriage, however.) The closing scene of the first act is set in the Venetian Senate, when Othello answers Brabantio's charges in a pseudotrial that vindicates Othello.

The second act opens in the daytime in Cyprus, to which Othello and Desdemona have sailed in

Desdemona convinces the Duke of her affection for Othello in Act I, Scene 3 of *Othello*. This is a plate from *Retzsch's Outlines to Shakespeare: Othello*, published in 1842. *(Illustration by Moritz Retzsch)*

separate ships, surviving a storm that drowned the Turkish fleet. From that scene until the end of the play, the action hurtles over two days and nights; this sense of speeding, telescoping time creates the audience's sense that Iago is driving Othello insane with jealousy of Desdemona and Cassio's supposed adultery. Frank Kermode argues that "the pivotal scene of the play is 3.3, which from the outset, with Iago's 'I like not that' as Cassio withdraws, to the end, when Othello has accepted the charge against Desdemona and planned her death and Cassio's, is fewer than five hundred lines long, probably less than half an hour of stage time" (173). Such speed emphasizes Othello's transformation from a calm, reasonable man into one possessed by rage and jealousy.

The third and fourth acts end with same-sex pairings that supplant the married couples of Othello and Desdemona, Iago and Emilia. The third act concludes with Iago swearing fealty to Othello in revenge on Desdemona and Cassio, and the fourth act closes with a domestic scene between Emilia and Desdemona, when the maid presents husbands' flaws from a more realistic view than the misogynistic stereotypes Iago used to manipulate Othello during the third act.

Two scenes contain songs. The first scene of the second act includes a drinking song that Iago performs, and the last scene of the fourth act includes a sad ditty sung by Desdemona about a woman whose lover betrays her. Both of those scenes also contain banter that is missing from most of the rest of the play—in 2.1, the joking talk is between Iago, Desdemona, and Emilia, and in 4.3, it is between Desdemona and Emilia.

Ironically, although Iago is the villain, he speaks the most lines in the play, including five soliloquies and two asides in the first, second, and fourth acts (1.3.374–395, 2.1.165–175 and 198, 2.1.286–312, 2.3.46–59, 2.3.336–362, and 4.1.95–105). By contrast, Othello, the hero of the play, has only two soliloquies (3.3.257–277 and 5.2.1–22). Perhaps Iago needs to have the most lines to allow him to achieve control of the other characters. Only Iago and Othello speak soliloquies, keeping the two soldiers in primary focus and eclipsing Desdemona, Cassio, and Emilia.

Style and Imagery

Though *Othello* is mostly written in poetry, the discussions between Roderigo and Iago are generally in prose, accentuating the informal, nasty content of their dialogue. Whereas Iago's cynical style suits his debased thoughts, G. Wilson Knight argues that the play's "supremely beautiful effects of style are all expressions of Othello's personal passion" (55). Knight notes the use of beautiful, unusual names in the play, such as "Anthropophagi, Ottomites, Arabian trees, 'the base Indian', the Egyptian, Palestine, Mauretania, the Sagittary, Olympus, Mandragora, Othello, Desdemona" (57). He also observes that "[t]here is no fusing of word with word, rather a careful juxtaposition of one word or image with another" (57).

Wordplay occurs in the very frequent use of the word *honest,* mostly to describe Iago misleadingly, but sometimes Desdemona and Cassio as well. The word *lie* is used as a double entendre for making love versus telling untruths (3.4.10–12 and 4.1.34–36). In his famous speech to Roderigo advising him to "Put money in thy purse" (1.3.335), Iago repeats the word *money* again and again, teaching the idle and slow-witted Roderigo to become Iago's bank. Frank Kermode also observes that *Othello* includes much hendiadys, "the habit of expansive doubling," such as "loving his own pride and purposes," "trimm'd in forms and visages of duty," "play and trifle with your reverence" and other examples during the mere "first 170 lines" of the play (168).

The meaning of the handkerchief, Othello's first gift to Desdemona (which he inherited from his mother), has often been discussed. Some critics have thought its whiteness symbolizes Desdemona's virgin purity, with the strawberries decorating it indicating her potential fertility after her marriage to Othello is consummated. The red strawberries also hint at Desdemona's blood that is spilled when Othello fails to kill her by strangulation and then presumably stabs her. Red as the color of lust and rage is suggested by the strawberries spotting the handkerchief. In 3.4.58–67, Othello implies through his mother's tale that Desdemona's handkerchief additionally symbolizes feminine power over men to civilize them through the bonds of love and trust; however, Iago's slander erodes that womanly power, as Othello's uncivilized, primal rage erupts against Desdemona.

References to Turks, the Venetians' enemies, draw attention to racial prejudice. Brabantio insultingly implies that Othello is a Turk (presumably because Moors are dark, of Muslim heritage, and from the East) when he says that letting Desdemona marry Othello would be like letting the Turks take Cyprus from Venice (1.3.205–206). Even Othello expresses prejudice against Turks when he asks, "Are we turned Turks?" (2.3.169) after the drunken Cassio attacks Montano. In his final speech, Othello refers to himself as both a Turk who deserves execution for his crime and as the executioner of that Turk (5.2.347–352). Harold C. Goddard contends that the frequent allusions to Turks in *Othello* set up Iago as the real Turk, though Othello may look like one (80–81).

Light and darkness, along with black and white, are repeatedly contrasted to question their stereotypical moral and racial associations. The play opens in the darkness of night, and most of its important scenes occur then. Iago says he will turn Desdemona's "virtue into pitch" (2.3.360) by making her kind efforts to help Cassio make her seem lascivious. When Othello speaks of murdering Desdemona during his soliloquy, he says, "Put out the light" (5.2.7) and then sadly ponders that he will not be able to relight her spirit once he kills her. Repeatedly, Othello is called a Moor, even by his wife, reminding the audience of his derided nationality and complexion. However, the Duke sees that "If virtue no delighted beauty lack / Your son-in-law is far more fair than black" (1.3.284–285).

Deceived by Iago, Othello feels the disgrace of becoming a cuckold has made his reputation "begrimed and black" like his skin (3.3.384); here he buys into European culture's racist blurring of dark colors with moral and physical ugliness. He is labeled "damned" by Brabantio (1.2.62), who insults him by mentioning his "sooty bosom" (1.2.69). Iago says women are "devils being offended" (2.1.110). Othello is dubbed a "blacker devil" by Emilia (5.2.130) after he repeatedly labels Desdemona one (3.3.475, 3.4.42, and 4.1.35). Emilia also calls Othello Desdemona's "most filthy bargain" (5.2.154), after labeling her an "angel" (5.2.129). Emilia says Othello is "ignorant as dirt" (5.2.161), confusing his mistaken sinful act with his racial darkness. After Othello finds he murdered Desdemona wrongly, since she was innocent, he says, "Whip me, ye devils" (5.2.274) and calls Iago a "demi-devil" (5.2.297). Othello then praises Desdemona as a "pearl" (5.2.343). Iago labels Othello "an old black ram" who "is tupping" Desdemona, a "white ewe" (1.1.85).

Disturbing animal imagery such as that of ram and ewe is common in the play, especially in the mouth of Iago. Iago brags that he will make Othello into an ass who is easily led (1.3.393) and driven mad (2.1.309). He similarly pictures his plot against Cassio in terms of a "web" to ensare "a fly," implying that Iago is the spider (2.1.166). Warning Othello (surprisingly enough), Iago compares jealousy to "a green-eyed monster" (3.3.166). Even

Desdemona uses animal imagery when she says of Othello, as though he were an animal, "I'll watch him tame" (3.3.23). Cassio says that drinking too much has made him and the other soldiers into "beasts" (2.3.290), which is what Iago manages to turn Othello into when he murders Desdemona. Iago's language transforms human feelings into base, bestial urges—love into lust, trustfulness into foolish gullibility, and so on, as when Iago conjures false pictures of Cassio committing adultery with Desdemona through images of goats, wolves, and monkeys in heat (3.3.400). Through such imagery, Iago transfers his disgusting view of the world onto Othello.

Othello then begins to use animal imagery, as when he says, "A horned man's a monster and a beast" (4.1.64), referring to cuckolds. Othello paints his love for Desdemona as defiled in calling it "a cistern for fouled toads" (4.2.63). Tainted by Iago's lies, Othello calls Desdemona "a lewd minx" (3.3.473) and "a fitchew," or stinky cat (4.1.146); Othello also describes women as "delicate creatures" full of "appetites" that husbands cannot control (3.3.268). Even Cassio, who is courteous toward upper-class women like Desdemona, mocks his lower-class lover Bianca (whom Iago labels a prostitute) by referring to her hopes of marrying Cassio as "the monkey's own giving out" (4.1.129). The language of prejudice, whether of sexism or racism, uses animal imagery to dehumanize the object of prejudice. This can be seen from the first scene of the play, when Iago inflames Brabantio's racism by comparing Othello to various animals, including a "Barbary horse" (1.1.107). When Othello himself says, "I'll tear her to pieces" (3.3.427), the audience knows that Iago has managed to dehumanize the noble general, making him into a brute.

Animal imagery plays a role in *Othello's* debate over what is natural and unnatural. In the play's second and third scene, Brabantio argues that Desdemona's attachment to a husband so unlike her in race, age, nationality, and background is unnatural. Iago uses this argument to convince Roderigo and Othello that it is natural for Desdemona to cheat

with Cassio, who is her like in age, race, and class. Othello echoes Iago's thinking with the phrase "nature erring from itself" (3.3.227).

"Throughout the play imagery of wind and weather is played against imagery of confinement," A. D. Nuttall observes (279). At the start of Act II, Othello and Desdemona survive the stormy sea, then enter the fortress at Cyprus. The stormy sea of 2.1, I believe, anticipates the mental storm Iago creates in Othello in Act III through activating his jealousy, thus causing seizures. Othello's emotional tempest crests when he kills Desdemona and himself in Act V.

Othello ties imagery of the ocean into that of freedom versus confinement when he says,

> But that I do love the gentle Desdemona,
> I would not my unhoused free condition
> Put into circumspection and confine
> For the sea's worth.
>
> (1.2.25–28)

Similarly, Othello later says Desdemona's fidelity would have been worth more than a jewel the size of the earth (5.2.140); this recalls Desdemona saying in 4.3 that she would not sell her chastity to give her husband all the riches in the world.

Slavery is another motif related to the imagery of confinement. Brabantio contends that Othello used witchcraft on Desdemona (1.3.168), in a kind of erotic enslavement. Othello says he once was sold into slavery (1.3.137). Iago ends up enslaving Othello with lies that confirm Othello's worries about his attractiveness to Desdemona, and Iago enslaves Roderigo by appealing to his lust for Desdemona.

Imagery of poison lets the audience see the corrupting effect of Iago's lies on Othello, as when Iago says the "Moor already changes with my poison" (3.3.322). Iago pours "pestilence into his ear" (2.3.355), poisoning Othello through slandering his wife. With irony, Iago brags of his cruelly effective gossip: "My med'cine works!" (4.1.46). At the play's end, Lodovico reacts to the bed containing the dead Othello, Desdemona, and Emilia by saying the "object poisons sight" (5.2.360). Lodovico here reminds the audience that Iago caused these deaths, while moving the imagery of poison from the mouth and ear to the eye.

Iago makes Cassio seem effeminate when he calls him a "spinster" (1.1.21), implies he is too pretty (1.1.17), and speaks of Cassio's "prattle" (1.1.24). Much as Cassio is put into feminine dress in a metaphorical sense, gender reversal cloaks Desdemona in military imagery. Othello calls her "fair warrior" (2.1.179), while Iago names her "our great captain's captain" (1.3.393) and states that "Our general's wife is now the general" (2.3.314). This military language suggests Desdemona is an unnatural threat to Othello's traditional supremacy as a husband and general. Iago feeds on Othello's fear of being ruled by his wife, making her seem monstrously bossy in her attempt to intercede for Cassio with her husband.

In contrast with this, Desdemona is earlier seen as property by her father, when Brabantio calls Othello a thief for stealing his daughter (1.1.75). From a more liberal stance than Brabantio's, Othello initially regards Desdemona as "free and bounteous to her mind" (1.3.260), before Iago corrupts Othello's view of her, making her seem like a possession contaminated by male lovers.

EXTRACTS OF CLASSIC CRITICISM
Thomas Rymer (ca. 1643–1713) [Excerpted from *A Short View of Tragedy* (1693), the first significant work of criticism about *Othello*. Rymer did not approve of the play.]

The character of that State [Venice] is to employ strangers in their Wars. But shall a Poet thence fancy that they will set a Negro to be their General; or trust a Moor to defend them against the Turk? With us a Black-amoor might rise to be a Trumpeter; but Shakespear would not have him less than a Lieutenant-General. With us a Moor might marry some little drab, or Small-coal Wench; Shake-spear would provide him the Daughter and Heir of some great Lord, or Privy-

Councellor: And all the Town should reckon it a very suitable match: Yet the English are not bred up with that hatred and aversion to the Moors, as are the Venetians, who suffer by a perpetual Hostility from them. . . .

There is in this Play, some burlesk, some humour, and ramble of Comical Wit, some shew, and some Mimickry to divert the spectators; but the tragical part is, plainly none other, than a Bloody farce, without salt or savour.

Samuel Johnson (1709–1784) [Excerpted from the preface to *The Plays of William Shakespeare* (1765). Among his many other achievements as one of the greatest literary critics, Dr. Johnson compiled a landmark edition of Shakespeare's plays. His writings on Shakespeare are still widely studied.]

The beauties of this play impress themselves so strongly upon the attention of the reader that they can draw no aid from critical illustration. The fiery openness of Othello, magnanimous, artless, and credulous, boundless in his confidence, ardent in his affection, inflexible in his resolution, and obdurate in his revenge; the cool malignity of Iago, silent in his resentment, subtle in his designs, and studious at once of his interest and his vengeance; the soft simplicity of Desdemona, confident of merit and conscious of innocence, her artless perseverance in her suit, and her slowness to suspect that she can be suspected, are such proofs of Shakespeare's skill in human nature as, I suppose, it is vain to seek in any modern writer. The gradual progress of which Iago makes in the Moor's conviction and the circumstances which he employs to inflame him are so artfully natural that, though it will perhaps not be said of him, as he says of himself, that he is *a man not easily jealous,* yet we cannot but pity him when at last we find him *perplexed in the extreme.* . . .

Even the inferior characters of this play would be very conspicuous in any other piece, not only for their justness but their strength. Cassio is brave, benevolent, and honest, ruined only by his want of stubbornness to resist an invidious invitation. Roderigo's suspicious credulity and impatient submission to the cheats which he sees practiced upon him, and which by persuasion he suffers to be repeated, exhibit a strong picture of a weak mind betrayed by unlawful desires to a false friend; and the virtue of Emilia is such as we often find, worn loosely but not cast off, easy to commit small crimes but quickened and alarmed at atrocious villainies.

[Johnson's remarks below are excerpted from James Boswell's classic *The Life of Samuel Johnson* (1791).]

I [Boswell] observed that the great defect of the tragedy of *Othello* was, that it had not a moral; for that no man could resist the circumstances of suspicion which were artfully suggested to Othello's mind.

JOHNSON. "In the first place, Sir, we learn from *Othello* this very useful moral, not to make an unequal match; in the second place, we learn not to yield too readily to suspicion. The handkerchief is merely a trick, though a very pretty trick; but there are no other circumstances of reasonable suspicion, except what is related by Iago of Cassio's warm expressions concerning Desdemona in his sleep; and that depended entirely on the assertion of one man. No, Sir, I think *Othello* has more moral than almost any other play."

Samuel Taylor Coleridge (1772–1834)
[Excerpted from *Notes and Lectures Upon Shakespeare, Vol. 1* (1849). Coleridge is today better

known as a poet, but his criticism has also been influential. His characterization of Iago as a "motiveless malignity" is justly famous.]

[1.3] Iago's speech:—
  Virtue? A fig! 'tis in ourselves that we are thus, or thus, &c.

This speech comprises the passionless character of Iago. It is all will in intellect; and therefore he is here a bold partisan of a truth, but yet of a truth converted into a falsehood by the absence of all the necessary modifications caused by the frail nature of man. And then comes the last sentiment,—

  Our raging motions, our carnal stings, our unbitted lusts,
  whereof I take this, that you call—love, to be a sect or scion!

Here is the true Iagoism of, alas! how many! Note Iago's pride of mastery in the repetition of "Go, make money!" to his anticipated dupe, even stronger than his love of lucre: and when Roderigo is completely won—
  I am chang'd. I'll go sell all my land—
when the effect has been fully produced, the repetition of triumph—

  Go to; farewell; put money enough in your purse!

The remainder—Iago's soliloquy—the motive-hunting of a motiveless malignity—how awful it is!

William Hazlitt (1778–1830)   [Excerpted from *A View of the English Stage* (1818). Along with Coleridge, Hazlitt was one of the leading critics of Shakespeare during the 19th century.]

Some persons more nice than wise, have thought the whole of the character of Iago unnatural. Shakespeare, who was quite as good a philosopher as he was a poet, thought otherwise. He knew that the love of power, which is another name for the love of mischief, was natural to man. He would know this as well or better than if it had been demonstrated to him by a logical diagram, merely from seeing children paddle in the dirt, or kill flies for sport. We might ask those who think the character of Iago not natural, why they go to see it performed—but from the interest it excites, the sharper edge which it sets on their curiosity and imagination? Why do we go to see tragedies in general? Why do we always read the accounts in the newspapers, of dreadful fires and shocking murders, but for the same reason? . . .

The general groundwork of the character of Iago, as it appears to us, is not absolute malignity, but a want of moral principle, or an indifference to the real consequences of the actions, which the modifying perversity of his disposition and love of immediate excitement lead him to commit. He is an amateur of tragedy in real life; and instead of exercising his ingenuity on imaginary characters, or forgotten incidents, he takes the bolder and more desperate course of getting up his plot at home, casts the principal parts among his nearest friends and connections, and rehearses it in downright earnest, with steady nerves and unabated resolution. The character is a complete abstraction of the intellectual from the moral being; or, in other words, consists in an absorption of every common feeling in the virulence of his understanding, the deliberate willfulness of his purposes, and in his restless untameable love of mischievous contrivance. . . .

The habitual licentiousness of Iago's conversation is not to be traced to the pleasure he takes in gross and lascivious images, but to a desire of finding out the worst side of every thing, and of proving himself an over-match for appearances.

Othello and Desdemona reunite while Iago (right) plots in Act II, Scene 1 of *Othello*. This is a print from the Boydell Shakespeare Gallery project, which was conceived in 1786 and lasted until 1805. *(Painting by Thomas Stothard; engraving by Thomas Ryder)*

A. C. Bradley (1851–1935) [Excerpted from *Shakespearean Tragedy* (1905). A. C. Bradley's book on Shakespeare is one of the most important of the 20th century.]

We are now in a position to consider the rise of Iago's tragedy. Why did he act as we see him acting in the play? What is the answer to that appeal of Othello's:

> Will you, I pray, demand that demi-devil
> Why he hath thus ensnared my soul and
>   body?

This question Why? is *the* question about Iago, just as the question Why did Hamlet delay? is *the* question about Hamlet. Iago refused to answer it; but I will venture to say that he *could* not have answered it, any more than Hamlet could tell why he delayed. But Shakespeare knew the answer, and if these characters are great creations and not blunders we ought to be able to find it too.

Is it possible to elicit it from Iago himself against his will? He makes various statements to Roderigo, and he has several soliloquies. From these sources, and especially from the latter, we should learn something. For with Shakespeare soliloquy generally gives information regarding the secret springs as well as the outward course of the plot; and, moreover, it is a curious point of technique with him that the soliloquies of his villains sometimes read almost like explanations offered to the audience. Now, Iago repeatedly offers explanations either to Roderigo or to himself. In the first place, he says more than once that he "hates" Othello. He gives two reasons for his hatred. Othello has made Cassio lieutenant; and he suspects, and has heard it reported, that Othello has an intrigue with Emilia. Next there is Cassio. He never says he hates Cassio, but he finds in him three causes of offence: Cassio has been preferred to him; he suspects *him* too of an intrigue with Emilia; and, lastly, Cassio has a daily beauty in his life which makes Iago ugly. In addition to these annoyances he wants Cassio's place. As for Roderigo, he calls him a snipe, and who can hate a snipe? But Roderigo knows too much; and he is becoming a nuisance, getting angry, and asking for the gold and jewels he handed to Iago to give to Desdemona. So Iago kills Roderigo. Then for Desdemona: a fig's end for her virtue! But he has no ill-will to her. In fact he "loves" her, though he is good enough to explain, varying the word, that his "lust" is mixed with a desire to pay Othello in his own coin. To be sure she must die, and so must Emilia, and so would Bianca if only the authorities saw things in their true light; but he did not set out with any hostile design against these persons.

Is the account which Iago gives of the causes of his action the true account? The answer of the most popular view will be, "Yes. Iago was, as he says, chiefly incited by two things, the desire of advancement, and a hatred of Othello due principally to the affair of the lieutenancy. These are perfectly intelligible causes; we have only to add to them unusual ability and cruelty, and all is explained. Why should Coleridge and Hazlitt and Swinburne go further afield?" To which last question I will at once oppose these; if your view is correct, why should Iago be considered an extraordinary creation; and is it not odd that the people who reject it are the people who elsewhere show an exceptional understanding of Shakespeare?

The difficulty about this popular view is, in the first place, that it attributes to Iago what cannot be found in the Iago of the play. Its Iago is impelled by *passions,* a passion of ambition and a passion of hatred; for no ambition or hatred short of passion could drive a man who is evidently so clear-sighted, and who must hitherto have been so prudent, into a plot so extremely hazardous. Why, then, in the Iago of the play do we find no sign of these passions or of anything approaching to them? Why, if Shakespeare meant that Iago was impelled by them, does he suppress the signs of them? Surely not from want of ability to display them. The poet who painted Macbeth and Shylock understood his business. Who ever doubted Macbeth's ambition or Shylock's hate? And what resemblance is there between those passions and any feeling that we can trace in Iago? The resemblance between a volcano in eruption and a flameless fire of coke; the resemblance between a consuming desire to hack and hew your enemy's flesh, and the resentful wish, only too familiar in common life, to inflict pain in return for a slight. Passion, in Shakespeare's plays, is perfectly easy to recognise. What vestige of it, of passion unsatisfied or of passion gratified, is visible in Iago? None: that is the very horror of him. He has *less* passion than an ordinary man, and yet he does these frightful things. The only ground for attributing to him, I do not say a passionate hatred, but anything deserving the name of hatred at all, is his own statement, "I hate Othello"; and we know what his statements are worth.

But the popular view, besides attributing to Iago what he does not show, ignores what he does show. It selects from his own account of his motives one or two, and drops the rest; and so it makes everything natural. But it fails to perceive how unnatural, how strange and suspicious, his own account is. Certainly he assigns motives enough; the difficulty is that he assigns so many. A man moved by simple passions due to simple causes does not stand fingering his feelings, industriously enumerating their sources, and groping about for new ones. But this is what Iago does. And this is not all. These motives appear and disappear in the most extraordinary manner. Resentment at Cassio's appointment is expressed in the first conversation with Roderigo, and from that moment is never once mentioned again in the whole play. Hatred of Othello is expressed in the First Act alone. Desire to get Cassio's place scarcely appears after the first soliloquy, and when it is gratified Iago does not refer to it by a single word. The suspicion of Cassio's intrigue with Emilia emerges suddenly, as an afterthought, not in the first soliloquy but the second, and then disappears for ever. The "love" of Desdemona is alluded to in the second soliloquy; there is not the faintest trace of it in word or deed either before or after. The mention of jealousy of Othello is followed by declarations that Othello is infatuated about Desdemona and is of a constant nature, and during Othello's sufferings Iago never shows a sign of the idea that he is now paying his rival in his own coin. In the second soliloquy he declares that he quite believes Cassio to be in love with Desdemona: it is obvious that he believes no such thing, for he never alludes to the idea again, and within a few hours describes Cassio in soliloquy as

an honest fool. His final reason for ill-will to Cassio never appears till the Fifth Act.

What is the meaning of all this? Unless Shakespeare was out of his mind, it must have a meaning. And certainly this meaning is not contained in any of the popular accounts of Iago.

Is it contained then in Coleridge's word "motive-hunting"? Yes, "motive-hunting" exactly answers to the impression that Iago's soliloquies produce. He is pondering his design, and unconsciously trying to justify it to himself. He speaks of one or two real feelings, such as resentment against Othello, and he mentions one or two real causes of those feelings. But these are not enough for him. Along with them, or alone, there come into his head, only to leave it again, ideas and suspicions, the creations of his own baseness or uneasiness, some old, some new, caressed for a moment to feed his purpose and give it a reasonable look, but never really believed in, and never the main forces which are determining his action. In fact, I would venture to describe Iago in these soliloquies as a man setting out on a project which strongly attracts his desire, and unconsciously trying to argue the resistance away by assigning reasons for the project. He is the counterpart of Hamlet, who tries to find reasons for his delay in pursuing a design which excites his aversion. And most of Iago's reasons for action are no more the real ones than Hamlet's reasons for delay were the real ones. Each is moved by forces which he does not understand; and it is probably no accident that these two studies of states psychologically so similar were produced at about the same period.

What then were the real moving forces of Iago's action? Are we to fall back on the idea of a "motiveless malignity"; that is to say, a disinterested love of evil, or a delight in the pain of others as simple and direct as the delight in one's own pleasure? Surely not. I will not insist that this thing or these things are inconceivable, mere phrases, not ideas; for, even so, it would remain possible that Shakespeare had tried to represent the inconceivability. But there is not the slightest reason to suppose that he did so. Iago's action is intelligible; and indeed the popular view contains enough truth to refute this desperate theory. It greatly exaggerates his desire for advancement, and the ill-will caused by his disappointment, and it ignores other forces more important than these; but it is right in insisting on the presence of this desire and this ill-will, and their presence is enough to destroy Iago's claims to be more than a demi-devil. For love of the evil that advances my interest and hurts a person I dislike, is a very different thing from love of evil simply as evil; and pleasure in the pain of a person disliked or regarded as a competitor is quite distinct from pleasure in the pain of others simply as others. The first is intelligible, and we find it in Iago. The second, even if it were intelligible, we do not find in Iago.

MODERN CRITICISM AND CRITICAL CONTROVERSIES

Modern critics have built on and reacted to critics of the past. The critic F. R. Leavis argues that the effect of A. C. Bradley's influential view of Othello and Desdemona as virtuous victims of Iago's evil plot "is to sentimentalize Shakespeare's tragedy and to displace its centre" (260). Leavis believes that Othello's flaws precipitate his tragedy:

Iago's power, in fact, in the temptation-scene is that he represents something that is in Othello—in Othello the husband of Desdemona: the essential traitor is within the gates. . . . The tragedy is inherent in the Othello-Desdemona relation, and Iago is a mechanism necessary for precipitating tragedy in a dramatic action. (264)

According to Leavis, what makes Othello effective as a heroic warrior and general is what makes him a flawed lover and husband—his "self-approving self-dramatization" (265). Othello excels at fighting battles and handling storms like the one that stops the Turkish fleet at Cyprus. Shakespeare's poetic language beautifully conveys Othello's heroic abilities. But when confronted with the debased, realistic language and worldview of Iago, Othello fails to cope. Through Othello, Shakespeare is showing the tragic limitations of the heroic man of action, in Leavis's view.

The critic Helen Gardner posits that Leavis's negative view of Othello stems from experiencing the horrors of World War I. In 1968, Gardner surveyed early 20th-century Shakespeare criticism such as Leavis's, explaining that "[it] became axiomatic in the twenties and thirties that professional soldiers were stupid" (*"Othello"*: A Retrospect, 1900–1967, 13). Even critics of the 1960s, according to Gardner, find it difficult to appreciate Othello. (I wonder if that is because heroism had again become unfashionable during the Vietnam War?)

A precursor to Leavis in seeing Othello critically, the great poet and critic T. S. Eliot thinks that Othello improperly justifies himself in his final speech in the play. Eliot calls Othello's self-justification an example of "bovarysme, the human will to see things as they are not" (132).

In 1930, G. Wilson Knight brought attention to the beauty of *Othello*'s poetry, which he calls "the *Othello* music" (57), deviating from the focus on character studies of A. C. Bradley and Samuel Taylor Coleridge. Knight notes that Othello often uses "rich, often expressly consonantal, outstanding words" (57) and says the play "possesses a unique solidity and precision of picturesque phrase or image, a peculiar chastity and serenity of thought. . . . The dominant quality is separation, not, as is more usual in Shakespeare, cohesion" (56).

In 1951, Harold C. Goddard linked *Othello* to *Hamlet* as revenge plays involving "motifs of eavesdropping, of pouring poison in the ear . . . and of the mousetrap" (69); also, in both tragedies, parent-child situations are central, while Desdemona serves as an "anti-Ophelia" who is willing to rebel against her father for the man she loves (70).

Goddard ties *Othello* to *The Merchant of Venice* as well as to *Hamlet,* not only due to their common setting and preoccupation with prejudice, but because the plays dramatize "the contrast between the inner and outer, depth and surface, the gilded that is mistaken for the golden, the precious that is hidden beneath the base. . . . The casket theme exactly!" (73).

Also in 1951, William Empson analyzed the frequent use of the word *honest* in the play, pointing out that Iago might resent being called honest, as it was a condescending term used to describe servants. Still, Iago manages to take advantage of his reputation for honesty when he manipulates his so-called superiors (218–249).

The renowned poet W. H. Auden argues that Iago is a practical joker who can be compared to a modern scientist; he experiments on Othello's psyche, exposing the frightening truth about him through Iago's cruel practical joke. Iago could also be compared to a psychoanalyst conducting research on Othello's mind (246–272).

In 1951, in *Othello,* Kenneth Burke insightfully discussed possessiveness in terms of Othello's sense of owning Desdemona sexually: "You have a tragic trinity of ownership in the profoundest sense of ownership, the property in human affections, as fetishistically localized in the object of possession, while the possessor is himself possessed by his very engagement" (166). Burke adds that "we should encounter in Othello as lover the theme of the newly rich, the marriage above one's station" (181).

Seeing Shakespeare as a forerunner of de Sade, existentialism, Ionesco's Theatre of the Absurd, and Artaud's Theatre of Cruelty in *Shakespeare: Our Contemporary* (1967), Jan Kott argues that Iago is a kind of stage manager who turns the world of the play away from the goodness of Othello and Desdemona and toward Iago's own evil.

> Is the world good or bad? What are the limits of suffering, what is the ultimate purpose of the few brief moments that pass between birth and death? . . . The world, in which Othello can believe in Desdemona's infidelity, in which treachery is possible, in which Othello murders Desdemona, in which there is no friendship, loyalty, or faith, in which Othello— by agreeing to the murder of Cassio—has consented to a secret assassination, such a world is bad. Iago is an accomplished stage manager. (87)

Iago takes control of the play, redefining its world according to his dark, sadistic nature. Such twisting also occurs in absurdist works of the 20th century by Beckett, Camus, and others.

In 1978, G. K. Hunter examined race in *Othello,* arguing against the racist critics who have seen Othello's murder of Desdemona as proof of his barbarian nature (69). Instead, Hunter thinks that "Othello was not the credulous and passionate savage that Iago has tried to make him, but that he was justified in his second, as in his first, self-defence: 'For nought I did in hate, but all in honour' [5.2.292]" (70). Hunter disagrees with many critics in seeing the end of the play as optimistic in affirming the reality of Desdemona and Othello's love, which defeats Iago's attempt to degrade them; Hunter speaks of "The wonderful recovery here of the sense of ethical meaning in the world, even in the ashes of all that embodied meaning" (70).

Peter Stallybrass applies the Russian critic Mikhail Bakhtin's ideas about the grotesque to *Othello,* examining the body as an enclosure defined by class and gender through which women's power at times erupts. Having married above him, Othello attempts to change Desdemona from being defined according to class as his superior, to having her defined according to gender. However, tinkering with Desdemona's identity makes her vulnerable to seeming untrustworthy, as though she were two people. As a lower-class foil to the aristocratic Desdemona, Emilia breaks the body's enclosure in being willing to entertain the possibility of committing adultery. Emilia is also the agent of truth in the play, suggesting truth's radical nature.

As a feminist critic, Karen Newman asks whether Shakespeare was a racist:

Shakespeare was certainly subject to the racist, sexist, and colonialist discourses of his time, but by making the black Othello a hero, and by making Desdemona's love for Othello, and her transgressions of her society's norms for women in choosing him, sympathetic, Shakespeare's play stands in a contestatory relation to the hegemonic ideologies of race and gender in early modern England. (77)

Newman says the ideology of race and gender that Shakespeare is challenging is that a black man would contaminate his white wife with "metaphorical blackness" and create a literally black child (75). Instead of seeing miscegenation as monstrous, Shakespeare shows miscegenation from a sympathetic perspective (77).

Another feminist, Carol Thomas Neely, categorizes *Othello* as a problem play like Shakespeare's most troubling comedies, in which friendship between men is at odds with romance:

As *Othello* begins, romantic love already dominates, but friendship is reasserted in perverted form. . . . The men's vanity and rivalry, their preoccupation with rank and reputation, and their cowardice render them as incapable of friendship as they are of love. (93)

In the comedies, women act as mediators, but when they try to do so in *Othello,* the men stop them.

The lost handkerchief becomes the emblem of the women's power and its loss. . . . The handkerchief is lost, literally and symbolically, not because of the failure of Desdemona's love, but because of Othello's loss of faith in that love. Once lost, the female power it symbolizes is degraded and constrained, and comedy gives way to tragedy. (98–99)

However, Emilia clings to vestiges of female power when she "moves from tolerating men's fancies to exploding them and from prudent acceptance to courageous repudiation" (103).

Winifred Godd as Iago, Marion Ivell as Emilia, Gerturde Rennyson as Desdemona, and Joseph Sheehan as Othello, in this photograph published by the Byron Company in 1903

Stanley Cavell speculates that *Othello* may be at some level about witchcraft trials. At the start of the play, Brabantio accuses Othello of bewitching Desdemona; the play ends with Desdemona proving her innocence through dying, like those tried for witchcraft via drowning; the names *Othello* and *Desdemona* allude to hell and demons, and Cavell provides other examples of witchery in the play (20–21). Cavell argues that subtle allusions to witch trials are fitting in a play about Othello's inability to accept his young wife due to the challenges she poses to his virility (19).

Stephen Greenblatt's *Renaissance Self-Fashioning* (1980) was an influential work for the critical movement called New Historicism, a rejection of a prior movement called the New Criticism, which advocated studying literary texts in isolation. Contending that in the 16th century the English became aware that they could shape their identities, Greenblatt argues that Othello uses narrative to create an identity that impresses the Venetian Senate and Desdemona; Iago echoes Othello's use of narrative as a form of power when he gets Othello to believe in his tales about Desdemona and Cassio's supposed adultery (*Renaissance:* 232–254).

In *Will in the World* (2004), Greenblatt notes that it is "Desdemona's full, bold presence in the marriage" that seems to "trigger her husband's homicidal jealousy" (132–133). He observes that *Othello* is unusual in being about a married couple, as most of Shakespeare's plays center upon widowers and sometimes widows (133). Greenblatt argues that *Othello*, like the other great tragedies written after Shakespeare's young son Hamnet's untimely death, shows the playwright's "preference for things untidy, damaged, and unresolved over things neatly arranged, well made, and settled" (324). This can be seen in the way Shakespeare portrays Iago's motives for destroying Othello as ambiguous and complex, unlike the play's source, a short story by Cinthio, which attributes Iago's cruel plot to his frustration over having been rejected by Desdemona (325). Greenblatt adds that Iago's refusal to explain his motives in 5.2.309–310 is another example of what he calls the "strategic opacity" that marks Shakespeare's great tragedies such as *Othello* and *King Lear* (327).

The feminist Lisa Jardine uses Elizabethan court records about the defamation of women for unchastity as a context for early audiences viewing *Othello*. Jardine writes that in 4.2, Othello "publicly defames Desdemona" by accusing her of unchastity (87). Instead of seeing jealousy as Othello's motive for killing Desdemona, Jardine argues that he "murders her for adultery" which he believed she had committed (90). This is a motive for Othello that would make sense to Elizabethan audiences.

Harvard professor Marjorie Garber observes that "Othello *looks* black, but it is Iago who becomes the pole of moral negativity (conventionally, 'blackness') in the play" (592). Iago "uses language . . . to insinuate, to imply, to pull out of people's imaginations the dark things that are already there" (606). Garber thinks that Iago creates "plays-within-the-play" that embody Othello's worst fantasies, as when Cassio speaks to Desdemona with Othello misconstruing their conversation since he cannot hear it; and when Cassio and Iago laugh about Bianca when Othello, who again cannot hear their words, thinks they are mocking Desdemona;

Iago also echoes Othello's words, while twisting them in 3.3.34–40 and 3.3.102–112 (606–607). Garber sees Iago as a "parasite" figure from classical drama, similar to Mosca in a play by Shakespeare's contemporary Ben Jonson, *Volpone;* Iago flatters, lives off, and ultimately destroys his "host," Othello (605–606).

THE PLAY TODAY

Othello is perhaps more popular than ever today, as readers find new contemporary meanings in its treatment of such ever-popular themes as racism, jealousy, and misogyny. In a 2003 article, Maurice Hunt argues that stereotyping leads to sadism in *Othello:* "Othello's hatred of Desdemona derives from Iago's accelerated persecution of him with the image of his wife as the stereotypic subtle whore of Venice, an identity whose mystery in the Moor's mind matches the enigma of a European people who have never completely accepted the warrior who yearns to be one of them" (163). Othello thus makes Desdemona a scapegoat for the painful stereotyping to which he has long been subjected as an outsider hired by Venice to fight for the city. Another stereotype Hunt sees in the play is the supposed effeminacy of Venetian men, a result of the city's excessive valuing of manners—hence, it sees the need to import warriors like Othello.

From a feminist perspective, Lynda E. Boose argues that *Othello* is revolutionary in featuring the bed "as a staging area for sexual violence" (25). Pornographic impulses are linked to misogynistic impulses in this play:

> [It] isn't just Othello who calls the woman
> he loves a "whore"—it is every male in the
> drama who has any narrative relationship
> with a woman. Moreover, it is always Iago's
> innuendoes, the Ensign's presence and its
> implicit call for the rallying of the male bond,
> that prompt each man to do so. (37)

The audience of *Othello* is implicated in voyeuristic misogyny, gaining pleasure from Iago's malignity, just as the male characters do (27). "By the final act, refracted incidents of misogynistic violence become so repetitious that they collectively constitute a moral demand for the masculine consciousness of the play's targeted audience to look, see and confront the image of a collective cultural guilt" (43).

Sharing Boose's feminist perspective, Emily C. Bartels sees the play "as a clash between a husband who would dominate his wife and a wife who would express her voice, will, and desire or between a military leader who is uncomfortable with his domestic and erotic roles and a woman" (73). Bartels's view, like F. R. Leavis's, contrasts with the traditional blaming of Iago for Othello's ruin.

In his final book, A. D. Nuttall, who died in 2007, connects *Othello* to other Shakespeare plays

Othello (Hubert Carter) shakes his fist at the sky after smothering Desdemona (Tita Brand) in *Othello*. This is an illustration of a 1905 production at the Shaftesbury Theatre. *(Illustration by Max Cowper)*

that involve "lateral causation"—that is, when one character manipulates another to the point of altering his personality. Such plays include *Henry VI, Part 1; Coriolanus; Julius Caesar;* and *Troilus and Cressida* (277, 290). Nuttall seems convinced by the critics who make a case for Iago's "latent homosexuality" (280). He compares Iago to Mercutio in *Romeo and Juliet* and Antonio in *The Merchant of Venice,* seeing in Othello's Ensign "a final perversion of the resistance put up by same-sex solidarity to heterosexual love" (181). Like S. T. Coleridge and A. C. Bradley, Nuttall thinks that "Othello was visibly a good artless man until Iago remade him, and the good Othello is still there at the end of the play" (298).

Theater productions of *Othello* are frequent, reflecting its continuing hold on the contemporary imagination. In addition, it has had an interesting filmic history. A 1922 silent film of *Othello,* directed by Dmitri Buchowetski, starred Emil Jannings. The film "chronicles the legacy of Victorian productions that insist on Desdemona's angel-like purity, whereas Janning's brooding performance creates a menacing Othello that communicates the period's abhorrence of miscegenation," writes Kathy M. Howlett (173). Breaking negative stereotypes of negritude seen in the 1922 silent film, the great Paul Robeson was the first African-American stage actor to perform as Othello in major theaters—in London in 1930 and New York in 1943. Robeson's performance inspired racist resentment from some critics but also admiring reviews that nonetheless contain racist undertones (Vaughan: 100–102).

In 1952, Orson Welles directed, wrote, produced, and starred as the Moor in a film adaptation of *Othello* that won the Palme d'Or at the Cannes Film Festival. (Welles's film was restored and rereleased in 1991 to acclaim.) Another 1950s version of *Othello* was directed by Sergei Yutkevich in Russia in 1955; it is available dubbed or with English subtitles.

In 1965, Stuart Burge directed a full-length film of *Othello* starring Laurence Olivier, Maggie Smith, and Frank Finlay (all three of whom were nominated for Oscars). Olivier's stage performance as Othello in 1964, upon which the 1965 film is based, was influenced by F. R. Leavis's view of Othello as an egotistical man of action (Snyder: 297). Welles's and Olivier's use of black-face dates their films.

In 1981, the British Broadcasting Corporation (BBC) filmed *Othello* under the direction of Jonathan Miller. In the film, a very tanned Anthony Hopkins plays Othello, and Bob Hoskins brilliantly plays Iago. Also in 1981, Franklin Melton directed a film version of *Othello* starring William Marshall and Ron Moody.

An acclaimed 1986 film of *Othello,* Verdi's great opera based on *Othello,* was directed by Franco Zeffirelli, featured Placido Domingo, and was nominated for an Oscar. In 1988, Janet Suzman bravely directed a noncommercial film of *Othello* in South Africa starring a black actor, John Kani. Based on a Royal Shakespeare Company theatrical performance, a 1990 film of *Othello* directed by Trevor Nunn starred the American opera singer Willard White as Othello and Ian McKellen as Iago.

Laurence Fishburne, Irène Jacob, and Kenneth Branagh starred in Oliver Parker's popular film of *Othello* (1995), the first commercial version to feature an African-American actor. "Unlike Janning's stylized, expressionist acting; Welles's understated, almost abstract realization of the role; or Olivier's overblown theatricality, Laurence Fishburne offers us our first naturalistic presentation of Othello," observes Kathy M. Howlett (176). Frederick Luis Aldama argues that director Parker foregrounds the issue of interracial relationships by beginning the film with a shot of an anonymous modern black man and white woman floating in a Venetian gondola: "This comparison and lack of exact match between the figures [who are not Fishburne and Jacob] allows Parker to subtly point to the more general occurrence of tragedy . . . in mixed-race romance—Othello and Desdemona's story is only a sliver of a widespread malady but a sliver that becomes archetypal because it is narrated under the impetus of an aesthetic will to make it permanently memorable" (203).

Finally, two innovative 21st-century movies should be mentioned. A 2001 film version of *Othello* directed by Geoffrey Sax uses contemporary dialogue, sets the play in modern London, and stars Eamonn Walker and Christopher Eccleston. Similarly, Tim Blake Nelson's *O* (2001) reworks the plot of *Othello* in contemporary times, but in America—"in relation to the fundamental American traumas of high school dating and athletic competition" (Aldama: 211).

FIVE TOPICS FOR DISCUSSION AND WRITING:

1. **Iago's motives:** Are Iago's motives merely what he says they are, such as thinking Othello slept with Emilia and wanting to get his revenge on Cassio for being promoted over Iago? Do you agree with the famous statement of the romantic poet Samuel Taylor Coleridge that Iago symbolizes "motiveless malignity"? How does Iago show that he enjoys manipulating Othello, Cassio, Desdemona, Roderigo, and Emilia? What is Iago's attitude toward Othello, Cassio, Roderigo, Emilia, and Desdemona?

2. **Youth and age:** What is the significance of age in this play? How does Othello's age affect his self-concept and his vulnerability to Iago's lies about Desdemona? How do Othello's preconceptions about the desires natural to youth affect his view of Desdemona? Why might Desdemona have chosen to elope with the middle-aged Othello instead of a handsome young man like Cassio? How is Brabantio portrayed as an aged father? How does Iago's view that seniority should be the basis of military promotion affect his feelings about young Cassio being named lieutenant?

3. **Moorish vs. Venetian:** What is the significance of race, nationality, and religion in this play? How do Iago's insults about Othello at the play's beginning resemble the ones he uses later to convince Othello that Desdemona could not truly love him? Why does Othello believe Iago's lies about Othello's unattractiveness in his Venetian wife's eyes? What is the significance of Othello being called the Moor by many characters, including

Desdemona? What do Othello's references to himself as a murderer of Turks in his final speech suggest about his view of himself as a Moor? Does the play support xenophobic stereotypes in dramatizing a Moor murdering his Christian wife?

4. **Gender:** What is the role of gender in this play? What expectations are there for upper-class Venetian women? To what extent does Desdemona adhere to and defy these expectations? She has defied her father to elope with a Moor, yet she refuses to accuse that Moor of murdering her. What ideas about lower-class womanhood arise through the characterizations of Emilia and Bianca, and how are these ideas different from those governing upper-class women? Consider also the bonding between military men that Othello comes to rely on in his alliance with Iago against Desdemona and Emilia. Is there a homoerotic subtext to the play? Note the gender reversal imagery concerning Desdemona and Cassio; what does it mean?

5. **Class:** What is the significance of class in this play? How does class intersect with race, gender, and nationality? When Iago slanders Othello to Brabantio, in what ways does he allude to Othello's class and nationality, as well as to his race and gender? Why do the Venetian noblemen who come to Cyprus address Desdemona as though she were one of their own? Why are they so shocked when Othello strikes Desdemona? How does the servant Emilia's ideas about marriage and chastity contrast with Desdemona's? Why does Iago think Cassio was promoted to lieutenant instead of himself? Why is Cassio made governor of Cyprus after Othello kills Desdemona, even though Cassio disgraced himself while he was drunk? How does Cassio treat Desdemona differently from the way he treats the lower-class Bianca? What images of animals, nature, monstrosity, and witchcraft embody the theme of class?

Bibliography

Aldama, Frederick Luis. "Race, Cognition, and Emotion: Shakespeare on Film." *College Literature* 33, no. 1 (2006): 197–213.

Auden, W. H. "The Joker in the Pack." In *The Dyer's Hand and Other Essays.* London: Faber, 1963, 246–272.

Barnet, Sylvan. Introduction to *Four Great Tragedies: Hamlet, Othello, King Lear, Macbeth.* New York: Penguin Signet, 1998, v–xxviii.

Bartels, Emily C. "Improvisation and *Othello:* The Play of Race and Gender." In *Approaches to Teaching Shakespeare's "Othello,"* edited by Peter Erickson and Maurice Hunt, 72–79. New York: Modern Language Association, 2005.

Boose, Lynda E. "'Let it be Hid': The Pornographic Aesthetic of Shakespeare's *Othello.*" In *New Casebooks: Othello by William Shakespeare,* edited by Lena Cowen Orlin, 22–48. New York: Palgrave, 2004.

Boswell, James. *The Life of Samuel Johnson.* London: Charles Dilly, 1791.

Bradley, A. C. *Shakespearean Tragedy.* London: Macmillan, 1905.

Bristol, Michael D. "Charivari and the Comedy of Abjection in Othello." In *New Casebooks: Othello by William Shakespeare,* edited by Lena Cowen Orlin, 78–102. New York: Palgrave, 2004.

Burke, Kenneth. "Othello: An Essay to Illustrate a Method." *The Hudson Review* 4 (1951): 165–203.

Cavell, Stanley. "Epistemology and Tragedy: A Reading of Othello." In *William Shakespeare's* Othello, edited by Harold Bloom, 7–22. New York: Chelsea House, 1987.

Coleridge, Samuel Taylor. *Notes and Lectures upon Shakespeare and Some Old Poets and Dramatists.* Vol. 1. Edited by H. N. Coleridge. London: William Pickering, 1849.

Eliot, T. S. "Shakespeare and the Stoicism of Seneca." In *Selected Essays, 1917–1932.* New York: Harcourt, 1932, 126–140.

Empson, William. "Honest in *Othello.*" In *The Structure of Complex Words.* New York: Random, 1951, 218–249.

Garber, Marjorie. *Shakespeare After All.* New York: Random House, 2004.

Gardner, Helen. "The Noble Moor." In *Othello: Critical Essays,* edited by Susan Snyder, 169–188. New York: Garland, 1988.

———. "*Othello:* A Retrospect, 1900–1967." *Shakespeare Survey* 21 (1968): 1–13.

Goddard, Harold C. *The Meaning of Shakespeare.* Vol. II. Chicago: University of Chicago Press, 1951.

Greenblatt, Stephen. *Renaissance Self-Fashioning: From More to Shakespeare.* Chicago: University of Chicago Press, 1980.

———. *Will in the World: How Shakespeare Became Shakespeare.* New York: Norton, 2004.

Hadfield, Andrew, ed. *A Routledge Literary Sourcebook on William Shakespeare's* Othello. London: Routledge, 2003.

Hazlitt, William. *A View of the English Stage.* London: 1818.

Hecht, Anthony. "*Othello.*" In *William Shakespeare's* Othello, edited by Harold Bloom, 123–142. New York: Chelsea House, 1987.

Hodgdon, Barbara. "Race-ing *Othello:* Re-Engendering White-Out." In *New Casebooks: Othello by William Shakespeare,* edited by Lena Cowen Orlin, 190–219. New York: Palgrave, 2004.

Howlett, Kathy M. "Interpreting the Tragic Loading of the Bed in Cinematic Adaptations of *Othello.*" In *Approaches to Teaching Shakespeare's* Othello, edited by Peter Erickson and Maurice Hunt, 169–179. New York: Modern Language Association, 2005.

Hunt, Maurice. "Shakespeare's Venetian Paradigm: Stereotyping and Sadism in *The Merchant of Venice* and *Othello.*" *Papers on Language and Literature* 39, no. 2 (March 1, 2003): 162–184.

Hunter, G. K. "*Othello* and Colour Prejudice." In *A Routledge Literary Sourcebook on William Shakespeare's* Othello, edited by Andrew Hadfield, 66–70. London: Routledge, 2003.

Jardine, Lisa. "'Why should he call her whore?': Defamation and Desdemona's Case." In *A Routledge Literary Sourcebook on William Shakespeare's* Othello, edited by Andrew Hadfield, 84–91. London: Routledge, 2003.

Johnson, Samuel. *The Plays of William Shakespeare.* 8 vols. London: J. & R. Tonson, 1765.

Kermode, Frank. *Shakespeare's Language.* New York: Farrar, Straus, & Giroux, 2000.

Knight, G. Wilson. "The *Othello* Music." In *A Routledge Literary Sourcebook on William Shakespeare's* Othello, edited by Andrew Hadfield, 55–56. London: Routledge, 2003.

Kott, Jan. *Shakespeare, Our Contemporary.* London: Routledge, 1967.

Leavis, F. R. "Diabolic Intellect and the Noble Hero: A Note on *Othello.*" In *The Common Pursuit.* London: Hogarth Press, 1984, 136–159.

Neely, Carol Thomas. "Women and Men in *Othello.*" In *William Shakespeare's* Othello, edited by Harold Bloom, 79–104. New York: Chelsea House, 1987.

Neill, Michael. "*Othello* and Race." In *Approaches to Teaching Shakespeare's* Othello, edited by Peter Erickson and Maurice Hunt, 37–52. New York: Modern Language Association, 2005.

Newman, Karen. "'And wash the Ethiop white': Femininity and the Monstrous in *Othello.*" In *A Routledge Literary Sourcebook on William Shakespeare's* Othello, edited by Andrew Hadfield, 74–77. London: Routledge, 2003.

Nuttall, A. D. *Shakespeare the Thinker.* New Haven, Conn.: Yale University Press, 2007.

Potter, Nicholas, ed. *William Shakespeare:* Othello. New York: Columbia University Press, 2000.

Rymer, Thomas. *A Short View of Tragedy.* 1693. Reprint, Manston, Yorkshire, U.K.: Scolar Press, 1970.

Shakespeare, William. *The Tragedy of Othello the Moor of Venice.* (Folio version). In *Four Great Tragedies: Hamlet, Othello, King Lear, Macbeth,* edited by Alvin Kernan, 167–295. New York: Penguin Signet, 1998. (All quotations in this chapter are taken from this version of *Othello.*)

Shapiro, James. *A Year in the Life of William Shakespeare, 1599.* New York: Harper Collins, 2005.

Snyder, Susan. "*Othello:* a Modern Perspective." In *The Tragedy of Othello, the Moor of Venice,* edited by Barbara A. Mowat and Paul Werstine, 287–298. New York: Simon & Schuster, 1993.

Spivack, Bernard. *Shakespeare and the Allegory of Evil.* New York: Columbia University Press, 1958.

Stallybrass, Peter. "Patriarchal Territories: The Body Enclosed." In *Rewriting the Renaissance,* edited by Margaret W. Ferguson, et al., 123–142 and 344–347. Chicago: University of Chicago Press, 1986.

Vaughan, Virginia Mason. "*Othello:* A Contextual History." In *A Routledge Literary Sourcebook on William Shakespeare's* Othello, edited by Andrew Hadfield, 100–103. London: Routledge, 2003.

Walen, Denise A. "Unpinning Desdemona." *Shakespeare Quarterly* 58, no. 4 (2007): 487–508.

FILM AND VIDEO PRODUCTIONS

Buchowetski, Dmitri, dir. *Othello*. With Emil Jannings, Werner Krauss, and Ica von Lenkeffy. Kino, 1922.

Burge, Stuart, dir. *Othello*. With Laurence Olivier, Maggie Smith, and Frank Finlay. British Home Entertainment, 1965.

Melton, Franklin, dir. *The Tragedy of Othello, The Moor of Venice*. With William Marshall, Ron Moody, and Jenny Agutter. Revelation Films, 1981.

Miller, Jonathan, dir. *The Complete Dramatic Works of William Shakespeare: Othello*. With Anthony Hopkins, Bob Hoskins, and Penelope Wilton. British Broadcasting Company (BBC), 1981.

Nelson, Tim Blake, dir. *O*. With Mekhi Phifer, Josh Hartnett, and Julia Stiles. Trimark Home Video: Lions Gate Entertainment, 2001.

Nunn, Trevor, dir. *Othello*. With Ian McKellen and Judi Dench. Primetime, 1990.

Parker, Oliver, dir. *Othello*. With Laurence Fishburne, Irène Jacob, and Kenneth Branagh. Culver City: Castle Rock Entertainment, 1995.

Sax, Geoffrey, dir. *Othello*. With Eamonn Walker, Christopher Eccleston, and Keeley Hawes. Acorn Media, 2001.

Suzman, Janet, dir. *Othello*. With John Kani, Richard Haddon Haines, and Joanna Weinberg. Arthaus Musik, 1989.

Welles. Orson, dir. *Othello*. With Orson Welles, Micheál MacLiammóir, and Suzanne Cloutier. Marceau Films/United Artists, 1952.

Yutkevich, Sergei, dir. *Othello*. With Sergie Bondarchuk, Irina Skobtseva, and Andrei Popov. Hendring, 1956.

Zeffirelli, Franco, dir. *Otello*. (Verdi's opera) With Placido Domingo, Katia Ricciarelli, and Justino Diaz. Kultur Video, 1986.

—Jeanette Roberts Shumaker

Pericles, Prince of Tyre

INTRODUCTION

Pericles is one of the least read and least performed of Shakespeare's plays. It was not even included in the landmark First Folio publication of Shakespeare's plays in 1623. Many scholars today regard the play as important only because it was apparently the first of Shakespeare's romances, though it is generally accepted that the play is not entirely Shakespeare's.

Nonetheless, *Pericles* can still charm audiences. Woven within the fabric of the play are fascinating "painful adventures" that Pericles experiences as he finds his identity and is reunited with his family. The reunion scene between Pericles and his daughter Marina inspired T. S. Eliot's poem "Marina" and is often compared to one of the most remarkable moments in Shakespearean drama: King Lear's reunion with his daughter Cordelia. Perilous seas and shipwrecks, riddles, severed heads, incest and revenge from the heavens, daughters born at sea, wives thrown in the sea, and dead wives revived are all featured in the play. The author of the chief source for the text, the English poet John Gower (ca. 1330–1408), plays a personal role: Rising from the ashes, he appears seven times to deliver narration at various points, including the play's epilogue.

In many ways, the blending of the tragic and the comic in *Pericles* offers an arresting depiction of death and rebirth, loss and recovery, good and evil. The principal characters overcome their misfortunes. Sold by pirates to a brothel, Pericles' daughter Marina nonetheless actively pursues virtue. The young function as a vehicle for the regeneration of the older generation. The silent Pericles, who has not had sustenance for months, is "revived" upon recognizing Marina; subsequently, her mother is "warmed" back to life. The complexities of love are brought to the forefront through an incestuous relationship between the character of Cleon and his daughter.

Overall, *Pericles,* a product of Shakespeare's late period, highlights life's ironies and unfairness. Its romances, miracles, dreams, and visions hint at the mystery of life and its inexplicable nature. Vengeance gives way to forgiveness and mercy. By extolling the power and significance of time—"Whereby I see that time's the king of men: / He's both their parent, and he is their grave, / And gives them what he will, not what they crave" (2.3.45–47; Sc.7. 45–47)—*Pericles* suggests that time can not only influence our lives but also act as a restorative force.

Pericles' adventures at sea take the audience to Antioch, Tarsus, Pentapolis, Ephesus, and Mytilene. The vast canvas of the play's setting, together with the sea voyages, is reminiscent of Homer's *Odyssey* as well as Shakespeare's *Othello,* set in Venice and Cyprus, and *Antony and Cleopatra.* The contrasting settings of the brothel where Marina works and the temple of Diana, where Thaisa becomes a priestess, attest to the range of the play's thematic concerns.

BACKGROUND

The chief source of *Pericles* is John Gower's story of Apollonius of Tyre, which appears in the 1393

Lychorida informs Pericles of Thaisa's death before presenting him with his daughter in Act II, Scene 5 of *Pericles, Prince of Tyre*. This illustration was designed for a 1918 edition of Charles and Mary Lamb's *Tales from Shakespeare*. *(Illustration by Louis Rhead)*

Confessio Amantis (Lover's Confession). This story was based on a Greek romance whose origins can be traced back to the fifth or sixth century C.E. Laurence Twine's *The Pattern of Painful Adventures* (1576) is also clearly a source, particularly for the brothel scenes.

The existence of a prose narrative, *The Painfull Adventures of Pericles Prince of Tyre* (1608) by George Wilkins, which follows *Pericles* closely, has led textual scholars into different camps: Some maintain that *The Painfull Adventures* is a subsequent novelization of *Pericles;* others argue that *Pericles* is a collaboration between Shakespeare and Wilkins. A small minority suggest that *The Painfull Adventures* is a source for the play. The first

and second part of *Pericles* exhibit such striking differences in terms of style, structure, and characterization that scholars have proposed the play is a collaboration with either Wilkins, William Rowley, Thomas Heywood, or John Day (or a combination of these). Many modern editors, such as Roger Warren of the Oxford Shakespeare Series, treat *Pericles* as a collaboration and employ *The Painfull Adventures* to reconstruct and amend the text that lies behind the quarto edition. This entry contains citations to Warren's reconstructed version, as well as to more traditional editions.

Date and Text of the Play

On May 20, 1608, Edward Blount registered *Pericles* in the Stationer's Register, which was a book kept by a trade guild, the Stationers' Company of London, responsible for ordering the professional activities of printers, bookbinders, publishers, and booksellers. Printers or publishers would register a book along with their name in the Stationer's Register, claiming their rights to the work. This functioned as an early form of copyright.

The textual history of *Pericles* is fraught with ambiguity. As with all Shakespearean plays, there is no original manuscript of *Pericles* written in his own hand. The quarto text of the play is considered a corrupt, pirated edition of the play made from a memorial reconstruction; that is, an actor or actors who performed in *Pericles* reconstructed it from memory. Some deficiencies of the quarto include mistakes and the printing of verse as prose and prose as verse. *Pericles* is not included in the 1623 First Folio collection of Shakespeare's plays (the first collected edition of the plays by Heminges and Condell), but it does appear in the later Third Folio. The absence of *Pericles* from the First Folio raises many questions. Some scholars maintain that *Pericles* was not included in the First Folio because parts of it were composed by another author, perhaps George Wilkins; others argue that Heminges and Condell did not have the printing rights for *Pericles*.

The much admired *Play*,

CALLED,

PERICLES, PRINCE of TYR

With the true Relation of the whole History, Adventures, and Fortunes of the said Prince.

VVritten by VV. SHAKESPEARE,

and publiſhed in his life time.

Actus Primus. Scena Prima.

Enter Gower.

TO ſing a ſong that old was ſung,
From aſhes ancient Gower is come,
Aſſuming mans infirmities,
To glad your ear and pleaſe your eyes;
hath been ſung at Feſtivals,
Ember eves, and holy-dayes,
nd Lords and Ladies in their lives,
ave read it for reſtoratives.
e purchaſe is to make men glorious.
bonum quo Antiquius, eo melius.
you, born in theſe latter times,
hen wits more ripe, accept my Rimes;
nd that to hear an old man ſing,
May to your wiſhes pleaſure bring:
life would wiſh, and that I might
ſte it for you like Taper-light.
his Antioch, then, Antiochus the great,
ilt up this City for his chiefeſt ſeat;
he faireſt in all Syria.
ell you what mine Authors ſay:
his King unto him took a Peer,
ho died, and left a female heir,
buckſome, blithe, and full of face,

To ſeek her as a bed-fellow,
In marriage pleaſures, play-fellow:
Which to prevent, he made a Law,
To keep her ſtill, and men in awe,
That who ſo askt her for his wife,
His Riddle told not, loſt his life:
So for her many a wight did die,
As yon grim looks do teſtiſie.
What enſues to the judgement of your eye,
I give my cauſe, who beſt can teſtiſie.

Enter *Antiochus, Prince Pericles, and follo*

Ant. Young Prince of *Tyre,* you have at large
The danger of the task you undertake.
Per. I have (*Antiochus*) and with a ſoul eml
With the glory of her praiſe, think death no haza
In this enterprize.
Ant. Muſick bring in our daughter, cloathed like
For embracements, even of *Jove* himſelf;
At whoſe conception, till *Lucina* reign'd,
Nature this dowry gave, to glad her preſence,
The Senate houſe of *Planets* all did ſit,
To knit in her their beſt perfections.

Title page of the Third Folio edition of *Pericles,* published in 1664. *Pericles* did not appear in the First Folio (1623) or the Second Folio (1632).

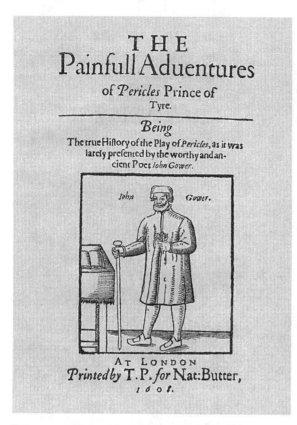

THE
Painfull Aduentures
of *Pericles* Prince of
Tyre.

Being

The true Hiſtory of the Play of *Pericles*, as it was
lately preſented by the worthy and an-
cient Poet *Iohn Gower*.

Iohn   *Gower*.

AT LONDON
Printed by T.P. *for* Nat: Butter,
1 6 0 8.

Title page of the original 1608 publication of the prose romance *The Painfull Adventures of Pericles Prince of Tyre* by George Wilkins. The image depicts John Gower. Some scholars believe that Shakespeare collaborated with Wilkins on the play *Pericles*.

Scholarly and critical opinions differ regarding the play's composition, but most believe it must have been written in 1607 or 1608. In the original quarto publication of the play, there were no act divisions, only scene divisions. Most modern editors do, however, divide the play into acts and scenes, but one prominent edition, Roger Warren's reconstructed Oxford edition (2003), provides only scene numbers, listed consecutively. This entry on *Pericles* provides citations to both the usual act and scene designations and also to the scene numbers given in the Warren edition. Line references are to the Warren edition.

SYNOPSIS
Brief Synopsis

Pericles opens with the medieval poet Gower rising from the dead to tell a tale. In Antioch in Syria, Pericles, Prince of Tyre, seeks to woo the daughter of King Antiochus. But the king has devised a riddle for suitors to solve, and they lose their lives if they fail. Surrounded by the heads of former suitors, Pericles realizes the riddle alludes to the incestuous relationship of Antiochus and his daughter. Pericles indirectly tells the king that he is aware of his secret but cannot publicly reveal it. Although the king grants him 40 days to solve the riddle, Pericles realizes that his life is in danger and flees. Returning to Tyre, he is overwhelmed with melancholy because he worries that his community will be harmed in Antiochus's effort to eliminate the threat he poses. Pericles takes Helicanus's advice to travel, and Antiochus dispatches Thaliart to Tyre to kill Pericles.

Arriving in Tarsus with flags of peace on his ships, Pericles provides corn for the community devastated by famine; the governor, Cleon, and his wife, Dionyza, are indebted to him. Pericles resumes his travels upon being informed that Thaliart is hunting him. A sea storm wrecks his ship, and he is cast ashore in Pentapolis, ruled by King Simonides. Fishermen recover his father's armor from the sea. Wearing this rusty armor and unaccompanied by a squire, Pericles competes along with five knights for the hand of Thaisa, the fair daughter of Simonides. The victorious Pericles introduces himself as a gentleman of Tyre, and after testing their love, Simonides allows Pericles and Thaisa to wed.

Letters inform Pericles that the gods have punished Antiochus and his daughter: Fire from the heavens shriveled up their bodies while they were in a lavish chariot. Pericles departs for Tyre with Thaisa because Helicanus will be crowned king if he does not return within six months. He fears that mutiny might break out. Pericles' misfortunes at sea continue. The pregnant Thaisa dies during childbirth, and her body is tossed overboard at the superstitious sailors' insistence so as to stop the storm. The infant is named Marina because she was born at sea. Fearing that Marina might not survive the voyage, Pericles heads for Tarsus.

In Ephesus, the lord of Ephesus brings a chest from the sea containing the body of Thaisa accompanied by jewels and a note from Pericles. Although Pericles requests burial befitting royalty for Thaisa, Cerimon realizes she is not dead and revives her. Entrusting Cleon and Dionyza with the care of Marina, Pericles returns to Tyre. The revived Thaisa recognizes the handwriting of Pericles in the note but does not remember giving birth to a daughter. She pleads to pursue the life of a priestess and is taken to the temple of Diana in Ephesus.

Rather than repay Pericles for his generosity, Dionyza hires a murderer, Leonine, to kill the charming Marina because she outshines her own daughter, Philoten. Marina is kidnapped by pirates as Philoten tries to kill her, and she is then sold to a brothel in Mytilene. The remorseful Cleon erects a monument in honor of Marina and shows the tomb to Pericles when he comes to Tarsus seeking his daughter.

Meanwhile, Marina refuses to break her virgin knot and influences the brothel-goers to undertake honorable activities. She even charms Lysimachus, the governor of Mytilene, who frequents the brothel. Pursuing a career in singing and embroidery, Marina finds an honest house.

Leaving Tarsus, the turbulent sea tosses Pericles on the shores of Mytilene. Father and daughter reunite as Lysimachus calls Marina to cure Pericles, who has not spoken or eaten for three months. Pericles goes to Ephesus after he dreams of the goddess Diana, who directs him to Ephesus to make a sacrifice at her temple and to narrate to those at the temple how he lost his wife. The priestess Thaisa initially faints when she recognizes Pericles, who recounts her death. They reunite joyfully. Cerimon explains to Pericles how he revived Thaisa. Thaisa learns that she has a daughter who will join hands in marriage with Lysimachus. Pericles' "unscissored" (3.3.29; Sc.13.29) hair, which was left uncut due to his mourning, will be trimmed for the nuptials.

Gower's epilogue articulates that evil is punished because the community rioted against Cleon and Dionyza and burned them in their palace. The virtuous at last find joy.

The headings below list both the traditional act and scene designations and also the corresponding consecutive scene numbers without act designations, as given in Roger Warren's reconstructed Oxford edition. Line references are to the Warren edition.

Act I, Scene 1 (Scene 1)

The play opens with Gower informing the audience that he has come from the dead and taken on the frail human condition to tell a riveting tale. He describes the setting and sets the scene. The setting is Antioch in Syria. King Antiochus the Great, whose wife has died, engages in a clandestine incestuous relationship with his daughter. To exchange marriage vows with the princess, suitors must decipher a riddle. If they fail, they lose their lives. The heads of former suitors appear. Gower exits, and King Antiochus, his followers, and Prince Pericles appear in the court of Antiochus. Prince Pericles has traveled to Antioch to win the hand of the princess in marriage. He declares his love for the princess, who is clad as a bride, and her father allows him to interpret the riddle. Pericles unravels the riddle, which alludes to Antiochus's incestuous relationship with the princess. He realizes that he is in danger. Whether he exposes the king's incest or pretends that he has failed to interpret the riddle, he faces the same fate: decapitation. He informs the king that he has solved the meaning of the riddle but that it is best if the truth remains hidden. Realizing that Pericles knows his secret and may stain his honor, Antiochus grants Pericles 40 days before his death sentence but later instructs Thaliart to kill him.

When all exit, Pericles renounces his love for the princess and launches a diatribe against incest. Fearing for his life, Pericles flees Antioch. No sooner does Antiochus offer Thaliart gold to kill Pericles than a messenger informs them that Pericles has fled. Antiochus reveals that his heart will not be at rest until Pericles is dead.

Act I, Scene 2 (Scene 2)

Returning to Tyre, Pericles is overcome by sadness, worried that Antiochus may wage war on Tyre because Pericles holds the secret of his incest. Pericles opens his heart to Helicanus, a councilor of Tyre, and confides in him about his troubles. Helicanus advises that Pericles bear his grief with patience. He also agrees that Pericles' fears are justified because Antiochus is a tyrant. "Go travel for a while," he suggests. The king listens to Helicanus's advice and reveals his intention to go to Tarsus.

Act I, Scene 3 (Scene 3)

Thaliart arrives in Tyre to kill Pericles, and he muses on the dangers of his actions. If he kills Pericles and is caught, he will be hanged in Tyre. If he returns to Antioch not having killed Pericles, a similar fate awaits him. Upon hearing Helicanus tell Aeschines and other lords that Pericles has left, Thaliart is relieved, certain that Pericles will perish at sea.

Act I, Scene 4 (Scene 4)

Tarsus is no longer the prosperous town it once was because it is steeped in famine. The governor, Cleon, tells his wife that they should recount sad tales so as to forget their misfortune. Informed that ships are approaching the shore, Cleon surmises that a neighboring nation has come to take advantage of their powerlessness and conquer them. Cleon insists that the ships bring enemies, although the lord informs him that the ships display white flags of peace. Pericles receives a warm welcome when he announces that his ships are not like the Trojan horse but are filled with corn. All he asks for is safe harborage for his men and his ships. His request is granted joyfully, and he delivers the town from famine.

Act II, Scene 1 (Scene 5)

Gower reappears and sums up what the audience has seen so far. Aided by a dumb show, Gower explains that Pericles is informed about Thaliart's arrival in Tyre to kill him and is advised to leave Tarsus. Pericles decides to continue his travels, but they are cut short by a sea storm that wrecks his ship. Cast ashore, Pericles craves to die in peace. Fishermen tell him that he is in Pentapolis, which is ruled by a good king, Simonides. Pericles entreats the fishermen and their master to pity him. They generously provide him with food and shelter, then help him recover his heritage by giving him his father's armor, bequeathed to him in the sea. Pericles will wear his father's armor to "joust and tourney" for the love of Simonides' fair daughter, whose birthday is on the following day.

Act II, Scene 2 (Scene 6)

In the presence of King Simonides and his daughter, Thaisa, five knights from Sparta, Macedon, Antioch, Athens, and Corinth parade in their armor. The king interprets their shields and the Latin mottoes. The sixth suitor, Pericles, is dressed in rusty armor and presents himself to Thaisa with the motto *In hac spe vivo,* meaning "In that hope I live." Although Pericles is mocked for his rusty armor, King Simonides points out to the lords that

Pericles presents his shield to King Simonides and Thaisa in Act II, Scene 2 of *Pericles, Prince of Tyre,* in this print published by Jennings and Chaplin in the 19th century. *(Painting by Henry Corbould; engraving by Frederick Bacon)*

an individual should not be judged by outward apparel. Simonides and Thaisa proceed to the gallery to watch the tournament, which takes place offstage.

Act II, Scene 3 (Scene 7)

Although Pericles triumphs at the tournament, he is overwhelmed with melancholy and does not eat at the celebratory banquet. Following her father's instructions, Thaisa is sent to Pericles to inquire about his identity. Pericles introduces himself as a gentleman of Tyre, not the prince of Tyre. Simonides pities him having been informed by Thaisa of the calamities that befell him.

Act II, Scene 4 (Scene 8)

In Tyre, Helicanus indicates that the gods have avenged themselves on Antiochus and his daughter. While Antiochus was in a chariot with his daughter, fire from the heavens shriveled up their bodies. In Helicanus's view, justice has been administered. Lords complain about the kingdom of Tyre being left without a ruler due to the protracted absence of Pericles. Although the lords offer Helicanus the crown, he rejects it and entreats them to seek out Pericles for another year.

Act II, Scene 5 (Scene 9)

Simonides enters, reading a letter. He implies it is written by his daughter, who expresses a wish not to marry in the next 12 months; as a result, the knights depart. Simonides then discloses that his daughter's letter informs him of her desire to marry the stranger knight, Pericles. But Simonides, concerned that Pericles is a traitor who has employed witchcraft to win the love of his daughter, attempts to test their love. When he is convinced of their love, he clasps their hands and gives them permission to wed.

Act III, Chorus (Scene 10)

Gower reenters to describe the marriage of Pericles and Thaisa and to announce that she is pregnant. He employs a dumb show to describe the ensuing events. Pericles learns of the death of Antiochus and his daughter. Upon hearing that Helicanus will be crowned king if Pericles does not return within six months, Pericles decides to return to Tyre lest mutiny break out. Simonides has mixed feelings, rejoicing that his son-in-law is royalty but grieving that he and his daughter will leave for Tyre. While Pericles is on a ship with Thaisa and her nurse, Lychorida, a storm breaks out. Gower appeals to the audience's imagination to imagine the stage as the ship, upon whose storm-battered deck Pericles appears and speaks.

Act III, Scene 1 (Scene 11)

Pericles laments his fate while Lychorida informs him that Thaisa has died during childbirth, leaving behind their infant daughter. Pericles mourns and complains to the gods that they bestow joyful gifts on him only to take them away. Although Pericles believes that it is merely a superstition when the master announces that Thaisa's body must be tossed overboard to appease the storm, he consents. Thaisa is placed in a casket with jewels and a note. Pericles then tells the ship's master to alter the course, heading now for Tarsus, because the infant may not survive the journey to Tyre.

Act III, Scene 2 (Scene 12)

The benevolent Cerimon, lord of Ephesus, provides food and fire to those affected by the storm. Philemon delivers a chest that looks like a coffin which had been tossed to the shore by the storm. Inside, Cerimon finds Thaisa's body and Pericles' note, which requests that Thaisa, as royalty, receive a proper burial. Realizing that she is not dead, Cerimon revives her.

Act III, Scene 3 (Scene 13)

In Tarsus, Pericles entrusts the care of the newborn, whom he has named Marina because she was born at sea, to Cleon and Dionyza. They vow to raise Marina as a princess following Pericles' request, since they are bound to him by duty. He generously provided help to them during the period of famine, and they wish to repay their gratitude.

Act III, Scene 4 (Scene 14)

Cerimon informs Thaisa that the casket she was found in contained jewels and a letter written by Pericles. Since she will not see her husband again, she wants to live as a priestess. Thaisa agrees with Cerimon's suggestion that his niece can take her to the nearby temple of Diana. Thaisa does not remember giving birth to Marina.

Act IV, Scene 1 (Scene 15)

Gower asks the audience to imagine that Pericles has arrived in Tarsus. Thaisa is a priestess, and Marina has grown up into a graceful and intelligent young lady. Murderously envious of the praise Marina receives for her perfections, Dionyza forgets that Pericles helped their community when they were devastated by famine. She is also concerned that Marina will overshadow her own daughter, Philoten. Dionyza commands Leonine to kill Marina at the seashore. When instructed to say her prayers, Marina realizes Leonine intends to kill her and passionately pleads with him to spare her innocent life: "I never killed a mouse nor hurt a fly" (l. 127). As soon as Leonine draws his sword to kill her, Marina is kidnapped by pirates. Leonine intends to lie to Dionyza that he has killed Marina at the seashore. He plans to see if the pirates will ravish Marina and abandon her.

Act IV, Scene 2 (Scene 16)

In Mytilene, a Pander and a Bawd complain that they are "too wenchless" (l. 5) and need "fresh" women for their trade. Bolt is sent to search for young women in the marketplace. The pirates inform Bolt that Marina is a virgin, and he buys her to initiate her to their profession. Marina mourns that Leonine spared her life. The Bawd instructs Bolt to advertise Marina's qualities and to announce that she is a virgin in the market so as to attract customers. The virtuous Marina insists that she will not lose her "virgin knot" (l. 139).

Act IV, Scene 3 (Scene 17)

Cleon is guilt-ridden that Marina has been "murdered" at his wife's orders. To hide her complicity in this "murder," Dionyza has also poisoned Leonine. A monument will be erected in memory of Marina. Dionyza says that she knows Cleon will follow her advice and keep quiet about Marina's murder.

Act IV, Scene 4 (Scene 18)

Gower says that Pericles, along with Helicanus and others, travels to reunite with his daughter, "all his life's delight" (l. 12), in order to take her back to Tyre. Old Aschines remains to govern Tyre. As presented in dumb show, Pericles laments when Cleon reveals Marina's tomb. He swears never to cut his hair or wash his face. He takes to the sea once again.

Act IV, Scene 5 (Omitted from Oxford edition)

Two Gentlemen of Mytilene, leaving a brothel, discuss the virtue of a prostitute there and vow to live virtuously in the future.

Act IV, Scene 6 (Scene 19)

The Pander and the Bawd regret having bought Marina for their brothel since she makes clients want to follow a path of virtuousness. Marina must either be ravished or they should get rid of her, the Bawd concludes. Marina entreats the governor of Mytilene, Lysimachus, who has come to the brothel in disguise, to act honorably and to spare her chastity. Making it clear to Lysimachus that she prefers death to being deflowered, Lysimachus is persuaded that she is a "piece of virtue" (l. 162). Although the Bawd instructs Bolt to take Marina's virginity and to use her as he pleases, she convinces him that sewing, weaving, and dancing are honorable activities she can engage in.

Act V, Chorus (Scene 20)

Marina escapes to an honest house, as Gower informs the audience, where she engages in singing and embroidery. Tossed by waves, Pericles' ship arrives in Mytilene.

Act V, Scene 1 (Scene 21)

Lysimachus learns through Helicanus that Pericles, who is now in Mytilene, has neither spoken nor eaten for three months. He inquires about Pericles' ill state. The noise of a sea battle is heard offstage. A lord of Mytilene suggests that a maid from Mytilene, Marina, can make the silent Pericles speak. Lysimachus instructs that she be brought to him. After she sings for him, he finally speaks, and she convinces him that her suffering equals his. Pericles weeps upon hearing of how Cleon's cruel wife conspired against Marina's life. Reunited with his daughter, Pericles experiences a rebirth: "thou that begett'st him that did thee beget" (l. 184). He hears the music of the spheres, and when all exit, the goddess Diana descends to him in his dream. Diana directs him to Ephesus to make a sacrifice at her temple and to narrate to the people gathered there how he lost his wife at sea.

Act 5, Scene 2 (Scene 22)
Gower introduces the final scene.

Act 5, Scene 3 (Scene 22 continued)
In Diana's temple in Ephesus, Pericles narrates how he married Thaisa, who died in childbed at sea. Upon hearing that Marina is still alive and recognizing Pericles, Thaisa faints. Cerimon

Thaisa faints upon recognizing Pericles in Act V, Scene 3 of *Pericles, Prince of Tyre,* in this print published by Jennings and Chaplin in the 19th century. *(Painting by T. Stothard; engraving by John Thompson)*

reveals to him that the nun who has fainted is his forlorn wife. Reunited with Thaisa, Pericles asks Cerimon how the supposed dead and drowned queen "re-lives." Marina does not speak in this scene, but Pericles informs Thaisa that their daughter will marry Lysimachus in Pentapolis. Pericles, who has not cut his hair for 14 years, will trim it for his daughter's nuptials. Gower's epilogue stresses that while virtue is "crowned with joy at last" (l. 112), evil is punished. Pericles, who experienced tremendous misfortunes, is now blessed with blissful joy.

CHARACTER LIST

John Gower Presenter of the play. He appears seven times.

Pericles, Prince of Tyre Noble prince who undergoes perilous adventures.

Antiochus King of Antioch who has a clandestine incestuous relationship with his daughter and has devised a riddle for suitors to solve in order to marry her. If a suitor fails, he is decapitated. Pericles unravels the riddle, which alludes to Antiochus's secret.

Antiochus's Daughter Pericles plans to marry her before he discovers the incestuous relationship between her and her father, Antiochus.

Thaliart Antiochus instructs him to murder Pericles.

Simonides The king of Pentapolis who initially tests Pericles and then gives him his consent to marry his daughter.

Thaisa The daughter of Simonides who marries Pericles.

Marina Pericles' daughter, who is born at sea during the tempest.

Cerimon Lord of Ephesus, who can perform miracles by reviving the dead.

Lysimachus Governor of Mytilene who frequents the brothel.

Helicanus Loyal follower and councilor of Tyre who advises Pericles to travel.

Aeschines A councilor of Tyre.

Cleon Governor of the famine-ridden Tarsus whose wife plots to have Marina killed.

Dionyza The wife of Cleon, who is envious of Marina and hires Leonine to kill her.

Leonine He plans to follow Dionyza's orders to kill Marina, but she is taken by pirates before he can comply with the evil plot.

Diana Goddess of chastity, who appears to Pericles in a dream and instructs him to make an offering at her temple in Ephesus.

Lychorida Thaisa's nurse.

Pander Owner of the brothel where Marina is sold.

Bawd Arranges prostitutes for clients.

Bolt Works for Pander and the Bawd.

Three Fishermen Subjects of Simonides in Pentapolis.

Master Ship's master who demands that Thaisa's body be thrown overboard to appease the storm.

Three Pirates They kidnap Marina and sell her to a brothel in Mytilene.

Five Knights Suitors of Simonides' daughter, Thaisa.

Sailor of Tyre On board the ship that takes Pericles and Helicanus to Mytilene.

Sailor of Mytilene Accompanies Lysimachus on board the ship that brings Pericles and Helicanus to Mytilene.

Lord of Mytilene Suggests that Marina can make Pericles speak.

CHARACTER STUDIES
Pericles

Pericles, who "look[s] for adventures in the world" (2.3.79; Sc.7.79), is a bold hero undaunted by the shipwrecks and hardships he suffers. From the outset, he proclaims: "Like a bold champion I assume the lists / Nor ask advice of any other thought / But faithfulness and courage" (1.1.104–106; Sc.1.104–106). His courage is brought to the fore when he risks his own life trying to solve the riddle while being surrounded by the decapitated heads of suitors. Although Antiochus tries to dissuade him from solving the riddle, he insists. Pericles' heroic demeanor is also registered in the words of his daughter: "My father, as nurse says, did never fear, / But cried 'Good seamen' to the mariners, / Gall-

ing his kingly hands with haling ropes" (4.1.103–105; Sc.15.103–105). Intrepid when confronted with the fierceness of nature, Pericles gradually becomes a man at the mercy of fate and is caught in a pattern of loss and recovery. Overwhelmed by misfortunes and reversals, he suspects that the gods are mocking him when he is finally reunited with his lost daughter.

Pericles' courage does not diminish, as shown when King Simonides accuses him of being a traitor and deploying witchcraft to win the love of his fair daughter. Pericles boldly defends himself: "Who calls me traitor, unless it be the King, / Even in his bosom will I write the lie" (2.5.51–52; Sc.9.51–52). He refuses to allow anyone to stain his honor: "And he that otherwise accounts of me, / This sword shall prove he's honour's enemy" (2.5.58–59, Sc.9.58–59). Hating hypocrisy, Pericles wishes that the truth could be told when he reveals to Antiochus that he knows his incestuous secret: "Few love to hear the sins they love to act" (1.1.135; Sc.1.135).

A sense of loyalty and responsibility toward his subjects dominates Pericles' character, as illustrated when he leaves Tyre not out of fear for his life but out of worry that Antiochus might endanger his people: "With hostile forces he'll o'erspread the land / And with th'ostent of war will look so huge / Amazement shall drive courage from the state, / Our men might be vanquished ere they do resist, / And subjects punished that ne'er thought offence / Which care of them, not pity myself" (1.2.24–29; Sc.2.24–29). His generosity is apparent with his support of Cleon and his community when their very existence is threatened by starvation. Expecting to be conquered, they are saved by Pericles' generosity. His princely qualities are highlighted as he nobly clarifies to Cleon that he does not "look for reverence but for love" (1.2.97; Sc.2.97).

Like King Lear, who realizes the supremacy and power of the elements and nature during a storm, Pericles pleads to the elements for mercy and announces his subservience to them: "Yet cease your ire, you angry starts of heaven! / Wind, rain, and thunder, remember earthly man / Is but a substance that must yield to you / And I, as fits my nature do obey you" (2.1.41–44; Sc.5.41–44). His helplessness in the face of nature and the gods is prominent in his words to the fishermen: "A man whom both the waters and the wind / In that vast tennis-court hath made the ball / For them to play the ball" (2.1.99–100; Sc.5.99–100). The violent disturbance in nature has made him realize the fragility of human nature.

Rather than lamenting his fate, Pericles displays gratitude toward fortune, as is evident when his father's armor is found: "Thanks fortune, yet that after all thy crosses / Thou giv'st me somewhat to repair my losses" (2.1.160–161; Sc.5.160–161). His humility is reinforced when he appears before Simonides and Thaisa in rusty armor and withholds his royal status by introducing himself as a "gentleman of Tyre" (2.3.77; Sc.7.77). His nobility and aristocratic upbringing shines through. He claims to have been educated in "arts and arms" (2.3.78; Sc.7.78). As Roger Warren points out, "if the audience sees [Pericles'] prowess—not only as a dancer, as in the quarto, but as a warrior too, in an onstage tournament—and *hears* him sing . . . then his claim is substantiated. He is in short, the Renaissance complete or universal man" (in Shakespeare, *Reconstructed Text*: 40–41).

As the play develops, Pericles exhibits extreme patience in the face of adversity. Having lost his beloved wife in "terrible childbed" (3.1.55; Sc.11.55), he obeys the sailors, who insist that she must be thrown overboard. Patiently bidding farewell—"[t]h' unfriendly elements / Forgot thee utterly, nor have I time / To give thee hallowed to thy grave" (3.1.56–58; Sc.11.56–58)—Pericles sacrifices his wife so the storm will cease. Some critics interpret his patience as passivity because he is not in control of the action and fortune appears to drive events. Other critics, such as Doreen DelVecchio and Antony Hammond, assert that Pericles' patience cannot be considered as passivity:

> In the world of romance, patience and readiness to endure are themselves actions of the highest order. . . . To choose patience and endurance, and thereby to accept suffering without demanding comprehension, requires willing and willed spiritual submission; the stress of doing so is great, and is itself active. (Shakespeare, *Pericles* [1998]: 56)

Patience is not enough to ward off melancholy from Pericles' spirit. Falsely informed that Marina has died, Pericles languishes in melancholy. For 14 years, he leaves his hair uncut. Setting aside the calamities that have befallen him, he is quick in thanking the gods, and he obeys their demands. He goes at once to Ephesus when the goddess Diana descends in a dream, asking him to make a sacrificial offering at her temple there. When reunited with Marina, he instructs his councillor Helicanus: "Down on thy knees, thank the holy gods as loud / As thunder threatens us, this is Marina!" (5.1.186–188; Sc.21.186–188). His misfortunes do not cloud his gratitude toward the gods when he discovers that his lost wife is alive: "[Y]our present kindness / Makes my past miseries sports" (5.2.61–62; Sc.22.61–62). Rewarded for his patience in suffering, Pericles is reminiscent of the biblical Job, who endures hardships but is reunited with his family and recompensed by God for his unwavering faith and patience. The benevolent do not perish in *Pericles*.

Marina

The second half of *Pericles* concentrates on Marina. Due to her spiritual and artistic qualities, Marina attracts the envy of women such as Dionyza and the admiration of men such as Lysimachus, who lose their licentiousness after they converse with her. Marina's sojourn in the brothel emphasizes her virtue and rhetorical skills. She offers lessons in morality as her virtuousness enables her to infuse virtue in the men who come to the brothel. Even Lysimachus, who aggressively comes to the brothel "meaning but to pay the price, / A piece of gold for [Marina's] virginity" (4.6.154–155; Sc.19.154–155), succumbs to the valiant virgin. Given the brothel's role as a seedy world of commercial sex, it is poignant that Marina treats it as a bastion of female and family honor by safeguarding her chastity. Hence, she plays a pivotal role in sanctifying female chastity, which was crucial to family honor. Enthralled by Marina's high moral standards, Lysimachus curses anyone who dares remove her honor: "Thou art a piece of virtue, / The best wrought up that ever nature made, / And I doubt not thy training hath been noble. / A curse upon him, die he like a thief, / That robs thee of thy honor" (4.6.162–166; Sc.19.162–166). The brothel scenes accentuate her high moral standards and juxtapose her values with those of the corrupt world of the sex trade. Confronted with the threat

Dionyza orders Leonine to kill Marina in Act IV, Scene 1 of *Pericles, Prince of Tyre*. This illustration was designed for a 1918 edition of Charles and Mary Lamb's *Tales from Shakespeare. (Illustration by Louis Rhead)*

to her chastity and honor in the brothel, Marina laments that "Leonine was so slack, so slow" (4.2.59; Sc.16.59) and that the pirates had not been "enough barbarous" throwing her overboard to "seek [her] mother" (4.2.62; Sc.16.62).

Rather than the brothel, Marina belongs to the honest house she finds by exercising her enduring virtue actively. A space far from the brothel, the honest house allows her to cultivate her musical, sewing, and dancing talents and to help others. Her eloquence, evident in the brothel scenes, also indicates that she is educated in classical rhetoric; as Jeanie Grant Moore puts forward, Marina is "the educated aristocratic lady of Renaissance humanism" (41). She stands in stark contrast to Antiochus's daughter, who engages in incest with her father. Janet Adelman writes that "the sacred and healing power of Marina is clearly an antidote to the poisonous monstrosity of Antiochus's daughter" (197). The valiant Marina espouses the values of Diana, the goddess of chastity, and asks for her aid when her chastity is under threat in the brothel: "Diana aid my purpose!" (4.2.140; Sc.16.140).

Marina can be related to Hermione in *The Winter's Tale* because both female figures undergo symbolic deaths. Hermione is accused by her sexually jealous husband, Leontes, that she engages in a promiscuous relationship with his best friend and that she is carrying his child. These unfounded accusations result in her "death." "Instead of an accusation of dishonesty producing a symbolic death," James L. Calderwood notes, "a literal attempt on [Marina's] life lands her in that graveyard of virginity, a brothel" (43). Rather than defiling Marina's honor, the brothel scenes accentuate her moral virtue. As Calderwood remarks, "so sacred is her honor, that when she carries it like a cross through the house of sin its glister sends whore after whore to her repentant knees" (43).

Marina is also linked to tropes of monuments. Pericles' words to Marina "like gazing on king's graves, and smiling" establish his daughter as a "funeral monument," in Amelia Zurcher's view (920). By becoming a monument, Marina can preserve her identity. Zurcher writes,

Marina becomes a monument before her time not because the past is a happier or simpler place than the present—in its extremity, quite the opposite—but because as a monument she can preserve an inviolability or integrity not available to the living. (920)

Innocent, yet dynamic, Marina is a complex character in a male patriarchal era. In the brothel scenes, she is instrumental in ensuring her success. She, alone, converts the customers, with no help, and incites them to aspire to ideals of virtue in their lives. Her marriage to Lysimachus complicates her character as it is a clear sign that she has taken a traditional role in a patriarchal society that ensures the domestic subjugation of women. However, her behavior in the brothel scenes challenges male authority because it delineates active features in her personality and alludes to the unconventional paths dynamic women can construct. Jeanie Grant Moore points out that:

The re-instatement of patriarchal order as the play closes has been momentarily challenged by the image of Marina, functioning outside the social convention of the protective nuclear family. Unlike her mother who retreats from life (or from a male-dominated world), Marina is forced into action and she shines for a moment as she suggests the potential for women. (43)

Overall, Marina's character is to be emulated. Having been sold into prostitution, through her rhetorical skills and charm, she turns every prospective customer into a reformed, born-again man. Her behavior constitutes an exalted expression of female virtue and determination.

Gower

The medieval poet is an extremely important character in *Pericles,* beginning the play and ending it. His significance in the play and the relationship he establishes with the audience is conveyed by F. David Hoeniger: "The effect [Gower] produces will not be forgotten, for in the course of the play he reappears seven times. Even when the play's action seems to be over, he enters once more, in order to summarize it, moralize in his characteristic manner about the characters, and wish the audience joy before announcing that the end of the play has really come" (463). Hoeniger argues, "There is no parallel for such a character in Shakespeare" (463). Gower relates events for the audience and plays a central role in bringing order to the chaotic and sprawling structure of the narrative. Although choruses appear in other Shakespearean plays, the chorus in *Pericles* is personalized and appears more frequently, seven times.

Gower's method is that of direct address: "Here have you seen a mighty king / His child, I wis, to incest bring" (2.1.1–2; Sc.5.1–2). He controls what the audience witnesses, manipulating the time and space of the world he constructs: "Thus time we waste, and long leagues make we short, / Sail seas in cockles, have an wish but for't, / Making to take imagination / From bourn to bourn, region to region" (4.4.1–4; Sc.17.1–4). He decides which events will be presented in dumb show ("What need I speak?" [2.1.16; Sc.5.16]) and where to stop the narration and to launch the audience into the action of the play: "What shall be next / Pardon old Gower; this 'longs text" (2.1.39–40; Sc.5.39–40); "I nill relate; action may / Conveniently the rest convey, / Which might not what by me is told" (3.1.55–57; Sc.11.55–57). It is noteworthy that he provides moral commentary on the events he narrates: "Although assailed with fortune fierce and keen, / Virtue preserved from fell destruction's blast / Led on by heaven, and crowned with joy at last" (5.2.110–112; Sc.22.110–112). Gower is revived for the purposes of the play, and his existence ends when the play does.

Lysimachus

Lysimachus is an ambiguous character. As the governor of Mytilene, he is considered noble, yet he is first introduced to us in a brothel, "a receptacle / Of all men's sins, and nurse of wickedness" (4.6.124–125; Sc.19.124–125), where he comes to take Marina's virginity. Exchanging marriage vows with Marina, it is unclear if Lysimachus has reformed. He is the vehicle for conveying themes concerning virginity, prostitution, honor, authority, and power. His notion of virginity is evident from his very first words: "How now, how a dozen of virginities? (4.6.28; Sc.19.28). As the governor of Mytilene, he should cater for the town's well-being and the prosperity, yet he appears insensitive toward the illnesses that prostitutes may have to endure: "'Tis the better for you that your resorters stand upon sound legs. How now, wholesome iniquity have you, that a man may deal withal and defy the surgeon?" (4.6.31–33; Sc.19.31–33).

Lysimachus's behavior in the brothel is contradictory. He initially appears aware of his power and freedom to misuse it if he so wishes: "I am the governor, whose authority / Can wink at blemishes, or on faults look friendly, / Or my displeasure punish at my pleasure" (4.6.95–98; Sc.19.95–98). His apparent deep-rooted prejudices regarding Marina and his threatening demeanor quickly make way for reverence and protection. Astounded by Marina's eloquence and virtue, he sees her as "virtue herself sent down from heaven a while / To reign on earth and teach us what we should be" (4.6.143–144; Sc.19.143–144). His sexually patronizing attitude toward Marina appears to disappear due to her influence, and he becomes more pure as illustrated by the use of the word *white*: "I came here with thoughts intemperate, / Foul and deformed, the which thy pains / So well hath laved that they are now white" (4.6.151–153; Sc.19.151–153). While he came to the brothel to exchange gold for Marina's virginity, believing that women are property to be bought, he is so overawed by her virtue and eloquence that he marries her. Further, by indicting Bolt for being associated with the brothel and corruption, "damned doorkeeper" (4.6.169; Sc.19.169), Lysimachus is presented as a transformed figure of purity.

Lysimachus is also instrumental in reuniting Pericles and Marina. He shows concern regarding Pericles' condition and has faith in Marina's spiritual powers, which can "make a battery through [Pericles'] deafened ports" (5.1.37; Sc.21.37). To support Pericles, he pretends that he hears the music of the spheres.

DIFFICULTIES OF THE PLAY

The study of *Pericles* involves many challenges, one being the play's complicated textual history. The play does not appear in the 1623 Folio, and the quarto text is haunted by inconsistencies. The precise date of the play's composition is not known, although scholars believe that it was composed around 1607. Not knowing the precise chronology of *Pericles* makes it difficult to relate the play to its immediate sociohistorical context.

Pericles also offers a number of complications for a contemporary audience. For example, today's readers may not be familiar with the 14th-century figure of John Gower and might be disoriented by his frequent presence in the play. The play's genre, combining tragedy and comedy, also poses challenges. The audience must suspend belief to experience the miraculous reunification of Pericles and Marina. As Paul Dean writes, "Marina's would-be killers construct a sham tomb for her, which Pericles is shown, so that her reappearance must indeed seem like a resurrection to him: and, of course . . . for Shakespeare's audience an *empty tomb* could mean only one thing" (128). A modern audience may have different assumptions than Shakespeare's had. Furthermore, dumb shows and the performance of restorative music are integral to *Pericles*. To grasp the full meaning of the text, the audience must be aware that the notion of romance was very different in Shakespeare's period.

The fragmented and episodic nature of *Pericles*, combined with the complex time scheme, can be confusing, as Cynthia Marshall remarks: "Modern readers, accustomed to causal action in drama, have been frustrated by the sparse or unlikely connections between events in *Pericles*" (62).

KEY PASSAGES
Act I, Scene 1 (Scene 1), 1–42
GOWER. To sing a song that old was sung
From ashes ancient Gower is come,

Assuming man's infirmities
To glad your ear and please your eyes.
It hath been sung at festivals,
On ember-eves and holy-ales,
And lords and ladies in their lives
Have read it for restoratives.
The purchase is to make men glorious,
Et bonum quo antiquius eo melious.
If you, born in these latter times
When wit's more ripe, accept my rhymes,
And to hear an old man sing
May to your wishes pleasure bring,
I life would wish, and that I might
Waste it for you, like taper-light.
This Antioch, then: Antiochus the Great
Built up this city for his chiefest seat,
The fairest in all Syria.
I tell you what mine authors say.
This king unto him took a fere
Who died, and left a female heir
So buxom, blithe, and full of face
As heaven had lent her all his grace,
With whom the father liking took,
And her to Incest did provoke.
Bad child, worse father, to entice his own
To evil should be done by none.
By custom what they did begin
Was with long use accounted no sin.
The beauty of this sinful dame
Made many princes thither frame
To seek her as a bedfellow,
Which to prevent he made a law
To keep her still, and men in awe,
That whoso asked her for his wife,
His riddle told not, lost his life.
So for her many a wight did die,
[The heads of former suitors are revealed]
What now ensues, to the judgement of
   your eye
I give my cause, who best can justify.

This opening speech by Gower frames the play's
narrative and introduces themes, characters, and
concerns that are elaborated throughout. In an act
of theatrical reference, Gower reminds the audience
that this is fiction. This metatheatrical device has
the effect of making the audience keep a distance
from the fictitious events they will witness. Gower
has risen "from ashes" to "sing a song," and he
directly addresses the audience, "to glad your ear
and please your eyes." The reference to *ear* draws
attention to the idea that the Elizabethan culture
was an acoustic culture, unlike our own, which is
dominated by the image. The presence of Gower
establishes a connection with other Shakespearean dramas that feature a chorus, such as *Henry
V, Romeo and Juliet,* and *Troilus and Cressida.* The
notable difference is that Gower appears more frequently—seven times—in *Pericles.* Thus, the play
extols his significance.

Shakespeare's debt to the medieval poet,
"ancient" Gower, and particularly his narrative
poem *Confessio Amantis,* is also explicitly evident
from the outset. Gower's *Confessio Amantis* had a
didactic aspect, a quality apparent in his epilogue:
"Virtue preserv'd from fell destruction's blast"
(5.2.111; Sc.22.111). In *Confessio Amantis,* Gower
spoke in octosyllabic verse, a characteristic that
is witnessed in his opening speech. The twofold
purpose of his speech, to please and entertain, is
articulated: "May to your wishes pleasure bring."
Gower whets the audience's appetite for the tale to
ensue. He is given life by the light of a taper that
gradually burns until it is extinguished when the
tale ends: "Waste it for you, like taper-light."

Gower provides information about the setting,
Antioch in Syria, so that the audience can employ
their imagination. But the play does not remain in
one static location; locations change frequently.
Gower's speech also articulates themes that are
developed and repeated throughout. His revival
from the dead activates the notion of death and resurrection, which is echoed through the revival of
Thaisa and the rebirth of Pericles. The incestuous
affair of Antiochus, which sparks Pericles' adventures on the perilous seas, is also given prominence
in the above speech, and it is a central preoccupation of the play.

By pronouncing moral judgment and articulat-
ing that the union of Antiochus and his daughter

is corrupted and shameful—"bad child, worse father to entice his own;" "sinful dame"—Gower prepares the ground for this father-daughter bond to function as a polar opposite to the graceful and innocent relationship between Simonides and Thaisa, and between Pericles and Marina. The possessiveness of Antiochus as father and illicit lover emerges through the riddle he has devised "[t]o keep her still, and men in awe." Antiochus fulfills his sexual passion with his daughter with no inhibitions, but the gods will punish him for his sexual and moral crime. The folktale convention that pervades the play is highlighted by the riddle and is further reinforced through Gower's reciting of a tale that has been narrated over the centuries.

Another important element in the opening speech is the complex chronology created through Gower's presence. Although firmly rooted in the medieval era, Gower has been reborn. His audience is from the future, and in his narration, he bridges time. This quality is also evident in *The Winter's Tale*, where a character named Time comes onstage to announce that 16 years have passed. Gower, as Paul Dean observes, is "a character in a story which is both later than the past which he is retelling, and earlier than those to whom he retells it" (126).

The passage offers vignettes into the events that will ensue. The danger posed by not solving the riddle is invoked, as many suitors have lost their lives in the pursuit of Antiochus's daughter. Gower prompts the audience to evaluate what will unfold before them, "to the judgement of your eye."

Act I, Scene 1 (Scene 1), 61–90

PERICLES. Like a bold champion I assume the lists,
Nor ask advice of any other thought
But faithfulness and courage.
[*He takes up and reads aloud the riddle*]
I am no viper, yet I feed
On mother's flesh which did me breed.
I sought a husband, in which labour
I found that kindness in a father.
He's father, son, and husband mild;
I mother, wife, and yet his child.

How they may be and yet in two,
As you will live resolve it.
Sharp physic is the last. [*Aside*] But O you powers
That gives heaven countless eyes to view men's acts,
Why cloud they not their sights perpetually
If this be true which makes me pale to read it?
[*He gazes on the Daughter*]
Fair glass of light, I loved you, and could still,
Were not this glorious casket stored with ill.
But I must tell you now my thoughts revolt,
For he's no man on whom perfections wait
That knowing sin within, will touch the gate.
You are a fair viol, and your sense the strings
Who fingered to make man his lawful music,
Would draw heaven down and all the gods to hearken,
But being played upon before your time,
Hell only danceth at so harsh a chime.
[*He turns to the Daughter*]
Good sooth, I care not for you.

ANTIOCHUS. Prince Pericles, touch not upon thy life,
For that's an article within our law.
As dangerous as the rest. Your time's expired.
Either expound now, or receive your sentence.

This key passage invokes one of the central preoccupations of *Pericles:* incest. King Antiochus refuses to relinquish his daughter to a husband and violates the sanctity of the father-daughter bond by engaging in incest. Pericles' behavior in this scene demonstrates his intelligence and bravery. The severed heads of former suitors does not impede his cause: to marry Antiochus's daughter. The text states that he is a "bold champion" of "faithfulness and courage." Angered by Pericles' insistence to decipher the riddle, even at the cost of his life, Antiochus has thrown the riddle on the floor. Pericles boldly picks it up to decipher it. The quickness and ease with which he interprets the riddle raises the question as to why former suitors could not solve it. Why does Pericles realize with such ease that the riddle hides the clandestine relationship of the king with his daughter?

As this passage vividly demonstrates, husband and father have become one because the father, Antiochus, has usurped the place of the husband in the same way the daughter has taken the place of the "mother" and "wife." Antiochus is not the only father reluctant to relinquish his daughter to a husband. Simonides ensures that Pericles undergoes a rite of passage by using the letter before he grants him the right to wed Thaisa.

No longer overwhelmed by the external beauty and the inward glamour of Antiochus's daughter, the "fair glass of light," Pericles is "pale" by what he has discovered, and his "thoughts revolt." His fervent love and desire for the daughter is replaced by repugnance. Having no feelings for her—"Good sooth, I care not for you"—he will not persist any longer because he now "know[s] sin [is] within." Of note is the sexually loaded language Pericles employs in relation to Antiochus's daughter. Imagery linked to penetration ("touch the gate") and fondling ("fingered") conveys his condemnation of the illicit union.

Finally, the passage under consideration outlines the danger Pericles faces because the king informs him that his time for deciphering the riddle has expired, and he runs the risk of decapitation.

Act V, Scene 1 (Scene 21), 143–204

MARINA. My name is Marina.

PERICLES. O I am mocked,
And thou by some incensèd god sent hither
To make the world to laugh at me.

MARINA. Patience, good, sir,
Or here I'll cease.

PERICLES. Nay, I'll be patient.
Thou little know'st how thou dost startle me
To call thyself Marina.

MARINA. The name
Was given me by one that had some power:
My father and a king.

PERICLES. How, a king's daughter,
And called Marina?

MARINA. You said would believe me,
But not to be a troubler of your peace,
I will end here.

PERICLES. But are you flesh and blood?
Have you a working pulse and are no fairy?
Motion as well? Speak on. Where were you born,
And wherefore called Marina?

MARINA. Called Marina
For I was born at sea.

PERICLES. At sea? What mother?

MARINA. My mother was the daughter of a king,
Who died when I was born, as my good nurse
Lychorida hath oft recounted weeping.

PERICLES. O, stop there a little! [*Aside*] This is the rarest dream,
That e'er dull sleep did mock sad fools withal.
This cannot be my daughter, buried. Well.
Where were you bred? I'll hear you more to th'bottom
Of your story, and never interrupt you.

MARINA. You'll scarce believe me, 'twere best I did give o'er.

PERICLES. I will believe you by the syllable
Of what you shall deliver. Yet give me leave.
How came you In these parts? Where were you bred?

MARINA. The king my father did in Tarsus leave me,
Till cruel Cleon, with his wicked wife,
Did seek to murder me, and wooed a villain
To attempt the deed; who having drawn to do't,
A crew of pirates came and rescued me.

To Mytilene they brought me. But good sir,
What will you of me? Why do you weep? It
   may be
You think me an impostor. No, good faith,
I am the daughter to King Pericles,
If good King Pericles be.

PERICLES [*rising*] Ho, Helicanus!
[*Enter Helicanus, Lysimachus, and attendants*]

HELICANUS. Calls my lord?

PERICLES. Thou art a grave and a noble
   councilor,
Most wise in general. Tell me if thou canst
What this maid is, or what is like to be,
That thus hath made me weep.

HELICANUS. I know not,
But here's the regent, sir, of Mytilene
Speaks nobly of her.

LYSIMACHUS. She would never tell
Her parentage. Being demanded that,
She would sit still and weep.

PERICLES. O Helicanus, strike me, honoured
   sir,
Give me a gash, put me to present pain,
Lest this great sea of joys rushing upon me
O'erbear the shores of my mortality
And drown me with their sweetness! [*To
   Marina*] O come hither,
Thou that begett'st him that did thee beget,
Thou that wast born at sea, buried at Tarsus,
And found at sea again!—O Helicanus,
Down on thy knees, thank the holy gods as loud,
As thunder threatens us, this is Marina!
[*To Marina*] What was thy mother's name? Tell
   me but that,
For truth can never be confirmed enough,
Though doubts did ever sleep.

This passage marks a rapid shift in the action, a
movement from crisis to extreme happiness. A part

Marina and Pericles reunite in Act V, Scene 1 of *Pericles, Prince of Tyre.* This illustration was designed for a 1918 edition of Charles and Mary Lamb's *Tales from Shakespeare. (Illustration by Louis Rhead)*

of the recognition scene, this passage involves tremendous emotional intensity because the separated father and daughter are finally reunited. Lysimachus has suggested that Marina be brought to heal Pericles, who has descended into physical and spiritual degradation. He attentively listens to the suffering she recounts. Only she can rouse him from his lethargic state. Pericles experiences a range of emotions at hearing Marina's sad story and the attempt made on her life. Having perceived Marina's physical resemblance to his wife—"My dearest wife was like this maid"—he is startled when she reveals her name (v.1. 146). Accustomed to being at the whims of fortune, Pericles fears that his encounter with Marina is a product of his imagination, a "rarest dream." His understandable pessimism is reflected in his reaction: "O I am mocked" by an angry god, "incensed." As Raphael Lyne emphasizes, "Pericles is portrayed as not ready for the good news, lost in his own suffering" (59). In the midst of tragedy, Pericles finds it inconceivable that he might be fortunate enough to experience such a miraculous reunification. His calamities have taught him to expect the worse, and he pleads to Helicanus to cause him physical pain so that he can be in touch with reality, which has not always been pleasant for him: "O Helicanus, strike me, honoured sir, / Give me a gash, put me to present pain, / Lest this great sea of joys rushing upon me / O'erbear the shores of my mortality / And drown me with their sweetness!" As Harold Bloom observes, "it is as though, emerging from trauma, he requires a proof of his own fleshly mortality" (612).

Pericles' questions signal his eagerness to inquire about the identity of Marina and his disbelief that she is a real human being: "But are you flesh and blood? / Have you a working pulse and are no fairy? / Motion as well? Speak on." Dazzled by the encounter, he perceives that she might be a spirit. Marina's discourse betrays her insecurity and fear that Pericles will "scarce believe me." She also surmises that he might be weeping because he feels that he is being mocked: "Why do you weep? It may be / You think me an impostor."

The passage also evokes Pericles' relationship with Helicanus. Throughout the play, Pericles has confided in and trusted Helicanus, who had advised him to leave Tyre upon hearing about the events in Antiochus. Acknowledging the qualities of Helicanus, Pericles attributes wisdom and nobility to him: "Thou art a grave and noble councillor, / Most wise in general." By asking for his aid in discerning Marina's identity, Pericles once again displays his trust in Helicanus.

Imagery related to the sea is dominant in Pericles' description of his overwhelming joy and his overall psychological state when he recognizes Marina as his lost daughter: Although connoting unexpected happiness, his words display a sadness arising from the cruel events he has experienced at sea. The sea has deprived him of his treasured wife. In contrast, for Marina, the sea is a life-giving force: "Thou that wast born at sea, buried at Tarsus / And found at sea again." His earlier disbelief—"This cannot be my daughter, buried"—has been replaced with his conviction that this is his lost daughter. Rather than displaying bitterness for his torments, he manifests his gratitude to the gods: "O Helicanus, / Down on thy knees, thank the holy gods as loud / As thunder threatens us, this is Marina!" The invocation of thunder interweaves joy with pain as it reminds the audience of the tempests Pericles has endured.

The regeneration of Pericles is largely achieved through Marina as reinforced by his own words: "Thou that begett'st him that did thee beget." Pericles undergoes a spiritual rebirth by being reunited with his daughter. His perplexing discourse, which intimates that the daughter has given birth to her father, echo the riddle in Antioch where the incestuous daughter was "mother, wife, and yet his child." Thaisa, the mother, is also reborn but only after the daughter has been found. The daughter has given birth both to mother and father. Lynda E. Boose explains the notion of begetting: "[T]he recreation is made possible by the daughter's regenerating both the mother and the father who generated her" (340).

The scene evokes overwhelming emotions, the joy of reuniting with the family. Life has triumphed over death. The sense that it is possible to recover what appeared irretrievably lost prevails.

DIFFICULT PASSAGES
Act IV, Scene 6 (Scene 19), 72–88

LYSIMACHUS. Now pretty one, how long have you been at this trade?

MARINA. What trade, sir?

LYSIMACHUS. Why, I cannot name it but I shall offend.

MARINA. I cannot be offended with my trade, please you to name it.

LYSIMACHUS. How long have you been of this profession?

MARINA. E'er since I can remember.

LYSIMACHUS. Did you go to't so young? Were you a gamester at five, or at seven?

MARINA. Earlier too, sir, if now I be one.

LYSIMACHUS. Why, the house you dwell in proclaims you to be a creature of sale.

MARINA. Do you know this house to be a place of such resort and will come into it? I hear say you're of
honourable parts, and are the governor of this place.

LYSIMACHUS. Why, hath your principal made known unto you who I am?

MARINA. Who is my principal?

LYSIMACHUS. Why, you're herb-woman, she that sets seeds and roots of shame and iniquity.
[*Marina weeps*]

LYSIMACHUS. O, you've heard something of my power, and so
Stand off aloof for a more serious wooing.
But pretty one, I do protest to thee
I am the governor, whose authority
Can wink at blemishes, or on faults look friendly,
Or my displeasure punish at my pleasure,
From which displeasure all thy beauty shall;
Not privilege thee, nor my affection
Which hath drawn me to this place abate,
If thou with further lingering withstand me.

This passage (here taken from the Warren edition, which is somewhat different from the others) sets up Lysimachus as a complex and contradictory character. The governor of Mytilene, who frequents the brothel, appears in disguise, and the virginal Marina is left alone with him to offer him sex. But while he is presented here as sexually threatening toward Marina, she will marry him later. This passage confirms Martin Orkin's belief that "the prospect of sexual violence and promiscuity in the (aristocratic or royal) male body, which sears Pericles' vision at Antioch, is extensively articulated [in Mytilene]" (70). Marina and Lysimachus have

diverging concepts of *trade*. In his discourse, trade means prostitution; in hers, it signifies honor and virginity. He goes as far as asking her if she became a prostitute ("gamester") at five or seven, but she perceives this as being a reference to her profession in honesty. Lysimachus appears hypocritical: While he will not name the trade for fear that he will "offend," he has visited the brothel for sex. Mistaking her reserved behavior as being part of a strategy to seduce him, he believes that she is seeking gain from him because he is in a position of authority: "You've heard something of my power, and so / Stand off aloof for a more serious wooing." Being blunt about his sexual passion, he makes it clear to Marina that he will harm her if she impedes him from fulfilling his passion. As governor, he expects satisfaction of his sexual urges and demands to be taken to "some private place." Overall, the passage is central to the characterization of Lysimachus and Marina, and it underscores the threats and dangers Marina faces.

Act III, Scene 2 (Scene 12), 26–46

CERIMON. I held it ever
Virtue and cunning were endowments greater
Than nobleness and riches. Careless heirs
May the two latter darken and dispend,
But immortality attends the former,
Making a man a god. 'Tis known I ever
Have studied physic, through which secret art,
By turning o'er authorities, I have,
Together with my practice, made familiar
To me and to my aid the blest infusions
That dwells in vegetives, in metals, stones,
And so can speak of the disturbances
That nature works, and of her cures, which doth give me
A more content and cause of true delight
Than to be thirsty after tottering honour,
Or tie my treasure up in silken bags
To please the fool and death.

SECOND GENTLEMAN. Your honour has
Through Ephesus poured forth your charity,

Cerimon and Philemon find Thaisa's body in a chest on the shore in Act III, Scene 2 of *Pericles, Prince of Tyre,* in this print published by Jacob Tonson in 1709.

And hundreds call themselves your creatures
   who by you
Have been restored. And not alone your
   knowledge,
Your personal pain, but even your purse still
   open
Hath built Lord Cerimon such strong renown
As time shall never—

In this climactic passage, Cerimon is introduced to the audience, and the coffin containing Thaisas's body is presented. Cerimon is a significant yet conflicting figure because of his magic, which can bring individuals back to life. The notion of healing is articulated in the play's prologue when Gower affirms that the story used to be narrated for "restoratives," namely for therapeutic purposes. In possessing magical powers ("secret art"), Cerimon is tremendously powerful, like Prospero in *The Tempest*. In this passage, Cerimon creates the atmosphere for the revival of Thaisa.

Cerimon ranks knowledge above wealth and social status because he possesses knowledge that has, in turn, granted him power. He has been studying "physic" to embrace immortality, to come closer to the divine in stature, "but immortality attends the former, / Making a man a god." A heightened sense of aura and honor is established around this character through the Gentleman's affirmation that Cerimon is renowned in Ephesus for restoring hundreds of individuals. Elizabeth Hart suggests that Cerimon is an "intercessor between human and divine" (317). The Gentleman says that Cerimon has used his power for benign purposes, namely restoring individuals. Some critics have suggested that Cerimon's magic derives from the occult. The process of reviving Thaisa involves a secret art that can also be suggestive of the playwright's artistry.

CRITICAL INTRODUCTION TO THE PLAY
The Romance Genre

Robert W. Uphaus declares that "*Pericles* is a magnificent outline of the conventions of romance" (34). The term *romance* was popularized by Edward Dowden, a 19th-century critic, to describe the late plays of Shakespeare: *Pericles, Cymbeline, The Winter's Tale,* and *The Tempest*. Romance can be broadly defined, as Howard Felperin contends, as "a success story in which difficulties of any number of kinds are overcome, and a tall story in which they are overcome against impossible odds or by miraculous means" (10).

These four plays share certain features that distinguish them from the rest of the Shakespearean canon. In each, the plot has an enchanting fairy tale quality. Their thematic concerns generally include journeys (literal or spiritual), regeneration and revival, loss and recovery of children, forgiveness and reconciliation, improbable reunions, oracles, dream visions, and father-daughter relationships. The salvation of the older generation is made possible through the actions of the younger generation. Time and geographical location are more flexible in the romances. Pericles travels throughout the Mediterranean. Gower, who functions as the chorus, announces the passage of years and the births and deaths of characters. In *The Winter's Tale,* Time comes onto the stage as a character, and the play is structured chronologically. The first three acts focus on the events before the passage of 16 years, and Acts IV and V are dramatized in the present.

Authority and Power

Pericles dwells on the notion of masculine authority and power and raises questions about the limits of authority. Regal power is expressed by Antiochus and Pericles. The power and authority of governors is expressed by Lysimachus, the governor of Mytilene, and Cleon, the governor of Tarsus. Carried away with the power of being king, Antiochus violates all laws and family values by engaging in sexual relations with his own daughter. His lust and sexual perversion is such that he punishes his daughter's suitors to keep his daughter for himself.

Lysimachus is also fully aware of the power he has due to his position as governor, and he communicates this to Marina in the brothel: "I am the governor, whose authority / Can wink at blemishes, or on faults look friendly, / Or my displeasure punish at my pleasure" (4.6.95–97; Sc.19.95–97). But what happens when authority is abused? Is power unrestrained? Kingship and power have their limits. Kings are not exempt from vengeance of the gods. Any abuse of power is likely to rebound on the perpetrator. The gods' rage at Antiochus and his daughter results in both of their deaths. Their retribution toward the "wicked Cleon," who participates in his wife's murderous scheme, is all too apparent: Cleon and Dionyza's palace, the symbol of their authority, is burned down by their sub-

jects while they, the figures of power, are in it. If Pericles is indeed confronted with his own illegitimate desire for his daughter in Antioch and flees from this desire, as many scholars have indicated, then his misfortunes can be viewed as a form of punishment. By presenting the incestuous relationship of Antiochus and his daughter, *Pericles* alerts us to the notion of regal duties and suggests that kingship involves not only communal but also personal morality. If a king cannot control his sexual appetite to the extent that he sleeps with his own daughter, it is doubtful that he can exercise control in running a state.

Although depicting the transgressions of figures of authority, *Pericles* is permeated by a sense of the overpowering potential of the futility of human existence. The powerlessness of humans in the face of nature and the gods is tied to the tempests Pericles endures: "Yet cease your ire, you angry stars of heaven! / Wind, rain, and thunder, remember earthly man / Is but a substance that must yield to you" (2.1.41–43; Sc.5.41–43). Pericles exhibits an understanding of this aspect of human existence in the first tempest: "And I, as fits my nature, do obey you" (2.1.44; Sc.5.44). The tempests in *Pericles* can be linked to *The Tempest* and *King Lear.* In *The Tempest,* the boatswain's ironic question "What care these roarers for the name of king?" (1.1.14) illustrates the theme of humanity's helplessness in the face of nature and conveys the idea that nature makes no exemptions. Similarly, left battling the elements in the storm and stripped of his authority and reason, King Lear contemplates human identity and realizes the limits of his power and authority: "Is man no more than this? . . . Unaccommodated man is no more but such a poor, bare, forked animal as thou art" (3.4.101–107). *Pericles* vividly demonstrates that the valiant do not perish and that the villainous are punished for their misdemeanours, as also crystallized in Cleon's welcome to Pericles: "The curse of heaven and men succeed their evils" (2.1.102; Sc.5.102). There is no place for evil in a kingdom since a kingdom can be strong only when there are close ties between members of the family or community: "When peers thus knit, a kingdom ever stands" (2.4.59; Sc.8.59).

Death and Rebirth

The theme of death and rebirth looms large in the romances and is intertwined with issues related to the family. In *The Winter's Tale,* Hermione falls apparently dead upon hearing that her son Mamillius has died. The deaths of mother and son are a result of the sexual jealousy of King Leontes, who believes his wife is pregnant with the child of his childhood friend. Hermione appears restored to life at the end of the play, and Leontes is reunited with her. In this play, Pericles undergoes a similar experience in that both his daughter and his wife are presumed dead, yet both are alive and the family reconciles at the end of the play. *Pericles* epitomizes the dreamlike quality of these reunions, as illustrated in Pericles' reactions when Marina begins disclosing her identity: "This is the rarest dream / That e'er dull sleep did mock sad fools withal. / This cannot be my daughter, buried" (5.1.150–152; Sc.21.150–152). When Pericles reunites with his wife, Thaisa, who was thought to be "dead and drowned" (5.2.57; Sc.22.57), Pericles asserts that this is a "great miracle" (5.2.80; Sc.22.80). Pericles, who became spiritually dead upon being informed of his daughter's supposed death, has been revived.

Cerimon's virtuous magic, engineering Thaisa's resurrection and the miraculous reunion between her and Pericles, imbues the play with a sense of wonder. *Pericles* stages a miracle, and the audience must suspend its disbelief when mother and daughter are recovered and the family is joyously together. Although Pericles regains his virtuous wife and daughter, the miracle also functions as a pessimistic commentary on marital and family life: Such relationships are extremely vulnerable. There are no unrestored losses at the end of the play, but the subdued shadows of loss leave an unsettling presence. In discussing *The Winter's Tale,* Catherine Belsey maintains that "they survive after all, but only by a miracle, a resurrection, an impossibility, the effect of a supernatural intervention in the institution our own culture fervently longs to

render inevitable and stable by attributing the family to natural cause" (120). In *Pericles,* like in *The Winter's Tale,* the concept of the family is weighted with ambivalences and ambiguities. *Pericles* stresses that the family is like a living organism that has to be kept alive through pure love and respect. Once its roots are cut off, it is difficult for the relationship to be restored to its former glory.

The Geography and Setting of the Play

Pericles involves journeys across the Mediterranean that reflect the hero's spiritual journey as he "look[s] for adventures in the world" (2.3.78; Sc.7.78). Afforded a symbolic dimension as in other Shakespearean plays, the settings articulate the play's themes. Antioch is a violent and dangerous world of corruption and incest. The severed heads of suitors—"martyrs slain in cupid's wars" (1.1.81; Sc.1.81), as Antiochus calls them—convey the theme of dismemberment and loss and evoke the immorality of the father and daughter. The decapitated heads crystallize the rank hypocrisy and ruthless violence of Antiochus's reign. Incest contaminates the family and the state; the unveiling of the incest brings deviant sexuality to the fore; and by violating and contaminating the sanctity of the father-daughter relationship, the miscreants bring wrath from the heavens.

Violence is not restricted to Antioch. In Tarsus, a world of deprivation and starvation, death has taken over, and the family unit itself has been affected. Mothers, traditionally viewed as providing sustenance to their infants, are portrayed as ready to devour their own children: "Those mothers who to nuzzle up their babes / Thought naught too curious are ready now / To eat those little darlings whom they loved" (1.4.42–44; Sc.4.42–44). Conscience, pity, and love have no place in the hearts of individuals such as Dionyza, who instructs Leonine to kill the innocent Marina. Dionyza states: "Let not conscience, / Which is but cold, or flaming love thy bosom / Enslave too nicely, nor let pity, which even women have cast off, melt thee" (4.1.56–59; Sc.15.56–59).

Pentapolis is an entirely different realm. Here is a world of feasting, gallant gentlemen, jousts, tournaments, and music. This is where Pericles finds a wife and begins his own family. In contrast to Antioch, in Pentapolis, father and daughter are honorable and the tournament, unlike the riddle, is not intended to kill the suitor but for the king's daughter to find a husband. Conspicuously absent from both royal families is the mother. The absence of the mother leads to the intensification of the father-daughter bond and is a theme dealt with in Janet Adelman's *Suffocating Mothers*.

Sexuality—and the economic gain that can accompany it—is abundant in Mytilene. Sexual corruption, the pox, and commercialism are rampant in the sphere of prostitution. The governor himself frequents the brothel. Meanwhile, there is no room for corruption in Ephesus, as this space is dominated by the "presence" of Diana, the goddess of chastity. Characterized by bliss, Ephesus is suggestive of reunion and reconciliation; it is where the entire family is whole again. Here, the marriage of Marina and Lysimachus is announced, and Pericles' family is reinstated. Marina and Lysimachus will reign in Tyrus. The one element that disrupts the familial joy in Ephesus is the news that Thaisa's father has died.

Style and Imagery

A range of images related to tempests, the sea, jewels, music, and eating appear in *Pericles*. The tempest imagery endorses the superiority of nature and the power of the gods over the human universe. Loss and peril, which are prominent in the play, are expressed in the storms that put Pericles at the whims of Fortune: "And he, good prince, having all lost, / By waves from coast to coast is tossed" (2.1.33–34; Sc.5.33–34). The shore functions as a place of safety and stability: "Till fortune, tired with doing bad, / Threw him ashore to give him glad" (2.1.37–38; Sc.5.37–38). The battle for dominance between nature and the human spirit are expressed in imagery of the tempest. It is impossible to overpower nature. David Solway writes:

The conflict in the dream that is *Pericles* is the eternal one going on between the destructive and capricious realm of Nature, the elemental world indifferent to human desires (signified by the tempest, the realm of the 'masked Neptune') and the world of the spirit or imagination, of human longing for harmony and election (signified by music and vision). (94)

Life and death interweave in relation to storms ("Did you not name a tempest, / A birth and death?" [Sc.22.53–54]). Pericles "thwart[s] the wayward seas" (4.4.10; Sc.18.10) on adventures that lead him on a spiritual journey. Thaisa dies during the storm while giving birth to Marina and receives a "watery" burial. Marina's whole existence appears to be marked by storms. The storm induces Thaisa's labor, which results in Marina's birth and her mother's death: "Thou hast a chiding nativity / As fire, air, water, earth, and heaven can make / To herald thee from the womb, poor inch of nature" (3.1.32–34; Sc.11.32–34). It also separates her from her loved ones. By fusing life and death, the storm functions as a device of separation, as illustrated when Marina laments her mother's death: "Ay me, poor maid, / Born in a tempest when my mother died, / This world to me is but a ceaseless storm / Whirring me from my friends" (4.1.69–72; Sc.15.69–72). Most notably, the sea also has a separating function when, according to the sailors' superstition, it demands the body of Thaisa in order for the storm to abate: "The sea works high, the wind is loud, and will not lie till the ship be cleared of the dead" (3.1.47–49; Sc.11.47–49). In this way, the dead are distanced from the living. The method of handling a storm, as Lychorida indicates to Pericles when Thaisa "dies," is patience, which impedes the storm from developing: "Patience, good sir, do not assist the storm" (3.1.19; Sc.11.19). By becoming forces of separation, the sea and the tempest also evoke a longing for reunion.

Eating and voracious hunger also feature prominently in *Pericles*. The riddle activates images of Antiochus's daughter eating her mother's flesh own offspring to avoid death. Hunger, in times of starvation, is depicted as having sharp teeth and being cannibalistic: "So sharp are hunger's teeth that man and wife / Draw lots who first shall die to lengthen life" (1.4.45–46; Sc.4.45–46). In contrast, Pericles forgoes sustenance when he loses his family. Notably, he employs imagery of feeding and hunger in his conversation with Marina just before he recognizes her: "Who starves the ears she feeds, and makes them hungry / The more she gives them speech" (5.1.102–103; Sc.21.102–103).

Jewels represent different ideas in the play. Marina's "jewel" in the brothel is her precious virginity, which is under threat, as signified in Bolt's angered words: "To take from you the jewel you hold so dear" (4.6.203; Sc.19.203). The beauty of Marina's eyes is crystallized in an image of jewels when Pericles notices that she looks like his wife, "her eyes as jewel-like" (5.1.100; Sc.21.100). While *jewel* signifies a precious item or quality, it can also suggest superficiality and pretentiousness. The discrepancy between appearance and reality is represented in the external lavishness of Antiochus and his daughter, which does not correspond to their internal corruption. "Appareled all in jewels" (2.3.9; Sc.7.9), the two were burnt by fire from heaven in "a chariot / Of an inestimable value" (2.3.7–8; Sc.7.7–8). Their self-aggrandizement and corruption was punished by the heavens because "sin had his reward" (2.3.16; Sc.7.16).

There are also important occurrences of music in *Pericles*. Pericles refers to the "harsh chime" (1.1.128; Sc.1.128), the discordant music, produced by Antiochus's daughter, who is presented as a stringed instrument that has been "fingered" (1.1.125; Sc.1.125) to produce lawful music but cannot due to transgressive desire. Music's function as a restorative and healing force is potently put forward in the revival and recognition scenes. Cerimon employs "rough and woeful music" (3.2.86; Sc.12.86) in combination with "secret art" (3.2.29; Sc.12.29) to revive Thaisa: "The rough and woeful music that we have, / Cause it to sound, beseech you! The vial once more. How thou stirr'st, thou block! / The music there!" (3.2.86–88; Sc.12.86–

Sailors toss Thaisa's body overboard in Act II, Scene 5 of *Pericles, Prince of Tyre*. This illustration was designed for a 1918 edition of Charles and Mary Lamb's *Tales from Shakespeare*. *(Illustration by Louis Rhead)*

("I am no viper, yet I feed / On mother's flesh which did me breed" [Sc1.107–109]) because she has usurped her mother's place sexually in bed. She degrades her mother through her illicit eating: "And she an eater of her mother's flesh / By the defiling of her parents' bed" (1.1.173–174; Sc.1.173–174). Serpentine qualities are attributed to father and daughter for transgressing moral boundaries: "And both like serpents are, who though they feed / On sweetest flowers, yet they poison breed" (1.1.175–176; Sc.1.175–176). The play also features images of mothers eating their

88). The benign qualities of music are extolled as "Nature awakes, a warmth / Breathes out of her" (3.2.90–91; Sc.12.90–91). Music is associated with harmony as Pericles hears the music of the spheres, celestial music, when he recognizes Marina. Music expresses his joy: "But hark, what music? / Tell Helicanus, my Marina, tell him / O'er point by point, for yet he seems to doubt, / How sure you are my daughter. But what music?" (5.1.211–214; Sc.21.211–214). Only Pericles can hear this music: "None? The music of the spheres, list, my Marina" (5.1.216; Sc.21.216). This suggests that the music is an internal harmony now that his inner turbulence has ceased. This brief image survey demonstrates that some of the image patterns of the play advance the articulation of the play's themes.

Prose and Its Functions in the Play

In Shakespearean drama, as in much of the drama of his era, the speech of low-status characters is predominantly in prose while that of high-status characters is in poetry. Shakespeare's use of prose in *Pericles* is exemplified by the scenes with the fishermen and the master in Pentapolis and in the brothel scenes in Mytilene.

The fishermen and their master eloquently voice truths and ironies of life. Their witty statements in prose offer insights into the nature of life. The master says that the world of the sea is similar to the world on earth because the same injustices pertain to both spaces. Powerful individuals dominate the less powerful ones: "Why, as men do a-land: the great ones eat up the little ones" (2.1.69–70; Sc.5.69–70). His comparison of "rich misers" to a whale that "plays and tumbles, driving the poor fry before him, and at last devours them all at mouthful" (2.1.71–72; Sc.5.71–72) aptly communicates the greediness and threatening nature of those high on the ladder of power.

Pericles realizes that the fishermen are full of mother wit and wisdom: "How from the finny subject of the sea / These fishers tell the infirmities of men" (2.1.88–89; Sc.5.88–89). The fishermen also advance the plot by informing Pericles about the tournament for the love of the princess Thaisa, and

they also deliver the armor of Pericles' father from the sea. Of utmost significance is the comment of the Second Fisherman upon finding the armor and struggling to take it out of the sea: "Here's a fish hangs in the net like a poor man's right in the law; 'twill hardly come out" (2.1.155–157; Sc.5.155–157). His words give sharp focus on the injustices of the law itself. The tone of unfairness that pervades this statement also alludes to the misfortunes Pericles has suffered.

The brothel scenes provide comic relief but also present the harsh realities of brothel life. Low characters such as Pander, the Bawd, and Bolt speak in prose, and their speech is marked by sexual innuendoes and bawdy language. The commercial aspect of the sex trade is underlined from the first scene in Mytilene, where Pander complains to the Bawd and Bolt: "We lost too much money this mart by being wenchless" (4.2.3–5; Sc.16.3–5). The hazards for both prostitutes and their clients are highlighted when Pander alludes to the death of the Transylvanian who slept with a diseased prostitute: "They're too unwholesome, o' conscience. The poor Transylvanian is dead that lay with the little baggage" (4.2.19–21; Sc.16.19–21). Syphilis was a daily reality and resulted in the death of customers and prostitutes, as indicated by the grotesque image Bolt provides: "Ay, she quickly popped him, she made him roast meat for worms" (4.2.22–23; Sc.16.22–23).

In the brothel scenes, Marina's verse outlines her virtue and nobility, while the prose of characters such as the Bawd and Bolt underscores their corruption. The Bawd's pragmatism is communicated in prose—"such a maiden head were no cheap thing if men / were as they have been" (4.2.56–57; Sc.16.56–57)—while Marina's lament is evoked in verse: "Alack that Leonine was so slack, so slow. / He should have struck, not spoke; or that these pirates, / Not enough barbarous, had but o'erboard thrown me / For to seek my mother" (4.2.59–62; Sc.16.59–62). The Bawd's prose is also full of images of physicality, illustrating the preoccupation with the body in the brothel. Marina is constructed as meat roasting on a spit—"Thou mayst cut a morsel off the spit" (4.2.124; Sc.16.124)—which Bawd and Bolt claim to "have bargained for the joint" (4.2.123; Sc.16.123).

Lysimachus's high upbringing is evident when he rebukes Bolt as he leaves the brothel: "Avaunt, thou damnèd doorkeeper! / Thy house, but for this virgin that doth prop it, / Would sink and overwhelm thee. Away" (4.6.169–171; Sc.19.169–171). His verse underscores that he, the governor of Mytilene, is a member of the aristocracy, as opposed to Bolt, who is of low social status. Lysimachus's anger at the brothel that houses Marina, delivered in verse, heightens the governor's indictment of the sex trade. Ironically, Lysimachus came to the brothel to take Marina's virginity, as he has previously told her.

Bolt's fury following Lysimachus's diatribe is in prose and is directed at Marina. Marina's virtuous virginity threatens his profession with ruin: "How's this? We must take another course with you. If your peevish chastity, which is not worth a breakfast in the cheapest country under the cope, shall undo a whole household, let me be gelded like a spaniel. Come your ways" (4.6.172–176; Sc.19.172–176). He threatens Marina's virginity, as indicated by the Bawd's instructions to him to "take her away, use her at [his] pleasure, crack the glass of her virginity, and make the rest malleable" (4.6.191–192; Sc.19.191–192). The Bawd reiterates that Marina means economic ruin for their trade: "She's born / to undo us" (4.6.197–198; Sc.19.197–198). Using verse, the speech pattern of the superior class, Marina defends herself and morally condemns Bolt, indicating that he is inferior not only to his master and mistress but also to the fiend of hell: "Neither of these can be so bad as thou art, / Since they do better in their command. / Thou hold'st a place for which the painèd'st fiend / Of hell would not in reputation change, / Thou damnèd doorkeeper to every coistrel / That comes enquiring for his Tib" (4.6.209–214; Sc.19.209–214). Her attack on Bolt appears successful; he promises to inform the Pander and the Bawd that she wishes to reside in a home for "honest women" (4.6.240; Sc.19.240).

The use of prose in the brothel sequences makes the scenes more realistic and may also, as Roger Warren indicates, "make it easier for an audience to participate in Marina's spiritual journey than in her father's, since her opponents are real people, not bogeymen like Antiochus" (Shakespeare, *Reconstructed Text:* 48).

EXTRACTS OF CLASSIC CRITICISM

Ben Jonson (1572–1637) [From "Ode to Himself" (1629). Shakespeare's great contemporary, Ben Jonson, was angered that his play *The New Inne* (1629) was less successful than he thought it should have been. Contemptuous of the popularity of *Pericles*, Jonson added an ode to his own play in which he defended his work and attacked *Pericles*. Jonson here directly criticizes the audience's tastes. His characterization of *Pericles* as a "mouldy tale" has been cited by scholars and critics over the centuries.]

COME leave the loathed stage,
And the more loathsome age:
Where pride and impudence (in faction
  knit)
Usurpe the chaire of wit!
Indicting, and arraigning every day
Something they call a Play.
Let their fastidious, vaine
Commission of the braine
Run on, and rage, sweat, censure, and
  condemn :
They were not made for thee, lesse thou
  for them.

Say, that thou pour'st them wheat,
And they will acornes eat :
'Twere simple fury, still, thy selfe to waste
On such as have no taste !
To offer them a surfeit of pure bread,
Whose appetites are dead !
No, give them graines their fill,
Huskes, draff to drink and swill.
If they love lees, and leave the lusty
  wine,

Envy them not, their palate's with the
swine.
No doubt some mouldy tale,
Like *Pericles;* and stale
As the Shrieve's crusts, and nasty as his
fish—
Scraps out of every dish
Throwne forth, and rak't into the com-
mon tub,
May keepe up the *Play-club:*
There, sweepings doe as well
As the best order'd meale.
For, who the relish of these guests will
fit,
Needs set them but the almes-basket of
wit.
And much good do 't you then:
Brave plush and velvet-men;
Can feed on orts: and safe in your
stage-clothes,
Dare quit, upon your oathes,
The stagers and the stage-wrights too
(your peeres)
Of larding your large eares
With their foule *comic* socks,
Wrought upon twenty blocks :
Which if they are torne, and turn'd, and
patch't enough,
The gamesters share your gilt, and you
their stuffe.—

Leave things so prostitute,
And take the *Alcaick* lute;
Or thine own *Horace* or *Anacreons* lyre;
Warm thee by *Pindares* fire:
And though thy nerves be shrunke, and
blood be cold,
Ere yeares have made thee old,
Strike that disdaineful heate
Throughout, to their defeate:
As curious fooles, and envious of thy
straine,
May, blushing, sweare no palsy 's in thy
braine.
But when they heare thee sing

The glories of thy *king,*
His zeale to *God,* and his just awe o'er
men :
They may, blood-shaken, then,
Feele such a flesh-quake to possesse their
powers,

William Watkiss Lloyd (1813–1893) [From
Essays on the Life and Plays of William Shakespeare
(1858). William Watkiss Lloyd worked in fields
such as biography, history, criticism, and classical
studies.]

Of Shakespeare's skill in the creation of individual character I think we may agree that
Pericles contains no indications whatever,
nothing therefore of his best excellence, but
in this respect it is not much inferior to the
Comedy of Errors, and it is perhaps not more
destitute than that play of the effusions of
his veins of impassioned and fanciful poesy.
Still the play has characteristics which have
led critics, without exception, to recognize
the hand of Shakespeare, and these have
been found in style and execution, and
principally in the fifth act. With this verdict
I cannot disagree, and I do not know that
I can give the grounds of it more definite
expression than they have hitherto found.
But the indications are quite as distinct of
a different pen or at least of the same at
a different time, and perhaps the choice
between these alternatives is the most difficult problem connected with the play.
Speaking from impression, I am disposed
to think Shakespeare remodeled a play of
another writer from beginning to end, and
that the discrepancies we observe are due to
his sometimes contenting himself with lop-
ping and abridging, sometimes taking the
trouble to alter and insert words and lines,
sometimes recasting speeches, and perhaps
scenes, entirely. We do not meet in the play
with the doggerel verses that are so frequent

in his known earlier plays, and what rhymed couplets occur are scarcely introduced with the judgment and system that are observable where he even is most lavish of them, but they seem rather interspersed and scattered like vestiges of an earlier half and only half obliterated creation. Again, the play is quite free from his youthful tendency to redundancy, and various and manifold as are its materials and incidents, its characters and combinations, its scenes and speeches have, to my mind, little of the goutiness, so to speak, and unwieldiness that are contrasted with the correctness and sweep of outline, the cleanness of limb and mastery of articulations that were realized by his pencil in his finished works. The style of the play is indeed remarkable for elliptical expressions that may in some instances have been the necessities of another writer in his metrical difficulties, but in others appear to result from a ruling feeling for conciseness sometimes carried to an extreme, terseness defying grammar in reliance on energy of thought.

MODERN CRITICISM AND CRITICAL CONTROVERSIES

The critic David Solway says that *Pericles* "resembles a kind of 'thought experiment' or imaginary voyage through time to an atemporal destination." (91) Though *Pericles* is hardly the most-discussed play in the Shakespearean canon, modern scholars have engaged in many lively debates over it—often over its merits. The characters in *Pericles* are generally regarded as simple and not fully developed in comparison to other Shakespearean plays. Doreen DelVecchio and Antony Hammond's perspective is representative of modern critical approaches to the play's characters:

> Pericles is not Prince Hamlet. . . . Moral action and character are pictures of simplicity like pieces on a black and white chess board, and the vagaries in the fortunes of the hero are resolved on the level of symbolic and

thematic action rather than on the level of plot and character. (Shakespeare, Pericles [1998]: 53).

Viewing the characters in *Pericles* as having merely emblematic functions, Robert W. Uphaus insists they are not fully fleshed-out individuals: "Characters throughout the play are viewed as either instruments or manifestations of providence; they are rarely, if ever, mimetically individuated" (37). In 1935, Caroline Spurgeon singled out *Pericles* as having no sustained motifs in its imagery (291). Other critics disagree, finding a range of imagery in the play.

The play's episodic and fragmented structure has also been the subject of controversy. According to Harold Goddard, the play lacks dramatic impact and fails to move the audience due to its structure and plot:

> . . . the work suffers from its loose structure and romantic plot. Take what is perhaps its greatest scene: the one in which Pericles and Marina are reunited. It is practically perfect as poetry and characterization. Why, then, does it fail to affect us as does the reunion scene between Lear and Cordelia of which it is in many respects an echo? (242)

On the other hand, as Northrop Frye contends, the play's episodic structure might be a part of Shakespeare's artistry, "a deliberate experiment in presenting a traditional archetypal sequence as nakedly and baldly as possible" (51).

In Frank Kermode's perspective, imagination is central to understanding the play as a coherent narrative because "after those early acts we find ourselves in a familiar environment, the Shakespearean drama in which all the action and suffering has a centre, and the work is an imaginative unity" (227). Inga-Stina Ewbank argues that the sprawling and discontinuous structure of the play and the impossibilities it depicts simply reflect real life: "The great events in life are discontinuous; they are not experienced as consequences of previous actions, or as logically connected" (128). The play aptly conveys the absurdities of life:

> When Pericles expresses his joy and wonder by simply telling the fable 'Thou that wast born at sea . . .' he is asserting the miraculous power of life to contain such discontinuities and illogicalities ('she is not dead at Tarsus, as she should have been'). (128–129)

The element of wonder that relates to the improbabilities represented in the play has been studied by several scholars. Peter G. Platt argues that the relationship between play and audience should be viewed as dynamic because "in late Shakespeare, a phase in many ways ushered in by *Pericles,* the audience experiences—and finally enables—the active, dynamic process of wonder" (138). For Suzanne Gossett, the structure of *Pericles* foregrounds the parallel attempts of father and daughter, Pericles and Marina, to find and construct a family (Shakespeare, *Pericles,* [2004]: 143).

The significance of the theme of incest has occupied various critics. Raphael Lyne supports the idea that the incest motif establishes a crux: "This episodic play starts with incest—this is the original sin of the play that starts the prince's wanderings. The play's structure juxtaposes beginning and end in a forceful contrast" (83). Lyne argues that Pericles is redeemed, but, he argues, "the fact that it was not his original sin, nor everybody's, is an imbalance in the equation" (83). Psychoanalytic and feminist readings of *Pericles* dwell on the incest motif. Pericles' desire for his daughter and his guilt are at the heart of the play, which, according to Ruth Nevo, can be seen in the representation of the sea. Nevo argues that the sea is Pericles' "beloved enemy" in the same way that Antiochus "as the sun-father is his envied and hostile rival" (53). She continues: "Antiochus represents at the outset, the threatening father figure, and whatever person Pericles seeks is a symbolic personage representing the mother, lost and forbidden" (53). Therefore, it is "always by the incest fear that

[Pericles] is haunted" (53). Illicit desire comes to the surface as "derivatives of these primal constellations erupt in language and situation throughout" and even more conspicuously "the very name he gives his daughter is the name of the sea" (53). According to Constance Jordan, the incest motif can also metaphorically represent a form of political tyranny, whereby the desire of Antiochus stands for Pericles' desire for absolute rule.

The genre of *Pericles* has also preoccupied scholars. The well-known Shakespearean scholar G. Wilson Knight argued against *Pericles* being categorized as a "romance" and emphasized that "it is a pleasure to observe that the term 'Final plays' is beginning to replace its misleading predecessor, 'the Romances'" (vii). Recent critical studies point out that although the play employs the conventions of romance, the resolution is unsatisfactory, as ambiguities remain. Jeanie Grant Moore calls the play a "riddled romance" and argues that its conclusion is not as harmonious as it seems, since it is unclear whether Pericles has learnt from his misfortunes. Marina, who was initially presented as independent, marries the partner her father has chosen for her, "the brothel frequenting Lysimachus" (42). More important, in Moore's view, is that the play does not adhere to the "picture of the monarchy" frequently evoked in romance because it presents a negative image of kingship, in the form of either Antiochus or Pericles (42).

The study of the symbolization in *Pericles* has taken a variety of avenues. For Heather Dubrow, the armor of Pericles' dead father resonates with a multitude of issues, including the recovery of Pericles' confidence and the restoration of his ability to protect others and to be protected. Dubrow also argues that the armor "represents representation itself [because] it is not the recovered father but a signifier of and surrogate for him" (192). In Cynthia Marshall's view, the play is "uniquely designed to incorporate the symbolic history of the human race into the history on one man" (65).

New historical approaches to *Pericles* primarily focus on the relationship between history and literature. Steven Mullaney maintains that *Pericles* is a statement on drama and constitutes "a radical effort to dissociate the popular stage from its cultural contexts and theatrical grounds of possibility— an effort to imagine, in fact, that popular drama could be a purely aesthetic phenomenon, free from history and from historical determination" (147). Margaret Healy takes a different approach in her article "Pericles and the Pox," claiming that *Pericles* functions as a critique of political marriages through the play's depiction of syphilis (pox). Other approaches that relate the play to history are Amelia Zurcher's examination of the monument as a trope in *The Winter's Tale* and *Pericles*. Zurcher argues that *Pericles* "rejects entirely the humanist notion of history's utility for the present, and with it any possibility for a dynamic relation between present and past" (904).

Some critics have discussed Shakespeare's choice of Pericles for the hero's name. J. M. S. Tompkins argues that the name *Pericles* refers to the noble Athenian statesman (whose biography would have been known to Shakespeare from Sir Thomas North's translation of Plutarch's *Lives of the Noble Grecians and Romans* [1579]) because of the remarkable patience he exhibits (317). In contrast, Roger Warren proposes that Shakespeare was inspired by Pyrocles and Musidorus in Sir Philip Sidney's *Arcadia;* these characters experience shipwreck together twice (Shakespeare, *Reconstructed Text:* 18).

THE PLAY TODAY

Though it is relatively neglected by readers, *Pericles* continues to inspire debate among scholars, particularly regarding its textual problems and collaborative nature. In fact, the general topic of "Shakespeare as cowriter" has fascinated many critics in recent years, with *Pericles* often providing a case in point.

This rarely staged play has been adapted for the screen only once: David Jones directed *Pericles* as part of the BBC Television Shakespeare Series, broadcast on December 8, 1984. Still, *Pericles* has recently appeared onstage in innovative ways.

Yukio Ninagawa's 2003 *Pericles,* produced at the Olivier stage of the National Theatre in Japanese with English subtitles, is considered a masterpiece. In the words of the *Daily Telegraph* reviewer Dominic Cavendish, it was a "visually ravishing Japanese *Pericles*." The director successfully "lent a universal aspect to the cataclysmic upheavals one man faces" while also managing to "make Shakespeare, . . . seem Japanese to the core." The play began and ended, according to Benedict Nightingale, "with a band of bedraggled, maimed refugees limping on stage to the sound of gunfire," and Ninagawa featured "actors dressed as masked puppets." Masaaaki Unchino's "handsome, striking, pig-tailed Pericles in warrior-dress and ornamental cloak" was "radiant with swaggering power and athletic vigour," according to the *Evening Standard* reviewer Nicholas de Jongh.

The visual aspect of performance was also striking in Mary Zimmerman's production of *Pericles,* performed at the Shakespeare Theatre in Washington, D.C., from November 2004 to January 2005 and at the Goodman Theatre in Chicago from January to February 2006. The color schemes were central to establishing the worlds of the play. As the *Washington Post* reviewer Peter Marks described it, Tarsus was "swathed in sunburnt linens and raiment of gold" while Mytilene was "adorned in decadent purples" and Pentapolis in "a sort of plush Ritz-Carlton of a city." The director's significant departure from Shakespeare's play, with Gower's lines distributed to most of the cast, decentralized the role of Gower. References to Marina's age were also altered, presenting her as 16 rather than 14.

Dominic Cooke's Royal Shakespeare Company production of *Pericles* (2006–07), at The Swan in Stratford-Upon-Avon, set the play in East Africa and explored issues of African dictatorship. Race became a prominent theme with a 25-actor cast that featured 10 black actors. The black actors used African pronunciation and wore African-themed costumes. Lucian Msamati, born in Zimbabwe, starred as Pericles. The inventive production even featured a pentathlon in Pentapolis.

FIVE TOPICS FOR DISCUSSION AND WRITING

1. **Kingship:** Discuss the concept of kingship in *Pericles*. Compare the different kings in the play. How does kingship relate to the family and to ideas of gender? How do issues of desire clash with those of duty and responsibility?

2. **Family relationships:** How are family dynamics depicted? How is the marital relationship of Pericles and Thaisa represented? How are father-daughter relationships (Antiochus-daughter, Pericles-Marina, Simonides-Marina) treated? To what extent is Pericles affected by his encounter with the incestuous relationship of Antiochus and his daughter? How does separation affect family members? How is reconciliation achieved? Why does Marina stay mostly silent at the end of the play?

3. **Setting:** How important are the geographical locations depicted in the play? How do these disparate settings affect the characters' worldviews, and how do they relate to their fortunes? How are the thematic concerns of the play developed through changes in setting?

4. **Happy ending:** Is there a harmonious resolution at the end of the play? What is your response to the miracle that *Pericles* dramatizes? Are there any unresolved contradictions? What do these contradictions arise from? Compare and contrast the endings in *The Winter's Tale* and *Pericles*.

5. **Pericles as a romance:** What are the artistic features of the romances? Provide examples from *Pericles*. What similarities does *Pericles* share with other plays in this genre (*The Tempest, The Winter's Tale, Cymbeline*)? In what ways does *Pericles* differ?

Bibliography

Adelman, Janet. "Masculine Authority and the Maternal Body: The Return to Origins in the Romances." In *Suffocating Mothers: Fantasies of the Maternal Origin in Shakespeare's Plays, Hamlet to the Tempest*. London: Routledge, 1992, 193–238.

Arthos, J. "*Pericles, Prince of Tyre:* A Study in the Dramatic Use of Romantic Narrative." *Shakespeare Quarterly* 4 (1953): 250–270.

Barber, C. L. "'Thou That Beget'st Him That Did Thee Beget': Transformation in *Pericles* and *The Winter's Tale.*" *Shakespeare Survey* 22 (1969): 59–67.

Belsey, Catherine. *Shakespeare and the Loss of Eden: The Construction of Family Values in Early Modern Culture*. Basingstoke, U.K.: Macmillan, 1999.

Berry, Ralph. *Shakespeare and Social Class*. Atlantic Highlands, N.J: Humanities Press International, 1988.

Billington, Michael. Review of *Pericles* by Yukio Ninagawa, *Guardian*, 31 March 2003. Available online. URL: http://www.nationaltheatre.org.uk/?lid=2909&dspl=reviews. Accessed January 12, 2011.

Bloom, Harold. "Pericles." In *Shakespeare: The Invention of the Human*. New York: Riverhead Books, 1998, 603–613.

Boose, Lynda E. "The Father and the Bride in Shakespeare." *PMLA* 97 (1982): 325–347.

Calderwood, James L. *Shakespeare and the Denial of Death*. Amherst: University of Massachusetts Press, 1987.

Cavendish, Dominic. Review of *Pericles* by Yukio Ninagawa, *Daily Telegraph*, 1 April 2003. Available online. URL: http://www.nationaltheatre.org.uk/?lid=2909&dspl=reviews. Accessed January 12, 2011.

Cobb, Christopher J. *The Staging of Romance in Late Shakespeare: Text and Theatrical Technique*. Newark: University of Delaware Press, 2007.

Craig, Hardin. "'Pericles' and 'The Painful Adventures.'" *Studies in Philology* 45 (1948): 600–605.

Dean, Paul. "Pericles' Pilgrimage." *Essays in Criticism* 50, no. 2 (2000): 125–144.

de Jongh, Nicholas. Review of *Pericles* by Yukio Ninagawa, *Evening Standard*, 31 March 2003. Available online. URL: http://www.nationaltheatre.org.uk/?lid=2909&dspl=reviews. Accessed January 12, 2011.

Dubrow, Heather. *Shakespeare and Domestic Loss*. Cambridge: Cambridge University Press, 1999.

Dunn, Catherine M. "The Function of Music in Shakespeare's Romances." *Shakespeare Quarterly* 20 (1969): 391–405.

Ewbank, Inga-Stina. "'My Name is Marina': The Language of Recognition." In *Shakespeare's Styles: Essays in Honour of Kenneth Muir,* edited by Philip Edwards, Inga-Stina Ewbank, and G. K. Hunter, 111–130. Cambridge: Cambridge University Press, 1980.

Felperin, Howard. *Shakespearean Romance.* Princeton, N.J.: Princeton University Press, 1972.

Frye, Northrop. *The Secular Scripture: A Study of the Structure of Romance.* Cambridge, Mass.: Harvard University Press, 1976.

Goddard, Harold C. *The Meaning of Shakespeare.* Vol. 1. Chicago: University of Chicago Press, 1951.

Hart, Elizabeth E. "'Great is Diana' of Shakespeare's Ephesus." *SEL: Studies in English Literature 1500–1900* 43, no. 2 (2003): 347–374.

Healy, Margaret. "*Pericles* and the Pox." In *Shakespeare's Late Plays: New Readings,* edited by Jennifer Richards and James Knowles, 92–107. Edinburgh: Edinburgh University Press, 1999.

Hoeniger, F. David. "Gower and Shakespeare in *Pericles.*" *Shakespeare Quarterly* 33 (1982): 461–479.

Jonson, Ben. "Ode (to himself)." In *The Oxford Book of Seventeenth Century Verse,* edited by H. J. C. Grierson and Geoffrey Bullough, 179–180. Oxford: Clarendon Press, 1934.

Jordan, Constance. "'Eating the Mother': Property and Propriety in *Pericles.*" In *Creative Imitation: New Essays on Renaissance Literature in Honor of Thomas M. Green,* edited by David Quint, Margaret W. Ferguson, G. W. Pigman III, and Wayne A. Rebhorn, 331–353. Binghamton, N.Y: Medieval & Renaissance Texts and Studies, 1992.

Kermode, Frank. *Shakespeare, Spenser, Donne: Renaissance Essays.* London: Routledge & Kegan Paul, 1971.

Knight, Wilson G. *The Crown of Life: Essays in Interpretation of Shakespeare's Final Plays.* London: Methuen, 1952.

Lloyd, William Watkiss. *Essays on the Life and Plays of Shakespeare, contributed to the edition of the poet by S. W. Singer, 1856.* London: C. Whittingham, 1858.

Lyne, Raphael. *Shakespeare's Late Work.* Oxford: Oxford University Press, 2007.

Marks, Peter. "A 'Pericles' with a Wind in its Sails," *Washington Post,* 16 November 2004, C01. Available online. URL: http://www.washingtonpost.com/wp-dyn/articles/A53024-2004Nov15.html. Accessed January 12, 2011.

Marshall, Cynthia. *Last Things and Last Plays: Shakespearean Eschatology.* Carbondale: Southern Illinois University Press, 1991.

Massai, Sonia. "From Pericles to Marina: 'While Women are to be had for Money, Love or Importunity.'" *Shakespeare Survey* 51 (1998): 67–77.

Moore, Jeanie Grant. "Riddled Romance: Kingship and Kinship in 'Pericles.'" *Rocky Mountain Review of Language and Literature* 57, no. 1 (2003): 33–48.

Mullaney, Steven. *The Place of the Stage: License, Play, and Power in Renaissance England.* Chicago: University of Chicago Press, 1988.

Nevo, Ruth. *Shakespeare's Other Language.* New York: Methuen, 1987.

Nightingale, Benedict. Review of *Pericles* by Yukio Ninagawa, *The Times,* 31 March 2003. Available online. URL: http://www.nationaltheatre.org.uk/?lid=2909&dspl=reviews. Accessed January 12, 2011.

Orkin, Martin. *Local Shakespeares: Proximations and Power.* New York: Routledge, 2005.

Platt, Peter G. "Pericles and the Wonder of Unburdened Proof." In *Reason Diminished: Shakespeare and the Marvelous.* University of Nebraska Press, 1997, 124–138.

Pericles, Prince of Tyre. Edited by Doreen DelVecchio and Antony Hammond. Cambridge: Cambridge University Press, 1998

———. *Pericles, Prince of Tyre.* Edited by Suzanne Gossett. London: Arden Shakespeare, 2004.

———. *A Reconstructed Text of Pericles, Prince of Tyre.* Edited by Roger Warren. Oxford: Oxford University Press, 2003.

Skeele, David, ed. *Pericles: Critical Essays.* New York: Garland, 2000.

———. *Thwarting the Wayward Seas: A Critical and Theatrical History of Shakespeare's Pericles in the Nineteenth and the Twentieth Centuries.* Newark: University of Delaware Press, 1998.

Solway, David. "'Pericles' as Dream." *Sewanee Review* 105, no. 1 (1997): 91–95.

Spurgeon, Caroline. *Shakespeare's Imagery and What It Tells Us.* Cambridge: Cambridge University Press, 1935.

Tompkins, J. M. S. "Why Pericles?" *Review of English Studies* 3, no. 12 (1952): 315–324.

Uphaus, Robert W. *Beyond Tragedy: Structure and Experience in Shakespeare's Romances.* Lexington: University of Kentucky Press, 1981.

Zurcher, Amelia. "Untimely Monuments: Stoicism, History, and the Problem of Utility in *The Winter's Tale* and *Pericles. ELH: English Literary History* 70, no. 4 (2003): 903–927.

FILM AND VIDEO PRODUCTIONS

Jones, David, dir. *Pericles.* With Mike Gwilym and Juliet Stevenson. BBC, 1984.

—Eleni Pilla

Richard II

INTRODUCTION

Richard II is the opening play of the four-part Henriad, which also includes the two parts of *Henry IV* and *Henry V.* The plays that Shakespeare wrote in 1595–96, among them *Romeo and Juliet* and *Richard II,* reflect a growing maturity in his poetics and intellectual depth. *Richard II* and the roughly contemporary *King John* are the only two plays in the Shakespeare canon entirely in verse; even the gardener in *Richard II* is poetic. The poetry of the play is, moreover, highly wrought, filled with metaphysical imagery.

The characters in *Richard II* possess a psychological depth absent in Shakespeare's plays of the early 1590s. The figures in the earlier *Henry VI* plays and *Richard III* (ca. 1593) seem interchangeable. Even Richard III himself lacks the psychological interest of Richard II. One may compare the opening soliloquy of *Richard III* with Richard II's soliloquy in 5.5 of the later work to see the difference. For all his charm, Richard III is a typical stage villain of the period: He announces intentions that exist before he utters them. Richard II appears to think as he speaks; his lines create the illusion that they are conceived on the spot, that thought and speech occur simultaneously. Richard II's psychological depth looks ahead to the great tragic heroes of Shakespeare's maturity, particularly Hamlet and Lear. Bolingbroke, though less well developed, still seems like a less articulate and less conscience-troubled Macbeth, whose ambition drives him to seize the throne and kill his prede-

cessor. Not all the characters in *Richard II* are as fully developed as they will be in the greater plays to come at the end of the 1590s. Still, many more figures are distinct from each other and, if not completely round, are more than mere devices to move the action forward.

Another mark of greater sophistication in *Richard II* is that the listener or reader must intuit the meaning behind the words. Characters show rather than tell what they are. In his soliloquy of 5.5, Richard does not say that he believes in a hierarchical world in which an individual's station is fixed; one must infer this outlook from the structure of his speech. He does not state that as king he appeared to be regal but did not act so; rather, he likens himself to a manikin that strikes the bell of a clock, a figure that looks alive but is not. Northumberland does not announce himself a flatterer of Bolingbroke. Instead, when, in 2.3, he praises the speeches of the taciturn Bolingbroke, he reveals his nature.

Richard II also demonstrates a more profound understanding of history than Shakespeare's earlier treatment of the Wars of the Roses. The plays of the first Henriad are chronicles: One might describe them as "one damn thing after another," with limited connection between events and little or no attempt to interpret them. *Richard II* concerns itself less with what happens—indeed, little does. Rather, the play presents the clash between Richard and Bolingbroke as a conflict between two worldviews, between the old medieval order and the modern world.

Sir Piers Exton murders King Richard II in Act V, Scene 5 of *Richard II*. This print is from Joseph Graves's *Dramatic Tales Founded on Shakespeare's Plays*, published by John Duncombe in the 19th century.

Although the events Shakespeare describes in the play occurred around 1400 and the play was written in the mid-1590s, the work raises questions of eternal relevance. To what extent does one owe allegiance to a bad government? This issue arose in the British colonies of North America in 1776. It underlies Henry David Thoreau's essay "Civil Disobedience," and it arose in the American South in the 1950s and 1960s, in Hungary in 1956, and in Poland in 1981. On a personal level, the play asks how identity is determined and what happens when one loses one's sense of self. What happens when private and public ties conflict? Because of his loyalty to the king, John of Gaunt refuses to avenge his brother's death. Bolingbroke does not hesitate to force his cousin Richard to separate from Richard's wife for political reasons.

Richard II delights even as it tells its audiences not what to think but what to think about.

BACKGROUND

History plays were a favorite form of a entertainment in the Elizabethan Age. Writing about English plays, Thomas Nash in *Pierce Penilesse His Supplication to the Divell* (1592) states,

First, for the subject of them (for the most part) it is borrowed out of our English Chronicles, wherein our fore-fathers valiant actes (that haue lyne long buried in rustie brasse and worme-eaten bookes) are revived, and they them selves raysed from the Grave of Oblivion . . . : then which, what can bee a sharper reproofe, to these degenerate, effeminate dayes of ours?

Between 1588 and 1600, some 200 historical dramas were staged. The popularity of this genre is reflected in Thomas Heywood's *An Apology for Actors* (1612), which observes,

Plays have made the ignorant more apprehensive [intelligent, discerning], taught the unlearned the knowledge of many famous histories, instructed such as cannot read in the discovery of all our English Chronicles: and what man have you now of such weak capacity that cannot discover of any notable thing recorded even from William the Conqueror, nay from the landing of Brute [mythical founder of Britain], until this day, being possessed of their true use.

In *The Arte of English Poesie* (1589) George Puttenham placed historical poetry just below religious verse "as well for the common benefit as for the speciall comfort euery man receiueth by it." Thomas Beard's 1612 preface to *The Theatre of Gods' Iudgements* (originally published in 1597) concurs:

Historie is accounted a verie necessarie and profitable thing, for that in recalling to mind the truth of things past, which otherwise would be buried in silence, it setteth before vs such effects (as warnings and admonitions touching good and euill) and layeth virtue and vice so naked before our eyes, with the punishments or rewards inflicted or bestowed upon the followers of each of them, that it may rightly be called an easie and profitable apprenticeship or schoole for euerie man to learne to get wisedome at another mans cost.

History had long been popular in England both on and off the stage. Medieval mystery plays (so named because they were staged by the various guilds, or mysteries), which continued to be performed into Shakespeare's lifetime, traced biblical stories from the Creation to the Last Judgment and were regarded as historical. The Hock Tuesday Play commemorating an 11th-century battle was performed annually at Coventry and staged for Queen Elizabeth when she visited Kenilworth in 1575. Shakespeare and his father may have traveled the dozen or so miles from Stratford to view the pageantry associated with her visit to Robert Dudley's estate.

John Bale's *Kynge Johan* (written before 1536) was played before Elizabeth at Ipswich in 1561. Another early historical drama, staged before the queen at Whitehall on January 18, 1562, is Thomas Norton and Thomas Sackville's *Gorboduc* (1565), which warns against evil counselors and shows the dangers of an unclear succession. Both themes appear in Shakespeare's *Richard II. The Life and Death of Jack Straw* (1593) deals with the Peasant's Revolt of 1381, early in the reign of Richard II. Other contemporary historical dramas include George Peele's *The Famous Chronicle of King Edward the First* (1593); Christopher Marlowe's *Edward II* (1594); *Thomas of Woodstock* (ca. 1592), an unfinished work that deals with the reign of Richard II; and *The Reign of King Edward the Third* (1596), in which Shakespeare almost certainly had a hand.

Shakespeare's first theatrical success had come with a history play, *Henry VI;* which part was performed first is unclear. The play opened in April 1592 at the Rose, Bankside, and continued through June with 15 performances. According to the diary of Philip Henslowe, manager of that theater, 16,344 people saw the play from the galleries; even more would have watched standing around the stage. Thomas Nash, with whom Shakespeare collaborated in writing *Henry VI, Part 1,* reflected on the popularity of that work when he observed,

How it would have joyed brave Talbot (the terror of the French) to think that after he had lain two hundred years in his tomb, he should triumph again on the stage, and have his bones new embalmed with the tears of ten thousand spectators at least . . . (at several times) who in the tragedian that represents his person, imagine they behold him fresh bleeding. (Wood 142–143)

Among nondramatic works of history published in the 16th century was Edward Hall's *The Union of the Two Noble and Illustrate Fameilies of Lancastre and Yorke* (1548), which drew heavily on Polydore Vergil's 1534 *Anglica Historia*. Hall's history covers the same period as Shakespeare's two tetralogies. *A Myrroure for Magistrates* (1559)—a collection of poems by William Baldwin, George Ferrers, Sir Thomas Chalconer, Thomas Phaer, and John Skelton—offers metrical monologues delivered by rulers and other prominent figures who suffered misfortunes. William Warner's *Albion's England* (1586–89) is another poetical treatment of English history. Samuel Daniel's *First Foure Bookes of the Civile War between the Two Houses of Lancaster and Yorke* (1595), with additional books appearing in 1596 and 1601, deals in verse with the same matter Edward Hall treated in prose. Raphael Holinshed published the first edition of his *Chronicles of England, Scotlande and Irelande* in 1577; the second edition was printed a decade later.

In writing *Richard II,* Shakespeare drew on many of these sources, and he may have read some other accounts as well. He chose in his play to concentrate on the final two years of Richard's reign. In 1397, Richard arrested the duke of Gloucester and the earls of Warwick and Arundel, who had long opposed his policies. Warwick was exiled, Arundel beheaded. Gloucester was imprisoned at the fortress of Calais, commanded by Thomas Mowbray, duke of Norfolk. Mowbray had been allied with Gloucester, as had Henry Bolingbroke, duke of Hereford. But while in Mowbray's custody, Gloucester died; Mowbray probably had him killed at the king's command.

In January 1398, Bolingbroke broke with Mowbray in Parliament, accusing him of treason, a charge he repeated before Richard II in April, when Shakespeare's play begins. The two men challenged each other to trial by combat. Failing to pacify the two, Richard ordered the trial by combat to occur in Coventry in September (Act I, Scene 3). There the king interrupted the duel. Acting on the advice of his council, he exiled both men. Mowbray, as stated in Act IV, Scene 1 of the play, died in Venice, though he did not, as the play states, fight in any crusade.

After John of Gaunt died on February 3, 1399, Richard seized Gaunt's property (2.1). In April, Richard set off for Ireland to confront the rebels; in July Bolingbroke returned (2.3). He executed Wiltshire, Bushy, and Green at the end of that month (3.1), and in August, he met with Richard at Flint Castle (3.3). Richard abdicated in September (4.1) and was imprisoned at Pomfret Castle, where he was killed in February 1400 (5.5–5.6), when the play ends.

John Dover Wilson postulated that in writing *Richard II* Shakespeare drew on an earlier play, which he adapted and pieced out using Samuel Daniel's *Civile Wars* (1609) and *Thoms of Woodstock* (1609). No such source play has been found, though, and Shakespeare probably drew on a wider range of materials than Dover Wilson allows. Christopher Marlowe had probably been influenced by Shakespeare's treatment of the weak Henry VI in writing his play about Edward II, and Marlowe's play in turn provided hints for *Richard II*. In Marlowe's play, the king attaches himself to three flatterers: Gaveston, Spencer, and Baldock. Richard also has three favorites: Bushy, Bagot, and Green. In each play, the duke of Lancaster (though not the same duke) warns the king about his misdeeds, and in each case, the king ignores him. Also in each play, the king grows more sympathetic as his fortunes decline. Shakespeare paid further tribute to Marlowe in Richard's "Was this face the face" speech at 4.1.281–286, a clear echo of Faustus's apostrophe to the shade of Helen: "Was this the face that launch'd a thousand ships, / And burnt the topless towers of Ilium?"

George Ferrers's account of Gloucester in *A Myrroure for Magistrates* shows the duke as prideful, but his death still calls for retribution. Thomas Chaloner wrote Richard's lament. He admits responsibility for Gloucester's death and for favoring parasites. His ghost declares,

I am a Kyng that ruled all by lust,
That forced not of virtue, right, or lawe,
But always put false Flatterers most in trust,
Ensuing such as could my vices clawe:
By faithful counsayle passing not a strawe.
What pleasure pryckt, that thought I to be
　just.

Shakespeare's Richard ignores the good advice of his uncles Lancaster and York. Although Bushy, Bagot, Green, and Scroop offer no suggestions about policy in the play, staging may show them whispering to the king as 1.4 begins and again when Richard visits John of Gaunt in 2.1.

Edward Hall's history contains many of the facts Shakespeare presents in his play, though Hall puts the trial by combat at Coventry in August. In Act I, Scene 4, Richard recounts Bolingbroke's courting of commoners as he leaves for exile in France. Hall reports, "Wonderful it is to write, and more strange to here, what nombre of people ranne in every towne and streete, lamenting and bewailing his departure" (387).

Shakespeare's chief source for the play, as for all his history plays, was the second edition of Raphael Holinshed's *Chronicles*. Holinshed notes that Richard alienated the nobility by threats and seizure of their property. According to Holinshed, the action in Shakespeare's 1.1 occurred at Shrewsbury rather than at Windsor, and the accusatory speeches were made by unnamed knights rather than by the principals, Mowbray and Bolingbroke. Shakespeare simplified history and heightened the tension by having the two dukes confront each other.

According to both Hall and Holinshed, Richard tried to reconcile the two men, but he did not order them to give up their quarrel, as he does in the opening of Shakespeare's play. Shakespeare thus makes Richard appear weaker when his two subjects refuse to heed his command. Shakespeare follows Holinshed's dating of the trial by combat; his description of the event resembles those in both Hall and Holinshed. Holinshed reports the death of Gaunt and the seizing of his property but says nothing about a final meeting between the king and his uncle. According to the play, Richard needs Gaunt's money to pay for the war in Ireland, a better reason than found in Holinshed, where the king uses these funds to pay for his extravagant life.

According to Holinshed, Bolingbroke returned from exile at the urging of "diverse of the nobilitie, as well prelates as other and like wise manie of the magistrates and rulers of the cities, townes and communaltie, here in England . . . promising him their aid, power and assistance, if he expelling K. Richard, as a man not meet for the office he bare, would take upon him the scepter, rule and obedience of his native land and religion." In the play, Bolingbroke does not receive—or need—any such encouragement. Holinshed notes that historians differ about how much of an army Bolingbroke brought with him when he returned to England. Shakespeare chose the version that claimed Bolingbroke came with eight ships and 3,000 men, a formidable force suggesting that Bolingbroke came back for more than just the legacy he was denied and that, in the play, he says is his sole purpose. The French chronicler Jean Froissart places Bolingbroke's landing at Plymouth; Shakespeare echoes Holinshed, who puts the landing at Ravenspurgh, Yorkshire, a Lancastrian stronghold.

At 2.3.135–136, Bolingbroke tells his uncle, York, that he has returned only to claim his inheritance, a claim that Shakespeare would have found in Holinshed. In the play, York replies that had he (York) been able to assemble a large enough force, he still would have opposed his nephew. Holinshed recounts that York gathered a large army, but his soldiers refused to fight against Bolingbroke. *A Myrroure for Magistrates* states that York defected. At 2.3.159, the duke says, "I do remain as neuter." However, at 3.2.200, Scroop tells the king, "Your uncle York is join'd with Bolingbroke." The failure

of the earl of Salisbury to prevent the Welsh forces from departing, shown in 2.4, appears in Holinshed. In both the *Chronicles* and the play, Richard initially hopes to defeat Bolingbroke's forces, but when he learns the magnitude of the rebellion, he despairs and disperses those troops still loyal to him (3.2.211–218).

According to Holinshed, Northumberland tricked Richard into going to Flint Castle, already held by forces loyal to Bolingbroke. Shakespeare omits this bit of treachery. Shakespeare's opening of 4.1 derives from Holinshed's account of the parliamentary investigation of the death of Gloucester in October 1399. Many lords accused the duke of Aumerle of involvement and challenged him. The bishop of Carlisle defended Richard and was arrested for his pains (4.1.150–151). Shakespeare invented the abdication scene itself. The conspiracy to restore Richard (4.1.321–334, 5.2, 5.6.1–16) is discussed in Holinshed. York's discovery of the plot and his son's involvement (5.2–5.3) comes from Holinshed, but Shakespeare gives the duchess of York a role here; Holinshed does not mention her because she had died six years before Richard's abdication. Holinshed offers various accounts of Richard's death, including the one Shakespeare uses in 5.5.

From Daniel's *Civile Wars,* Shakespeare probably got the idea to make Isabella an adult; she was, in fact, barely 10 when Richard died. York's description of Richard's disgrace in 5.2 resembles Daniel's rendering: The king, Daniel writes, was "Most meanely mounted on a simple steed: / Degraded of all grace and ease beside, / Thereby neglect of all respect to breed." Daniel implicates Henry IV more strongly in Richard's death than does Shakespeare. In the poem, the new king "eies a knight, that then was by, / Who soone could learne his lesson by his eie." Daniel's footnote identifies the knight as Sir Pierce of Exton. At 5.6.39, Henry IV admits only to wishing Richard dead but not to inciting Sir Pierce Exton to regicide. Daniel gives Richard a soliloquy before his death, as does Shakespeare. In Daniel's version, the deposed ruler envies the cowherd he sees grazing his flock.

Shakespeare's Richard regards no life as content. Daniel's speech finds echoes in *Henry IV, Part 2,* 3.1.4–31 and 4.5.21–31, as well as in *Henry V,* 4.1.230–284. Richard's valiant defense of his life against Sir Pierce and his servants in 5.5 also appears in Daniel.

Thomas of Woodstock covers far more time than Shakespeare's play, beginning in 1382 on the eve of Richard's marriage to Anne of Bohemia and ending after the death of Gloucester in 1397. The play opens with a tumultuous scene in which the dukes of Lancaster and York, the earls of Arundel and Surrey, Sir Thomas Cheney, and others flee a banquet at which Richard has plotted to poison them. Just as York does in *Richard II,* 2.1.17–30, York and Sir Thomas Cheney in *Woodstock* blame Richard's flatterers for the king's misdeeds. Northumberland in Shakespeare's play similarly states, "The King is not himself, but basely led / By flatterers" (2.1.241–242). York in Shakespeare's play remarks that Richard is obsessed with "Report of fashions in proud Italy" (2.1.21); in *Woodstock,* Richard and his flatterers appear in 3.1 "Very Richly Attyr'd In newe fashions." Woodstock as Lord Protector during the king's minority promises to remove these favorites, but instead the king dismisses Woodstock. At 3.2.1,404–1,405 in that earlier play, Woodstock says, "I would my death might end the miserye / my feare presageth to my wretched country." John of Gaunt echoes this speech at 2.1.67–68 of Shakespeare's work: "Ah, would the scandal vanish with my life, / How happy then were my ensuing death!"

Green in *Thomas of Woodstock* asks for and receives the right to collect the king's revenues in exchange for 7,000 pounds a month that he will give the king. Richard agrees to this farming out of his country and acknowledges that he thus becomes "A landlord to this warlike realm," that he has "Rent out our kingdome like a pelting [paltry] Farme / That erst was held, as fair as Babilon / The mayden conquerors to all the world" (4.1.1,887–1,890). Shakespeare's John of Gaunt declaims to Richard, "Landlord of England art thou now, not king" (2.1.113), and just before Richard enters, Gaunt laments to his brother York that

> This land of such dear souls, this dear dear land,
> Dear for her reputation through the world,
> Is now leas'd out—I die pronouncing it—
> Like to a tenement or pelting farm.
>
> (2.1.57–60)

Willoughby complains that Richard has extorted money through "blanks" (*Richard II,* 2.1.250)—that is, blank charters to which subjects were forced to sign their names; afterward, the king's officers turned these into debentures. *Woodstock* shows Richard's officers engaging in this practice.

While the poetry of *Thomas of Woodstock* is far beneath that of Shakespeare, the play employs much horticultural imagery that also appears in *Richard II.* Arundel blames the dukes for not purging the court of Richard's flatterers: "You all are princes of the royal blood / Yett like great oakes ye lett the Ivye growe / To eate your hartes out with his falce Imbraces" (*Woodstock,* 1.1.175–177). Richard refers to Gloucester's house as "the cave that keepes the tusked boar / That rootes up Englands vinards [vineyards] uncontrould" (ibid., 4.2.2,162–2,163). At the end of *Woodstock,* Lancaster and York order the execution of Richard's favorites "to purge faire Englands plessant feild / Of all those ranckorous weeds that choakt the grownds / & left hir pleasant meads like barron hills" (5.6.2,960–2,962). In *Richard II,* the Gardener similarly refers to the king's flatterers as weeds (3.4.50).

The most famous passage in *Richard II* is John of Gaunt's paean to England at 2.1.31–68. Samuel Taylor Coleridge called these lines "the most magnificent, and, at the same time, the truest eulogism of our native country that the English language can boast." Such patriotic effusions are common in English history plays of the period. Though none attain to the grandeur of Gaunt's great speech, his sentiments echo those of the Queen Mother's in George Peele's *The Famous Chronicle of King Edward the First* (1593):

> Illustrious England, ancient seat of kings,
> Where chivalry hath royaliz'd thy fame,

That sounding bravely through terrestrial vale,
Proclaiming conquests, spoils, victories,
Rings glorious echoes through the farthest
    world. (Read 118)

From these materials, and perhaps from three French manuscript sources (*La Chronique de la Traïson et Mort de Richart Deux Roy Dengleterre* [ca. 1412], Jean Le Beau's *Chronique de Richard II depuis l'an 1399* [1399], and Jean Créton's metrical *Histoire du Roy d'Angleterre Richard II* [early 15th century]), Shakespeare fashioned his historical tragedy. To these he added his poetical genius and his deep insight into the human condition to create a work that has lived on the page and on the stage for more than four centuries.

Date and Text of the Play

On December 7, 1595, Sir Edward Hoby wrote to Sir Robert Cecil, son of Queen Elizabeth's chief adviser,

> Sir, findinge that you wer not convenientlie to be at London to morrow night I am bold to send to knowe whether Teusdaie [December 9] may be anie more in your grace to visit poore Channon [Canon] rowe where as late as it shal please you a gate for your supper shal be open: & K. Richard present him selfe to your vewe. Pardon my boldness that ever love to be honored with your presence nether do I importune more then your occasions may willingly assent unto, in the meanetime & ever restinge At your command Edw. Hoby. (qtd. in Chambers 2: 320–321)

It is not clear whether Hoby, a collector of historical prints, was referring to a picture or a play, or even which Richard is intended. Still, the Shakespeare scholar E. K. Chambers includes this letter among references to performances of *Richard II*. As son-in-law to the Lord Chamberlain, patron of Shakespeare's theatrical company, Hoby could have arranged a private performance of the work, which probably was composed in 1595–96. Stylistically it resembles *King John* and *Romeo and Juliet,* works that also date from this period.

The play was first printed by Andrew Wise in quarto in 1597 (Q1), "as it hath beene publikely acted by the right Honourable the Lord Chamberlaine his Seruants." The work was entered in the Stationers' Register on August 29 that year and probably appeared in print shortly thereafter. Two more quartos followed in 1598 (Q2, Q3); Q4 appeared in 1608, Q5 in 1615. Each quarto was printed from the edition immediately preceding it, except that Q4, printed by William White for Matthew Law, for the first time includes the deposition scene (4.1.154–318), though in a form that suggests memorial reconstruction.

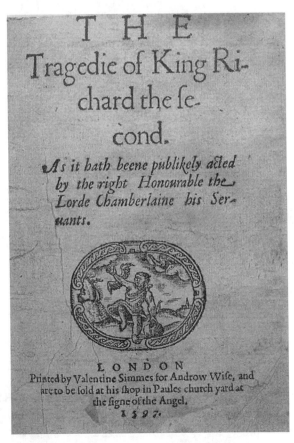

Title page of the first quarto edition of *Richard II,* published in 1597

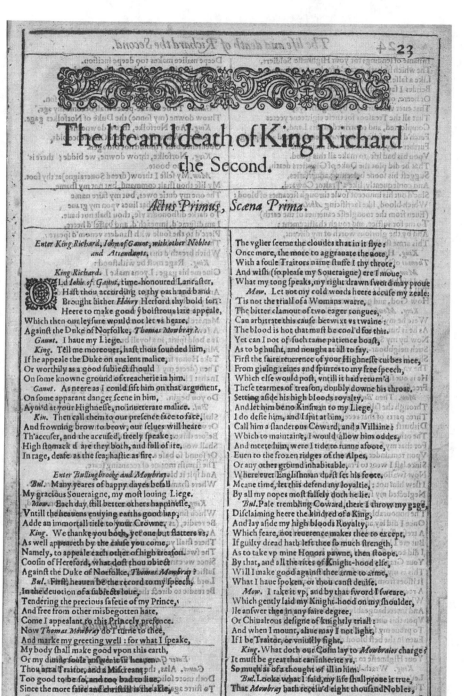

Title page of the First Folio edition of *Richard II*, published in 1623

The play was printed in the 1623 First Folio based on Q3, and perhaps Q5, collated with a prompt book. The Folio version provides an accurate version of the deposition scene and offers fuller stage directions than the earlier editions. A sixth quarto appeared in 1634, based on the text of the Second Folio (1632). Modern editions of the play essentially follow the act and scene divisions of the 1623 printing, except that 5.4 was included in the Folio's 5.3. Hence, the Folio's 5.4 has become the modern 5.5, and the Folio's 5.5 appears now as 5.6. (Citations below are from the *Riverside Shakespeare,* 2nd ed. Boston: Houghton Mifflin, 1996.)

SYNOPSIS
Brief Synopsis
The play covers the period April 1398 to February 1400. In 1398, Thomas Mowbray, duke of Norfolk, and Henry Bolingbroke, duke of Hereford, former political allies, quarreled. As the play opens, the two accuse each other of treason and challenge each other to trial by combat. Bolingbroke also blames Mowbray for the death of Thomas of Woodstock, duke of Gloucester, uncle to both King Richard and Bolingbroke, and for keeping for himself funds intended for the English soldiers stationed at Calais. The king, having failed to pacify them, sets a date for the duel, but when the two men meet for this encounter, Richard instead banishes them.

Richard faces a challenge from Irish rebels, who have killed his heir apparent, Roger, fourth earl of March, in a rebellion. To finance his Irish wars, Richard exacts money from his subjects and seizes the lands of the recently deceased John of Gaunt, duke of Lancaster, which Henry Bolingbroke should legally inherit.

As soon as Richard sails for Ireland, Bolingbroke comes back to England, ostensibly to claim his inheritance, though he may already have a more ambitious plan, since he brings with him an army of 3,000. By the time Richard returns to England, Bolingbroke has won over most of the nobility and has begun to act as ruler by executing Richard's political allies. Richard, without an army, announces that he will abdicate. Ever the opportunist, Bolingbroke seizes the throne, orders Richard to Pomfret Castle in Yorkshire, and sends Queen Isabella back to France. Richard's supporters launch various attempts to restore him, but in February 1400, the former king is killed. Though Henry wanted Richard dead, he feels guilty for the murder, banishes Richard's killer, and vows a pilgrimage to the Holy Land to atone for the killing.

Act I, Scene 1
The play opens at Windsor Castle in April 1398. Henry Hereford, also known as Bolingbroke (derived from his birthplace in Lincolnshire) and later still as King Henry IV, has, before the first scene, accused Thomas Mowbray, duke of Norfolk, of treason for his involvement in the death of Thomas of Woodstock, duke of Gloucester, uncle to both King Richard and Bolingbroke. Now, in front of Richard, Bolingbroke repeats this accusation, adds others, and challenges Mowbray to trial by combat. Mowbray accepts. The king tries to pacify them and enlists the aid of John of Gaunt (named for his birthplace, Ghent), duke of Lancaster, who is Bolingbroke's father. But the antagonists refuse to be reconciled. The scene ends with Richard's ordering them to meet in a trial by combat at Coventry "upon Saint Lambert's Day" (1.1.199)—September 17.

Act I, Scene 2
The scene shifts to the duke of Lancaster's palace in London, where John of Gaunt discusses the death of his brother Gloucester with Gloucester's widow. Gaunt's first speech responds to his sister-in-law's implied plea offstage for him to avenge Gloucester's murder. Both blame the king. Gaunt urges the duchess to leave vengeance to God, since Richard is God's regent on Earth.

Act I, Scene 3
At the tourney at Coventry, Mowbray and Bolingbroke again accuse each other of treason. Just as the two, having armed, prepare to fight, Richard stops the duel by throwing down his warder, or

King Richard presides over the tourney at Coventry in this 19th-century depiction of Act I, Scene 3 of *Richard II*. (Illustration by John Jellicoe)

baton, symbol of his office as judge of the trial by combat. Still seeking to avoid bloodshed, he banishes both men from England, Bolingbroke for a decade, a sentence quickly reduced to six years, and Mowbray forever.

Act I, Scene 4

In London, Richard, Green, Bagot, and Aumerle talk about Bolingbroke's departure from England. Richard comments disdainfully on Bolingbroke's courtesy to commoners, as though Bolingbroke regarded himself as next in line for the throne. The conversation then turns to the rebels in Ireland and Richard's need for money to finance the war against them, a war he will lead in person. When news arrives that John of Gaunt is dying, Richard regards the event as an opportunity to seize Gaunt's property to pay for the Irish campaign.

Act II, Scene 1

With his brother, the duke of York, Gaunt, dying at Ely House, awaits Richard's arrival to warn the king against continuing the ruinous financial and political course Richard has been pursuing. While Gaunt waits, he delivers his great paean to England, which, according to Gaunt, Richard has turned into "a tenement or pelting [paltry] farm" (2.1.60). When Richard arrives, Gaunt criticizes

the king's behavior. As York had predicted, Richard disregards Gaunt's warning. Before being carried off to his deathbed, Gaunt accuses Richard of killing Gloucester. Northumberland soon reenters to announce the death of Gaunt. Richard seizes Gaunt's property despite York's protests. After the king departs, Northumberland, Willoughby, and Ross remain to discuss the king's exactions against commoners and the nobility. The latter two see no hope for redress, but Northumberland informs them that Bolingbroke is on his way back to England with an army of 3,000 men. He will land as soon as Richard sails for Ireland. Willoughby and Ross agree to join Northumberland in defecting to Bolingbroke.

Act II, Scene 2

At Windsor Castle, Queen Isabella tells Bushy and Bagot that she misses Richard and fears impending misfortune. Bushy tries to reassure her. Green enters to confirm the queen's fears: He informs her that Bolingbroke has landed with his army at Ravenspurgh, and many of the nobility have thrown their support to him. York enters. Richard has left him as regent to guard the country, but his allegiance is torn between the rightful king, Richard, and his wronged nephew, Bolingbroke. Bushy and Green flee for what they regard as the safety of Bristol Castle, while Bagot sets off to join the king in Ireland.

Act II, Scene 3

Before Berkeley Castle, Gloucestershire, Bolingbroke and his supporters confront Berkeley and York. York reprimands Bolingbroke for returning to England against the king's orders and for raising an army against his sovereign. Bolingbroke insists that he has returned only to claim his rightful title as Duke of Lancaster and his properties that Richard expropriated illegally. York sympathizes with his nephew but says he would still oppose Bolingbroke if he could. Since his forces are too weak, York invites Bolingbroke to stay at Berkeley Castle; York at this time will "remain as neuter" (2.3.159)—that is, neutral. Bolingbroke declines the offer of hospitality. Instead, he leaves for Bristol to confront Bushy, Bagot, and their associates.

Act II, Scene 4

At a camp in Wales, the Earl of Salisbury tries to persuade a Welsh captain not to disband his army, which Richard needs to oppose Bolingbroke. The Captain replies that the soldiers believe the king is dead; they therefore will not remain even for a day.

Act III, Scene 1

At Bristol, Bolingbroke orders the execution of Bushy and Green

Act III, Scene 2

Richard returns to Wales from Ireland. He is initially confident that he will defeat Bolingbroke, but when Salisbury enters to announce that the Welsh army has disbanded, Richard despairs. His mood continues to fluctuate, but he gives up hope even before Scroop arrives to inform him that Wiltshire, Bushy, and Green are dead. When Carlisle and Aumerle urge Richard to appeal to York for help, Richard again becomes hopeful, but Scroop tells them that York, too, has gone over to Bolingbroke. Richard dismisses the few soldiers he still has and sets off for Flint Castle to "pine away" (3.2.209).

Act III, Scene 3

Bolingbroke and his army appear before Flint Castle. Bolingbroke instructs Northumberland to tell Richard that if the king revokes his sentence of banishment and returns Bolingbroke's lands, Bolingbroke will lay down his arms. Otherwise, he will fight. Richard, standing on the battlements above Bolingbroke, agrees to these conditions, then considers defiance. Finally, unbidden, he offers to abdicate. In a symbolic gesture, Richard descends from the top of the castle into "the base court" (3.3.176). When the king meets Bolingbroke face-to-face, the latter kneels in a sign of obedience, but again Richard says he is prepared to give up the throne.

Queen Isabella and her ladies in the garden in Act III, Scene 4 of *Richard II,* in this print published by Virtue & Company in the 19th century *(Painting by George Henry Boughton; engraving by Thomas Sherratt)*

Act III, Scene 4

In the Duke of York's garden at Langley, the queen and two of her ladies try to beguile the time. When a gardener and two of his assistants enter, the women withdraw to eavesdrop on the men's conversation. The gardener instructs his helpers to prop up the weak branches, prune those that have grown too vigorously, and remove the weeds choking the plants. The first assistant asks why they should cultivate this garden when England itself is left untended. The head gardener replies that Richard's flatterers, whom the gardener likens to weeds, have been killed, and the neglectful king himself is to be deposed. The queen emerges from hiding to chide the gardener for meddling in state affairs. He apologizes for his bad news but adds that if she goes to London, she will learn that he has spoken the truth. She and her attendants leave. The gardener, pitying her, says he will plant a bank of rue where one of her tears fell.

Act IV, Scene 1

At Westminster Hall, London, Bolingbroke investigates the murder of his uncle Gloucester. Bagot blames Aumerle for Gloucester's death. Aumerle then challenges Bagot to trial by combat. Fitzwater also accuses Aumerle and challenges him, as do Henry Percy and an unnamed lord. Surrey defends Aumerle and challenges Fitzwater. Fitzwater declares that Mowbray told him that Aumerle sent two men to execute Gloucester. Aumerle challenges the absent Mowbray. Bolingbroke orders Mowbray's repatriation, but the Bishop of Carlisle informs him that Mowbray is dead. Bolingbroke replies that he will assign dates for the various pending trials by combat.

York enters to tell Bolingbroke that Richard has agreed to abdicate. Bolingbroke now prepares to ascend the symbolically vacant throne, but the Bishop of Carlisle protests. He calls Bolingbroke a traitor and predicts civil war if Richard is deposed. Northumberland responds by arresting the bishop for treason.

Bolingbroke orders that Richard be brought forth to surrender his crown in public. Richard, as usual, vacillates before yielding. Northumberland tells Richard to read out a list of charges justifying his deposition. Richard evades this demand, and Bolingbroke at length withdraws it. Richard calls for a mirror to see how his misfortunes have changed him in appearance as he has changed in station. After gazing at his face, Richard flings the mirror to the ground, shattering the crystal. As the scene ends, Richard is to be taken to the Tower of London, Bolingbroke plans his own coronation, and the Abbot of Westminster, Carlisle, and Aumerle plot to restore Richard to the throne.

Act V, Scene 1
The queen awaits Richard's passage on his way to the Tower of London. She and Richard exchange tearful farewells. Northumberland enters to order Richard to Pomfret (Pontefract) Castle in Yorkshire and the queen to France. Richard echoes Carlisle's prediction of civil war between Northumberland and Bolingbroke, a prophecy fulfilled in the two parts of *Henry IV*. The scene ends with the separation of the royal couple.

Act V, Scene 2
At his palace, the Duke of York tells his wife how Bolingbroke was cheered and Richard abused as

they passed through London's streets. York's son enters. Formerly the Duke of Aumerle, he has been reduced by Bolingbroke to the rank of Earl of Rutland for his alleged role in the death of Gloucester. York discovers that Rutland is carrying a letter about a plot to assassinate Bolingbroke, now Henry IV, at Oxford and return Richard to the throne. Despite the duchess's protests, York sets off to warn the new king. She orders her son to go to Henry and beg forgiveness before York arrives. She will follow as quickly as possible to support her son.

Act V, Scene 3
At Windsor Castle, Henry IV asks about his prodigal son, Prince Hal. Rutland enters. He asks for and receives a private audience with the king and locks the door. York arrives and pounds on the door while warning Henry that Rutland is a traitor. Henry admits York, who gives the king his son's treasonous letter. The duchess joins the group. All three kneel before the king. York urges his son's execution, while Rutland seeks pardon and his mother pleads for him. Henry agrees to forgive Rutland but intends to execute the other conspirators.

Act V, Scene 4
At Windsor, Sir Pierce Exton tells his servants of his plan to kill Richard to please Henry. They set off for Pomfret Castle.

Act V, Scene 5
Alone at Pomfret, Richard soliloquizes about his situation. Exton and his servants enter. Richard slays two of his assailants before Exton kills the former king.

Act V, Scene 6
At Windsor Castle, Henry learns that civil war has erupted; rebels have destroyed Cirencester in Gloucershire. Northumberland, Fitzwater, and Percy report the executions of various plotters against Henry. Henry grants Carlisle his life but tells the bishop to spend it in a religious retreat. Exton enters with the news of Richard's death. When Henry condemns Exton's deed, Exton replies

that Henry said he wanted Richard dead. Henry concedes the point but still banishes Exton. As the play ends, Henry vows to undertake a pilgrimage to the Holy Land to expiate the sin of Richard's death.

CHARACTER LIST

King Richard the Second Richard came to throne at the age of 10 in 1377 and was deposed in 1399. Shakespeare presents Richard as a weak though legitimate ruler who refuses to heed good advice. He is also a poet.

John of Gaunt Duke of Lancaster, uncle of Richard and father of Bolingbroke, Gaunt tries to save Richard from himself. An embodiment of English virtues, Gaunt dies in Act II, Scene 1.

Edmund of Langley Duke of York, another of Richard's uncles, brother to John of Gaunt. Like his brother, he is loyal to Richard but recognizes the king's errors. Left behind to protect England when Richard goes to Ireland to fight rebels there, he initially tries to prevent Bolingbroke from seizing power. He soon shifts his allegiance, though, and devotes himself to the new ruler.

Henry Bolingbroke Son of John of Gaunt and cousin of Richard, initially he is Duke of Hereford. Later he becomes Duke of Lancaster and then King Henry IV. Ambitious and opportunistic, he says little. Unlike his royal cousin, he appeals to the populace and proves himself efficient.

Duke of Aumerle The son of the Duke of York, Aumerle remains loyal to Richard even after the king is deposed. He joins a plot to kill Henry IV, though when the conspiracy is discovered, he abandons his colleagues and begs the new king's forgiveness.

Thomas Mowbray The Duke of Norfolk was historically an opponent of Richard but turned loyalist. As governor of the castle at Calais, he bore some responsibility for the murder of Thomas of Woodstock, which occurred there. In the play, he dies in exile in Venice.

Duke of Surrey Supporter of Aumerle.

Earl of Salisbury A supporter of Richard II. He tries to keep the Welsh troops from dispersing before Richard returns from Ireland and later encourages Richard to resist Bolingbroke.

Lord Berkeley A supporter of Richard II.

Sir John Bushy One of the king's favorites; executed by Bolingbroke.

Sir John Bagot Another of Richard's favorites. In 4.1, he accuses Aumerle of involvement in the death of the Duke of Gloucester.

Sir Henry Green A supporter of Richard who is executed by Bolingbroke.

Earl of Northumberland An early supporter of Bolingbroke.

Henry Percy Also known as Hotspur, the son of Northumberland is another early adherent to Bolingbroke's cause.

Lord Ross Supporter of Bolingbroke.

Lord Willoughby Supporter of Bolingbroke.

Lord Fitzwater Supporter of Bolingbroke; one of Aumerle's many accusers in Act IV, Scene 1.

Bishop of Carlisle Loyal to Richard II.

Abbot of Westminster Supporter of Richard II, conspirator against Henry IV.

Lord Marshal Presides over the trial by combat between Mowbray and Bolingbroke in 1.3.

Sir Stephen Scroop Loyal to Richard II; in 3.2, he brings much bad news to the king.

Sir Pierce of Exton Slayer of Richard II, banished by Henry IV for his pains.

Captain of a Band of Welshmen Refuses to wait for Richard's return from Ireland (2.4).

Two Gardeners They discuss the political situation in 3.4.

Isabella Queen to Richard II.

Duchess of York Mother of Aumerle. She pleads for his life in 5.3 after his part in the plot against Henry IV is discovered.

Duchess of Gloucester The widow of Thomas of Woodstock; in 1.2, she urges her brother-in-law, John of Gaunt, to avenge her husband's death.

CHARACTER STUDIES
Richard II

When Richard first appears onstage in the opening scene, he seems to embody all the elements of kingship. Seated on his throne, he listens impartially to the accusations and counterattacks of the Dukes of Hereford and Norfolk. He tells the latter that though Bolingbroke (the Duke of Hereford) is cousin to the king, "Such neighbor nearness to our sacred blood / Should nothing privilege him nor partialize / The unstooping firmness of my upright soul" (1.1.119–121). He tries to reconcile the two dukes without bloodshed, ordering each in turn to reject the other's challenge. When neither does his bidding, he declares,

> We were born not to sue, but to command,
> Which since we cannot do to make you friends,
> Be ready, as your lives shall answer it,
> At Coventry upon Saint Lambert's Day.

By the end of this scene, Shakespeare has revealed the hollowness—*hollow* is a key word in the play—of Richard's kingship. Though born to command, he cannot: His nobles ignore his order to reconcile with each other. He claims to possess an "upright soul," but many in Shakespeare's audience would know from the same sources the playwright used that Richard had ordered the killing of his uncle Gloucester; those unfamiliar with this incident would learn of it in 1.2. Richard's speaking of his "sacred blood" exposes another flaw. He regards himself as God's agent on Earth. In the painting know as the Wilton Diptych, a young Richard is shown being presented to the Virgin Mary, who is surrounded by angels. After Bolingbroke returns to England at the head of an army, Richard comments, "For every man that Bolingbroke hath press'd / To lift shrewd steel against our golden crown / God for his Richard hath in heavenly pay / A glorious angel" (3.2.58–61). This speech may allude to the painting; the lines certainly show how deeply Richard believes in the divine right of kings.

This was orthodox Tudor doctrine. The 1571 *Homilie against Disobedience and Wilful Rebellion* asks, "What shall we then do to an evil, to an unkind Prince, an enemy to us, hated of God, hurtful to the Common-wealth?" The answer offered is: "Lay no violent hands upon him, saith good David, but let live until God appoint, and work his ends, either by natural death, or in war by lawful enemies, not by traitorous subjects." By 1595, history, and Shakespeare's earlier history plays, had shown that whatever the theoretical merits of this sentiment, it had been more honored in the breach than the observance. In the few years before *Richard II* was staged, theater audiences had seen depictions of the deposition of Edward II, Henry VI, and Richard III. Weak or tyrannical rulers had come to bad ends, and Shakespeare's Richard II unhappily combines both traits. These plays, and the history that underlies them, side with Peter Wentworth's sentiment in his *Pithie Exhortation to Her Maiestie for Establishing Her Successor* (1589), which states that a usurper who rules well is to be preferred over the legitimate ruler who endangers the state through "great misgovernment."

In 1.3, Richard, having ordered the trial by combat he cannot prevent, stops the duel before it begins. Samuel Daniel's *Civile Wars* claims that Richard stopped the fight because he feared that a Bolingbroke victory would make the duke more popular than ever. Banishing both men may have been sound policy at the moment, but as Shakespeare presents the event, Richard's action seems capricious. According to Edward Hall's account, after Richard interrupted the fight, he consulted with his council for two hours. In Shakespeare's play, Richard mentions that his decision was made with the advice of that council (1.3.124), and later in the scene, the king observes that John of Gaunt had concurred (1.3.233–235). Still, Richard gives the impression that he has acted as he has merely to seize the attention that has been directed at the combatants. Richard's has been a coup de théâtre by a theatrical ruler, a show king rather than the thing itself. In *Henry IV, Part 1*, 3.2.60–84, Bolingbroke, now Henry IV, tells his son, Prince Hal, how Richard repeatedly made himself a spectacle. By interrupting the trial by combat, Richard has also violated the laws of chivalry on which his kingship depends.

According to Henry IV, Richard "Enfeoff'd himself to popularity" (*Henry IV, Part 1*, 3.2.69). Yet

The commons hath he pill'd [stripped] with
  grievous taxes,
And quite lost their hearts; the nobles hath he
  fin'd
For ancient quarrels, and quite lost their
  hearts. (II.1.249–251)

Despite these exactions, Richard has "grown bankrupt" (2.1.257) through his extravagances and so must seize John of Gaunt's property to finance the Irish wars. York warns the king of the illegality of this action, which calls into question his own legitimacy, "for how art thou a king / But by fair sequence and succession?" (2.1.198–199). By denying Bolingbroke his rightful inheritance, York declares, "You pluck a thousand dangers on your head, / You lose a thousand well-disposed hearts" (2.1.205–206). Richard rejects this good counsel and persists in his illegal course, which will cost him his throne.

By the time Richard reappears an act later, in 3.2, England is in revolt. In his first long speech, Richard calls upon the land itself to repel the rebels. Carlisle and Aumerle urge the king to embrace less metaphysical aid; Richard replies that "heaven still guards the right" (3.2.62). Immediately, Salisbury enters with the news that the Welsh army has disbanded. Richard now shifts from excessive confidence to despair and urges his supporters to fly him for safety. Aumerle replies, "Comfort, my liege, remember who you are" (3.2.82). Once more, Richard's hopes soar, only to be dashed again by the bad news that Scroop brings. Throughout the scene, Richard's mood changes repeatedly, but in the end despair prevails. Circumstances are grim, but Richard revels in the role he has chosen. He chides Aumerle for trying to encourage him to resistance: "Beshrew thee, cousin, which didst lead me forth / Of that sweet way I was in to despair!" (3.2.204–205). He finds resignation more comfortable than opposition to Bolingbroke. When he thinks that Bushy, Bagot, and Green have deserted him—Scroop reports that they have been executed by Bolingbroke (though Bagot is alive in 4.1)—he likens them to Judases, implying that he himself is

King Richard between Bolingbroke and Mowbray in Act I, Scene 3 of *Richard II (Illustration by William Hatherell)*

in 1.4, the king contemptuously describes Bolingbroke as seeking the goodwill of the populace. Such courtesy to commoners will not strike modern audiences as a flaw, but even in Shakespeare's time, Richard's attitude was anachronistic. Machiavelli had observed in *The Prince* (1532) that no ruler can succeed without the goodwill of his subjects. Lord Burghley, Queen Elizabeth's chief adviser, urged his son Robert Cecil to "show much humility and some familiarity" to inferiors: "Yet do I advise thee not to affect nor neglect popularity too much." In *Fragmenta Regalia* (1641), Sir Robert Naunton described Elizabeth as "a Courtier of the people, yea of the Commons." She "stooped and declined lowe in presenting her person to the publique view as she passed in her Progresse and perambulations."

Rather than earning the love of his subjects, as Naunton writes that Elizabeth sought to do, Richard alienates them. As Ross states in the play,

Christ. He will cling to this role for much of the rest of the play, though his mind is too chameleonlike to stay steadfast to any one position for very long.

At Flint Castle, Bolingbroke and Richard meet. Bolingbroke asserts his allegiance to the king and asks only that his banishment be revoked and his lands restored. At first, Richard is again defiant, again asserts that "God omnipotent / Is mustering in his clouds on our behalf / Armies of pestilence" (3.3.85–87) to strike down the rebels' children, thus recalling the 10th and final plague that God visited upon the Egyptians in Exodus. Some 35 lines later, Richard accepts Bolingbroke's conditions, only to turn to Aumerle immediately thereafter and ask whether he should defy his cousin. Aumerle urges the king to buy time until he can oppose Bolingbroke effectively, but Richard instead resolves to abdicate. According to Holinshed's *Chronicles*, Richard was already virtually a prisoner in Flint Castle. Shakespeare changed his source to show Richard as self-dramatizing and despairing in giving up the crown before Bolingbroke asked—or compelled—him to do so.

York had commented shortly before that Richard still looks kingly and adds, "Alack, alack for woe, / That any harm should stain so fair a show" (3.2.70–71). These lines imply that Richard possesses the image of kingship but lacks the substance. Having for the moment decided to give up the throne, Richard dramatizes himself in a highly rhetorical speech. He uses language beautifully, and his poetry is as metaphysical as that of John Donne, who was beginning to write in the mid to late 1590s. After some 25 lines of highly polished verse, even Richard recognizes that he is merely spinning out words: "Well, well, I see I talk but idly, and you laugh at me" (3.3.170–171). This is one of the few moments in the play in which Richard exhibits a glimmer of self-knowledge, and it does not last. As he descends to the courtyard to meet Bolingbroke, he likens himself to Phaeton, son of Apollo, whose mismanagement of the chariot of the sun led to his death. Richard, in the play and, indeed, in the effigy on his tomb at Westminster Abbey, is associated with the sun. Yet just

as he is a show king rather than a true ruler, he is Phaeton rather than Apollo and has mishandled his office. As the scene ends, Richard again agrees to abdicate.

In the deposition scene itself, however, Richard again wavers. In his first speech in 4.1, he once more likens himself to Christ and compares his nobles, who have defected to Bolingbroke, as Judases. Though he lacks power to retain his crown, he seizes control of the scene as director and chief actor. "God save the King!" he proclaims (4.1.172). When no one responds, he adds, "amen" (4.1.173), playing, as he says, the roles of both priest and clerk.

Though he had said he would abdicate, he now holds the crown and forces Bolingbroke to seize it, giving visual confirmation of the usurpation. His language is again highly wrought as he develops the metaphysical conceit of the crown as a well, himself and Bolingbroke as twin buckets, one rising (Bolingbroke) as the other sinks, full of water (himself). "I thought you had been willing to resign" (4.1.190), Bolingbroke tersely responds, and 10 lines later, he again asks, "Are you contented to resign the crown?" Richard characteristically provides a wavering reply, "Ay, no, no, ay" (l. 201), and then launches into another highly wrought flight of rhetoric. Of the 160 lines in the abdication section of 4.1, Bolingbroke speaks 13, Richard 119. He steals the scene, and when Northumberland tries to make him read out a list of accusations against himself, he deftly avoids doing so by claiming his eyes are too filled with tears for him to see the writing.

Richard calls for a mirror to see how much he has changed in appearance since he has changed so much in station, and he launches into a speech echoing Faust's praise of Helen. Shakespeare is not merely paying tribute to Marlowe here. Faust's Helen is a spirit without substance, as Richard has been the image of kingship without the reality, a reflection of kingship only. Unlike Richard, Bolingbroke rarely indulges in metaphor—Richard calls him "silent king" (4.1.290)—but he makes a telling comment after Richard dashes the mirror to the ground and laments that "sorrow hath destroy'd my face" (4.1.291). Bolingbroke retorts, "The shadow of your sorrow hath destroy'd / The shadow of your face" (4.1.292–293). Richard has indeed been a king of shadows.

Richard accepts Bolingbroke's revision in a speech that anticipates Hamlet's response to Gertrude when she asks why he "seems" to take his father's death so personally. Hamlet says,

> Seems, madam? Nay, it is, I know not "seems."
> 'Tis not alone my inky cloak, good mother,
> Nor customary suits of solemn black,
> Nor windy suspiration of forc'd breath,
> No, nor the fruitful river of the eye,
> Nor the dejected havior of the visage,
> Together with all forms, moods, shapes of
>   grief,
> That can denote me truly. These indeed seem,
> For they are actions that a man might play,
> But I have that within that passes show,
> These but the trappings and the suits of woe.
>   (1.2.76–86)

Richard tells Bolingbroke,

> My grief lies all within,
> And these external manners of laments
> Are merely shadows to the unseen grief
> That swells with silence in the tortur'd soul.
>   (4.1.295–298)

As Richard's fortunes ebb, he begins to develop an interiority that makes him more sympathetic than he had been in the first two acts. Yet he is still consciously playing a part: As soon as he leaves the stage, the Abbot of Westminster, loyal to Richard, comments, "A woeful pageant have we here beheld" (4.1.321). Richard will remain self-absorbed until his death and will seek to be the cynosure of every scene. Nonetheless, beneath the beautiful plumage of his language, the audience comes to recognize and pity the dying bird.

Shakespeare took from Daniel's *Civile Wars* the invented scene of the parting of Richard and Isabella in London (5.1). This transformation of the playwright's source again exposes Richard's self-absorption. In Daniel's poem, Richard tries to cheer his queen, the center of his concern. In the play, Richard urges Isabella, "Tell thou the lamentable tale of me, / And send the hearers weeping to their beds" (5.1.44–45). He casts himself as the tragic hero of a fiction, the role he has played throughout the final three acts of the play.

Yet Richard also demonstrates a newfound grasp of political reality here when he tells Northumberland that his alliance with the new king will be short-lived. Henry IV will fear the earl; the earl will regard Henry as ungrateful no matter what the king grants him. The truth of this prediction is evidenced at the start of *Henry IV, Part 1*.

It is apt that Richard's final long speech is a soliloquy, for he has been trapped in his own imagination for the entire play. In another flight of metaphysical verse, he peoples his prison with his thoughts. "Thus play I in one person many people, / And none contented" (5.5.31–32). He is still the player king, still solipsistic, fittingly ending his life as a solitary man wrapped up in his imaginings. In this soliloquy, he likens himself to the figure that strikes the bell of a clock, a simulacrum—a show rather than reality. Only at the last, when he kills two of his assailants before dying, does he exhibit the lion-like quality of kingship that Isabella urged upon him at their parting.

The first printed version of the play bears the title *The Tragedie of King Richard the second*. Richard emerges as a tragic figure who brings about his own downfall. In his final scene, he even attains a measure of self-knowledge when he says, "I wasted time, and now doth time waste me" (5.5.49). As a king, he elicits no compassion, but as a man, he emerges as deeply sympathetic as well as deeply flawed.

Henry Bolingbroke

Bolingbroke is Richard's antagonist and antithesis, the ant to Richard's grasshopper. Richard's poetry is metaphysical, and in his speeches he creates an alternate reality that it is his tragedy to mistake for truth. Bolingbroke never deludes himself in that way. When Richard banishes Bolingbroke, his father, John of Gaunt, tries to console him: "Think not the King did banish thee, / But thou the King" (1.3.279–280). Gaunt adds that Bolingbroke can imagine that his father has sent him to the Continent to win honor, or that he is leaving England to escape the plague. Gaunt continues,

> Suppose the singing birds musicians,
> The grass whereon thou tread'st the presence strow'd,
> The flowers fair ladies, and thy steps no more
> Than a delightful measure or a dance.
> (1.3.288–291)

Ever the realist, Bolingbroke rejects such counsel:

> O, who can hold a fire in his hand
> By thinking on the frosty Caucasus?
> Or cloy the hungry edge of appetite
> By bare imagination of a feast?
> (1.3.294–297)

Bolingbroke is also an opportunist. When he returns from exile, he claims that he does so to secure the titles and property that Richard has wrongfully taken from him. Shakespeare subtly alters his sources to cast doubt on that claim. In 2.1, immediately after Richard seizes John of Gaunt's estate, Northumberland says that Bolingbroke already has assembled a fleet and army and intends to land as soon as Richard and his army embark for Ireland. Bolingbroke must therefore have made these preparations before Richard had denied him his inheritance. In Shakespeare's sources, Bolingbroke does not prepare to return until after Richard denies him his rightful inheritance. Also, Shakespeare chose the account claiming that Bolingbroke returned with an army rather than the version that states he came back alone. Richard's expropriation gives Bolingbroke the perfect pretext to justify his return, but Shakespeare's timing makes clear that the duke's thoughts are more ambitious.

The crowd cheers as "bareheaded" Bolingbroke, "upon a hot and fiery steed," enters London with Richard behind him, as described by the Duke of York in Act V, Scene 2 of *Richard II*. This is a print from the Boydell Shakespeare Gallery project, which was conceived in 1786 and lasted until 1805. *(Painting by James Northcote; engraving by Robert Thew)*

Bolingbroke's playing to the crowds as he was leaving England also reveals his royal longings. Richard had noted that Bolingbroke had acted "As were our England in reversion his, / And he our subjects' next degree in hope" (1.4.35–36). He flatters Northumberland and Percy, and when York condemns his unlawful return, Bolingbroke, who had first appealed to him as his uncle, calls him his father. Bolingbroke thus shows that he knows how and when to cajole, but he also recognizes that words alone cannot win him his rights, let alone the throne. York yields not to his nephew's good words but to Bolingbroke's larger army. Again, Shakespeare has altered the historical accounts he read to demonstrate Bolingbroke's understanding of the need for power, that might makes right rather than the reverse. As he tells Richard in 3.3, if the king will not grant his wishes, "I'll use the advantage of my power" (3.3.42).

Bolingbroke's willingness to manipulate language to his advantage is evident in his condemnation of Bushy and Green in 3.1. He accuses them, inter alia, of separating the king from his queen and thus drawing tears from the queen's eyes. In 5.1, once Bolingbroke has gained power, he really does separate Richard from Isabella, sending her back to France, Richard to imprisonment in Yorkshire. He also claims that he exiles them to reform the realm, but he devotes only three lines of his accusation to their misleading the king, a dozen to their offenses against Bolingbroke personally.

For all his self-absorption, Richard recognizes the iron fist that lies beneath Bolingbroke's velvet glove. When Bolingbroke says to him at Flint Castle, "So far be mine, my most redoubted lord, / As my true service shall deserve your love" (198–199), Richard replies, "[T]hey well deserve to have / that know the strong'st and surest way to get" (3.3.200–201). Richard understands that at this point, he is Bolingbroke's prisoner, not his king any longer, because Bolingbroke has the power and the willingness to use it. As Richard says, "[W]e must do what force will have us do" (3.3.207).

As long as Bolingbroke remains the wronged party seeking justice, he retains the sympathy of the audience. Even when he executes some of Richard's favorites, his actions may appear as an attempt to reform the realm, though his chief charge against Bushy and Green is personal, not political. At Flint Castle, however, his ambition manifests itself, and as he gains power, he loses something of his humanity. Richard is right when he warns Northumberland that Bolingbroke will turn on him, as he will on other former allies. "The love of wicked men converts to fear, / That fear to hate, and hate turns one or both / To worthy [merited] danger and deserved death," Richard says (5.1.66–68). The two *Henry IV* plays will show how Bolingbroke as king destroys those who helped him to power and whom he had professed to love. Too late, they will discover that Bolingbroke is, as Henry Hotspur calls him, a "vile politician" (*Henry IV, Part 1*, 1.3.241).

Having deposed Richard, Bolingbroke orders the former king to Pomfret Castle, the queen to France. Isabella asks that both be exiled, to which Northumberland replies, "That were some love, but little policy" (5.1.81). Whatever professions of love or duty Bolingbroke may offer, his guiding

principle remains the politically expedient. Learning of the plot against him in 5.2, Bolingbroke pardons Aumerle and spares the life of the Bishop of Carlisle. He will execute the other conspirators, though. Although he will not order the execution of Richard, he asks aloud, "Have I no friend to rid me of this living fear?" (5.4.2). Sir Pierce Exton understands Henry IV's desire to have Richard killed. Then, having achieved his goal of ridding himself of Richard, Henry IV denounces Exton. A true Machiavellian, he uses others and then discards them as scapegoats when he no longer needs them. He will serve other of his supporters, including Northumberland and Hotspur, similarly. The new king claims that he regrets the killing of Richard, and to expunge his guilt, he vows to make a pilgrimage to the Holy Land, a vow that remains unkept.

John of Gaunt, Duke of Lancaster

In the play's opening line, Richard addresses his uncle as "Old John of Gaunt, time-honored Lancaster" (1.1.1). Gaunt is indeed old: he was 58 in 1398, and he dies in 2.1. More significantly, his values are old. Even though he knows that Richard is ruling badly and has ordered the death of Gaunt's brother, Gloucester, he refuses to act against Richard. He tells his sister-in-law, Gloucester's widow, that Richard is God's anointed and therefore only God can punish him.

Like Richard, then, Gaunt believes in the divine right of kings even when they govern wrongly. He also shares with his king the sense that language corresponds to reality, a view, as noted above, that the realist Bolingbroke does not share. At the same time, he recognizes the limitations of words. He tells the king, "Thy word is current with him [time] for my death, / But dead, thy kingdom cannot buy my breath" (1.3.231–232). The king ignores this truth about how far the writ of his words extends, as he ignores Gaunt's warning in 2.1 that Richard has yielded to flatterers and is destroying England. A true patriot, Gaunt would give his life to save king and country. It is fitting that Shakespeare gives him the greatest encomium to England ever penned. Such selflessness is out of fashion in the world of the play, though, and Gaunt's death early in the work reflects the loss of the values he embodies.

Edmund of Langley, Duke of York

York shares his brother's concern for the king's welfare. He urges Gaunt to "deal mildly with his youth" (2.1.69), though Richard is already over 30 when the play opens. Still, compared to York and Gaunt, he is relatively young. York is less optimistic than Gaunt that the king will listen to good advice, but he cannot refrain from offering some any more than Gaunt could. York, another embodiment of old values, warns the king that seizing Gaunt's property will prove disastrous: "You pluck a thousand dangers on your head, / You lose a thousand well-disposed hearts" (2.1.205–206). York is the last survivor of the world of Edward III, a golden age for England. He explicitly links himself to that world when he confronts his nephew in 2.3:

> Were I but now lord of such hot youth
> As when brave Gaunt, thy father, and myself
> Rescued the Black Prince, that young Mars of
>   men,
> From forth the ranks of many thousand
>   French,
> O then how quickly should this arm of mine,
> Now prisoner to the palsy, chastise thee,
> And minister correction to thy fault!
>   (2.3.99–105)

He would like to restore to England the power and good government it then enjoyed (and that Shakespeare may already have dramatized in *Edward III*). The young king, however, will not heed his uncle's warning.

Richard does, however, appoint him regent when the king goes to Ireland, and York, despite his recognition that Richard has governed badly, musters such forces as he can to oppose his nephew Bolingbroke's invasion. He even sends a servant to get a thousand pounds of his own money to pay the soldiers and to gather for them such armor as he owns.

York is one of the few characters not taken in by Bolingbroke's fine words. When the two meet near Berkeley Castle, Bolingbroke kneels to him, as later he kneels to Richard just before taking him prisoner. York tells his nephew, "Show me thy humble heart, and not thy knee, / Whose duty is deceivable and false" (2.3.83–84), as indeed it is. To Bolingbroke's flattering appeal of "My gracious uncle," York retorts, "Grace me no grace, nor uncle me no uncle. / I am no traitor's uncle, and that word 'grace' / In an ungracious mouth is but profane" (2.3.87–89). All the appeals of Bolingbroke and his supporters do not change York's view that his nephew and his adherents are rebels. He would arrest them all if he could. Since he lacks a large enough army to do so, he yields to necessity and remains neutral, though Scroop later reports that York has "join'd with Bolingbroke" (3.2.200) and surrendered all the king's northern castles.

York still hopes to keep Richard on the throne, though. When Northumberland refers to the king as plain "Richard" without a title (3.3.6), recognizing the reality that Richard no longer has any authority, York chides the earl: "It would beseem the Lord Northumberland / To say King Richard" (3.3.7–8). York still insists that Richard receive the respect a monarch deserves. Bolingbroke tries to gloss over Northumberland's reference, but again York is not fooled by his nephew's words. He warns Bolingbroke that "the heavens are over our heads" (3.3.17) and watching over the anointed ruler. When Richard appears atop the walls of Flint Castle, York remarks on Richard's kingly appearance and laments that any harm should befall him.

York's tearful account of Richard's humiliation in London shows how deeply the duke still sympathizes with the deposed monarch, and he still refers to Richard's "sacred head" (5.2.30). Like his brother Gaunt, though, he yields to what he sees as God's will. Gaunt would not avenge his brother's death, leaving punishment to God. York sees the hand of heaven in Richard's downfall and has sworn allegiance to the new king. Having done so, he will remain as loyal to him as he had been to Richard. Thus, when he learns of his son's role in the plot against Henry IV, he rushes to expose the young man and even urges the king to execute him. Such disinterested loyalty is out of fashion in the new world of Henry IV. The play does not indicate what becomes of York, but he has no part in the remaining plays of the second Henriad; the Duke of York in *Henry V* is a different character.

Henry Percy, Earl of Northumberland

Northumberland is Bolingbroke's chief supporter. He incites Ross and Willoughby to rebellion, telling them, after Richard seizes Gaunt's property,

> Now, afore God, 'tis shame such wrongs are
>   borne
> In him, a royal prince, and many moe
> Of noble blood in this declining land.
> The King is not himself, but basely led
> By flatterers, and what they will inform,
> Merely in hate, 'gainst any of us all,
> That will the King severely prosecute
> 'Gainst us, our lives, our children, and our
>   heirs.
>
> (2.1.238–245)

He has been conspiring with Bolingbroke even before Richard appropriated Gaunt's estate, as is evident from his knowledge that Bolingbroke has mustered an army and navy and is preparing to invade England as soon as Richard takes his own army to Ireland.

When Bolingbroke and Northumberland meet in Gloucestershire, the latter flatters the man Richard aptly calls the "silent king," remarking,

> These high wild hills and rough uneven ways
> Draws out our miles and makes them
>   wearisome,
> And yet your fair discourse hath been as sugar,
> Making the hard way sweet and delectable.
>
> (2.3.4–7)

He defends Bolingbroke against York's charge of treason, claiming that "The noble Duke hath been too much abused" (2.3.37).

Shakespeare omitted Northumberland's betrayal of Richard by luring him to Flint Castle, which historically was already occupied by troops loyal to Bolingbroke. However, Northumberland is the first to dethrone Richard linguistically when he refers to him as plain "Richard" without any prefix. When York rebukes him, Northumberland shows some of Bolingbroke's skill at manipulating language by claiming that he omitted the word *king* only for the sake of brevity (3.3.10–11). He serves as Bolingbroke's messenger to Richard at Flint Castle, repeating the claim that Bolingbroke seeks only his rights as duke of Lancaster and confirms his belief in the duke's claims. In the deposition scene, he arrests the Bishop of Carlisle for speaking against Bolingbroke's usurpation, and he acts as Bolingbroke's agent in dispatching Richard to Pomfret Castle. When he last appears in the play, he is still a devoted flatterer of Henry IV, wishing "all happiness" to Bolingbroke's "sacred state" (5.6.6). In the first act of *Henry IV, Part 1*, however, he confirms Richard's prophecy that, having been instrumental in securing the crown for Bolingbroke, Northumberland will always feel under-rewarded and so seek more.

Hotspur (Henry Percy)

The son of Northumberland, Hotspur in *Richard II* provides intimations of his fiery nature and absent-mindedness, which is much more evident in *Henry IV, Part 1*. When his father chides him for ignoring Bolingbroke, asking, "Have you forgot the Duke of Hereford, boy?" Percy replies that he has no memory of ever meeting the man (2.3.36–39). Once introduced, he offers his youthful service, which he loyally provides. Historically, Hotspur was three years older than Bolingbroke. Shakespeare portrays him as a young man to make him the contemporary and foil of Prince Hal, Bolingbroke's son.

Duke of Aumerle

The son of the Duke of York, Aumerle supports and flatters Richard, and after Richard is deposed, he joins a conspiracy to restore the deposed monarch. His chief devotion, however, is to himself. After Mowbray and Bolingbroke are banished, he feigns fondness for both. He urges Mowbray to write to him from the Continent, but he also escorts Bolingbroke on his way. He tells Richard that he does not say "Farewell" to Bolingbroke, pretending that he is so overcome with emotion that he cannot speak (1.4.11–19).

When Richard returns from Ireland, Aumerle tries unsuccessfully to rally the king to action. According to Holinshed, Aumerle had persuaded Richard to stay in Ireland longer than the king should have; as a result, the Welsh army awaiting Richard's return disbanded, so Aumerle's bad advice may have cost Richard his throne and his life. Shakespeare omits this detail, making him a better councilor. In 4.1, he denies any responsibility for the death of the Duke of Gloucester, instead blaming Mowbray, once his ally. Shakespeare does not note that Richard gave Aumerle much of the dead Gloucester's property and made him Duke of Albemarle (Aumerle), but in the play, Bolingbroke demotes him to Earl of Rutland for his suspected role in Gloucester's death (5.2.43).

When York discovers his son's role in the conspiracy against Henry IV and threatens to expose him, Aumerle hastens to the new king to admit his guilt, plead for forgiveness, and expose his coconspirators. Bolingbroke pardons him, and he lives to become Duke of York in *Henry V*.

Thomas Mowbray, Duke of Norfolk

Although historically Mowbray had been Bolingbroke's political ally, he first appears in the play as Bolingbroke's antagonist. As governor of the English fortress at Calais, he is guilty, as Bolingbroke charges, of complicity in the death of Gloucester, though he never admits his role in the killing. He also protects Richard by never disclosing the king's responsibility for Gloucester's murder. He serves as another exemplar of the vanishing old order of idealistic knighthood invoked by Gaunt in his paean to England in 2.1. There Gaunt speaks of English kings

Renowned for their deeds as far from home,
For Christian service and true chivalry,

As is the sepulcher in stubborn Jewry
Of the world's ransom, blessed Mary's son.
                                        (2.1.53–56)

In 4.1, the Bishop of Carlisle reports that Mowbray died after serving in various crusades. (Mowbray in fact did not serve in any.) As with the death of Gaunt, Mowbray's demise signals the demise of the old order.

Sir John Bushy, Sir John Bagot, Sir Henry Green

These unfortunately named historical figures appear in the play rather like Rosencrantz and Guildenstern in *Hamlet* as essentially indistinguishable favorites and flatterers of Richard. In 2.2, Bushy seeks to console the queen, who is lamenting Richard's absence. His language here resembles that of Richard in its metaphysical imagery, as he likens the effect of tears to the distortion of a painting meant to be glanced sideways. Bushy and Green are executed by Bolingbroke in 3.1. In 3.2, Scroop reports the death of Bagot as well, but he appears in 4.1 to accuse Aumerle, a former ally, of complicity in the death of Gloucester. He then vanishes from the play. Shakespeare diminished their roles from what he found in his sources, thus emphasizing Richard's responsibility for his own bad decisions.

Bishop of Carlisle

A supporter of Richard, he urges the king to action when Richard despairs after returning from Ireland. He is one of the few to remain loyal to Richard throughout the play, and he is the only character to object to Bolingbroke's seizing the throne in 4.1, correctly predicting civil war if Richard is deposed. In his speech, he articulates the view of Richard, Gaunt, and York that Richard as king is "the figure of God's majesty" on Earth (4.1.125). After Bolingbroke becomes king, Carlisle joins the plot against him and is banished to a monastery at the end of the play. Henry IV spares his life in recognition of Carlisle's "High sparks of honor" (5.6.29).

Sir Pierce of Exton

Sir Pierce embodies the opportunism of Boling-broke and the new king's world. Seeking to curry favor with the new ruler, he seizes on Henry IV's expressed wish for Richard's death, goes to Pomfret Castle with his servants, and murders the deposed ruler. Immediately, he suspects that he has acted wrongly, but he takes Richard's body from Pomfret Castle to Windsor to present to Henry. For his pains, he is banished.

Isabella

Historically, Isabella was 10 years old when the events of the play occur. Shakespeare, following Samuel Daniel's *Civile Wars,* made her an adult so she could demonstrate more powerful emotions. She provides a different perspective on Richard,

Queen Isabella (Lily Brayton) and her attendants in Act III, Scene 4 of an early 20th-century production of *Richard II,* in this photograph published by Virtue & Company *(Photographed by J. & L. Caswall Smith)*

calling him "sweet" (2.2.9) immediately after he has illegally seized the dead Gaunt's property. In the three scenes in which she appears (2.2, 3.4, 5.1), she expresses her love for her husband. In 5.1, she tries to cheer him, and she asks Northumberland to banish them both so they can remain together. Her grief and bereavement render Richard more sympathetic, and they show the human cost of Bolingbroke's usurpation.

Duchess of Gloucester, Duchess of York

These two characters, who never appear onstage together, may have been played by the same actor, who may also have played Isabella, since she is never on stage with either of the duchesses. Like Isabella, these women concern themselves with the private rather than the public world of the play. Their focus is on family. Thus, Gloucester's widow urges her brother-in-law Gaunt to avenge her husband's death. Gaunt refuses. The Duchess of York more successfully pleads for her son's life while her husband urges his death for treason. Like Isabella, the duchesses illustrate the human costs of male-dominated politics. The Duchess of Gloucester dies of grief (2.2.97). Her sister-in-law survives, but her pleas for her son are ignored by her husband, just as Gaunt ignored the Duchess of Gloucester's desire to avenge her dead husband.

None of the women in this play, or, indeed, in the second tetralogy, wield power. The domestic world is pushed aside, as is evidenced by the small roles the women play. Hotspur sums up the world of the second tetralogy when he tells his wife in *Henry IV, Part 1,* "This is no world / To play with mammets [dolls, toy or human] and to tilt with lips. / We must have bloody noses and crack'd crowns, / And pass them current too" (2.3.91–94).

DIFFICULTIES OF THE PLAY

Richard II is a history play, but students should keep in mind that, to write it, Shakespeare had to draw on the histories available at the time. Therefore, a modern history of Richard II, such as Nigel Saul's 1997 edition, will be useful but will not reflect Shakespeare's story as much as Raphael Holinshed's *Chronicles* and other 16th-century accounts of Richard's reign. These provide a clearer sense of the play's antecedents.

Shakespeare's selective use of these sources can also be puzzling. In some instances, he selected from varying versions (e.g., Bolingbroke's return to England). In others, he changed what he found to suit his dramatic purposes (e.g., Northumberland's tricking Richard to go to Flint Castle). An awareness of these changes will help students evaluate how Shakespeare intended his audiences to understand characters, themes, and action.

Nonetheless, while such background knowledge is useful, it is not essential. *Macbeth* and *King Lear* derive from the same primary source—Holinshed—as *Richard II*. Since these first two plays are labeled tragedies, students are more willing to examine them as independent works. *Richard II* is similarly accessible on its own terms. When it first appeared on the stage of the Curtain or the Rose in 1595 or 1596, the events it depicts were 200 years in the past. Some in the audience, such as members of the Inns of Court, would have been familiar with the story. Some would have seen *Thomas of Woodstock,* a probable source for Shakespeare's work. Many in the audience, though, would have been illiterate and ignorant of the history on which Shakespeare drew.

Shakespeare does not require any prior knowledge for an appreciation of *Richard II*. Everything that the audience needs to know, Shakespeare provides. As The French philosopher Michel Foucault remarked, "Il n'y a pas hors de texte"—there is nothing outside the text. It is also important to remember that Shakespeare may be writing a history, though the earliest printed versions of the play refer to *Richard II* as a tragedy, as does Francis Meres in *Palladis Tamia* (1598)—but he is not writing history. The events in the play unfold over a period of two years, yet they seem to follow each other in close succession. Compression creates intensity, an essential ingredient in drama. Shakespeare also has shaped the characters, through the speeches he invented for them, for his own dramatic purposes. The Richard of this play, the Bolingbroke, and the John of Gaunt bear the names of historical figures. Their characters, however, are the creation of the dramatist. Like many movies, this play could carry the epigraph "Based on the true story."

More challenging, and more important, than correlating events in the play to the historical record is discerning Shakespeare's vision of history as reflected in the work. Does he subscribe to the Lancastrian myth that Richard was a bad ruler who needed to be deposed for the good of the country? John of Gaunt, though he accepts the view that only God can punish a king, foresees Richard's deposition. From *A Myrroure for Magistrates* (1559) to William Warner's *The Second Part of Albion's England* (1589), 16th-century writers criticized Richard's actions. Peter Wentworth's *Pithie Exhortation to Her Maiestie for Establishing Her Successor* (1589) argued that a usurper who governs well is better than a rightful king who endangers the state through "great misgovernment." Ross, Willoughby, and Northumberland in Act II, Scene 1 justify their rebellion by highlighting Richard's dangerous behavior at home and his concessions to the French abroad.

Yet Shakespeare's plays epitomize what the Russian philosopher and literary critic Mikhail Bakhtin calls "dialogism," the presentation of multiple viewpoints. The Bishop of Carlisle and Richard predict that Bolingbroke's usurpation of the throne will result in civil war, as indeed happens. Are these civil wars in the *Henry IV* plays and the Wars of the Roses depicted in Shakespeare's earlier tetralogy divine retribution for rebellion against God's anointed ruler? Are they the consequence of the all-too-human lust for power? If Henry IV and his grandson (Henry VI) had governed better, would these wars have been avoided? In other terms, does Shakespeare posit a providential world in which rebels are punished for disturbing the divinely ordained order? Or is history secular, with events determined solely by human action?

Another, related, question concerns Shakespeare's attitude toward the old order and the new. Whatever Richard's faults may be, his is a poetic, chivalric world in which even the gardener speaks in verse. When Mowbray and Bolingbroke challenge each other in 1.1, they do so formally, ritualistically. In 4.1, after Richard has effectively been deposed and Bolingbroke rules, the challenges multiply so thickly that the scene descends to parody. Similarly, when the Duke and Duchess of York plead before Henry IV, the king remarks, "Our scene is alt'red from a serious thing, / And now is chang'd to 'The Beggar and the King'" (5.3.79–80). Falstaff's catechism concerning honor in *Henry IV, Part 1,* 5.1.127–141 reflects the values of Bolingbroke's regime. England under Henry IV is a more practical but also more prosaic country, prosaic both literarily and figuratively.

Shakespeare's language may also seem difficult initially. Shakespeare wrote in Early Modern English and, moreover, in highly metaphoric language. Richard refers to Mowbray and Bolingbroke as "high-stomached" (1.1.18)—that is, proud. Mowbray says he would confront Bolingbroke "were I tied to run afoot / Even to the frozen ridges of the Alps" (1.1.63), using *tied* to mean compelled. Bolingbroke calls his glove, or "gage," his "honor's pawn"—that is, pledge (1.1.74). Almost every modern edition of the play will provide notes that gloss such terms. Students should also consult the *Oxford English Dictionary,* which traces the historical meanings of words; they may enjoy working out the origins of various words and phrases. The play's language is artificial. No one at the time really spoke as Shakespeare's characters did. It is also beautiful. Terms such as "neighbor nearness" (1.1.119) and "Wrath-kindled gentlemen" (1.1.152) create images that plainer language cannot. One must read Shakespeare slowly and thoughtfully, but the effort will be richly rewarded.

KEY PASSAGES
Act II, Scene 1, 31–68

JOHN OF GAUNT. Methinks I am a prophet new inspir'd,
And thus expiring do foretell of him:
His rash fierce blaze of riot cannot last,
For violent fires soon burn out themselves;
Small show'rs last long, but sudden storms are
short;
He tires betimes that spurs too fast betimes;
With eager feeding food doth choke the
feeder;
Light vanity, insatiate cormorant,
Consuming means, soon preys upon itself.
This royal throne of kings, this sceptred isle,
This earth of majesty, this seat of Mars,
This other Eden, demi-paradise,
This fortress built by Nature for herself
Against infection and the hand of war,
This happy breed of men, this little world,
This precious stone set in a silver sea,
Which serves it in the office of a wall,
Or as a moat defensive to a house,
Against the envy of less happier lands;
This blessed plot, this earth, this realm, this
England,
This nurse, this teeming womb of royal kings,
Fear'd by their breed, and famous by their
birth,
Renowned for their deeds as far from home,
For Christian service and true chivalry,
As is the sepulchre in stubborn Jewry
Of the world's ransom, blessed Mary's Son;
This land of such dear souls, this dear dear
land,
Dear for her reputation through the world,
Is now leas'd out—I die pronouncing it—
Like to a tenement or pelting farm.
England, bound in with the triumphant sea,
Whose rocky shore beats back the envious
siege
Of wat'ry Neptune, is now bound in with
shame,
With inky blots and rotten parchment bonds;
That England, that was wont to conquer others,
Hath made a shameful conquest of itself.
Ah, would the scandal vanish with my life,
How happy then were my ensuing death.

This is the most famous speech in the play. Many who have never read *Richard II* will recognize John of Gaunt's praise of England. These sentiments reveal Gaunt's true patriotism, as distinct from Bolingbroke's seeming concern for the realm. As Gaunt says at the end of the speech, he would give his life for England. He looks back on a golden, idealistic age that has passed. This is the world to which he and his belief belong. That world is dead, and he is about to die.

This speech thus illuminates the character of John of Gaunt while also setting forth the plight of England. Richard's poor government has ruined the country. Gaunt rightly foresees that if the king does not alter his course, he will destroy himself. Gaunt casts himself in the mold of the biblical prophets who warned Israel to repent or meet destruction. Richard will, as Gaunt predicts, lose his throne because of his refusal to act as a good ruler.

The imagery of this speech encapsulates Richard's fall. Gaunt begins by linking Richard to fire, an equation made elsewhere in the play as well. Fire, one of the four elements of the Elizabethan periodic table, purifies and ascends. Gaunt then likens Richard to rain, or water, another of the four elements. Unlike fire, water descends; it is also less pure than fire. In shifting the imagery linked to Richard, Gaunt shows the king's decline. The metaphor of the self-consuming cormorant also foreshadows Richard's self-destruction.

In describing England, Gaunt also uses the image of the garden, specifically the Garden of Eden. This is another trope that pervades the play. Under Richard, England has become a lost Eden, a fallen world in need of redemption. The references to the Holy Sepulcher and to the crusades reinforce the imagery of salvation. Richard likes to compare himself to Christ, but the king has proved to be a destroyer rather than a redeemer. At the end of *Richard II*, Bolingbroke, now Henry IV, promises to undertake a pilgrimage to the Holy Land (changed at the beginning of *Henry IV, Part 1* to an armed pilgrimage, i.e., a crusade), but he never fulfills that pledge because he, too, will not redeem England from the chaos that bad rule has created. The role of England's redeemer will be left to Henry V.

Act III, Scene 2, 143–177

AUMERLE. Where is the Duke my father
  with his power?

KING RICHARD. No matter where—of
  comfort no man speak:
Let's talk of graves, of worms, of epitaphs,
Make dust our paper, and with rainy eyes
Write sorrow on the bosom of the earth.
Let's choose executioners and talk of wills;
And yet not so, for what can we bequeath
Save our deposed bodies to the ground?
Our lands, our lives, and all are Bolingbroke's,
And nothing can we call our own but death,
And that small model of the barren earth
Which serves as paste and cover to our bones.
For God's sake let us sit upon the ground
And tell sad stories of the death of kings:
How some have been depos'd, some slain in war,
Some haunted by the ghosts they have
  deposed,
Some poisoned by their wives, some sleeping
  kill'd,
All murthered—for within the hollow crown
That rounds the mortal temples of a king
Keeps Death his court, and there the antic sits,
Scoffing his state and grinning at his pomp,
Allowing him a breath, a little scene,
To monarchize, be fear'd, and kill with looks,
Infusing him with self and vain conceit,
As if this flesh which walls about our life
Were brass impregnable; and humor'd thus,
Comes at the last and with a little pin
Bores through his castle wall, and farewell king!
Cover your heads, and mock not flesh and
  blood
With solemn reverence, throw away respect,
Tradition, form, and ceremonious duty,
For you have but mistook me all this while.
I live with bread like you, feel want,
Taste grief, need friends: subjected thus,
How can you say to me I am a king?

Throughout this scene, as throughout the play, Richard vacillates between hope and despair. Having learned of the deaths of his favorites at the hand of Bolingbroke at Bristol, Richard abandons hope; he begins his speech by saying that he does not care where the Duke of York and his army are, even though these forces would, if loyal to the king, allow Richard to fight and perhaps defeat Bolingbroke.

Richard then launches into an elaborate lament embellished with metaphysical conceits and hyperbole. Even though Richard does not yet know Bolingbroke's intent, the king already imagines himself deposed. Assuming that he will be both deposed and killed (as, indeed, he will be), he envisions himself the subject of a tragic tale; perhaps Shakespeare has in mind *A Myrroure for Magistrates,* in which Richard's ghost appears. His desire to be the focus of a sad story belies his seeming sense that death is all that anyone finally can claim as his own.

Similarly, his distinction between kingship and mortality indicates his lack of self-knowledge, making his speech a plea for sympathy from his audience rather than an epiphany. This speech looks ahead to Lear's understanding that "unaccommodated man is no more but . . . a poor, bare, fork'd animal" (*King Lear* 3.4.106–108), that his hand smells of mortality (4.6.133), that he is not ague-proof (4.6.105). Whereas for Lear such reflections signal his transformation, Richard's sense of himself as God's agent on Earth remains. In the next scene, he will declare to Bolingbroke, "my master, God omnipotent, / Is mustering in his clouds on our behalf / Armies of pestilence, and they shall strike / Your children yet unborn and unbegot" (3.3.85–88). At least part of Richard's tragedy is his inability to learn. Yet his speeches are filled with beautiful imagery, such as that of death's keeping his court in the king's crown. Richard may be thinking of depictions of the Dance of Death. Such macabre scenes are fittingly medieval in a play about the shift from an older to a newer conception of monarchy.

Act III, Scene 3, 143–170

KING RICHARD: What must the King do now? Must he submit?

The King shall do it. Must he be depos'd?
The King shall be contented. Must he lose
The name of king? a' God's name let it go.
I'll give my jewels for a set of beads,
My gorgeous palace for a hermitage,
My gay apparel for an almsman's gown,
My figur'd goblets for a dish of wood,
My scepter for a palmer's walking staff,
My subjects for a pair of carved saints,
And my large kingdom for a little grave,
A little little grave, an obscure grave—
Or I'll be buried in the king's high way,
Some way of common trade, where subjects'
    feet
May hourly trample on their sovereign's head;
For on my heart they tread now whilst I live,
And buried once, why not upon my head?
Aumerle, thou weep'st, my tender-hearted
    cousin!
We'll make foul weather with despised tears;
Our sighs and they shall lodge [beat down] the
    summer corn,
And make a dearth in this revolting land.
Or shall we play the wantons with our woes
And make some pretty match with shedding
    tears?
And thus to drop them still upon one place,
Till they have fretted us a pair of graves
Within the earth, and therein laid—there lies
Two kinsmen digg'd their graves with weeping
    eyes.
Would not this ill do well?

As in the speech just discussed above, Richard truly plays the wanton with his woes. Bolingbroke still has not asked for the crown. On the contrary, he has insisted on his desire only for a revocation of his banishment and the recognition of his right to his father's property and titles. It is Richard, not Bolingbroke, who first broaches the issue of deposition. Richard's use of anaphora (repetition of the same word in succeeding clauses) and isocolon (parallel construction) reveals that he is speaking for effect. The repetition in "a little grave, / a little little grave" suggests sentimentality rather than sincerity. So, too, do his hyperbolic images, which he employs here as he did in the previous scene. Thus, here he imagines carving out graves with tears, as metaphysical a conceit as any in the poetry of John Donne or Andrew Marvell.

Richard delivers this speech to Aumerle and Northumberland while Bolingbroke awaits an interview with him. Repeatedly, Richard delays action with speech. In this quality, he anticipates Hamlet, though he lacks Hamlet's intelligence. Even Richard recognizes at length that he has talked overlong—"I talk but idly" (3.3.171), he concedes—and notes that instead of eliciting tears from Aumerle, his cousin is laughing at him. In two lines devoid of imagistic flourishes, Northumberland, agent of Bolingbroke, then reminds the king of the business at hand.

Act IV, Scene 1, 113–149

BOLINGBROKE. In God's name I'll ascend
  the regal throne.

BISHOP OF CARLISLE. Marry, God forbid!
Worst in this royal presence may I speak,
Yet best beseeming me to speak the truth.
Would God that any in this noble presence
Were enough noble to be upright judge
Of noble Richard! Then true noblesse would
Learn him forbearance from so foul a wrong.
What subject can give sentence on his king?
And who sits here that is not Richard's subject?
Thieves are not judg'd but they are by to hear,
Although apparent [obvious] guilt be seen in
  them,
And shall the figure of God's majesty,
His captain, steward, deputy elect,
Anointed, crowned, planted many years,
Be judg'd by subject and inferior breath,
And he himself not present? O, forfend it,
  God,
That in a Christian climate souls refin'd
Should show so heinous, black, obscene a
  deed!
I speak to subjects, and a subject speaks,
Stirr'd up by God, thus boldly for his king.

My Lord of Hereford here, whom you call
  king,
Is a foul traitor to proud Hereford's king,
And if you crown him, let me prophesy,
The blood of English shall manure the ground,
And future ages groan for this foul act.
Peace shall go to sleep with Turks and infidels,
And in this seat of peace tumultuous wars
Shall kin with kin and kind with kind
  confound.
Disorder, horror, fear, and mutiny
Shall here inhabit, and this land be call'd
The field of Golgotha and dead men's skulls.
O, if you raise this house against this house,
It will the woefullest division prove
That ever fell upon this cursed earth.
Prevent it, resist it, let it not be so,
Lest child, child's children, cry against you
  "woe."

York has just brought the news that Richard has surrendered the throne to Bolingbroke. As Bolingbroke prepares to assume the kingship, Carlisle objects in words that express the orthodox Tudor view that the king—any king—is God's substitute

Richard surrenders his crown to Bolingbroke in Act IV, Scene I of *Richard II*. This is a print from the Boydell Shakespeare Gallery project, which was conceived in 1786 and lasted until 1805. *(Painting by Mather Brown; engraving by Benjamin Smith)*

on Earth, and therefore, no matter how badly he governs, only God can remove him. This is the view that John of Gaunt and York also express, as representatives of the older order, though York is assuaged by his sense that God has deposed Richard (5.2.37–40). Hence, York can shift his allegiance.

Carlisle lacks York's conscience. He remains faithful to Richard and warns of the consequences that will ensue if Richard is deposed. He declares that the sins of the fathers who depose Richard will be visited on their children and their children's children, a fitting biblical allusion from a churchman. Like York at 2.1.31, Carlisle thinks himself inspired to utter his warning. This speech, like York's, will also go unheeded. Yet the civil wars that Carlisle foretells begin at once (5.6), continue in the next two plays of the tetralogy (*Henry IV, Part 1* and *Part 2*), and form the basis of Shakespeare's earlier Henriad (*Henry VI, Part 1, Part 2,* and *Part 3* and *Richard III*). As Shakespeare knew, Edward Hall began his 1548 history of the Wars of the Roses with Richard's deposition. If they wished, Shakespeare's audiences could see in Carlisle's speech and in the subsequent unfolding of his prophecy an endorsement of a providential universe and the divine right of kings. Still, Richard is deposed, and Henry IV would die in his bed after defeating all who opposed him.

Act IV, Scene 1, 200–221

BOLINGBROKE. Are you contented to resign the crown?

KING RICHARD. Ay, no, no ay; for I must nothing be;
Therefore no no, for I resign to thee.
Now mark me how I will undo myself:
I give this heavy weight from off my head,
And this unwieldy sceptre from my hand,
The pride of kingly sway from out my heart;
With mine own tears I wash away my balm,
With mine own hands I give away my crown,
With mine own tongue deny my sacred state,
With mine own breath release all duteous oaths;

All pomp and majesty I do forswear;
My manors, rents, revenues I forgo;
My acts, decrees, and statutes I deny;
God pardon all oaths that are broke to me!
God keep all vows unbroken are made to thee!
Make me, that nothing have, with nothing griev'd,
And thou with all pleas'd, that hast all achiev'd!
Long mayst thou in Richard's seat to sit,
And soon lie Richard in an earthy pit!
God save King Henry, unking'd Richard says,
And send him many years of sunshine days!

According to the modern rendering of his opening words, Richard's speech begins with his typical vacillation. In the First Folio, the spelling differs: "I no; no I." This older spelling carries an added meaning. In surrendering his kingship, Richard is yielding his very identity. Medieval and Renaissance political theory held that the king had two bodies: One is that of the mortal ruler, the other of the undying office. Throughout the play, Richard has conflated these two. Despite the occasional speech to the contrary, he has envisioned himself as the embodiment of the role he has played. To lose his role is to lose his sense of self. Later in this scene, he will call for a mirror, capture his image in it, and then dash the crystal to the ground in a symbolic shattering of himself. He has undone himself politically but also existentially. He has become nothing.

Even as he divests himself of royalty and identity, Richard is still the actor who wants to be the observed of all observers. He orders everyone else, "Now mark me." Dethroning himself, Richard employs anaphora and isocolon as he plays to his audience. Earlier in the play, he had said, "Not all the water in the rough rude sea / Can wash the balm off from an anointed king" (3.2.54–55). Now he says that a few tears may do so. His speech descends to couplets and sentimentality as he anticipates a speedy death; his phrase "earthy pit" is bathetic. In the last line, he transfers the image of the sun, which had been associated with Richard

Rich. I, no; no, I: for I muſt nothing bee:
Therefore no, no, for I reſigne to thee.
Now, marke me how I will vndoe my ſelfe.
I giue this heauie Weight from off my Head,
And this vnwieldie Scepter from my Hand,
The pride of Kingly ſway from out my Heart,
With mine owne Teares I waſh away my Balme,
With mine owne Hands I giue away my Crowne,
With mine owne Tongue denie my Sacred State,
With mine owne Breath releaſe all dutious Oathes;
All Pompe and Maieſtie I doe forſweare;
My Manors, Rents, Reuenues, I forgoe;
My Acts, Decrees, and Statutes I denie:
God pardon all Oathes that are broke to mee,
God keepe all Vowes vnbroke are made to thee.
Make me, that nothing haue, with nothing grieu'd,
And thou with all pleas'd, that haſt all atchieu'd.
Long may'ſt thou liue in *Richards* Seat to ſit,
And ſoone lye *Richard* in an Earthie Pit.
God ſaue King *Henry*, vn-King'd *Richard* ſayes,
And ſend him many yeeres of Sunne-ſhine dayes.
What more remaines?

North. No more: but that you reade
Theſe Accuſations, and theſe grieuous Crymes,
Committed by your Perſon, and your followers,
Againſt the State, and Profit of this Land:
That by confeſſing them, the Soules of men
May deeme, that you are worthily depos'd.

Rich. Muſt I doe ſo? and muſt I rauell out
My weau'd-vp follyes? Gentle *Northumberland*,
If thy Offences were vpon Record,
Would it not ſhame thee, in ſo faire a troupe,
To reade a Lecture of them? If thou would'ſt,
There ſhould'ſt thou finde one heynous Article,
Contayning the depoſing of a King,
And cracking the ſtrong Warrant of an Oath,
Mark'd with a Blot, damn'd in the Booke of Heauen.
Nay, all of you, that ſtand and looke vpon me,
Whil'ſt that my wretchedneſſe doth bait my ſelfe,
Though ſome of you, with *Pilate*, waſh your hands,
Shewing an outward pittie: yet you *Pilates*
Haue here deliuer'd me to my ſowre Croſſe,
And Water cannot waſh away your ſinne.

North. My Lord diſpatch, reade o're theſe Articles.

Rich. Mine Eyes are full of Teares, I cannot ſee:
And yet ſalt-Water blindes them not ſo much,
But they can ſee a ſort of Traytors here.
Nay, if I turne mine Eyes vpon my ſelfe,
I finde my ſelfe a Traytor with the reſt:
For I haue giuen here my Soules conſent,
T'vndeck the pompous Body of a King;
Made Glory baſe; a Soueraigntie, a Slaue;
Prowd Maieſtie, a Subiect; State, a Peſant.

North. My Lord.

Rich. No Lord of thine, thou haught-inſulting man;
No, nor no mans Lord: I haue no Name, no Title;
No, not that Name was giuen me at the Font,
But 'tis vſurpt: alack the heauie day,
That I haue worne ſo many Winters out,
And know not now, what Name to call my ſelfe.
Oh, that I were a Mockerie, King of Snow,
Standing before the Sunne of *Bullingbrooke*,
To melt my ſelfe away in Water-drops.
Good King, great King, and yet not greatly good,
And if my word be Sterling yet in England,
Let it command a Mirror hither ſtraight,

That it may ſhew me what a Face I haue,
Since it is Bankrupt of his Maieſtie.

Bull. Goe ſome of you, and fetch a Looking-Glaſſe.

North. Read o're this Paper, while ỹ Glaſſe doth come.

Rich. Fiend, thou torments me, ere I come to Hell.

Bull. Vrge it no more, my Lord *Northumberland*.

North. The Commons will not then be ſatisfy'd.

Rich. They ſhall be ſatisfy'd: Ile reade enough,
When I doe ſee the very Booke indeede,
Where all my ſinnes are writ, and that's my ſelfe.

Enter one with a Glaſſe.

Giue me that Glaſſe, and therein will I reade.
No deeper wrinckles yet? hath Sorrow ſtrucke
So many Blowes vpon this Face of mine,
And made no deeper Wounds? Oh flatt'ring Glaſſe,
Like to my followers in proſperitie,
Thou do'ſt beguile me. Was this Face, the Face
That euery day, vnder his Houſe-hold Roofe,
Did keepe ten thouſand men? Was this the Face,
That like the Sunne, did make beholders winke?
Is this the Face, which fac'd ſo many follyes,
That was at laſt out-fac'd by *Bullingbrooke*?
A brittle Glory ſhineth in this Face,
As brittle as the Glory, is the Face,
For there it is, crackt in an hundred ſhiuers.
Marke ſilent King, the Morall of this ſport,
How ſoone my Sorrow hath deſtroy'd my Face.

Bull. The ſhadow of your Sorrow hath deſtroy'd
The ſhadow of your Face.

Rich. Say that againe.
The ſhadow of my Sorrow: ha, let's ſee,
'Tis very true, my Griefe lyes all within,
And theſe externall manner of Laments,
Are meerely ſhadowes, to the vnſeene Griefe,
That ſwells with ſilence in the tortur'd Soule.
There lyes the ſubſtance: and I thanke thee King
For thy great bountie, that not onely giu'ſt
Me cauſe to wayle, but teacheſt me the way
How to lament the cauſe. Ile begge one Boone,
And then be gone, and trouble you no more.
Shall I obtaine it?

Bull. Name it, faire Couſin.

Rich. Faire Couſin? I am greater then a King:
For when I was a King, my flatterers
Were then but ſubiects; being now a ſubiect,
I haue a King here to my flatterer:
Being ſo great, I haue no neede to begge.

Bull. Yet aske.

Rich. And ſhall I haue?

Bull. You ſhall.

Rich. Then giue me leaue to goe.

Bull. Whither?

Rich. Whither you will, ſo I were from your ſights.

Bull. Goe ſome of you, conuey him to the Tower.

Rich. Oh good: conuey: Conueyers are you all,
That riſe thus nimbly by a true Kings fall.

Bull. On Wedneſday next, we ſolemnly ſet downe
Our Coronation: Lords, prepare your ſelues.   *Exeunt.*

Abbot. A wofull Pageant haue we here beheld.

Carl. The Woes to come, the Children yet vnborne,
Shall feele this day as ſharpe to them as Thorne.

Aum. You holy Clergie-men, is there no Plot
To rid the Realme of this pernicious Blot?

Abbot. Before I freely ſpeake my minde herein,
You ſhall not onely take the Sacrament,
To bury mine intents, but alſo to effect

What

A page from the First Folio edition of *Richard II*, published in 1623. In this edition, Richard's speech begins with "I no; no I."

as king, to Bolingbroke to highlight the transposition of the two men, one from subject to ruler, the other from ruler to subject.

Act V, Scene 5, 1–66

KING RICHARD. I have been studying how
  I may compare
This prison where I live unto the world;
And for because the world is populous,
And here is not a creature but myself,
I cannot do it; yet I'll hammer it out.
My brain I'll prove the female to my soul,
My soul the father, and these two beget
A generation of still-breeding thoughts;
And these same thoughts people this little
  world,
In humors like the people of this world:
For no thought is contented. The better sort,
As thoughts of things divine, are intermix'd
With scruples, and do set the word itself
Against the word,
As thus, "Come, little ones," and then again,
"It is as hard to come as for a camel
To thread the postern of a small needle's eye."
Thoughts tending to ambition, they do plot
Unlikely wonders: how these vain weak nails
May tear a passage through the flinty ribs
Of this hard world, my ragged prison walls;
And for they cannot, die in their own pride.
Thoughts tending to content flatter themselves
That they are not the first of fortune's slaves,
Nor shall not be the last—like seely [silly, i.e.,
  simple] beggars
Who sitting in the stocks refuge their shame,
That many have and others must sit there;
And in this thought they find a kind of ease,
Bearing their own misfortunes on the back
Of such as have before endur'd the like.
Thus play I in one person many people,
And none contented. Sometimes am I king;
Then treasons make me wish myself a beggar,
And so I am. Then crushing penury
Persuades me I was better when a king;
Then am I king'd again, and by and by
Think that I am unking'd by Bolingbroke,

And straight am nothing. But what e'er I be,
Nor I, nor any man that but man is,
With nothing shall be pleas'd, till he be eas'd
With being nothing. [*Music plays*] Music do I
  hear?
Ha, ha, keep time! How sour sweet music is
When time is broke, and no proportion kept!
So is it in the music of men's lives.
And here have I the daintiness of ear
To check time broke in a disordered string;
But for the concord of my state and time
Had not an ear to hear my true time broke.
I wasted time, and now doth time waste me;
For now hath time made me his numb'ring
  clock:
My thoughts are minutes, and with sighs they
  jar
Their watches on unto mine eyes, the outward
  watch,
Whereto my finger, like a dial's point,
Is pointing still, in cleansing them from tears.
Now, sir, the sound that tells what hour it is
Are clamorous groans, which strike upon my
  heart,
Which is the bell. So sighs, and tears, and
  groans
Show minutes, times, and hours; but my time
Runs posting on in Bolingbroke's proud joy,
While I stand fooling here, his Jack of the
  clock.
This music mads me, let it sound no more,
For though it have holp mad men to their wits,
In me it seems it will make wise men mad.
Yet blessing on his heart that gives it me!
For 'tis a sign of love; and love to Richard
Is a strange brooch in this all-hating world.

It is apt that Richard, so self-engrossed, should end his life in solitary confinement and deliver his final long speech to an audience of one: himself. The imagery here is characteristically metaphysical, as when he turns his brain to the mother, his soul to the father of his reflections. As he did in earlier speeches, Richard here questions his identity. If he is not king, then he is also not Richard, not himself, and so is nothing. That word echoes throughout this work as it will again in *King Lear,* another tragic tale of a self-deposed monarch. Also characteristic in this speech is Richard's fluctuating mind, as he imagines himself king, beggar, king again, then nothing, and finding contentment nowhere.

Just as, while looking at his image in the mirror (4.1.281–286), he echoed Marlowe's Faust's encomium to the shade of Helen, so here he recalls Faust's reflections on biblical passages in the opening scene of Marlowe's play. There Faust rejected one profession after another, as Richard here fails to find contentment in any of the imaginary states he considers. Although he had earlier spoken of the leveling effect of mortality, his speech follows the social ranking from king to beggar, showing that he retains a belief in hierarchy.

Though he thus shows that, unlike Shakespeare's later and greater tragic heroes, Richard has learned little from his experience, he has gained one insight, that he squandered his opportunities: "I wasted time, and now doth time waste me." He does not dwell on the lesson, though. Instead, he returns to self-dramatization in his conceit that he is like a manikin tolling the hours. The comparison is appropriate, for Richard, like the figures of a clock, has throughout the play been an image without substance. At the end of this soliloquy, Richard shows a glimmer of concern for another when he blesses the unknown player of the music he hears. Even here, though, he cannot escape solipsism in assuming that the music is being played for him. And in his conclusion, he returns to bathos and sentimentality in claiming that the entire world hates him.

DIFFICULT PASSAGES
Act I, Scene 1, 152–156
KING RICHARD. Wrath-kindled gentlemen, be rul'd by me,
Let's purge this choler without letting blood.
This we prescribe, though no physician;
Deep malice makes too deep incision.
Our doctors say this is no month to bleed.

Richard here employs the imagery of medieval and Renaissance medicine, which posited that illness derived from an imbalance of the four humors, or fluids in the body: melancholy, or black bile; phlegm; blood; and choler, or yellow bile. An excess of this last fluid caused anger, and one way to restore a healthful balance was to bleed the patient to eliminate the superfluity. The medical practice of the day was linked to astrology; certain dates were designated as *dies male* (the origin of the word "dismal"), or bad days for undertaking procedures or business. Richard wants to remove the anger of Bolingbroke and Mowbray, which he attributes to their excess of yellow bile, without blood-letting, which in this case would mean a duel.

Richard's attempt to pacify the two dukes without trial by combat seems commendable. He admits, though, that he is not a physician, and his prescription is ill-advised. He may fear that Bolingbroke will defeat Mowbray, thus confirming the latter's guilt (and by implication Richard's) and adding to Bolingbroke's already substantial popularity. Still, Mowbray might have killed Bolingbroke had the king allowed the duel, and Richard then would not have been deposed. Moreover, Richard is rejecting an established chivalric practice and so is subverting the very code that makes him king.

Act I, Scene 4, 42–52
KING RICHARD. We will ourself in person to this war,
And for our coffers, with too great a court
And liberal largess, are grown somewhat light,
We are enforc'd to farm our royal realm,
The revenue whereof shall furnish us
For our affairs in hand. If that comes short,
Our substitutes at home shall have blank charters,
Whereto, when they shall know what men are rich,
They shall subscribe them for large sums of gold,
And send them after to supply our wants,
For we will make for Ireland presently.

There is historical context to this passage. Facing a rebellion in Ireland, Richard needed money to pay his troops. Since his extravagances and excessive generosity to his flatterers had left his treasury depleted, he needed to raise money. One method he adopted was to allow someone (in this case the earl of Wiltshire) to collect the revenues owed the king in exchange for a fixed payment, a practice known as farming the realm. The king thereby got the money he needed, but the earl took more money from the king's subjects than he had promised to pay the king. Such a practice was therefore unpopular.

Also unpopular was the use of blank charters. The king's agents compelled people to sign their names to blank pieces of paper or parchment. Later, these documents would be converted to promissory notes requiring the undersigned to pay to the king whatever sum had been written above their names. These methods of extorting money cost Richard the support of the nobility and commons, who turned to Bolingbroke for redress.

CRITICAL INTRODUCTION
TO THE PLAY
Imagery

Richard II employs a rich variety of imagery that underscores the work's action, characterization, and themes. One of the key verbal and visual image patterns is that of up and down. As the play opens, the audience sees Richard seated on his throne, which is placed on a dais and so is elevated above the other characters. Thus, he is up, and his fortunes seem so, too. Yet as soon as the action begins with Bolingbroke's challenge to Mowbray, and by implication the king, regarding the death of Gloucester, a threat to Richard's position becomes evident in the play's language. "How high a pitch his resolution soars!" Richard remarks of Bolingbroke's challenge to Mowbray (1.1.109).

Bolingbroke's crest includes the falcon, a soaring bird, and Bolingbroke plays on this symbol when Richard asks him to surrender Mowbray's glove as a sign of reconciliation: "Shall I seem

King Richard (Herbet Beerbohm Tree) listens to Bolingbroke (Oscar Asche) impeaching Norfolk (William Haviland) in Act I, Scene I of *Richard II*. This is an illustration of a 1903 production at His Majesty's Theatre. *(Illustration by Paul Thiriat)*

crestfallen in my father's sight? / Or with pale beggar-fear impeach my height / Before this outdar'd dastard?" he asks (1.1.188–190). Bolingbroke refuses to stoop by yielding to the king. By appropriating the language of height, he already implicitly challenges Richard's elevated station. In 1.3, Bolingbroke again links himself to the soaring falcon (1.3.61) and says that his father's presence lifts him up "to reach at victory above my head" (1.3.71–72).

Conversely, Richard—who, in 1.3 again initially appears elevated above his subjects—descends to embrace his cousin Bolingbroke, and when he interrupts the trial by combat, he throws his baton, or warder, down. In *Henry IV, Part 2*, Lord Mowbray, son of the Mowbray in this play, remarks,

O, when the king did throw his warder down
(His own life hung upon the staff he threw),
Then threw he down himself and all their lives
That by indictment and by dint of sword
Have since miscarried under Bolingbroke.

(4.1.123–127)

In this speech, Lord Mowbray clarifies the significance of the imagery Shakespeare uses in the earlier play. Shakespeare links Richard to descent in 1.3, Bolingbroke to rising. In the following scene, even though Richard has banished Bolingbroke, the king still refers to him as "high Hereford" (1.4.2).

Richard's association with descent continues as the play proceeds. After the Welsh soldiers desert, Salisbury likens Richard to a meteor: "I see thy glory like a shooting star / fall to the base earth from the firmament" (2.4.19). The word *base* also links itself to Richard, another foreshadowing of his approaching fall.

Richard tries to cling to the language of ascent. Temporarily fighting off despair, he tells his followers that despite the loss of the Welsh army, "Look not to the ground, / Ye favorites of a king, are we not high? / High be our thoughts" (3.2.87–89). This optimistic mood soon passes after Scroop again links Bolingbroke with height. Scroop compares Bolingbroke to a storm that causes rivers to overflow and adds, "So high above his limits swells the rage / Of Bolingbroke" (3.2.109–110). Richard's spirit and language now descend: "For God's sake let us sit upon the ground / And tell sad stories of the death of kings" (3.2.155–156).

In the climactic scene at Flint Castle, Richard again begins in an elevated position, the last time he will so appear. He stands on the battlements while Bolingbroke and his supporters wait below. Bolingbroke sends word that "on both his knees [he] doth kiss King Richard's hand" (3.3.36), but it is clear from Richard's speech when the king appears that Bolingbroke does not kneel. Even while still physically elevated, Richard imagines himself "buried in the king's high way" (3.3.155) and talks of carving out his grave with tears. His fallen fortunes are rendered visually when he

descends from the top of the castle to "the base court" (3.3.182), the courtyard where Bolingbroke is standing. "Down, down I come, like glist'ring Phaeton," Richard declares (3.3.178), assuming the language of descent and hence defeat. "Down court! Down king!" (3.3.182).

For the last time in the play, Bolingbroke kneels to Richard. The next time anyone kneels, it will be to Bolingbroke as Henry IV. Richard recognizes the hollowness of Bolingbroke's gesture and urges him to rise. "Up, cousin, up, your heart is up, I know, / Thus high at least [*touching his crown*], although your knee be low" (3.3.194–195). The fortunes of the two have reversed themselves, as the imagery demonstrates. This reversal is reflected in the speech of the Gardener in 3.4, when he observes that the king has "met with the fall of leaf" (3.4.49). He also uses the image of a scale in which Richard's side sinks as Bolingbroke's rises (3.4.84–89).

Richard echoes this simultaneous action of rising and falling in the deposition scene. Richard is holding one side of the crown, Bolingbroke the other. "Now is this golden crown like a deep well," Richard declares in one of his many brilliant similes,

That owes [has] two buckets, filling one another,
The emptier ever dancing in the air,
The other down, unseen, and full of water:
That bucket down and full of tears am I,
Drinking my griefs, whilst you mount up on
  high.

(4.1.184–189)

As he is being taken to Pomfret Castle, Richard once more refers to "mounting Bolingbroke" (5.1.56). The audience has already seen Bolingbroke literally mount; in 4.1, he ascends the throne that once was Richard's. Richard's descent culminates in 5.5, when he who had begun the play on a dais ends his life in a dungeon. Yet at the play's end, Shakespeare offers a countermovement. As Richard's fortunes have declined, he has grown more sympathetic. He fights bravely against his attackers, and when they overcome him, he at last reappropriates the language of ascent: "Mount, mount, my soul! Thy seat is up on high, / Whilst my gross flesh sinks downward, here to die" (5.5. 111–112). Perhaps Shakespeare here offers another of his Faustian references, inviting his audience to contrast the damnation of Faust, whose soul is carried down to hell, with the salvation of Richard, whose soul ascends to heaven. Shakespeare's imagery thus reveals Richard's redemption as a human being.

Another set of images, consisting of fire/sun and water, underscores the conflict between Richard and Bolingbroke and reflects their changing circumstances. Richard associates himself with the sun in 3.2 when Aurmerle urges him to act against Bolingbroke's growing rebellion. Richard replies,

> Discomfortable cousin, know'st thou not
> That when the searching eye of heaven is hid
> Behind the globe, that lights the lower world,
> Then thieves and robbers range abroad unseen
> In murthers and in outrage boldly here,
> But when from this terrestrial ball
> He fires the proud tops of the eastern pines
> And darts his light through every guilty hole,
> Then murthers, treasons, and detested sins,
> The cloak of night being pluck'd from off their
>   backs,
> Stand bare and naked, trembling at
>   themselves?
> So when this thief, this traitor Bolingbroke,
> Who all this while hath revell'd in the night,
> Shall see us rising in our throne, the east,
> His treasons will sit blushing in his face,
> Not able to endure the sight of day,
> But self-affrighted tremble at his sin.
>   (3.2.36–53)

John of Gaunt had earlier linked the element of fire with Richard when he warned that the king's "rash fierce blaze of riot cannot last, / For violent fires soon burn out themselves" (2.1. 33–34). Bolingbroke, too, likens Richard to the sun when the king appears on the battlements of Flint Castle:

> See, see, king Richard doth himself appear,
> As doth the blushing discontented sun
> From out the fiery portal of the east,
> When he perceives the envious clouds are bent
> To dim his glory and to stain the track
> Of his bright passage to the occident.
>   (3.3.62–67)

Conversely, Bolingbroke is linked to the element of water. Scroop, describing Bolingbroke's invasion, compares it to a stormy day that "makes the silver rivers drown their shores, / As if the world were all dissolv'd to tears" (3.2.107–108). Bolingbroke himself appropriates this element when he remarks,

> Methinks King Richard and myself should
>   meet
> With no less terror than the elements
> Of fire and water, when their thund'ring shock
> At meeting tears the cloudy cheeks of heaven.
> Be he the fire, I'll be the yielding water;
> The rage be his, whilst on the earth I rain
> My waters—on the earth, and not on him.
>   (3.3.54–60).

Bolingbroke here speaks in the metereological terms of the Renaissance, which maintained that thunderstorms resulted from the encounter of water and fire. On one level, he also grants Richard the higher and purer element of fire. Yet water extinguishes fire, as Bolingbroke will put Richard out of his throne and then out of the world. The language here thus foreshadows the play's subsequent events.

In this same scene, Shakespeare has the two men exchange the imagery of sun/fire and water to signify a transfer of power. In descending from Flint's battlements to the base court, Richard likens himself not to the true sun but to Phaeton, the impostor driver of the sun's chariot who is killed for his presumption, another foreshadowing of Richard's fate. Richard remarks that "night-owls shriek where mounting larks should sing" (3.3.183), signifying his eclipse. Just prior to his descent, the king takes to himself the imagery of water, saying, "We'll make foul weather with despised tears, / . . . Or shall we play the wanton with our woes / And make some pretty match with shedding tears?" (3.3.161, 164–165).

Even earlier in the play, Shakespeare provides hints of this transformation. When Richard banishes Bolingbroke, the latter remarks, "The sun that warms you here shall shine on me, / And those his golden beams to you here lent / Shall point on me and gild my banishment" (1.3.145–147). The sunshine is only lent to Richard; Bolingbroke already claims this symbol of royalty. Salisbury sees Richard's fortunes declining with the desertion of the Welsh soldiers, observing that his sun "sets weeping in the lowly west" (2.4.21). Richard, too, foretells his downfall when at the end of 3.2 he urges his followers to go "From Richard's night to Bolingbroke's fair day" (3.2.218).

In the deposition scene, the transfer of imagery, like the transfer of power, is complete. "God save King Henry, unking'd Richard says, / and send him many years of sunshine days!" (4.1.220–221). Richard wishes that he were a snow king facing the sun of Bolingbroke, "To melt myself away in water drops!" (4.1.262). When he looks at himself in the mirror, Richard wonders, "Was this face the face / That like the sun did make beholders wink?" (4.1.283–284). Once upon a time, it was, but the play's language shows that it is so no longer.

Richard's metamorphosis from fire to water continues to manifest itself in the play's last act. When the queen sees her deposed husband, she wishes her attendants would "dissolve to dew / And wash him fresh again with true-love tears" (5.1.8–10). In his last moments, Richard observes that his finger keeps pointing to his eyes "in cleansing them from tears" (5.5.54). In death, the king becomes another liquid still. Learning of Richard's murder, Henry IV laments, "That blood should sprinkle me to make me grow" (5.6.46).

Garden imagery pervades the play as a comment on the fate of England. John of Gaunt famously compares England to "this other Eden, demi-paradise" (2.1.42), which Richard's bad government has converted "to a tenement [property held by a tenant] or a pelting [paltry] farm" (2.1.60). Richard is both a bad gardener/caretaker of his country and a "fair rose" (5.1.8) who is destroyed by his parasitic favorites. They contribute to the destruction of paradise; Bolingbroke calls them "The caterpillars of the commonwealth, / Which I have sworn to wed and pluck away" (2.3. 166–167). Later, the Gardener refers to these favorites as weeds (3.4.50).

At the center of the play, Shakespeare places a scene that does nothing to advance the plot but, through the image of the garden, encapsulates the history of England under Richard, Richard's own fate, and the ideal future under Bolingbroke. Here, the Gardener and his assistants create order in their little plot. An assistant highlights the macrocosm-microcosm connection when he asks why they should properly maintain their plot of land when the entire kingdom "Is full of weeds, her fairest flowers chok'd up" (3.4.44), the trees unpruned, and herbs overrun with caterpillars (echoing Bolingbroke's use of that word). The Gardener replies that for his neglect, the king suffers "the fall of leaf" (3.4.48), which he could have prevented had he tended his kingdom properly. After Richard's deposition, the queen likens him to a withered rose (5.1.8).

Under Bolingbroke, England may recover. Richard discharges his supporters that they may "ear [plow] the land that hath some hope to grow, / For I have none" (3.2.212–213). In 3.4, the Gardener says that Bolingbroke has weeded the English garden by executing the Earl of Wiltshire, Bushy, and Green. Carlisle fears that Richard's deposition will not restore an English Eden. Rather, he prophesies that "The blood of English shall manure the ground," and the country will be called "The field of Golgotha and dead men's skulls" (4.1.137, 144). Bolingbroke's final speech suggests, however, that Richard's death will lead to regeneration: The former king's blood will make the new king grow (5.6.46).

Structure

Like the play's imagery, its structure underscores the action, reflecting the shift in power from Richard to his antagonist. The work is perfectly balanced, the climax coming at the play's midpoint—Act III, Scene 3—when the two main characters confront each other at Flint Castle in the third of their five encounters. Richard dominates the opening acts of the work. He appears in 1.1, 1.3, 1.4, 2.1, 3.2, and 3.3 and is the subject of discussion in 1.2 (as John of Gaunt and Gloucester's widow discuss Gloucester's death, ordered by the king), 2.2 (where Bushy and the queen discuss the king's absence), and 2.4 (in which Salisbury tries unsuccessfully to keep the Welsh army intact for Richard). The only scenes in which he is absent either in person or through reference are 2.3 and the short 3.1.

In each of the scenes in which he appears in the first half of the play, Richard controls the action. In 1.1, he presides over the quarrel between Mowbray and Bolingbroke. In 1.3, he is umpire of their trial by combat, which he interrupts by exiling the two opponents. In 1.4, he announces his intention of going to Ireland and his plans for paying for the war. He seizes John of Gaunt's property in 2.1, and in 3.2, he dismisses his followers.

By contrast, Bolingbroke appears in 1.1 and 1.3, vanishes into exile until 2.3, is absent again until 3.1, and resurfaces in 3.3. In the first two of these scenes, he is visually and verbally subject to Richard, who is elevated on his throne and who commands his actions. In 2.3 and 3.1, he acts independently of the king, as the king does of him. Only in 3.3 do the two men exchange condition, as Bolingbroke compels the king to accompany him to London.

In the second half of the play, the situation is reversed. In 4.1, Richard and Bolingbroke appear. Richard speaks more than the "silent king," even though he is present for only about half the scene; indeed, he enters at precisely the midpoint of 4.1. But Bolingbroke now controls the action, forcing Richard to abdicate. In the following scene, Richard appears again, this time without Bolingbroke but still under his power as the deposed monarch is led first to the Tower of London and then to Pomfret Castle. Richard appears only once more in the play, 5.5, when he is killed.

Richard surrenders his crown to Bolingbroke in Act IV, Scene I of *Richard II*. This is a print from Malcolm C. Salaman's 1916 edition of *Shakespeare in Pictorial Art*. (Painting by Sir John Gilbert)

The second half of the work belongs to Bolingbroke, who appears in 4.1, 5.3, and 5.6, and is the subject of conversation in 5.2 (York's description of Bolingbroke's entry into London, in which Bolingbroke is the star and Richard the supernumerary) and 5.4 (as Sir Pierce Exton sets off to kill Richard to please the new king). He also controls the action in every scene, even when he is absent, whether, as just noted, he orders Richard's imprisonment and Isabella's exile, or Sir Pierce Exton acts on what he believes to be the king's wish for Richard's death.

The play thus begins again with 4.1. Nevertheless, the two parts mirror each other in such a way as to raise questions about the nature of Bolingbroke's rule. The first scene opens with Richard's presiding over the mutual recriminations of Mowbray and Bolingbroke centering on the death of Gloucester. Similarly, 4.1 begins with charges and countercharges regarding Bagot's and Aumerle's roles in Gloucester's death. In 1.1, Richard tries to end the argument, ordering Bolingbroke to surrender Mowbray's glove as a token of reconciliation. Bolingbroke refuses. In 4.1, Bolingbroke orders Bagot not to accept Aumerle's challenge. Bagot ignores him. Unable to effect a reconciliation between Mowbray and Bolingbroke in 1.1, Richard orders a trial by combat that never transpires. In 4.1, Bolingbroke orders various trials by combat because so many challenges have been issued, but these trials never occur in the play.

At the end of 2.1, after Richard has exiled Bolingbroke and seized the estate of John of Gaunt, the king seems firmly in control of his realm and the play's action. After Richard departs, Northumberland, Willoughby, and Ross lament the state of the country, and Northumberland reveals a plot to restore Bolingbroke. At the end of 4.1, after Richard has been deposed, Carlisle has been arrested for opposing this action, and Bolingbroke has planned his coronation, he appears to have eliminated all opposition to his realm. Again, three characters remain behind: the Abbot of Westminster, Carlisle, and Aumerle, who bewails Bolingbroke's actions, while the Abbot tells the others of a plot to restore Richard.

In 3.2, Richard learns of Bolingbroke's rebellion. In 5.3, Bolingbroke learns of a plot against his life, and in 5.6, he is told that rebels have burned the town of Cirencester. At the opening of the play, Richard is tainted with the blood of Gloucester; at the end, Bolingbroke is tainted with the blood of Richard. In 1.3, Richard perpetually exiles Mowbray, his agent in the killing of Gloucester. In 5.6, Henry IV permanently banishes Exton, his instrument in the killing of the deposed king. In 2.1, John of Gaunt foretells a grim future for Richard and England under him. In 4.1 and 5.1, Carlisle and Richard, respectively, offer similar predictions about Bolingbroke's kingship.

From one perspective, then, the play's structure is linear. There is a clear progression from the reign of Richard II to that of Bolingbroke as Henry IV. From another point of view, the play's action is circular. A new king sits on the throne, but his reign may be as troubled as that of his predecessor, his governance no better.

From Medieval to Modern

The play's structure calls into question the extent to which Shakespeare endorses the Lancastrian myth of the good ruler Henry IV replacing the bad king Richard II. One king may be very much like the other. The play shows, however, that the shift from Plantagenet to Lancastrian ruler marks more than a dynastic shift: It signifies nothing less than the death of an established medieval order to a world in which, in the words of John Donne, all coherence is gone. It is a world that allows for self-fashioning, but it is also a world ruled by time, chance, and mutability.

The play opens in a medieval world in which word matches thing, and identity is fixed. Richard is king, and "king" refers to Richard, who reigns by right of birth. He has inherited the throne through the legitimate claim of his father, the Black Prince, oldest son of Edward III. John of Gaunt, a representative of this old world, argues for hierarchy, order, and degree when, in 1.2, he insists that only God can punish Richard for any evil actions because only God is above the king, God's deputy. Even as Mowbray and Bolingbroke meet in mutual accusation and anger, they observe the rituals of chivalric challenge.

When they confront each other at the trial by combat, Bolingbroke declares he is "As confident as is the falcon's flight / Against a bird" (1.3.61–62); his crest of a falcon is apt symbol for him. Again, sign (signifier) matches reality (signified). In that scene, the power of the king's word is apparent when he banishes Mowbray and Bolingbroke. The latter he exiles for 10 years, a sentence he later reduces to six with a speech—"such is the breath of kings," Bolingbroke observes (1.3.215). When John of Gaunt pleads for his son, Richard replies, "Six years we banish him, and he shall go" (1.3.248). The king's words banish Mowbray for life, and Mowbray never sees England again. John of Gaunt suggests that Bolingbroke say he is traveling on the Continent to gain honor or to escape the plague, but Bolingbroke insists that banishment is that thing and nothing else.

Aumerle accompanies Bolingbroke as the latter sets off on his travels. Richard asks what Bolingbroke said to his cousin. Aumerle replies that Bolingbroke said, "Farewell" (1.4.11), but Aumerle did not say farewell to him. Although the word is customary at parting, it conveys a wish for prosperity that Aumerle will not utter because he does not want his cousin to fare well. Aumerle comments that if the word might somehow have lengthened Bolingbroke's exile, then he would have uttered it. But in a world of fixed meaning, "farewell" can express only a desire for success. Because Aumerle does not feel that desire, he will not say the word.

In 2.1, John of Gaunt puns on his name, noting that it matches his condition: "Gaunt am I for the grave, gaunt as the grave" (2.1.82). Just as Bolingbroke's crest truly represents him, so Gaunt's name represents the reality of his situation. Richard clings to this view that name and reality are one. Returning to England from Ireland, he claims that the name of king is worth 20,000 men. He orders Earth itself to attack Bolingbroke. "This earth shall have a feeling, and these stones / Prove armed soldiers, ere her native king / Shall falter under foul rebellion's arms" (3.2.24–26).

Yet Richard himself has undermined his medieval world. John of Gaunt says that Richard has ceased to act as England's king but rather has transmuted himself into England's landlord (2.1.113). Name and station do not match. After Richard seizes Bolingbroke's inheritance, York chides the king for warring against his countrymen rather than against England's traditional enemy, France. Worse, by denying Bolingbroke his right to his father's lands and titles, the king destroys the very order and degree according to which he takes his power:

Take Hereford's rights away, and take from
 Time
His charters and his customary rights;

Let not to-morrow then ensue to-day;
Be not thyself; for how art thou a king
But by fair sequence and succession?
                              (2.1.195–199)

The consequences of Richard's actions soon appear. Northumberland refers to Richard without giving him the title of king (3.3.6), indicating that name and identity have become separated. Richard had sought to deny Bolingbroke his identity as Duke of Lancaster, and the instruction he has taught has returned to plague the inventor. Bolingbroke had capitalized on that breach of custom to gain the support of the nobility. Whether or not they wanted Richard deposed, they could not stand by idly to watch the basis of their society eroded and so had rallied to Bolingbroke. York insists that "King" and "Richard" not be separated, but his is a minority view. Percy tells Bolingbroke that Flint Castle "royally is mann'd." Bolingbroke replies, "Why, it contains no king" (3.321, 324). On one level, Bolingbroke's speech reveals his ignorance of the king's location. It also implies, however, that although Richard is within, no king resides there because Richard no longer is de facto king and soon will not be king de jure either.

In the world of Bolingbroke, identity is mutable. Richard no longer knows who or what he is. The Duke of Lancaster can make himself king. Carlisle, another representative of the dying medieval order, argues that Bolingbroke is Richard's subject and cannot change his condition: "My Lord of Hereford here, whom you call king, / Is foul traitor to proud Hereford's king" (4.1.134–135). The word *king*, Carlisle argues, is not a counter to be moved about at will; it must be linked to *Richard*. In the new world, such an archaic view is "capital treason," as Northumberland states (4.1.151). Bolingbroke, who makes himself king, will change Aumerle into Rutland, as he demotes Richard from ruler to prisoner to nothing.

Just before his death, Richard puns in a distorted echo of Gaunt's playing on his name. A groom reports that Bolingbroke rode the former king's horse, and the horse seemed proud to carry

Henry IV banishes Exton in this 19th-century depiction of Act V, Scene 6 of *Richard II*. *(Painting by Friedrich Pecht; engraving by Alfred Krausse)*

him. Richard rails at the animal for not throwing off the new king but then apologizes. Horses, after all, are supposed to bear their riders. Richard continues, "I was not made a horse, / And yet I bear a burthen like an ass, / Spurr'd, gall'd, and tir'd by jauncing Bolingbroke" (5.5.92–94). Whereas, in the old world, Gaunt's identity and condition were one, in the new world, these are no longer linked. Richard, though a man, is treated by Bolingbroke as if he were a beast.

Another indicator of the shifting significance of words appears when the Duchess of York pleads with Henry IV for her son's life. "Say 'pardon,' King, let pity teach thee how" (5.3.116). Her husband, who opposes her request, urges Henry to use the word in its French sense, turning it into a polite

refusal to do as she asks. The Duchess retorts, "Dost thou teach pardon pardon to destroy? / Ah, my sour husband, my hard-hearted lord, / That sets the word itself against the word!" (5.3.120–122). When Henry says he pardons her son, she asks that he repeat the word so she can feel certain he means what he says.

Sir Pierce Exton experiences the divorce of word from reality. Expecting thanks from Henry for killing Richard, he receives a rebuke instead. Exton replies, "From your own mouth, my lord, did I this deed." Henry replies casuistically,

They love not poison that do poison need,
Nor do I thee. Though I did wish him dead,
I hate the murtherer, love him murthered.
(5.6.37–40)

To atone for the guilt of Richard's death, Henry promises a pilgrimage to the Holy Land; his words will prove meaningless.

EXTRACTS OF CLASSIC CRITICISM

Samuel Johnson (1709–1784) [Excerpted from *The Plays of William Shakespeare* (1765). Johnson's "short stricture" appears at the conclusion of *Richard II* in his important edition of Shakespeare's plays. He raises issues here about the extent of Shakespeare's fidelity to his historical sources and his indebtedness to *Thomas of Woodstock*, an anonymous play attributed to Shakespeare by the 21st-century scholar Michael Egan. Comparisons between Shakespeare and Ben Jonson, which almost always favored the former, were commonplace in the 17th and 18th centuries. In calling the work a tragedy, Johnson raises questions about the play's genre, and his observation about passion in the play has been explored more fully by later commentators. Johnson's reservations about the play's ending are not widely shared by critics. In the theater, however, much of Act V is often cut.]

This play is extracted from the Chronicle of *Holingshead*, in which many passages may be found which *Shakespeare* has, with very little alteration, transplanted into his scenes; particularly a speech of the bishop of *Carlisle* in defence of King *Richard*'s unalienable right, and immunity from human jurisdiction.

[Ben] *Johnson,* who, in his *Catiline* and *Sejanus,* has inserted many speeches from the *Roman* historians, was, perhaps, induced to that practice by the example of *Shakespeare,* who had condescended sometimes to copy more ignoble writers. But *Shakespeare* had more of his own than *Johnson,* and, if he sometimes was willing to spare his labour, shewed by what he performed at other times, that his extracts were made by choice or idleness rather than necessity.

This play is one of those which *Shakespeare* has apparently revised; but as success in works of invention is not always proportionate to labour, it is not finished at last with the happy force of some other of his tragedies, nor can be said much to affect the passions, or enlarge the understanding.

August Wilhelm von Schlegel (1767–1845)
[Excerpted from *A Course of Lectures on Dramatic Art and Literature* (1815). Schlegel's translation of Shakespeare is a masterpiece of German literature and did much to popularize Shakespeare on the Continent. Schlegel's literary criticism influenced Samuel Taylor Coleridge and his fellow English romantics.]

In *Richard the Second,* Shakespeare exhibits a noble kingly nature, at first obscured by levity and by the errors of an unbridled youth, and afterwards purified by misfortune, and rendered by it more highly and splendidly illustrious. When he has lost the love and reverence of his subjects, and is on the point of losing also his throne, he then feels with a bitter enthusiasm the high vocation of the kingly dignity and its transcendental rights, independent of personal merit or changeable institutions. When the earthly crown is fallen from his head, he first appears a king whose innate nobility no humiliation can annihilate. . . . The political incident of the deposition is sketched with extraordinary knowledge of the world;—the ebb of fortune, on the one hand, and on the other, the swelling tide, which carries every thing along with it. While Bolingbroke acts as a king, and his adherents behave towards him as if he really were so, he still continues to give out that he has come with an armed band merely to demand his birthright and the removal of abuses. The usurpation has been long completed, before the word is pronounced and the thing publicly avowed. The old John of Gaunt is a model of chivalrous honour: he stands there like a pillar of the olden times which he has outlived. His son, Henry IV, was altogether unlike him: his character is admirably sustained throughout the three pieces in which he appears. We see in it that mixture of hardness, moderation, and prudence, which, in fact, enabled him to secure the possession of the throne which he had violently usurped; but without openness, without true cordiality, and incapable of noble ebullitions, he was so little able to render his government beloved, that the deposed Richard was even wished back again.

Samuel Taylor Coleridge (1772–1834)
[Excerpted from an anonymous report in the *Bristol Gazette* of November 18, 1813, of a lecture Coleridge delivered on November 11, 1813, at the White Lion, Broad Street. More famous today as a poet, Coleridge was also an important critic. His observations focus on Shakespeare's psychological insights and imaginative language.]

Shakespeare shewed great judgment in his first scenes, they contained the germ of the ruling passion which was to be developed hereafter; thus Richard's hardiness of mind, arising from kingly power, his weakness and debauchery from continual and unbounded flattery, and the haughty temper of the Barons; one and the other alternately forming the moral of the Play, are glanced at in the first scenes. An historic play requires more excitement than a tragic, thus Shakespeare never loses an opportunity of awakening a patriotic feeling; for this purpose Old Gaunt accuses Richard of having *"farmed* out the island." What could be a greater rebuke to a King than to be told that

> This realm, this England
> Is now leased out . . .
> Like to a tenement, or pelting farm . . .
>   [2.1.50–60]

This speech of Gaunt is most beautiful; the propriety of putting so long a speech into the mouth of an old dying man might easily be shown, it thence partook of the nature of prophecy;

> Methinks I am a prophet new inspired,
> And thus expiring, do foretell of him.
>   [2.1.31–32]

. . . The beautiful *keeping of the character of the Play* is conspicuous in the Duke of York. He, like Gaunt, is old; and, full of a religious loyalty struggling with indignation at the King's vices and follies, is an evidence of a man giving up all energy under a feeling of despair. The Play throughout is a history of the human mind, when reduced to ease its anguish with words instead of action, and the necessary feeling of weakness which such a state produces. The scene between the Queen, Bushy, and Bagot [2.2], is also worthy of notice, from the characters all talking high, but performing nothing; and from Shakespeare's tenderness to those presentiments, which, wise as we will be, will still adhere to our nature.

Shakespeare has contrived to bring the character of Richard, with all his prodigality and hard usage of his friends, still within the compass of our pity, for we find him much beloved by those who knew him best, the Queen is passionately attached to him, and his good Bishop (Carlisle) adheres to the last: he is not one of those whose punishment gives delight; his failings appear to arise from outward objects, and from the poison of flatterers around him; we cannot, therefore, help pitying, and wishing he had been placed in a rank where he would have been less exposed, and where he might have been happy and useful.

William Hazlitt (1778–1830) [Excerpted from *Characters of Shakespeare's Plays* (1817). Hazlitt exemplifies romantic criticism's focus on Shakespeare's characters. His image of Richard II as a tragic poet-king has been popular both on the stage and in critical appraisals. Hazlitt also considers the political implications of the play, a subject of much discussion in late 20th- and early 21st-century analyses.]

Richard II is a play little known compared with *Richard III* which last is a play that every unfledged candidate for theatrical fame chuses to strut and fret his hour upon the stage in; yet we confess that we prefer the nature and feeling of the one to the noise and bustle of the other; at least, as we are so often forced to see it acted. In *Richard II* the weakness of the king leaves us leisure to take a greater interest in the misfortunes of the man. After the first act, in which the arbitrariness of his behaviour only proves his want of resolution, we see him staggering under the unlooked-for blows of fortune, bewailing his loss of kingly power, not preventing it, sinking under the aspiring genius of Bolingbroke, his authority trampled on, his hopes failing him, and his pride crushed and broken down under insults and injuries, which his own misconduct had provoked, but which he has not courage or manliness to resent. The change of tone and behaviour in the two competitors for the throne according to their change of fortune, from the capricious sentence of banishment passed by Richard upon Bolingbroke, the suppliant offers and modest pretensions of the latter on his return, to the high and haughty tone with which he accepts Richard's resignation of the crown after the loss of all his power, the use which he makes of the deposed king to grace his triumphal progress through the streets of London, and the final intimation of his wish for his death, which immediately finds a servile executioner, is marked throughout with complete effect and without the slightest appearance of effort. The steps by which Bolingbroke mounts the throne are those by which Richard sinks into the grave. We feel neither respect nor love for the deposed monarch; for he is as wanting in energy as in principle: but we pity him, for he pities himself. His heart is by no means hardened against himself, but bleeds afresh at every new stroke of mischance, and his sensibility, absorbed in his own person, and unused to misfortune, is not only tenderly alive to its own sufferings, but without the fortitude to bear them. He is, however, human in his distresses; for to feel pain, and sorrow, weakness, disappointment, remorse and anguish, is the lot of humanity, and we sympathize with him accordingly. The sufferings of the man make us forget that he ever was a king.

The right assumed by sovereign power to trifle at its will with the happiness of others as a matter of course, or to remit its exercise as a matter of favour, is strikingly shewn in the sentence of banishment so unjustly pronounced on Bolingbroke and Mowbray, and in what Bolingbroke says when four years of his banishment are taken off, with as little reason.

How long a time lies in one little word!
Four lagging winters and four wanton
  springs

End in a word: such is the breath of
  kings.

[1.3.213–215]

A more affecting image of the loneliness of a state of exile can hardly be given than by what Bolingbroke afterwards observes of his having "sighed his English breath in foreign clouds" [3.1.20]; or than that conveyed in Mowbray's complaint at being banished for life. [Quotes 1.3.159–171] How beautiful is all this, and at the same time how *English* too!

Richard II may be considered as the first of that series of English historical plays, in which "is hung armour of the invincible knights of old" [William Wordsworth, "It Is Not To be Thought Of That the Flood," ll. 9–10] in which their hearts seem to strike against their coats of mail, where their blood tingles for the fight, and words are but the harbingers of blows. Of this state of accomplished barbarism the appeal of Bolingbroke and Mowbray is an admirable specimen. Another of those "keen encounters of their wits" [*Richard III,* 1.2.115] which serve to whet the talkers' words, is where Aumerle answers in the presence of Bolingbroke to the charge which Bagot brings against him of being an accessory in Gloster's death. [Quotes 4.1.33–79] . . .

The characters of old John of Gaunt and of his brother York, uncles to the King, the one stern and foreboding, the other honest, good-natured, doing all for the best, and therefore doing nothing, are well kept up. The speech of the former, in praise of England, is one of the most eloquent that ever was penned. . . . [Quotes 2.1.40–66]

The character of Bolingbroke, afterwards Henry IV is drawn with a masterly hand:— patient for occasion, and then steadily availing himself of it, seeing his advantage afar off, but only seizing on it when he has it within his reach, humble, crafty, bold, and aspiring,

Bolingbroke and Richard enter London, as described in Act V, Scene 2 of *Richard II*. This is an illustration of a 1903 production at His Majesty's Theatre. (*Illustration by Frederick Henry Townsend*)

encroaching by regular but slow degrees, building power on opinion, and cementing opinion by power. His disposition is first unfolded by Richard himself, who however is too self-willed and secure to make a proper use of his knowledge. [Quotes 1.4.23–36] Afterwards he [Bolingbroke] gives his own character to Percy, in these words:

> I thank thee, gentle Percy, and be sure
> I count myself in nothing else so happy
> As in a soul rememb'ring my good
> friends,

And as my fortune ripens with thy love,
It shall be still thy true love's
recompense.

[2.3.45–49]

We know how he afterwards kept his promise. His bold assertion of his own rights, his pretended submission to the king, and the ascendancy which he tacitly assumes over him without openly claiming it, as soon as he has him in his power, are characteristics of this ambitious and politic usurper. But the part of Richard himself gives the chief interest to the play. His folly, his vices, his misfortunes, his reluctance to part with the crown, his fear to keep it, his weak and womanish regrets, his starting tears, his fits of hectic passion, his smothered majesty, pass in succession before us, and make a picture as natural as it is affecting.

Sir Edmund Kerchever Chambers (1866–1954) [Excerpted from the introduction to *The Tragedy of King Richard the Second*, 1891. In addition to providing character analysis and examining Shakespeare's language and the play's structure, Chambers contextualizes the play within its literary and historical milieu. This selection offers an astute analysis of Richard.]

The central idea of *Richard II* is a tragical one; it is a tragedy of failure, the necessary failure of a king, however rightfully he may reign, however "fair a show" [3.3.71] he may present, if he is weak and self-seeking and lawless. The action of the play presents the working out of this tragedy; it traces the downfall of Richard from the scenes where he appears as a powerful monarch, disposing with a word of the lives of his subjects, to that where his unkinged, murdered corpse is borne on to the stage. The instrument of his ruin is his cousin Henry, and therefore Bolingbroke's rise becomes a natural parallel to Richard's fall. The king's own image of the two buckets [4.1.184–189] holds good: in the first act Richard is supreme, Henry at the lowest depth; gradually one sinks, the other ascends, until they are on a level, when they meet at Flint Castle. As is often the case, the turning-point of the action is put precisely in the middle of the play. Still the same process continues, and when the final catastrophe of the last act occurs, the original positions of the two are exactly reversed; it is now Henry's word that is potent to doom Richard. Whether the play has been revised or not, it is at least a marvel of careful workmanship; situations and phrases constantly occur in the second half of the play which are pointed inversions of others at the beginning. The moving forces of the play are thus to be found in the characters of the chief personages, in the clash of the two spirits, one capable, the other incapable, of making circumstances the stepping stones to his own end. . . .

On the delineation of Richard all the resources of Shakespeare's genius have been poured: it is a work of art and love. We have presented to us the portrait of a finely tempered man, gifted and graced in mind and body. He "looks like a king" [3.3.368] for beauty and majesty, with his fair face in which the blood comes and goes. His marvelous wealth of eloquent imaginative speech irradiates the play. . . . The very root of his nature is an exquisite sensitiveness, intellectual and emotional; he reads his cousin's thoughts in his face; he is a lover of music and pageantry, of regal hospitality and luxurious slendour. And withal there are lacking in him the elements which go to make up the backbone of a character. This beautiful, cultured king, for all his delicate half-tones of feeling and thought, is a being devoid of moral sense, treacherous, unscrupulous, selfish; he murders his uncle, robs his cousin, and oppresses his people; he trails the fair name of England in the dust; even in the days of his captivity he regrets his follies, but scarcely regards his crimes. It is not in moral sense only that he is deficient, but in moral and intellectual fibre. . . . In prosperity he yields himself to flatterers; in adversity he puts an idle confidence in a supposed God-given commission to reign. Contrary events are for him not a spur to action, but an incentive to imagination; he plays around them with lambent words; he is always "studying how to compare" [5.5.1]. The best side of him appears when he is fallen; he becomes the part of victim better than that of tyrant; the softer qualities in him move our pity, the sterner ones that he has not are less needed. True, he strikes no blow, and finds a ready comfort in despair, but he keeps his plaining and poetic laments for his friends, and meets the rebel lords with subtle scorn and all the dignity of outraged royalty. Yet even here he betrays, like another of Shakespeare's characters—Orsino in *Twelfth Night*—what we are accustomed to think of as essentially modern faults; he is a shade too self-conscious, a touch too theatrical in his attitude.

MODERN CRITICISM AND CRITICAL CONTROVERSIES

Modern criticism of *Richard II* began with two works: E. M. W. Tillyard's *The Elizabethan World Picture* (1943) and Caroline F. E. Spurgeon's *Shakespeare's Imagery and What It Tells Us* (1935). The former opened an ongoing debate about the play's political outlook and historical context. The latter inaugurated close textual readings of the play as a self-contained artifact.

Tillyard's groundbreaking work, followed the next year by *Shakespeare's History Plays* (1944), claimed that the histories endorsed the orthodox Tudor political doctrine of the divine right of kings to govern badly. This view finds expression in *Richard II* in the speeches of John of Gaunt in Act I, Scene 3; York; the Bishop of Carlisle in Act IV, Scene 1; and Richard. The rebellions that Henry IV faces at the end of *Richard II* and throughout the next two plays, and the Wars of the Roses dramatized in the first Henriad, are punishment for the deposition of the rightful king, according to Tillyard's reading of Shakespeare. Tillyard saw in Shakespeare's histories an endorsement of the ideal of order. In these works, audiences see the working out of a divine plan for the triumph of the Tudor dynasty and a warning against any attempt to remove Elizabeth.

Tillyard thus broke with the 19th-century focus on character in the plays. He placed these works squarely in their historical and intellectual context. For him, Shakespeare was using the English past to comment on the English present, making Shakespeare a humanist historian who regarded the past as a teacher of universal lessons as well as a conservative upholder of Tudor orthodoxy.

Lily B. Campbell's *Shakespeare's Histories* (1947) went even further in Tillyard's contextualizing direction, linking events in the play to those of Elizabeth's reign. The death of Gloucester, ordered by Richard in the play, would recall the death of Mary, Queen of Scots, ordered by Elizabeth. Both actions were of questionable legality. Elizabeth was also accused of listening to favorites (the earl of Leicester and later the earl of Essex) to the detriment of her kingdom and of farming out her realm to them, the same charges that were leveled at Richard. However, just as John of Gaunt declares that only God can judge and punish Richard, so Shakespeare's play argues that Elizabeth's subjects were bound to obedience. Campbell thus situated the play squarely in the late 16th century despite its setting of nearly 200 years earlier.

Some later critics have endorsed the views of Tillyard and Campbell, at least regarding Shakespeare's use of history as commentary on contemporary politics. Coppélia Kahn's *Man's Estate* (1981) reads Shakespeare's plays about medieval society as statements about the early modern world in which he was living. Other critics, such as Graham Holderness in *Shakespeare's History* (1985), dissent. According to Holderness, Shakespeare, like some 16th-century historians, recognized that, as L. P. Hartley wrote, the past is another country;

they do things differently there. Holderness claims: "The plays are not thinly disguised studies of Tudor England in the 1590s. . . . Nor do they obediently mime the official ideology of the state, reshaping the past into Tudor apology" (131). Rather, Shakespeare's plays about feudalism treat that period and have no connection with Tudor England.

Tillyard's interpretation of the histories as endorsements of a providential universe has also been challenged. Norman Rabkin in *Shakespeare and Common Understanding* (1967) agrees with Tillyard that *Richard II* poses the question of what to do about a legitimate ruler who governs badly. Richard and John of Gaunt believe that the king is sacrosanct, yet Richard's supporters Aumerle and Carlisle urge him to use earthly means to retain the throne and not to rely on providence. The civil wars that ensue after Richard's deposition may not result from divine retribution, and the plays show that Henry IV and Henry V governed better than did Richard. Deposing a legitimate but bad king may not be sinful after all. Rabkin argues that *Richard II* and Richard II are ambiguous. The latter earns the audience's sympathy as a character even as he fails as a monarch. Alvin Kernan's essay "*The Henriad: Shakespeare's Major History Plays*" (1969), which coined the term *Henriad,* regards the four plays as an ambiguous epic that moved from the fixed world of feudalism to the mutability of the Renaissance.

Henry Ansgar Kelly's *Divine Providence in the England of Shakespeare's Histories* (1970) also challenges Tillyard's assumption of a monolithic world view in Tudor England. Kelly finds three competing myths in Renaissance historiography: a Lancastrian myth, a Yorkist myth, and a Tudor myth. The French chronicler Jean Froissart (ca. 1337–ca. 1405) and the historian and poet Jean Creton (fl. 1386–1420) sympathized with Richard II. The English chronicler Thomas Walsingham (d. 1422) regarded Richard's downfall as just punishment for the murder of Thomas of Woodstock and saw Henry IV as God's anointed. Walsingham thus endorsed the Lancastrian view of history. Yorkists viewed the Lancastrian Henries (IV, V, VI) as usurpers justly dispossessed by Richard III. The

Tudor myth favored the Lancastrians but integrated Yorkist aspirations through the marriage of Henry VII with the Yorkist Elizabeth.

Jan Kott (*Shakespeare, Our Contemporary* [1964]), Moody E. Prior (*The Drama of Power* [1973]), and John Wilders (*The Lost Garden*, [1978]) interpret *Richard II* as rejecting a providential universe. For Kott, Shakespeare is modern because he understands that power, not providence, determines history. Prior acknowledges that Shakespeare used history to draw lessons for his contemporaries, but those lessons deal with the secular issues of how to govern. For Wilders, the histories depict the repeated failure of flawed humans to create a perfect world, thereby enacting a secular fall of humanity.

Caroline Spurgeon's groundbreaking study looks back to 19th-century attempts to use the plays to discover Shakespeare's moods and mind. For Spurgeon, Shakespeare's use of garden imagery reveals his love of the English countryside. Yet her focus on the texts rather than on their context and on language rather than character marks a break with earlier analyses and anticipates New Critical studies. She points out the thematic significance of the garden scene at the center of *Richard II* (3.4). Even though it does nothing to advance the plot, it highlights the play's central concern through its metaphors: the loss of Eden through Richard's destructive behavior. Spurgeon also notes the play's references to Richard as sun king, to birth and regeneration, and to inheritance, and she relates these images to a central concern of both tetralogies: the legacy of discord inherited from civil unrest.

Richard D. Altick's New Critical article "Symphonic Imagery in *Richard II*" (1947) catalogs a dozen images that wind through the play. Altick argues that these terms, such as earth, gardens, blood, pallor, the sun, tears, dark blots, generation, and the crown work together to unify the play structurally. For Arthur Suzman, in "Imagery and Symbolism in *Richard II*" (1956), the playwright uses images of rising and falling to convey the play's theme, establish character, and carry the action. Katherine Montgomery Harris similarly examines another set of conceits in her article "Sun and Water Imagery in *Richard II*" (1970). Yet another such study is Clayton G. Mackenzie's "Paradise and Paradise Lost in *Richard II*" (1986), which looks at images of life and health versus imagery of death in the play as well as references to gardens. Such close readings illuminate the work.

THE PLAY TODAY

Richard II is recognized today as one of Shakespeare's greatest history plays, but it is generally admired somewhat less than the subsequent plays in the Henriad tetralogy—*Henry IV, Part 1* and *Henry IV, Part 2*. Nonetheless, its complex portrayal of a flawed leader—though much less flawed than the monstrous Richard in *Richard III*—has an obviously timeless appeal for those interested in the role of politics in society. The play has appeared onscreen only in small-scale productions, including a BBC version with Ian McKellen in 1970, a 1978 BBC version with Derek Jacobi, and a 2001 avant-garde film directed by John Farrell. Perhaps the major 21st-century stage presentation was the 2005 production at the Old Vic in London, starring Kevin Spacey.

Recent criticism of the play has built on close reading and historical contextualization even as it has incorporated the influences of feminism, cultural materialism, New Historicism, and deconstruction that have added concerns of gender, linguistic ambiguity, and political power. These approaches emphasize the indeterminacy of the text itself as well as its multiple possible meanings.

An example of criticism's concern with the play's anatomizing of power is Christopher Pye's 1988 article "The Betrayal of the Gaze: Theatricality and Power in Shakespeare's *Richard II*" (1988). Pye examines the ways in which Richard and Bolingbroke create power and subvert it at the same time. In the deposition scene, Richard asserts his kingship by giving it away. Only the legitimate ruler can remove himself from the throne. Yet Richard cannot prevent Bolingbroke's usurpation; even as Richard asserts and Bolingbroke acknowledges Richard's power to depose himself, Richard's power shifts to the new ruler.

Richard (Herbert Beerbohm Tree) and the Queen (Lily Brayton) exchange tearful farewells in Act V, Scene 1 of *Richard II*. This is an illustration of the 1903 production at His Majesty's Theatre. *(Illustration by Balliol Salmon)*

Catherine Belsey's essay "Making Histories Then and Now: Shakespeare from *Richard II* to *Henry V*" (1989) offers a twist on Tillyard's view of the Tudor rage for order and unity and also on New Criticism's focus on the play's language. She argues that *Richard II* opens with the illusion of Tillyard's Elizabethan World Picture. Kings go on crusades. Words are faithful representations of things. Names and their meaning are one. John of Gaunt, who represents this old order, puns on his name to show that he is gaunt/Gaunt indeed (2.1). Richard, however, has divorced word and thing. Though he has the title of king, he has reduced himself to landlord of England. He also tries to

separate Bolingbroke, rightful duke of Lancaster, from his title. Richard's actions lead to his deposition. The name of king, which Richard thought was worth 20,000 men, becomes valueless.

Consequently, Richard cannot survive. If he is not king, he says, "I must nothing be" (4.1.201). He likens himself to a snowman melting before the sun of Bolingbroke, an apt image for his disintegrating identity. He will not just die; he will vanish. This separation of word and thing persists throughout the tetralogy. Only power creates reality. Richard was the legitimate king because he inherited the throne. Henry IV and the succeeding Lancastrians are legitimate kings only if they can defeat their rivals.

Jean E. Howard and Phyllis Rackin's *Engendering a Nation* (1997) demonstrates how feminist criticism can add to an understanding of the play and also to the period in which it was composed. In the first Henriad and in *King John,* women play important roles. In *Richard II,* women are relegated to minor parts, and their concerns are domestic rather than dynastic. Isabella laments her separation from her husband. She would accept his deposition if she and Richard could be exiled together. The Duchess of Gloucester wants revenge against the king because he ordered her husband killed. She does not concern herself with the legality or political implications of her desire. When the Duchess of York pleads for her son's life, she is not thinking about the consequences of his attempted treason. John of Gaunt's male response to his sister-in-law and York's to his wife emphasize public rather than private implications: An anointed king can be punished only by God; treason must not go unpunished.

The grieving women in the play—and all the women grieve—expose the cost of male action over which they have no control. The Duchess of Gloucester dies of grief. Isabella, separated from Richard, goes into exile. The Duchess of York achieves her goal of saving her son but then vanishes from the play.

The marginality of women in the play appears in the triumph of the manly Bolingbroke. Richard shows himself effeminate. Shakespeare does not raise the issue of the king's homosexuality the way Marlowe did that of Edward II, though Bolingbroke hints at it when he accuses Bushy and Green of separating Richard from Isabella. Shakespeare's audiences would nonetheless regard Richard's behavior as feminine. He cries; he talks rather than acts. In Deborah Warner's 1995 production of the play, Fiona Shaw played Richard to highlight the king's effeminacy.

Bolingbroke appears onstage with a strong father, and late in the work, he asks about his son. Bolingbroke has neither mother nor wife; Richard has no father or son. Lord Ross says that Richard's seizing of Bolingbroke's inheritance has left Bolingbroke "bereft and gelded of his patrimony" (2.1.237). Bolingbroke returns to England to regain not just his property but also his masculinity. Howard and Rackin argue that the play reflects male concerns about female rule. Elizabeth I valued courtly display over military prowess. They thus contextualize the play quite as much as Tillyard had, but their focus adds another dimension to the work.

FIVE TOPICS FOR DISCUSSION AND WRITING

1. **Bolingbroke versus Richard:** Does Bolingbroke prove in this play to be a better ruler than Richard? Does he prove to be a better human being? Does the play suggest that power tends to corrupt, and that absolute power tends to corrupt absolutely, as Lord Acton observed?

2. **Imagery:** Choose one or more image patterns in the play and trace Shakespeare's use of them to reveal character and thematic concerns. You might start with what many critics consider to be the finest passage in the play: the speech by Richard that begins, "I have been studying how I may compare / This prison where I live unto the world." How does the prison imagery inform our understanding of Richard's condition, both before and after he is imprisoned?

3. **Tragedy:** The 1597 quarto edition of this play refers to it as a tragedy. Is this play truly the tragedy of Richard II? If so, what kind of tragedy is it? Is it an Aristotelian tragedy in which a good person is destroyed because of a tragic flaw? Is it more of a tragedy than Shakespeare's other history plays?

4. **The hero:** William Makepeace Thackeray subtitled his *Vanity Fair* piece "A Novel without a Hero." Does *Richard II* have a hero? If so, who is it? Some have suggested the hero is England itself. Is that true, or is Bolingbroke or even Richard more a true hero?

5. **Politics:** Does *Richard II* endorse a Machiavellian view of the world? Bolingbroke is certainly a more successful politician. Will his success benefit England?

Bibliography

Altick, Richard D. "Symphonic Imagery in *Richard II.*" *PMLA* 62, no. 2 (June 1947): 339–365.

Beard, Thomas. *The Theatre of God's Judgements.* London: Adam Islip, 1612.

Belsey, Catherine. "Making Histories Then and Now: Shakespeare from *Richard II* to *Henry V.*" In *Uses of History: Marxism, Postmodernism and the Renaissance,* edited by Francis Barker, Peter Hulme, and Margaret Iverson, 24–46. Manchester, U.K.: Manchester University Press, 1991.

Bloom, Harold. *Shakespeare: The Invention of the Human.* New York: Riverhead, 1998.

Brooke, Nicholas, ed. *Shakespeare: Richard II: A Casebook.* London: Macmillan, 1973.

Bullough, Geoffrey. *Earlier English History Plays: Henry VI, Richard III, Richard II.* Volume 3 of *Narrative and Dramatic Sources of Shakespeare.* London: Routledge and Kegan Paul; New York: Columbia University Press, 1960.

Calderwood, James L. *Metadrama in Shakespeare's Henriad.* Berkeley: University of California Press, 1979.

Campbell, Lily B. *Shakespeare's "Histories": Mirrors of Elizabethan Policy.* San Marino, Calif.: Huntington Library, 1947.

Chambers, E. K. *William Shakespeare: A Study of Facts and Problems.* 2 vols. Oxford: Clarendon, 1930.

Coyle, Martin, ed. *William Shakespeare: Richard II.* New York: Columbia University Press, 1998.

Daniel, Samuel. *Civile Wars.* New Haven, Conn.: Yale University Press, 1958.

Forker, Charles R. *Shakespeare: The Critical Tradition: Richard II.* London: Athlone Press, 1998.

Garber, Marjorie. *Shakespeare After All.* New York: Pantheon Books, 2004.

Hall, Edward. *The Union of the Two Noble and Illustrate Famelies of Lancastre and Yorke.* London: R. Graftoni, 1548.

Harris, Katherine Montgomery. "Sun and Water Imagery in *Richard II.*" *Shakespeare Quarterly* 21, no. 2 (Spring 1970): 157–165.

Heywood, Thomas. *An Apology for Actors.* London: N. Okes, 1612.

Hodgdon, Barbara. *The End Crowns All: Closure and Contradiction in Shakespeare's History.* Princeton, N.J.: Princeton University Press, 1991.

Holderness, Graham. *Shakespeare: The Histories.* New York: St. Martin's Press, 2000.

———. *Shakespeare's History.* New York: St. Martin's Press, 1985.

Holinshed, Raphael. *Holinshed's Chronicles of England, Scotland, and Ireland.* 6 vols. London: Johnson, 1807.

Howard, Jean E., and Phyllis Rackin. *Engendering a Nation: A Feminist Account of Shakespeare's English Histories.* London: Routledge, 1997.

Kahn, Coppélia. *Man's Estate: Masculine Identity in Shakespeare.* Berkeley: University of California Press, 1981.

Kantorowicz, Ernst H. *The King's Two Bodies: A Study in Medieval Political Theology.* Princeton, N.J.: Princeton University Press, 1957.

Kelly, Henry Ansgar. *Divine Providence in the England of Shakespeare's Histories.* Cambridge, Mass.: Harvard University Press, 1970.

Kenan, Alvin. "*The Henriad:* Shakespeare's Major History Plays." *Yale Review* 59 (1969): 3–32.

Kott, Jan. *Shakespeare, Our Contemporary.* Translated by Boleslaw Taborski. Garden City, N.Y.: Doubleday, 1964.

MacKenzie, Clayton G. "Paradise and Paradise Lost in *Richard II.*" *Shakespeare Quarterly* 37, no. 3 (Autumn 1986): 318–339.

Nash, Thomas. *Pierce Penilesse: His Supplication to the Divell.* 1592. Reprint, Edinburgh: Edinburgh University Press, 1966.

Newlin, Jeanne T., ed. *Richard II: Critical Essays.* New York: Garland, 1984.

Ornstein, Robert. *A Kingdom for a Stage: The Achievement of Shakespeare's History Plays.* Cambridge, Mass.: Harvard University Press, 1972.

Pearlman, E. *William Shakespeare: The History Plays.* New York: Twayne, 1992.

Prior, Moody E. *The Drama of Power: Studies in Shakespeare's History Plays.* Evanston, Ill.: Northwestern University Press, 1973.

Pugliatti, Paola. *Shakespeare the Historian.* London: Macmillan, 1996.

Pye, Christopher. "The Betrayal of the Gaze: Theatricality and Power in Shakespeare's *Richard II*." *ELH: English Literary History* (1988): 575—598.

Rabkin, Norman. *Shakespeare and the Common Understanding.* New York: Free Press, 1967.

Rackin, Phyllis. *Stages of History: Shakespeare's English Chronicles.* London: Routledge, 1991.

Read, Herbert Edward. *The English Vision: An Anthology.* London: Eyre, 1933.

Reese, M. M. *The Cease of Majesty.* London: Edward Arnold, 1961.

Richmond, H. M. *Shakespeare's Political Plays.* New York: Random House, 1967.

Ribner, Irving. *The English History Play in the Age of Shakespeare.* London: Methuen, 1957.

Saccio, Peter. *Shakespeare's English Kings: History, Chronicle, and Drama.* 2nd ed. Oxford: Oxford University Press, 2000.

Saul, Nigel. *Richard II.* New Haven, Conn.: Yale University Press, 1997.

Shakespeare, William. *King Richard II.* Updated ed. Edited by Andrew Gurr. Cambridge: Cambridge University Press, 2003.

———. *King Richard II.* Edited by John Dover Wilson. Cambridge University Press, 1968.

———. *Shakespeare's History Plays: Richard II to Henry V.* Edited by Graham Holderness. London: Macmillan, 1992.

Shewring, Margaret. *King Richard II.* Shakespeare in Performance Series. Manchester, U.K.: Manchester University Press, 1996.

Siemon, James R. *Word against Word: Shakespearean Utterance.* Amherst: University of Massachusetts Press, 2002.

Smidt, Kristian. *Uncomformities in Shakespeare's History Plays.* Atlantic Highlands, N.J.: Humanities Press, 1982.

Sprague, Arthur Colby. *Shakespeare's Histories: Plays for the Stage.* London: Society for Theatre Research, 1964.

Spurgeon, Caroline F. E. *Shakespeare's Imagery and What It Tells Us.* Cambridge: Cambridge University Press, 1935.

Suzman, Arthur. "Imagery and Symbolism in *Richard II.*" *Shakespeare Quarterly* 21, no. 2 (Spring 1970): 157–165.

Thayer, C. G. *Shakespearean Politics: Government and Misgovernment in the Great Histories.* Athens: Ohio University Press, 1983.

Thomas in Woodstock. Edited by Peter Curbin and Douglas Sedge. Manchester: Manchester University Press, 2009.

Tillyard, E. M. W. *The Elizabethan World Picture.* London: Chatto & Windus, 1943.

———. *Shakespeare's History Plays.* London: Chatto & Windus, 1944.

Traversi, Derek. *Shakespeare: From Richard II to Henry V.* Stanford, Calif.: Stanford University Press, 1957.

Wilders, John. *The Lost Garden: A View of Shakespeare's English and Roman History Plays.* Totowa, N.J.: Rowman and Littlefield, 1978.

Wood, Michael. *Shakespeare.* New York: Basic, 2003, 142–143.

FILM AND VIDEO PRODUCTIONS

Bardwell, Jenny, dir. *Richard II: Casting a King.* With Derek Jacobi, Ian McKellan, and Fiona Shaw. Films for the Humanities and Sciences, 2002.

Bogdanov, Michael, dir. *Richard II.* Films for the Humanities and Sciences, 1990.

Cottrell, Richard, and Toby Robertson, dirs. *The Tragedy of Richard II.* With Ian McKellen, Timothy West, David Calder, Andrew Crawford, Lucy Fleming, and Paul Hardwick. BBC, 1970.

Farrell, John, dir. *Richard the Second.* With Matte Osian, Kadina de Elejalde, and Frank O'Donnell. Farrellmedia, 2001.

Giles, David, dir. *Richard II.* With Derek Jacobi, John Gielgud, Charles Keating, and Wendy Hiller. BBC, 1978.

Menmuir, Raymond, dir. *The Life and Death of Richard II.* With Ric Hutton, Richard Parry, and Hugh Stewart. Australian Broadcasting Corporation, 1960.

Morley, Royston, dir. *Richard II.* With Alan Wheatley and Brian Nissen. BBC, 1950.

Woodman, William, dir. *Richard II.* With David Birney and Paul Shenar. Bard Productions, 1982.

—Joseph Rosenblum

Richard III

INTRODUCTION

Richard III concludes Shakespeare's first tetralogy, or group of four plays, treating the Wars of the Roses. The play hearkens back to events and characters from the three parts of *Henry VI,* which Shakespeare wrote immediately before *Richard III.* Yet it demonstrates a major development in Shakespeare's stagecraft. Richard is Shakespeare's first great character, and this is the first of his histories to focus on an individual rather than on events. In some ways, the play is still an apprentice piece. It contains 40 named characters, rendered more confusing by multiple Richards, Edwards, and Elizabeths. By contrast, *Richard II,* dating from a few years later, has only 29 named characters, and they are more easily distinguished. *Richard III* is highly rhetorical in a self-conscious way. Shakespeare would rely on rhetorical tropes throughout his career, but in his early plays, these call attention to themselves. Later he would learn to conceal these devices and to particularize speech patterns. Richard, Anne, the Duchess of York, and Margaret employ the same balanced sentences, stichomythia, and puns.

Shakespeare had also not yet fully learned how to portray characters from the inside out, to show them thinking. Richard's early soliloquies amuse with their wit, but his words sound rehearsed. He usually knows what he will say before he speaks, though in his final soliloquy as well as that at the end of 1.2, he finds his meaning as he talks. Still, Richard is a powerful presence onstage, and he anticipates the more psychologically complex villains of the tragedies: Iago, Edmund, and Macbeth. What Richard lacks in interiority, he makes up for with wit and cunning, and he energizes the play. He is never absent from the stage for long, and when he is, the play flags until he reappears.

None of the other male characters can rival Richard's interest, but Shakespeare creates a virtual Greek chorus of women who repeatedly challenge the duke/king. They cannot defeat him, but he does not prevail either, and Queen Elizabeth beats him at his own Machiavellian game of pretense. *Titus Andronicus* and the *Henry VI* plays contain powerful women as well, but Tamora and Margaret in those works anticipate Lady Macbeth in their cruelty. Here, for the first time, Shakespeare offers women who are both powerful and sympathetic.

As the chorus of women as well as avenging ghosts (5.3) suggest, the classical influence remains strong. Shakespeare's first comedy, *The Comedy of Errors,* and first tragedy, *Titus Andronicus,* clearly reveal their Roman models. *Richard III* draws heavily on Seneca for language and characterization, but Shakespeare blends the Roman with native theatrical traditions and subject matter to produce something rare and strange. A powerful piece in itself, *Richard III* shows Shakespeare feeling his way to the greater artistry that will manifest itself in his second tetralogy of English histories and the great tragedies that follow.

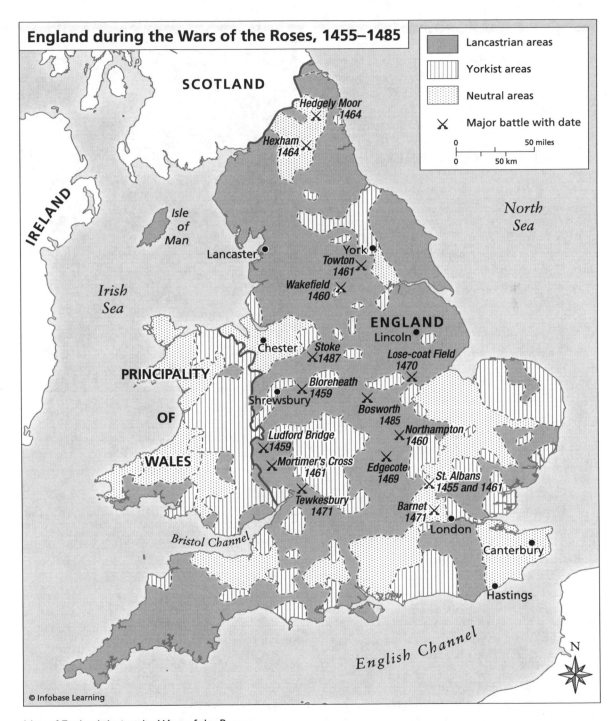

England during the Wars of the Roses, 1455–1485

▨	Lancastrian areas
▥	Yorkist areas
░	Neutral areas
✕	Major battle with date

SCOTLAND

IRELAND

Isle of Man

Lancaster

Irish Sea

North Sea

Hedgely Moor *1464*

Hexham *1464*

York
Towton 1461

Wakefield 1460

ENGLAND
Lincoln

Chester

PRINCIPALITY

Shrewsbury

Stoke 1487

Bloreheath 1459

Lose-coat Field *1470*

Bosworth 1485

OF

Ludford Bridge 1459

Northampton 1460

WALES

Mortimer's Cross 1461

Edgecote 1469

St. Albans 1455 and 1461

Tewkesbury 1471

Barnet 1471

London

Bristol Channel

Canterbury

Hastings

English Channel

N

© Infobase Learning

Map of England during the Wars of the Roses

BACKGROUND

Richard III culminates with the triumph of Henry Tudor, Queen Elizabeth's grandfather. The play's subject was therefore significant to the reigning monarch, whose legitimacy depended on the justice of Richard's overthrow. The Queen's Men, the acting company created by the monarch herself, performed a play on this subject, *The True Tragedie of Richard the Third* (pub. 1594), an important source for Shakespeare's work. *The True Tragedie* covers the same period, with many of the same incidents, as Shakespeare's Acts II–V.

The prologue to *The True Tragedie* opens with the Ghost of Clarence calling for revenge; Shakespeare shows the death of Clarence in 1.4 and brings back his ghost in 5.3. Truth in the prologue describes Richard as "A man ill-shaped, crooked backed, lame armed, withal valiantly minded, but tyrannous in authority" (ll. 50–51). Physically and psychologically, Shakespeare's Richard mirrors this image. In the opening scene of *The True Tragedie,* the dying Edward IV tries to reconcile the rival factions on his court, as he does in 2.1 of Shakespeare's work. In the following scene, citizens discuss the king's death; that is the subject of Shakespeare's 2.3. Richard's royal ambition manifests itself in *True Tragedie*'s third scene; Shakespeare had made his aspiration plain in *Henry VI, Part 3,* 3.2. In a soliloquy in that scene, Richard speaks of disguising his intentions. The Richard of *True Tragedie* similarly depicts himself as an actor: "I will so plaie my part, / That ile be more than I am, and not much lesse then I looke for" (Scene 3).

Richard's usurpation proceeds similarly in both works; Shakespeare even borrows some of the imagery from the earlier play. In Scene 7 of *True Tragedie,* Richard tells Rivers, "Nay ouer boord al such mates I hurl, whilst I do guid the helme." At 1.4.18–20 of Shakespeare's play, Clarence dreams that as he and his brother are sailing to France, "Methought that Gloucester [Richard] stumbled, and in falling / Strook me (that thought to stay him) overboard / Into the tumbling billows of the main." At the council at the Tower of London in Scene 10 of *True Tragedie,* Richard accuses Queen

The murder of the princes in the Tower of London in Act IV, Scene 3 of *Richard III.* This is a print from the Boydell Shakespeare Gallery project, which was conceived in 1786 and lasted until 1805. *(Painting by James Northcote; engraving by William Skelton)*

Elizabeth and Jane Shore of bewitching him. Hastings, Shore's lover, tries to defend her. Richard interrupts Hastings's "If" with "If villain, feedst thou me with Ifs & ands" and orders Hastings's execution. In 3.4, Hastings declares, "If they have done this deed, my noble lord—" and Richard replies, "If? Thou protector of this damned strumpet, / Talk'st thou to me 'ifs'? Thou art a traitor. / Off with his head!" (ll. 73–76).

The True Tragedie shows the killing of the princes in the Tower, which Shakespeare only reports. In this scene (12) of *True Tragedie,* Jack Denten hesitates to perform the murder, and Will Slawter chides him. Afterward, Myles Forest remarks, "a bloody deed we have performed."

Shakespeare uses this material in the killing of Clarence. The second murderer in 1.4 suffers pangs of conscience, for which the first murderer chides him. After Clarence is dead, the second murderer calls the action "a bloody deed, and desperately dispatch'd" (1.4.271). Just before the princes are killed, Forest, talking to Edward V, refers to Richard as king. Edward retorts, "Am not I King?" Forest corrects himself: "I would have said my Lord your uncle the Protector." Brackenbury similarly slips in this Freudian manner and then corrects himself at 4.1.17–19 in talking to Queen Elizabeth.

After Buckingham's revolt in *True Tragedie*, Richard acknowledges his guilt and considers repentance, only to reject that thought, just as Shakespeare's Richard does after his dream of his victims (5.3). *True Tragedie* does not include this dream sequence, but as the Battle of Bosworth looms, a page remarks there, "Those Peeres which he unkindly murthered, / Doth crie for justice at the hands of God" (Scene 16). Richard himself acknowledges,

> Clarence complaines, and crieth for reuenge,
> My Nephues blood, Reuenge, reuenge, doth
>   crie.
> The headlesse Peeres come pressing for reuenge.
>   (Scene 18)

Both plays show the prebattle interview between Richmond and his stepfather, Stanley. In *True Tragedie,* Stanley observes of Richard's army, "The chiefest of his company are liker to flie to thee, then to fight against thee" (Scene 17). Shakespeare gives similar words to Blunt: "He hath no friends, but what are friends for fear, / Which in his dearest need will fly from him" (5.2.24–25).

In *True Tragedie*'s battle, the wounded Richard cries, "A horse, a horse, a fresh horse" (Scene 19). Shakespeare transformed this line into his famous "A horse, a horse, my kingdom for a horse" (5.4.10). A page in *True Tragedie* urges Richard to flee, but the king refuses. Shakespeare shows Catesby asking Richard to withdraw, but Richard continues to fight. In both plays, Richmond kills Richard.

True Tragedie and Shakespeare drew on a century of historical writing, virtually all of it vilifying Richard and thus strengthening the Tudor claim to the throne. The antiquarian John Rous, writing during Richard's short reign (June 1483–August 1485), was apparently the first to record that Richard was born with teeth (*Henry VI, Part 3* 5.6.75; *Richard III* 2.4.28, 4.4.49) and shoulder-length hair after a two-year gestation. The duchess mentions Richard's difficult delivery at 4.4.162–167. Rous also charged Richard with killing his nephews (4.2–4.3) and first wife (hinted at in *Richard III* 4.2.50–52) and ordering if not carrying out the execution of Henry VI (as shown in *Henry VI, Part 3* 5.6). In the English version of his *History of the Earls of Warwick* (written 1483–85), Rous praised Richard as "a mighty prince and especial good lord . . . in his realm full commendably punishing offenders of the laws, especially oppressors of the Commons, and cherishing those who were virtuous, by the which discreet guiding he got great thanks and love of all his subjects great and poor." These lines do not appear in the Latin version, written perhaps to gain favor with Richard's successor.

Henry VII commissioned Polydore Vergil to write *Angliche Historiae* (completed 1513, pub. 1534). Vergil describes Richard as "little of stature, deformed of body, the one shoulder higher than the right . . . a short and sour countenance, which seemed to savour of mischief, and utter evidently craft and deceit." Vergil repeatedly ascribes ambition and deceit to Richard. Thus, when Richard summons people in York to swear allegiance to Edward V, Vergil claims that Richard was insincere. Yet Vergil also recognized Richard's abilities: "Truly, he had a sharp wit, provident and subtle, apt both to counterfeit and dissemble; his courage also high and fierce." Shakespeare probably did not read Vergil's history, but his play presents all these facets of the Yorkist king.

Shakespeare did read Thomas More's *History of King Richard III* (written 1513, pub. 1543), probably in Edward Hall's *The Union of the Noble and Illustre Famelies of Lancastre and Yorke* (1548) or

Raphael Holinshed's *Chronicles of England, Scotland, and Ireland* (2nd ed., 1587). Hall and Holinshed served as Shakespeare's chief sources for all his history plays. Both writers essentially copy More's account for the period to October 1483, where More's work ends, and supplement this material with Polydore Vergil's account and Richard Grafton's *Continuation of Hardyng's Chronicle* (1543). Holinshed also relied on Grafton's *A Chronicle at Large and Mere History of the Affairs of England and the Kings of the Same* (1569). More grew up in the household of John Morton, who deserted Richard for the future Henry VII. Morton supplied information about Richard and may even have written the Latin life attributed to More. In any event, More's was hardly an unbiased account. However, as John Jowett writes in the introduction to his edition of *The Tragedy of King Richard III* (2000), "More's *History* had various qualities that anticipate Shakespeare's play: interest in the psychology of human motivation, political insight, ethical perspective, depth of texture, subtle irony, and dramatic immediacy" (21).

Like Vergil, More describes Richard as misshapen: "eivill featured of limnes, croke backed, the left shulder muche higher than the righte, harde favoured of visage." Shakespeare has Richard mention his limp (1.1.23) and his withered arm (3.4.73–74), and York alludes to the hump on Richard's back (3.1.130–131). For More, Richard's exterior reveals his character. "He was malicious, wrothfull and envious. . . . He was close and secrete, a depe dissimuler, lowlye of countenaunce, arrogante of herte, outwardely familier where he inwardely hated, not lettynge to kisse whom he thought to kill, despiteous and cruell." More claims that Richard killed Henry VI in the Tower of London and conspired to kill Clarence (*Richard III,* 1.1 and 1.4). More also writes that Richard wanted to be king even while Edward IV lived, as Richard declares in his soliloquy in *Henry VI, Part 3* (3.2). Once Edward IV died, Richard plotted to kill the king's sons. In Shakespeare's play, as in *The True Tragedie,* Edward on his deathbed tries to reconcile the Woodvilles and Yorkist factions (2.1). According to More, Richard arranged for

Edward V to be brought from Ludlow to London with only a small guard so the new king would be easier to seize (2.2.117–140). More reported the executions of Rivers, Grey, and Vaughn at Pomfret Castle (3.3 in Shakespeare), the citizens' forebodings (2.3), the queen taking sanctuary with her younger son (2.4), and Richard removing the boy from her.

In both More and Shakespeare, Buckingham maintains that the youth has no right to seek refuge. In More, the duke argues, "And verily I have harde [heard] of sanctuarye menne, but I never harde before of sanctuary children." Shakespeare translates this speech into blank verse: "Oft have I heard of sanctuary men, / But sanctuary children never till now" (3.1.55–56). Shakespeare mentions Richard's divided councils at Crosbie Place and Baynard's Castle (3.1.179, 3.2.12–14), about which he learned from More. More also recounts Stanley's menacing dream and fear of Richard, the warning Stanley sends to Hastings, and Hastings's dismissal of Stanley's concern (3.2.1–34). Shakespeare's description of the council meeting at the Tower (3.4) derives from More, as does Hastings's belated noting of the omens preceding his arrest for treason.

Shakespeare adapted from More the conversations that Hastings has on his way to that ill-fated meeting. According to More, Hastings stops to talk with a priest. Sir Thomas Howard, whom Richard has sent to accompany Hastings, remarks, "What my lord I pray you come on, wherefore talke you so long with that priest, you have no need of a priest yet." In Shakespeare, Buckingham says much the same thing to Hastings at 3.2.113–115:

> What, talking with a priest, Lord
>   Chamberlain?
> Your friends at Pomfret [Rivers, Grey, and
>   Vaughn, about to be executed],
> they do need the priest,
> Your honor hath no shriving work in hand.

More also mentions Hastings's encounter with a pursuivant (server of warrants) with whom he had spoken when Edward IV was angry with the Lord

Chamberlain. (Shakespeare imagines that Edward had Hastings imprisoned in the Tower [1.1.66–69], though this episode has no historical basis.) In More's account, Hastings observes, "I never in my life [was] merrier nor never in so great surety." Shakespeare uses More's dramatic irony as Hastings declares, "I am in better state than e'er I was" (3.2.104).

More relates that Richard summoned prominent citizens to hear Hastings proclaimed a traitor. To show their fear of Hastings's supposed plot, More writes that Richard and Buckingham donned "olde evill favored briganders" that they would wear only if "some sodeyne neccesitie had constraigned them." In Shakespeare, at the beginning of 3.5, the stage direction calls for the two men to appear "in rotten armor." Richard sends a herald to proclaim Hastings's treason. More reflects, "Nowe was thys proclamacion made within twoo houres after he was beheaded, and it was so curiously endyted and so fayre written in Parchement in a fayre sette hande, . . . that every child might perceive that it was prepared and studied before." Shakespeare's scrivener makes this same point in 3.6.

More claims that the Lord Mayor, Edward Shaw, was complicit in Richard's usurpation and tries to win over the citizenry. Richard also engages the clergymen Raffe Shaw (brother to the mayor) and "Freer Pynkie," (Friar Penker). Both are mentioned in the First Folio version at 3.5.103–104, though not in the quarto. According to More, Richard circulated the story that his brother Edward IV and Edward's children are illegitimate (3.5.74–94), but he urges that his brother's bastardry "should be lesse and more finely & closely handled, not even fully playne and directely, but touched a slope craftily" (More). Shakespeare's Richard says of this matter, "Yet touch this sparingly, as 'twere far off" (3.5.93).

In 3.7, Buckingham reports his speech to the citizens at the Guildhall.

> I did infer your lineaments,
> Being the right idea of your father,
> Both in your form and nobleness of mind.
>   (3.7.12–14)

This irony derives from More, who reports Raffe Shaw's preaching to the citizens that Richard "as well in all princely behaveour as in liniamentes and favour of his visage representeth the very face of the noble duke his father."

The citizens are not impressed; More writes: "They stoode as they had been turned into stones." In Shakespeare, Buckingham compares them to "dumb statues, or breathing stone" (3.7.25). The next day, the citizens are summoned to Baynard's Castle, where Richard appears between two bishops. Shakespeare took this staging from More. The scene unfolds as More described it, though Shakespeare heightens the drama and perhaps the comedy by having the citizens withdraw and Richard recall them. More writes that when Richard accepts the crown, "there was a greate cry and shoute, crying kyng Richard." In the Folio version, the citizens say "Amen" to Buckingham's "Long live Richard, England's worthy king!" (3.7.240–241). In the quarto, only the Lord Mayor responds to Buckingham. Shakespeare thus implies that Richard never enjoyed popular support.

Once Richard becomes king, he and Buckingham fall out. More ponders the reason for this rift. In the play, Shakespeare implies that the killing of the princes (which he copies from More) was a cause, as was Richard's denying Buckingham the earldom of Hereford he had previously promised to give the duke (3.1.194–196). Both explanations appear in More, who adds yet another: Buckingham's jealousy of Richard's glory. Shakespeare does not so darken Buckingham's character, since the duke supports the future Henry VII's claim to the throne.

Shakespeare hastens over the various uprisings against Richard in September and October 1483 (4.4.498–538) and conflates the two attempts by Richmond (the future Henry VII) to claim the throne (4.4.521, 4.5.532–533, Act V) in October 1483 (failed) and August 1485 (succeeded). On the eve of battle, Hall and Holinshed, continuing More's *History,* report, "The fame went out that he [Richard] had the same night a dreadful and a terrible dreame, for it seemed to hym beynge a slepe that he sawe diverse ymages lyke terrible develles which pulled and hauled hym, not sufferynge hym to take any quyet or rest." In 5.3, Shakespeare shows the dream, which he peoples not with devils but with Richard's victims (perhaps inspired by Richard's speech in Scene 18 of *True Tragedie* as noted above). Hall speculates that the dream was prompted by pangs of conscience, which Shakespeare also shows in Richard's last soliloquy (5.3.177–206).

Hall further states that on the eve of battle, the duke of Norfolk received a warning: "Jack of Norfolke be not to bolde / For Dykon thy maister is bought and solde." This couplet appears in 5.3.304–305 as "Jockey of Norfolk, be not so bold, / For Dickon thy master is bought and sold." Richard had taken George Stanley hostage to ensure Stanley's loyalty. When Stanley refused to bring his troops to attack Richmond, Richard ordered George's beheading. According to Hall, unnamed councillors persuaded Richard to defer the execution until the end of the battle. Shakespeare credits the duke of Norfolk with this advice, which results in George's survival, since Richard is defeated and killed. Shakespeare took the order of battle and probably the casualty list (5.5.13–14) from Hall and Holinshed, though the names of the noble dead also appear in *True Tragedie*.

While Holinshed largely copied More and Hall, he added a few elements that Shakespeare used. Hastings's remark at 1.1.136–137, "The king is sickly, weak, and melancholy, / And his physicians fear him mightily," echoes Holinshed's "There was little hope of recouerie in the cunning of his physicians." The bleeding of Henry VI's corpse in the presence of Richard (1.2.55–56) comes from Holinshed, as does the reference to Richard's ominous visit to Rougemont (4.2.104–105) and Richard's error at 5.3.324 stating that Richmond was supported "at our mother's cost." Holinshed had written "mother" rather than the correct "brother." Holinshed describes Richard's sheathing and unsheathing his dagger, which may prompt York's request for this weapon at 3.1.110.

In shaping his play, Shakespeare drew on literary models, particularly the Roman tragedian Seneca and Christopher Marlowe. He would have read Seneca in school, and Seneca's *Tenne Tragedies* appeared in English (translated by Thomas Newton) in 1581. The theme of revenge, use of stichomythia, the appearance of ghosts (5.3), and the play's highly rhetorical balanced sentences all reflect Senecan influence. In a 1980 article, Harold F. Brooks reveals specific debts to the Roman playwright. From Seneca's *Troades*, Shakespeare adapted the roles of the Duchess of York (modeled on Hecuba); Queen Elizabeth (like Andromache); Anne (based on Polyxena); and Margaret, who assumes the role of Helen. Elizabeth, like Andromache, has lost her son. Anne and Polyxena marry an enemy and are sacrificed. Margaret and Helen belong to the opposing side (Lancaster/Greek) but join in the lamentations of their former foes. Like Hecuba, the Duchess of York has seen multiple children killed and, like her, gave birth to the man who would bring destruction to her family (Paris/Richard). Richard's wooing of Anne in 1.2 recalls Lycus's pursuit of Megara in Seneca's *Hercules Furens*. Lycus is an enemy who takes advantage of Hercules' absence to try to win a woman who hates him. Lycus's suit fails, but Shakespeare used his arguments as he invented Richard's more successful attempt. Richard's offering Anne his sword to kill him in that scene resembles Hippolytus's action: He draws his sword but cannot kill Phaedra, who confesses her love for him. In his wooing, Richard attributes his evil actions to love just as Seneca's Medea does in her play.

Though Richard is a historical figure, Shakespeare's presentation of him owes something to Christopher Marlowe's Barabas in *The Jew of Malta* (ca. 1589). Both Richard and Barabas open their respective eponymous plays with a revealing, self-justifying soliloquy. In the prologue to Marlowe's play, Machiavel introduces Barabas as a disciple; Richard's first speech marks him as Machiavellian as well. Both are outsiders, Barabas because of his religion, Richard because of his deformity, and each seeks to avenge himself on the society that has ostracized him. Buckingham assumes the same role as Ithamore: Richard calls Buckingham "My other self" (2.2.120), as Barabas refers to Ithamore as "my second self" (*Jew of Malta* 3.4.15). After rendering faithful service, both Buckingham and Ithamore fall out with their masters and are killed by them. Richard's final soliloquy (5.3.177–206) resembles Faustus's final speech, and the ghosts' repeated "Despair and die!" echo Faustus's words in 5.1.56 of *Doctor Faustus* (ca. 1592).

Eight tragedies in *A Myrrour for Magistrates* (1559; expanded ed., 1563) deal with characters associated with Richard III. Clarence's account, written by William Baldwin, tells of the prophecy that someone whose name begins with G will supplant Edward IV's children on the throne (1.1.53–59). Clarence reports drowning in a butt of malmsey, in which, he says, he was "New Christened." At 1.1.50, Richard tells his brother, "O, belike his Majesty hath some intent / That you should be new christ'ned in the Tower." Thomas Sackville's induction to the duke of Buckingham's tragedy in *A Myrrour* includes a description of Hades that may have provided hints for Clarence's speech in *Richard III*'s 1.4.43–63, though Seneca's plays contain about 25 depictions of hell, Ovid recounts Juno's descent into hell, and in Virgil's *Aeneid*, book 6 is devoted to Hades. In Shakespeare, the treasures that Clarence sees at the bottom of the ocean (1.4.26–33) recall the Cave of Mammon in Edmund Spenser's *Faerie Queene*, 2.7 (1590).

Medieval mystery and morality plays and their 16th-century imitators also influenced Shakespeare's treatment of Richard. Richard resembles Herod of the mystery plays (and the Bible from which these plays derive) in killing the innocent children of Edward IV. Richard also describes himself as a vice of the medieval morality plays: "Thus, like the formal Vice, Iniquity, / I moralize two meanings in one word" (3.1.82–83). This character carried a dagger of lath, as Richard toys with his. Like Richard, too, the Vice disguised his true nature in his interaction with other characters. Hypocrisy in the morality play *Lusty Juventus* (1550) masquerades as Friendship. Perverse Doctrine in *New Custom* (1563) calls himself Sound Doctrine. The Vice took the audience into his con-

fidence, just as Richard does in his soliloquies, and reveled in his evil like Richard, only to be defeated at the end of the play, as Richmond overcomes Richard.

Date and Text of the Play

Under the date of October 20, 1597, the Stationers' Register C, folio 25 recto, records, "Andrew wise / Entred for his copie vnder thandes of mr Barlowe, and mr warden man. / The tragedie of kinge Richard the Third with the death of the duke of Clarence[.]" The first quarto (Q1) of *Richard III* appeared shortly thereafter, bearing the date 1597 on the title page. A second quarto (Q2) appeared in 1598, a third (Q3) in 1602. On June 25, 1603, Wise transferred ownership of *Richard III*, *Richard II*, and *Henry IV, Part 1* to Matthew Law, who brought out further quartos of the play in 1605 (Q4), 1612 (Q5), and 1622 (Q6). *Richard III* was printed among the histories in the 1623 Folio (F), which collected 36 of Shakespeare's plays. Further quartos of the play appeared in 1629 (Q7) and 1634 (Q8). Only *Henry IV, Part 1* was printed in more early quartos than *Richard III*, a testament to the play's popularity. The play probably was written in 1592–93. It may have been first staged then or when the theaters reopened in 1594 after being closed for a long period from mid-1593 to late 1594 because of sedition and plague.

The text of each quarto after the first was based on that of the preceding edition, though with occasional modifications. Q2, for example, adds two lines missing in Q1, and Q3 includes additional stage directions. Q5 was printed from both Q3 and Q4. F derives from Q3, Q6, and a manuscript. F contains about 190 lines more than Q1; F runs to about 3,800 lines, second only to *Hamlet* in length. Q and F differ in more than a thousand readings. Either version was probably too long to perform uncut. The printed version of the 3,000-line John Webster's *Duchess of Malfi* (written ca. 1613, pub. 1623) declares itself "The perfect and exact Coppy, with diverse things Printed, that the length of the Play would not beare in the Presentment."

173

The Tragedy of Richard the Third:
with the Landing of Earle Richmond, and the Battell at Bosworth Field.

Actus Primus. Scœna Prima.

Enter Richard Duke of Gloster, solus.

Ow is the Winter of our Discontent,
Made glorious Summer by this Son of Yorke:
And all the clouds that lowr'd vpon our house
In the deepe bosome of the Ocean buried.
Now are our browes bound with Victorious Wreathes,
Our bruised armes hung vp for Monuments;
Our sterne Alarums chang'd to merry Meetings;
Our dreadfull Marches, to delightfull Measures.
Grim-visag'd Warre, hath smooth'd his wrinkled Front:
And now, in stead of mounting Barbed Steeds,
To fright the Soules of fearfull Aduersaries,
He capers nimbly in a Ladies Chamber,
To the lasciuious pleasing of a Lute.
But I, that am not shap'd for sportiue trickes,
Nor made to court an amorous Looking-glasse:
I, that am Rudely stampt, and want loues Maiesty,
To strut before a wonton ambling Nymph:
I, that am curtail'd of this faire Proportion,
Cheated of Feature by dissembling Nature,
Deform'd, vn-finish'd, sent before my time
Into this breathing World, scarse halfe made vp,
And that so lamely and vnfashionable,
That dogges barke at me, as I halt by them.
Why I (in this weake piping time of Peace)
Haue no delight to passe away the time,
Vnlesse to see my Shadow in the Sunne,
And descant on mine owne Deformity.
And therefore, since I cannot proue a Louer,
To entertaine these faire well spoken dayes,
I am determined to proue a Villaine,
And hate the idle pleasures of these dayes.
Plots haue I laide, Inductions dangerous,
By drunken Prophesies, Libels, and Dreames,
To set my Brother *Clarence* and the King
In deadly hate, the one against the other:
And if King *Edward* be as true and iust,
As I am Subtle, False, and Treacherous,
This day should *Clarence* closely be mew'd vp:
About a Prophesie, which sayes that G,
Of *Edwards* heyres the murtherer shall be.
Diue thoughts downe to my soule, here *Clarence* comes.

Enter Clarence, and Brakenbury, guarded.

Brother, good day: What meanes this armed guard

That waites vpon your Grace?
  Cla. His Maiesty tendring my persons safety,
Hath appointed this Conduct, to conuey me to th'Tower
  Rich. Vpon what cause?
  Cla. Because my name is *George.*
  Rich. Alacke my Lord, that fault is none of yours:
He should for that commit your Godfathers,
O belike, his Maiesty hath some intent,
That you should be new Christned in the Tower,
But what's the matter *Clarence*, may I know?
  Cla. Yea *Richard*, when I know: but I protest
As yet I do not: But as I can learne,
He hearkens after Prophesies and Dreames,
And from the Crosse-row pluckes the letter G:
And sayes, a Wizard told him, that by G,
His issue disinherited should be.
And for my name of *George* begins with G,
It followes in his thought, that I am he.
These (as I learne) and such like toyes as these,
Hath moou'd his Highnesse to commit me now.
  Rich. Why this it is, when men are rul'd by Women:
'Tis not the King that sends you to the Tower,
My Lady *Grey* his Wife, *Clarence* 'tis shee,
That tempts him to this harsh Extremity.
Was it not shee, and that good man of Worship,
Anthony Woodeuille her Brother there,
That made him send Lord *Hastings* to the Tower?
From whence this present day he is deliuered?
We are not safe *Clarence*, we are not safe.
  Cla. By heauen, I thinke there is no man secure
But the Queenes Kindred, and night-walking Heralds,
That trudge betwixt the King, and Mistris *Shore.*
Heard you not what an humble Suppliant
Lord *Hastings* was, for her deliuery?
  Rich. Humbly complaining to her Deitie,
Got my Lord Chamberlaine his libertie.
Ile tell you what, I thinke it is our way,
If we will keepe in fauour with the King,
To be her men, and weare her Liuery.
The iealous ore-worne Widdow, and her selfe,
Since that our Brother dub'd them Gentlewomen,
Are mighty Gossips in our Monarchy.
  Bra. I beseech your Graces both to pardon me,
His Maiesty hath straightly giuen in charge,
That no man shall haue priuate Conference
(Of what degree soeuer) with your Brother.
  Rich.

Title page of the First Folio edition of *Richard III,* published in 1623

Q was long regarded as a "bad" quarto—that is, a corrupt version of the play Shakespeare wrote, which F reproduced accurately. The most popular view of Q was set forth by David Lyall Patrick in *The Textual History of Richard III* (1936). He argued that the Lord Chamberlain's Men lost their prompt-book while touring the provinces. Together, they reconstructed the play from memory, and Q1 is the result. The textual scholar W. W. Greg endorsed this view in his review of Patrick's book (*The Library*, 4th ser., 19 [1938–39]: 118–120). As late as 1996, Peter Davidson, who edited Q1 for Cambridge University Press, repeated Patrick's theory.

In a meticulous study of Q1 and F, Kristian Smidt challenged the prevailing orthodoxy (*Iniurious Impostors and Richard III* [1964]). Smidt argued that Q1 shows no signs of memorial reconstruction. It may be based on the manuscript used for F, but in many places it improves on the Folio text. At 1.4.72, Q omits Clarence's prayer to spare his wife and children. Clarence was killed in 1478, two years after his wife died. According to F, Sir Richard Ratcliffe presides over the executions of Rivers, Grey, and Vaughn at Pomfret (3.3) and Hastings in London (3.4) on the same day, a physical impossibility. Q replaces Ratcliffe with Catesby, Hastings's former servant and friend, in 3.4. Not only is this change sensible, it also shows Richard's ability to seduce Hastings's onetime ally. F shows the Archbishop of York helping Queen Elizabeth seek sanctuary for herself and her son York and the Archbishop of Canterbury convincing her to let York join his brother in the Tower of London. In Q, the Archbishop of York becomes Richard's instrument for securing York, again revealing Richard's power to persuade. F has Edward IV reconciling Rivers and Dorset, who were not enemies; Q correctly has the king asking Hastings and Rivers to shake hands (2.1.7). At 3.2.89 in F, Stanley says, "What, shall we toward the Tower? The day is spent." The action occurs in the morning, so Q's "But come my Lo: shall we to the tower" is more logical. F omits the fine "clock" passage in 4.2.99–116. Elsewhere, F offers better readings. Smidt therefore concludes,

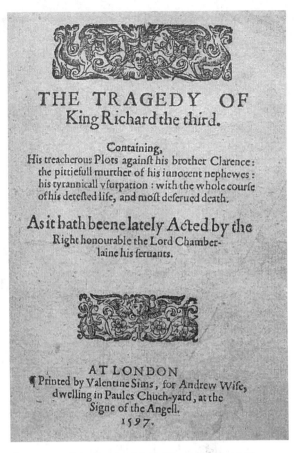

THE TRAGEDY OF
King Richard the third.

Containing,
His treacherous Plots against his brother Clarence:
the pittiefull murther of his innocent nephewes:
his tyrannicall vsurpation: with the whole course
of his detested life, and most deserued death.

As it hath beene lately Acted by the
Right honourable the Lord Chamberlaine his seruants.

AT LONDON
Printed by Valentine Sims, for Andrew Wise,
dwelling in Paules Chuch-yard, at the
Signe of the Angell.
1597.

Title page of the first quarto edition of *Richard III*, published in 1597

[T]he quarto variants have all the appearance of having at some time been produced by a fairly systematic process of revision. . . . [T]he quarto may have been revised for sense and accuracy. The Folio, on the other hand, in addition to avoiding profanity [banned in 1606 under penalty of a heavy fine], may have been revised especially for euphony. . . . There is no doubt that there are many more unmetrical lines in the quarto than in the Folio. (100–102)

Both Q and F are probably revisions of Shakespeare's original draft, perhaps altered by Shakespeare, possibly by other hands, or by a combination of author, actors, and editors.

SYNOPSIS
Brief Synopsis

The play covers the period 1471–85. It opens with the arrest of George, Duke of Clarence, in 1477, part of Richard, Duke of Gloucester's plan to remove all those who stand between him and the throne. The next scene moves back to 1471, three months after the Battle of Tewkesbury, which ended Lancastrian opposition to Edward IV. Shakespeare invents Richard's wooing of Anne Neville as she accompanies the body of her father-in-law, Henry VI, to burial. Scene 1.3 reveals the deep fissures within the court of Edward IV, divisions Richard will exploit. In 1.4, Clarence is killed (1478).

The remaining four acts unfold between 1483 and 1485. Following Edward's unsuccessful effort to reconcile his wife's relatives and his own (2.1), the king dies (2.2). Richard moves to seize the throne. As Lord Protector, he arrests Rivers, Grey, and Vaughn (2.4) and lodges the sons of Edward IV in the Tower of London (3.1). At a council that is supposed to prepare for the coronation of Edward V, Richard arrests Hastings, who opposes Richard's usurpation, and Hastings is executed (3.4). With the help of Buckingham, Richard then tries to persuade the citizens of London to name him king (3.5, 3.7). Despite a lack of popular support, Richard is crowned at Westminster (4.1).

To strengthen his hold on the throne, Richard asks Buckingham to kill the princes in the Tower of London. Instead, Buckingham revolts (4.2, 4.4), but James Tyrrel arranges for the boys' execution (4.3). Richard wants to marry his niece, the daughter of Edward IV, to legitimize his reign. The play implies that Richard is responsible for the death of his first wife, Anne. Queen Elizabeth seems to agree to the match between Richard and her daughter (also named Elizabeth), but the young woman will marry Henry VII instead.

Richard's failure to secure his niece's hand is but one of his growing problems. Messengers report uprisings against him throughout England (4.4),

and Lord Stanley secretly defects to Richmond (5.1), who invades the country to topple Richard. The play's fifth act shows Richard and Richmond preparing for war (5.2–5.3); the play culminates with the Battle of Bosworth (August 22, 1485; 5.4–5.5), in which Richard is killed.

Act I, Scene 1

In his opening soliloquy, Richard declares himself a villain and predicts the imminent arrest of his brother George, Duke of Clarence. As Richard ends his speech, Clarence enters, guarded by Sir Robert Brackenbury, lieutenant of the Tower of London. Feigning ignorance, Richard asks why Clarence is being locked up. Clarence replies that their brother, King Edward IV, has been warned by a wizard that someone with a name starting with the letter G will supplant his children on the throne; Edward assumes that the prophecy points to George, though the audience recognizes that the G refers to Richard, Duke of Gloucester.

Richard blames the queen and her brother, Anthony Woodville, for Clarence's predicament, and he promises to intercede for his brother. Once Clarence departs, Richard declares his intention to have Clarence executed, his hope that Edward IV will die soon, and his plan to wed Anne Neville.

Act I, Scene 2

Anne Neville enters alongside the coffin of Henry VI, whom Richard has recently killed. Richard enters. Anne rails against him; he responds by praising her. To her accusation that he has killed Henry VI and her husband, Edward of Lancaster, Richard replies that her beauty drove him to commit those crimes. He gives Anne his sword and bares his breast, saying that she is free to avenge herself if she wishes, but she should remember that his actions resulted from his love for her. She cannot kill him. He offers to perform the deed himself, but again she demurs. By the end of the scene, Anne has accepted an engagement ring from Richard and agreed to go to Crosby House, one of his London properties, to wait for him. Once she leaves, Richard expresses his amazement that he has won her hand. He informs the audience that he will wed her, but he "will not keep her long" (1.2.256).

Act I, Scene 3

Elizabeth Woodville, wife of the king, laments her husband's illness. Lords Rivers and Grey try to comfort her, as does the Duke of Buckingham. Buckingham announces that Edward wants to make peace between the Woodvilles and Richard. Richard enters complaining that he has been unjustly accused of hating the queen's relatives. Richard and the queen exchange accusations while Queen Margaret, widow of Henry VI, bitterly glosses Richard's speeches. Margaret then comes forward to accuse all the Yorkists of disloyalty to her Lancastrian husband and herself. She thereby achieves what Edward has not: uniting the squabbling factions, who join to condemn her. She curses all except Buckingham, whom she warns to beware of Richard. Catesby enters to summon everyone to the king. Richard remains behind to meet with two murderers he has hired to kill Clarence.

Act I, Scene 4

Clarence tells his jailer of a frightening dream he has had. In this vision, as he and Richard are sailing from England to France, Richard bumps Clarence overboard. After drowning, Clarence crosses the River Styx to Hades, where his father-in-law, Warwick, and Edward of Lancaster, Prince of Wales, denounce him for betraying them. They summon fiends to seize Clarence, and the fiends' howling awakens him.

While Clarence sleeps again, two murderers enter. The duke, awakened, tries to dissuade them from killing him. He assures them that Richard will reward them for their pity. They respond that Richard has sent them. Clarence's pleas convince one murderer to relent, but the other stabs him and then drowns him in a butt of malmsey.

Act II, Scene 1

The ailing King Edward IV believes that he has reconciled the rival factions in his court. His wife urges him to pardon Clarence. Richard responds angrily, accusing her of mockery, since Clarence has been executed at Edward's command. Edward says that he rescinded the order, but Richard retorts that the pardon came too late. Edward blames everyone for Clarence's death, but chiefly himself.

Act II, Scene 2

Clarence's children, Edward and Margaret Plantagenet, discuss their father's death with their grandmother, the Duchess of York. Queen Elizabeth enters to announce that Edward IV has died. Buckingham urges that Edward's son, also named Edward, be brought to London from Ludlow. To avoid strife, Buckingham argues that only a small retinue should escort the prince on his journey. Richard and Buckingham intend to be part of that group.

Act II, Scene 3

Three citizens discuss the king's death and England's prospects.

Act II, Scene 4

In London, the Archbishop of York, the young Duke of York (brother to the Prince of Wales), Queen Elizabeth, and the Duchess of York await the

Queen Elizabeth and the Duke of York in Act II, Scene 4 of *Richard III,* in this print published by Virtue & Company in the 19th century *(Painting by Edward Matthew; engraving by John Henry Robinson)*

arrival of Edward. A messenger arrives to announce that Rivers, Grey, and Vaughan, relatives and allies of the queen, have been arrested at the order of Richard and Buckingham. Elizabeth foresees the downfall of her family. Aided by the Archbishop of York, she flees with her younger son to sanctuary in Westminster Abbey.

Act III, Scene 1

Upon reaching London, Edward asks for his mother and brother. Lord Hastings informs him and his attendants that they have sought sanctuary. Buckingham sends Cardinal Bourchier to take the Duke of York from his mother by persuasion or force. Edward asks Richard where he and his brother are to lodge until the coronation; Richard recommends the Tower of London. The cardinal returns with Edward's brother, who makes some witty observations at Richard's expense. The boys exit for the Tower.

Buckingham, Catesby, and Richard plot to put Richard on the throne. Catesby is commissioned to sound out Hastings and Stanley to learn whether they will support Richard's usurpation.

The young Duke of York reunites with his brother, Prince Edward, before Gloucester, Hastings, Buckingham, Cardinal Bourchier, and Catesby in Act III, Scene I of *Richard III*. This is a print from the Boydell Shakespeare Gallery project, which was conceived in 1786 and lasted until 1805. *(Painting by James Northcote; engraving by Robert Thew)*

Act III, Scene 2

A messenger from Lord Stanley urges Hastings to flee because Stanley has had an ominous dream. Hastings dismisses Stanley's fears. Catesby enters and broaches the plot to depose Edward V. Hastings rejects the idea. Stanley and Catesby leave for a council meeting at the Tower; Buckingham and Hastings follow.

Act III, Scene 3

At Pomfret Castle, where Richard II had been killed, Rivers, Grey, and Vaughan are brought forth to be executed.

Act III, Scene 4

At the council in the Tower, Buckingham, Stanley, Hastings, and the others discuss the upcoming coronation. Richard enters briefly, then leaves with Buckingham. When they return, Richard accuses the queen and Jane Shore, formerly Edward's IV's mistress and now Hastings's, of using witchcraft to wither his arm. Hastings begins to reply, but Richard cuts him off with an accusation of treason and orders his immediate execution. Too late, Hastings recognizes that he should have heeded Stanley's warning and other ominous signs.

Act III, Scene 5

Richard and Buckingham appear on the Tower walls in rusty armor, suggesting that they have armed hastily out of fear of Hastings. They discuss counterfeiting their emotions. Catesby brings the Lord Mayor; Lovell and Ratcliffe arrive with Hastings's head. Richard and Buckingham claim that Hastings intended to kill them in the council chamber that day. Buckingham lies that he had wanted to await the arrival of the Lord Mayor before executing Hastings, so the mayor could have heard the traitor's confession. The mayor replies that Buckingham's assurance of Hastings's treason suffices. After the mayor departs, Richard sends Buckingham after him to imply that Edward's children are bastards, as was Edward himself, and to remind the citizens that Edward mistreated them. Richard intends to isolate the children of Edward and Clarence.

Act III, Scene 6

A Scrivener enters with the indictment he has copied against Hastings. The Scrivener notes the palpable falsehood of the charges but adds that no one is brave enough to challenge them.

Act III, Scene 7

Buckingham reports that the citizens of London have responded coldly to the proposal to crown Richard. London's mayor, aldermen, and citizens gather before Baynard's Castle, where Richard appears to be meditating with two churchmen. Buckingham begs Richard to accept the throne, which Richard initially refuses, protesting that Edward's son is the rightful heir.

Buckingham retorts that Edward's marriage to Elizabeth Woodville was not legal, so his children are illegitimate; hence, Richard should agree to become king. Catesby and the mayor add their pleas. When Richard still declines, Buckingham declares that he will find another person to rule the country, but Edward IV's son will never reign. Buckingham, the mayor, and the others depart. Catesby urges Richard to recall them, which he does. He now agrees to be crowned the next day.

Act IV, Scene 1

Queen Elizabeth; the Duchess of York; Marquess of Dorset; Anne, Duchess of Gloucester; and Lady Margaret Plantagenet (Clarence's daughter) meet before the Tower of London. The queen wants to see her children, but Brackenbury tells them that the king has forbidden visitors to the children. Elizabeth queries the word *king,* which Brackenbury then amends to Lord Protector. Stanley arrives to take Anne to Westminster to be crowned, removing any doubt as to Richard's intention to usurp the throne. Elizabeth urges her son, Dorset, to flee England; Stanley concurs. As the women depart, Elizabeth prays for the welfare of her children in the Tower.

Act IV, Scene 2

King Richard III tells Buckingham to kill the princes in the Tower. Buckingham requests time

The murder of the princes, as described by Tyrrel, in this 19th-century depiction of Act IV, Scene 3 of *Richard III (Engraving by Gustav Lüderitz)*

to consider. Richard sends for Sir James Tyrrel to commit the murders. Stanley announces Dorset's flight.

Richard tells Catesby that Queen Anne is sick and about to die. The king intends to marry Clarence's daughter to a commoner so she will not be a threat to him. To strengthen his claim to the throne, Richard wants to marry Edward IV's daughter.

When Tyrrel appears, Richard instructs him to kill Edward IV's sons. Tyrrel agrees to do so. Buckingham returns to ask for the earldom of Hereford, which Richard has promised him. Richard initially ignores this request and then denies it. After Richard and his supporters depart, Buckingham announces his intention to flee the court.

Act IV, Scene 3

Tyrrel reports the death of the princes. Richard says that he has imprisoned Clarence's son, married Clarence's daughter to a commoner, and killed Anne and Edward's sons. He again declares his desire to wed Edward IV's daughter. Catesby enters to tell the king that John Morton, Bishop of Ely, has fled to Henry Tudor, Earl of Richmond, and Buckingham has raised an army against Richard.

Act IV, Scene 4

In front of the palace, Queen Margaret, widow of Henry VI, hides to overhear and comment upon the laments of the Duchess of York and Queen Elizabeth. Margaret at length comes forward to join the other women in recounting their grief and cursing Richard. Margaret departs, and Richard enters with his attendants on their way to fight Buckingham. The Duchess and Elizabeth condemn the king. After the Duchess departs, Richard tries to persuade Elizabeth to agree to his marriage with her daughter. Their lengthy debate ends equivocally. Richard thinks that he has succeeded, but he will be proved wrong.

Ratcliffe enters to say that Richmond is about to land with an army. Stanley confirms this report. Richard orders Stanley to raise an army to oppose Richmond. Fearing Stanley's loyalty, Richard intends to keep Stanley's son hostage. Once Stanley leaves, a series of messengers arrive to tell of uprisings in various parts of the country and of Richmond's landing at Milford Haven, Wales. Buckingham, however, has been captured.

Act IV, Scene 5

Stanley asks Sir Christopher Urswick to tell Richmond that because Richard holds George Stanley hostage, the earl cannot openly support the rebellion. Urswick should also report that Elizabeth wants her daughter to marry Richmond.

Act V, Scene 1

Buckingham is led forth to execution. He acknowledges that for his treachery to Edward and Edward's family, he deserves his fate.

Act V, Scene 2

At a camp near Tamworth, Richmond urges his forces onward to confront Richard.

Act V, Scene 3

On one side of Bosworth Field, Richard and his army make their camp, while Richmond and his forces camp on the other. Stanley visits Richmond and promises to help him, but not too openly lest Richard kill George. After Stanley departs, Richmond prays and sleeps.

Richard and Richmond dream of the ghosts of those Richard has killed. Each spirit curses Richard and wishes success to Richmond. In the morning, each leader addresses his soldiers. As the scene ends, a messenger tells Richard that Stanley refuses to bring his up forces. Richard wants to kill George Stanley immediately, but Norfolk persuades Richard to wait until after the battle.

Act V, Scene 4

In the midst of the battle, Richard calls for a horse, his own having been killed. Catesby urges the king to withdraw, but Richard refuses.

Act V, Scene 5

Richard and Richmond fight; Richard is killed. Stanley hands Richmond the crown. Richmond declares a pardon to all of Richard's supporters who accept the new regime. He says he will marry Elizabeth of York, thereby uniting the houses of York and Lancaster and ending the Wars of the Roses.

CHARACTER LIST

King Edward IV Ruler of England as the play begins, but he appears physically and emotionally weak, no match for his clever brother Richard.

George, Duke of Clarence Brother of the king; too trusting of his other brother, Richard.

Edward, Prince of Wales Son of Edward IV. A clever youth but at 13 too young to govern or to understand his uncle Richard's political machinations.

Richard, Duke of York Younger brother of the Prince of Wales. A shrewd youth but powerless and marked for destruction.

Edward Plantagenet Son of Clarence.

Richard, Duke of Gloucester Brother to the king; clever, charming, and deadly. He will become Richard III.

Henry Tudor, Earl of Richmond He will defeat Richard at the Battle of Bosworth and so become Henry VII, founder of the Tudor line.

Cardinal Bourchier   Archbishop of Canterbury, manipulated by Richard.

Thomas Rotherham   Archbishop of York. He tries unsuccessfully to shield Queen Elizabeth and her son, the Duke of York, from Richard.

John Morton   Bishop of Ely, who defects to Richmond.

Duke of Buckingham   Richard's cat's paw and then his victim.

Duke of Norfolk   A loyal supporter of Richard who pays for his loyalty with his life.

Earl of Surrey   Norfolk's son.

Anthony Woodville, Earl Rivers   Brother to Queen Elizabeth, one of Richard's many opponents who will be eliminated during Richard's march to the throne.

Marquess of Dorset   Son of Elizabeth, supporter of Richmond.

Lord Grey   Son of Elizabeth and another of Richard's victims.

Earl of Oxford   Richmond supporter.

Lord Hastings   Edward IV's Lord Chamberlain, too trusting of Richard.

Lord Stanley   Also called anachronistically the Earl of Derby, a title he acquired under Henry VII. Ostensibly a backer of Richard, he commits his forces to Richmond.

Lord Lovel   Supporter of Richard III.

Sir Thomas Vaughan   Another of Richard's victims.

Sir Richard Ratcliffe   Part of Richard's inner circle.

Sir William Catesby   Another close ally of Richard.

Sir James Tyrrel   Leader of the murderers of the princes in the Tower of London.

Sir James Blunt   Backer of Richmond.

Sir Walter Herbert   Backer of Richmond.

Sir Robert Brackenbury   Lieutenant of the Tower of London, where the princes are kept and killed.

Sir William Brandon   Richmond's standard bearer at the Battle of Bosworth. He is killed in the fighting.

Christopher Urswick   A priest.

Hastings   A server of warrants who shares the name of Lord Hastings, with whom he speaks in 3.2.

Lord Mayor of London   Eager to please Buckingham and Richard.

Queen Elizabeth   Wife of Edward IV.

Queen Margaret   Widow of Henry VI.

Duchess of York   Mother of Edward, Clarence, and Richard.

Lady Anne   Widow of Edward, the son of Henry VI, and later married to Richard.

Margaret Plantagenet   Daughter of Clarence.

CHARACTER STUDIES
Richard

The role of Richard was the first great part that Shakespeare wrote for Richard Burbage, who would play all the leading characters that Shakespeare created: Romeo, Hamlet, Othello, King Lear, Macbeth, Antony, Coriolanus, Pericles, Prospero. Richard dominates the stage as he controls the action of his play. He speaks 1,145 lines in the Folio version, 1,070 lines in the shorter quarto text, or about a third of the play. Among Shakespeare's characters, only Hamlet has more lines. Richard appears in 14 of the play's 25 scenes, and of the 11 in which he is absent, four contain fewer than 20 lines.

Actors have craved the role at least since 1699, when Colley Cibber, who played the lead, rewrote the play to make Richard an even more dominant figure; in Cibber's revision, Richard delivers 40 percent of the lines. David Garrick, using Cibber's version, debuted in the part on October 19, 1741, in Goodman's Fields; while he managed Drury Lane Theatre, he presented the play 100 times. In the late 18th and 19th centuries, every leading actor played the character: John Philip Kemble, George Cooke, Edmund Kean, Junius Brutus Booth and his son Edwin, and Henry Irving. This trend continued in the 20th century. In his first Shakespearean role, John Barrymore played Richard. Laurence Olivier famously starred in the part on both stage and screen. Among other leading actors to appear as this character were Alec Guiness (Stratford, Ontario,

Junius Brutus Booth as Richard in *Richard III,* in this print published by Gebbie & Husson Company in 1887 *(Illustration by Rouse)*

1953), Christopher Plummer (Royal Shakespeare Theatre, 1961), Alan Bates, Ian Holm, George C. Scott, Anthony Sher (Royal Shakespeare Company, 1984), and Ian McKellen (Royal National Theatre, 1989; film version, 1995).

By the time Shakespeare wrote *Henry VI, Part 3,* he had begun to shape the character of Richard for the final play of the tetralogy. In 1.1 of *Henry VI, Part 3,* Richard urges his father to seize the throne, and by 3.2 of that work, he already speaks of his ambition to become king himself. He reveals his cruelty in killing both Henry VI and Henry's son, and he also boasts of his skills in duplicity: "Why, I can smile, and murther whiles I smile, / And cry 'Content' to that which grieves my heart,

/ And wet my cheeks with artificial tears, / And frame my face to all occasions" (3.2.182–185). In the final scene of *Henry VI, Part 3,* Richard kisses his nephew, whom he loathes. He then likens himself to Christ's betrayer: "so Judas kissed his master, / And cried 'All hail!' when as he meant all harm" (5.7.33–34). In *Richard III,* Richard continues to dissimulate, and in his soliloquies, he shares with the audience his delight in doing so.

Though he lacks psychological depth, Richard is nonetheless a complex character, compounded of diverse elements. One of these is the Machiavel, a figure already popular on the Elizabethan stage. In *The Prince* (1514), Niccolo Machiavelli wrote that a ruler "should appear to be compassionate, faithful to his word, guileless, and devout. And indeed he should be. But his disposition should be such that, if he needs to be the opposite, he knows how. . . . And he should have a flexible disposition, varying as fortune and circumstance dictate."

The motto of the Machiavel is the opposite of Hamlet's: to seem rather than to be. The Machiavel indeed knows "seems," as does Richard, whose speech in *Henry VI, Part 3* quoted above demonstrates. As George Lyman Kittredge writes in his edition of the plays, "Richard may be termed Shakespeare's dramatic interpretation of the Machiavellian villain" (Shakespeare, *Complete Works:* 788). E. E. Stoll makes this point even more forcefully, describing Richard as "charged to the muzzle with Machiavellian principles of egoism, promptitude and resolution, violence and fraud. Like other Machiavels he boasts and gloats, fawns upon and fondles the minions of his villainy, and he plays the hypocrite as egregiously as Barabas" in Christopher Marlowe's *The Jew of Malta* (Stoll: 344).

Every action he undertakes advances Richard's quest for the crown. He begins by eliminating his older brother Clarence (1.1, 1.4). He pursues Anne Neville not because he loves her but because she was betrothed to (in Shakespeare's play married to) the Lancastrian heir to the throne and hence valuable politically (1.2). Later, Richard decides that Edward IV's daughter, Elizabeth, would prove more useful than Anne. Shakespeare implies that

Richard kills his wife so that he can remarry, and he pursues Elizabeth with the same false protestations of love that he employed to win Anne (4.4).

Once Edward IV dies, Richard uses his power as Lord Protector to arrest and execute those who support the dead king's son, Edward V, and he cunningly lodges both of Edward's children in the Tower of London, then a palace as well as a prison. He does not kill only Edward V because he knows that by revealing his ambition while Richard, Edward's other son lives, he would provoke the crowning of that youth. So he waits until both boys are in his power. He suborns powerful figures like the Lord Mayor of London and the Duke of Buckingham, to whom he promises the earldom of Hereford (3.1) to assist in his usurpation. By the beginning of the fourth act, he has so outmaneuvered his opponents that he is crowned king at Westminster.

To the ruthless renaissance prince, Shakespeare, as noted in the Background section, adds the medieval Vice and his 16th-century avatars. Richard compares himself to this figure at 3.1.82–83 in his ability to "moralize two meanings in one word." He demonstrates this skill when he, who is responsible for Clarence's death, declares, "God pardon them that are the cause thereof!" (1.3.314). He appears to refer to the queen, though he actually is speaking of himself. Similarly, when his royal nephew objects to Richard's arrest of Rivers, Richard warns the prince,

> The untainted virtue of your years
> Hath not yet dived into the world's deceit,
> Nor more can you distinguish of a man
> Than that of his outward show, which, God he
>   knows,
> Seldom or never jumpeth with the heart.
> (3.1.7–11)

Though Richard seems to be speaking of Rivers, he is describing himself.

He also boasts that he seems "a saint, when most I play the devil" (1.3.337). Urged to avenge the death of Clarence, he responds by saying that

"God bids us do good for evil" (1.3.334). He arranges to be found between two bishops when the citizens of London call upon him in 3.7, and he pretends to have no desire to be king, though he has summoned the people precisely to be chosen ruler. Though he rejects providence, he repeatedly invokes God's name here. Earlier, he blames Margaret's misfortunes on an avenging God in whom he does not believe (1.3.173–180).

The Vice often represents what is wrong with society. Richard exemplifies the corruption of 15th-century England. Though he is the worst offender, Clarence, Hastings, and Buckingham have all betrayed their oaths, some more than once. Margaret is sympathetic in this play, but in *Henry VI, Part 3,* York aptly describes her as having a "tiger's heart wrapp'd in a woman's hide" (1.4.137). She shows herself as capable of child killing, and man killing, as Richard. Queen Elizabeth snatched the crown from Margaret, just as Richard takes it from Edward V. Richard succeeds not because he is fox among chickens but because he is the cleverest fox in the skulk.

Like the Vice a corrupter and misleader of others, Richard also exhibits the Vice's comedic side. When Clarence laments that he is imprisoned because his name, George, begins with *G*, Richard jests that Edward intends to rechristen him in the Tower (1.1.49–50). When Rivers praises Richard's apparent rejection of revenge against those whom he accuses of killing Clarence, Richard replies in a humorous aside, "had I curs'd now, I had curs'd myself" (1.3.318). Speaking to Brackenbury, Richard observes,

> We say that Shore's wife hath a pretty foot,
> A cherry lip, a bonny eye, a passing pleasing
>   tongue;
> And that the Queen's kindred are made
>   gentlefolk.
> How say you, sir? Can you deny all this?

Brackenbury replies, "With this, my lord, myself have nought to do." Richard puns on Brackenbury's "nought":

Naught to do with Mistress Shore? I tell thee,
   fellow,
He that hath naught to do with [has sex with]
   her (excepting one)
Were best to do it secretly alone.

Since Jane Shore was the king's mistress, Brackenbury inquires, "What one, my lord?" Richard cleverly responds, "Her husband, knave" (1.193–102).

In a 1995 Royal Shakespeare Company production of the play under the direction of Steven
Pimlott, David Troughton's Richard first appears
onstage dressed as a jester. Troughton thus indicates how Richard thinks others see him, but this
costume also emphasizes the comic aspect of the
part. Pimlott and Troughton may have borrowed
the idea of the jester from the Tbilisi, Georgia's,
Rustavelli Company's production from the late
1970s and early 1980s, in which Ramaz Chkh-
ikvadze played Richard as both clown and psychopath and the set used a modified torn circus tent.
This interpretation influenced Antony Sher's acting
of Richard III with the Royal Shakespeare Company (1984–86). Sher's Richard wants power but
also enjoys attaining it, joking with the princes
even as he plans their deaths.

Richard's great appeal to audiences and actors,
and the source of his ability to deceive so many
others on stage, lies in his being a consummate
actor. He revels in the role-playing, and he shares
that enjoyment with audiences in a way that makes
them complicit with him. As already noted, he
stage manages the scene with the citizens (3.7).
Earlier, he gives Buckingham the lines he is to
speak to the assembled Londoners and offers the
duke a Machiavellian version of Hamlet's advice to
the players:

Come, cousin, canst thou quake and change
   thy color,
Murther thy breath in middle of a word,
And then again begin, and stop again,
As if thou were distraught and mad with
   terror?

                                   (3.5.1–4)

Richard's excellence at dissimulation is evidenced by Hastings's assertion that "there's never a
man in Christendom / Can lesser hide his love or
hate than he" (3.4.52). Hastings is therefore convinced that at the council in the Tower, Richard
bears no animosity toward anyone because if Richard were angry with anyone, "he had shown it in
his looks" (3.4.57). In fewer than 20 lines more,
Richard will shout, "Off with his [Hastings's]
head!" (3.4.76). With Anne he can play the devoted
suitor, with Clarence the loyal brother, with the
Woodvilles a reconciled opponent, with the princes
a caring uncle. All believe him, and all end up dead.

He is a monster, but his wit, intelligence, and
charm make him an attractive one. In his essay
"On the Tragedies of Shakespeare" (1811), Charles
Lamb objected to the way George Frederick Cooke
played Richard. Lamb wrote that Cooke clearly
showed Richard's evil side but failed to present
the amiableness of Shakespeare's character. Lamb
writes that in the text,

> A horror of his crimes blends with the effect
> which we feel, but how is it qualified, how is
> it carried off, by the rich intellect which he
> displays, his resources, his wit, his buoyant
> spirits, his vast knowledge and insight into
> characters, the poetry of his part. (Lamb, 252)

Cooke, Lamb concludes, captured only the murderer, whereas Shakespeare mingled with that aspect
"the lofty genius, the man of vast capacity,—the
profound, the witty, accomplished Richard[.]" (252).

Once he attains the throne, though, Richard's energy flags. Antony Sher played Richard on
crutches, but through the first three acts, he is in
constant motion. Michael Coveney, writing in the
Financial Times for June 21, 1984, observed, "His
speed is genuine and frightening. . . . Stunned
momentarily by Queen Margaret's . . . curses,
he springs into a pew and settles, stock still, like
a frog on a stone" (qtd. in Colley, 239–241). In
Sher's interpretation, Richard as king abandons his
crutches and is carried by others. Only in the climactic battle does he move on his own again, his

crutches replaced by a sword and mace. But he is killed as he kneels, not fighting Richmond.

John Barrymore's 1920 performance of Richard also showed disintegration. A review in the *New York World* for March 8, 1920, contrasted the two wooing scenes: "When he woos Lady Anne[,] Richard is on the rising crest of good fortune and is in the best of spirits. But when he interviews the widowed ex-Queen he is beset with fears and is fighting for his Kingdom and his life" (qtd. in Colley, 823). Alexander Woollcott's review for the *New York Times* of that same date also noted Richard's mental disintegration as the play proceeds.

Richard's loss of control appears even as he ascends the throne at the beginning of 4.2. In his first speech as king, he asks Buckingham, "But shall we wear these glories for a day? / Or shall they last, as we rejoice in them?" (4.2.5–6). Richard's first royal request is that Buckingham kill the princes in the Tower; Buckingham refuses, and in 4.3, a messenger reports that the duke is leading a rebellion against his former friend. The same messenger informs Richard that John Morton has joined Henry Tudor. In 4.4, Richard seeks to win the hand of Elizabeth, Edward IV's daughter, just as he had wooed Anne in the first act. Whereas his earlier effort succeeded, this one does not. The scene closes with the arrival of a series of messengers reporting uprisings throughout the country, and Richard orders Ratcliffe to go to the Duke of Norfolk. Changing his mind, he sends Catesby but is so flustered that he forgets to tell the man what he wants done. He also instructs Ratcliffe to go to Salisbury ahead of the king's forces, then reverses himself.

Richard's doubts increase on the eve of battle. Pitching his tent at the edge of Bosworth Field he says, "Here will I lie tonight—/ But where tomorrow?" (5.3.7–8). Even before his harrowing dream, he reflects, "I have not that alacrity of spirit / Nor cheer of mind that I was wont to have" (5.3.73–74). As the battle looms, he tells Ratcliffe that he fears his forces will not remain loyal (5.3.214). This concern is well-founded. Stanley refuses to fight for Richard; instead, his forces join Richmond's, and Richard is defeated.

Richard on the battlefield at Bosworth Field in this 19th-century depiction of Act V, Scene 4 of *Richard III* (*Illustration by Arthur Hopkins; engraving by C. Carter*)

Not all actors playing Richard have followed this arc of rise and fall. Colley Cibber presented a Richard undaunted to the end. Just before the climactic battle, he shakes off his horrible dream and declares, "Conscience avaunt; Richard's himself again" (5.3.85). Olivier's Richard retains Cibber's "Richard's himself again," and he dies fighting savagely. Still, the Barrymore-Sher interpretation is truer to Shakespeare's text, however much some actors want to remain heroic and dominant throughout the play.

Richmond

Evil is always more attractive than good: Satan is more fascinating than Christ in *Paradise Lost;* Dante's *Inferno* is read more than is his *Paradiso.*

Richmond thus begins with a handicap from which he never recovers. Though in the play and historically he defeats Richard on the battlefield, his role cannot rival Richard's for interest or engagement with the audience. He offers no confiding soliloquies. He has no sense of humor. He triumphs not because of his clever planning but rather because Richard finally alienates too many powerful figures who turn to Richmond as the only potentially legitimate alternative.

Just as Shakespeare laid the foundation of Richard's character in *Henry VI, Part 3*—John Barrymore incorporated five scenes from that play into his 1920 *Richard III*—so he was already thinking of Richmond's triumph. At 4.6.67 of that play, Henry VI calls Richmond "England's hope" and puts his hand on the earl's head in benediction. Richard recalls the prediction that he would not live long after seeing Richmond as well as Henry's prediction that Richmond would be king (*Richard III*, 4.2.95–97, 106–107).

Shakespeare sanitizes the Richmond he found in Hall and Holinshed. According to Hall, in his speech to his troops before the Battle of Bosworth, Richmond reminded his followers that they had long been poor, and victory would gain them wealth. This section of the address does not appear in the play. Hall also records Richmond's making a hereditary claim to the throne. Shakespeare omitted this part of his speech as well because it would not withstand scrutiny. Some of Richmond's lines in Hall are given to Blunt, Oxford, and Herbert to show that they share his convictions and are inspired by him.

Whereas Richard speaks of God only when playing to the galleries or disguising his real thoughts, Shakespeare's Richmond is meant to be sincerely pious. His first word after killing Richard is *God.* (5.5.1). In his oration to his soldiers (5.3.237–270), Richmond mentions God six times. Richard in his (5.3.314–341) does not mention God once. Richmond is the unifier; by marrying Edward IV's daughter, he joins the houses of Lancaster and York. His final speech recalls Shakespeare's depiction of the beginning of the Wars of the Roses

(*Henry VI, Part 1*, 2.4) and the horrors of civil war in which fathers and children kill each other (*Henry VI, Part 3*, 2.5). Now the disasters shown in the three *Henry VI* plays yield to Richmond's final words, to "smiling plenty and fair prosperous days!" (5.5.34). Richmond brings peace, but his is a diminished, less heroic, and less entertaining world.

Buckingham

The Duke of Buckingham is Richard's chief supporter in the first three acts of the play. Shakespeare expanded his role from what he found in his sources. For example, in More, Hall, and Holinshed, Richard is chiefly responsible for arranging that Edward, Prince of Wales, should come to London with a small guard, making him and his Woodville relatives more vulnerable. In 2.2, Buckingham makes this proposal; Richard pretends to follow Buckingham's lead (2.2.151–154). As in the chronicles, Buckingham argues against granting sanctuary to Edward V's brother once Richard has imprisoned Edward's IV's older son in the Tower. Shakespeare again expands Buckingham's role by having him instruct Catesby to determine whether Hastings will support Richard's usurpation. Hall writes that Richard "moved Catesby to prove with some wordes cast out a farre of[f], whether he could think it possible to wynne the lorde Hastynges to their part."

In 3.5, Buckingham imagines himself Richard's equal as a thespian:

> Tut, I can counterfeit the deep tragedian,
> Speak and look back, and pry on every side,
> Tremble and start at wagging of a straw;
> Intending deep suspicion, ghastly looks
> Are at my service, like enforced smiles;
> And both are ready in their offices
> At any time to grace my stratagems.
>
> (3.5.5–11)

He and Richard play this scene to convince the Lord Mayor of Hastings's treachery, and in 3.7, Buckingham stage manages the citizens' granting Richard the throne. Buckingham here regards

Richard III asks Buckingham to consent to the murder of the princes in this 19th-century depiction of Act II, Scene 2 of *Richard III. (Painting by W. Nicholas; engraving by John Sartain)*

himself as the director, Richard as his actor, as Buckingham tells Richard how to dissemble. He even gives instructions about props ("get a prayer-book in your hand," 3.7.47) and blocking ("stand between two churchmen," 3.7.48).

Though Buckingham imagines himself in control, he discovers that he is merely another of Richard's pawns. Moreover, he lacks Richard's persuasive powers. In the chronicles, the Londoners acclaim Richard king, but in the play they show no such enthusiasm. In the Royal Shakespeare Theatre (RST) production with Antony Sher as Richard, Buckingham at the beginning of 3.7 reports his failure to move the citizens and then laughs to show that he was joking, implying that he has in fact succeeded with them. Buckingham

thus becomes a jester like Richard. In the RST production, Buckingham also intimidates the Lord Mayor. Historically, though, Buckingham did not secure the people's assent to Richard's rule, and the text reflects that outcome.

Although Buckingham may think himself Richard's equal as politician and actor, Richard has merely used him to gain the throne. Once Buckingham ceases to be useful, Richard dismisses him. Margaret had warned Buckingham not to trust Richard:

> . . . take heed of yonder dog!
> Look when he fawns he bites; and when he
>   bites,
> His venom tooth will rankle to the death.
>   (1.3.288–290)

Too late, Buckingham recognizes the truth of her warning. As he is led to execution on Richard's orders, he recalls her words, "he shall split thy very heart with sorrow" (1.3.299; 5.1.26).

Margaret

As Buckingham learns to his cost, no one can rival Richard. Margaret, widow of Henry VI, comes as close as anyone can. Historically, she had returned to France in November 1475 and died in 1482, so she could not have been present in either of the scenes in which Shakespeare places her. She is the only character to appear in all four plays of the first tetralogy, and she remains a powerful figure throughout. She is the most forceful character in the three *Henry VI* plays, leading the Lancastrian forces. She is also adulterous and cruel. In *Richard III*, she is the lone vestige of the old regime and is left with only the power to curse. This she uses freely.

Margaret is no mere harridan, though. Rather, she embodies Nemesis, vengeance. In 1.3, she curses the Woodvilles and Yorkists, who, much as they distrust and hate each other, unite against her. She curses Elizabeth, "Long mayst thou live to wail thy children's death, / And see another, as I see thee now, / Deck'd in thy rights as thou art stall'd in mine!" She wishes that Rivers, Dorset, and Hastings be "by some unlook'd accident cut off!" (1.3.203–205, 213). She warns Buckingham that if he trusts Richard, Richard will break his heart, and she invokes the heavens to "hurl down their indignation" on Richard (1.3.219).

By the time she reappears in 4.4, many of her curses have been fulfilled. Rivers and Hastings are dead; Queen Elizabeth's sons are as well, and Anne reigns in Elizabeth's stead. Like a Senecan avenging ghost, she overhears the lamentations of her opponents, the Duchess of York and Queen Elizabeth. (By the time this scene supposedly unfolds, 1483, Margaret was, in fact, a ghost). The wheel of fortune has turned, and she witnesses "the waning of mine enemies" (4.4.4). She emerges to triumph verbally over the once victorious Yorkists and to curse Richard one last time before she returns to her native France to smile at England's woes.

Edward, Prince of Wales, and Richard, Duke of York

The sons of Edward IV appear in only three scenes. York appears without his brother in Scene 2.4; both boys share Scenes 3.1 and 5.3, though in the latter they have only a cameo role as avenging ghosts haunting Richard's nightmare and beneficent spirits blessing Richmond. Speaking of their deaths, Tyrrel quotes Dighton's description of them as "gentle babes" (4.3.9), but Edward was 13 and Richard 11 when they were killed. Edward is a bright youth who stands up to his uncle Richard. When Richard suggests that the trip from Ludlow to London has tired the prince and made him melancholy, Edward replies that he is sad because his uncle Rivers has been arrested, along with Grey and Vaughan. Richard replies that they were traitors. Perhaps casting a gimlet eye on Richard, the boy retorts, "God keep me from false friends!—but they were none" (3.1.16). He greets the Lord Mayor and Hastings with courtesy and shows keen intellectual curiosity about the history of the Tower of London.

His inquiry into the Tower's classical origins marks him as an antiquarian and humanist in the manner of Erasmus and Thomas More. The Tower itself further ties him to More, since both were imprisoned and executed there. Shakespeare contrasts the Renaissance prince Edward with Richard, the medieval Vice. The matter of the Tower's history was in question as Shakespeare was writing *Richard III*. John Stow in his *Annals of England* (1592) rejected the view, expressed by Buckingham in the play, that Julius Caesar built the original Tower. Stow thus reversed his earlier position in *Summary of English Chronicles* (1565) and *Chronicles of England* (1580). Like any good Renaissance humanist scholar, Edward asks for documentary evidence to support Buckingham's claim, though he is willing to credit oral report, too.

Edward expresses another Renaissance value as well: the desire for fame. He links himself to the conquering Caesar and promises to imitate him and his own ancestors, Edward III and Henry V, by conquering France "if I live until I be a man" (3.1.91). Richard's asides indicate that Edward will not reach adulthood.

York first appears in 2.4, where he displays his precociousness. When his mother remarks that he has grown almost as big as his older brother, he replies that he hopes not because his uncle says that only weeds grow rapidly; gracious plants mature slowly. Richard's mother observes that if that were true, Richard should be gracious. York contradicts her, saying he heard that Richard "grew so fast / That he could gnaw a crust at two hours old" (2.4.27–28). York wishes he had recalled that story because he could have rounded on his uncle.

When York reappears in 3.1, he does just that. Whereas Edward displays seriousness with his discussion of history and fame, York plays the jester and repeatedly scores off Richard. He reminds Richard that he had said, "idle weeds are fast in growth" (3.1.103). York does not refer to Richard's teeth. Rather, York notes that Edward has grown taller than he. Will Richard then say that the prince is idle? After placing Richard in the awkward position of maligning his supposed sovereign or recanting, York now asks for Richard's dagger, perhaps

The murder of the princes, as described by Tyrrel in Act IV, Scene 3 of *Richard III*. This is a print from the Boydell Shakespeare Gallery project, which was conceived in 1786 and lasted until 1805. *(Painting by James Northcote; engraving by Francis Legat)*

reflecting on Richard's habit of playing with that weapon. Richard tries to evade the request by promising something weightier. The quick-witted York then asks for Richard's sword. When Richard says his sword is too heavy for the young man, York turns Richard's words against him yet again: "O then I see you will part but with light gifts!" (3.1.118). The prince notes York's wordplay and remarks to Richard, "Your grace knows how to bear with him" (3.1.127).

Instantly, York parries with "You mean to bear me" (3.1.128). York appears to be self-deprecating in saying that because he is little, Edward calls him an ape and thinks that Richard should carry York on his shoulder. York clearly is referring to Richard's hump. In an aside, even Buckingham expresses his admiration for York's cleverness.

When York learns that he is to lodge in the Tower, he reverts to being a child, saying that he fears the place because it may be haunted by Clarence's ghost. Edward again shows maturity in asserting that he fears "no uncles dead." Richard adds, "Nor none that live, I hope." Edward astutely counters, "And if they live, I hope I need not fear" (3.1.146–148). Through their witty and clever speeches, Shakespeare endears both children to the audience and so begins to erode Richard's appeal.

Clarence

Historically, Clarence repeatedly plotted against his older brother, Edward IV, and in *Henry VI, Part 3,* he turned against him to help reinstate Henry VI on the throne before again shifting his loyalty back to the Yorkist cause. Like Margaret, Clarence undergoes melioration in this play. He is Richard's first victim, and, like all subsequent ones, he trusts his brother, whom he should fear. Even in his ominous dream in Act I, in which Richard knocks him overboard and he drowns, he thinks that Richard strikes him accidentally (1.4.18).

His dream vision, anticipating Mercutio's in the same location in *Romeo and Juliet* (1.4), reflects Clarence's poetical nature, filled as it is with lovely images of the sea bottom. These lines also look ahead to Ariel's song "Full fathom five your father lies" in *The Tempest* (1.2.397–405). More ominously, Clarence in his sleep sees Warwick and Edward of Lancaster, both of whom he betrayed. Clarence thus becomes not only Richard's first victim but also the first to suffer vengeance for crimes he has committed. His death establishes the pattern on the play, as characters learn too late of Richard's treachery and suffer for previous actions. Richard is both scourge and avenger. Since his victims seem in this play more sinned against than sinning, Richard increasingly alienates audiences that initially, like those he betrays on stage, find him attractive.

DIFFICULTIES OF THE PLAY

Because *Richard III* is known as a history play, students may believe that to understand the work they need to acquaint themselves with Richard's life. Reading a modern biography of Richard such as Charles Ross's *Richard III* (1981) may prove helpful. It is important to remember, however, that Shakespeare drew on the histories of his own time, not modern histories. Hence, reading Raphael Holinshed's *Chronicles* and other 16th-century accounts of Richard's reign will provide a clearer sense of the play's antecedents.

Furthermore, Shakespeare did not slavishly copy from his sources. He changed what he found to suit his dramatic purposes (e.g., introducing Margaret, conflating the various rebellions against Richard). An awareness of these changes will help students evaluate how Shakespeare intended his audiences to understand characters, themes, and action.

While such background knowledge is useful, it is not essential. *Macbeth* and *King Lear* derive from the same primary source as *Richard III*: Holinshed's *Chronicles*. Since these first two works are labeled tragedies, students are more willing to examine them as independent artifacts. *Richard III* is similarly accessible on its own terms. Indeed, though it was placed among the histories in the First Folio, the title page of the quarto reads *The Tragedy of King Richard the third*, which is also the running title throughout. Even the Folio title page calls the play *The Tragedy of Richard the Third*.

The events depicted in the play were more than 100 years old by the time Shakespeare presented them on stage. Some in the audience, such as members of the Inns of Court, would have been familiar with the story. Some would have seen *The True Tragedie of Richard III*, an important source for Shakespeare's work. Many in the audience, though, would have been illiterate and ignorant of the history on which Shakespeare draws.

Hence, Shakespeare does not require any prior knowledge of history for an appreciation of *Richard III*. Indeed, given how fast and loose he plays with events and characters, knowledge of the history of the period may confuse rather than clarify.

Act I moves vertiginously from 1477 (1.1) back to 1471 (1.2) to 1483 (1.3) to 1478 (1.4). Margaret's presence in Edward's court seems to puzzle even Richard, who asks her, "Wert thou not banished on pain of death?" (1.3.166). At 4.4.521–527, a messenger announces that Richmond's invading fleet has been dispersed by a storm (as it was in October 1483) and has returned to Brittany. Five lines later, Catesby declares that Richmond has landed in Wales (as he did in August 1485). Nearly two years elapse in that short interval.

Rather than trying to match the play with reality, viewers and readers should accept the work for what it is: a creative fiction. Shakespeare is not writing history. The events in the play unfold over a period of 14 years, yet they seem to follow each other in close succession. Compression creates intensity, an essential ingredient in drama. Shakespeare also has shaped the characters, through the speeches he invented for them, for his own dramatic purposes. Richard, Buckingham, Clarence, Anne Neville, Queen Margaret, and the others bear the names of historical figures. Their actions and speeches, however, are the creation of the dramatist. Like many movies, this play could carry the epigraph "Based on the true story."

While familiarity with history is not necessary, those unacquainted with the *Henry VI* plays may be at a disadvantage. Why in Clarence's dream does Warwick, identified only as Clarence's father-in-law, call him "false Clarence"? (1.4.51). In 5.1 of *Henry VI, Part 3*, Clarence abandons Warwick and Henry VI and joins his brothers rebelling against that monarch. This fact does not resurface in *Richard III*. Margaret repeatedly refers to characters and events depicted in the earlier plays of the tetralogy. Reading only *Richard III* without knowledge of the *Henry VI* plays may be likened to reading one Sherlock Holmes story. One can understand the events, but the characters and actions gain depth from a familiarity with the entire oeuvre.

Shakespeare drew not only on history but also on literary sources in writing this play. As noted in the Background section, Clarence's vision of the underworld in Scene 1.4 draws on classical and

Renaissance texts. Clarence's encounter with Warwick recalls Aeneas's confrontation with the shade of Dido in book 6 of the *Aeneid*, which describes Aeneas's descent into Hades. Aeneas betrayed Dido, thus causing her death. The dream meeting with Edward of Lancaster probably was suggested by Aeneas's seeing his dead Greek enemies a few lines after Dido's ghost departs. The implicit linking of Clarence to Aeneas deepens his character. Aeneas is flawed, like Clarence, but also heroic and admirable.

One may read *Richard III* as a retelling of the Trojan War: One founding myth of Britain is that it took its name from Brut, a great-grandson of Aeneas who founded Troynovant (London). Eliza-beth, Anne, and the Duchess of York are conquered Trojan women; the princes are Astyanax, son of Andromache and Hector, whom the Greeks kill. Yet from defeated Troy the Roman Empire will rise to conquer Greece. Raging, warlike Richard will, like Achilles, triumph for a time, but ultimately he and the Yorkists will be defeated. The marriage of Richmond and Elizabeth, like that of Aeneas and Lavinia, will join former enemies to create a peaceful and powerful state. Knowledge of the classics will thus enrich the appreciation of Shakespeare's plays.

Shakespeare's language may pose difficulties initially. He wrote in Early Modern English, and, moreover, in highly metaphoric language. The play's language is artificial. No one at the time really spoke like Shakespeare's characters. Furthermore, he employs many rhetorical devices that any Elizabethan schoolboy would recognize but that most college graduates today know nothing of. The more one knows of classical and Renaissance tropes, the more one can appreciate Shakespeare's artistry. Yet even if one cannot distinguish anaphora from epistrophe, one can appreciate the power and the beauty of the speeches. One must read Shakespeare slowly and thoughtfully, but the effort will be richly rewarded. As his first editors, John Heminge and Henry Condell, wrote in "To the great Variety of Readers" introducing the First Folio, "to your divers capacities, you will finde enough, both to draw, and hold you: for his wit can no more lie hid, then it can be lost. Reade him, therefore; and againe, and againe."

Lady Anne in Act I, Scene 2 of *Richard III*. This is a print from Charles Heath's 1848 edition of *The Heroines of Shakspeare: Comprising the Principal Female Characters in the Plays of the Great Poet. (Painting by J. W. Wright; engraving by W. H. Egleton)*

KEY PASSAGES
Act I, Scene 1, 1–41

RICHARD. Now is the winter of our
  discontent
Made glorious summer by this sun of York;
And all the clouds that low'rd upon our house
In the deep bosom of the ocean buried.
Now are our brows bound with victorious
  wreaths,
Our bruised arms hung up for monuments,
Our stern alarums chang'd to merry meetings,

Our dreadful marches to delightful measures.
Grim-visag'd War hath smooth'd his wrinkled
  front;
And now, in stead of mounting barbed steeds
To fright the souls of fearful adversaries,
He capers nimbly in a lady's chamber
To the lascivious pleasing of a lute.
But I, that am not shap'd for sportive tricks,
Nor made to court an amorous looking-glass;
I, that am rudely stamp'd, and want love's
  majesty
To strut before a wanton ambling nymph;
I, that am curtail'd of this fair proportion,
Cheated of feature by dissembling nature,
Deform'd, unfinish'd, sent before my time
Into this breathing world, scarce half made up,
And that so lamely and unfashionable
That dogs bark at me as I halt by them—
Why, I, in this weak piping time of peace,
Have no delight to pass away the time,
Unless to see my shadow in the sun
And descant on mine own deformity.
And therefore, since I cannot prove a lover
To entertain these fair well-spoken days,
I am determined to prove a villain
And hate the idle pleasures of these days.
Plots have I laid, inductions dangerous,
By drunken prophecies, libels, and dreams,
To set my brother Clarence and the King
In deadly hate the one against the other;
And if King Edward be as true and just
As I am subtle, false, and treacherous,
This day should Clarence closely be mew'd up
About a prophecy, which says that G
Of Edward's heirs the murtherer shall be.
Dive, thoughts, down to my soul, here
  Clarence comes!

Of all Shakespeare's plays, only *Richard III* opens with a soliloquy, which shows Richard's isolation. As he declared in *Henry VI, Part 3*, 5.6.83, "I am myself alone." Having no confidant on stage, he gives the audience that role. He presents himself as clever, witty, even sympathetic because of his deformities; and though he threatens, he seems

Lena Ashwell as Margaret in *Richard III (Photographed by Window & Grove)*

more the comic villain here than the psychopath he will later reveal himself to be. With his striking opening metaphors, he shows his command of language. He also exhibits his skill at moralizing "two meanings in one word" (3.1.83). The surface meaning of the opening lines is that unhappiness has yielded to joy. But for Richard, now is the season of discontent because, as he will soon explain, he has no part to play in this peaceful world. He puns on the word *sun*, as he will play with language throughout the work. The sun traditionally represents royalty but is a particularly apt metaphor for Edward IV because at the Battle of Mortimer's Cross (1461), Edward, who triumphed, saw three suns (*Henry VI, Part 3*, 2.1.26–40).

Richard's speech is divided into three almost equal portions. Lines 1–13 describe the current situation. Picking up on the Yorkist victory at Tewkesbury that ends *Henry VI, Part 3* (though *Richard III* opens almost seven years later), Richard shows the effects of the end of the civil wars between the houses of York and Lancaster. This portion of the soliloquy ends with the alliterative and scornful reference to "the lascivious pleasing of a lute," or, as the quarto reads, "of a love" (l. 13).

Lines 14–27 explain why Richard hates "this weak piping time of peace" (l. 24): He is physically and temperamentally unsuited to it. Richard, the great dissembler, links himself to nature even as he describes himself as unnatural, again packing a double meaning into one word. Sigmund Freud commented on Richard's sense of being "Cheated . . . by dissembling nature" (l. 19; see Freud's comments in the Extracts of Classic Criticism section). Those who feel cheated, Freud reflects, regard themselves as entitled to compensation. By emphasizing his physical deformities, Richard is playing not only to the audience's sympathy but also to its desire, as well as his own, for recompense for wrongs suffered. "I may do wrong myself, since wrong has been done to me," Freud imagines the audience thinking.

Hence, the third part of the speech, lines 28–40, in which Richard announces his plot against his brother, seems almost justified. His use of the words *therefore* and *prove* imply a logical argument. An unwary listener or reader will be beguiled by this demonic reasoning. Moreover, while Richard appears to be confiding in the audience, he conceals more than he reveals; he does not indicate here that Clarence is to be but one victim of many in his march to the throne. Richard had made this point in *Henry VI, Part 3*, 5.6.80–91, but here he plays down his malice, again showing his skill at seduction, though he denies such ability.

The speech's balanced tripartite structure, with its thesis, antithesis, and synthesis, is mirrored in the balance and contrast of images: winter of discontent and glorious summer, "stern alarums chang'd to merry meetings," "dreadful marches" turned to "delightful measures." Shifting from his description of the times to his self-portrait, he changes his syntax and meter to make the audience hear how he, unlike the times, lacks symmetry and balance. Lines 16 and 18 begin with trochees rather than iambs, breaking the standard meter. Line 23, "That dogs bark at me as I halt by them," itself halts. Lines 28 and 30 are hypermetric, containing additional syllables.

Richard appears active and vigorous, in control of the action. He has laid a plot for Clarence's arrest, and as the soliloquy ends, Clarence appears under guard to be taken to the Tower. Richard's statement that he is "determined to prove a villain" (1.1.30) is, however, more ambiguous than he recognizes. Is he the one who determines his deeds? Or is his behavior determined for him by providence? The entire play may be read as a debate about the meaning of this "determined."

Act I, Scene 2, 228–264

RICHARD. Was ever woman in this humor woo'd?
Was ever woman in this humor won?
I'll have her, but I will not keep her long.
What? I, that kill'd her husband and his father,
To take her in her heart's extremest hate,
With curses in her mouth, tears in her eyes,
The bleeding witness of my hatred by,
Having God, her conscience, and these bars
  against me,
And I no friends to back my suit at all
But the plain devil and dissembling looks?
And yet to win her! All the world to nothing!
Hah!
Hath she forgot already that brave prince,
Edward her lord, whom I, some three months
  since,
Stabb'd in my angry mood at Tewksbury?
A sweeter and a lovelier gentleman,
Fram'd in the prodigality of nature—
Young, valiant, wise, and (no doubt) right
  royal—
The spacious world cannot again afford.
And will she yet abase her eyes on me,
That cropp'd the golden prime of this sweet
  prince

And made her widow to a woeful bed?
On me, whose all not equals Edward's moi'ty?
On me, that halts and am misshapen thus?
My dukedom to a beggarly denier,
I do mistake my person all this while!
Upon my life, she finds (though I cannot)
Myself to be a marv'llous proper man.
I'll be at charges for a looking glass,
And entertain a score or two of tailors
To study fashions to adorn my body:
Since I am crept in favor with myself,
I will maintain it with some little cost.
But first I'll turn yon fellow in his grave,
And then return lamenting to my love.
Shine out, fair sun, till I have bought a glass,
That I may see my shadow as I pass.

This soliloquy ends an unhistorical scene of Shakespeare's invention in which Richard confronts Anne Neville as she is accompanying the corpse of Henry VI to burial. At the end of *Henry VI, Part 3*, Richard killed that king, as he earlier had killed Anne's fiancé, Edward of Lancaster. Shakespeare makes Edward her husband. Though Anne has every reason to hate Richard, and though he encounters her in the most inauspicious of moments, he wins her consent to marry him.

As soon as she departs, Richard expresses to the audience his own astonishment at his success. Whereas in his first two soliloquies that frame the opening scene, he was stating what he already had thought out, here Shakespeare presents a man speaking as the ideas come to him. What delights him is not that he has gained the love of a woman he desires. As he makes clear, his affections do not tend that way. To the extent that he wants Anne, he values her for her political connections as the daughter of the powerful Earl of Warwick and wife of the now-dead Lancastrian heir to the throne.

Rather, Richard revels in his ability to dissemble and persuade. He recapitulates the obstacles that should have barred the path to success: his villainy and his physical appearance. Samuel Taylor Coleridge observed, "The inferiority of his person made Richard seek compensation in the superior-

Richard wins over Lady Anne in Act I, Scene 2 of *Richard III*, in this print published by Petter & Galpin Cassell in the 19th century. *(Painting by John Dawson Watson; engraving by J. A. Wright)*

ity of his intellect." It is that superiority that he is celebrating. He echoes his first soliloquy ironically in saying that he will buy a mirror in which to view himself. Both here and in the opening scene, though, he speaks of his shadow rather than his substance, as if he were an evil spirit. He links himself not to the sun but to the clouds that lower over the house of York. Shakespeare demonstrates Richard's excitement by giving him a line with 12 syllables and another with one. Meter and rhythm break down to indicate the passion that overwhelms him.

At the end of this soliloquy, Richard speaks contemptuously of the body of Henry, who not only was a king but also was regarded by many English people as a saint. Richard had promised Anne he would solemnly inter "this noble king, / And wet his grave with my repentant tears" (1.2.214–215). Once he is alone, he reveals how far those words were from his thoughts. He dismissively calls the saintly king "yon fellow," whom he will quickly deposit in the grave without ceremony and then return to Anne in what will clearly be pretended sorrow.

Act V, Scene 3, 177–206

RICHARD. Give me another horse! Bind up
  my wounds!
Have mercy, Jesu! Soft, I did but dream.
O coward conscience, how dost thou
  afflict me!
The lights burn blue. It is now dead midnight.
Cold fearful drops stand on my trembling
  flesh.
What do I fear? Myself? There's none else by.
Richard loves Richard, that is, I am I.
Is there a murtherer here? No. Yes, I am.
Then fly. What, from myself? Great reason
  why—
Lest I revenge. What, myself upon myself?
Alack, I love myself. Wherefore? For any good
That I myself have done unto myself?
Oh, no! Alas, I rather hate myself
For hateful deeds committed by myself.
I am a villain; yet I lie, I am not.
Fool, of thyself speak well; fool, do not flatter:
My conscience hath a thousand several
  tongues,
And every tongue brings in a several tale,
And every tale condemns me for a villain.
Perjury, perjury, in the highest degree;
Murther, stern murther, in the direst degree;
All several sins, all us'd in each degree,
Throng to the bar, crying all, "Guilty! guilty!"
I shall despair; there is no creature loves me,
And if I die no soul will pity me.
And wherefore should they, since that I myself
Find in myself no pity to myself?
Methought the souls of all that I had
  murther'd

Came to my tent, and every one did threat
To-morrow's vengeance on the head of
  Richard.

Before returning to France, Queen Margaret declares that Richard's end is near: "Earth gapes, hell burns, fiends roar, saints pray, / To have him suddenly convey'd from hence" (4.4.75–76). This imagery and language recall the damnation of Marlowe's Faustus, who, in his final speech, pleads, "Earth gape!" that he may hide (*Doctor Faustus,* 5.2.153). At the end of that speech, devils appear to convey him to hell. One scene earlier, Faustus, contemplating suicide, tells himself, "Damned art thou, Faustus, damned; despair and die!" (5.1.56). Many of the ghosts who appear in Richard's dream in 5.3 use those last three words.

Richard's final soliloquy also draws on the damnation of Faustus. From Marlowe, Shakespeare was learning to create introspective characters. This speech shows that he was mastering this art. Richard has just awakened from a dream in which he has seen his victims' ghosts and heard them curse him. His first words suggest that he also had another dream dealing with the impending battle. His call for another horse anticipates his cry during the actual fighting: "A horse, a horse! My kingdom for a horse!" (5.4.7, 13). With his next line, Richard begins to echo Faustus's last speech. Even the time, midnight, is identical as Richard, like Faustus, begins by invoking Jesus and then quickly recants. The "cold, fearful drops" of sweat that cover his flesh (5.3.181) recall Christ's blood that Faustus sees streaming above him. "One drop would save my soul, half a drop!" (*Doctor Faustus,* 5.2.144). Like Faustus, he speaks of flight, only to change his mind. Throughout the speech, Richard imitates Faustus's vacillation, his staccato speech that indicates his shifting thoughts, his fear and despair. Just as Faustus's bargain with the devil brought him success and then damnation, Richard's Machiavellian behavior first gained and then cost him his kingship.

The speech contrasts markedly with Richard's opening soliloquy, given that speech's logical construction and happy scheming. These lines

Ghosts of the people he murdered haunt Richard in his dreams in this 19th-century depiction of Act V, Scene 3 of *Richard III. (Painting by Friedrich Pecht; engraving by Tobias Bauer)*

in Act V expose his disintegration. In *Henry VI, Part 3*, Richard had boasted, "I am myself alone." (5.6.83). In that play and through most of *Richard III*, he had reveled in his solitude, rejecting love and friendship. His first words as king are: "Stand all apart" (4.2.1). Now he recognizes the price he has paid. This Aristotelian epiphany makes Richard a tragic figure and earns him a modicum of audience sympathy. As F. S. Boas writes in *Shakspere and His Predecessors* (1896),

> As Richard starts from his slumber, there is wrung at last from his lips the agonized cry of homage to the moral law. The horror of his isolation from humanity falls upon him, echoing, as it were, the grim burden of the spectral chorus; he shrieks aloud: "There is no

creature loves me." He to whom love had been only foolishness clutches at it convulsively as he hangs over the darkness of the abyss, and with the imploring cry for pity from his fellows, his scheme of self-centered life crumbles into the dust. That is the "true tragedy" of Richard III, the real and significant Nemesis of which his death in battle at the hands of Richmond, God's representative, is only the outward, though dramatically and historically imperative, confirmation. (155)

DIFFICULT PASSAGES
Act III, Scene 6, 1–14

SCRIVENER. Here is the indictment of the
  good Lord Hastings,
Which in a set hand fairly is engross'd
That it may be to-day read o'er in Paul's.
And mark how well the sequel hangs together:
Eleven hours I have spent to write it over,
For yesternight by Catesby was it sent me;
The precedent was full as long a-doing,
And yet within these five hours Hastings liv'd,
Untainted, unexamin'd, free, at liberty.
Here's a good world the while! Who is so gross
That cannot see this palpable device?
Yet who so bold but says he sees it not?
Bad is the world, and all will come to nought,
When such ill dealing must be seen in thought.

The Scrivener, one who copies documents, has just labored for 11 hours to write out a fair copy of the charges against Hastings, who was executed while the Scrivener was working on the document. The indictment, which the Scrivener received from Catesby, must have taken nearly as long to write out. Thus, Richard's claim in the previous scene that Hastings's guilt manifested itself only on the day of his execution cannot be true. Everyone is afraid to point out this contradiction, though it is apparent to all.

The Scrivener's insight shows that while Clarence, Anne Neville, and Hastings remain blind to Richard's machinations, the citizenry penetrate his masquerade. Regardless of what the Scrivener has had to write under compulsion, to him Hastings is still good. This scene anticipates Buckingham's speech at the beginning of 3.7, in which the Duke reports the people's lack of response to his speech favoring Richard's coronation. Even before Richard gains the throne, his plots begin to fail. Like the garden scene in *Richard II* (3.4) and Katherine's English lesson in *Henry V* (3.4), this seemingly insignificant episode at the midpoint of the play conveys much meaning in foreshadowing Richard's downfall.

Act IV, Scene 4, 35–78

MARGARET. If ancient sorrow be most
  reverent,
Give mine the benefit of seniority,
And let my griefs frown on the upper hand.
If sorrow can admit society [*she sits with the
  other women*]
Tell over your woes again by viewing mine:
I had an Edward, till a Richard kill'd him;
I had a Harry, till a Richard kill'd him:
Thou hadst an Edward, till a Richard kill'd
  him;
Thou hadst a Richard, till a Richard kill'd him.

DUCHESS OF YORK. I had a Richard, too,
  and thou didst kill him;
I had a Rutland too, thou holp'st to kill him.

MARGARET. Thou hadst a Clarence too, and
  Richard kill'd him.
From forth the kennel of thy womb hath crept
A hell-hound that doth hunt us all to death:
That dog, that had his teeth before his eyes
To worry lambs and lap their gentle blood,
That foul defacer of God's handiwork,
That excellent grand tyrant of the earth
That reigns in galled eyes of weeping souls,
Thy womb let loose to chase us to our graves.
O upright, just, and true-disposing God,
How do I thank thee that this carnal cur
Preys on the issue of his mother's body,
And makes her pew-fellow with others' moan!

DUCHESS OF YORK. O Harry's wife,
  triumph not in my woes!
God witness with me, I have wept for thine.

MARGARET. Bear with me; I am hungry for
  revenge,
And now I cloy me with beholding it.
Thy Edward, he is dead, that kill'd my Edward;
Thy other Edward dead, to quit my Edward;
Young York he is but boot, because both they
Match'd not the high perfection of my loss.
Thy Clarence he is dead that stabb'd my
  Edward,
And the beholders of this frantic play,
Th' adulterate Hastings, Rivers, Vaughan,
  Grey,
Untimely smoth'red in their dusky graves.
Richard yet lives, hell's black intelligencer,
Only reserv'd their factor to buy souls
And send them thither; but at hand, at hand,
Ensues his piteous and unpitied end.
Earth gapes, hell burns, fiends roar, saints pray,
To have him suddenly convey'd from hence.
Cancel his bond of life, dear God, I pray,
That I may live and say, "The dog is dead."

Queen Margaret has concealed herself to eavesdrop on the laments of Queen Elizabeth and the Duchess of York, her former enemies. This exchange recapitulates events shown in *Henry VI, Part 3* and this work. It also continues the debate this play stages about the role of providence in human affairs. The husband of the Duchess of York had tried to supplant Henry as king and died in the Wars of the Roses, but her son Edward had gained the throne and her son Richard had killed Henry. Elizabeth had married Edward and thus reigned as queen instead of Margaret. As Yorkists, the Duchess and Elizabeth had defeated the Lancastrian Margaret, but now all three women have cause to grieve.

Margaret comes forward to join her onetime opponents to recount her losses: her husband Henry and her son Edward. In her earlier appearance in 1.3, she had cursed her Yorkist enemies, and she now points out that justice or Nemesis has caught up with them. In her first speech here, she notes that the murder of the princes in the Tower balances the murder of her husband and son. The Duchess of York retorts that her husband and son were killed by Margaret; the hatred between the houses of York and Lancaster persists despite the terrible cost to both sides.

Margaret replies that the Duchess is to blame for the present horrors because she gave birth to Richard. In a conciliatory effort that anticipates the union of York and Lancaster at the end of the play, the Duchess asks for and offers mutual sympathy, and Margaret moderates her tone. She still maintains that the deaths of Edward IV, Edward V, the young Duke of York, Clarence, and the others whom Richard has killed represent divine punishment for the evils they committed. Margaret posits a providential universe, and she regards Richard as an agent of revenge. But vengeance will fall on him as well. In imagery borrowed from the damnation of Doctor Faustus, she looks forward to his downfall, which ensues in the next act.

CRITICAL INTRODUCTION
TO THE PLAY
Themes

A central concern throughout Shakespeare's work is the contrast between appearance and reality. Although Shakespeare lived in the Renaissance, with its scientific revolution and emphasis on empiricism, his plays repeatedly depict the limits of observation. Clarence believes Richard's protestations of love and his assertion that the queen and Jane Shore, Edward IV's lover, rule the country. When the murderers come to kill him, Clarence tells them that Richard will better reward them for sparing him than Edward will for killing him. Clarence will not believe the second murderer's statement that Richard hates him. The first murderer, too, tells Clarence that Richard will not weep for his death.

"O, do not slander him, for he is kind," Clarence insists (1.4.241). The first murderer informs him that Richard, not Edward, has sent them. Clarence remains incredulous: "It cannot be, for

Richard Mansfield as Richard III and Beatrice Cameron as Lady Anne in *Richard III,* in this photograph published by Gebbie & Husson Company in 1890

he bewept my fortune, / And hugg'd me in his arms, and swore with sobs / That he would labor my delivery" (1.4.244–246). Clarence has had the ocular and auricular proof of Richard's love. Too late, he learns the truth that Richard has hidden so well.

The same fate befalls Anne Neville in the next scene. Richard's words, tears, and offer to kill himself confuse her. He has killed her husband and father-in-law, but he claims he is contrite and acted out of love for her. "I would I knew thy heart," she says, and he replies, "'Tis figur'd in my tongue" (1.2.193–194). Though she remains wary, she believes his show of penitence and agrees to marry him. Only later does she discover her error; her ghost declares she "never slept a quiet hour" with him (5.3.160).

In the third scene, Richard again fools everyone with his seeming, convincing the Woodvilles that he is reconciled with them. As Richard comments to the audience, "And thus I clothe my naked villainy / With odd old ends stol'n forth of holy writ, / And seem a saint, when most I play the devil" (1.3.335–337). Hastings believes he can judge Richard's mood from his appearance. Just before Richard accuses Hastings of treason and orders Hastings's execution, he asks the Bishop of Ely for some of the bishop's famous strawberries (3.3). Shakespeare took this incident from the chronicles, but he uses it for its symbolic function: Strawberries conceal the deadly serpent lurking beneath the plants. Like Anne and Clarence, Hastings learns to his cost that he cannot trust appearances.

Another key concern deals with the role of providence. In 1.3, Queen Margaret curses the Woodvilles and the York family they support. She prays that Elizabeth's husband will die "by surfeit" to atone for the death of Henry VI, whom Edward supplanted (1.3.196). For her son Edward murdered, Elizabeth's son Edward will be killed, and all those who stood by when the Lancastrian Prince of Wales was murdered will die unnaturally.

Many of Margaret's prayers are answered. Edward IV dies soon after she curses him, and Richard kills Elizabeth's sons, Hastings, Rivers, Vaughan, and Grey. Buckingham, who denies the power of providence, promises Elizabeth on All Souls' Day to be loyal to her and her children. If he is not, "God punish me / With hate in those where I expect most love" (2.1.34–35). On a later All Souls' Day, he remembers those words as he is about to be executed by Richard, whom he helped to the throne by betraying Elizabeth and her children. Richard, another who denies providence, meets retribution at the Battle of Bosworth.

Elizabeth remains unconvinced, though. Mourning her dead sons, she asks, "Wilt thou, O God, fly from such gentle lambs, / And throw them in the entrails of the wolf? / When didst thou sleep when such a deed was done?" (4.4.22–24). Mar-

garet, who believes in divine justice, acknowledges that nothing hindered the killing of her husband and son, either. Elizabeth's prayer for her children's welfare (4.1.98–102) goes unanswered. Not all malefactors in the play are punished: The murderers of Clarence and of the princes in the Tower do not suffer for their actions. Margaret curses Dorset, but he survives, as does Stanley, who plays a double game with Richard and Richmond. As is true so often in Shakespeare's works, two contradictory truths are told at once.

Shakespeare's plays repeatedly anatomize the nature of political power. On one level, Richard exemplifies tyranny. He gains the throne illegally and abuses his authority. Richmond's triumph at the end of the play marks the return of legitimate and good government. The tetralogy opens with Bedford's lament, "Hung be the heavens with black, yield day to night!" (*Henry IV, Part 1*, 1.1.1). The play's last line inverts this imagery as it anticipates "fair prosperous days" (*Richard III*, 5.5.34).

Yet as Margaret repeatedly declares, Edward IV is a usurper, and his son, whom Richard supplants, therefore has no more legitimate claim to the throne than Richard himself. Richmond's right to the throne is even more tenuous. In the course of the first tetralogy, Edward usurps the throne from Henry, Richard seizes the throne from Edward's son, and Henry wins the crown from Richard. Might makes right, and those who oppose this viewpoint are executed, like Hastings, or are powerless to act, like Margaret. Shakespeare uses the same summertime, sunshine imagery for Edward at the beginning of the play as for Henry at the end. The arc of history is long. Does it bend toward justice or back upon itself? The play poses the question but offers no definitive response.

Structure

Although *Richard III* deals with history, it handles chronology creatively. As noted in the section on difficulties, the first act plays hopscotch with time, jumping from 1477 (1.1) back to 1471 (1.2), forward to 1483 (1.3), and then back again to 1478

(1.4). The remainder of the play proceeds more linearly, but the two-month period between Edward's death and Richard's coronation occupies more lines than Richard's two-year reign, which seems to end as soon as it begins. Shakespeare conflates the 1483 and 1485 rebellions against Richard, and he shows Richard wooing Elizabeth's daughter on his way to fight Buckingham. Anne Neville did not die until 1484, many months after Buckingham's uprising was defeated.

Shakespeare structures his play for maximum dramatic effect, employing what has come to be known as the Freytag pyramid, named for Gustave Freytag, author of *Technique of the Drama* (1863). This pyramid serves as a standard literary model in which tension in a narrative builds toward a climax and then relaxes. As Shakespeare tells the story of Richard's rise and fall, he begins with the elimination of Richard's older brother, Clarence, whose claim to the throne was better and who would probably prove an ally to Edward IV's children. Marriage with Anne Neville, though it occurred in 1472, well before Clarence's death, appears as Richard's next step. In 1.3, he lulls the Woodvilles into trusting him; in Scene 2.4, a messenger announces that the queen's brother (Rivers), son (Grey), and ally (Vaughan) have been arrested.

Richard then moves to secure both sons of Edward IV (3.1) and to remove Hastings, another impediment to his own coronation. With all potential claimants killed or neutralized and other powerful nobles, like Buckingham, won to his side, Richard manipulates public opinion sufficiently to claim the throne (3.7, 4.1). As soon as he is crowned, though, his fortunes begin to decline. He has reached the zenith on the wheel of fortune and Freytag pyramid and has nowhere to go but down. Buckingham refuses to kill the princes (4.2) and rebels against Richard. In 4.4, Richard fails to win the hand of Elizabeth's daughter, rebellions spread across the land, and Stanley secretly defects; also, Richmond lands at Milford Haven. The play's final act shows Richard's defeat and death at the Battle of Bosworth, thus completing the revolution of fortune's wheel.

Like the play's language (see the section on Style and Imagery), the structure of the work relies on parallelism and antitheses. The opening scene begins with a soliloquy by Richard, who declares that he has laid plots, "inductions dangerous" (1.1.32), to remove Clarence as an obstacle to his gaining the throne. Mirroring this scene, Margaret, Richard's nemesis and chief opponent through the first four acts of the play, begins 4.4 with a soliloquy in which she states, "Here in these confines slily I have lurk'd, / To watch the waning of mine enemies. A dire induction I am witness to" (4.4.5). With this second induction, the play moves from Richard's successful plotting to his failures.

These begin in that very scene. The act and scene divisions are not Shakespeare's, but the echoes are. In 1.2, Richard successfully woos Anne. In 4.4, he thinks he has convinced Elizabeth to let him marry her daughter, but he has not. He also believes he has ensured Stanley's loyalty by taking Stanley's son George hostage. Again, his ploy fails; Stanley's forces will join Richmond's in the climactic battle. Before he becomes king, Richard repeatedly deceives others. Once he gains the crown, others deceive him.

In 1.3, Margaret's first scene, the Woodvilles and Yorkists join to attack her. In 4.4, the Duchess of York and Elizabeth Woodville unite with Margaret to curse Richard. Through Buckingham, Richard manipulates the Cardinal in 3.1 ("My lord, you shall overrule my mind for once," 3.1.57), and in 3.4, he sends the Bishop of Ely to fetch him strawberries. In 4.4, churchmen prove less pliant. The Bishop of Exeter rebels against Richard, and the Bishop of Ely joins Richmond. Clarence's fearful dream in 1.4 anticipating his death is matched by Richard's in 5.3 that presages his demise. The second murderer hesitates to kill Clarence (1.4), just as Forrest later almost changes his mind about killing the princes (4.3.15).

This parallelism exists even within scenes. In 1.3, the Yorkists and Woodvilles quarrel with each other, then join to attack Margaret. In 3.1, Edward V speaks seriously with Gloucester. Then his younger brother enters and repeatedly taunts his uncle, thereby showing the difference in the two boys' character. In 5.3, each ghost who curses Richard then blesses Richmond. That scene keeps shifting between Richard and Richmond, giving them equal space to show that Richard, who has heretofore dominated the stage, has now met his match.

Revolving within the circuit of Richard's turning wheel of fortune are the cycles of other characters. In 3.2, Hastings boasts of his prosperity, saying that he is "in better state than e'er I was" (3.2.104). In 3.4, he is arrested for treason and executed. Buckingham in 2.1 tells Elizabeth that if he betrays her, "God punish me / With hate in those where I expect most love" (2.1.34–35). Facing execution late in the play, Buckingham recalls that promise: "That high All-Seer, which I dallied with, / Hath turn'd my feigned prayer on my head" (5.1.20–21). In 1.3, Rivers wants to imprison Margaret (1.3.304). In 2.4, he is arrested, and he is executed in 3.3.

The play may also be viewed as enacting Margaret's curses in 1.3.187–302. She begins by calling for the death of Edward IV, which occurs in 2.2, and of Edward V (death reported in 4.3). She prays that Elizabeth will "outlive thy glory like my wretched self" (1.3.202). In 4.1, Elizabeth is denied entrance to the Tower to see her sons and learns that Richard will be crowned king, Anne to become queen. She sends her son Dorset away to join Richmond, "Lest thou increase the number of the dead, / And make me thrall to Margaret's curse, / Nor mother, wife, nor England's counted queen" (4.1.44–46). Margaret prays for the deaths of Rivers, who is executed in 3.3, and Hastings, who dies in 3.4. She warns Buckingham that Richard will destroy him; this prophecy comes true in 5.1. She also foretells Richard's downfall; he is killed at the beginning of 5.5.

Style and Imagery

Shakespeare would have learned many rhetorical tropes in school, and he employs these profusely in *Richard III*. Brian Vickers's article "Shakespeare's Use of Rhetoric" (1971) discusses these devices. Among those recurring in the play is anaphora, the repetition of words at the beginning of clauses. An example occurs as Rivers goes to execution and recalls Margaret's verbal attacks: "Then curs'd she Richard, then curs'd she Buckingham, / Then curs'd she Hastings" (3.3.18–19). Earlier in the play, Richard, having won the hand of Anne Neville, exclaims to the audience and himself, "Was ever woman in this humour woo'd? / Was ever woman in this humour won?" (1.2.227–228). As these two instances illustrate, anaphora lends itself to parallel sentence structure, or parison.

A variation on parison is isocolon, in which corresponding clauses are of equal length. Claiming that her grief exceeds that of the widowed Queen Elizabeth and Clarence's orphaned children, the Duchess of York declares,

> She for an Edward weeps, and so do I;
> I for a Clarence weep, so doth not she;
> These babes for Clarence weep, and so do I;
> I for an Edward weep, so do not they.
> (2.2.82–85)

Another device that the play employs is epistrophe, in which consecutive clauses end with the same word. On his way to the Tower, Clarence tells Richard that Edward IV

> From the cross-row plucks the letter G,
> And says a wizard told him that by G
> His issue disinherited should be;
> And for my name of George begins with G,
> It follows in his thought that I am he.
> (1.1.55–59)

Richard uses epistrophe in his first soliloquy:

> And therefore, since I cannot prove a lover
> To entertain these fair well-spoken days,
> I am determined to prove a villain
> And hate the idle pleasures of these days.
> (1.1.28–31)

Richard's language also displays antimetabole, the repetition of words in inverted order. Reflecting on the rise of the Woodvilles to the ranks of the aristocracy, he says, "Since every Jack became a gentleman, / There's many a gentle person made a Jack" (1.3.71–72). Here, Richard also is punning on two different meanings of the word *Jack*. In the first clause, it is a common name. (As Gwendolyn remarks in Act I of Oscar Wilde's *The Importance of Being Earnest*, "There is very little music in the name Jack, if any at all, indeed. It does not thrill. It produces absolutely no vibrations. . . . Besides, Jack is a notorious domesticity for John!") In the second clause, *Jack* means a worthless person.

This type of punning is called antanaclasis, in which the same word takes on different meanings. Anne uses this device, combined with anaphora, when she attacks Richard for killing Henry VI: "Cursed the heart that had the heart to do it! / Cursed the blood that led his blood from hence!" (1.2.14–15). Paronomasia, another form of punning, echoes a word with a variant. When Richard refers to the dead princes as his cousins, by which he means they are related to him, Elizabeth retorts, "Cousins indeed, and by their uncle cozen'd" (4.4.222). Asteismus involves the use of the same or similar word by two different people in two different ways. Brackenbury replies to Richard's questioning him about Jane Shore, "With this, my lord, myself have nought to do." Richard pretends to misunderstand "nought," nothing, as "naught," sex. "Naught to do with Mistress Shore? I tell thee, fellow, / He that doth naught with her (excepting one) / Were best to do it secretly alone" (1.1.97–100). Richard also uses syllepsis, which he defines when he likens himself to the Vice, who will "moralize two meanings in one word" (3.1.82–83).

Other rhetorical devices in the play include ploce and epizeuxis. The former repeats a word within a clause or line. The Duchess of York notes that her sons, having defeated Henry VI, "themselves, the conquerors, / Make war upon themselves, brother to brother, / Blood to blood, self against self" (2.4.61–63). In the latter trope, a word is even more closely iterated, as when Rivers invokes his prison: "O Pomfret, Pomfret!" (3.3.9). A special form of this repletion, in which the last word of one clause

begins the next, is called anadiplosis. Hastening to confront the rebellious Buckingham, Richard declares, "Come, I have learn'd that fearful commenting / Is leaden servitor to dull delay; / Delay leads impotent and snail-pac'd beggary" (4.3.51–53). When anadiplosis is used in three or more clauses it becomes climat or gradatio; both words mean ladder. Richard, reflecting on his dream on the eve of the Battle of Bosworth says, "My conscience hath a thousand several tongues, / And every tongue brings in a several tale, / And every tale condemns me for a villain" (5.3.193–195).

When Anne Neville addresses Henry VI's corpse as "Thou bloodless remnant of that royal blood" (1.2.7), echoing a word with a variant, her speech exemplifies polyptoton. Richmond says of hope, "Kings it makes gods, and meaner creatures kings" (5.2.24). Such repetition of the same word at the start and end of a clause is epanalepsis.

One reason that *Richard III* is so long is that its characters employ copia, demonstrating their fertile imaginations. In his *Institutio Oratoria,* the Roman Quintilian wrote that the rhetorician should possess *copia rerum ac verborum*—a good supply of thoughts and words. Richard displays this quality in his opening soliloquy when he conjures up a variety of images to describe Edward's peaceful reign (1.1.1–13). Margaret's attack on Richard also shows her copia as she calls him

> Thou elvish-mark'd, abortive, rooting hog!
> Thou that was seal'd in thy nativity
> The slave of nature and the son of hell!
> Thou slander of thy heavy mother's womb!
> Thou loathed issue of thy father's loins!
> Thou rag of honor! Thou detested—
>   (1.3.227–232)

Contrasting with these elaborations on a theme are the pithy exchanges between Richard and Anne in 1.2 and Elizabeth in 4.4. Their rapid-fire one-line dialogue, stichomythia, was a staple of Senecan tragedy and so is appropriate for this play.

Although the play often employs these ornate linguistic flourishes, it can stoop to plain speech that is the more shocking for its rarity. When Buckingham asks Richard what they should do if Hastings does not agree to depose Edward V, Richard replies, "Chop off his head!" (3.2.193). When Buckingham seems to misunderstand Richard's murderous thoughts about the princes, Richard says, "Shall I be plain? I wish the bastards dead" (4.2.18). Learning that Stanley will not lead his army to join Richard's, the king exclaims, "Off with his son George's head!" (5.3.344).

The play's figures of speech serve for more than ornamentation. Henry Peacham, in the 1593 edition of his *Garden of Eloquence,* noted that they "do attend upon affections [passion], as ready handmaids of commandment to express most aptly whatsoever the heart doth affect or suffer." They also affect the audience's emotional response. For Sir Philip Sidney, eloquence impels to moral action (*The Defence of Poesie,* ca. 1581). The modern literary scholar John Jowett discovers a thematic function in these formal tropes as well: "The web of rhetoric in *Richard III* effectively suggests a world in which events, as much as language, are locked into patterns of grim inevitability" (26).

The play's heavy use of rhetoric consorts well with the many debates staged here. In school, Shakespeare would have practiced *disputatio in utramque partem*—arguing both sides of a question. The confrontation between Anne and Richard in 1.2 is more argument than courtship, and Richard wins. In 1.3, Margaret confronts Edward's wife and her supporter. In 1.4, the two murderers argue between themselves about conscience, and Clarence tries to persuade both of them to spare him. After Edward IV dies, Rivers and Buckingham consider whether to provide a large escort to bring Edward V to London. Again, Richard's view prevails. In the next scene, three citizens take different views on what the future holds. Buckingham persuades Cardinal Bourchier not to allow the Duke of York to claim the right of asylum (3.1). Stanley tries unsuccessfully to convince Hastings to flee Richard, and Catesby cannot persuade him to support Richard's usurpation (3.2). Richard then secures Hastings's execution and the Lord Mayor's belated acquiescence (3.4–3.5). In 3.7, Buckingham seems to persuade Richard to accept the crown.

Richard cannot persuade Buckingham to kill the princes but has no difficulty getting James Tyrrel to do his bidding (4.2). He debates with Queen Elizabeth about his marrying her daughter. He thinks he has won again, but he has not. In the fifth act, Richard and Richmond urge their supporters to fight for them. Once more, Richard, who triumphed so easily in the debates of the first three acts, proves less successful than Richmond, who wins not only the rhetorical battle but also, as a result, the military one. The entire play enacts a debate about the nature of providence and the role of the individual in determining events. Is Richmond an agent of God or a good and lucky leader? How much free will can one exercise? Hastings can heed Stanley's warning or not, can support Richard's usurpation or oppose it. Yet once he chooses to ignore Stanley's dream and to oppose Richard's becoming king, his fate is sealed. Rivers, Grey, and Vaughan are never given the chance to support or oppose Richard; they are arrested and executed because they are of the Woodville faction. Richard may be a self-willed Machiavel or an instrument of divine retribution on the houses of Lancaster and York.

While the play's language is highly rhetorical, it is also poetic. Only about 80 of its 3,800 lines are in prose. Many image patterns pervade the work, often clustering around Richard to serve as commentary on him. Chief among these are references to animals. Richard's crest includes a white boar; various characters refer to him less flatteringly as a pig. Margaret calls him "Thou elvish-mark'd, abortive, rooting hog" (1.3.227). Stanley tells Sir Christopher Urswick that George Stanley is imprisoned "in the sty of the most deadly boar" (4.5.2). Richmond calls Richard "The wretched, bloody, and usurping boar" and "this foul swine" (5.2.7, 10). Stanley dreams that the boar "rased off his helm" (3.2.11), meaning that Richard will cut off his head. The ghosts of the dead princes pray for Richmond, "Good angels guard thee from the boar's annoy" (5.3.151). Anne uses a variation on this motif when she refers to Richard as a hedgehog (1.2.102).

Richard also is repeatedly compared to a dog. His mother calls him a "hell-hound" (4.4.48). Margaret describes him as biting and venom-toothed and warns Buckingham, "Take heed of yonder dog" (1.3.290, 288). Triumphant, Richmond announces, "The day is ours, the bloody dog is dead" (5.5.2). Toads and spiders were regarded as venomous as well as ugly; these images, too, surround Richard. Margaret calls him "a bottled spider" and "poisonous bunch-back'd toad" (1.3.241, 245). Elizabeth, too, calls him both toad and spider (4.4.81). After spitting on him, Anne Neville declares, "Never hung poison on a fouler toad" (1.2.147). His mother addresses him, "Thou toad, thou toad" (4.4.145). Richard is also likened to a tiger (2.4.50) and a cockatrice (4.1.54). Anne speaks of him more generically as a beast (1.2.71).

Drawing on the play's spider image, Antony Sher appeared on stage with crutches painted black and depending black coattails to create the image of "a scuttling, multilimbed creature," as Sher described himself in the *Times* (London) for July 29, 1986. Reviewing one of Sher's performances in the role, Ros Asquith likened him to "a tarantula on elastic legs" (*Observer,* May 12, 1985, qtd. in Colley, 237). When John Barrymore was preparing to play Richard in 1920, he studied a red tarantula in the Bronx Zoo and onstage mimicked what he perceived as the spider's walk.

Further highlighting Richard's bloodthirsty character are references to Richard as butcher. Pointing to the corpse of Henry VI, whom Richard killed, Anne tells him, "Behold this pattern of thy butcheries" and declares that Richard never dreams "on aught but butcheries" (1.2.54, 100). Sending her son Dorset to join Richmond, Elizabeth charges him, "Go hie thee, hie thee from this slaughter house" (4.1.43). Elizabeth tells Richard, "The parents live whose children thou hast butcher'd" (4.4.397). In Richmond's dream, the ghost of Edward of Lancaster says, "The wronged souls / Of butchered princes fight in thy behalf" (5.3.121–122).

Imagery links Richard with the demonic. Anne calls him a fiend, devil, "dreadful minister of hell" and "foul devil" (1.2.34, 45, 46, 50). Margaret uses similar language, attacking him as devil, cacodemon, and "son of hell" (1.3.117, 143, 29). She prays that Richard will sleep only "while some tormenting dream / Affrights thee with a hell of ugly devils" (1.3.223–224) and claims that all the minister of hell attend upon him (1.3.293), thus again linking Richard with the diabolical. Later, she calls him "hell's black intelligencer" (4.4.71). Elizabeth urges her son Dorset to "live with Richmond, from the reach of hell" (4.1.42), and when Richard tries to win her consent for her daughter to marry him, she asks, "Shall I be tempted of the devil thus?" Richard accepts the characterization, responding, "Ay, if the devil tempt you to do good" (4.4.418–419). Earlier, he says that he plays the devil (1.3.357).

Yet another set of images highlights Richard's acting skills, which he uses to deceive. In his opening speech, he tells the audience, "Plots have I laid, inductions dangerous" (1.1.32), using the language of the theater. A plot is not just an evil plan but also the outline of a play, and an induction is the opening of a drama. For Richard, all the world is a stage. Anne calls Richard a dissembler, and he confesses to "dissembling looks" (1.2.184, 236). Richard stages the action in 3.5 to persuade the Lord Mayor of Hastings's treason and in 3.7 to win the citizens' consent to his becoming king. He instructs Buckingham in how to sway the people. The council at the Tower (3.4) is a performance. Richard intentionally arrives late, and Buckingham remarks, "Had you not come upon your cue, my lord, / William Lord Hastings had pronounc'd your part" (3.4.26–27). Richard exits, then returns to pretend that the queen and Jane Shore used witchcraft to wither his arm. His accusations against them and Hastings are pure performance, as everyone onstage as well as in the audience knows, but everyone plays along. Richard's acting turns others into players. His murder of the princes makes Elizabeth a "painted queen," "flattering index of a dire pageant," "queen in jest, only to fill the scene" (4.4.83, 85, 91). He drives Buckingham to "counterfeit the deep tragedian" (3.5.5).

Shakespeare's plays are filled with images drawn from nature. An important image in this play is the sun, which first appears in the play's second line as a pun. The sun serves as a symbol of royalty, and it is especially apt for Edward IV, "this sun of York," because, as noted above, in *Henry VI, Part 3*, just before the Battle of Mortimer's Cross, he sees three suns (2.1.25), presaging victory. Later in that play, Henry VI likens Edward to the sun (5.6.23–24). Richard twice speaks of viewing his "shadow in the sun" (1.1.26, 1.2.263), indicating that he will eclipse Edward. Margaret says that Richard "turns the sun to shade" (1.3.265) and speaks of his "cloudy wrath" (1.3.267). Antony Sher's decision to dress in black provides a visual confirmation of Richard's power to bring darkness. Following Edward's death, the third citizen warns, "When the sun sets, who doth not look for night?" (2.3.34).

At the play's opening, Richard declares, "All the clouds that low'r'd upon our house / In the deep bosom of the ocean [lie] buried" (1.1.3–4). On the day of the Battle of Bosworth, he notes, "The sky doth frown and low'r upon our army" (5.3.283). The clouds have returned to block the sun of the house of York. Solar imagery shifts to Richmond, who observes on the eve of battle, "The weary sun hath made a golden set, / And by the bright tract of his fiery car / Gives token of a goodly day to-morrow" (5.3.19–21). This linking of Richmond with the sun foretells his gaining the crown.

In his opening soliloquy, Richard also speaks of winter's giving way to summer under Edward (1.1.1–2). With Richard's reign, winter, the season of death and infertility, returns. As Richard maneuvers to become king, the third citizen remarks, "When great leaves fall, then winter is at hand" (2.3.33). The first murderer describes Richard as "snow in harvest" (1.4.242). Richard observes, "Short summers lightly have a forward spring" (3.1.94), foreshadowing that the summer of Yorkist rule will not last. As Richard's fortunes begin to change, Margaret notes, "So now prosperity begins to mellow / And drop into the rotten mouth of death" (4.4.1–2), indicating the onset of winter for Richard himself. Soon it will be summertime for Richmond, who condemns Richard for spoiling England's "summer fields and fruitful vines" (5.2.8). Richard observes that Richmond "never in his life / Felt so much cold as overshoes in snow" (5.3.325–326). Richard intends this description to portray Richmond as "a milksop" (5.3.325), but Shakespeare uses the imagery to distance Richmond from winter's cold. Richmond's final speech ends with the promise of summer's "smiling plenty, and fair prosperous days!" (5.5.34). The winter of discontent that Richard inaugurated has been made glorious summer by the Tudor triumph. This transformation is made evident linguistically through the contrast between Richard's line 1.1.1 and Richmond's 5.5.34.

EXTRACTS OF CLASSIC CRITICISM
William Richardson (1743–1814) [Excerpted from *Essays on Some of Shakespeare's Dramatic Characters*, 5th ed. (1797). Richardson's examination of Richard's appeal anticipates later studies of the play, including Freud's, quoted below. In writing about the play as a tragedy, Richardson raises the question of genre that later critics have considered.]

The catastrophe of a good tragedy is only the completion of our pleasure, and not the chief cause of it. The fable, and the view which the poet exhibits of human nature, conducted through a whole performance, must produce our enjoyment. But in the work now before us there is scarcely any fable; and there is no character of eminent importance but that of Richard. He is the principal agent; and the whole tragedy is an exhibition of guilt, where abhorrence for the criminal is much stronger than our interest in the sufferers, or esteem for those who, by accident rather than great exertion, promote his downfall. We are pleased no doubt with his punishment; but the display of his enormities, and their progress to this completion,

Edmund Kean as Richard III in *Richard III (Painting by John James Halls; engraving by Charles Turner)*

is produced, not by veiling or contrasting offensive features and colours, but by so connecting them with agreeable qualities residing in the character itself, that the disagreeable effect is entirely suppressed, or by its union with coalescing qualities, is converted into a pleasurable feeling. In particular, though Richard has no sense of justice, nor indeed of any moral obligation, he has an abundant share of those qualities which are termed intellectual. Destitute of virtue, he possesses ability. He shows discernment of character; artful contrivance in forming projects; great address in the management of mankind; fertility of resource; a prudent command of temper; much versatility of deportment; and singular dexterity in concealing his intentions. He possesses, along with these, such perfect consciousness of the superior powers of his own understanding above those of other men, as leads him not ostentatiously to treat them with contempt, but to employ them, while he really contemns their weakness, as engines of his ambition. Now, though these properties are not the objects of moral approbation, and may be employed as the instruments of fraud no less than of justice, yet the native and unmingled effect which *most* of them produce on the spectator, independent of the principle that employs them, is an emotion of pleasure. The person possessing them is regarded with deference, with respect, and with admiration. Thus, then, the satisfaction we receive in contemplating the character of Richard, in the various situations in which the poet has shown him, arises from a mixed feeling; a feeling compounded of horror, on account of his guilt; and of admiration, on account of his talents. By the concurrence of these two emotions the mind is thrown into a state of unusual agitation; neither painful nor pleasant, in the extremes of pain or of pleasure, but strangely delightful. Surprise and amazement, excited by the striking

are the chief objects of our attention. Thus Shakespeare, in order to render the shocking vices of Richard an amusing spectacle, must have recourse to other expedients than those usually practiced in similar situations. Here, then, we are led to enquire into the nature of these resources and expedients: for why do we not turn from the Richard of Shakespeare, as we turn from his Titus Andronicus? Has he invested him with any charm, or secured him by any talisman from disgust and aversion? The subject is curious and deserves our attention. Here, then, we may observe in general that the appearance conjunctures which he himself very often occasions, and which give exercise to his talents, together with astonishment at the determined boldness and success of his guilt, give uncommon force to the general impression. . . . We may also observe that suspense, wonder, and surprise, occasioned by the operation of great abilities, under the guidance of uncontrolled inhumanity, by their awful effects and the postures they assume, together with anxiety to see an union so unworthy dissolved, give poignancy to our indignation, and annex to it, if I may use the expression, a certain wild and alarming delight. . . .

The other excellencies of this tragedy, besides the character of Richard, are, indeed, of an inferior nature, but not unworthy of Shakespeare. The characters of Buckingham, Anne, Hastings, and Queen Margaret are executed with lively colouring and striking features; but, excepting Margaret, they are exhibited indirectly; and are more fully known by the conduct of Richard towards them, than by their own demeanor. They give the sketch and outlines in their own actions; but the picture appears finished in the deportment of Richard. This, however, of itself is a proof of very singular skill. The conduct of the story is not inferior to that in Shakespeare's other historical tragedies. It exhibits a natural progress of events, terminated by one interesting and complete catastrophe. Many of the episodes have uncommon excellence. Of this kind are, in general, all the speeches of Margaret. Their effect is awful; they coincide with the style of the tragedy; and by wearing the same gloomy complexion, her prophecies and imprecations suit and increase its horror. There was never in any poem a dream superior to that of Clarence. It pleases, like the prophecies of Margaret, by a solemn anticipation of future events, and by its consonance with the general tone of the tragedy. It pleases, by being so simple, so natural, and so pathetic, that every reader seems to have felt the same or similar horrors; and is inclined to say, with Brackenbury: "No wonder, Lord, that it affrighted you; I am afraid methinks to hear you tell it [1.4.64–65]."

This tragedy, however, like many works of Shakespeare, has many faults; and in particular, it seems to have been too hastily written. Some incidents are introduced without any apparent reason, or without apparent necessity in the conduct of the performance. . . . We see a good, prudential reason for the marriage of Richard with Elizabeth, but none for his marriage with Lady Anne. We almost wish that the first courtship had been omitted and that the dialogue between Richard and Anne had been suited and appropriated to Richard and the Queen. Neither are we sufficiently informed of the motives that, on some occasions, influenced the conduct of Buckingham. . . . The young princes bear too great a share in the drama. It would seem the poet intended to interest us very much in their misfortunes. The representation, however, is not agreeable. The Princes have more smartness than simplicity; and we are more affected with Tyrrell's description of their death, than pleased with anything in their own conversation. Nor does the scene of the ghosts, in the last act, seem equal in execution to the design of Shakespeare. There is more delightful horror in the speech of Richard awakening from his dream, than in any of the predictions denounced against him. . . . Yet, with these imperfections, this tragedy is a monument of striking genius; and the success of the poet, in delineating the character of Richard, has been as great as the singular boldness of the design.

William Hazlitt (1778–1830) [Excerpted from *Characters of Shakespeare's Plays* (1817). Hazlitt was one of the great romantic critics of Shakespeare.

In addition to providing a trenchant psychological analysis of Richard well before Freud, Hazlitt here discusses the practical matter of production, a concern for every actor and director of this long and complex play.]

The Richard of Shakespeare is towering and lofty; equally impetuous and commanding; haughty, violent, and subtle; bold and treacherous; confident in his strength as well as in his cunning; raised high by his birth, and higher by his talents and his crimes; a royal usurper, a princely hypocrite, a tyrant and a murderer of the house of Plantagenet. . . . The restless and sanguinary Richard is not a man striving to be great, but to be greater than he is; conscious of his strength of will, his power of intellect, his daring courage, his elevated station; and making use of these advantages to commit unheard-of crimes, and to shield himself from remorse and infamy. . . .

The play itself is undoubtedly a very powerful effusion of Shakespeare's genius. The ground-work of the character of Richard, that mixture of intellectual vigour with moral depravity, in which Shakespeare delighted to show his strength—gave full scope as well as temptation to the exercise of his imagination. The character of his hero is almost everywhere predominant, and marks its lurid track throughout. The original play is, however, too long for representation, and there are some few scenes which might be better spared than preserved, and by omitting which it would remain a complete whole. The only rule, indeed, for altering Shakespeare is to retrench certain passages which may be considered either as superfluous or obsolete, but not to add or transpose anything. The arrangement and development of the story, and the mutual contrast and combination of the *dramatis personae,* are in general as finely managed as the development of the characters or the expression of the passions.

Nathan Drake (1766–1836) [Excerpted from *Shakespeare and His Times* (1817). While emphasizing Richard's demonic nature, Drake explains why the role is so attractive. He also recognizes the importance of Margaret, whose part is too often cut in productions.]

The character of Richard the Third . . . is a picture of a demoniacal incarnation, moulding the passions and foibles of mankind, with superhuman precision, to its own iniquitous purposes. Of this isolated and peculiar state of being Richard himself seems sensible when he declares: "I am myself alone [*Henry VI, Part 3,* 5.6.83]." From a delineation like this [John] Milton must have caught many of the most striking features of his Satanic portrait. The same union of unmitigated depravity

Frank Robert Benson as Richard in *Richard III,* in this print published by Virtue & Company in 1901 (*Photographed by J. & L. Caswall Smith*)

and consummate intellectual energy characterizes both, and renders what would otherwise be loathsome and disgusting, an object of sublimity and shuddering admiration. Richard, stript as he is of all the softer feelings, and all the common charities, of humanity, possessed of "neither pity, love, nor fear," and loaded with every dangerous and dreadful vice, would, were it not for his unconquerable powers of mind, be insufferably revolting. But, though insatiate in his ambition, envious and hypocritical in his disposition, cruel, bloody, and remorseless in all his deeds, he displays such an extraordinary share of cool and determined courage, such alacrity and buoncy of spirit, such constant self-possession, such an intuitive intimacy with the workings of the human heart, and such matchless skill in rendering them subservient to his views, as so far to subdue our detestation and abhorrence of his villainy, that we, at length, contemplate this fiend in human shape with a mingled sensation of intense curiosity and grateful terror. The task, however, which Shakespeare undertook was, in one instance, more arduous than that which Milton subsequently attempted; for, in addition to the hateful constitution of Richard's moral character, he also had to contend against the prejudices arising from personal deformity, and yet, in spite of striking personal defects, which were considered, also, as indicatory of the depravity and wickedness of his nature, the poet has contrived, through the medium of the high mental endowments just enumerated, not only to obviate disgust, but to excite extraordinary admiration. One of the most prominent and detestable vices indeed, in Richard's character, his hypocrisy, connected, as it always is, in his person, with the most profound skill and dissimulation, has, owing to the various parts which it induces him to assume, most materially contributed to the popularity of this play, both on the stage, and in the closet. He is one who can "frame his face to all occasions," and accordingly appears, during the course of his career, under the contrasted forms of a subject and a monarch, a politician and a wit, a soldier and a suitor, a sinner and a saint; and in all with such apparent ease and fidelity to nature that while to the explorer of the human mind he affords, by his penetration and address, a subject of peculiar interest and delight, he offers to the practiced performer a study well calculated to call forth his fullest and finest exertions. He, therefore, whose histrionic powers are adequate to the just exhibition of this character, may be said to have attained the highest honours of his profession; and, consequently, the popularity of *Richard III.,* notwithstanding the moral enormity of its hero, may be readily accounted for, when we recollect that the versatile and consummate hypocrisy of the tyrant has been embodied by the talents of such masterly performers as [David] Garrick, [John Philip] Kemble, [George Frederick] Cooke, and [Edmund] Kean. So overwhelming and exclusive is the character of Richard that the comparative insignificancy of the other persons of the drama may be necessarily inferred; they are reflected to us, as it were, from his mirror, and become more or less important, and more or less developed, as he finds it necessary to act upon them; so that our estimate of their character is entirely founded on his relative conduct, through which we may very correctly appreciate their strength or weakness. The only exception to this remark is in the person of Queen Margaret, who, apart from the agency of Richard, and dimly seen in the darkest recesses of the picture, pours forth, in union with the deep tone of the tragedy, the most dreadful curses and imprecations, with such a wild and prophetic fury, indeed, as to involve the whole scene in tenfold gloom and horror. We have to add that the moral of this play is great and impressive.

John Philip Kemble (1757–1823) [Excerpted from *Macbeth and King Richard the Third: An Essay, In Answer to Remarks on Some of the Characters of Shakspeare*, 2nd ed. (1817). This is Kemble's response to Thomas Whately. Like Whately, Kemble, who played the role of Richard, notes *Macbeth*'s indebtedness to the earlier history play. Typical of so much romantic criticism, Kemble focuses on character. He understands Richard's heroic side as well as his villainy.]

Macbeth and Richard are, both, as intrepid as man can be; yet it may be said of each, without any diminution of that praise, that he is sometimes terror-struck at the recollection of his crimes. The characters that Shakspeare draws, are human creatures; and however their peculiarities may individuate them, yet they are always connected with the general nature of man by some fine link of universal interest, and by some passion to which they are liable in common with their kind. On the eve of the battle that is to decide his doom, Richard acknowledges a conscience: Bold in supernatural assurances of security from all peril, Macbeth sighs for the protection of his former popularity.

Ambition is the sole impulse that directs every action of Richard's life: his heart, in which every malignant and violent passion reigns uncontrolled, is hardened in wickedness: his mind is sunk into that depth of hopeless depravity, where the bad believe all other men to be as abandoned as themselves: he attains the crown by hypocrisy habitual to him, and by murders, that entail no remorse in the stern valour with which he maintains his ill-acquired sovereignty. . . .

The character of Richard is simple; that of Macbeth is mixed: Richard is only intrepid; Macbeth intrepid and feeling. Richard's crimes are the suggestions of his own disposition, originally bad, and at last confirmed in evil; he knows no "compunctious visitings of nature;" alive only to the exigencies of his situation, he is always at full leisure to display his valour.

Sigmund Freud (1856–1939) [Excepted from "Some Character Types Met with in Psycho-Analytic Work" (1916). Freud here offers a psychological interpretation of Richard and explains the character's appeal to audiences.]

In the opening soliloquy to Shakespeare's *Richard III,* Gloucester, who subsequently becomes King, says:

> But I, that am not shap'd for sportive tricks,
> Nor made to court an amorous looking-glass;
> I, that am rudely stamp'd, and want love's majesty
> To strut before a wonton ambling nymph;
> I, that am curtail'd of this fair proportion,
> Cheated of feature by dissembling nature,
> Deform'd, unfinish'd, sent before my time
> Into this breathing world, scarce half made up,
> And so lamely and unfashionable,
> That dogs bark at me as I halt by them;
> ***
> And therefore, since I cannot prove a lover,
> To entertain these fair well-spoken days,
> I am determined to prove a villain,
> And hate the idle pleasures of these days.
> [1.1.14–23, 28–31]

At a first glance this tirade may perhaps seem unrelated to our present theme. Richard seems to say nothing more than: "I find these idle times tedious, and I want to enjoy myself. As I cannot play the lover on account of my deformity, I will play the villain; I will intrigue, murder and do anything else I please." Such a frivolous motivation could not but stifle any stirring of sympathy in the audience, if it were not a screen for something much more serious. Otherwise the play would be psychologically impossible, for the writer must know how to furnish us with a secret background of sympathy for his hero, if we are to admire his boldness and adroitness without inward protest; and such sympathy can only be based on understanding or on a sense of a possible inner fellow-feeling for him.

I think, therefore, that Richard's soliloquy does not say everything; it merely gives a hint, and leaves us to fill in what it hints at. When we do so, however, the appearance of frivolity vanishes, the bitterness and minuteness with which Richard has depicted his deformity make their full effect, and we clearly perceive the fellow-feeling which compels our sympathy even with a villain like him. What the soliloquy thus means is: "Nature has done me a grievous wrong in denying me the beauty of form which wins human love. Life owes me reparation for this, and I will see that I get it. I have a right to be an exception, to disregard the scruples by which others let themselves be held back. I may do wrong myself, since wrong has been done to me." And now we feel that we ourselves might become like Richard, that on a small scale, indeed, we are already like him. Richard is an enormous magnification of something we find in ourselves as well. We all think we have reason to reproach Nature and our destiny for congenital and infantile disadvantages; we all demand reparation for early wounds to our narcissism, our self-love. . . .

It is, however, a subtle economy of art in the poet that he does not permit his hero to give open and complete expression to all his secret motives. By this means he obliges us to supplement them; he engages our intellectual activity, diverts it from critical reflection and keeps us firmly identified with his hero.

MODERN CRITICISM AND CRITICAL CONTROVERSIES

Modern criticism of Shakespeare's histories begins with E. M. W. Tillyard's *Shakespeare's History Plays* (1944). Tillyard argues that Shakespeare's two tetralogies (the three parts of *Henry VI* and *Richard III; Richard II,* the two parts of *Henry IV,* and *Henry V*) embodied the Tudor myth, which maintained that the killing of Richard II unleashed God's vengeance in the Wars of the Roses. The death of Richard III and the ascension of the Tudor dynasty that restored order were divinely ordained. As Tillyard states, "the main business of the play [*Richard III*] is to complete the national tetralogy and to display the working out of God's plan to restore England to prosperity" (199). He regards the first tetralogy as unified by "the steady political theme: the theme of order and chaos, of proper political degree and civil war, of crime and punishment, of God's mercy finally tempering his justice, of the belief that such had been God's way with England" (201).

Much subsequent writing about the histories in general and *Richard III* in particular has supported or dissented from Tillyard's study. Among those sharing Tillyard's view are M. M. Reese in *The Cease of Majesty* (1961); A. P. Rossiter in *Angel with Horns,* edited by Graham Storey (1961); C. A. Patrides, *The Phoenix and the Ladder* (1964); Nicholas Brooke, *Shakespeare's Early Tragedies* (1968); Wilbur Sanders, *The Dramatist and the Received Idea* (1968); Robert G. Hunter, *Shakespeare and the Mystery of God's Judgments* (1976); Emrys Jones, *The Origins of Shakespeare* (1977); and R. Chris Hassel, Jr., *Songs of Death: Performance, Interpretation, and the Text of Richard III* (1987). Hassel writes of the play's conclusion: "After the excruciating uncertainties of seemingly random destiny, of chance and change, that have been vividly dramatized in this world of time, God's providence has finally been manifested and vindicated" (121).

Other critics have challenged this interpretation. David L. Frey maintains in *The First Tetralogy* (1976), "Shakespeare rejected the theme of divine providence as found in the sources" (87). John Wilders expresses the same view in *The Lost Garden* (1978). Another of this persuasion is A. L. French in his 1974 article "The Mills of God and Shakespeare's Early History Plays." Hassel claims that the curses, prayers, and prophecies in the play come true, thus revealing divine oversight. French disputes this reading; he finds no moral sense informing the play. Edward IV, who usurped the throne, dies in his bed. His innocent children are killed. While some curses are fulfilled, others are not. Margaret condemns all members of the house of York, but Dorset thrives, and Elizabeth lives to see her daughter become queen. In the *Henry VI* plays, Margaret is guilty of murder, but she survives in the play to see her enemies destroyed. Rather than finding in the tetralogy a restoration of providential order, French sees the opposite. He writes, "Starting off from a world of simple, heroic patriotism, embodied in Talbot and others, it moves towards a final world in which morality has ceased to have any meaning at all—where death has become totally capricious, striking down the innocent and sparing the guilty and sometimes, for no obvious reason, doing the reverse" (qtd. in Smidt) Henry A. Kelly's *Divine Providence in the England of Shakespeare's Histories* (1970) claims that *Richard III* satirizes rather than accepts a providential reading of history.

Some have tried to reconcile these two views. For Wilbur Sanders, the play's conclusion endorses a providential universe, but the rest of the play does not. Shakespeare tacks on an orthodox ending to a heterodox work. Moody Prior also steers a middle course in *The Drama of Power* (1973). Here he maintains that

Shakespeare, like all his contemporaries of whatever intellectual bias, approached *Richard III* through the providential idea of history, but he left the idea more complex, less rigid, more humane than he found it in any of his sources.

He was thus liberated of its conventional pieties and mechanistic rigor. (58)

Though Sanders and Brooke regard the play as endorsing the providential reading of history, they regard Richard as heroic for opposing divine determinism.

Another challenge to Tillyard came from critics who regard the history plays as "mirrors of Elizabethan policy" (Campbell). W. A. Armstrong's 1946 article "The Elizabethan Conception of the Tyrant" examines *Richard III* in light of contemporary distinctions between legitimate rulers who had to be obeyed and usurpers who could be overthrown. Sharing this view that the plays comment on contemporary issues is David Bevington's *Tudor Drama and Politics: A Critical Approach to Topical Meaning* (1968). According to Alexander Leggatt's *Shakespeare's Political Drama* (London: 1988), the histories anatomize power. Such a reading of history plays has a long history. On November 12, 1589, the Privy Council asked the Archbishop of Canterbury, the Lord Mayor of London, and the Master of the Revels to examine all plays staged in and near London because these works were treating "certain matters of divinity and state unfit to be suffered."

The character of Richard continues to fascinate 20th-century critics quite as much as it interested 18th- and 19th-century readers. According to A. L. French in his 1968 article "The World of Richard III," Shakespeare made of Richard a figure more complex than the cardboard villain he found in his sources. Waldo McNeir's "The Masks of Richard III" (1971) examines Richard's skill at manipulating others, including the audience, through his theatrical abilities. Ralph Berry, in "Richard III: Bonding the Audience," finds that Richard proves attractive because he does what the audience wants him to do. Early in the play, he courts the audience with his soliloquies and asides and makes them his accomplices. He also bonds with the audience by using many images drawn from their bourgeois world. As the play progresses, Richard stops talking to the audience. Shakespeare thus distances the audience from the character, preparing them to accept and indeed celebrate his downfall.

As the excerpt from Freud quoted in Extracts of Classic Criticism above indicates, Richard lends himself to psychological interpretations. Charles A. Adler's "Richard III: His Significance as a Study in Criminal Life-Style" (1936) presents a sympathetic reading of his character. Drawing on the *Henry VI* plays as well as *Richard III*, Adler finds in Richard a youngest child trying to catch up to his siblings and, indeed, to surpass them. Adler regards Richard as close to his father but alienated from his mother. This distance from the Duchess leads to his hostility to all women. According to Adler, Richard wants to befriend others (a dubious proposition) but fears rejection and hence remains aloof.

In "Some Shakespearean Characters in the Light of Present Day Psychologies" (1942), Ira S. Wile expands on Adler's interpretation. Like Adler, Wile views Richard as responding to a sense of inferiority. Wile also uses Alfred Adler's theory that an inferiority complex can generate a compensatory sense of superiority such as Richard demonstrates. Wile explains Richard's misogyny as resulting from his subordinating his desire for sex to his desire for power, and that will to power in turn springs from Richard's attempt to compensate for his deformity.

Murray Krieger in "The Dark Generations of Richard III" (1959), disagrees. Krieger claims that Richard wants power so that he can succeed as a lover. "He invariably couples the assertion of political power with the sexual assertion of manliness," Krieger writes (33). He goes on to argue that Richard "pursues power so that he may coerce a mistress—one who will have to play the game of treating him as a lover and who, though it only aggravates her revulsion, will painfully sport with him as with one 'fram'd in the prodigality of nature [1.2.243]'" (37). Krieger also offers a psychological explanation of Richard's victims. They know he is a villain, but they, like him, are hypocrites. "His victories can be attributed not so much to the fact that he is more villainous than the rest, as to the fact that he is more

consistently and self-admittedly villainous" (39). Richard offers power that the others want; they side with him, but then he destroys them.

For Gerald H. Zuk in "A Note on Richard's Anxiety Dream" (1957), "Richard is not in any sense a leader; rather he is one who would destroy authority and leadership" (38). Hence, he succeeds as long he opposes authority, but once he gains power himself, he disintegrates. Zuk concludes, "This great character study of Shakespeare represents an archetype of the individual who suddenly experiences a powerful wish-fulfillment, who undergoes severe ego stress as a result of the fulfillment, and whose ego may be threatened with total dissolution in trying to bring under control previously repressed superego forces" (39).

Richard III contains four significant roles for women: Margaret, Elizabeth, Anne, and the Duchess of York. Feminist critics have provided helpful insights into these characters. Jean E. Howard and Phyllis Rackin's *Engendering a Nation: A Feminist Account of Shakespeare's English Histories* (1997) contends that *Richard III* treats women more sympathetically than *Henry VI, Parts 1, 2,* and *3* do, but the women in *Richard III* lack the power they previously had in the earlier plays of the tetralogy. Howard and Rackin write:

> The subversive theatrical energy of the peasant Joan [in *Henry VI, Part 1*] is replaced by the pathos of suffering English queens. Margaret, the adulterous wife and bloodthirsty warrior of the Henry VI plays, is transformed into a bereaved and suffering prophet of divine vengeance for the crimes of the past. In the Henry VI plays, the female characters are defined as opponents to the masculine project of English history-making. In *Richard III*, all of the women support the desired conclusion of the historical plot, the foundation of the Tudor dynasty. (106)

Howard and Rackin argue that at the beginning of *Richard III*, Richard appropriates "Margaret's power of subversive speech," and at the end of the play, Richmond assumes "the moral authority of bereaved and suffering women to authorize this victory" (116). The women lose not only power but also individuality. They are transformed into a single "chorus of ritual lamentation, curse, and prophecy that enunciates the play's providential agenda" (116).

Madonne M. Miner's "'Neither Mother, Wife, nor England's Queen': The Role of Women in *Richard III*" (1980) presents a different interpretation of the play's treatment of women. Richard's opening speech declares that the Edwardian world belongs to the "wanton ambling nymph" (1.1.17) rather than to warriors and political plotters like himself. To Richard, war is manly, peace feminine.

The Duchess of York speaks with Edward and Margaret Plantagenet about their father's death in this 19th-century depiction of Act II, Scene 2 of *Richard III*. (*Painting by Henry Corbould; engraving by Henry Rolls*)

Richard blames women for the various evil deeds he commits. He says that the queen is responsible for Clarence's imprisonment and then his death. He tells Anne that she is responsible for his killing Henry VI and Prince Edward, as later he will claim that he murdered the princes for love of Elizabeth. He accuses the queen and Jane Shore of deforming him through witchcraft.

Although Richard seems to ascribe power to women, he values them only for their male associations. Anne Neville interests him because she is the daughter of the Earl of Warwick and daughter-in-law of Henry VI. Later, he wants to marry his niece Elizabeth, Edward IV's daughter. By killing husbands, fathers, and children, Richard thinks that he deprives women of power and identity. The women defeat Richard by uniting. Though they oppose each other early in the play, in Act IV they unite to oppose Richard. Women do not appear in Act V (except for the ghost of Anne). But Richmond recognizes that England's peace requires a master-mistress. Only by uniting the masculine and feminine—that is, by his marrying Elizabeth—can "these bloody days" end (5.5.36).

Paul N. Siegel's "Richard III as Businessman" (1978) offers a Marxist reading of the play. Like Berry, Siegel discusses Richard's use of bourgeois imagery. Having contemplated marrying Anne Neville, Richard reminds himself, "But yet I run before my horse to market: / Clarence still breathes, Edward still lives and reigns; / When they are gone, then must I count my gains" (1.1.160–162). After he gains Anne's hand, Richard expresses his surprise at his success and numbers among the obstacles he has overcome the lack of "friends to back my suit" (1.2.235). He tells Queen Elizabeth that after he has defeated Buckingham, he will "retail my conquest won" to her daughter (4.4.335). When Richard learns the number of Richmond's soldiers opposing him, he rejoices, "Why, our battalia trebles that account" (5.3.11). Ralph Berry's essay discussed above regards these images as part of Shakespeare's attempt to make Richard sympathetic to a bourgeois audience. Siegel interprets these images as a critique of both Richard and emerging capitalism. Siegel writes, "Shakespeare saw the Tudor order threatened by the rampant individualism of both the old nobility with its tradition of feudal prerogatives that superseded the national state, and the most aggressive section of the bourgeoisie, which was already in the 1590s beginning to challenge the monarchy" (101). For Siegel, Richard embodies the latter with its capitalist rapacity.

THE PLAY TODAY

Though set in the 15th century, *Richard III* presents a timeless anatomy of the lust for power. In "A Country of the Mind" (1990), Lois Potter writes that despite the historical setting, the play seems modern in its treatment of politics and propaganda. Certainly its appeal continues to be powerful today. Modern critics and theatergoers continue to be fascinated by this improbably successful hero-villain. Some are preoccupied with examining *Richard III*'s status as Shakespeare's first "great" play (not everyone agrees with this designation). A relatively new slant is to examine Richard and his physical deformity in light of the increasingly popular field of disability studies.

Productions emphasize Richard's charisma and Machiavellian nature, and often implicitly compare him to tyrants of the present day or recent past. A review published on April 8, 1939, in the *Birmingham Evening Dispatch* found in John Laurie's Richard "the ruthless singleness of purpose observed to-day in the Dictators." Donald Wolfit, who played Richard in the late 1930s and 1940s, said that the more he studied Richard, the more the medieval monarch seemed to him to resemble Hitler. Ian McKellen's 1995 movie of the play, based on his stage version, is set in the 1930s, with Richard as a fascist. Many other famous actors have played Richard, including John Barrymore, Simon Russell Beale, Laurence Olivier, and Ian Richardson. The 1996 documentary *Looking for Richard* featured Al Pacino and other famous actors commenting on their roles in *Richard III*.

The character of Richard continues to captivate actors and audiences, not only as a study of power and of evil but also as an individual at once dam-

Publicity photo for the 1955 film version of *Richard III*, with Laurence Olivier (center) as Richard

aged and charming. Does he, like Iago, exemplify motiveless malignity? Wherein lies his power to fascinate those onstage and off? He is one of Shakespeare's great creations, one of the many enduring monuments to the playwright's artistry, insight into the human psyche, and understanding of politics, not just of his age but for all time.

FIVE TOPICS FOR DISCUSSION AND WRITING

1. **Theatricality:** What are some examples of theatricality in the play? Which characters are actors within the work? How do all the allusions to playacting comment on kingship and power?
2. **Tragedy:** Is this play a tragedy? Does it include a tragic hero? Does it include a hero of any kind?
3. **Fate:** Who controls the play's action? What does the play say about individuals' ability to determine their fates? What role do curses and providence play here?
4. **Women:** In this play, are women merely pawns to be manipulated by men? Do women determine the outcome of the play?
5. **Politics:** What does the play say about the nature of government? Can principle prevail over power?

Bibliography

Adler, Charles A. "Richard III: His Significance as a Study in Criminal Life-Style." *International Journal of Individual Psychology* 3 (1936): 55–60.

Armstrong, W. A. "The Elizabeth Conception of the Tyrant." *Review of English Studies* 22 (1946): 161–181.

Berry, Edward. *Patterns of Decay: Shakespeare's Early Histories.* Charlottesville: University of Virginia Press, 1975.

Berry, Ralph. "Richard III: Bonding the Audience." In *Mirror up to Shakespeare,* edited by J. C. Gray, 114–127. Toronto: University of Toronto Press, 1984.

Bevington, David. *Tudor Drama and Politics: A Critical Approach to Topical Meaning.* Cambridge, Mass.: Harvard University Press, 1968.

Blanpied, John W. *Time and the Artist in Shakespeare's English Histories.* Newark: University of Delaware Press, 1983.

Bloom, Harold. *Shakespeare: The Invention of the Human.* New York: Riverhead, 1998.

Boas, Frederick Samuel. *Shakspere and His Predecessors.* London: J. Murray, 1896; New York: Charles Scribner's Sons, 1904.

Brooke, Nicholas Stanton. *Shakespeare's Early Tragedies.* London: Methuen, 1968.

Brooks, Harold F. "*Richard III,* Unhistorical Amplifications: The Women's Scenes and Seneca." *Modern Language Review* 75, no. 4 (October 1980): 721–737.

Bullough, Geoffrey. *Earlier English History Plays: Henry VI, Richard III, Richard II.* Volume 3 of *Narrative and Dramatic Sources of Shakespeare.* London: Routledge and Kegan Paul, 1966.

Campbell, Lily Bess. *Shakespeare's "Histories": Mirrors of Elizabethan Policy.* San Marino, Calif.: Huntington Library, 1947.

Clemen, Wolfgang H. *A Commentary on Shakespeare's Richard III.* Translated by Jean Bonheim. London: Methuen, 1968.

Colley, Scott. *Richard's Himself Again: A Stage History of Richard III.* Westport, Conn.: Greenwood Press, 1992.

Dessen, Alan C. *Shakespeare and the Late Moral Plays.* Lincoln: University of Nebraska Press, 1986.

French, A. L. "The Mills of God and Shakespeare's Early History Plays." *English Studies* 55 (1974): 313–324.

———. "The World of Shakespeare." *Shakespeare Studies* 4 (1968): 25–39.

Frey, David L. *The First Tetralogy.* The Hague: Mouton, 1976.

Garber, Marjorie. *Shakespeare After All.* New York: Pantheon Books, 2004.

———. *Shakespeare's Ghost Writers: Literature as Uncanny Causality.* New York: Methuen, 1987.

Haeffner, Paul A. *A Critical Commentary on Shakespeare's Richard the Third.* London: Macmillan, 1966.

Hall, Edward. *The Union of the Two Noble and Illustrate Famelies of Lancastre and Yorke.* London: R. Graftoni, 1548.

Hankey, Julie, ed. *Richard III: Plays in Performance.* London: Junction Books, 1981.

Hassel, R. Chris, Jr. *Songs of Death: Performance, Interpretation, and the Text of Richard III.* Lincoln: University of Nebraska Press, 1987.

Heilman, Robert. "Satiety and Conscious: Aspects of *Richard III.*" *Antioch Review* 24 (1964): 57–73.

Holderness, Graham. *Shakespeare's History.* New York: St. Martin's Press, 1985.

Holinshed, Raphael. *Holinshed's Chronicles of England, Scotland, and Ireland.* 6 vols. London: Johnson, 1807.

Howard, Jean E., and Phyllis Rackin. *Engendering a Nation: A Feminist Account of Shakespeare's English Histories.* London: Routledge, 1997.

Hunter, Robert G. *Shakespeare and the Mystery of God's Judgments.* Athens: University of Georgia Press, 1976.

Jones, Emrys. *The Origins of Shakespeare.* Oxford: Clarendon Press, 1977.

Jones, Robert C. *These Valiant Dead: Renewing the Past in Shakespeare's Histories.* Iowa City: University of Iowa Press, 1991.

Kelly, Henry A. *Divine Providence in the England of Shakespeare's Histories.* Cambridge, Mass.: Harvard University Press, 1970.

Krieger, Murray. "The Dark Generations of Richard III." *Criticism* 1 (1959): 32–48.

Lamb, Charles. *Essays of Ella, and Other Pieces.* London: Routledge, 1886.

Leggatt, Alexander. *Shakespeare's Political Drama: The History Plays and the Roman Plays.* London: Routledge, 1988.

Logan, Robert A. *Shakespeare's Marlowe: The Influence of Christopher Marlowe on Shakespeare's Artistry.* Aldershot, U.K.: Ashgate, 2007.

Machiavelli, Niccolò. *The Prince.* Edited by Robert M. Adams. New York, 1977.

McNeir, Waldo. "The Masks of Richard III." *Studies in English Literature* 11 (1971): 167–186.

Miner, Madonne M. "'Neither Mother, Wife, nor England's Queen': The Role of Women in Richard III." In *The Woman's Part: Feminist Criticism of Shakespeare,* edited by Carolyn Ruth Swift Lenz. et al,, 35–55. Urbana: University of Illinois Press, 1980.

More, Thomas. *History of King Richard III.* New Haven, Conn.: Yale University Press, 1976.

Muir, Kenneth. *The Sources of Shakespeare's Plays.* New Haven, Conn.: Yale University Press, 1978.

Ornstein, Robert. *A Kingdom for a Stage: The Achievement of Shakespeare's History Plays.* Cambridge, Mass.: Harvard University Press, 1972.

Patrick, David Lyall. *The Textual History of Richard III.* Stanford, Calif.: Stanford University Press, 1936.

Patrides, C. A. *The Phoenix and the Ladder: The Rise and Decline of the Christian View of History.* Berkeley: University of California Press, 1964.

Peacham, Henry. *The Garden of Eloquence.* London, 1593.

Polter, Lois. "A Country of the Mind." *Times Literary Supplement* (August 3, 1990): 825.

Polydori, Vergilli. *Angliche historiae.* Basileae [Basel, Switzerland]: Guarinum, 1570.

Prior, Moody E. *The Drama of Power: Studies in Shakespeare's History Plays.* Evanston, Ill.: Northwestern University Press, 1973.

Rackin, Phyllis. *Stages of History: Shakespeare's English Chronicles.* Ithaca, N.Y.: Cornell University Press, 1990.

Reed, Robert Rentoul, Jr. *Crime and God's Judgment in Shakespeare.* Lexington: University of Kentucky Press, 1984.

Reese, M. M. *The Cease of Majesty.* London: Edward Arnold, 1961.

Ribner, Irving. *The English History Play in the Age of Shakespeare.* Rev. ed. New York: Barnes & Noble Books, 1965.

Richmond, Hugh M. *King Richard III.* Manchester, U.K.: Manchester University Press, 1989.

Rons, John. *History of the Earls of Warwick.* London: n.p., 1485.

Ross, Charles. *Richard III.* New Haven, Conn.: Yale University Press, 1981.

Rossiter, A. P. *Angel with Horns, and Other Shakespeare Lectures.* Edited by Graham Storey. New York: Theatre Arts Books, 1961.

Saccio, Peter. *Shakespeare's English Kings: History, Chronicle, and Drama.* 2nd ed. Oxford: Oxford University Press, 2000.

Sanders, Wilbur. *The Dramatist and the Received Idea: Studies in the Plays of Marlowe & Shakespeare.* London: Cambridge University Press, 1968.

Shakespeare, William. *The Complete Works of Shakespeare.* Edited by George Lyman Kittredge. Boston and New York: Ginn and Co., 1936.

———. *King Richard III.* Edited by Alan S. Downer. London: Society for Theatre Research, 1959.

———. *King Richard III.* Updated ed. Edited by Janis Lull. Cambridge: Cambridge University Press, 2009.

———. *The Tragedy of King Richard III.* Edited by John Jowett. Oxford: Oxford University Press, 2000.

Siegel, Paul N. "Richard as Businessman." *Shakespeare Jahrbuch* 114 (1978): 101–106.

Smidt, Kristian. *Iniurious Impostors and Richard III.* New York: Humanities Press, 1964.

———. *Unconformities in Shakespeare's History Plays.* London: Macmillan, 1982.

Spurgeon, Caroline F. E. *Shakespeare's Imagery and What It Tells Us.* Cambridge: Cambridge University Press, 1935.

Stoll, Elmer Edgar. *Shakespeare Studies, Historical and Comparative in Method.* New York: Macmillan, 1927.

Tanner, Tony. *Prefaces to Shakespeare.* Cambridge, Mass.: Harvard University Press, Belknap Press, 2010.

Thomas, Sidney. *The Antic Hamlet and Richard III.* New York: King's Crown Press, 1943.

Tillyard, E. M. W. *Shakespeare's History Plays.* London: Chatto & Windows, 1944.

The True Tragedie of Richard the Third. London, 1594.

Vickers, Brian. "Shakespeare's Use of Rhetoric." In *A New Companion to Shakespeare Studies,* edited by Kenneth Muir and Samuel Schoenbaum, 83–98. Cambridge: Cambridge University Press, 1971.

Watson, Donald G. *Shakespeare's Early History Plays: Politics at Play on the Elizabethan Stage.* Athens: University of Georgia Press, 1990.

Wilders, John. *The Lost Garden: A View of Shakespeare's English and Roman Plays.* London: Macmillan, 1978.

Wile, Ira S. "Some Shakespearean Characters in the Light of Present Day Psychologies." *Psychiatric Quarterly* 16 (1942): 62–90.

Wilson, F. P. *Marlowe and the Early Shakespeare.* Oxford: Clarendon Press, 1954.

Zuk, Gerald H. "A Note on Richard's Anxiety Dream." *American Image* 14 (1957): 37–39.

FILM AND VIDEO PRODUCTIONS

Bogdanov, Michael, dir. *Richard III.* With Andrew Jarvis and Michael Pennington. Portman Productions, 1990.

Howell, Jane, dir. *Richard III.* With Ron Cook, Rowena Cooper, and Michael Byrne. BBC/Time-Life, 1982.

Loncraine, Richard, dir. *Richard III.* With Ian McKellen, Annette Bening, Robert Downey, Jr., Kristin Scott Thomas, and Maggie Smith. MGM/United Artists, 1995.

Olivier, Laurence, dir. *Richard III.* With Laurence Olivier, Ralph Richardson, John Gielgud, and Claire Bloom. L.O.P., 1955.

—Joseph Rosenblum